THE GREATEST SUPERMAN STORIES EVER TOLD

DC Comics, Inc.

President and Publisher **Jenette Kahn**

V.P.-Editorial **Dick Giordano**

Co-Editor **Mike Gold**

Co-Editor **Robert Greenberger**

Design Director **Richard Bruning**

Managing Editor **Terri Cunningham**

Production Director **Bob Rozakis**

Executive V.P. **Paul Levitz**

V.P.-Creative Director **Joe Orlando**

Marketing Director **Bruce Bristow**

Circulation Director **Matt Ragone**

Advertising Director **Tom Ballou**

Controller **Pat Caldon**

Published by **DC Comics, Inc.**, 666 Fifth Avenue, New York, NY 10103

Printed in Canada

Cover Illustration by Dean Motter

Back Cover Illustration by John Byrne and Jerry Ordway

Fourth Printing – Trade Paperback Edition

To Jerry Siegel
and Joe Shuster,
who started it all,
To the memories of
Wayne Boring
and E. Nelson Bridwell,

and

To the dozens of talented
men and women whose efforts
over the past fifty years
combined to make
The Man of Steel
a true American legend.

TABLE OF CONTENTS

HE ORIGINS OF SUPERMAN

As befits a character whose exploits would rapidly assume the mantle of legend, his beginnings were both humble and cataclysmic.

Cataclysmic, for he was born out of the death of a world. Hurled into a cold, forbidding universe, an orphaned babe suddenly more alone than any other being had ever been. He rode a plume of fire, tucked inside the metal womb of a tiny spaceship. And behind him, unseen as he slept the untroubled sleep of the innocent, the dying planet exploded into a billion fragments. Green, glowing fragments that spread across the universe. Radioactive. Lethal. Waiting for him.

Humble, for that planet-shattering blast was born in the minds of two teenagers, growing up in the heartland of America. Raised on science-fiction pulp magazines and dreams of the world beyond Ohio.

Their names were Jerry Siegel and Joe Shuster, writer and artist respectively. In their imaginations was born a character of almost unequalled appeal. A character who reached into the American psyche, and pressed all the right buttons. A character called Superman.

It was the 1930s. The precise moment of Superman's conception can only be guessed, but it was certainly no later than 1934. Jerry Siegel first used the name in 1933 in a short story he wrote for his fanzine (a fan-produced, amateur magazine) Science Fiction. The story was "The Reign of the Superman," and had little to do with the character we know by that name today. It was the tale of a man who gained and misused fantastic mental powers. It was illustrated by Joe Shuster.

Five more years passed before the public saw the name applied to the greatest of costumed adventurers. In that time Siegel and Shuster would try without success to interest many publishers in their creation. Originally envisioned as a newspaper strip, Superman was first presented to the syndicates in that form. The reaction was resoundingly negative, and rejection after rejection led to rewriting and recutting with no success. Exhausting American syndicates, they even tried Cana-

dian publishers. Joe Shuster had relatives north of the forty-ninth parallel. He'd spent many summers in and around the Toronto area. In fact, the embryonic Superman's first job was with the *Daily Star*, modelled on the *Toronto Star*. The general consensus? The character would have "no lasting appeal."

Meanwhile Siegel and Shuster were not without work. Although Superman would become their most famous creation, eclipsing all others almost completely, his early adventures were not the first comic material they produced. Their careers reached back to the very beginnings of the Industry—mostly at DC Comics.

Armed with a successful track record, they sold Superman. Credit for finally bringing Superman into the world should properly lie with All-American editor Sheldon Mayer. Superman was recut to comic book form and shown to Harry Donenfeld, president of DC Comics, who authorized its final publication. And as the saying has it, a Legend was born.

Superman would see print in *Action Comics* number one, cover-dated June 1938, and it was there the Depression-weary, war-leery nation got its first glimpse of the character who would become an American icon. Although he received star billing on that landmark issue, Superman did not reappear on the cover until the seventh issue. He did not take possession of the cover position until *Action Comics* number 19, by which time he had won his own title, *Superman*. At the height of his popularity he would star in more than half a dozen titles, including *Superboy, Adventure Comics, World's Finest Comics*, and *Justice League of America*, among others.

The first Superman story was simple enough, and even contained elements that writer Siegel had developed in other stories written earlier, and reused in stories created after the genesis of Superman.

The story: Out in the reaches of space there once existed a great and proud planet, Krypton. In the earliest versions, Krypton was a planet within our own solar system. Siegel and Shuster may well have been inspired by then-prevalent concepts of the asteroid belt as the remnants of a tenth planet, destroyed in some terrible cataclysm. Astronomers and astrophysicists of the 1970s would give a less dramatic reason for the band of mountain-sized boulders circling the sun: the gravitational pull of mighty Jupiter, swinging round on a regular schedule, never gave a planet the chance to form in the gulf between itself and Mars. But in the 1930s, science fiction was full of tales of that long ago vanished world.

Krypton was an ideal world, far advanced beyond the planet Earth of 1938. A world of supreme technological advancement. A world of humanlike beings raised to physical and mental perfection. Men and women alike, a race of supermen.

But a doomed race. As we first saw it, tremors in the planet's crust shook the mighty towers of Krypton. Gusts of flame burst through the cracking mantle. The sky darkened. The people trembled. They had conquered their world, harnessed it to their will. Now that world was rebelling, and they could not understand. They could not believe. One man acted to learn the truth. He was Jor-L, a brilliant scientist. He, and he alone, realized the ultimate fate of the planet. The pressures building within the core would soon shatter the planet completely.

As a name, "Jor-L" had seen print in another of Siegel's stories, written after the conception of Superman, but published before.

Bounding across the city, each leap carrying him across the space of several blocks, Jor-L raced home, to find his beautiful wife Lora waiting. Waiting with their son. When we first met the child who would become Superman he was a nameless newborn babe. It would not be until 1957 that the audience following his adventures learned Superman's real name, the name given him by his Kryptonian parents. By then his father's nomenclature would have changed, slightly, to Jor-El, and Superman would be Kal-El, meaning "Star Child" in the language of the planet.

Fearing the ultimate destruction of Krypton, Jor-L conceived a mad gamble, a chance for survival for his son. Anticipating the doom that hurtled towards them all, Jor-L had built a model, a single, small prototype of the fleet of giant rockets he hoped could be built to carry all the race of Krypton to a safe haven in distant space.

The people had rejected his plan, refusing to believe his prediction of destruction. The little model, fully functional, was all that had been built. Jor-L decided to place his infant son in the miniature rocket. To snatch for him a hope of life, out of the very jaws of death. Lora agreed. The baby was placed in the rocket, and as the final surge of earthquakes blasted through the towering cities of Krypton, the craft was hurled on its long journey towards Earth.

There, after a rough landing, the sole survivor was found by passing motorists. Originally unidentified, they later became Jonathan and Martha Kent. Their names, too, varied in some of the earlier retellings. In 1942 George Lowther wrote a Superman novel, detailing the origin much as stated in the comics, but finally giving the adoptive parents-to-be the names Sarah and Eben Kent. (These names they would be known by in the 1948 *Superman* serial and in the pilot episode of *The Adventures of Superman* television series.) The Lowther novel was also the first to give Superman's Kryptonian family name the full "El" spelling, rather than the single letter "L," and change the first vowel in Superman's mother's name from "o" to "a."

In the 1938 comic book version, the nameless Kents, an elderly couple without children of their own, took the foundling to a nearby "orphan asylum," returning later to apply to adopt the baby. In subsequent retellings, it was revealed this return was the Kents' intention all along. By the time the Kents returned, the staff was more than happy to see the baby go. Already possessing the fabulous powers of a native of Krypton, the tiny babe had all but demolished the orphanage before the Kents' return.

Named Clark Kent, the child grew to manhood before donning the familiar red-blue-and-yellow costume of Superman. There are conflicting versions of how Clark got his name. In the stories themselves, it has been revealed as his mother's maiden name, but in the minds of Siegel and Shuster, no one can say for sure. One version has him being named, simply enough, for actors Clark Gable and Kent Taylor. Another version gives the name as a roundabout salute to the old pulp magazines which fired the imaginations of Superman's creators: Doc Savage, the crusading "Man of Bronze," was christened Clark Savage Jr., and his creator was author of Lester Dent.

Young Clark was cautioned to keep his powers a secret. In the first issue of *Superman*, Pa Kent warned him, saying, "Now listen to me, Clark! This great strength of yours—you've got to hide it from people or they'll be scared of you!" Ma was less fretful, adding that "when the proper time comes you must use it to assist humanity."

Establishing himself in Metropolis, Clark sought out his job at the *Daily Planet*, and thus encountered the longest-lasting member of the supporting cast, Lois Lane. Lois is the only character other than Superman who can lay claim to being there from the very beginning. She entered Clark Kent's life in *Action #1*, already a crusading reporter for the Metropolis *Daily Star* (later renamed "Planet"). The other well-known cast members, Jimmy Olsen and Perry White, would come later, both born out of Superman's adventures on radio.

Later development of the character added Superboy to the legend (in 1945), revealing that it was not as an adult that Clark Kent first demonstrated his Kryptonian abilities to the world, but as a youth in Smallville. From these tales, appearing mostly in *Superboy* and *Adventure Comics*, we learned most of what we know about the kindly Kents. Beginning as a farmer, Jonathan Kent would later buy a general store in Smallville, and this cozy setting would serve as the starting point for many adventures over the years to come. (In one of the curious confusions of continuity that has beset DC Comics occasionally over the years, it was several years before the existence of Superboy was acknowledged within the Superman titles.)

It was in Smallville, too, that we met Lana Lang. A vivacious redhead and Superboy's sometime girlfriend, Lana occupied a role in his childhood and adolescence similar to that assumed in later years by Lois. The Superboy chronicles became as complex as Superman's, over the thirty-odd years of their publishing history. No one seemed especially bothered by the contradictions inherent in the appearance of Superboy as a major element of Superman's

past. Perhaps readers were less fussy about stringent continuity in those days. More likely, they simply welcomed anything that presented them with an avenue to more adventures of their favorite hero.

Out of the Superboy stories came more details of Superman's past life on Krypton. Using his super-memory, young Clark was able to recount much of the day-to-day goings-on of his native world. Much more than one might expect a newborn to remember. And, indeed, as the chronicles progressed, Superman's age at his departure from Krypton advanced. He became a toddler, eventually, not only fully conscious of his surroundings, but actually able to speak Kryptonian. Again, the contradictions were happily ignored by the readers. As long as the stories were exciting, no one cared much about the details.

So, as Superman's career proceeded, the texture changed, the details changed. Even the personalities changed. But Superman remained more or less the same, the rock around which all other things orbited.

Kryptonian culture and technology may have been ideals, far advanced beyond Earth, but Kryptonians themselves became more like us. Krypton was revealed to have been a gigantic planet, closer perhaps to Jupiter than Earth in size, and Superman's strength was explained as coming from this source, as muscles evolved to deal with the crushing weight of Krypton's gravity become superpowerful on earth.

Here, too, was the origin of Superman's ability to fly. Earth's gravity was simply not sufficient to restrain him. His invulnerability also held as a remnant of his planet of birth. All Kryptonians, it seems, have super-dense molecular structures.

This season of alteration in the legend also brought an increased focus on Krypton itself. The planet had gone almost unmentioned for the first decade of Superman's life, but in the years that followed it became a vital cog in the working machinery of the character.

This reached its most significant point fairly early, in 1949, when Superman for the first time encountered a glowing fragment of his native planet. Colored red in the comic debut, kryptonite was actually born on the Superman radio series, and would remain for the rest of his career as the single most dangerous threat to his existence. The lethal kryptonite assumed its green hue as of the second appearance. Later red kryptonite would be introduced, but its effects on Superman were profoundly different, as we shall see.

The introduction of kryptonite also added to the role of the prime villain in Superman's Rogues' Gallery. Lex Luthor, the maddest of mad scientists, quickly learned not only of the existence of this ultimate bane to Superman, but also how to create it artificially. (In one story adapted from both the radio show and the second movie serial, he actually tricked Superman into gathering the necessary elements himself.)

This focus on Krypton could not continue long, of course, before the ultimate contact is made with Superman's past: live Kryptonians. In the August 1950 issue, Superman confronted three Kryptonian criminals, fired into orbit by Jor-El, and thus allowed to escape the destruction of the planet. Jor-El, it became increasingly apparent, had more than one rocket tucked away in his lab. He was also more deeply involved in the handing down of Kryptonian justice than might be expected from someone whose claim to fame was as a simple scientist, however great. As the legend progressed, one began to get an image of Albert Einstein being invited to sit on the Supreme Court, Jor-El's involvement with every level of Kryptonian social structure became so great.

Eventually Jor-El was revealed as the inventor/discoverer of a device which, over the years, would prove almost as great a thorn in Superman's side as kryptonite: The Phantom Zone. This ghostly other-dimensional realm was seen by the populace of Krypton as a more benevolent punishment than the traditional exile into orbit. In a significant scene, Jor-El was seen promising a condemned criminal that he would create something kinder than a hundred years in suspended animation. The reader can judge whether the Phantom Zone was really a greater kindness. Projected into this "twilight dimension" criminals became disembodied spirits, able to see and hear all that transpired on their native world, but unable to touch, taste, smell, or in any way make contact with anyone outside the Zone.

Learning of the existence of the Zone, Superman also discovered that many of the criminals interred there were at the end of their sentences, and he felt naturally compelled to release them. Most had not learned the error of their ways however, and, possessing Superman's powers, set off on super-villainous campaigns. Invariably they ended up back in the Zone, gnashing their incorporeal teeth at Superman, and vowing revenge.

By this point, Siegel and Shuster were gone. They'd departed by 1947, in fact, and control of their creation passed to various editors, writers, and artists. The first of these to make a measurable impact on Superman's legend was Mort Weisinger, who assumed control of the editorial reins after World War II. Under Weisinger's influence the Superman most clearly identified in the minds of the public began to take shape.

Weisinger, it has been reported, had a habit of conferring with neighborhood children, asking them what they would like to see

happening with the character whose adventures were, after all, still aimed almost entirely at their young minds. It was in this period then that the proliferation of superpowers began. Whether directly because of the suggestions of children, or because of a canny awareness of what kids like to see, the Superman stories of this era filled up with a multitude of characters possessing powers identical to Superman's. First to arrive, retroactively, was Krypto the Superdog.

It seems Jor-El had a model of that prototype rocket in which he launched his son to Earth. And, being a dutiful and caring father, Jor-El did not wish to risk his son's life in an untried rocket, so first launched the family's pet dog into space in the model rocket.

Krypto appears at random times throughout the stories, both in Smallville and Metropolis, and even out in deep space, his favorite romping grounds. His longevity speaks well for Superman's probable lifespan, since nothing in the text has ever indicated Kryptonian dogs have a lifespan greater than their earthly equivalents.

Krypto was followed with the introduction of a more significant character in the chronicles, Superman's cousin Kara, known to the world as Supergirl. First appearing in May of 1959, Supergirl would quickly develop an origin almost as complex as Superman's. Here an entire city survived the destruction of Krypton, a bubble of air somehow clinging to this spaceborne fragment. Later retellings added an airtight "weather dome" which really contained the air.

Among the residents of this so-called Argo City were Zor-El and his wife Alura. Zor-El, it should be clear, was the younger brother of Jor-El. Some years after the destruction of Krypton the inhabitants of Argo City discovered the chunk of planet on which they were riding through space was turning into Anti-Kryptonite, through some strange delayed reaction. Attempts were made to cover the ground beneath them with lead, to block the deadly radiation, but like their parent planet before them, the space-faring people of Argo City realized they were doomed.

Imitating his illustrious brother, Zor-El placed his daughter, a teenager, in a rocket, and sent her off to Earth. After being found by Superman, she adopted the identity of Linda Lee. Supergirl operated in secret for years, until Superman judged her training period to be complete, and revealed her existence to an amazed and delighted world in February 1962.

The stream of tragedy has always run deep in the Superman legend. Beginning as it did with the deaths of billions of people, how could it be otherwise? Curiously, in this period of stories we might now view as increasingly silly, that tragic theme was developed more and more, with the repeated emphasis on Krypton, and Superman's lost heritage. The role of Superman as a "stranger in a strange land" was introduced and developed during this time. Never mind the fact he had been raised as a human being, with all the human values of his Bible-belt upbringing. Superman increasingly longed for the lost life of Krypton. He swore by the planet's name ("Great Krypton!") and, in his Fortress of Solitude, built a huge shrine to the memory of his parents and planet.

Then, too, there was Kandor. The original capital of the world government of Krypton (replaced by Kryptonopolis, birthplace of the Babe of Steel), Kandor was a city of some one billion inhabitants, reduced to the size of a phone book and imprisoned in a bottle by the evil alien Brainiac. Years later, when Brainiac came to Earth and began stealing our major cities, Superman discovered this remnant of his heritage, complete with thriving population, and set it in a place of honor in his arctic Fortress, promising the Kandorians he would spare no effort in discovering a way to restore them to full size.

Later, when Jimmy Olsen was granted three wishes by a magical source, he elected to use one to send Superman back for a brief visit to Krypton. Not wanting his super-friend to know what he was planning, Jimmy typed his wish, rather than speaking it aloud. His intent was for Superman to "meet his parents," but upon arriving on Krypton Superman found Lara about to marry someone else, and in a precursor to *Back to the Future*, was forced to engineer the circumstances under which his parents would meet and marry. Jimmy, it seems, inadvertently typed "mate" instead of "meet."

Over the years almost everyone ended up on Krypton, in one way or another. And, in their shared title, *World's Finest Comics*, Superman and Batman had a few adventures in the shrunken city of Kandor, in the long years before Superman found a way to finally keep his promise and restore the city to full size. In one such adventure, set upon by Luthor's thugs, Superman defended himself against a half dozen toughs. Having no powers in the Kryptonian environment of Kandor, Superman nevertheless held his own, prompting one of the thugs to comment, "Even without his super-powers, this guy's tough!" The readers never doubted he would be.

During this stretch of adventures Superman's chroniclers also included noted science-fiction writers Edmond Hamilton and Otto Binder. It was Binder who added Supergirl and Brainiac to the legend and created one of the best of the Superboy stories of the period, one which would spin off a character into the legend of the adult Superman.

Created as a Frankenstein Monster analog, the first creature to be called "Bizarro" was an imperfect duplicate of the Boy of Steel, born in a laboratory accident. A scientist friend of Superboy's was trying to create artificial uranium, for use in atomic medicine. His attempts were failures, however, as his "duplicator ray" produced uranium that was not radioactive. The machine was jostled, at one point, and Superboy himself was exposed to the rays. The machine exploded, but the result of the exposure was an almost crystalline version of the young hero, white-faced and chisel-featured, with an unruly mop of coarse black hair.

As typical of many Superboy stories of the time this was a much-modified retelling of a tale originally presented in the Superman newspaper strip. Many stories from that source were watered down and presented in the comic books themselves.

Meanwhile, Superman's story continued to expand backwards into his past. As Lana Lang was eventually brought forward into the Superman legend, so too were other well-known characters carried back into the early adventures. The villainous Luthor was revealed, in 1960, to have once been Superboy's friend, back in Smallville. His hatred of the Man of Steel grew out of events of those younger days. His first name, Lex, was revealed in this story, some twenty years after his debut.

Smallville, as it developed over the years, became a busy place, as comic realities go. The *World's Finest* teaming of Superman and Batman was shown to have had its genesis in Smallville, when Thomas and Martha Wayne passed through with their son Bruce. This meeting occurred more than once, as stories were told and retold to develop the legend further. In one version young Bruce even donned a bat-like costume, calling himself the Flying Fox, and briefly battling crime in Smallville.

The 1960s came as hard times for Superman. A time of cultural upheaval for America and the world, the clear-cut, some might say simpleminded, good-versus-evil philosophies of Superman stories seemed hoary indeed. Attempts to address the world situation seemed no more than trendy throwaways, often as not missing the mark by some distance. Comic books have always followed society's fads, trying as best they could to cash in on popular movements. But for Superman, somehow, the topicality seemed more a failed attempt to shoehorn the character into a mold for which he was not intended.

Clark Kent could grow long sideburns, and Lois Lane could turn black to explore the inner city experience of Metropolis, but somehow it was all too hard to believe. The Metropolis of Superman simply did not seem a place that could have ghettoes or poor people, of any color. Too long the city had been the gleaming gemstone in the diadem of DC's imaginary cities. New York without the graffiti, Chicago without the political machine, Los Angeles without the smog.

The elements of Superman's tragic past were played up during the sixties and seventies, but with an alienating effect. The pining for Krypton became almost offensive, each exclamation of "Great Krypton!" almost an insult to the world which had been Superman's home for most of his life. A downward spiral was begun, and it seemed unlikely much could be done to alter its course towards oblivion.

The legend continued to grow with retroactive revisionism. As the planet Krypton was moved about in space, relocating to positions further and further from Earth at the discretion of a succession of writers and editors, more and more clever and complex justifications were needed to get that tiny rocket across the gulf of space to its target. In 1938 it was enough that Jor-L had built a fairly large Fourth of July skyrocket, into which he placed his son, and which he simply pointed at Earth. No one quibbled distance or trajectory. Wonderment was king over all, and the cruel master of logic could be kept at bay if a story was paced fast enough. With an entire planet about to blow up around them, even the canniest reader could be forgiven for easily accepting Siegel's simplistic vision of space-navigation.

By the 1970s the rocket was equipped with a "star drive," and the warp, or rip in space, that this strange engine opened also accounted for a veritable deluge of Kryptonian artifacts which followed Superman to Earth. By then so much debris of the explosion had arrived in the solar system it sometimes seemed the destruction of Krypton must have been uni-directional, and all aimed at Earth. By having the tiny rocket generate a kind of mini–black-hole, a whirlpool in space, later writers were able to justify much that had gone before.

In another revision the rocket was made to explode upon arrival on Earth, before the effects of solar radiation rendered the metal, plastic, and glass invulnerable. This explosion was used to create the two nearly perfectly circular pieces of super-glass for Clark to use in his spectacles. Someone had finally realized Clark would not be able to cut the glass with his fingernail, however super the nail might be. To have him do so was like having a normal man cut regular glass with his normal fingernail.

In a final attempt to update the image, Clark Kent finally left the *Daily Planet*. The paper had been bought by Morgan Edge, a cross between Rupert Murdoch and Don Corleone. Swallowed whole by Edge's Galaxy Communications the, venerable *Planet* became only a tiny cog in a great media empire, and Clark Kent found himself a TV journalist and anchorman for WGBS. With blow-dried hair and wide, flashy ties, the "new" Clark seemed a far cry from the creation of Siegel and Shuster. And for many the concept of Clark as a TV personality seemed flawed from the start. If, say, Peter Jennings was secretly Superman, how could he cover a live story of a natural disaster or terrorist hijacking, and still do his chosen duty as Superman? Clark's job as a newspaper reporter gave him exactly the mobility he needed to simultaneously cover fast-breaking stories and save the day as Superman. Being on camera served instead to curtail his much-needed freedom.

During this era, all too briefly, another comic book legend entered the Superman picture. Jack Kirby had been as much a founding father of the industry as Siegel and Shuster, and in the almost half-century of his career had created or helped to create a troupe of characters with appeal almost as lasting as Superman's.

He was approached to work on a revamping for Superman but, according to Kirby, preferred to work more peripherally, pointing the way, rather than actually steering the flagship book. He took on a supporting title in the Superman Family, *Superman's Pal, Jimmy Olsen*. Both Lois and Jimmy had had their own books since the fifties, and into the *Olsen* title, beginning with #133, October 1970, Kirby poured a major helping of his astonishing creative genius. The result was an almost staccato burst of brilliance in a previously pedestrian title. The stories in *Jimmy Olsen* had never been less than the Superman stories they really were, but under Kirby's tutelage the character jumped feet first into the Age of Aquarius.

Kirby resurrected the Newsboy Legion, characters he had created with Joe Simon in the 1940s, and with them sent Jimmy on a wild roller coaster ride through an almost hallucinogenic vision of the counterculture world of the late sixties and early seventies. Here were the Hairies, a quasi-tribal group of hippie/bikers who dwelled in an arboreal city in the Wild Area. Here was The Project, a super-secret DNA experiment that produced genetically altered super-creatures of all shapes and sizes, including the core group of special agents, the DNAliens. Here, too, was the Mountain of Judgment, a motorized colossus sent roaring across the countryside on a mission of arcane mystery. Kirby threw away concepts in three panels that a less gifted writer would have labored over for three or four books.

In *The Forever People* Kirby introduced Superman to the Gods of New Genesis. For the first time the Man of Tomorrow encountered beings who were truly his equals, and perhaps, because of their legitimate claim to godhood, even his betters.

Sadly, this surge of creativity was short-lived. Kirby's main interest and drive was directed toward his Fourth World cycle, The New Gods, The Forever People, and Mister Miracle. This intricately woven tapestry of a New Ragnarok, a truly Cosmic War of beings no less than Gods, occupied most of even Kirby's giant talent. In time his turn on *Jimmy Olsen* was ended. He had contributed Morgan Edge to the scheme of things, but not enough of his effect reached the other titles. Superman still looked to be in serious trouble.

Then writer Dennis O'Neil pinpointed what he believed to be the major flaw in Superman. The Man of Tomorrow had simply become too powerful. O'Neil claimed it was impossible to do exciting, dynamic stories with a being so awesome he could potentially annihilate an entire alien race simply by listening hard. With editor Julius Schwartz and longtime artist Curt Swan, O'Neil set about reshaping the Super-man character.

It would have been difficult to select a better team. Schwartz was already one of the Grand Old Men of both comic books and science fiction. His career was as long as Superman's, and he was already known for revamping established characters. His directions for the book had been as innovative as the structure would allow. Superman was a character trap-ped within his own legend, but Schwartz had done some good work with him nonetheless.

Swan had begun drawing Superman in the mid-1950s, his work on Superman was among the best, and his clean, realistic style had become more closely identified with the Man of Steel than almost any other inheritor of Shuster's mantle. O'Neil was an award-win-ning writer who had already worked a stun-ning revitalization of DC's *Green Lantern* series and an equally successful series of dynamic Batman stories that recaptured much of the original power of that much-maligned character.

His approach to Superman was simple enough: strip the character of a third of his power. This was accomplished, beginning in the January, 1971 *Superman*, #233, by a time-tested method, the creation of a duplicate Superman. Into this ersatz creature went one third of Superman's power, and out of the loss came a more manageable hero. Luckily for the de-powered Superman, all the kryptonite on Earth was turned to harmless iron by a chain reaction generated in the same accident that created the double. By the end of this cycle the duplicate had drained off a full half of the Man of Steel's powers.

Schwartz humanized Clark Kent somewhat, letting him grow his sideburns and wear suits of a color other than blue. He also set about integrating Superman more fully into the "DC Universe." Largely because of the cohesive, cross-referenced "reality" created by Marvel Comics, readers everywhere were demanding more complex and sustained backgrounds for the characters and stories. Weisinger had created a coherent cross-continuity within the individual Superman titles. Schwartz now set about spreading that continuity.

After O'Neil departed, Superman quickly regained his lost powers. After all, there were many who insisted his powers, as with any Kryptonian, were infinite, and two-thirds of infinity is, well, still infinity. (This infinite reading to Superman's powers had the unfor-tunate side effect of implying that Krypto and Beppo the super monkey were just as power-ful as Superman, but since neither appeared much anymore, the potential problem was neatly side-stepped.)

By the beginning of the eighties another re-evaluation was in progress. Managing editor Dick Giordano and publisher Jenette Kahn realized the whole DC line had become hope-lessly convoluted. A massive house-cleaning was called for.

It was to be done in a twelve-part series without the preceding history. The title was *Crisis on Infinite Earths*, and it was nothing less than a calculated massacre. The readers were left gasping for breath. And, more importantly, they were primed for change. It was time to do another "fix" on Superman. The most sweep-ing "fix" of all. Dick Giordano approached me and, in close collaboration with editors Mike Carlin and Andrew Helfer, I set up the parameters of a "new" Superman.

He debuted in 1986, and in point of fact, he wasn't "new" at all. He was thematically closer to the Superman of Siegel and Shuster than he had been for decades. Gone were the godlike powers. Gone too was his career as Superboy. Krypton was redesigned and redefined. Jor-El and Lara looked different. Ma and Pa Kent were younger when they found the baby. They told the world he was their natural child, rather than going through the elaborate ritual of adoption.

Again, as in the very beginning, he grew to manhood without taking on the identity of Superboy. In fact, because in this version his super-powers developed slowly, as his Krypto-nian cells absorbed solar radiation over the years, young Clark felt no need to hide his abilities. When first seen, at age eighteen, he had become champion of the Smallville High football team, much to the chagrin of the other players. Seeing the distress of Clark's team-mates prompted Pa Kent to tell his son the true story of his beginnings, and impress upon Clark that he must never use his great gifts to make himself superior to others, only, and always, to help them.

Humbled by Pa's words, Clark resolved to set out into the world and assume the responsibilities inherent in his powers—but secretly. He did not want the world to know there was a "guardian angel" looking out for their welfare.

Only after he was forced to act openly to save a crashing space-plane at Metropolis Airport did Clark return to Smallville and, with the help of Ma and Pa Kent, create the costumed identity of Superman. Then, too, did he first conceive of altering his appearance as Clark, ending with the traditional slicked-back hair and horn-rimmed spectacles.

In a major philosophical inversion, Clark Kent had become the "real" character, who posed as Superman, instead of the reverse. Further, no one on Earth, save Ma and Pa Kent, had even the slightest inkling of Superman's dual identity. Freed of the driving compulsion to pretend he wasn't Superman, Clark was able to become a more dynamic character in his own right. He proudly displayed his football trophies in his Metropolitan apartment, and even kept a Nautilus machine to explain his magnificent physique.

Lois, too, was free to become the intelligent, self-assured character she'd been almost fifty years before. With no one suspecting Superman's dual identity, Lois needed to waste no more time trying to reveal it.

The *Daily Planet* was restored to its original place in the chronicles. Perry White was introduced as managing editor, rather than editor-in-chief, making more logical his close relationship with his reporters.

Perhaps the biggest change of all was born out of fellow writer Marv Wolfman's suggested "fix" for Lex Luthor. No longer a mad scientist, Luthor became a super-businessman, the most powerful man in Metropolis, until Superman arrived. His need to destroy the Man of Steel was due to the much more human motivation of jealousy. Superman cost Luthor his position in the world. Like the Salieri of *Amadeus*, recognizing the genius of Mozart, Luthor knew that to be Number One again he must eliminate the competition. Unlike Salieri, Luthor cannot acknowledge that Superman is truly his better, and this is why he must always fail.

And so Superman takes flight into his second half-century. He'd weathered some rough seas in the first five decades of his life. He'd flown high, higher than any other character. But he'd also sunk low. He'd gloried in dynamic, exciting stories, and he'd wallowed in silliness and pretension. He'd been a proud emblem of the nation, and he'd been embarrassed by the nation's excesses. Campy, cultish, classic.

All these things and more, he'd been. But above all, he'd always been Superman.

And he always will be.

GATHERING THE GREATEST

Assembling *The Greatest Superman Stories Ever Told* is an honor and a privilege, but taking on such a task is really asking for trouble. The Man of Steel isn't simply more powerful than a locomotive—he's got about as much momentum as a Japanese Bullet train, and everybody's got his or her own idea as to what should be incorporated into such a project. No matter how many stories we include, we're going to miss several of your favorites.

This makes sense. There were something in the neighborhood of 5,000 Superman stories in the past fifty years, not counting "crossover" appearances in other characters' stories. Being the seminal comic book super-hero, Superman gave birth to an entire type of entertainment that previously was unavailable.

I suspect the stories each of us finds most enjoyable are those that represent the best of the material published when we were in our preadolescent years. Nostalgia plays heavily in our memories, and Superman—like virtually all comic book features created in the United States during its early decades—was perceived by its original editors as children's entertainment.

In working on this book, we were pleased to discover that most of the stories suggested for inclusion truly stand the test of time: they are as entertaining today as they were back when first they were published. Indeed, the only type of story that didn't live up to expectation was the "origin" story in which a major character was introduced or, in many cases (villain Lex Luthor comes to mind), the motivation behind the character's existence first was revealed. What we remember about these stories are the events and not the surrounding context.

This led us to our first and most important criterion in selecting the stories in this book: we wanted to present the greatest stories, and not necessarily the most significant stories from the standpoint of continuity.

The goal of *The Greatest Superman Stories Ever Told* is to represent the best of the entire range of stories during Superman's first fifty years.

Artistically, we chose to divide Superman's career into four distinctive "eras." We started with the initial Joe Shuster period, with its lighter lines and coy touches. A number of artists contributed to the feature during this period—in addition to Shuster, the work of Jack Burnley, John Sikela and Wayne Boring dominated the series.

The end of World War II brought about the Wayne Boring period, with its more heroic posturing and dynamic cityscapes. Al Plastino, Dick Sprang, George Papp and others joined Boring in providing the look and feel to this period.

The 1960s brought another look to the feature, as the clean, slick lines of Curt Swan dominated the appearance of The Man of Steel. Of all the major Superman artists, Swan had—and continues to have—the most enduring impact on how we see the character, joined by such talents as Ross Andru, Jose Luis Garcia-Lopez, and Neal Adams.

1986 saw a complete overhaul on the Superman myth, with John Byrne's action-packed work to be found on two of the three monthly Superman titles during the first two post-revision years. His friend and collaborator, Jerry Ordway, handles Superman's third monthly title.

Having divided the Superman legend into four artistic eras, it became important to represent as many of the major supporting characters as possible. We attempted to illustrate the breadth of the Superman myth (Superboy, Smallville, the Fortress, Bizarros) as well as certain concepts in the rest of the DC Universe that had an equally significant impact.

At this point, I should offer a word of warning. Periodically, the Superman editors and creators would do a bit of "house-cleaning" and revise or even ignore sundry elements in the continuity. Interestingly, in the late 1950s then-editor Mort Weisinger kept true to his own continuity but would publish contradictory sagas as "imaginary stories," many of which appear in this book. Readers did not take continuity as religiously back then as they do today, and while the device might seem silly by today's standards, many of the most enduring Superman sagas of this period were "imaginary stories."

Don't get confused by this device, as when the entire Superman continuity was revised in 1986, all previous tales retroactively became "imaginary stories."

In selecting the greatest Superman stories ever told, we also kept an eye on previous reprint projects: we attempted to avoid including stories that have been reprinted a great many times in the past. The seminal two-part story from *Action Comics* #1 and #2, for example, first was reprinted several months later in *Superman* #1 and has been put to ink at least a dozen times since. Quite a number of the stories included in *The Greatest Superman Stories Ever Told* appear for the second time anywhere—many others never before have been reprinted in color.

We decided to allow nominations from all of Superman's various comic *book* appearances, no matter which publication the story might have come from. I say this because nearly all the stories herein are from either *Superman* or *Action Comics*; believe me, we considered stories from *Superman's Pal Jimmy Olsen, Superman's Girl Friend Lois Lane, World's Finest Comics*, and from the many other titles that featured The Man of Steel and his cohorts.

We were forced to eliminate from consideration the Superman newspaper strip, as we do not have high-quality reproduction material available. That's a shame, as the original long-running newspaper series featured some great stories, and have not been seen in this form in several decades. However, a number of the stories in this volume, including "The Battle with Bizarro" and "The Girl from Superman's Past," first were written for the newspaper strip and later were adapted into comics form (even if they were actually *published* in comic book form first).

Having established an organizational procedure, we selected a nominating committee of creators, historians, and longtime fans to suggest stories.

Man of Steel creators Jerry Siegel and Joe Shuster, of course, headed our list. Unfortunately, Joe was in poor health and could not offer his suggestions. Jerry, however, was quick and forthcoming, making some interesting and unique selections.

Longtime DC Comics editor Julius Schwartz, who edited Superman from 1970 until the 1986 revitalization, joined our committee. Julie is the man who—appropriately—resurrected the super-hero from its own post-War depression, rejuvenating such renowned features as Batman, The Flash, Green Lantern, The Atom, Hawkman, and the Justice League (nee Society) of America. He also is responsible for training a great many of the most formidable writers and artists to apply their talents to this medium during the past three generations.

Artist Curt Swan, another committee member, has been among the prime Superman pencillers for the past thirty years. Curt has drawn more Superman pages than any other artist; I would guess that when people see a drawing of Superman in their mind's eye, 90 percent of them see a Superman that was drawn by Curt Swan.

As for our historians, Dr. Jerry Bails has dedicated much of his free time to the scholarly study of comic books, indexing the careers of several armies of writers, artists and editors. Jerry is also one of the founding fathers of comic art fandom, and is responsible (along-with fan-turned-comics-writer Roy Thomas) for encouraging Julie Schwartz in his work at reviving many of the classic 1940s super-heroes and themes.

Michael L. Fleisher is best known for his work as a comics writer (Jonah Hex, Conan the Barbarian, The Spectre, and The Warlord, among many other characters), but his credits also include researching and authoring definitive looks at the lives of Superman, Batman and Wonder Woman. This work led Michael to spend years in the DC library reading (and taking notes on) virtually every Superman story published during The Man of Steel's first three decades. His *The Great Superman Book* was published by Warner Books (DC's sister-company) on the occasion of Superman's fortieth anniversary.

Don Rosa rounds out our list of historians. Today best known for his work writing and drawing new Uncle Scrooge stories (following in Carl Barks' webprints is an act of incredible courage), for years Don has written—and continues to write—the definitive question-and-answer column on comics history, presently appearing in *Amazing Heroes* magazine.

I think that in order to excel in any creative medium, you must have a true appreciation for the form. In this, Jenette Kahn sets the standard for the entire staff: long before she was appointed DC Comics' president and publisher, Jenette was a dedicated comics enthusiast. She heads our list of comics fans.

Elizabeth Smith Flynn has been active in organized comics fandom for more than a decade, and had written a handful of Superman stories for editor Julie Schwartz in the mid-1970s while attending Columbia University in New York.

Perhaps the most vocal of the Superman fans are those who are dedicated to the futuristic Legion of Super-Heroes, of which Superboy was a member (back when Superboy was an aspect of the Superman continuity). Harry Broertjes was a co-founder of Legion fandom; to pay the rent, Harry is on the editorial staff of *The Miami Herald*.

Al and Barbara Shroeder were among the many extremely vocal Superman fans who met through editor Schwartz's letter columns; unlike the rest of their contemporaries, Al and Barb got married and raised a family—of future comics fans, no doubt.

Armed with the committee's nominations, Robert Greenberger and I met with John Byrne to select the line-up, following the criteria outlined above. Since I'm in the biography-section of this treatise, Robert is a member of DC Comics' editorial staff, where he serves as editor of several titles, a member of the Development team, and the Official House Historian.

Once the three of us came up with a master list, we had to eliminate certain stories because high-quality reproduction material could not be located, or the only reproduction material available was heavily edited. At all times, we have attempted to present these stories as they had originally appeared.

The stories surviving the final cut were then re-colored by a squadron of the top colorists available, taking advantage of the expanded color palette available for use on the whiter, thicker and more opaque Baxter-quality paper used in this book.

It is genuinely unfortunate that a number of major Superman contributors are not represented in this book. Writers and artists like Cary Bates, Jose Luis Garcia-Lopez, Neal Adams, Jerry Ordway, Marv Wolfman, Edmond Hamilton and Dennis O'Neil (to name but a few) had an enormous impact on the Superman saga; we deeply regret space did not allow us to include representations of their work.

It is equally unfortunate that we were unable to determine the writers of several stories in this volume. The concept of listing creative credits goes back to the earliest days of the medium, but across-the-board credits on virtually all stories became tradition only in the past two decades. Complete credits did not appear on the sundry Superman stories until the mid-1960s. Whereas it is fairly easy to determine the identity of the uncredited artists, it is impossible to determine the writers of these stories.

If we had ten times the page count, we still would not be able to represent fully the entire scope of the Superman legend—but within the confines of this, we've given it a good shot.

It is important to remember that the greater Superman myth includes the Fleischer/Paramount theatrical cartoons, the long-running radio show, two movie serials, six feature-length movies, several long-running television shows (including the various cartoon series), two different newspaper comic strips (plus guest appearances in a third), and thousands upon thousands of toys, merchandising items, novels, coloring and activity books, and magazines. But before all of this, during all of this, and after all of this, there was Superman— The Comic Book.

We hope *The Greatest Superman Stories Ever Told* will serve as the definitive starting point for any research, be it motivated by scholarly, nostalgic or merely entertainment desires.

Sit back and enjoy this, a mere sampling of *The Greatest Superman Stories Ever Told*.

—Mike Gold

(Active in the comics field for a mere one-fourth of Superman's fifty years, Mike Gold serves as DC Comics' Senior Editor/Director of Development.)

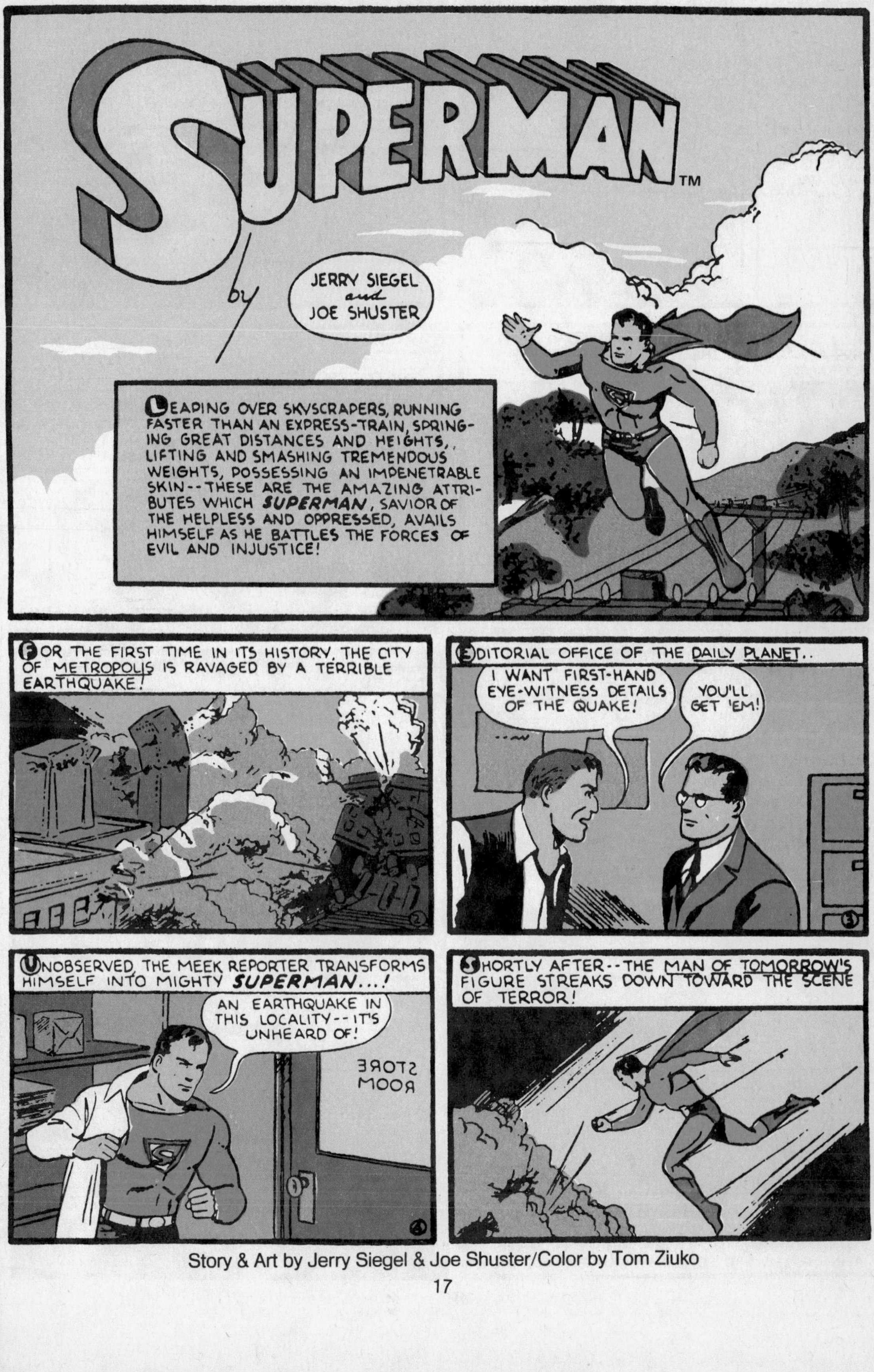
SUPERMAN™
by
JERRY SIEGEL and JOE SHUSTER
LEAPING OVER SKYSCRAPERS, RUNNING FASTER THAN AN EXPRESS-TRAIN, SPRINGING GREAT DISTANCES AND HEIGHTS, LIFTING AND SMASHING TREMENDOUS WEIGHTS, POSSESSING AN IMPENETRABLE SKIN--THESE ARE THE AMAZING ATTRIBUTES WHICH SUPERMAN, SAVIOR OF THE HELPLESS AND OPPRESSED, AVAILS HIMSELF AS HE BATTLES THE FORCES OF EVIL AND INJUSTICE!
FOR THE FIRST TIME IN ITS HISTORY, THE CITY OF METROPOLIS IS RAVAGED BY A TERRIBLE EARTHQUAKE!
EDITORIAL OFFICE OF THE DAILY PLANET..
I WANT FIRST-HAND EYE-WITNESS DETAILS OF THE QUAKE!
YOU'LL GET 'EM!
UNOBSERVED, THE MEEK REPORTER TRANSFORMS HIMSELF INTO MIGHTY SUPERMAN...!
AN EARTHQUAKE IN THIS LOCALITY--IT'S UNHEARD OF!
STORE ROOM
SHORTLY AFTER--THE MAN OF TOMORROW'S FIGURE STREAKS DOWN TOWARD THE SCENE OF TERROR!

Story & Art by Jerry Siegel & Joe Shuster/Color by Tom Ziuko

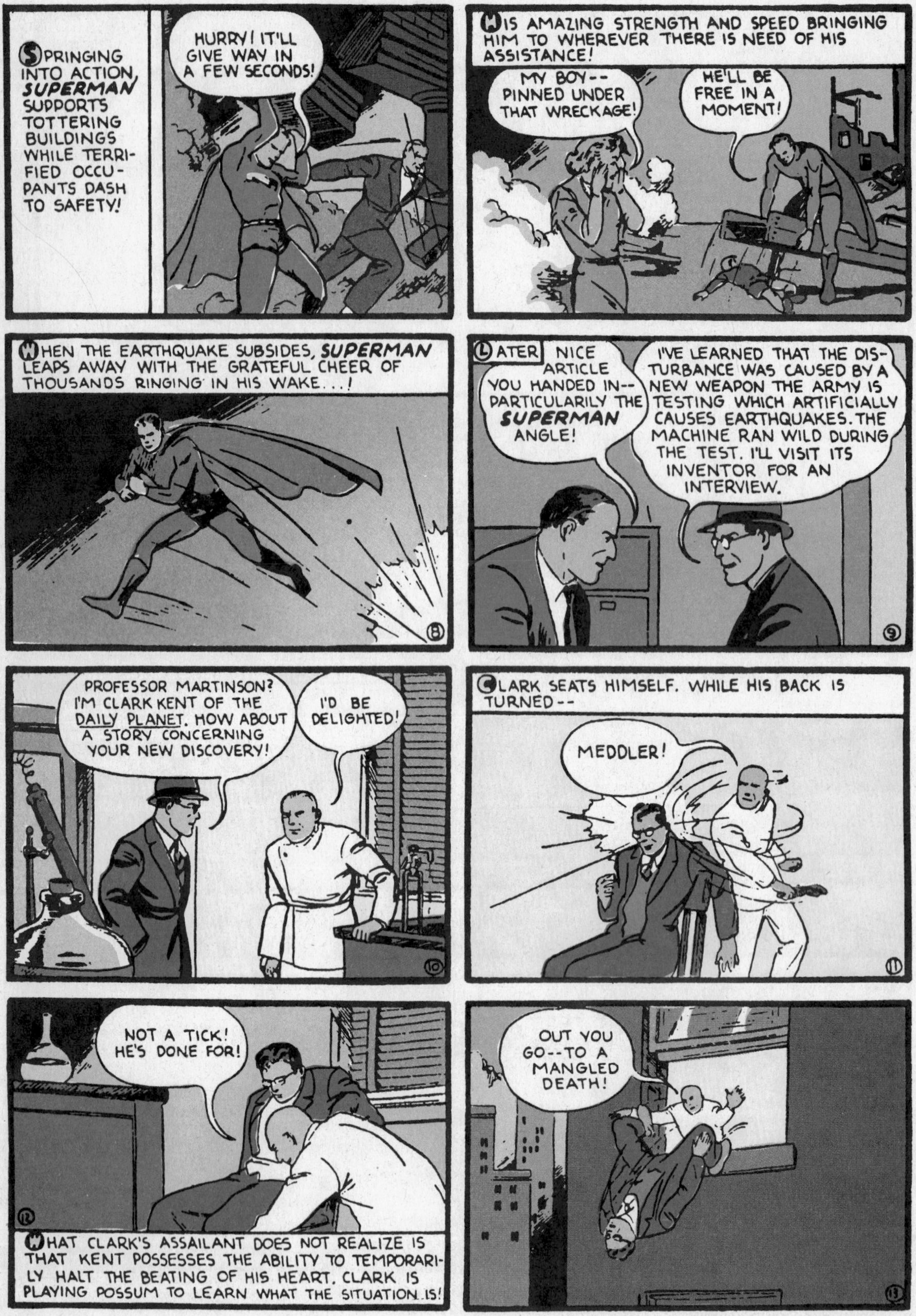

SPRINGING INTO ACTION, SUPERMAN SUPPORTS TOTTERING BUILDINGS WHILE TERRIFIED OCCUPANTS DASH TO SAFETY!
HURRY! IT'LL GIVE WAY IN A FEW SECONDS!
HIS AMAZING STRENGTH AND SPEED BRINGING HIM TO WHEREVER THERE IS NEED OF HIS ASSISTANCE!
MY BOY-- PINNED UNDER THAT WRECKAGE!
HE'LL BE FREE IN A MOMENT!
WHEN THE EARTHQUAKE SUBSIDES, SUPERMAN LEAPS AWAY WITH THE GRATEFUL CHEER OF THOUSANDS RINGING IN HIS WAKE...!
LATER
NICE ARTICLE YOU HANDED IN-- PARTICULARILY THE SUPERMAN ANGLE!
I'VE LEARNED THAT THE DISTURBANCE WAS CAUSED BY A NEW WEAPON THE ARMY IS TESTING WHICH ARTIFICIALLY CAUSES EARTHQUAKES. THE MACHINE RAN WILD DURING THE TEST. I'LL VISIT ITS INVENTOR FOR AN INTERVIEW.
PROFESSOR MARTINSON? I'M CLARK KENT OF THE DAILY PLANET. HOW ABOUT A STORY CONCERNING YOUR NEW DISCOVERY!
I'D BE DELIGHTED!
CLARK SEATS HIMSELF. WHILE HIS BACK IS TURNED--
MEDDLER!
NOT A TICK! HE'S DONE FOR!
WHAT CLARK'S ASSAILANT DOES NOT REALIZE IS THAT KENT POSSESSES THE ABILITY TO TEMPORARILY HALT THE BEATING OF HIS HEART. CLARK IS PLAYING POSSUM TO LEARN WHAT THE SITUATION IS!
OUT YOU GO--TO A MANGLED DEATH!

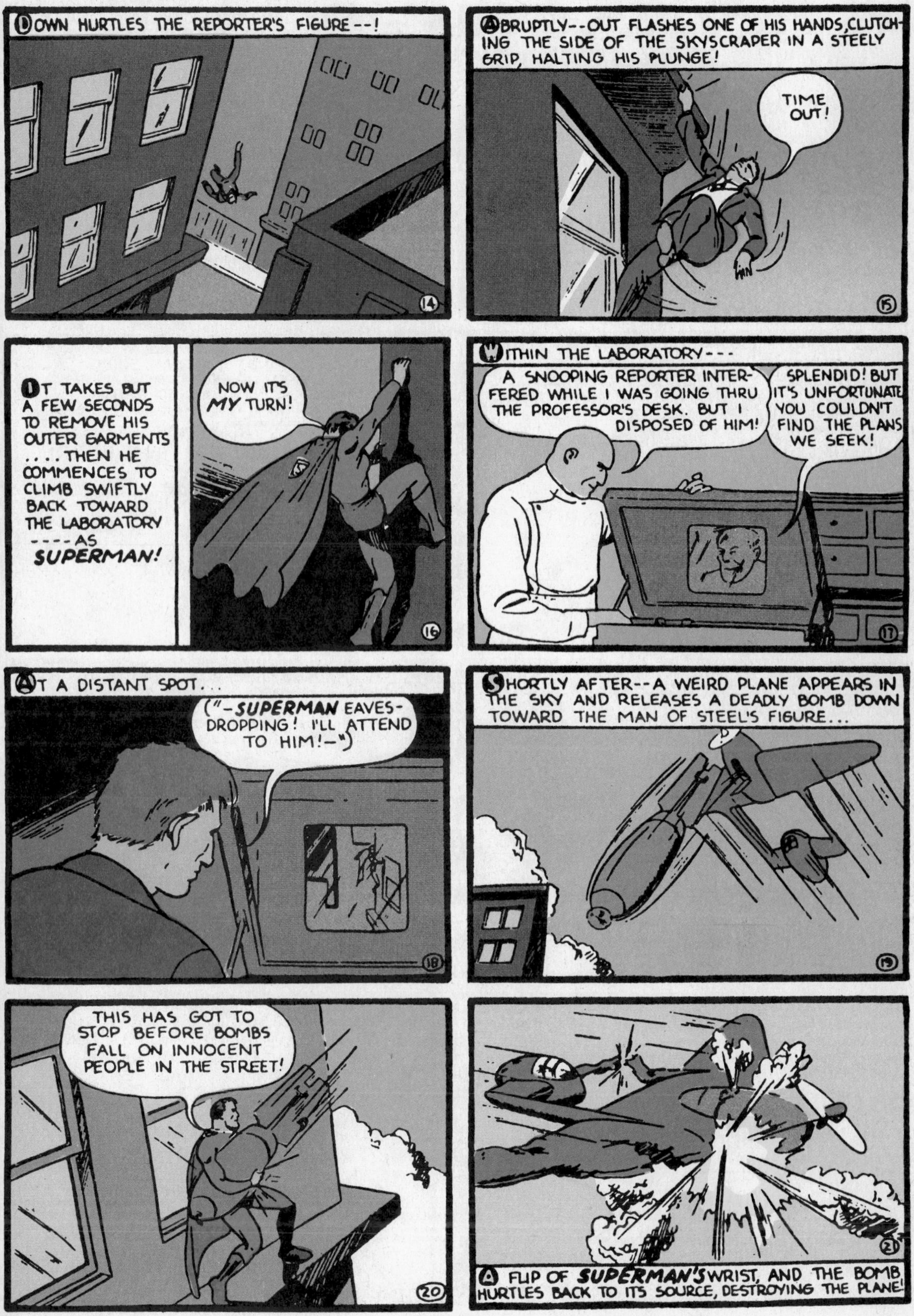
DOWN HURTLES THE REPORTER'S FIGURE--!
ABRUPTLY--OUT FLASHES ONE OF HIS HANDS, CLUTCHING THE SIDE OF THE SKYSCRAPER IN A STEELY GRIP, HALTING HIS PLUNGE!
TIME OUT!
IT TAKES BUT A FEW SECONDS TO REMOVE HIS OUTER GARMENTS ....THEN HE COMMENCES TO CLIMB SWIFTLY BACK TOWARD THE LABORATORY ----AS **SUPERMAN!**
NOW IT'S *MY* TURN!
WITHIN THE LABORATORY---
A SNOOPING REPORTER INTERFERED WHILE I WAS GOING THRU THE PROFESSOR'S DESK. BUT I DISPOSED OF HIM!
SPLENDID! BUT IT'S UNFORTUNATE YOU COULDN'T FIND THE PLANS WE SEEK!
AT A DISTANT SPOT...
("-**SUPERMAN** EAVES-DROPPING! I'LL ATTEND TO HIM!-")
SHORTLY AFTER--A WEIRD PLANE APPEARS IN THE SKY AND RELEASES A DEADLY BOMB DOWN TOWARD THE MAN OF STEEL'S FIGURE...
THIS HAS GOT TO STOP BEFORE BOMBS FALL ON INNOCENT PEOPLE IN THE STREET!
A FLIP OF **SUPERMAN'S** WRIST, AND THE BOMB HURTLES BACK TO ITS SOURCE, DESTROYING THE PLANE!

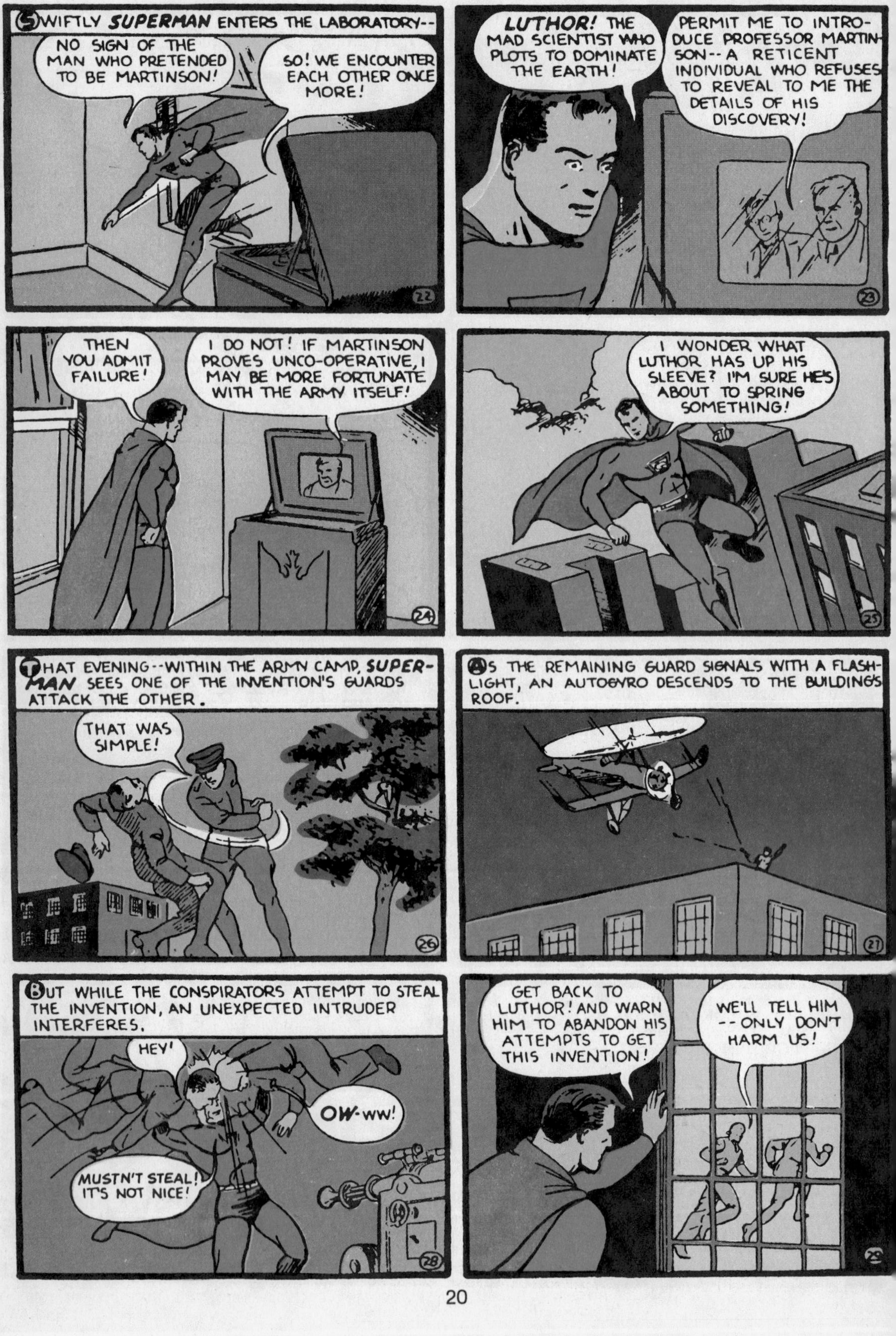
SWIFTLY SUPERMAN ENTERS THE LABORATORY--
NO SIGN OF THE MAN WHO PRETENDED TO BE MARTINSON!
SO! WE ENCOUNTER EACH OTHER ONCE MORE!
22
LUTHOR! THE MAD SCIENTIST WHO PLOTS TO DOMINATE THE EARTH!
PERMIT ME TO INTRODUCE PROFESSOR MARTINSON--A RETICENT INDIVIDUAL WHO REFUSES TO REVEAL TO ME THE DETAILS OF HIS DISCOVERY!
23
THEN YOU ADMIT FAILURE!
I DO NOT! IF MARTINSON PROVES UNCO-OPERATIVE, I MAY BE MORE FORTUNATE WITH THE ARMY ITSELF!
24
I WONDER WHAT LUTHOR HAS UP HIS SLEEVE? I'M SURE HE'S ABOUT TO SPRING SOMETHING!
25
THAT EVENING--WITHIN THE ARMY CAMP, SUPERMAN SEES ONE OF THE INVENTION'S GUARDS ATTACK THE OTHER.
THAT WAS SIMPLE!
26
AS THE REMAINING GUARD SIGNALS WITH A FLASH-LIGHT, AN AUTOGYRO DESCENDS TO THE BUILDING'S ROOF.
27
BUT WHILE THE CONSPIRATORS ATTEMPT TO STEAL THE INVENTION, AN UNEXPECTED INTRUDER INTERFERES.
HEY!
OW-WW!
MUSTN'T STEAL! IT'S NOT NICE!
28
GET BACK TO LUTHOR! AND WARN HIM TO ABANDON HIS ATTEMPTS TO GET THIS INVENTION!
WE'LL TELL HIM --ONLY DON'T HARM US!
29

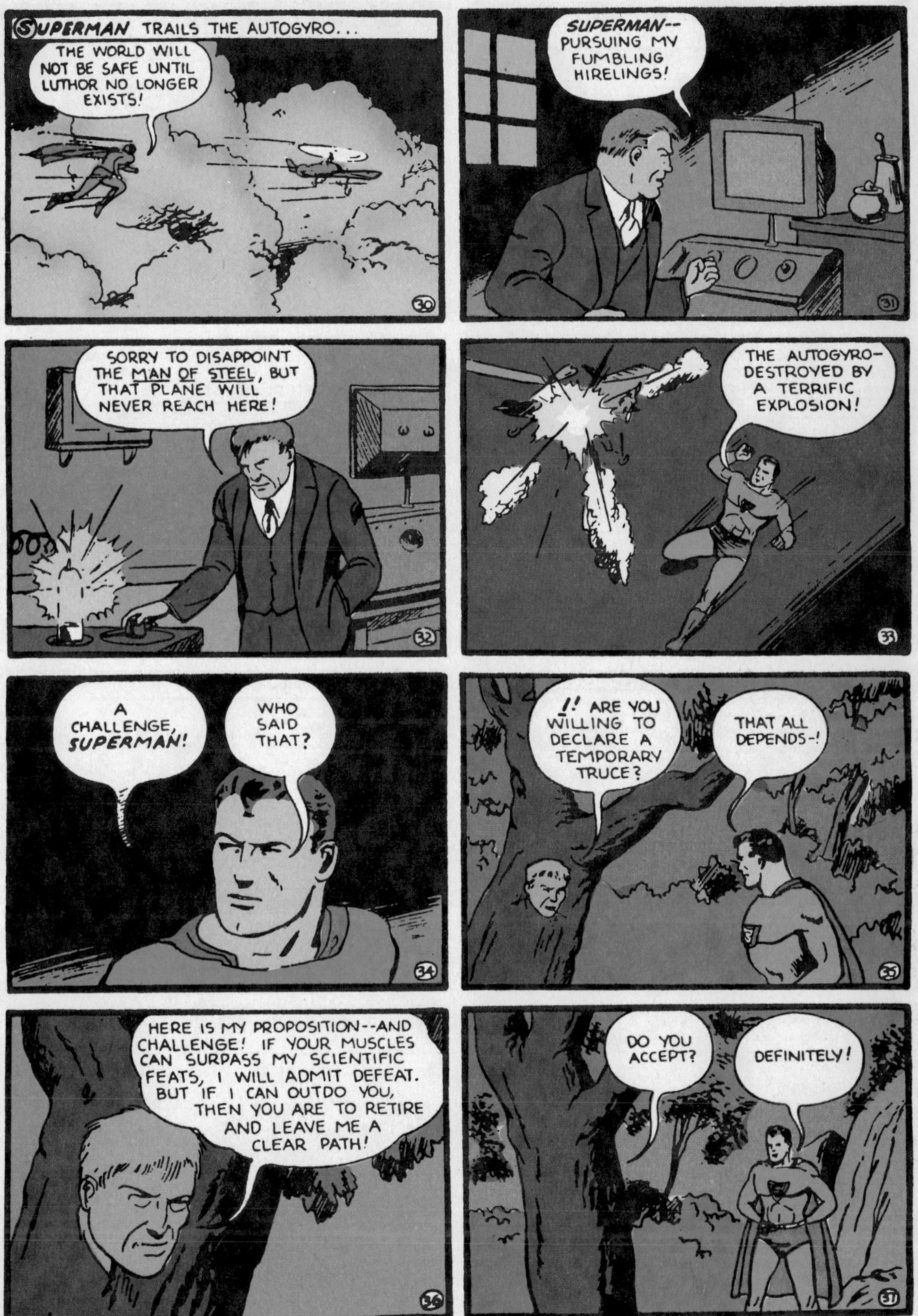
SUPERMAN TRAILS THE AUTOGYRO...
THE WORLD WILL NOT BE SAFE UNTIL LUTHOR NO LONGER EXISTS!
SUPERMAN-- PURSUING MY FUMBLING HIRELINGS!
SORRY TO DISAPPOINT THE MAN OF STEEL, BUT THAT PLANE WILL NEVER REACH HERE!
THE AUTOGYRO- DESTROYED BY A TERRIFIC EXPLOSION!
A CHALLENGE, SUPERMAN!
WHO SAID THAT?
!! ARE YOU WILLING TO DECLARE A TEMPORARY TRUCE?
THAT ALL DEPENDS-!
HERE IS MY PROPOSITION--AND CHALLENGE! IF YOUR MUSCLES CAN SURPASS MY SCIENTIFIC FEATS, I WILL ADMIT DEFEAT. BUT IF I CAN OUTDO YOU, THEN YOU ARE TO RETIRE AND LEAVE ME A CLEAR PATH!
DO YOU ACCEPT?
DEFINITELY!

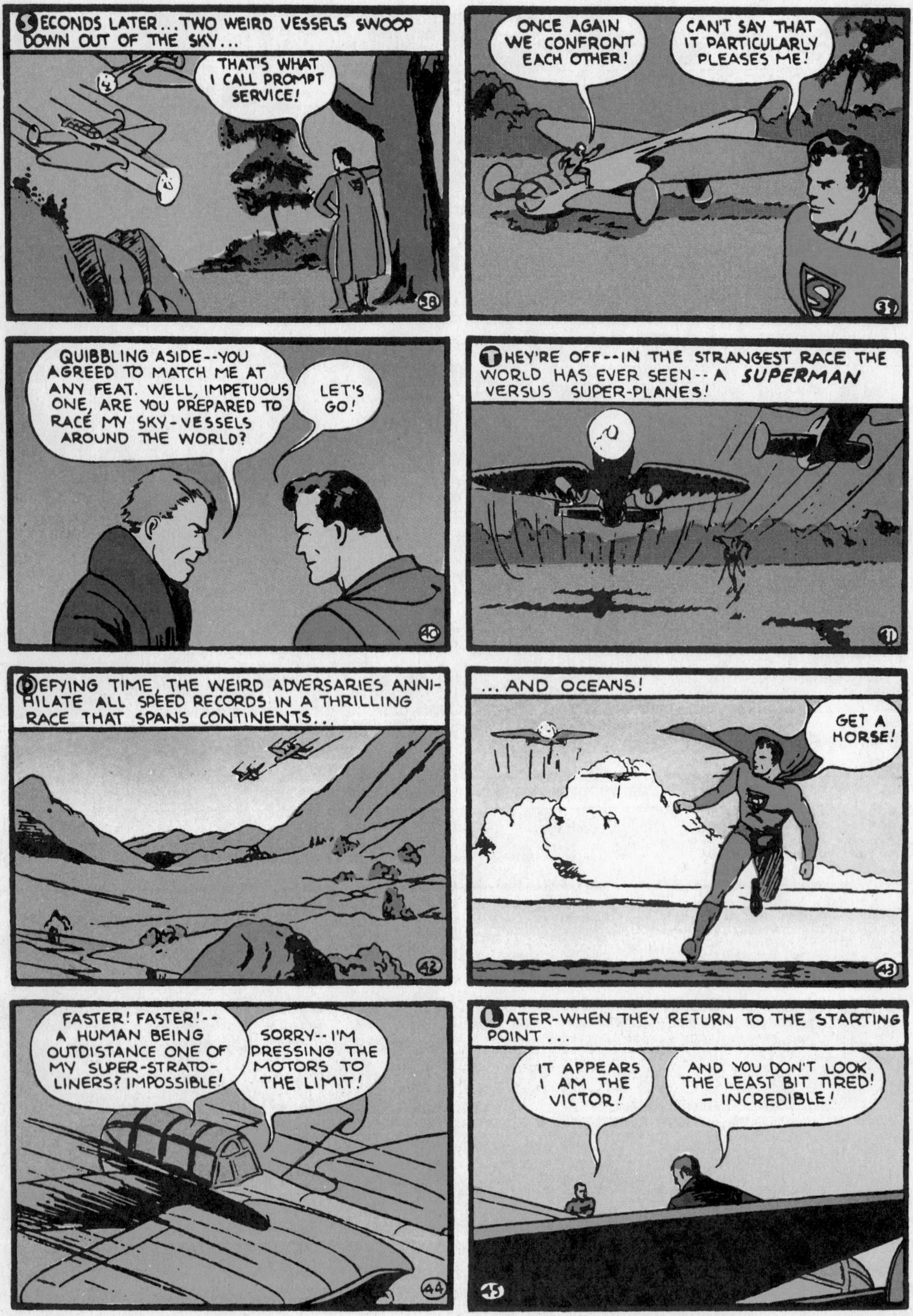
SECONDS LATER... TWO WEIRD VESSELS SWOOP DOWN OUT OF THE SKY...
THAT'S WHAT I CALL PROMPT SERVICE!
ONCE AGAIN WE CONFRONT EACH OTHER!
CAN'T SAY THAT IT PARTICULARLY PLEASES ME!
QUIBBLING ASIDE--YOU AGREED TO MATCH ME AT ANY FEAT. WELL, IMPETUOUS ONE, ARE YOU PREPARED TO RACE MY SKY-VESSELS AROUND THE WORLD?
LET'S GO!
THEY'RE OFF--IN THE STRANGEST RACE THE WORLD HAS EVER SEEN--A SUPERMAN VERSUS SUPER-PLANES!
DEFYING TIME, THE WEIRD ADVERSARIES ANNIHILATE ALL SPEED RECORDS IN A THRILLING RACE THAT SPANS CONTINENTS...
...AND OCEANS!
GET A HORSE!
FASTER! FASTER!--A HUMAN BEING OUTDISTANCE ONE OF MY SUPER-STRATO-LINERS? IMPOSSIBLE!
SORRY--I'M PRESSING THE MOTORS TO THE LIMIT!
LATER-WHEN THEY RETURN TO THE STARTING POINT...
IT APPEARS I AM THE VICTOR!
AND YOU DON'T LOOK THE LEAST BIT TIRED! - INCREDIBLE!

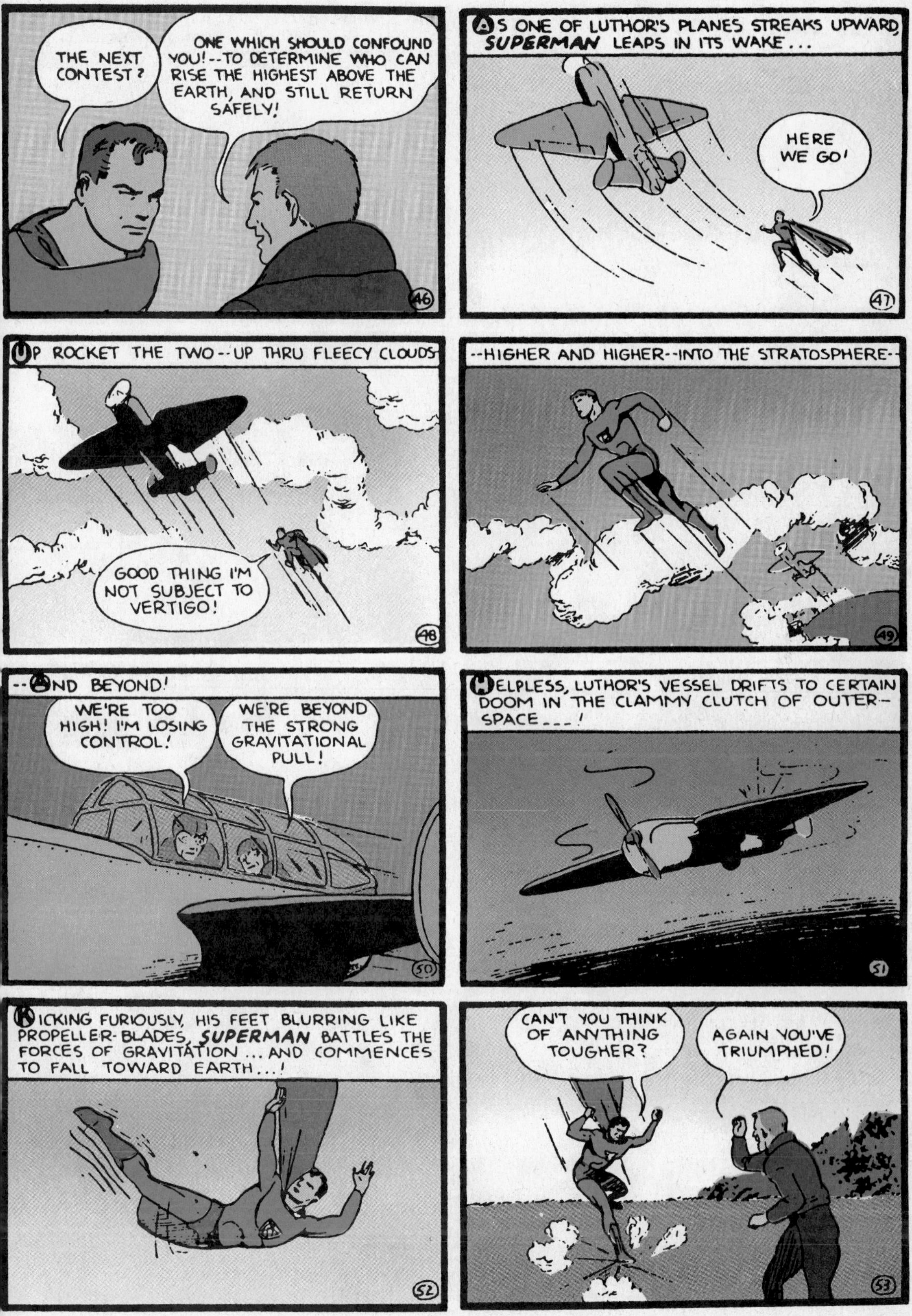
THE NEXT CONTEST?
ONE WHICH SHOULD CONFOUND YOU!--TO DETERMINE WHO CAN RISE THE HIGHEST ABOVE THE EARTH, AND STILL RETURN SAFELY!
AS ONE OF LUTHOR'S PLANES STREAKS UPWARD, SUPERMAN LEAPS IN ITS WAKE...
HERE WE GO!
UP ROCKET THE TWO--UP THRU FLEECY CLOUDS-
GOOD THING I'M NOT SUBJECT TO VERTIGO!
--HIGHER AND HIGHER--INTO THE STRATOSPHERE--
--AND BEYOND!
WE'RE TOO HIGH! I'M LOSING CONTROL!
WE'RE BEYOND THE STRONG GRAVITATIONAL PULL!
HELPLESS, LUTHOR'S VESSEL DRIFTS TO CERTAIN DOOM IN THE CLAMMY CLUTCH OF OUTER-SPACE---!
KICKING FURIOUSLY, HIS FEET BLURRING LIKE PROPELLER-BLADES, SUPERMAN BATTLES THE FORCES OF GRAVITATION ... AND COMMENCES TO FALL TOWARD EARTH...!
CAN'T YOU THINK OF ANYTHING TOUGHER?
AGAIN YOU'VE TRIUMPHED!

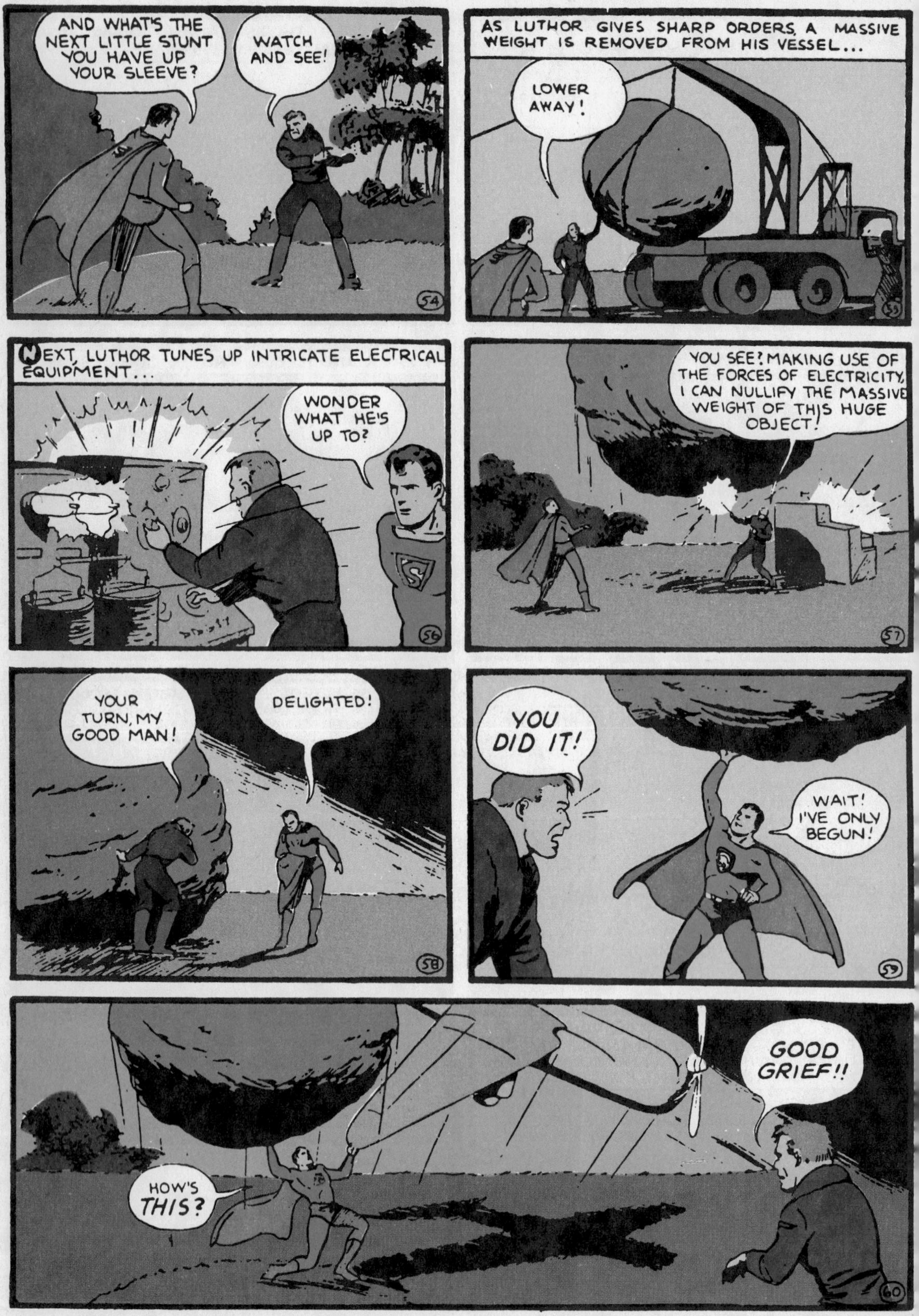
AND WHAT'S THE NEXT LITTLE STUNT YOU HAVE UP YOUR SLEEVE?
WATCH AND SEE!
54
AS LUTHOR GIVES SHARP ORDERS, A MASSIVE WEIGHT IS REMOVED FROM HIS VESSEL...
LOWER AWAY!
55
NEXT, LUTHOR TUNES UP INTRICATE ELECTRICAL EQUIPMENT...
WONDER WHAT HE'S UP TO?
56
YOU SEE? MAKING USE OF THE FORCES OF ELECTRICITY, I CAN NULLIFY THE MASSIVE WEIGHT OF THIS HUGE OBJECT!
57
YOUR TURN, MY GOOD MAN!
DELIGHTED!
58
YOU DID IT!
WAIT! I'VE ONLY BEGUN!
59
GOOD GRIEF!!
HOW'S THIS?
60

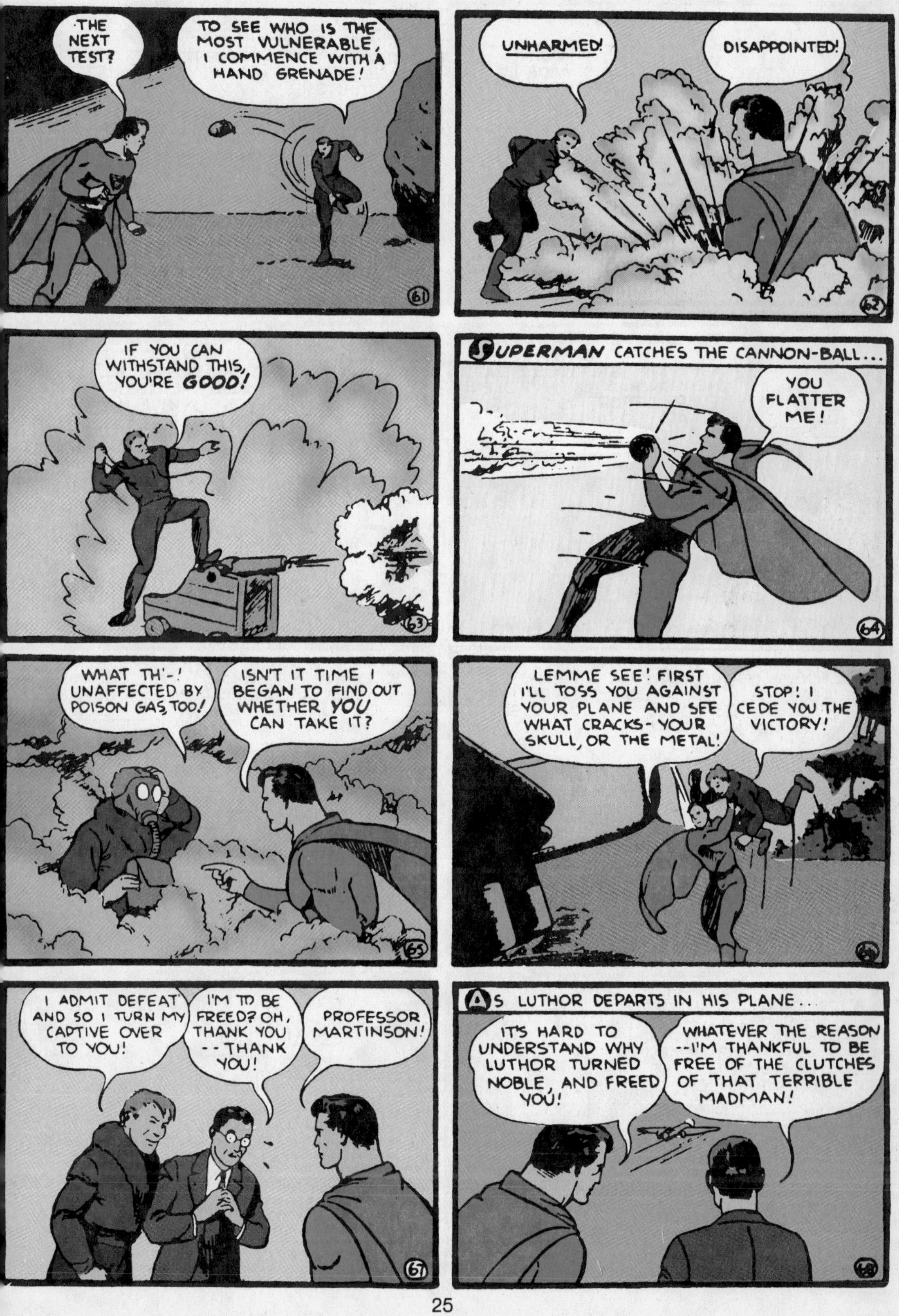
THE NEXT TEST?
TO SEE WHO IS THE MOST VULNERABLE, I COMMENCE WITH A HAND GRENADE!
61
UNHARMED!
DISAPPOINTED!
62
IF YOU CAN WITHSTAND THIS, YOU'RE GOOD!
63
SUPERMAN CATCHES THE CANNON-BALL...
YOU FLATTER ME!
64
WHAT TH'-! UNAFFECTED BY POISON GAS, TOO!
ISN'T IT TIME I BEGAN TO FIND OUT WHETHER YOU CAN TAKE IT?
65
LEMME SEE! FIRST I'LL TOSS YOU AGAINST YOUR PLANE AND SEE WHAT CRACKS- YOUR SKULL, OR THE METAL!
STOP! I CEDE YOU THE VICTORY!
I ADMIT DEFEAT AND SO I TURN MY CAPTIVE OVER TO YOU!
I'M TO BE FREED? OH, THANK YOU --THANK YOU!
PROFESSOR MARTINSON!
67
AS LUTHOR DEPARTS IN HIS PLANE..
IT'S HARD TO UNDERSTAND WHY LUTHOR TURNED NOBLE, AND FREED YOU!
WHATEVER THE REASON --I'M THANKFUL TO BE FREE OF THE CLUTCHES OF THAT TERRIBLE MADMAN!

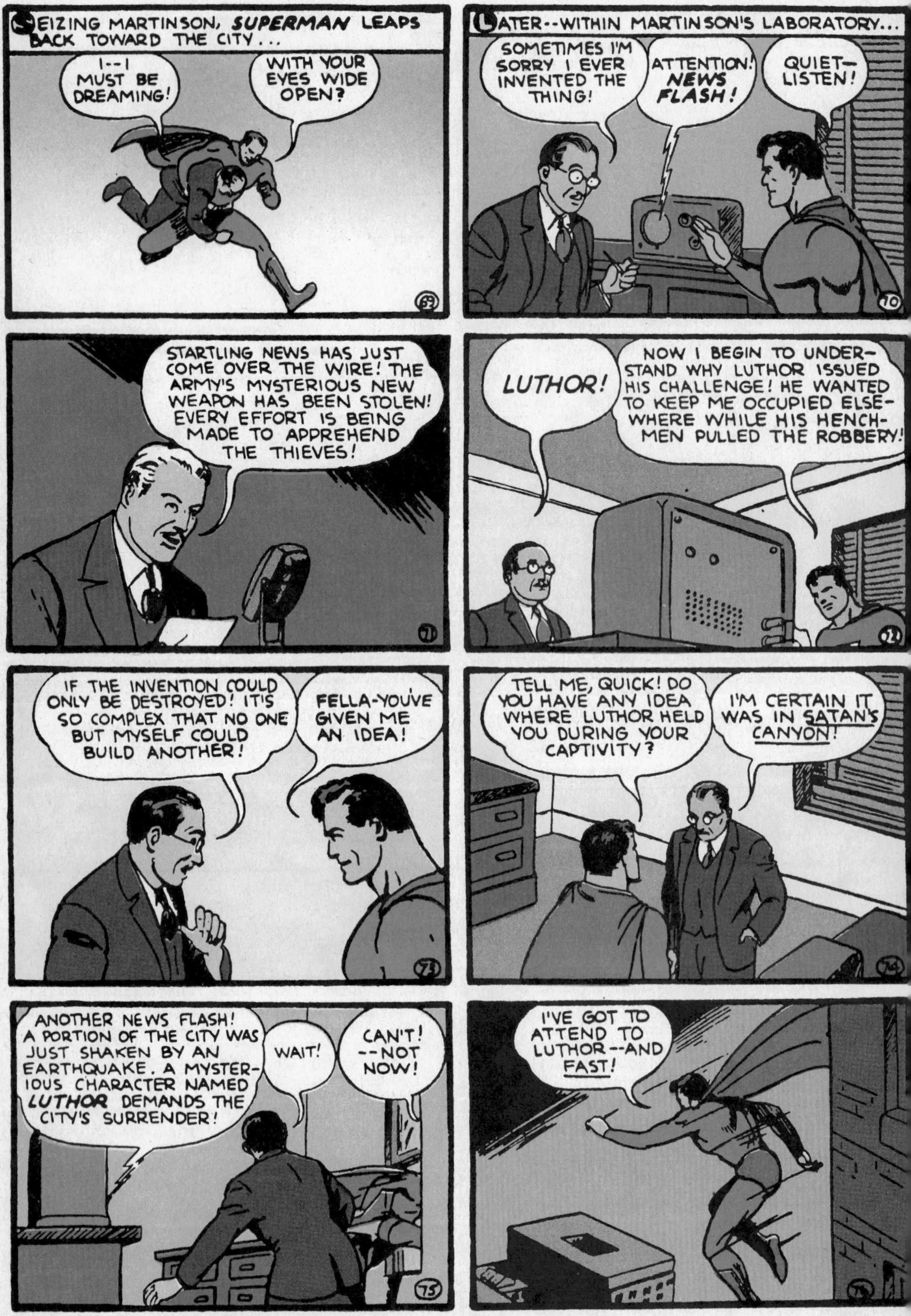
SEIZING MARTINSON, SUPERMAN LEAPS BACK TOWARD THE CITY...
I--I MUST BE DREAMING!
WITH YOUR EYES WIDE OPEN?
LATER--WITHIN MARTINSON'S LABORATORY...
SOMETIMES I'M SORRY I EVER INVENTED THE THING!
ATTENTION! NEWS FLASH!
QUIET— LISTEN!
STARTLING NEWS HAS JUST COME OVER THE WIRE! THE ARMY'S MYSTERIOUS NEW WEAPON HAS BEEN STOLEN! EVERY EFFORT IS BEING MADE TO APPREHEND THE THIEVES!
LUTHOR!
NOW I BEGIN TO UNDERSTAND WHY LUTHOR ISSUED HIS CHALLENGE! HE WANTED TO KEEP ME OCCUPIED ELSEWHERE WHILE HIS HENCHMEN PULLED THE ROBBERY!
IF THE INVENTION COULD ONLY BE DESTROYED! IT'S SO COMPLEX THAT NO ONE BUT MYSELF COULD BUILD ANOTHER!
FELLA-YOU'VE GIVEN ME AN IDEA!
TELL ME, QUICK! DO YOU HAVE ANY IDEA WHERE LUTHOR HELD YOU DURING YOUR CAPTIVITY?
I'M CERTAIN IT WAS IN SATAN'S CANYON!
ANOTHER NEWS FLASH! A PORTION OF THE CITY WAS JUST SHAKEN BY AN EARTHQUAKE. A MYSTERIOUS CHARACTER NAMED LUTHOR DEMANDS THE CITY'S SURRENDER!
WAIT!
CAN'T! --NOT NOW!
I'VE GOT TO ATTEND TO LUTHOR--AND FAST!

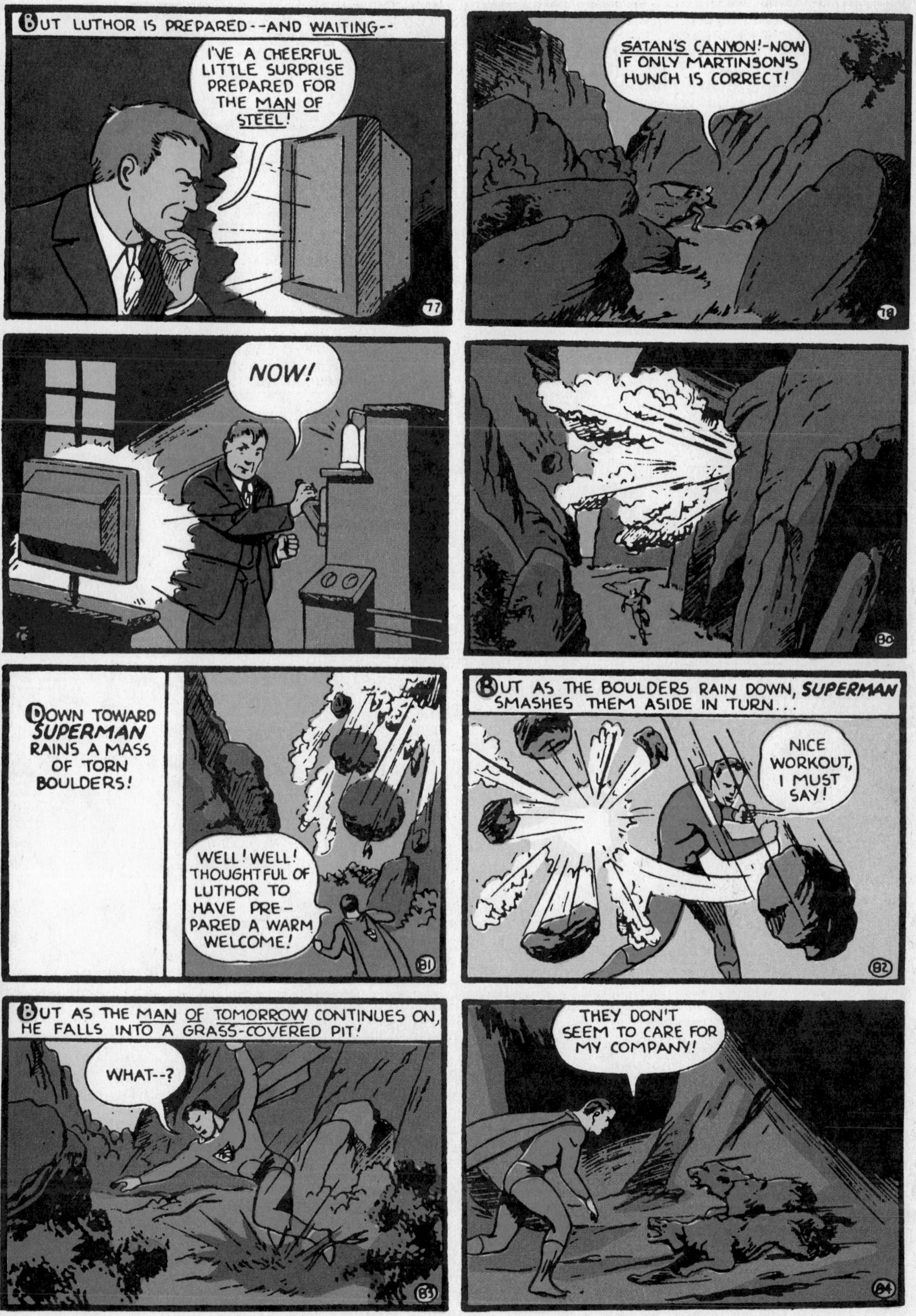
BUT LUTHOR IS PREPARED--AND WAITING--
I'VE A CHEERFUL LITTLE SURPRISE PREPARED FOR THE MAN OF STEEL!
SATAN'S CANYON!-NOW IF ONLY MARTINSON'S HUNCH IS CORRECT!
NOW!
DOWN TOWARD SUPERMAN RAINS A MASS OF TORN BOULDERS!
WELL! WELL! THOUGHTFUL OF LUTHOR TO HAVE PRE-PARED A WARM WELCOME!
BUT AS THE BOULDERS RAIN DOWN, SUPERMAN SMASHES THEM ASIDE IN TURN...
NICE WORKOUT, I MUST SAY!
BUT AS THE MAN OF TOMORROW CONTINUES ON, HE FALLS INTO A GRASS-COVERED PIT!
WHAT--?
THEY DON'T SEEM TO CARE FOR MY COMPANY!

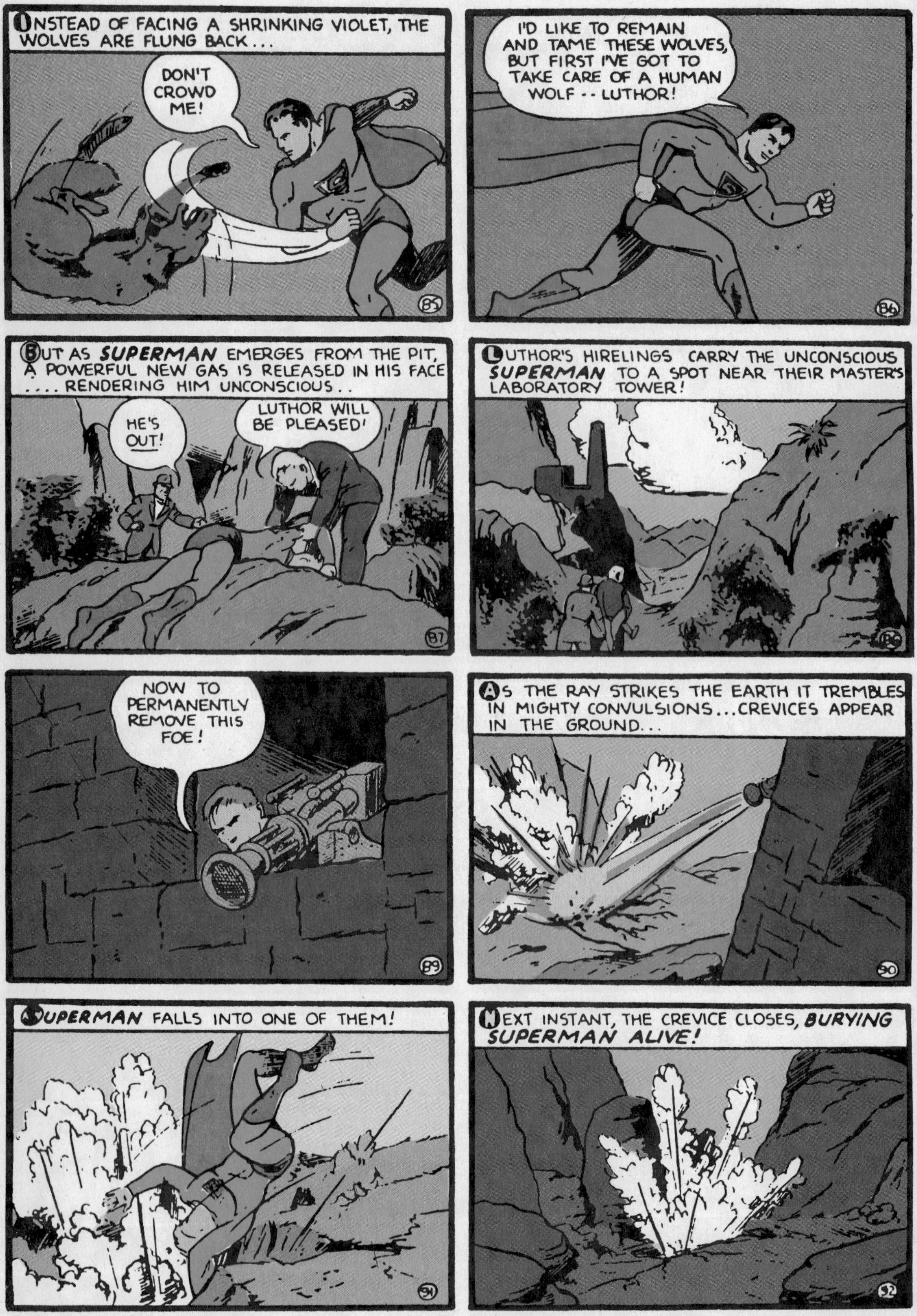
INSTEAD OF FACING A SHRINKING VIOLET, THE WOLVES ARE FLUNG BACK...
DON'T CROWD ME!
I'D LIKE TO REMAIN AND TAME THESE WOLVES, BUT FIRST I'VE GOT TO TAKE CARE OF A HUMAN WOLF -- LUTHOR!
BUT AS SUPERMAN EMERGES FROM THE PIT, A POWERFUL NEW GAS IS RELEASED IN HIS FACE .... RENDERING HIM UNCONSCIOUS..
HE'S OUT!
LUTHOR WILL BE PLEASED!
LUTHOR'S HIRELINGS CARRY THE UNCONSCIOUS SUPERMAN TO A SPOT NEAR THEIR MASTER'S LABORATORY TOWER!
NOW TO PERMANENTLY REMOVE THIS FOE!
AS THE RAY STRIKES THE EARTH IT TREMBLES IN MIGHTY CONVULSIONS...CREVICES APPEAR IN THE GROUND...
SUPERMAN FALLS INTO ONE OF THEM!
NEXT INSTANT, THE CREVICE CLOSES, BURYING SUPERMAN ALIVE!

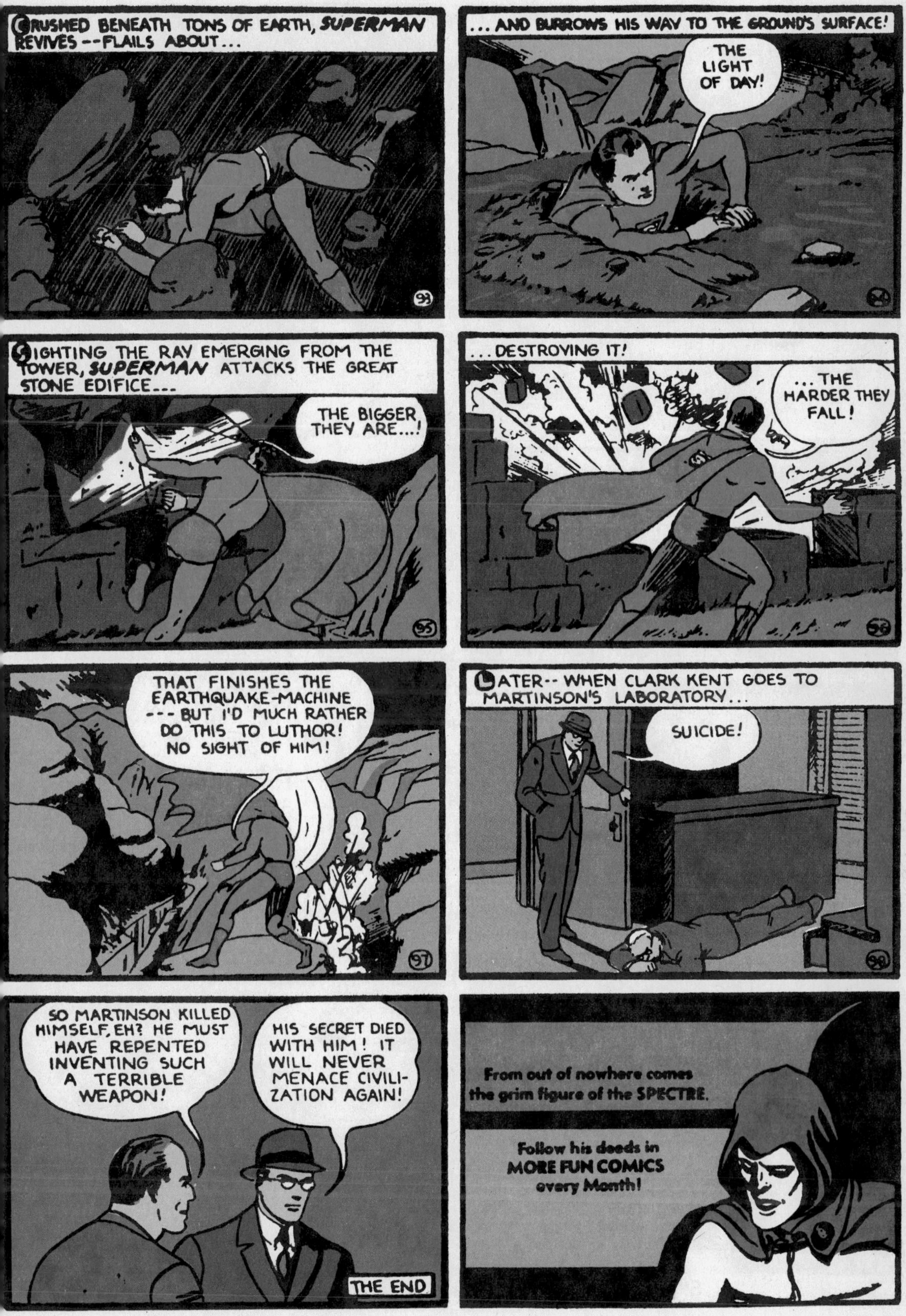
CRUSHED BENEATH TONS OF EARTH, SUPERMAN REVIVES --FLAILS ABOUT...
... AND BURROWS HIS WAY TO THE GROUND'S SURFACE!
THE LIGHT OF DAY!
SIGHTING THE RAY EMERGING FROM THE TOWER, SUPERMAN ATTACKS THE GREAT STONE EDIFICE...
THE BIGGER THEY ARE...!
...DESTROYING IT!
... THE HARDER THEY FALL!
THAT FINISHES THE EARTHQUAKE-MACHINE --- BUT I'D MUCH RATHER DO THIS TO LUTHOR! NO SIGHT OF HIM!
LATER-- WHEN CLARK KENT GOES TO MARTINSON'S LABORATORY...
SUICIDE!
SO MARTINSON KILLED HIMSELF, EH? HE MUST HAVE REPENTED INVENTING SUCH A TERRIBLE WEAPON!
HIS SECRET DIED WITH HIM! IT WILL NEVER MENACE CIVILIZATION AGAIN!
THE END
From out of nowhere comes the grim figure of the SPECTRE.
Follow his deeds in MORE FUN COMICS every Month!

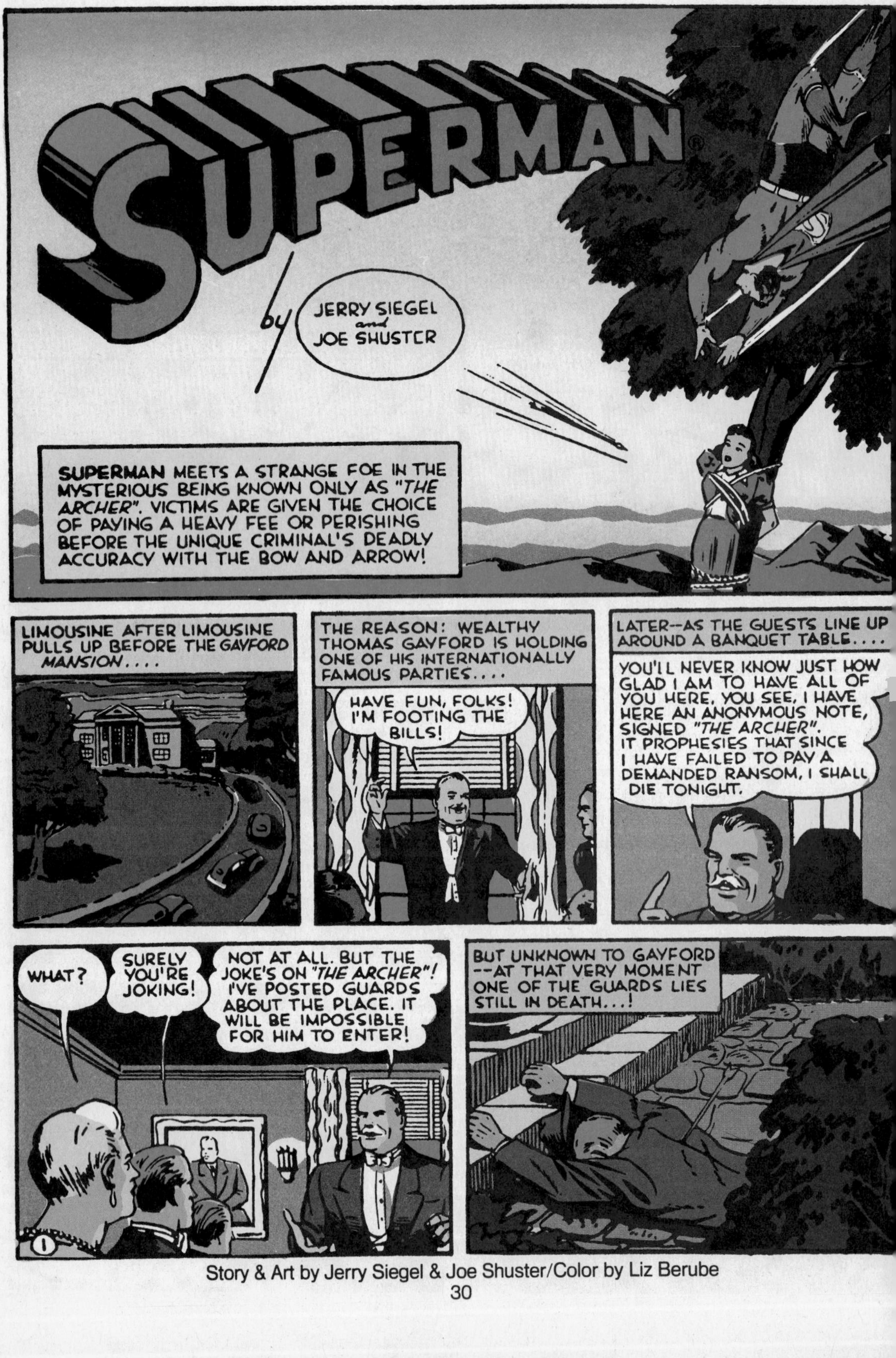

SUPERMAN
by JERRY SIEGEL and JOE SHUSTER
SUPERMAN MEETS A STRANGE FOE IN THE MYSTERIOUS BEING KNOWN ONLY AS "THE ARCHER". VICTIMS ARE GIVEN THE CHOICE OF PAYING A HEAVY FEE OR PERISHING BEFORE THE UNIQUE CRIMINAL'S DEADLY ACCURACY WITH THE BOW AND ARROW!
LIMOUSINE AFTER LIMOUSINE PULLS UP BEFORE THE GAYFORD MANSION....
THE REASON: WEALTHY THOMAS GAYFORD IS HOLDING ONE OF HIS INTERNATIONALLY FAMOUS PARTIES....
HAVE FUN, FOLKS! I'M FOOTING THE BILLS!
LATER--AS THE GUESTS LINE UP AROUND A BANQUET TABLE....
YOU'LL NEVER KNOW JUST HOW GLAD I AM TO HAVE ALL OF YOU HERE. YOU SEE, I HAVE HERE AN ANONYMOUS NOTE, SIGNED "THE ARCHER". IT PROPHESIES THAT SINCE I HAVE FAILED TO PAY A DEMANDED RANSOM, I SHALL DIE TONIGHT.
WHAT?
SURELY YOU'RE JOKING!
NOT AT ALL. BUT THE JOKE'S ON "THE ARCHER"! I'VE POSTED GUARDS ABOUT THE PLACE. IT WILL BE IMPOSSIBLE FOR HIM TO ENTER!
BUT UNKNOWN TO GAYFORD --AT THAT VERY MOMENT ONE OF THE GUARDS LIES STILL IN DEATH...!
1

Story & Art by Jerry Siegel & Joe Shuster/Color by Liz Berube

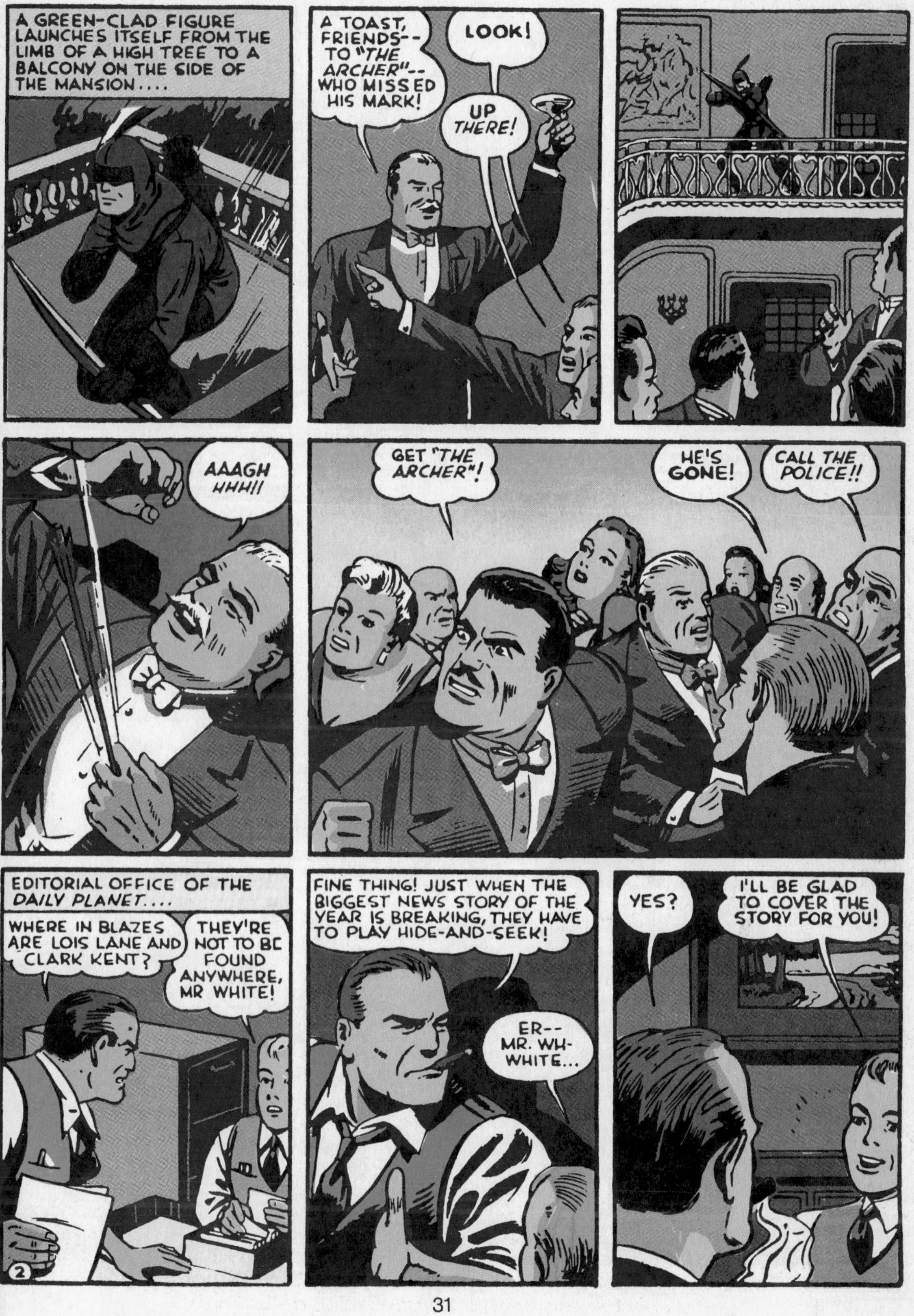
A GREEN-CLAD FIGURE LAUNCHES ITSELF FROM THE LIMB OF A HIGH TREE TO A BALCONY ON THE SIDE OF THE MANSION....
A TOAST, FRIENDS-- TO "THE ARCHER"-- WHO MISSED HIS MARK!
LOOK!
UP THERE!
AAAGH HHH!!
GET "THE ARCHER"!
HE'S GONE!
CALL THE POLICE!!
EDITORIAL OFFICE OF THE DAILY PLANET....
WHERE IN BLAZES ARE LOIS LANE AND CLARK KENT?
THEY'RE NOT TO BE FOUND ANYWHERE, MR WHITE!
2
FINE THING! JUST WHEN THE BIGGEST NEWS STORY OF THE YEAR IS BREAKING, THEY HAVE TO PLAY HIDE-AND-SEEK!
ER-- MR. WH-WHITE...
YES?
I'LL BE GLAD TO COVER THE STORY FOR YOU!

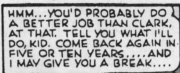
YOU'LL COVER IT?

I--I'D LIKE TO BECOME A REAL REPORTER-- LIKE CLARK KENT, AND IF YOU'D ONLY GIVE ME A CHANCE...

HMM...YOU'D PROBABLY DO A BETTER JOB THAN CLARK, AT THAT. TELL YOU WHAT I'LL DO, KID. COME BACK AGAIN IN FIVE OR TEN YEARS....AND I MAY GIVE YOU A BREAK....

T-TEN YEARS? --THAT'S A LONG TIME!

CLARK AND LOIS RETURN TO THE NEWSPAPER OFFICE....

SO HERE YOU ARE! WHERE HAVE YOU TWO BEEN?

OUT LOOKING FOR MATERIAL --BUT NOT A THING IS STIRRING!

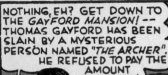

NOTHING, EH? GET DOWN TO THE GAYFORD MANSION! -- THOMAS GAYFORD HAS BEEN SLAIN BY A MYSTERIOUS PERSON NAMED "THE ARCHER". HE REFUSED TO PAY THE AMOUNT DEMANDED!

WHAT --?!

"THE ARCHER"! SOUNDS MELO-DRAMATIC!

--AND EXCITING

YOU, EH? IT DOESN'T TAKE YOU LONG TO SHOW UP WHEREVER NEWS IS BEING MADE!

THAT'S OUR BUSINESS!

HAVE YOU ANY IDEA WHO THIS "ARCHER" MAY BE, CASEY?

NONE AT ALL--YET, BUT WE HAVE SOME INTERESTING CLUES.

WHY DON'T YOU COOK UP A NEW COME-BACK?

THAT ONE'S A LITTLE SHOP-WORN!

QUIET, YOU TWO--OR I'LL HAVE YOU RUN OFF THE PLACE!

3

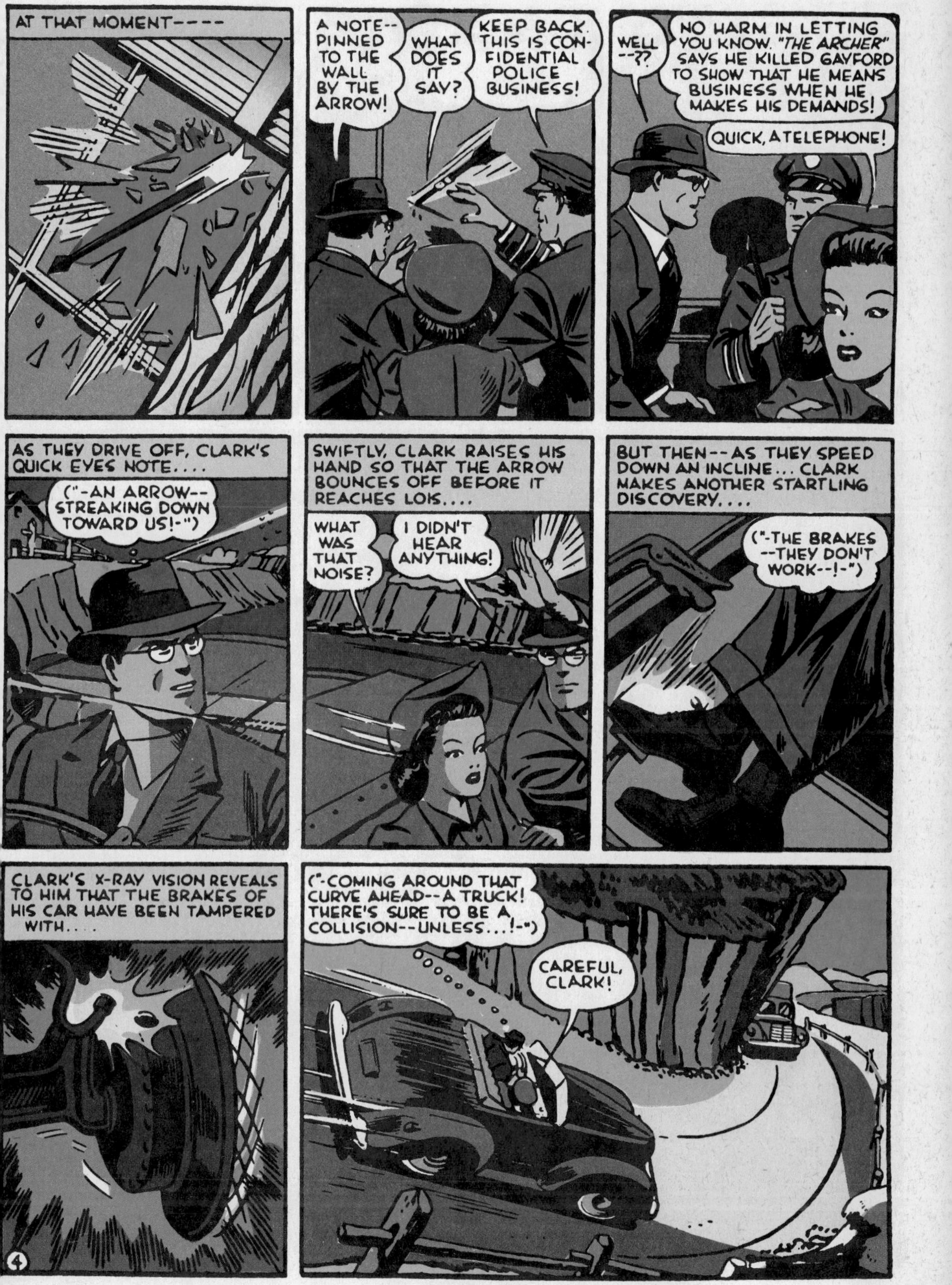

AT THAT MOMENT----
A NOTE--PINNED TO THE WALL BY THE ARROW!
WHAT DOES IT SAY?
KEEP BACK. THIS IS CONFIDENTIAL POLICE BUSINESS!
WELL --??
NO HARM IN LETTING YOU KNOW. "THE ARCHER" SAYS HE KILLED GAYFORD TO SHOW THAT HE MEANS BUSINESS WHEN HE MAKES HIS DEMANDS!
QUICK, A TELEPHONE!
AS THEY DRIVE OFF, CLARK'S QUICK EYES NOTE....
("-AN ARROW--STREAKING DOWN TOWARD US!-")
SWIFTLY, CLARK RAISES HIS HAND SO THAT THE ARROW BOUNCES OFF BEFORE IT REACHES LOIS....
WHAT WAS THAT NOISE?
I DIDN'T HEAR ANYTHING!
BUT THEN--AS THEY SPEED DOWN AN INCLINE... CLARK MAKES ANOTHER STARTLING DISCOVERY....
("-THE BRAKES --THEY DON'T WORK--!-")
CLARK'S X-RAY VISION REVEALS TO HIM THAT THE BRAKES OF HIS CAR HAVE BEEN TAMPERED WITH....
("-COMING AROUND THAT CURVE AHEAD--A TRUCK! THERE'S SURE TO BE A COLLISION--UNLESS...!-")
CAREFUL, CLARK!
4

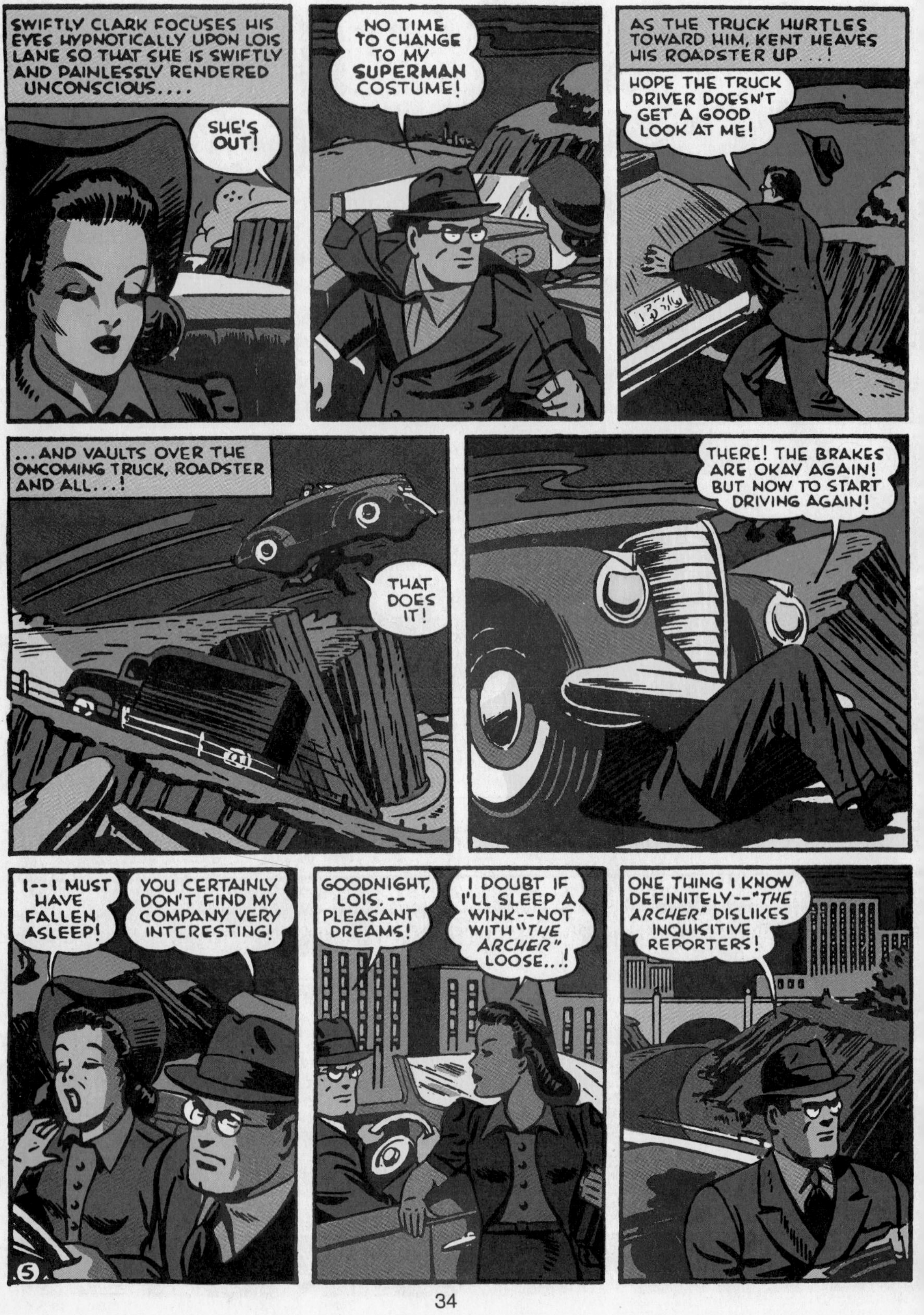
SWIFTLY CLARK FOCUSES HIS EYES HYPNOTICALLY UPON LOIS LANE SO THAT SHE IS SWIFTLY AND PAINLESSLY RENDERED UNCONSCIOUS....
SHE'S OUT!
NO TIME TO CHANGE TO MY SUPERMAN COSTUME!
AS THE TRUCK HURTLES TOWARD HIM, KENT HEAVES HIS ROADSTER UP...!
HOPE THE TRUCK DRIVER DOESN'T GET A GOOD LOOK AT ME!
...AND VAULTS OVER THE ONCOMING TRUCK, ROADSTER AND ALL...!
THAT DOES IT!
THERE! THE BRAKES ARE OKAY AGAIN! BUT NOW TO START DRIVING AGAIN!
I--I MUST HAVE FALLEN ASLEEP!
YOU CERTAINLY DON'T FIND MY COMPANY VERY INTERESTING!
GOODNIGHT, LOIS.--PLEASANT DREAMS!
I DOUBT IF I'LL SLEEP A WINK--NOT WITH "THE ARCHER" LOOSE...!
ONE THING I KNOW DEFINITELY--"THE ARCHER" DISLIKES INQUISITIVE REPORTERS!
5

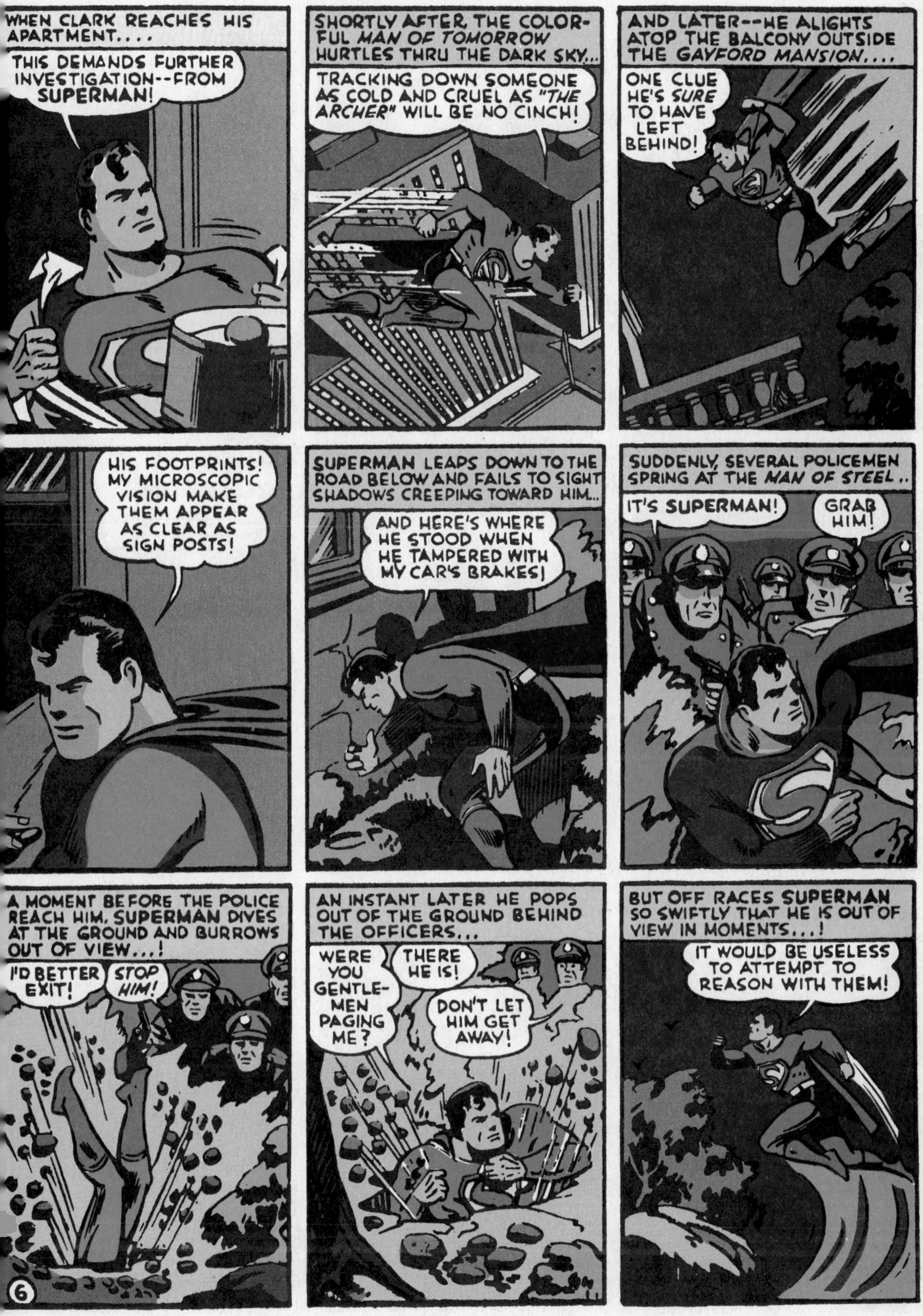
WHEN CLARK REACHES HIS APARTMENT....
THIS DEMANDS FURTHER INVESTIGATION--FROM SUPERMAN!
SHORTLY AFTER THE COLORFUL MAN OF TOMORROW HURTLES THRU THE DARK SKY...
TRACKING DOWN SOMEONE AS COLD AND CRUEL AS "THE ARCHER" WILL BE NO CINCH!
AND LATER--HE ALIGHTS ATOP THE BALCONY OUTSIDE THE GAYFORD MANSION....
ONE CLUE HE'S SURE TO HAVE LEFT BEHIND!
HIS FOOTPRINTS! MY MICROSCOPIC VISION MAKE THEM APPEAR AS CLEAR AS SIGN POSTS!
SUPERMAN LEAPS DOWN TO THE ROAD BELOW AND FAILS TO SIGHT SHADOWS CREEPING TOWARD HIM...
AND HERE'S WHERE HE STOOD WHEN HE TAMPERED WITH MY CAR'S BRAKES!
SUDDENLY, SEVERAL POLICEMEN SPRING AT THE MAN OF STEEL..
IT'S SUPERMAN!
GRAB HIM!
A MOMENT BEFORE THE POLICE REACH HIM, SUPERMAN DIVES AT THE GROUND AND BURROWS OUT OF VIEW...!
I'D BETTER EXIT!
STOP HIM!
6
AN INSTANT LATER HE POPS OUT OF THE GROUND BEHIND THE OFFICERS...
WERE YOU GENTLEMEN PAGING ME?
THERE HE IS!
DON'T LET HIM GET AWAY!
BUT OFF RACES SUPERMAN SO SWIFTLY THAT HE IS OUT OF VIEW IN MOMENTS...!
IT WOULD BE USELESS TO ATTEMPT TO REASON WITH THEM!

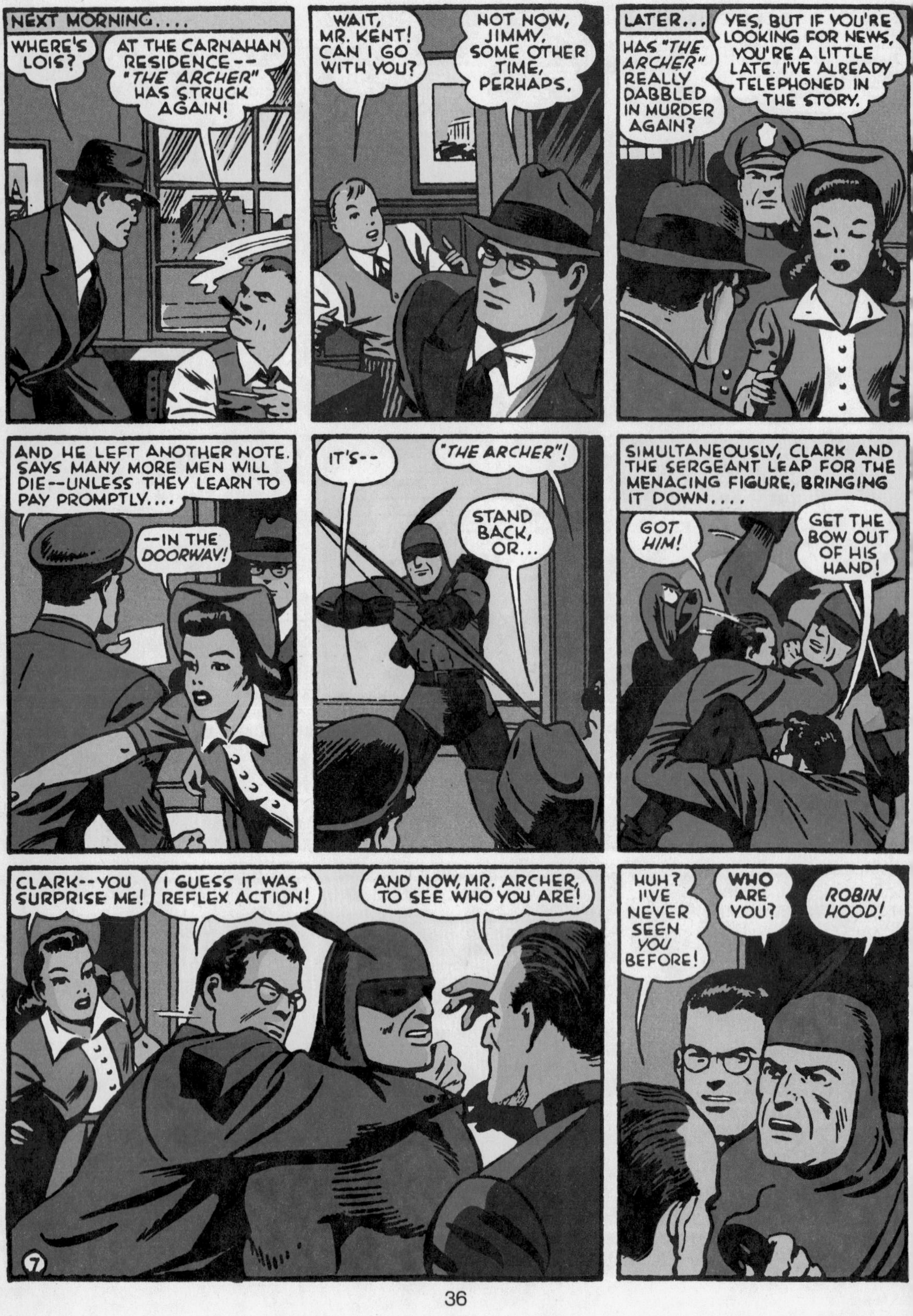

NEXT MORNING....
WHERE'S LOIS?
AT THE CARNAHAN RESIDENCE-- "THE ARCHER" HAS STRUCK AGAIN!
WAIT, MR. KENT! CAN I GO WITH YOU?
NOT NOW, JIMMY, SOME OTHER TIME, PERHAPS.
LATER...
HAS "THE ARCHER" REALLY DABBLED IN MURDER AGAIN?
YES, BUT IF YOU'RE LOOKING FOR NEWS, YOU'RE A LITTLE LATE. I'VE ALREADY TELEPHONED IN THE STORY.
AND HE LEFT ANOTHER NOTE. SAYS MANY MORE MEN WILL DIE--UNLESS THEY LEARN TO PAY PROMPTLY....
--IN THE DOORWAY!
IT'S--
"THE ARCHER"!
STAND BACK, OR...
SIMULTANEOUSLY, CLARK AND THE SERGEANT LEAP FOR THE MENACING FIGURE, BRINGING IT DOWN....
GOT HIM!
GET THE BOW OUT OF HIS HAND!
CLARK--YOU SURPRISE ME!
I GUESS IT WAS REFLEX ACTION!
AND NOW, MR. ARCHER, TO SEE WHO YOU ARE!
7
HUH? I'VE NEVER SEEN YOU BEFORE!
WHO ARE YOU?
ROBIN HOOD!

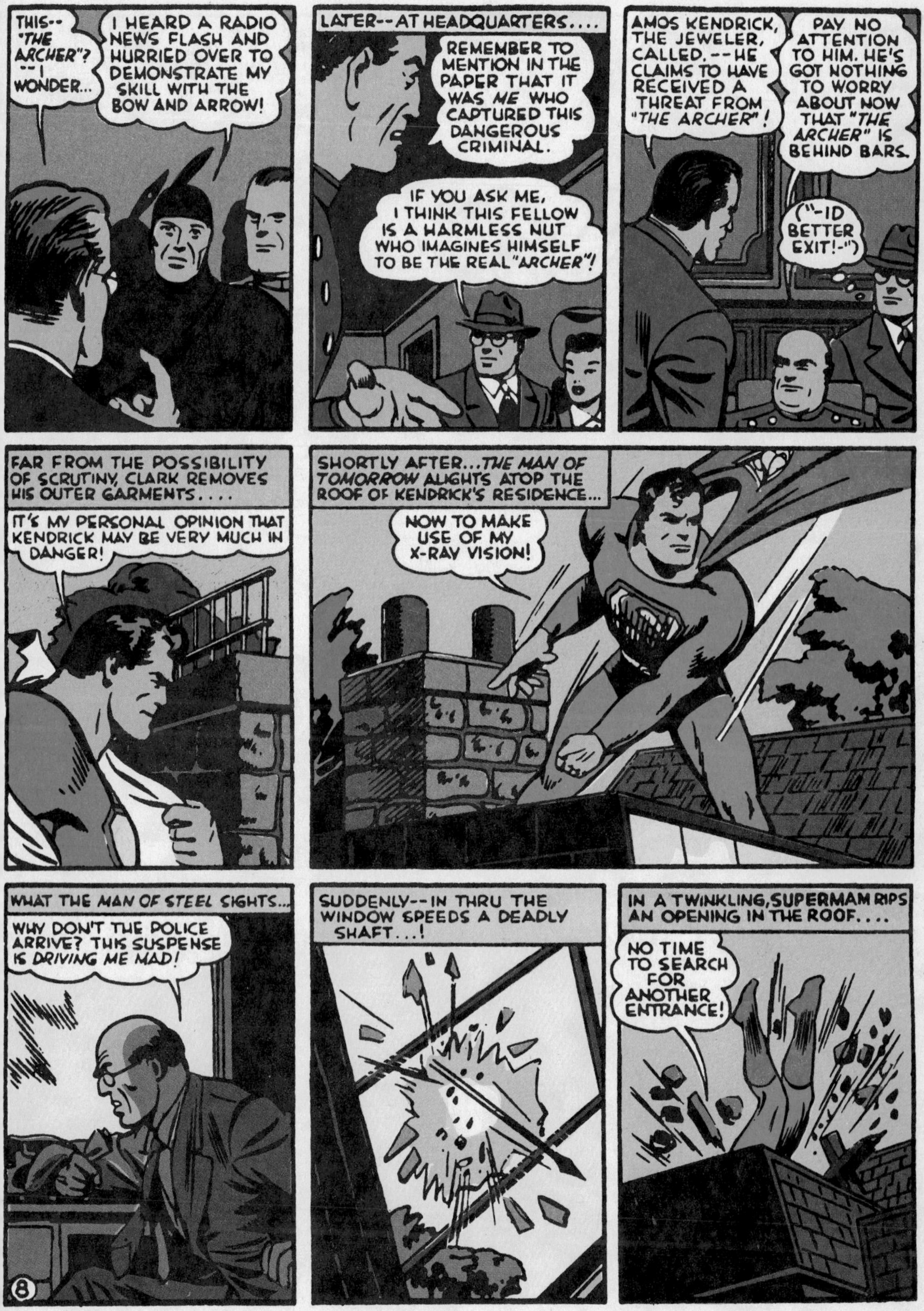

THIS--"THE ARCHER"?--I WONDER...
I HEARD A RADIO NEWS FLASH AND HURRIED OVER TO DEMONSTRATE MY SKILL WITH THE BOW AND ARROW!
LATER--AT HEADQUARTERS....
REMEMBER TO MENTION IN THE PAPER THAT IT WAS *ME* WHO CAPTURED THIS DANGEROUS CRIMINAL.
IF YOU ASK ME, I THINK THIS FELLOW IS A HARMLESS NUT WHO IMAGINES HIMSELF TO BE THE REAL "ARCHER"!
AMOS KENDRICK, THE JEWELER, CALLED.--HE CLAIMS TO HAVE RECEIVED A THREAT FROM "THE ARCHER"!
PAY NO ATTENTION TO HIM. HE'S GOT NOTHING TO WORRY ABOUT NOW THAT "THE ARCHER" IS BEHIND BARS.
("-ID BETTER EXIT!-")
FAR FROM THE POSSIBILITY OF SCRUTINY, CLARK REMOVES HIS OUTER GARMENTS....
IT'S MY PERSONAL OPINION THAT KENDRICK MAY BE VERY MUCH IN DANGER!
SHORTLY AFTER...*THE MAN OF TOMORROW* ALIGHTS ATOP THE ROOF OF KENDRICK'S RESIDENCE...
NOW TO MAKE USE OF MY X-RAY VISION!
WHAT THE *MAN OF STEEL* SIGHTS...
WHY DON'T THE POLICE ARRIVE? THIS SUSPENSE IS *DRIVING ME MAD!*
8
SUDDENLY--IN THRU THE WINDOW SPEEDS A DEADLY SHAFT...!
IN A TWINKLING, SUPERMAM RIPS AN OPENING IN THE ROOF....
NO TIME TO SEARCH FOR ANOTHER ENTRANCE!

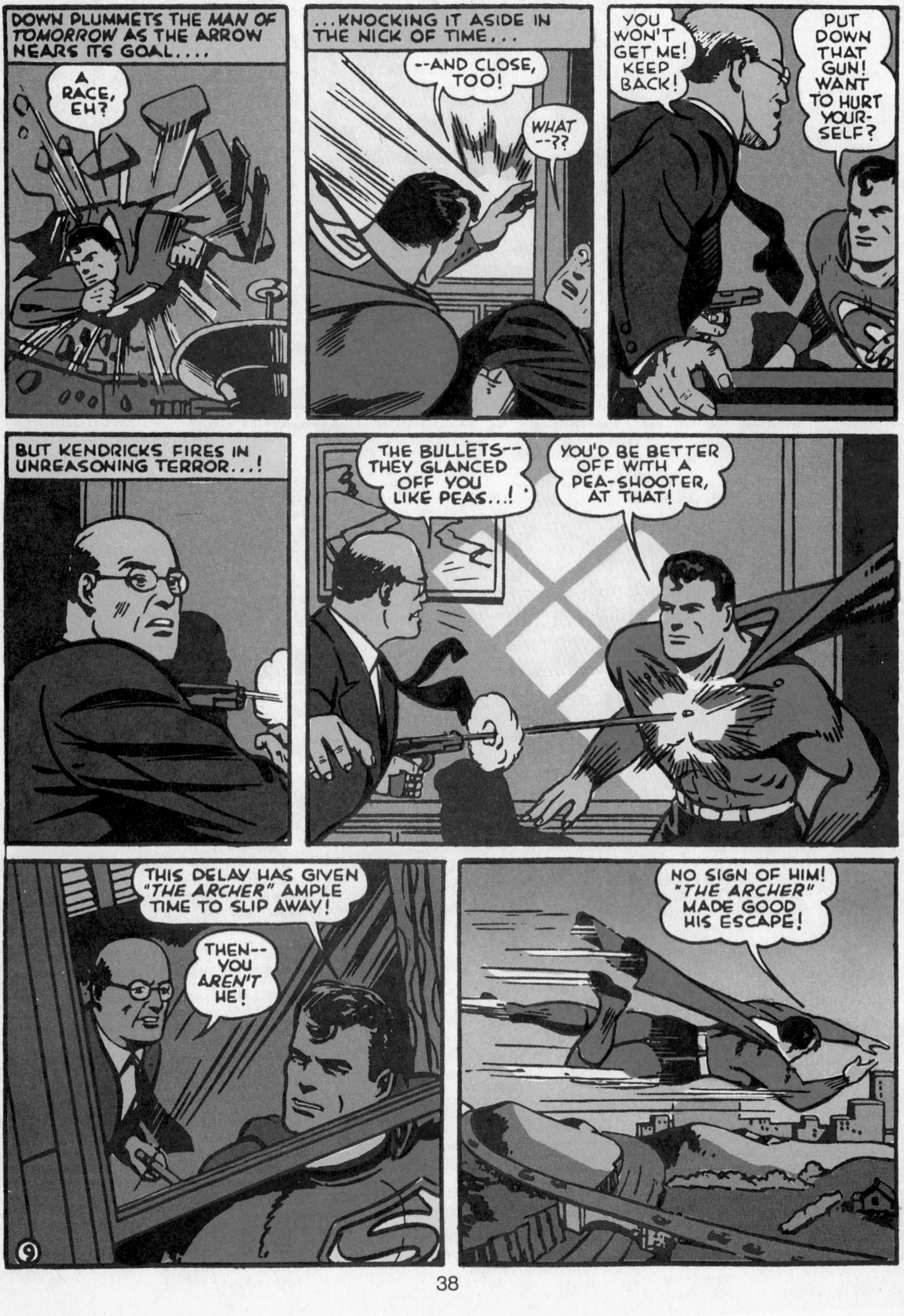

DOWN PLUMMETS THE MAN OF TOMORROW AS THE ARROW NEARS ITS GOAL....
A RACE, EH?
...KNOCKING IT ASIDE IN THE NICK OF TIME...
--AND CLOSE, TOO!
WHAT --??
YOU WON'T GET ME! KEEP BACK!
PUT DOWN THAT GUN! WANT TO HURT YOURSELF?
BUT KENDRICKS FIRES IN UNREASONING TERROR...!
THE BULLETS-- THEY GLANCED OFF YOU LIKE PEAS...!
YOU'D BE BETTER OFF WITH A PEA-SHOOTER, AT THAT!
THIS DELAY HAS GIVEN "THE ARCHER" AMPLE TIME TO SLIP AWAY!
THEN-- YOU AREN'T HE!
9
NO SIGN OF HIM! "THE ARCHER" MADE GOOD HIS ESCAPE!

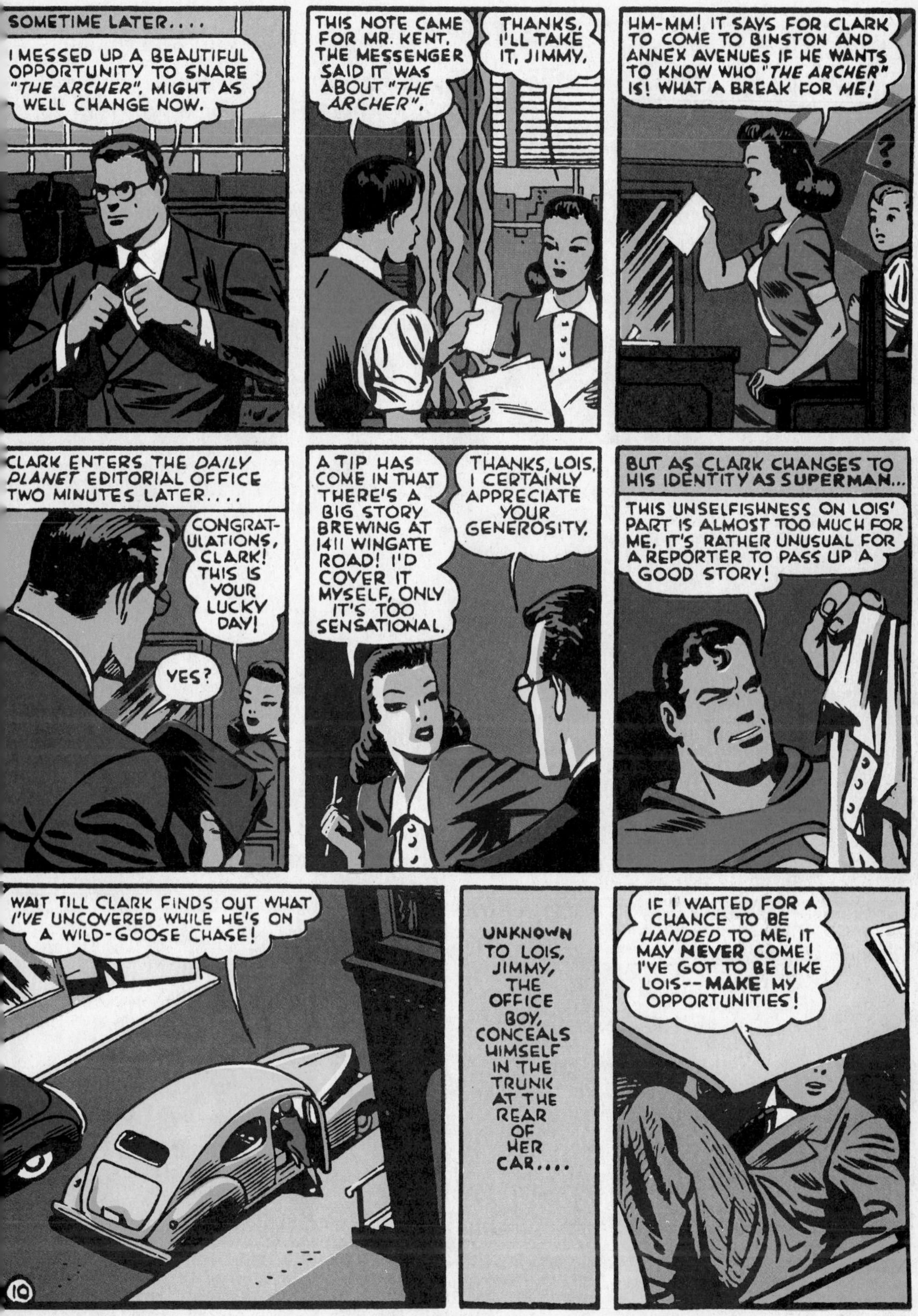
SOMETIME LATER....
I MESSED UP A BEAUTIFUL OPPORTUNITY TO SNARE "THE ARCHER". MIGHT AS WELL CHANGE NOW.
THIS NOTE CAME FOR MR. KENT. THE MESSENGER SAID IT WAS ABOUT "THE ARCHER".
THANKS. I'LL TAKE IT, JIMMY.
HM-MM! IT SAYS FOR CLARK TO COME TO BINSTON AND ANNEX AVENUES IF HE WANTS TO KNOW WHO "THE ARCHER" IS! WHAT A BREAK FOR ME!
?
CLARK ENTERS THE DAILY PLANET EDITORIAL OFFICE TWO MINUTES LATER....
CONGRATULATIONS, CLARK! THIS IS YOUR LUCKY DAY!
YES?
A TIP HAS COME IN THAT THERE'S A BIG STORY BREWING AT 1411 WINGATE ROAD! I'D COVER IT MYSELF, ONLY IT'S TOO SENSATIONAL.
THANKS, LOIS. I CERTAINLY APPRECIATE YOUR GENEROSITY.
BUT AS CLARK CHANGES TO HIS IDENTITY AS SUPERMAN...
THIS UNSELFISHNESS ON LOIS' PART IS ALMOST TOO MUCH FOR ME. IT'S RATHER UNUSUAL FOR A REPORTER TO PASS UP A GOOD STORY!
WAIT TILL CLARK FINDS OUT WHAT I'VE UNCOVERED WHILE HE'S ON A WILD-GOOSE CHASE!
10
UNKNOWN TO LOIS, JIMMY, THE OFFICE BOY, CONCEALS HIMSELF IN THE TRUNK AT THE REAR OF HER CAR....
IF I WAITED FOR A CHANCE TO BE HANDED TO ME, IT MAY NEVER COME! I'VE GOT TO BE LIKE LOIS--MAKE MY OPPORTUNITIES!

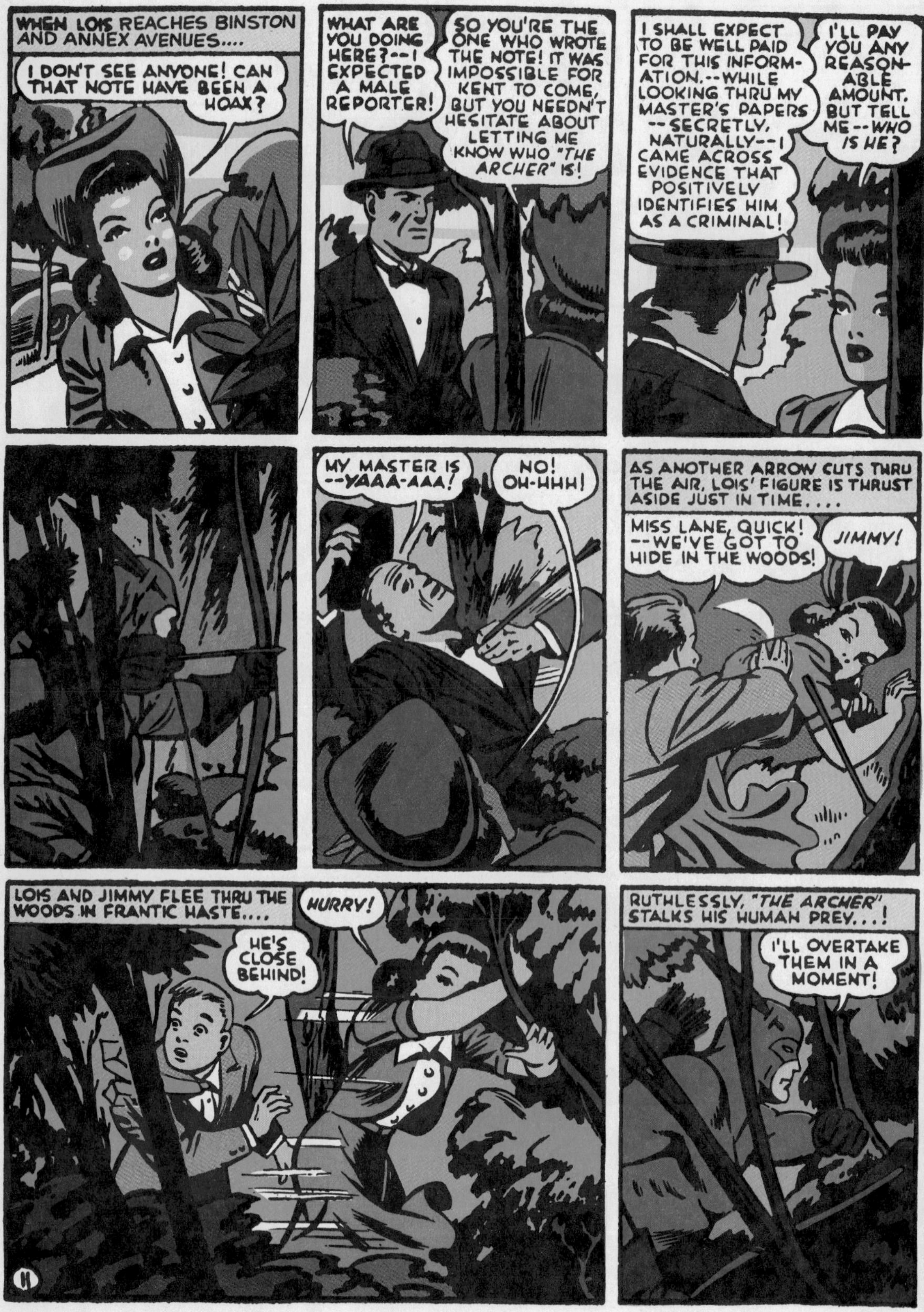
WHEN LOIS REACHES BINSTON AND ANNEX AVENUES....
I DON'T SEE ANYONE! CAN THAT NOTE HAVE BEEN A HOAX?
WHAT ARE YOU DOING HERE?--I EXPECTED A MALE REPORTER!
SO YOU'RE THE ONE WHO WROTE THE NOTE! IT WAS IMPOSSIBLE FOR KENT TO COME, BUT YOU NEEDN'T HESITATE ABOUT LETTING ME KNOW WHO "THE ARCHER" IS!
I SHALL EXPECT TO BE WELL PAID FOR THIS INFORMATION.--WHILE LOOKING THRU MY MASTER'S PAPERS --SECRETLY, NATURALLY--I CAME ACROSS EVIDENCE THAT POSITIVELY IDENTIFIES HIM AS A CRIMINAL!
I'LL PAY YOU ANY REASONABLE AMOUNT. BUT TELL ME--WHO IS HE?
MY MASTER IS --YAAA-AAA!
NO! OH-HHH!
AS ANOTHER ARROW CUTS THRU THE AIR, LOIS' FIGURE IS THRUST ASIDE JUST IN TIME....
MISS LANE, QUICK! --WE'VE GOT TO HIDE IN THE WOODS!
JIMMY!
LOIS AND JIMMY FLEE THRU THE WOODS IN FRANTIC HASTE....
HURRY!
HE'S CLOSE BEHIND!
11
RUTHLESSLY, "THE ARCHER" STALKS HIS HUMAN PREY...!
I'LL OVERTAKE THEM IN A MOMENT!

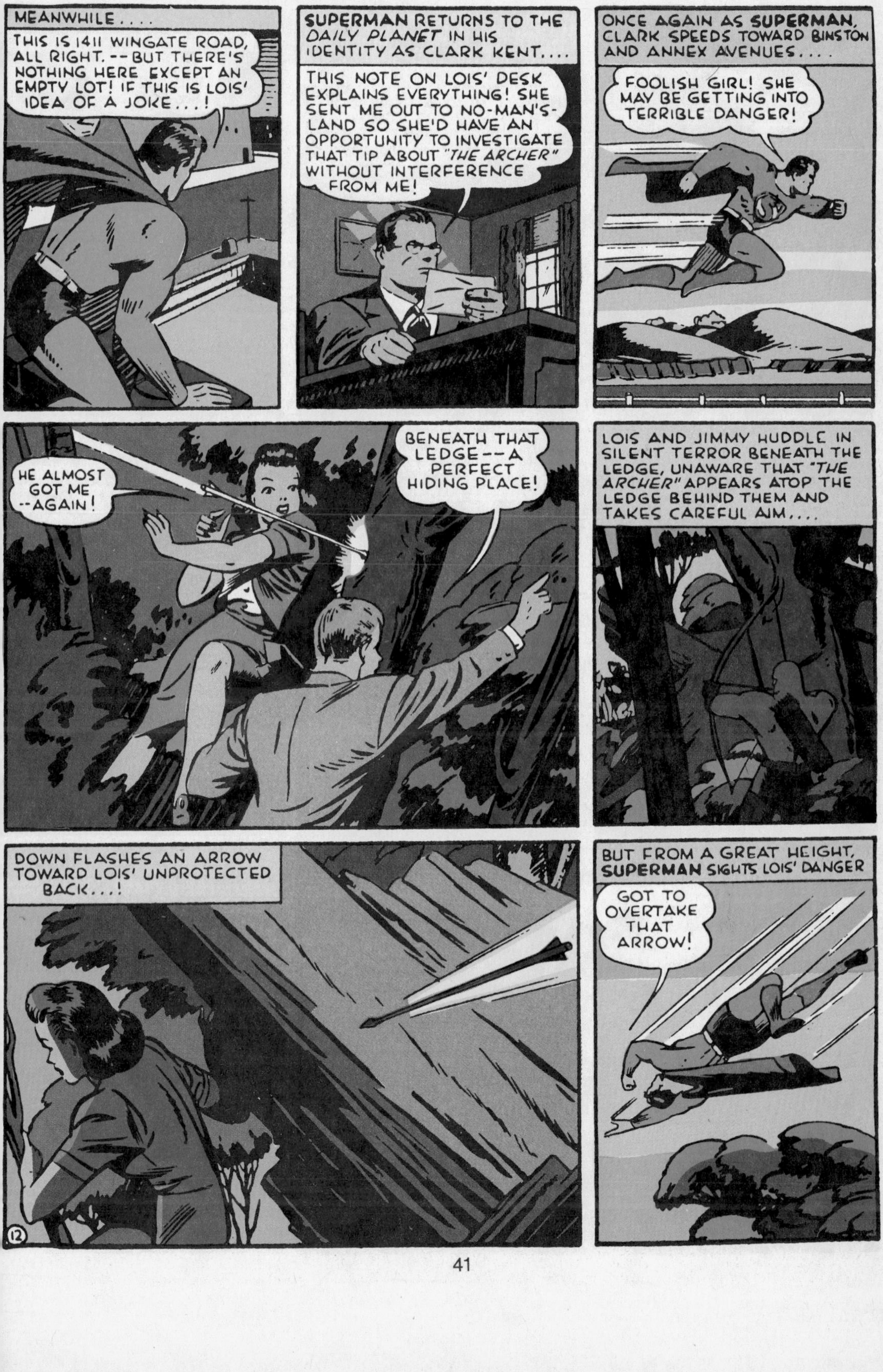
MEANWHILE....
THIS IS 1411 WINGATE ROAD, ALL RIGHT. -- BUT THERE'S NOTHING HERE EXCEPT AN EMPTY LOT! IF THIS IS LOIS' IDEA OF A JOKE...!
SUPERMAN RETURNS TO THE DAILY PLANET IN HIS IDENTITY AS CLARK KENT....
THIS NOTE ON LOIS' DESK EXPLAINS EVERYTHING! SHE SENT ME OUT TO NO-MAN'S-LAND SO SHE'D HAVE AN OPPORTUNITY TO INVESTIGATE THAT TIP ABOUT "THE ARCHER" WITHOUT INTERFERENCE FROM ME!
ONCE AGAIN AS SUPERMAN, CLARK SPEEDS TOWARD BINSTON AND ANNEX AVENUES....
FOOLISH GIRL! SHE MAY BE GETTING INTO TERRIBLE DANGER!
HE ALMOST GOT ME --AGAIN!
BENEATH THAT LEDGE--A PERFECT HIDING PLACE!
LOIS AND JIMMY HUDDLE IN SILENT TERROR BENEATH THE LEDGE, UNAWARE THAT "THE ARCHER" APPEARS ATOP THE LEDGE BEHIND THEM AND TAKES CAREFUL AIM....
DOWN FLASHES AN ARROW TOWARD LOIS' UNPROTECTED BACK...!
12
BUT FROM A GREAT HEIGHT, SUPERMAN SIGHTS LOIS' DANGER
GOT TO OVERTAKE THAT ARROW!

NECK AND NECK!

THE *MAN OF TOMORROW* SWOOPS DOWN BEHIND LOIS, RECEIVING THE ARROW UPON HIS OWN SUPER-TOUGH SKIN....

SUPERMAN!

WHAT A GENIUS YOU ARE, LOIS-- FOR GETTING INTO TROUBLE!

OFF RACES *"THE ARCHER"* IN FRANTIC FLIGHT....

IF I CAN ONLY REACH MY CAR...!

UP WITH YOU!

FLUNG BY THE *MAN OF STEEL'S* TREMENDOUSLY POWERFUL MUSCLES, THE HUGE BOULDER SMASHES THE CRIMINAL'S AUTO TO BITS!

LET GO!

THAT MASK IS COMING OFF!

IT'S QUIGLEY --THE FAMOUS BIG-GAME HUNTER!

I--I THOUGHT HUNTING HUMAN BEINGS WOULD PROVE MORE PROFITABLE!

ANY KID COULD TELL YOU THAT CRIME DOESN'T PAY, MR. QUIGLEY.

I'LL BIND HIM FOR YOU-- THEN SEE TO IT THAT POLICE GET HERE PROMPTLY!

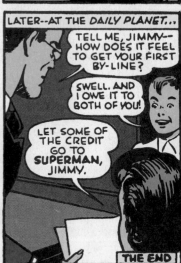

LATER--AT THE *DAILY PLANET*...

TELL ME, JIMMY-- HOW DOES IT FEEL TO GET YOUR FIRST BY-LINE?

SWELL. AND I OWE IT TO BOTH OF YOU!

LET SOME OF THE CREDIT GO TO SUPERMAN, JIMMY.

THE END

SUPERMAN

JERRY SIEGEL AND JOE SHUSTER

THE NAZIS CLAIM THE WESTWALL IS INVULNERABLE—WELL, HERE'S WHERE I FIND OUT!

TOWARD THE SIEGFRIED LINE RACES **SUPERMAN,** SAVIOR OF THE HELPLESS AND OPPRESSED, AS SHELLS BURST ON ALL SIDES OF HIM!

WITHIN THE UNDERGROUND FORTIFICATIONS...

IT'S INCREDIBLE! WE'VE SCORED DIRECT HITS AND STILL HE KEEPS COMING ON!

KEEP FIRING! ACH! THAT INHUMAN CREATURE HAS **GOT TO BE STOPPED!**

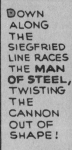

DOWN ALONG THE SIEGFRIED LINE RACES THE **MAN OF STEEL,** TWISTING THE CANNON OUT OF SHAPE!

JUST LET 'EM TRY FIRING NOW!

...THEN TEARING THE TOP OFF THE CONCRETE WESTWALL, SHOUTS AN INVITATION BACK TOWARD THE MAGINOT LINE TO THE FRENCH FORCES...

COME AND GET 'EM!

A TERRIFIC LEAP CARRIES **SUPERMAN** FAR INTO GERMANY... BUT AS HE HURTLES THRU THE AIR, A FIGHTING PLANE SWOOPS TOWARD HIM GUNS BLAZING...

LOOKING FOR TROUBLE, EH?

WELL, HERE IT IS!

HIMMEL! VOS IS DISS?

SHORTLY AFTER, THE **MAN OF TOMORROW** STREAKS DOWN THROUGH THE CEILING OF HITLER'S RETREAT...

ZOOM-M

Story & Art by Jerry Siegel & Joe Shuster/Color by Liz Berube

43

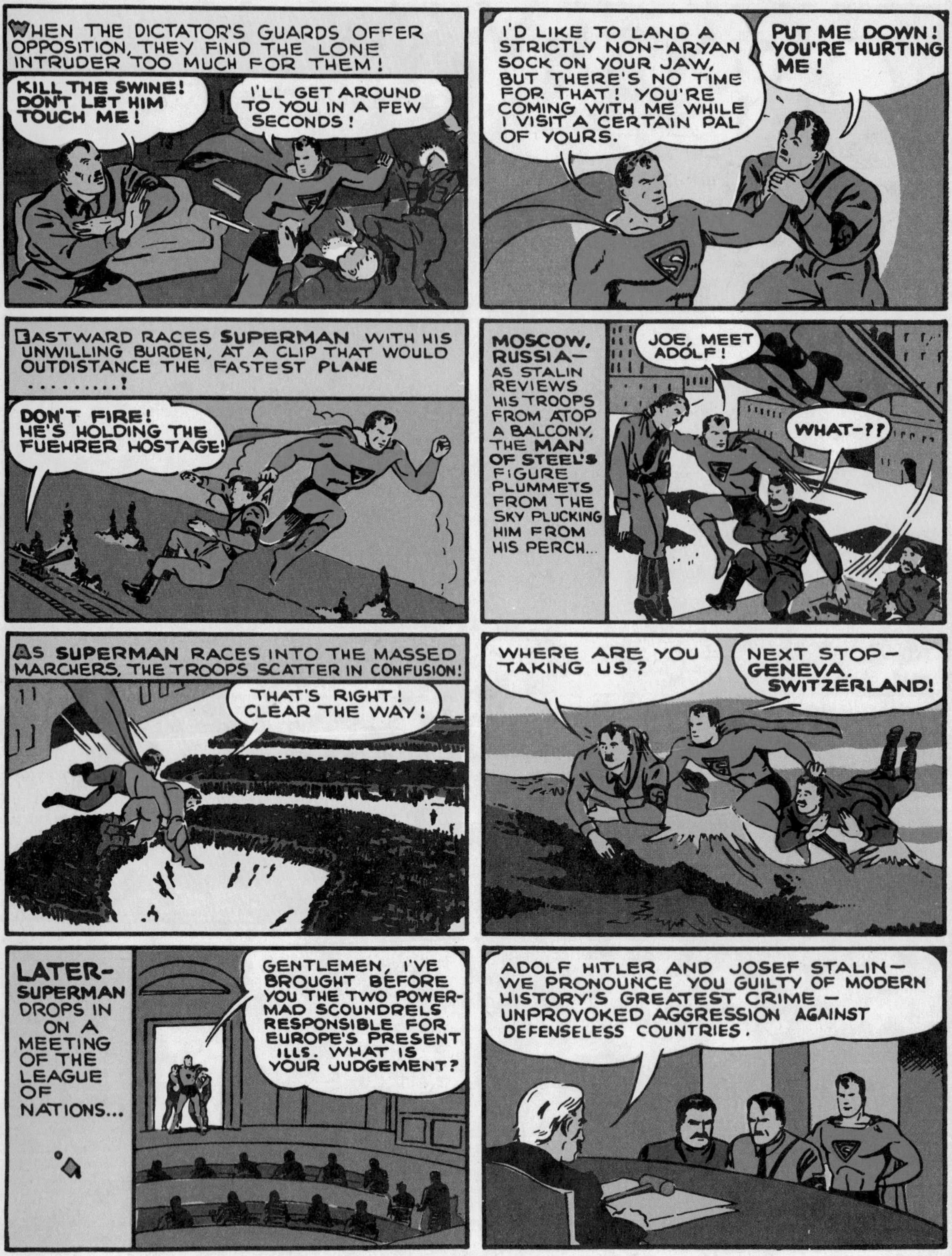
WHEN THE DICTATOR'S GUARDS OFFER OPPOSITION, THEY FIND THE LONE INTRUDER TOO MUCH FOR THEM!
KILL THE SWINE! DON'T LET HIM TOUCH ME!
I'LL GET AROUND TO YOU IN A FEW SECONDS!
I'D LIKE TO LAND A STRICTLY NON-ARYAN SOCK ON YOUR JAW, BUT THERE'S NO TIME FOR THAT! YOU'RE COMING WITH ME WHILE I VISIT A CERTAIN PAL OF YOURS.
PUT ME DOWN! YOU'RE HURTING ME!
EASTWARD RACES SUPERMAN WITH HIS UNWILLING BURDEN, AT A CLIP THAT WOULD OUTDISTANCE THE FASTEST PLANE ....!
DON'T FIRE! HE'S HOLDING THE FUEHRER HOSTAGE!
MOSCOW, RUSSIA— AS STALIN REVIEWS HIS TROOPS FROM ATOP A BALCONY, THE MAN OF STEEL'S FIGURE PLUMMETS FROM THE SKY PLUCKING HIM FROM HIS PERCH...
JOE, MEET ADOLF!
WHAT-??
AS SUPERMAN RACES INTO THE MASSED MARCHERS, THE TROOPS SCATTER IN CONFUSION!
THAT'S RIGHT! CLEAR THE WAY!
WHERE ARE YOU TAKING US?
NEXT STOP— GENEVA, SWITZERLAND!
LATER— SUPERMAN DROPS IN ON A MEETING OF THE LEAGUE OF NATIONS...
GENTLEMEN, I'VE BROUGHT BEFORE YOU THE TWO POWER-MAD SCOUNDRELS RESPONSIBLE FOR EUROPE'S PRESENT ILLS. WHAT IS YOUR JUDGEMENT?
ADOLF HITLER AND JOSEF STALIN— WE PRONOUNCE YOU GUILTY OF MODERN HISTORY'S GREATEST CRIME — UNPROVOKED AGGRESSION AGAINST DEFENSELESS COUNTRIES.

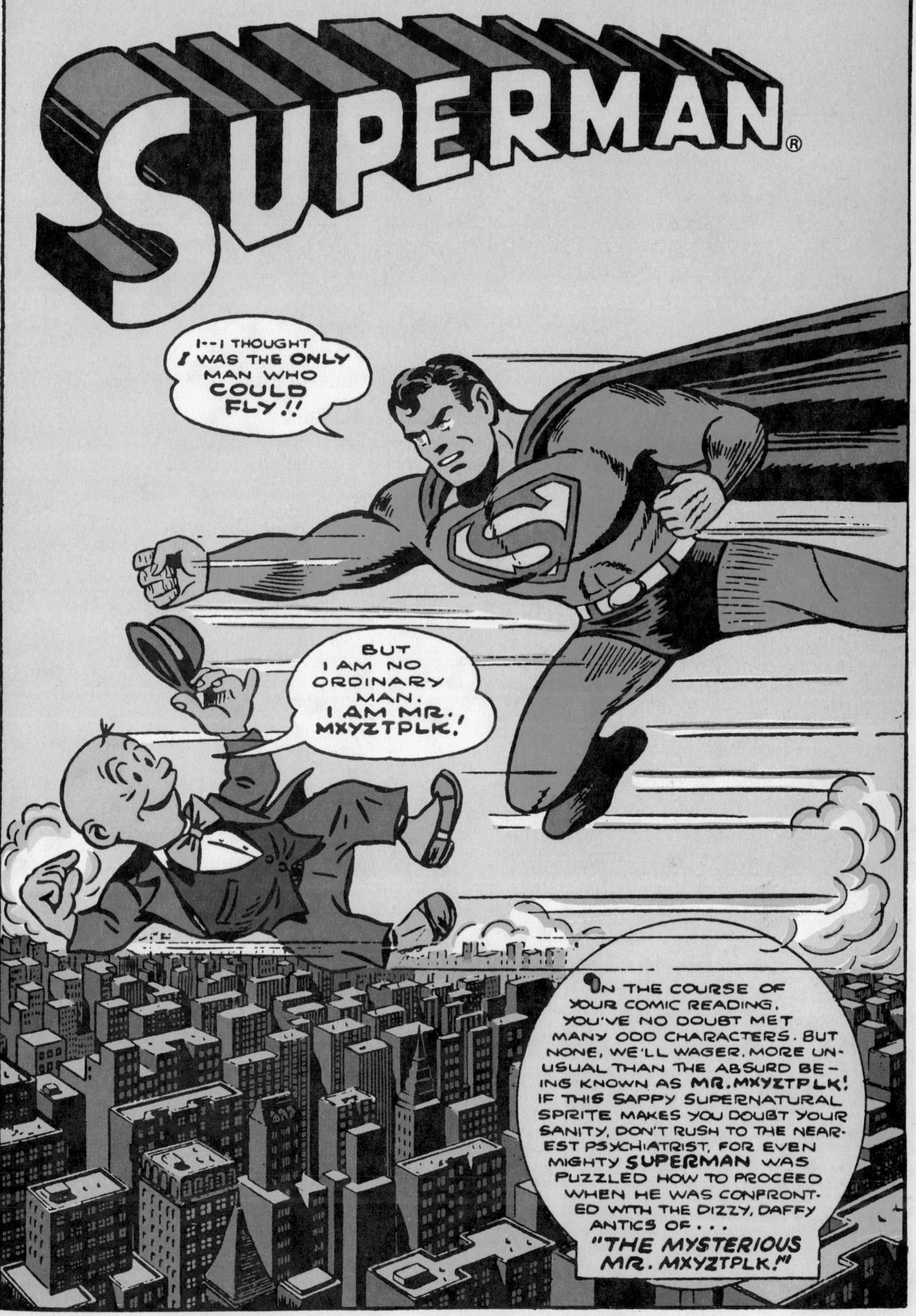
SUPERMAN®
I--I THOUGHT I WAS THE ONLY MAN WHO COULD FLY!!
BUT I AM NO ORDINARY MAN. I AM MR. MXYZTPLK!
IN THE COURSE OF YOUR COMIC READING, YOU'VE NO DOUBT MET MANY ODD CHARACTERS. BUT NONE, WE'LL WAGER, MORE UNUSUAL THAN THE ABSURD BEING KNOWN AS MR. MXYZTPLK! IF THIS SAPPY SUPERNATURAL SPRITE MAKES YOU DOUBT YOUR SANITY, DON'T RUSH TO THE NEAREST PSYCHIATRIST, FOR EVEN MIGHTY SUPERMAN WAS PUZZLED HOW TO PROCEED WHEN HE WAS CONFRONTED WITH THE DIZZY, DAFFY ANTICS OF . . .
"THE MYSTERIOUS MR. MXYZTPLK!"

Story by Jerry Siegel/Art by John Sikela/Color by Michele Wolfman

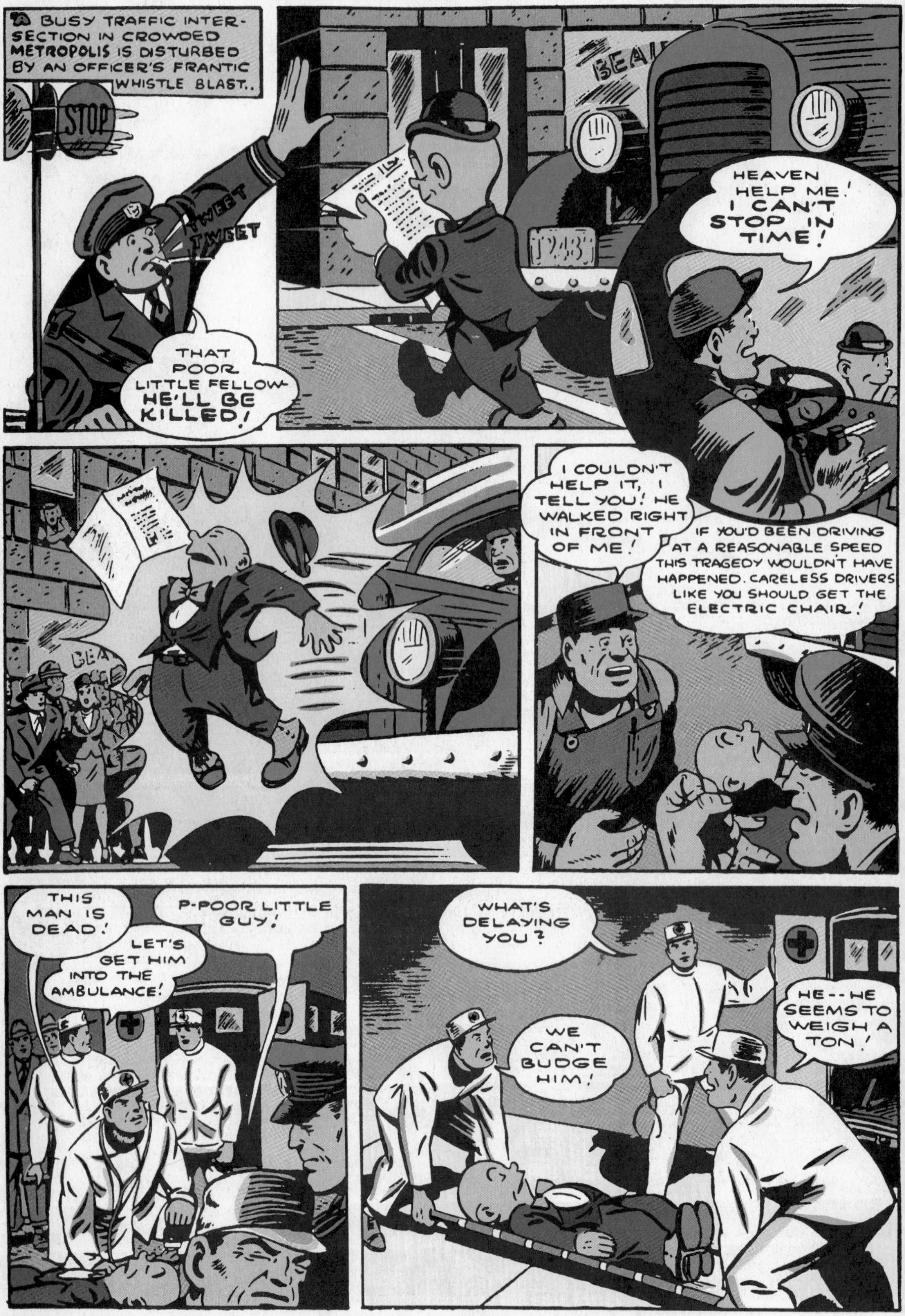
A BUSY TRAFFIC INTERSECTION IN CROWDED METROPOLIS IS DISTURBED BY AN OFFICER'S FRANTIC WHISTLE BLAST..
STOP
TWEET TWEET
THAT POOR LITTLE FELLOW-- HE'LL BE KILLED!
HEAVEN HELP ME! I CAN'T STOP IN TIME!
I COULDN'T HELP IT, I TELL YOU! HE WALKED RIGHT IN FRONT OF ME!
IF YOU'D BEEN DRIVING AT A REASONABLE SPEED THIS TRAGEDY WOULDN'T HAVE HAPPENED. CARELESS DRIVERS LIKE YOU SHOULD GET THE ELECTRIC CHAIR!
THIS MAN IS DEAD!
P-POOR LITTLE GUY!
LET'S GET HIM INTO THE AMBULANCE!
WHAT'S DELAYING YOU?
WE CAN'T BUDGE HIM!
HE--HE SEEMS TO WEIGH A TON!

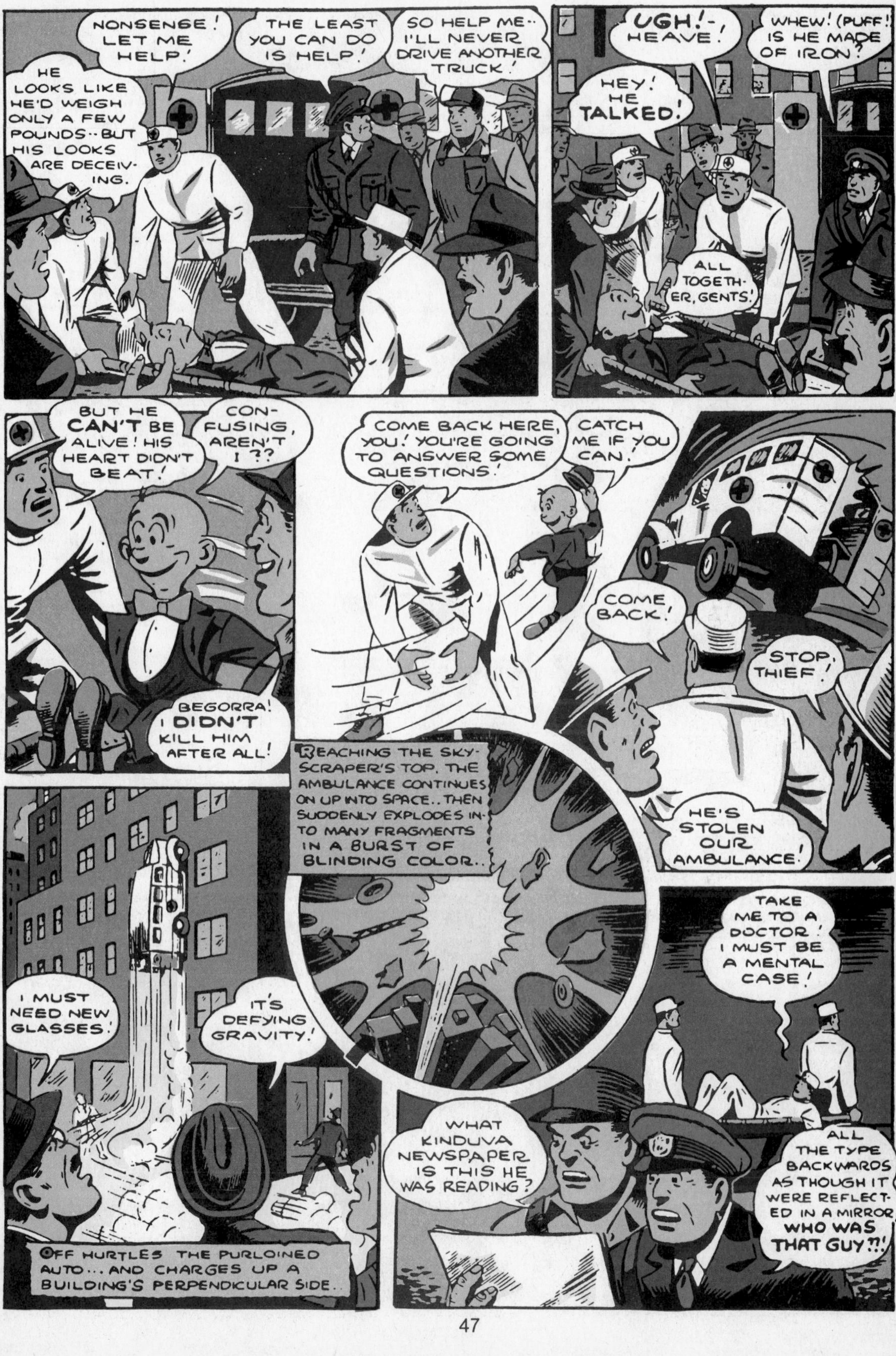
NONSENSE! LET ME HELP!
HE LOOKS LIKE HE'D WEIGH ONLY A FEW POUNDS.. BUT HIS LOOKS ARE DECEIV-ING.
THE LEAST YOU CAN DO IS HELP!
SO HELP ME.. I'LL NEVER DRIVE ANOTHER TRUCK!
UGH!-, HEAVE!
WHEW! (PUFF!) IS HE MADE OF IRON?
HEY! HE TALKED!
ALL TOGETH-ER, GENTS!
BUT HE CAN'T BE ALIVE! HIS HEART DIDN'T BEAT!
CON-FUSING, AREN'T I ??
BEGORRA! I DIDN'T KILL HIM AFTER ALL!
COME BACK HERE, YOU! YOU'RE GOING TO ANSWER SOME QUESTIONS!
CATCH ME IF YOU CAN!
COME BACK!
STOP, THIEF!
HE'S STOLEN OUR AMBULANCE!
I MUST NEED NEW GLASSES!
IT'S DEFYING GRAVITY!
OFF HURTLES THE PURLOINED AUTO... AND CHARGES UP A BUILDING'S PERPENDICULAR SIDE.
REACHING THE SKY-SCRAPER'S TOP, THE AMBULANCE CONTINUES ON UP INTO SPACE.. THEN SUDDENLY EXPLODES IN-TO MANY FRAGMENTS IN A BURST OF BLINDING COLOR..
TAKE ME TO A DOCTOR! I MUST BE A MENTAL CASE!
WHAT KINDUVA NEWSPAPER IS THIS HE WAS READING?
ALL THE TYPE BACKWARDS AS THOUGH IT WERE REFLECT-ED IN A MIRROR WHO WAS THAT GUY?!

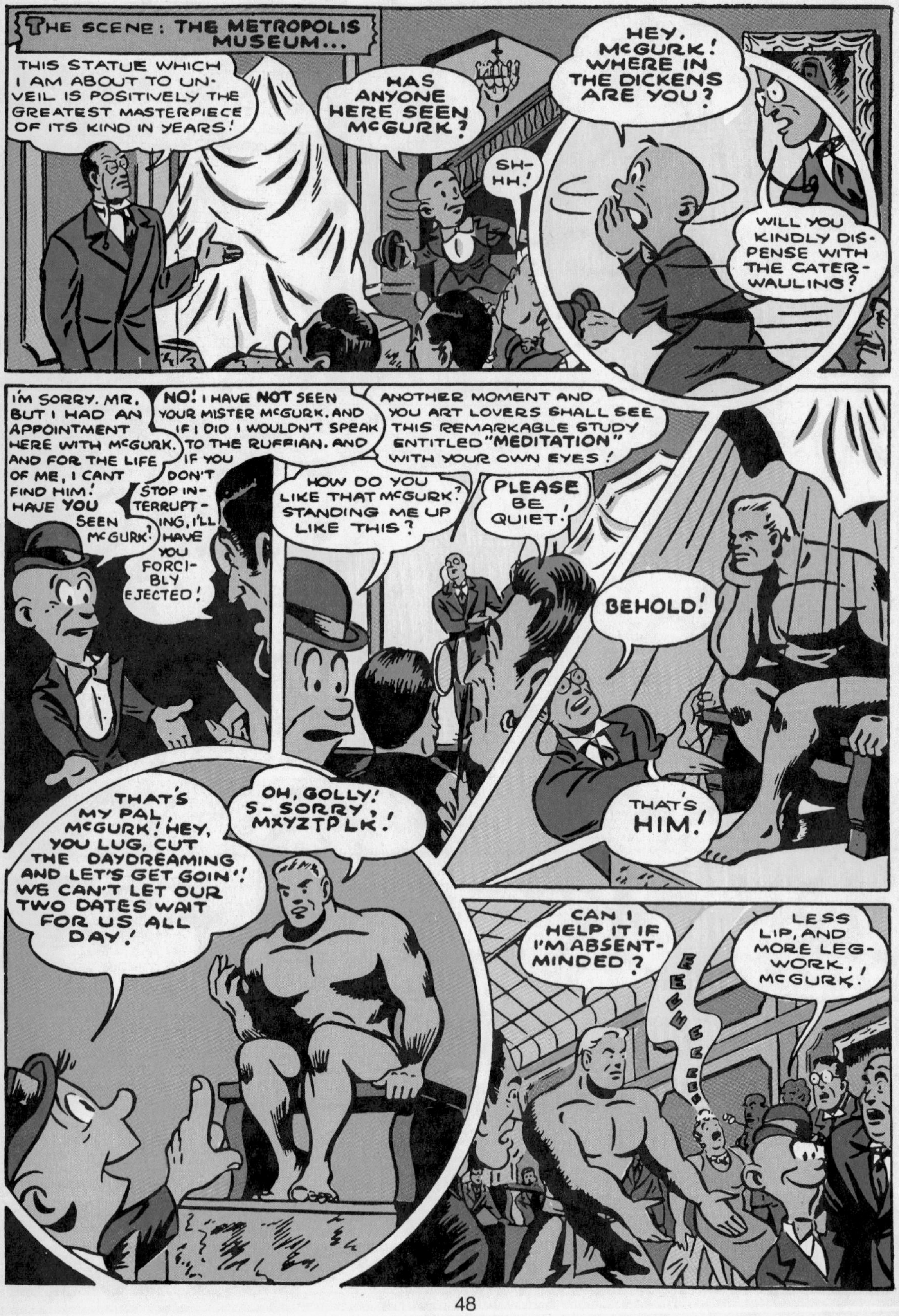

THE SCENE: THE METROPOLIS MUSEUM...
THIS STATUE WHICH I AM ABOUT TO UN-VEIL IS POSITIVELY THE GREATEST MASTERPIECE OF ITS KIND IN YEARS!
HAS ANYONE HERE SEEN McGURK?
SH-HH!
HEY, McGURK! WHERE IN THE DICKENS ARE YOU?
WILL YOU KINDLY DIS-PENSE WITH THE CATER-WAULING?
I'M SORRY, MR. BUT I HAD AN APPOINTMENT HERE WITH McGURK. AND FOR THE LIFE OF ME, I CANT FIND HIM! HAVE YOU SEEN McGURK?
NO! I HAVE NOT SEEN YOUR MISTER McGURK. AND IF I DID I WOULDN'T SPEAK TO THE RUFFIAN. AND IF YOU DON'T STOP IN-TERRUPT-ING, I'LL HAVE YOU FORCI-BLY EJECTED!
ANOTHER MOMENT AND YOU ART LOVERS SHALL SEE THIS REMARKABLE STUDY ENTITLED "MEDITATION" WITH YOUR OWN EYES!
HOW DO YOU LIKE THAT McGURK? STANDING ME UP LIKE THIS?
PLEASE BE QUIET!
BEHOLD!
THAT'S HIM!
THAT'S MY PAL, McGURK! HEY, YOU LUG, CUT THE DAYDREAMING AND LET'S GET GOIN'! WE CAN'T LET OUR TWO DATES WAIT FOR US ALL DAY!
OH, GOLLY! S-SORRY, MXYZTPLK!
CAN I HELP IT IF I'M ABSENT-MINDED?
LESS LIP, AND MORE LEG-WORK, McGURK!

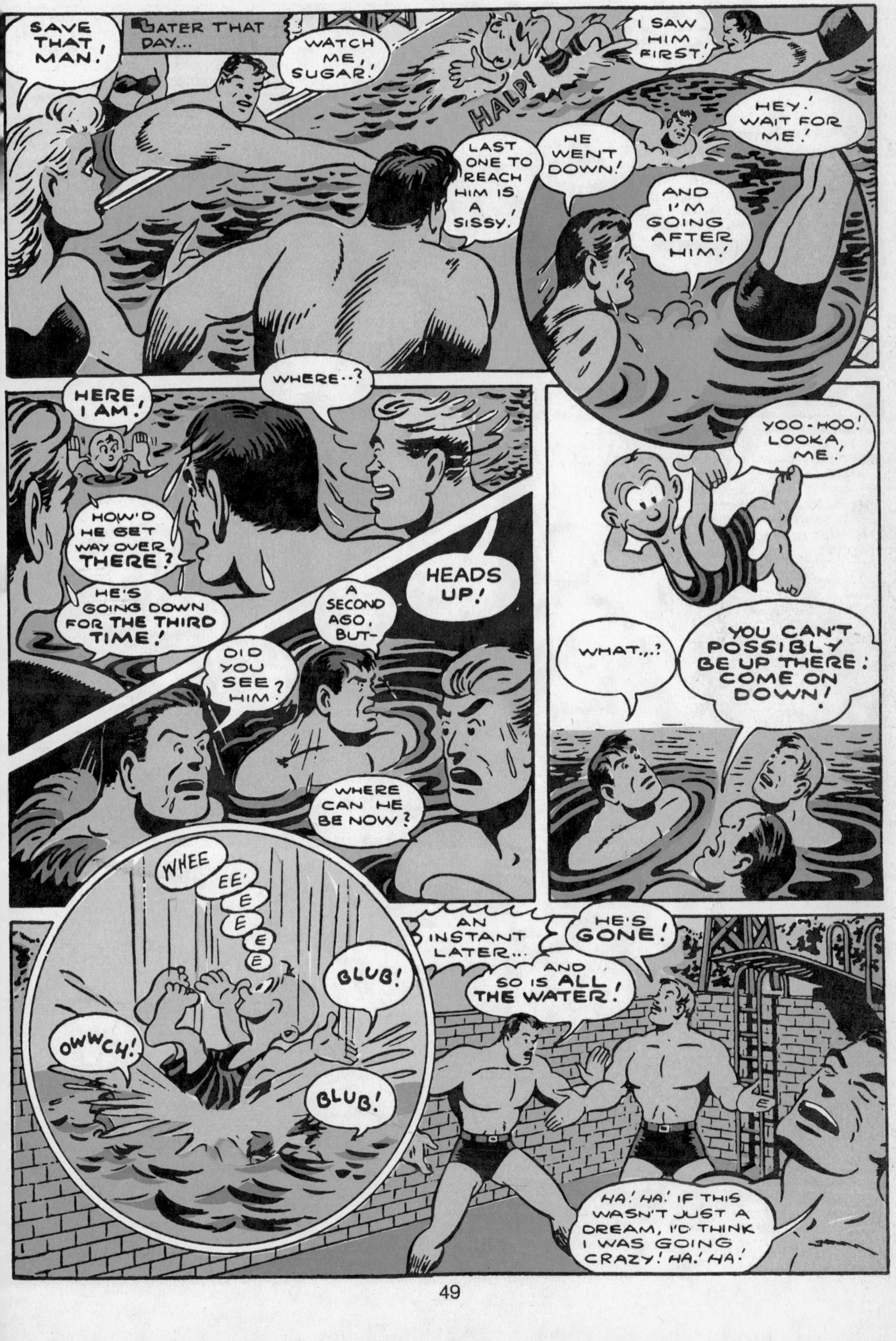

SAVE THAT MAN!
LATER THAT DAY...
WATCH ME, SUGAR!
HALP!
I SAW HIM FIRST!
HEY! WAIT FOR ME!
HE WENT DOWN!
LAST ONE TO REACH HIM IS A SISSY!
AND I'M GOING AFTER HIM!
WHERE..?
HERE, I AM!
HOW'D HE GET WAY OVER THERE?
HE'S GOING DOWN FOR THE THIRD TIME!
YOO-HOO! LOOKA, ME.
HEADS UP!
A SECOND AGO, BUT-
DID YOU SEE HIM?
WHERE CAN HE BE NOW?
WHAT...?
YOU CAN'T POSSIBLY BE UP THERE: COME ON DOWN!
WHEE
EE
E
E
E
E
BLUB!
OWWCH!
BLUB!
AN INSTANT LATER...
HE'S GONE!
AND SO IS ALL THE WATER!
HA! HA! IF THIS WASN'T JUST A DREAM, I'D THINK I WAS GOING CRAZY! HA! HA!

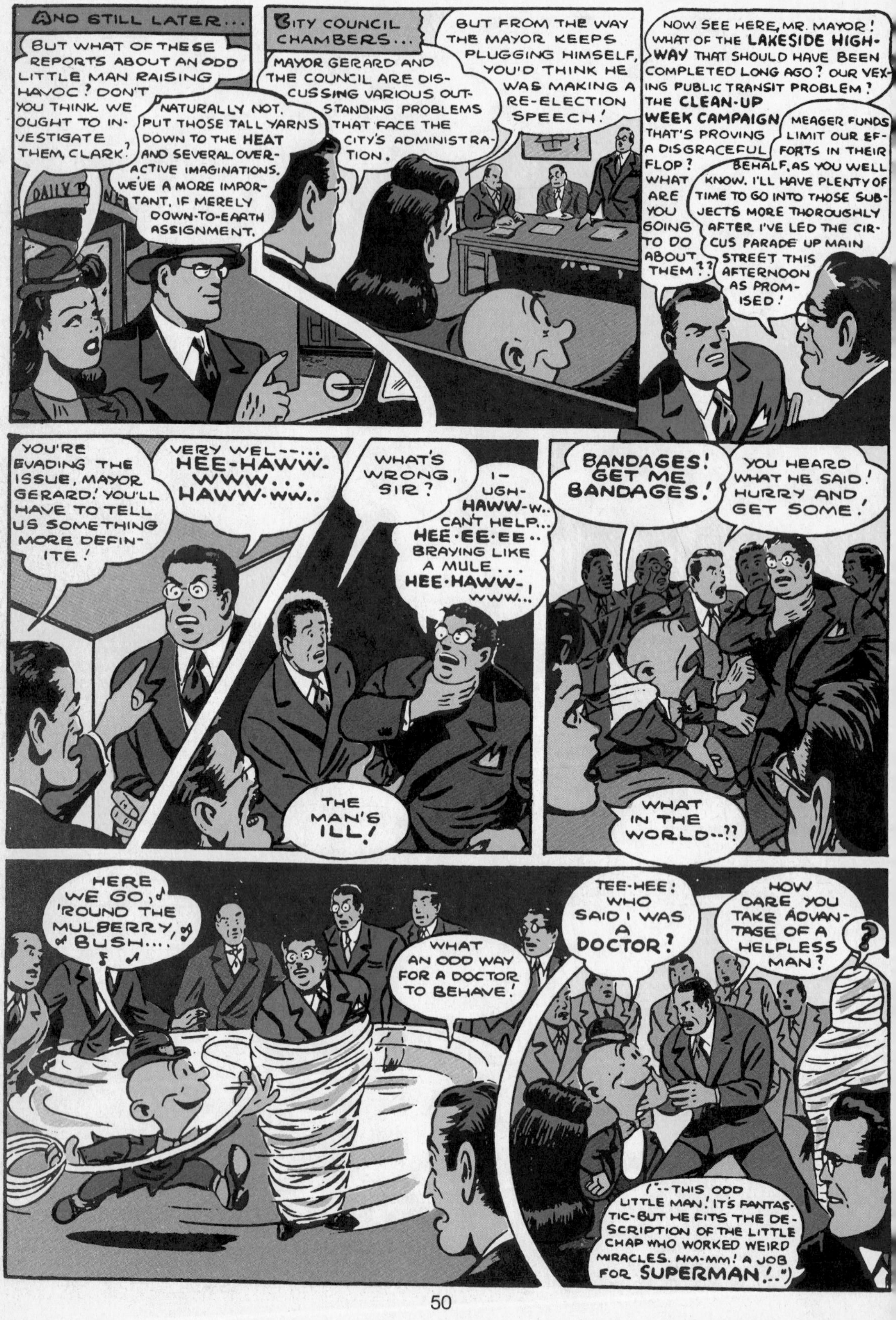
AND STILL LATER...
BUT WHAT OF THESE REPORTS ABOUT AN ODD LITTLE MAN RAISING HAVOC? DON'T YOU THINK WE OUGHT TO INVESTIGATE THEM, CLARK?
NATURALLY NOT. PUT THOSE TALL YARNS DOWN TO THE HEAT AND SEVERAL OVER-ACTIVE IMAGINATIONS. WE'VE A MORE IMPORTANT, IF MERELY DOWN-TO-EARTH ASSIGNMENT.
CITY COUNCIL CHAMBERS...
MAYOR GERARD AND THE COUNCIL ARE DISCUSSING VARIOUS OUTSTANDING PROBLEMS THAT FACE THE CITY'S ADMINISTRATION.
BUT FROM THE WAY THE MAYOR KEEPS PLUGGING HIMSELF, YOU'D THINK HE WAS MAKING A RE-ELECTION SPEECH!
NOW SEE HERE, MR. MAYOR! WHAT OF THE LAKESIDE HIGHWAY THAT SHOULD HAVE BEEN COMPLETED LONG AGO? OUR VEXING PUBLIC TRANSIT PROBLEM? THE CLEAN-UP WEEK CAMPAIGN THAT'S PROVING A DISGRACEFUL FLOP? WHAT ARE YOU GOING TO DO ABOUT THEM??
MEAGER FUNDS LIMIT OUR EFFORTS IN THEIR BEHALF, AS YOU WELL KNOW. I'LL HAVE PLENTY OF TIME TO GO INTO THOSE SUBJECTS MORE THOROUGHLY AFTER I'VE LED THE CIRCUS PARADE UP MAIN STREET THIS AFTERNOON AS PROMISED!
YOU'RE EVADING THE ISSUE, MAYOR GERARD! YOU'LL HAVE TO TELL US SOMETHING MORE DEFINITE!
VERY WEL---... HEE-HAWW-WWW... HAWW-WW..
WHAT'S WRONG, SIR?
I- UGH- HAWW-W.. CAN'T HELP... HEE-EE-EE.. BRAYING LIKE A MULE... HEE-HAWW-WWW..!
THE MAN'S ILL!
BANDAGES! GET ME BANDAGES!
YOU HEARD WHAT HE SAID! HURRY AND GET SOME!
WHAT IN THE WORLD--??
HERE WE GO, 'ROUND THE MULBERRY BUSH....
WHAT AN ODD WAY FOR A DOCTOR TO BEHAVE!
TEE-HEE! WHO SAID I WAS A DOCTOR?
HOW DARE YOU TAKE ADVANTAGE OF A HELPLESS MAN?
?
("--THIS ODD LITTLE MAN! IT'S FANTASTIC-BUT HE FITS THE DESCRIPTION OF THE LITTLE CHAP WHO WORKED WEIRD MIRACLES. HM-MM! A JOB FOR SUPERMAN!..")

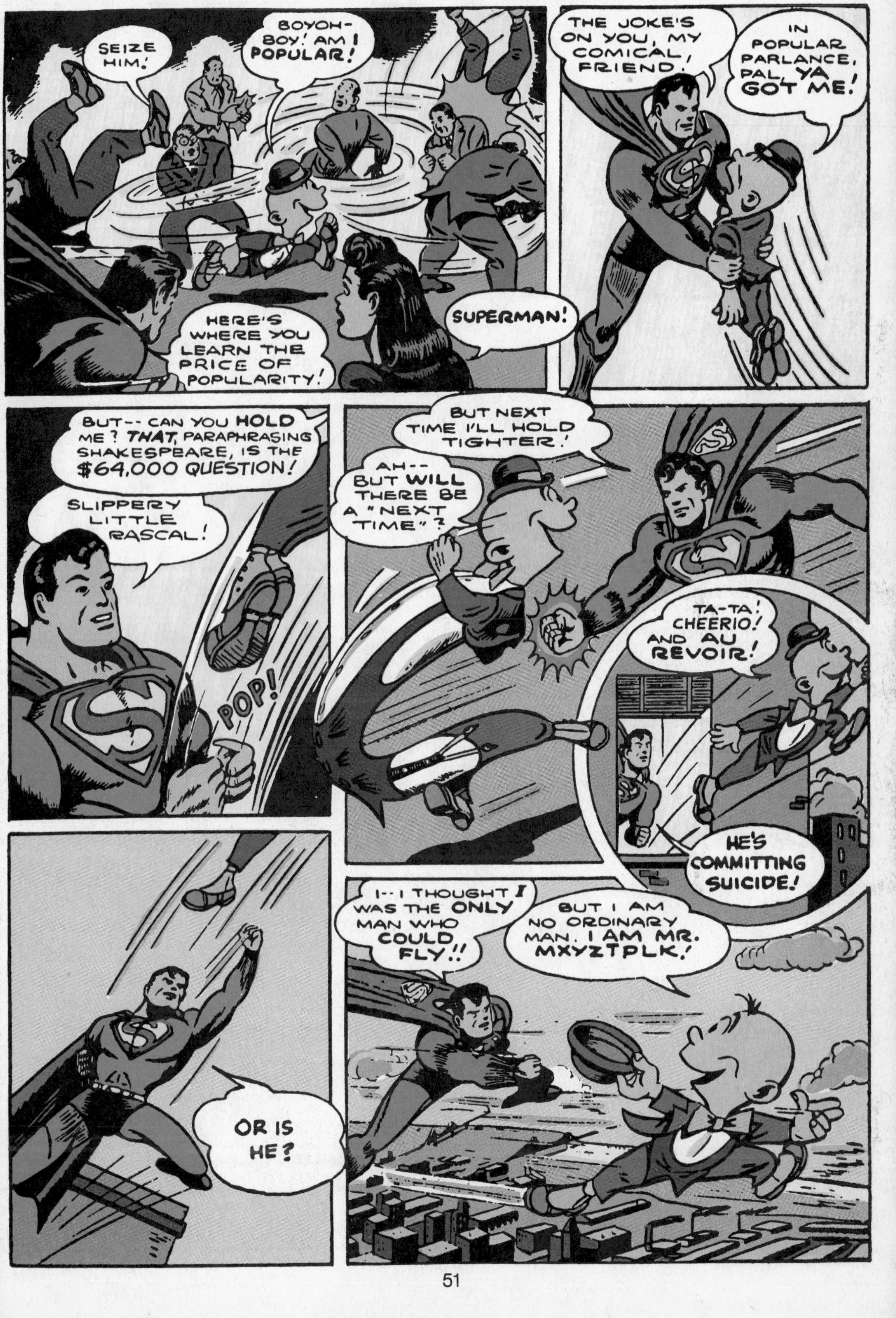
SEIZE HIM!
BOYOH-BOY! AM I POPULAR!
HERE'S WHERE YOU LEARN THE PRICE OF POPULARITY!
SUPERMAN!
THE JOKE'S ON YOU, MY COMICAL FRIEND!
IN POPULAR PARLANCE, PAL, YA GOT ME!
BUT-- CAN YOU HOLD ME? THAT, PARAPHRASING SHAKESPEARE, IS THE $64,000 QUESTION!
SLIPPERY LITTLE RASCAL!
POP!
BUT NEXT TIME I'LL HOLD TIGHTER!
AH-- BUT WILL THERE BE A "NEXT TIME"?
TA-TA! CHEERIO! AND AU REVOIR!
HE'S COMMITTING SUICIDE!
OR IS HE?
I-- I THOUGHT I WAS THE ONLY MAN WHO COULD FLY!!
BUT I AM NO ORDINARY MAN. I AM MR. MXYZTPLK!

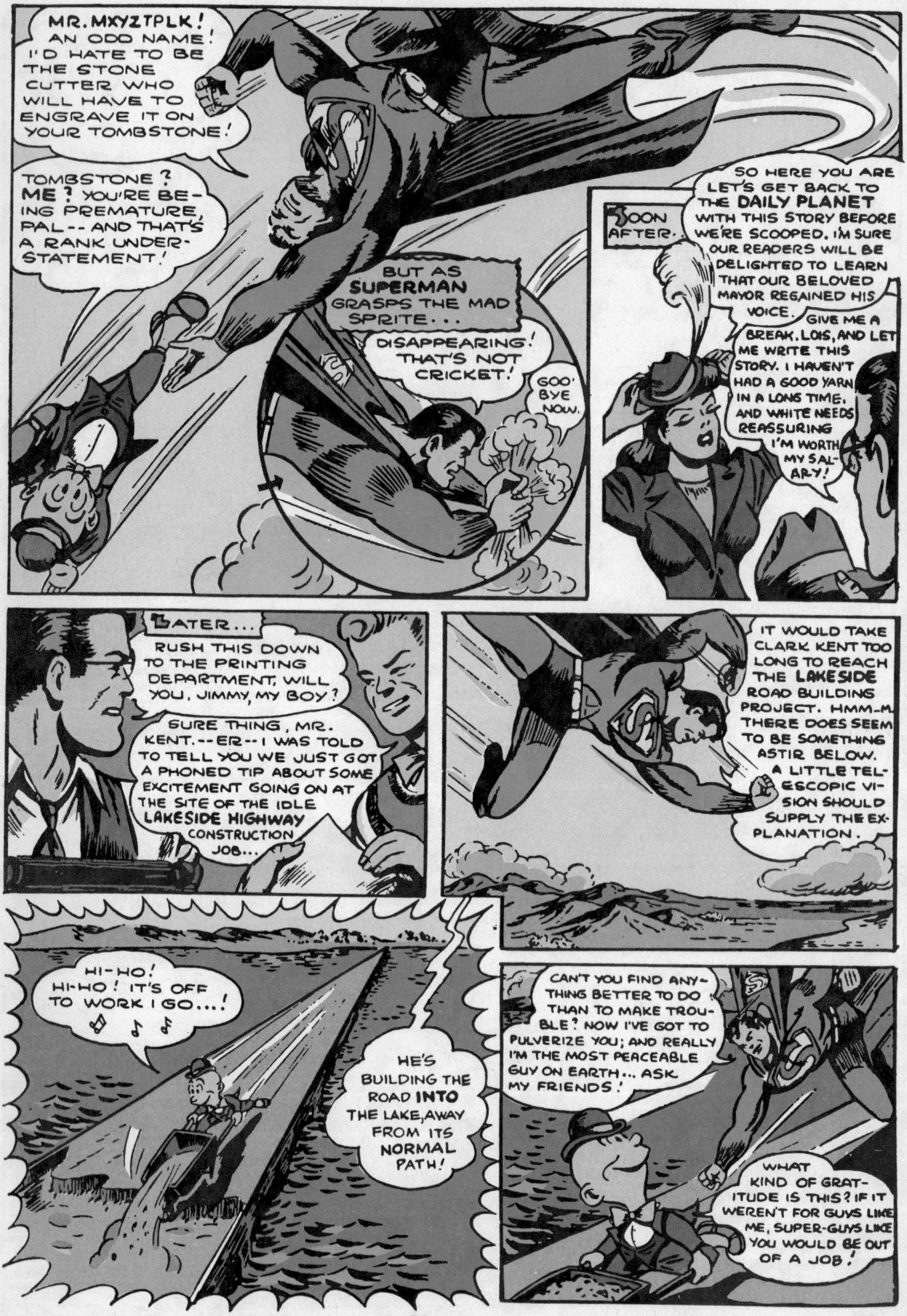
MR. MXYZTPLK! AN ODD NAME! I'D HATE TO BE THE STONE CUTTER WHO WILL HAVE TO ENGRAVE IT ON YOUR TOMBSTONE!
TOMBSTONE? ME? YOU'RE BE-ING PREMATURE, PAL-- AND THAT'S A RANK UNDER-STATEMENT!
BUT AS SUPERMAN GRASPS THE MAD SPRITE...
DISAPPEARING! THAT'S NOT CRICKET!
GOO' BYE NOW.
SOON AFTER.
SO HERE YOU ARE LET'S GET BACK TO THE DAILY PLANET WITH THIS STORY BEFORE WE'RE SCOOPED. I'M SURE OUR READERS WILL BE DELIGHTED TO LEARN THAT OUR BELOVED MAYOR REGAINED HIS VOICE.
GIVE ME A BREAK, LOIS, AND LET ME WRITE THIS STORY. I HAVEN'T HAD A GOOD YARN IN A LONG TIME. AND WHITE NEEDS REASSURING I'M WORTH MY SAL-ARY!
LATER...
RUSH THIS DOWN TO THE PRINTING DEPARTMENT, WILL YOU, JIMMY, MY BOY?
SURE THING, MR. KENT.--ER--I WAS TOLD TO TELL YOU WE JUST GOT A PHONED TIP ABOUT SOME EXCITEMENT GOING ON AT THE SITE OF THE IDLE LAKESIDE HIGHWAY CONSTRUCTION JOB...
IT WOULD TAKE CLARK KENT TOO LONG TO REACH THE LAKESIDE ROAD BUILDING PROJECT. HMM-M. THERE DOES SEEM TO BE SOMETHING ASTIR BELOW. A LITTLE TEL-ESCOPIC VI-SION SHOULD SUPPLY THE EX-PLANATION.
HI-HO! HI-HO! IT'S OFF TO WORK I GO...!
HE'S BUILDING THE ROAD INTO THE LAKE, AWAY FROM ITS NORMAL PATH!
CAN'T YOU FIND ANY-THING BETTER TO DO THAN TO MAKE TROU-BLE? NOW I'VE GOT TO PULVERIZE YOU; AND REALLY I'M THE MOST PEACEABLE GUY ON EARTH... ASK MY FRIENDS!
WHAT KIND OF GRAT-ITUDE IS THIS? IF IT WEREN'T FOR GUYS LIKE ME, SUPER-GUYS LIKE YOU WOULD BE OUT OF A JOB!

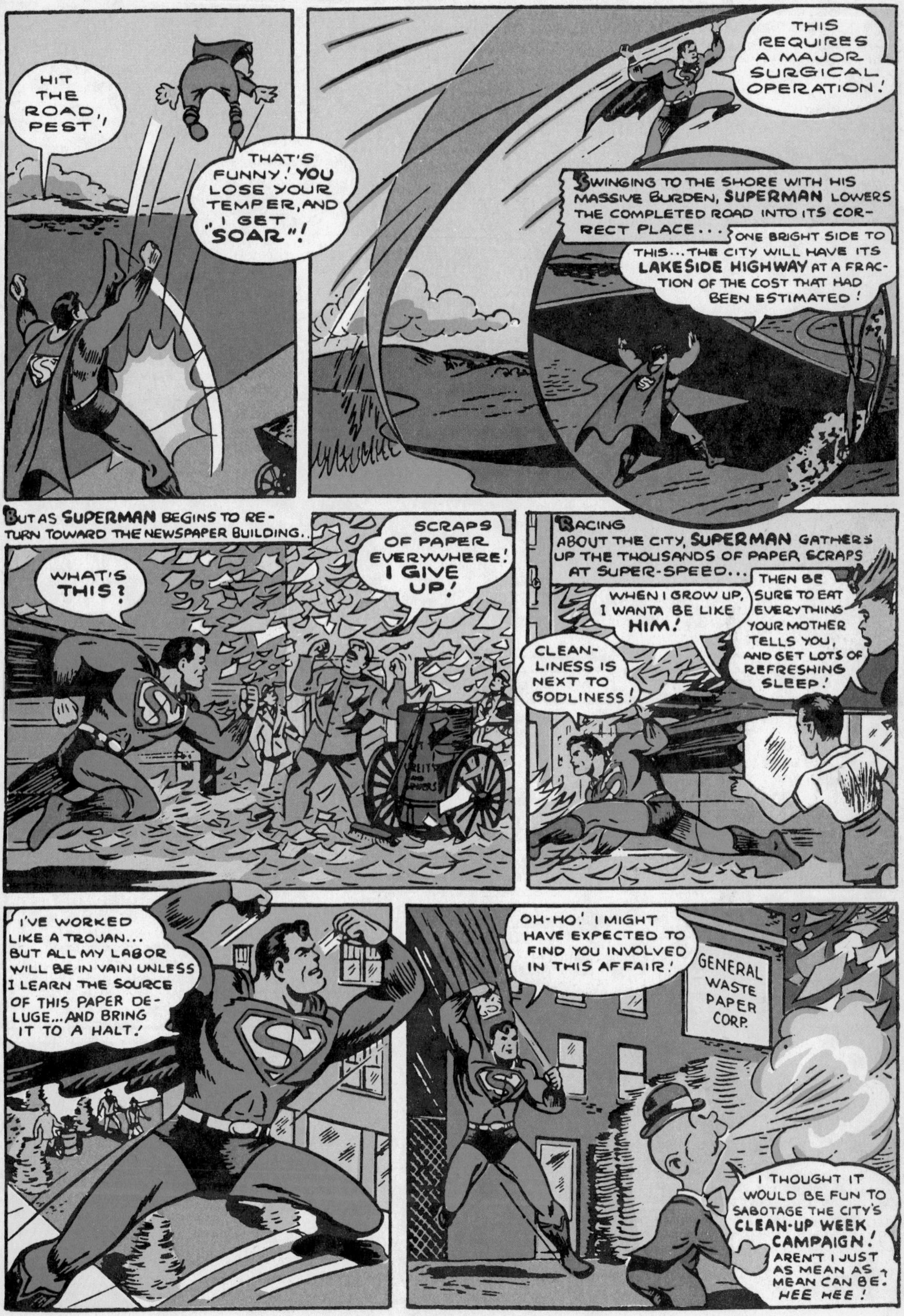
HIT THE ROAD, PEST!
THAT'S FUNNY! YOU LOSE YOUR TEMPER, AND I GET "SOAR"!
THIS REQUIRES A MAJOR SURGICAL OPERATION!
SWINGING TO THE SHORE WITH HIS MASSIVE BURDEN, SUPERMAN LOWERS THE COMPLETED ROAD INTO ITS CORRECT PLACE...
ONE BRIGHT SIDE TO THIS... THE CITY WILL HAVE ITS LAKESIDE HIGHWAY AT A FRACTION OF THE COST THAT HAD BEEN ESTIMATED!
BUT AS SUPERMAN BEGINS TO RETURN TOWARD THE NEWSPAPER BUILDING..
WHAT'S THIS?
SCRAPS OF PAPER EVERYWHERE! I GIVE UP!
RACING ABOUT THE CITY, SUPERMAN GATHERS UP THE THOUSANDS OF PAPER SCRAPS AT SUPER-SPEED...
WHEN I GROW UP, I WANTA BE LIKE HIM!
THEN BE SURE TO EAT EVERYTHING YOUR MOTHER TELLS YOU, AND GET LOTS OF REFRESHING SLEEP!
CLEANLINESS IS NEXT TO GODLINESS!
I'VE WORKED LIKE A TROJAN... BUT ALL MY LABOR WILL BE IN VAIN UNLESS I LEARN THE SOURCE OF THIS PAPER DELUGE... AND BRING IT TO A HALT!
OH-HO! I MIGHT HAVE EXPECTED TO FIND YOU INVOLVED IN THIS AFFAIR!
GENERAL WASTE PAPER CORP.
I THOUGHT IT WOULD BE FUN TO SABOTAGE THE CITY'S CLEAN-UP WEEK CAMPAIGN! AREN'T I JUST AS MEAN AS MEAN CAN BE? HEE HEE!

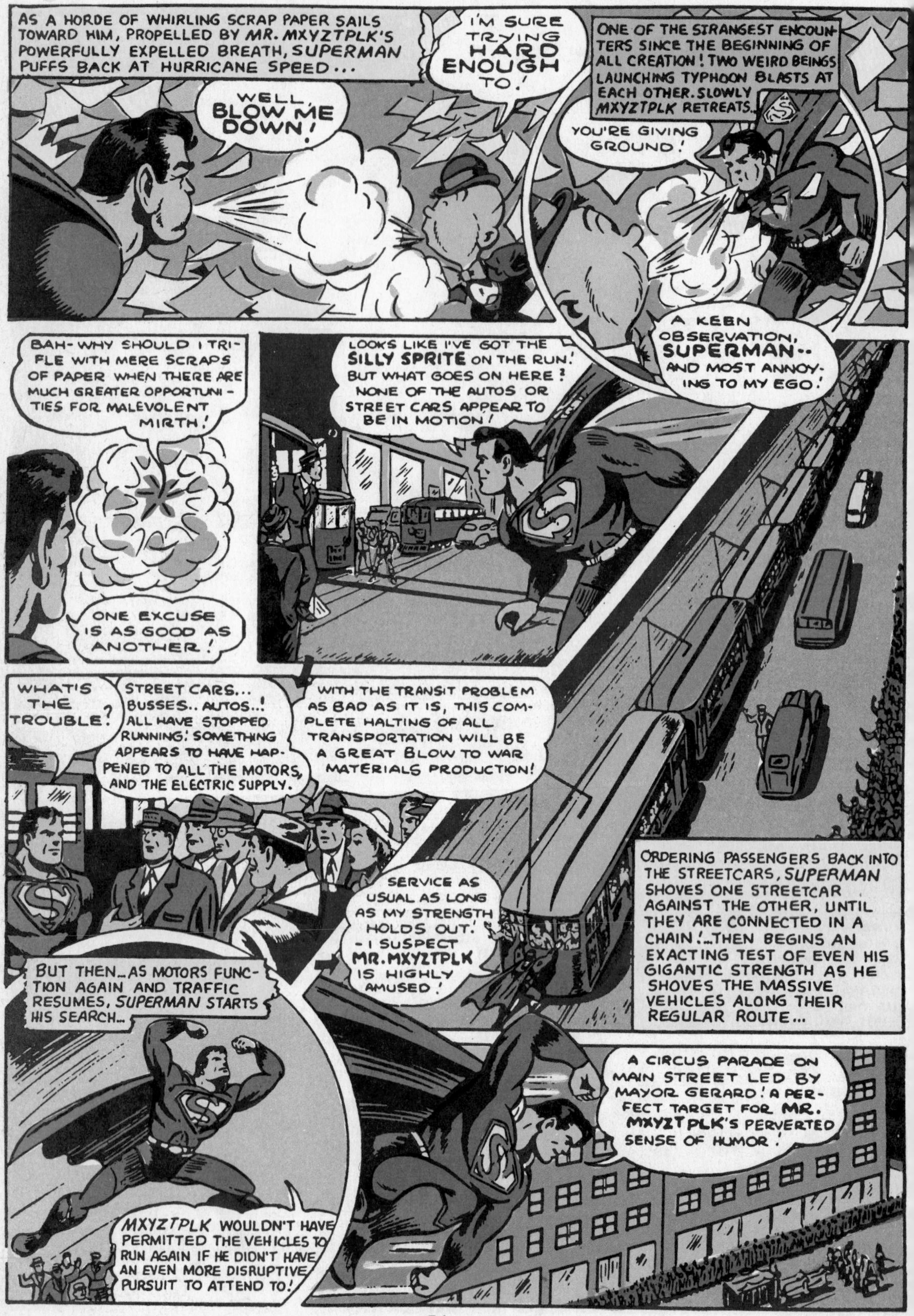

AS A HORDE OF WHIRLING SCRAP PAPER SAILS TOWARD HIM, PROPELLED BY MR. MXYZTPLK'S POWERFULLY EXPELLED BREATH, SUPERMAN PUFFS BACK AT HURRICANE SPEED...
I'M SURE TRYING HARD ENOUGH TO!
WELL, BLOW ME DOWN!
ONE OF THE STRANGEST ENCOUNTERS SINCE THE BEGINNING OF ALL CREATION! TWO WEIRD BEINGS LAUNCHING TYPHOON BLASTS AT EACH OTHER. SLOWLY MXYZTPLK RETREATS...
YOU'RE GIVING GROUND!
A KEEN OBSERVATION, SUPERMAN-- AND MOST ANNOYING TO MY EGO!
BAH- WHY SHOULD I TRIFLE WITH MERE SCRAPS OF PAPER WHEN THERE ARE MUCH GREATER OPPORTUNITIES FOR MALEVOLENT MIRTH!
ONE EXCUSE IS AS GOOD AS ANOTHER!
LOOKS LIKE I'VE GOT THE SILLY SPRITE ON THE RUN! BUT WHAT GOES ON HERE? NONE OF THE AUTOS OR STREET CARS APPEAR TO BE IN MOTION!
WHAT'S THE TROUBLE?
STREET CARS... BUSSES.. AUTOS...! ALL HAVE STOPPED RUNNING! SOMETHING APPEARS TO HAVE HAPPENED TO ALL THE MOTORS, AND THE ELECTRIC SUPPLY.
WITH THE TRANSIT PROBLEM AS BAD AS IT IS, THIS COMPLETE HALTING OF ALL TRANSPORTATION WILL BE A GREAT BLOW TO WAR MATERIALS PRODUCTION!
ORDERING PASSENGERS BACK INTO THE STREETCARS, SUPERMAN SHOVES ONE STREETCAR AGAINST THE OTHER, UNTIL THEY ARE CONNECTED IN A CHAIN!...THEN BEGINS AN EXACTING TEST OF EVEN HIS GIGANTIC STRENGTH AS HE SHOVES THE MASSIVE VEHICLES ALONG THEIR REGULAR ROUTE...
SERVICE AS USUAL AS LONG AS MY STRENGTH HOLDS OUT! - I SUSPECT MR. MXYZTPLK IS HIGHLY AMUSED!
BUT THEN...AS MOTORS FUNCTION AGAIN AND TRAFFIC RESUMES, SUPERMAN STARTS HIS SEARCH...
MXYZTPLK WOULDN'T HAVE PERMITTED THE VEHICLES TO RUN AGAIN IF HE DIDN'T HAVE AN EVEN MORE DISRUPTIVE PURSUIT TO ATTEND TO!
A CIRCUS PARADE ON MAIN STREET LED BY MAYOR GERARD! A PERFECT TARGET FOR MR. MXYZTPLK'S PERVERTED SENSE OF HUMOR!

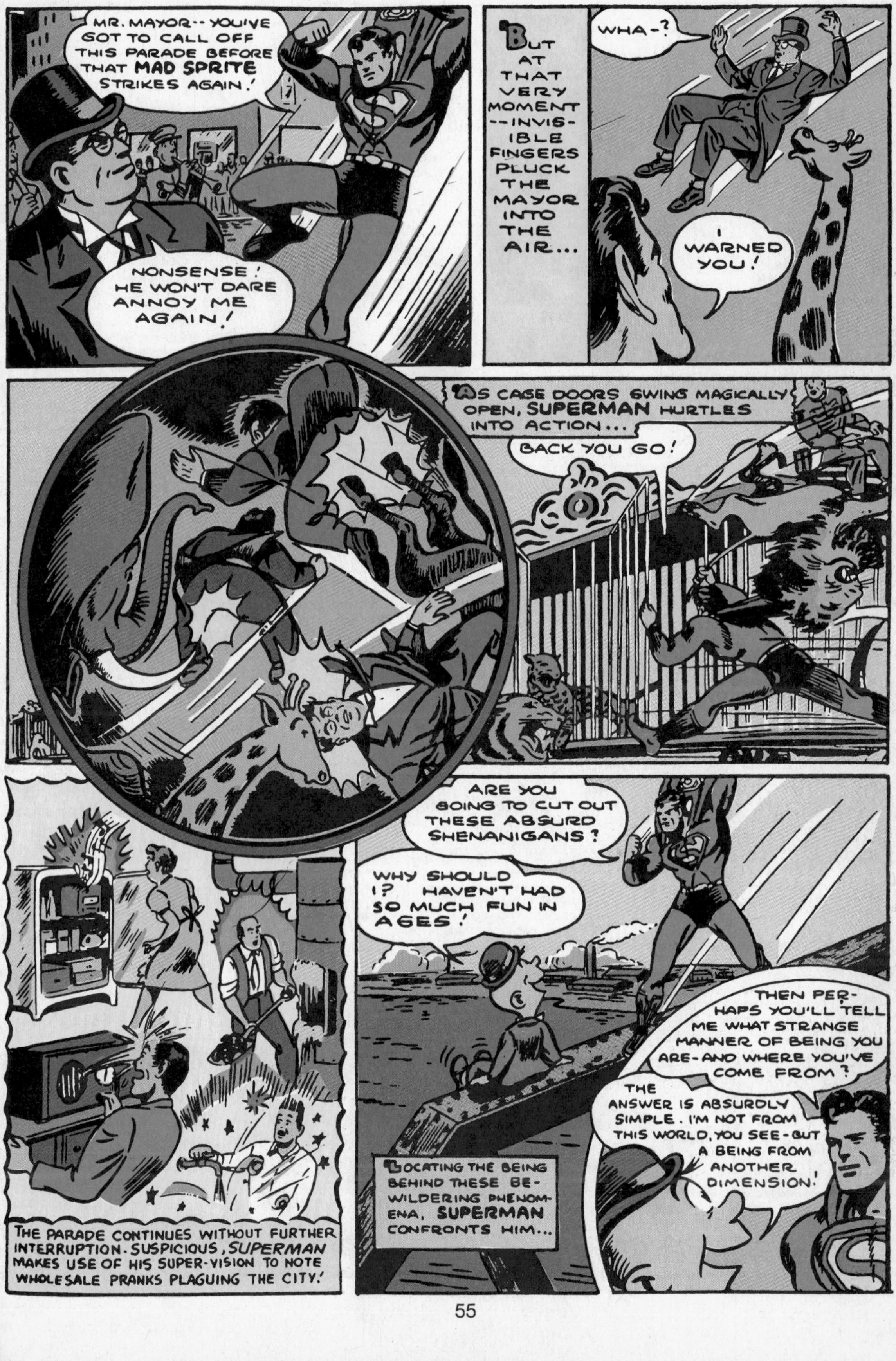
MR. MAYOR--YOU'VE GOT TO CALL OFF THIS PARADE BEFORE THAT MAD SPRITE STRIKES AGAIN!
NONSENSE! HE WON'T DARE ANNOY ME AGAIN!
BUT AT THAT VERY MOMENT--INVISIBLE FINGERS PLUCK THE MAYOR INTO THE AIR...
WHA-?
I WARNED YOU!
AS CAGE DOORS SWING MAGICALLY OPEN, SUPERMAN HURTLES INTO ACTION...
BACK YOU GO!
THE PARADE CONTINUES WITHOUT FURTHER INTERRUPTION. SUSPICIOUS, SUPERMAN MAKES USE OF HIS SUPER-VISION TO NOTE WHOLESALE PRANKS PLAGUING THE CITY!
ARE YOU GOING TO CUT OUT THESE ABSURD SHENANIGANS?
WHY SHOULD I? HAVEN'T HAD SO MUCH FUN IN AGES!
LOCATING THE BEING BEHIND THESE BEWILDERING PHENOMENA, SUPERMAN CONFRONTS HIM...
THEN PERHAPS YOU'LL TELL ME WHAT STRANGE MANNER OF BEING YOU ARE-AND WHERE YOU'VE COME FROM?
THE ANSWER IS ABSURDLY SIMPLE. I'M NOT FROM THIS WORLD, YOU SEE-BUT A BEING FROM ANOTHER DIMENSION!

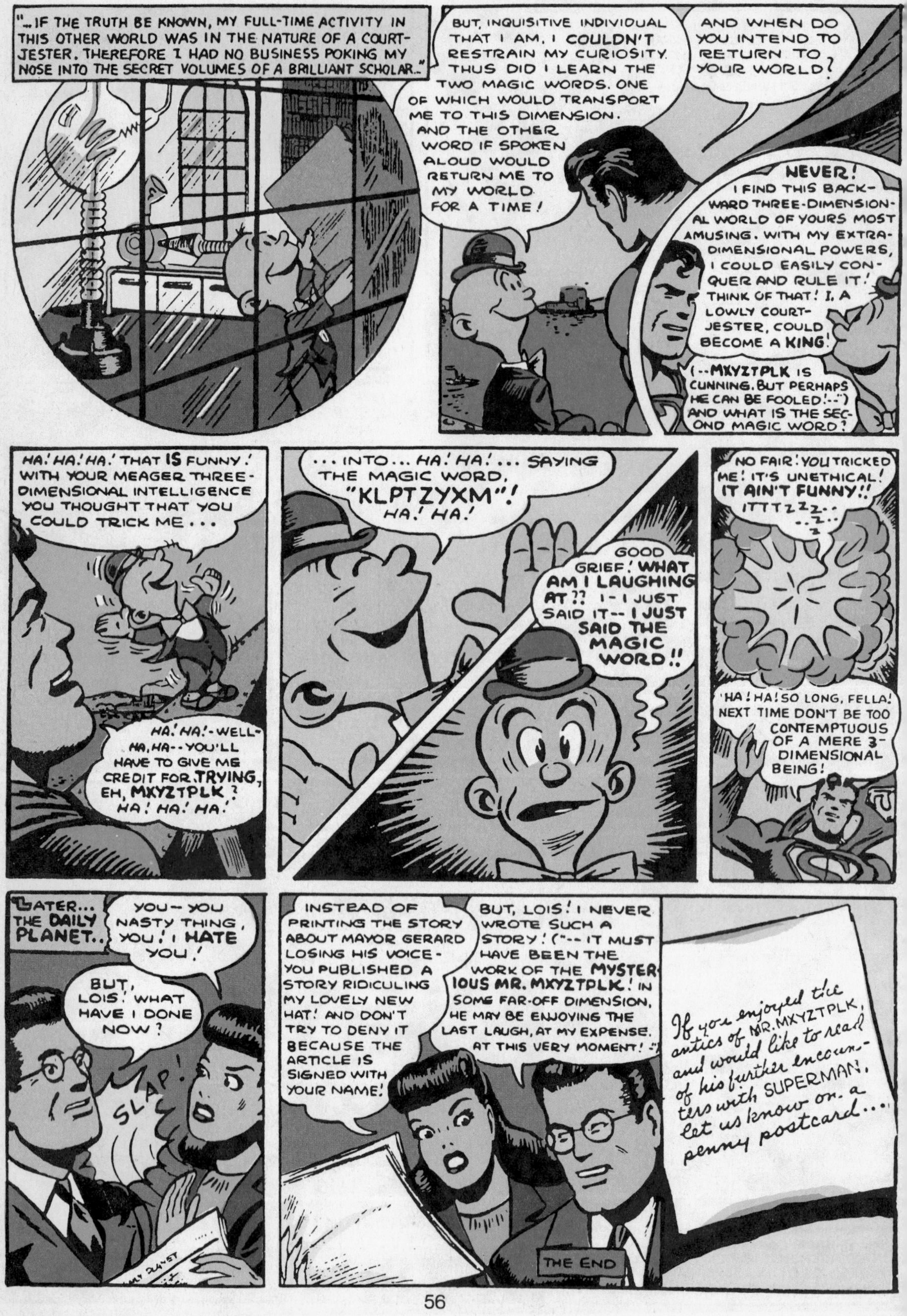
"...IF THE TRUTH BE KNOWN, MY FULL-TIME ACTIVITY IN THIS OTHER WORLD WAS IN THE NATURE OF A COURT-JESTER. THEREFORE I HAD NO BUSINESS POKING MY NOSE INTO THE SECRET VOLUMES OF A BRILLIANT SCHOLAR..."
BUT, INQUISITIVE INDIVIDUAL THAT I AM, I COULDN'T RESTRAIN MY CURIOSITY. THUS DID I LEARN THE TWO MAGIC WORDS. ONE OF WHICH WOULD TRANSPORT ME TO THIS DIMENSION. AND THE OTHER WORD IF SPOKEN ALOUD WOULD RETURN ME TO MY WORLD FOR A TIME!
AND WHEN DO YOU INTEND TO RETURN TO YOUR WORLD?
NEVER! I FIND THIS BACKWARD THREE-DIMENSIONAL WORLD OF YOURS MOST AMUSING. WITH MY EXTRA-DIMENSIONAL POWERS, I COULD EASILY CONQUER AND RULE IT! THINK OF THAT! I, A LOWLY COURT-JESTER, COULD BECOME A KING!
(--MXYZTPLK IS CUNNING. BUT PERHAPS HE CAN BE FOOLED!--") AND WHAT IS THE SECOND MAGIC WORD?
HA! HA! HA! THAT IS FUNNY! WITH YOUR MEAGER THREE-DIMENSIONAL INTELLIGENCE YOU THOUGHT THAT YOU COULD TRICK ME...
HA! HA!-WELL-HA, HA--YOU'LL HAVE TO GIVE ME CREDIT FOR TRYING, EH, MXYZTPLK? HA! HA! HA!
...INTO...HA! HA!...SAYING THE MAGIC WORD, "KLPTZYXM"! HA! HA!
GOOD GRIEF! WHAT AM I LAUGHING AT?? I-I JUST SAID IT--I JUST SAID THE MAGIC WORD!!
NO FAIR! YOU TRICKED ME! IT'S UNETHICAL! IT AIN'T FUNNY!! ITTTZZZ...
HA! HA! SO LONG, FELLA! NEXT TIME DON'T BE TOO CONTEMPTUOUS OF A MERE 3-DIMENSIONAL BEING!
LATER... THE DAILY PLANET..
YOU-YOU NASTY THING, YOU! I HATE YOU!
BUT, LOIS! WHAT HAVE I DONE NOW?
SLAP!
INSTEAD OF PRINTING THE STORY ABOUT MAYOR GERARD LOSING HIS VOICE-YOU PUBLISHED A STORY RIDICULING MY LOVELY NEW HAT! AND DON'T TRY TO DENY IT BECAUSE THE ARTICLE IS SIGNED WITH YOUR NAME!
BUT, LOIS! I NEVER WROTE SUCH A STORY! ("--IT MUST HAVE BEEN THE WORK OF THE MYSTERIOUS MR. MXYZTPLK! IN SOME FAR-OFF DIMENSION, HE MAY BE ENJOYING THE LAST LAUGH, AT MY EXPENSE, AT THIS VERY MOMENT!--")
If you enjoyed the antics of MR. MXYZTPLK, and would like to read of his further encounters with SUPERMAN, let us know on a penny postcard...
THE END

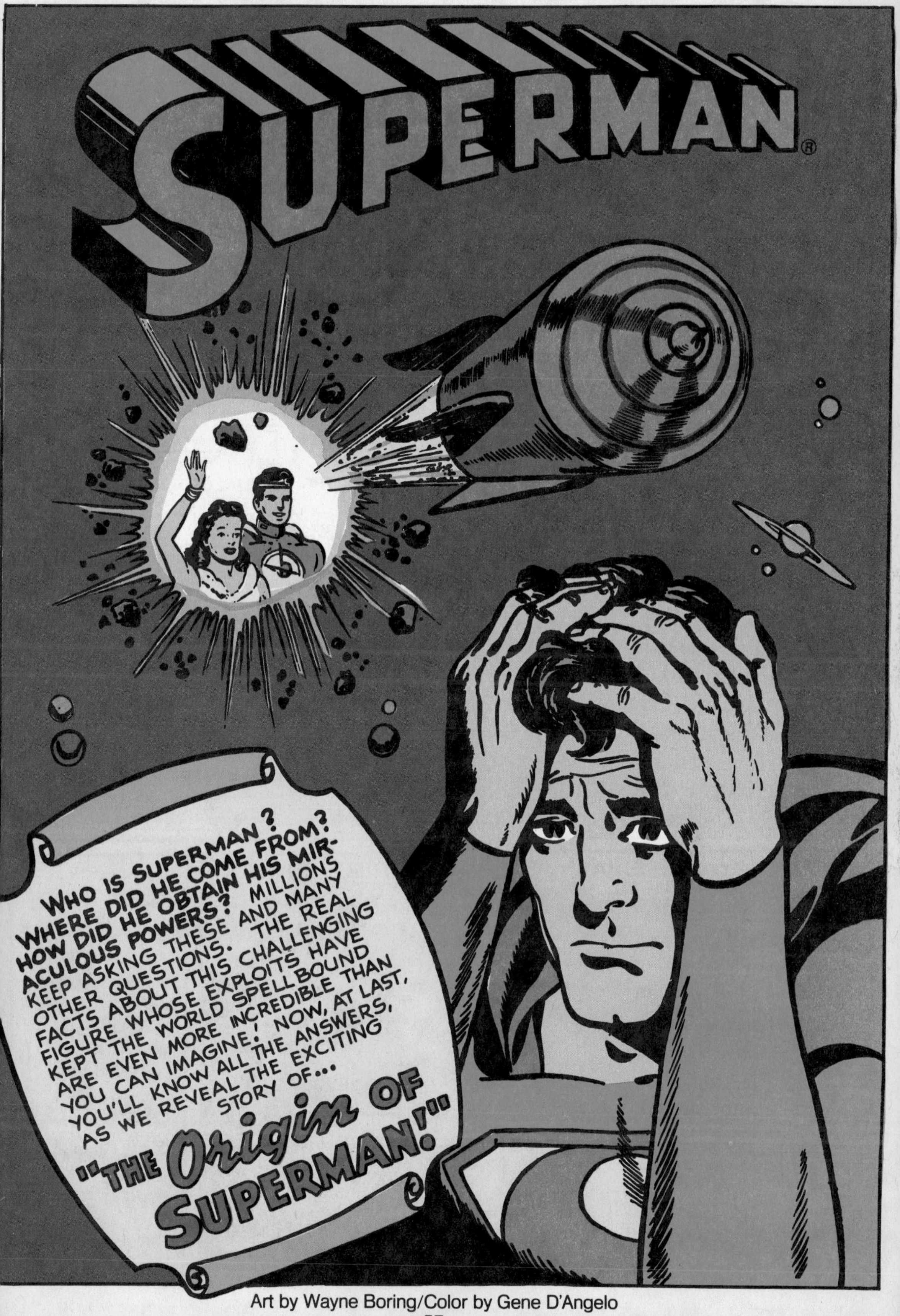
SUPERMAN®
WHO IS SUPERMAN? WHERE DID HE COME FROM? HOW DID HE OBTAIN HIS MIRACULOUS POWERS? MILLIONS KEEP ASKING THESE AND MANY OTHER QUESTIONS. THE REAL FACTS ABOUT THIS CHALLENGING FIGURE WHOSE EXPLOITS HAVE KEPT THE WORLD SPELLBOUND ARE EVEN MORE INCREDIBLE THAN YOU CAN IMAGINE! NOW, AT LAST, YOU'LL KNOW ALL THE ANSWERS, AS WE REVEAL THE EXCITING STORY OF...
"THE Origin OF SUPERMAN!"
Art by Wayne Boring/Color by Gene D'Angelo

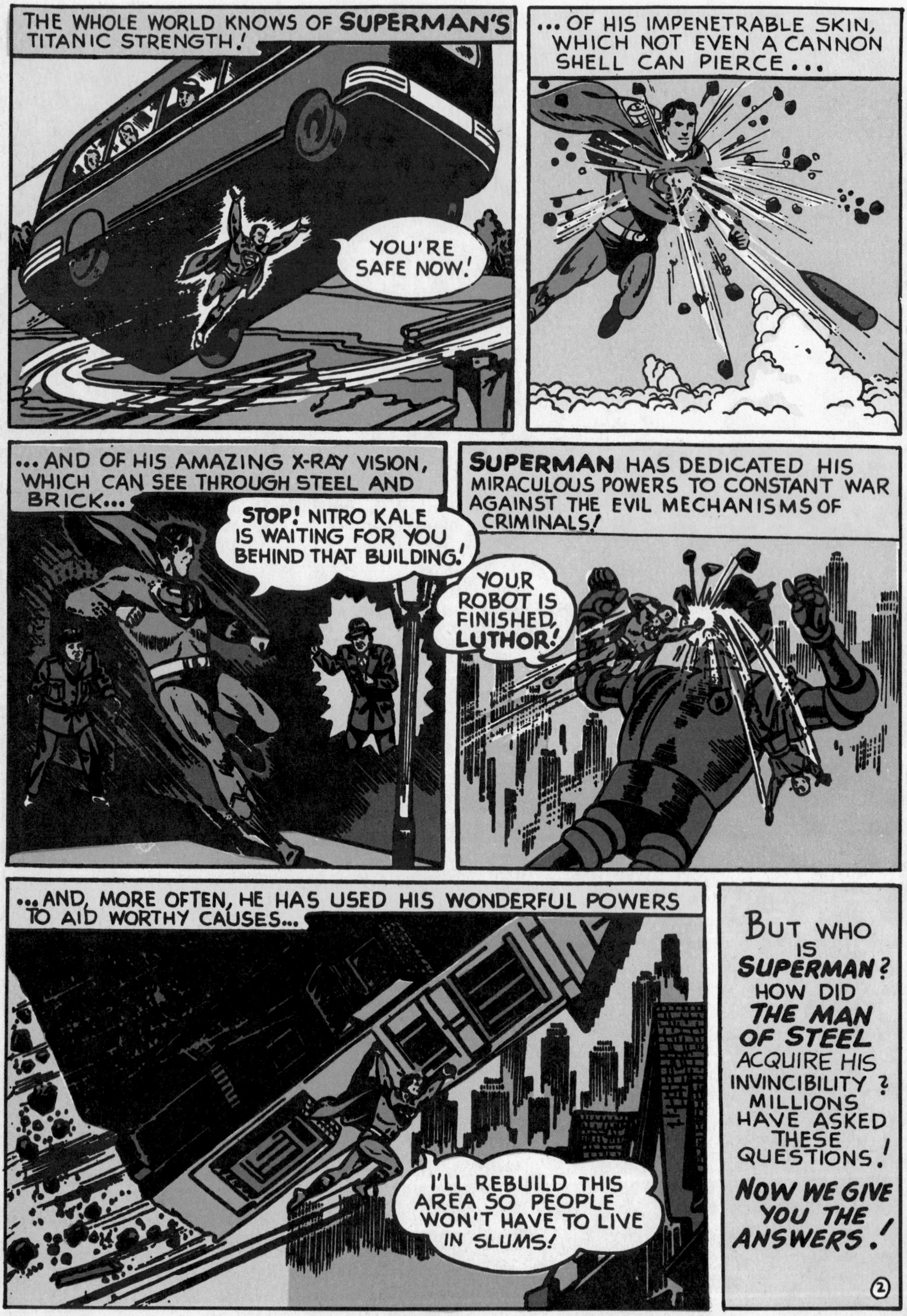
THE WHOLE WORLD KNOWS OF SUPERMAN'S TITANIC STRENGTH!
YOU'RE SAFE NOW!
...OF HIS IMPENETRABLE SKIN, WHICH NOT EVEN A CANNON SHELL CAN PIERCE...
...AND OF HIS AMAZING X-RAY VISION, WHICH CAN SEE THROUGH STEEL AND BRICK...
STOP! NITRO KALE IS WAITING FOR YOU BEHIND THAT BUILDING!
SUPERMAN HAS DEDICATED HIS MIRACULOUS POWERS TO CONSTANT WAR AGAINST THE EVIL MECHANISMS OF CRIMINALS!
YOUR ROBOT IS FINISHED, LUTHOR!
...AND, MORE OFTEN, HE HAS USED HIS WONDERFUL POWERS TO AID WORTHY CAUSES...
I'LL REBUILD THIS AREA SO PEOPLE WON'T HAVE TO LIVE IN SLUMS!
BUT WHO IS SUPERMAN? HOW DID THE MAN OF STEEL ACQUIRE HIS INVINCIBILITY? MILLIONS HAVE ASKED THESE QUESTIONS!
NOW WE GIVE YOU THE ANSWERS!
2

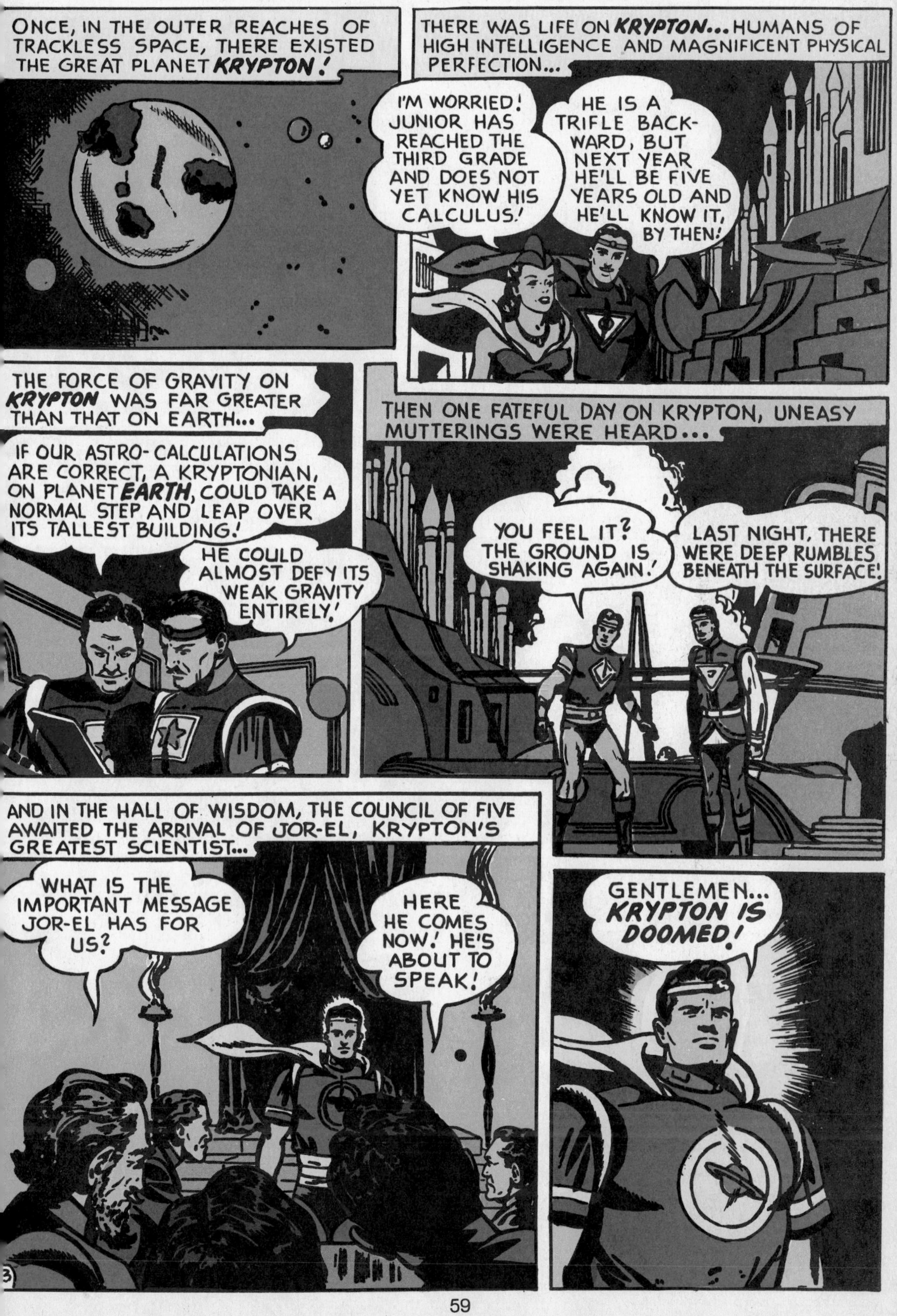
ONCE, IN THE OUTER REACHES OF TRACKLESS SPACE, THERE EXISTED THE GREAT PLANET KRYPTON!
THERE WAS LIFE ON KRYPTON... HUMANS OF HIGH INTELLIGENCE AND MAGNIFICENT PHYSICAL PERFECTION...
I'M WORRIED! JUNIOR HAS REACHED THE THIRD GRADE AND DOES NOT YET KNOW HIS CALCULUS!
HE IS A TRIFLE BACKWARD, BUT NEXT YEAR HE'LL BE FIVE YEARS OLD AND HE'LL KNOW IT, BY THEN!
THE FORCE OF GRAVITY ON KRYPTON WAS FAR GREATER THAN THAT ON EARTH...
IF OUR ASTRO-CALCULATIONS ARE CORRECT, A KRYPTONIAN, ON PLANET EARTH, COULD TAKE A NORMAL STEP AND LEAP OVER ITS TALLEST BUILDING!
HE COULD ALMOST DEFY ITS WEAK GRAVITY ENTIRELY!
THEN ONE FATEFUL DAY ON KRYPTON, UNEASY MUTTERINGS WERE HEARD...
YOU FEEL IT? THE GROUND IS SHAKING AGAIN!
LAST NIGHT, THERE WERE DEEP RUMBLES BENEATH THE SURFACE!
AND IN THE HALL OF WISDOM, THE COUNCIL OF FIVE AWAITED THE ARRIVAL OF JOR-EL, KRYPTON'S GREATEST SCIENTIST...
WHAT IS THE IMPORTANT MESSAGE JOR-EL HAS FOR US?
HERE HE COMES NOW! HE'S ABOUT TO SPEAK!
3
GENTLEMEN... KRYPTON IS DOOMED!

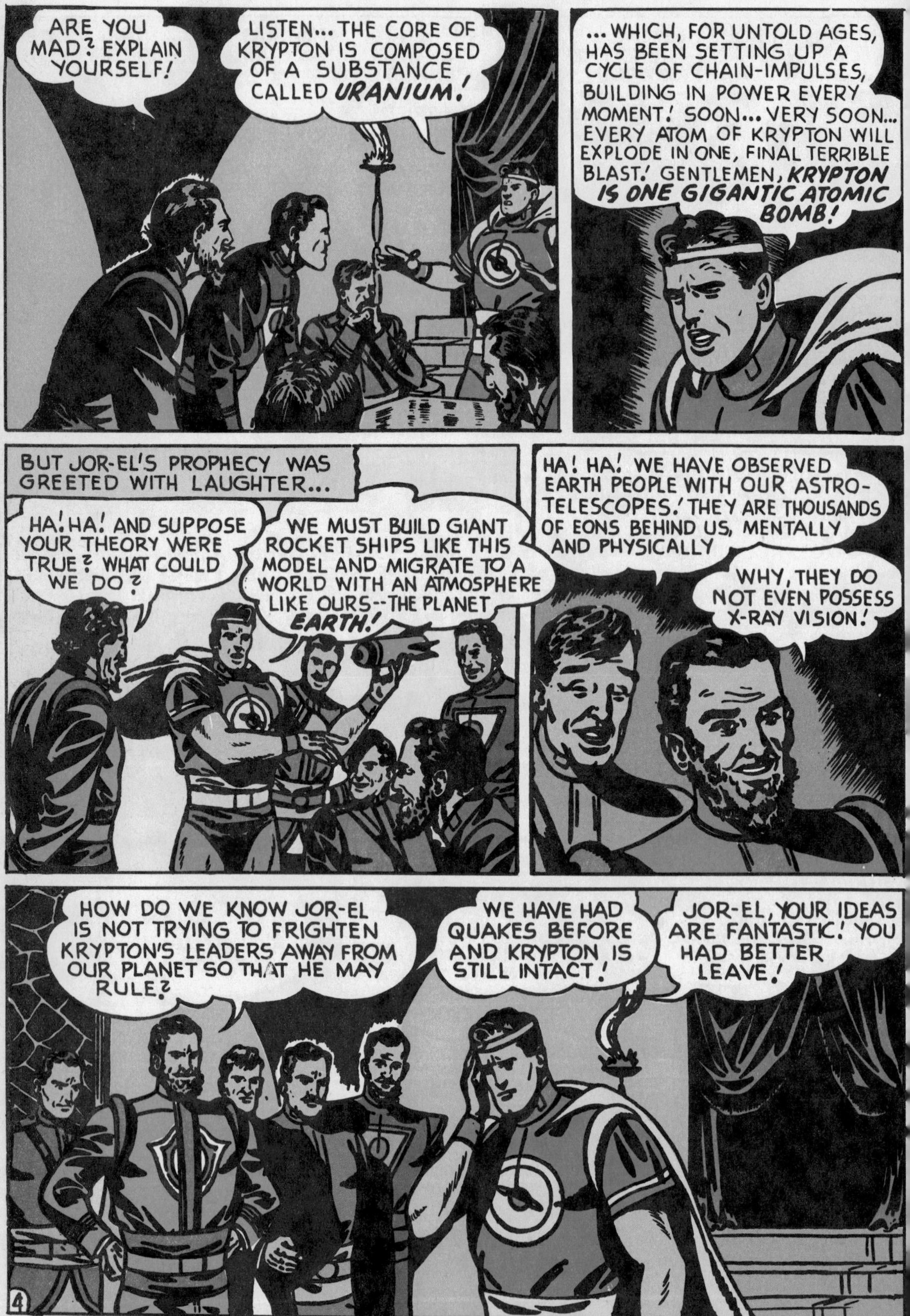
ARE YOU MAD? EXPLAIN YOURSELF!
LISTEN... THE CORE OF KRYPTON IS COMPOSED OF A SUBSTANCE CALLED URANIUM!
...WHICH, FOR UNTOLD AGES, HAS BEEN SETTING UP A CYCLE OF CHAIN-IMPULSES, BUILDING IN POWER EVERY MOMENT! SOON... VERY SOON... EVERY ATOM OF KRYPTON WILL EXPLODE IN ONE, FINAL TERRIBLE BLAST! GENTLEMEN, KRYPTON IS ONE GIGANTIC ATOMIC BOMB!
BUT JOR-EL'S PROPHECY WAS GREETED WITH LAUGHTER...
HA! HA! AND SUPPOSE YOUR THEORY WERE TRUE? WHAT COULD WE DO?
WE MUST BUILD GIANT ROCKET SHIPS LIKE THIS MODEL AND MIGRATE TO A WORLD WITH AN ATMOSPHERE LIKE OURS--THE PLANET EARTH!
HA! HA! WE HAVE OBSERVED EARTH PEOPLE WITH OUR ASTRO-TELESCOPES! THEY ARE THOUSANDS OF EONS BEHIND US, MENTALLY AND PHYSICALLY
WHY, THEY DO NOT EVEN POSSESS X-RAY VISION!
HOW DO WE KNOW JOR-EL IS NOT TRYING TO FRIGHTEN KRYPTON'S LEADERS AWAY FROM OUR PLANET SO THAT HE MAY RULE?
WE HAVE HAD QUAKES BEFORE AND KRYPTON IS STILL INTACT!
JOR-EL, YOUR IDEAS ARE FANTASTIC! YOU HAD BETTER LEAVE!
4

JOR-EL LEFT, A TRAGIC, BEATEN FIGURE... WHILE KRYPTON'S RUMBLINGS AND QUAKINGS INCREASED...

FOOLS... BLIND FOOLS! THEY ARE ALL DOOMED! I PRAY I MAY YET HAVE TIME TO SAVE MY WIFE ...AND THE BABY!

AT HOME, JOR-EL'S BRAVE WIFE LOOKED AT HIM AND UNDERSTOOD...

I SEE IT IN YOUR FACE! THEY REFUSED TO BELIEVE YOU!

I TRIED, LARA ...BELIEVE ME, I TRIED!

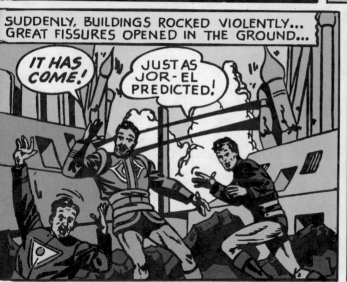

SUDDENLY, BUILDINGS ROCKED VIOLENTLY... GREAT FISSURES OPENED IN THE GROUND...

IT HAS COME!

JUST AS JOR-EL PREDICTED!

QUICKLY, LARA--THE SPACE SHIP! THERE IS JUST ROOM IN IT FOR YOU AND THE BABY!

NO, MY HUSBAND...MY PLACE IS HERE WITH YOU! BUT OUR SON... LET HIM HAVE HIS CHANCE FOR LIFE!

LARA... MY DEAR... MY DEAR...

THE HELPLESS INFANT WAS PLACED INTO THE SPACE-SHIP--AND MOMENTS LATER THE TINY CRAFT ROCKETED INTO THE VOID!

FAREWELL, MY SON!

GOOD LUCK!

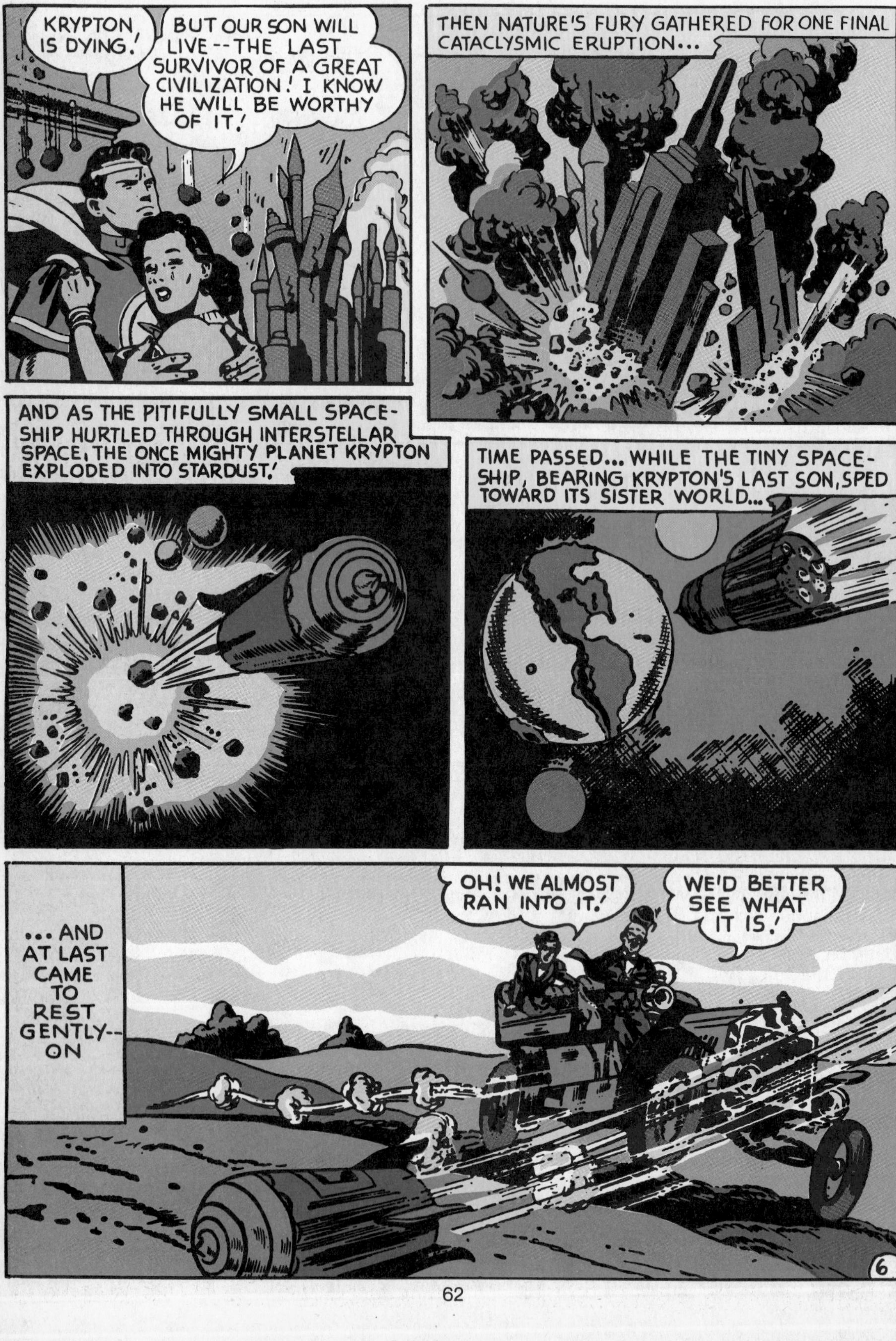

KRYPTON IS DYING!
BUT OUR SON WILL LIVE--THE LAST SURVIVOR OF A GREAT CIVILIZATION! I KNOW HE WILL BE WORTHY OF IT!
THEN NATURE'S FURY GATHERED FOR ONE FINAL CATACLYSMIC ERUPTION...
AND AS THE PITIFULLY SMALL SPACE-SHIP HURTLED THROUGH INTERSTELLAR SPACE, THE ONCE MIGHTY PLANET KRYPTON EXPLODED INTO STARDUST!
TIME PASSED... WHILE THE TINY SPACE-SHIP, BEARING KRYPTON'S LAST SON, SPED TOWARD ITS SISTER WORLD...
... AND AT LAST CAME TO REST GENTLY--ON
OH! WE ALMOST RAN INTO IT!
WE'D BETTER SEE WHAT IT IS!
6

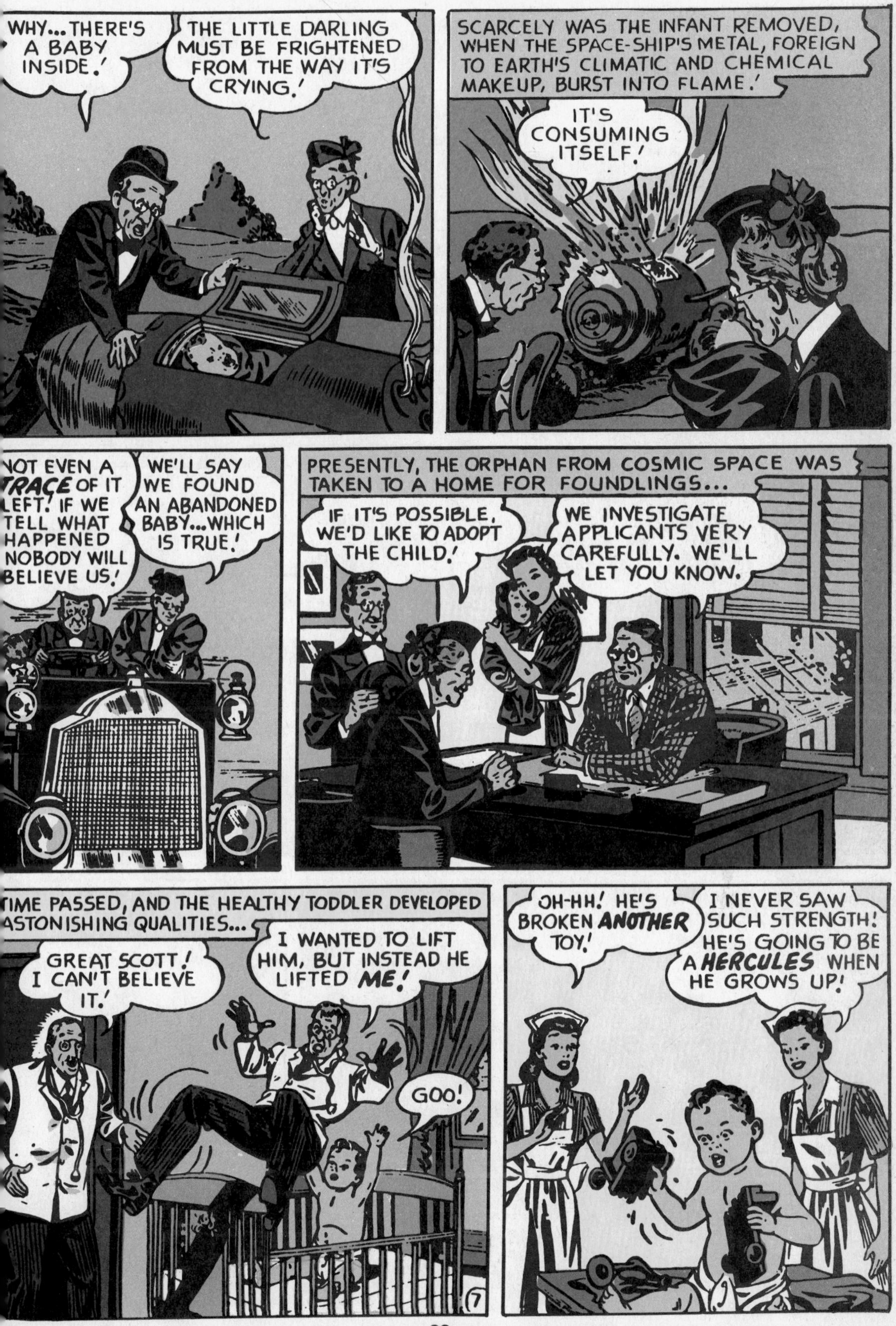
WHY...THERE'S A BABY INSIDE.'
THE LITTLE DARLING MUST BE FRIGHTENED FROM THE WAY IT'S CRYING.'
SCARCELY WAS THE INFANT REMOVED, WHEN THE SPACE-SHIP'S METAL, FOREIGN TO EARTH'S CLIMATIC AND CHEMICAL MAKEUP, BURST INTO FLAME.'
IT'S CONSUMING ITSELF.'
NOT EVEN A TRACE OF IT LEFT! IF WE TELL WHAT HAPPENED NOBODY WILL BELIEVE US!
WE'LL SAY WE FOUND AN ABANDONED BABY...WHICH IS TRUE.'
PRESENTLY, THE ORPHAN FROM COSMIC SPACE WAS TAKEN TO A HOME FOR FOUNDLINGS...
IF IT'S POSSIBLE, WE'D LIKE TO ADOPT THE CHILD.'
WE INVESTIGATE APPLICANTS VERY CAREFULLY. WE'LL LET YOU KNOW.
TIME PASSED, AND THE HEALTHY TODDLER DEVELOPED ASTONISHING QUALITIES...
GREAT SCOTT! I CAN'T BELIEVE IT.'
I WANTED TO LIFT HIM, BUT INSTEAD HE LIFTED ME!
GOO!
7
OH-HH! HE'S BROKEN ANOTHER TOY!
I NEVER SAW SUCH STRENGTH! HE'S GOING TO BE A HERCULES WHEN HE GROWS UP!

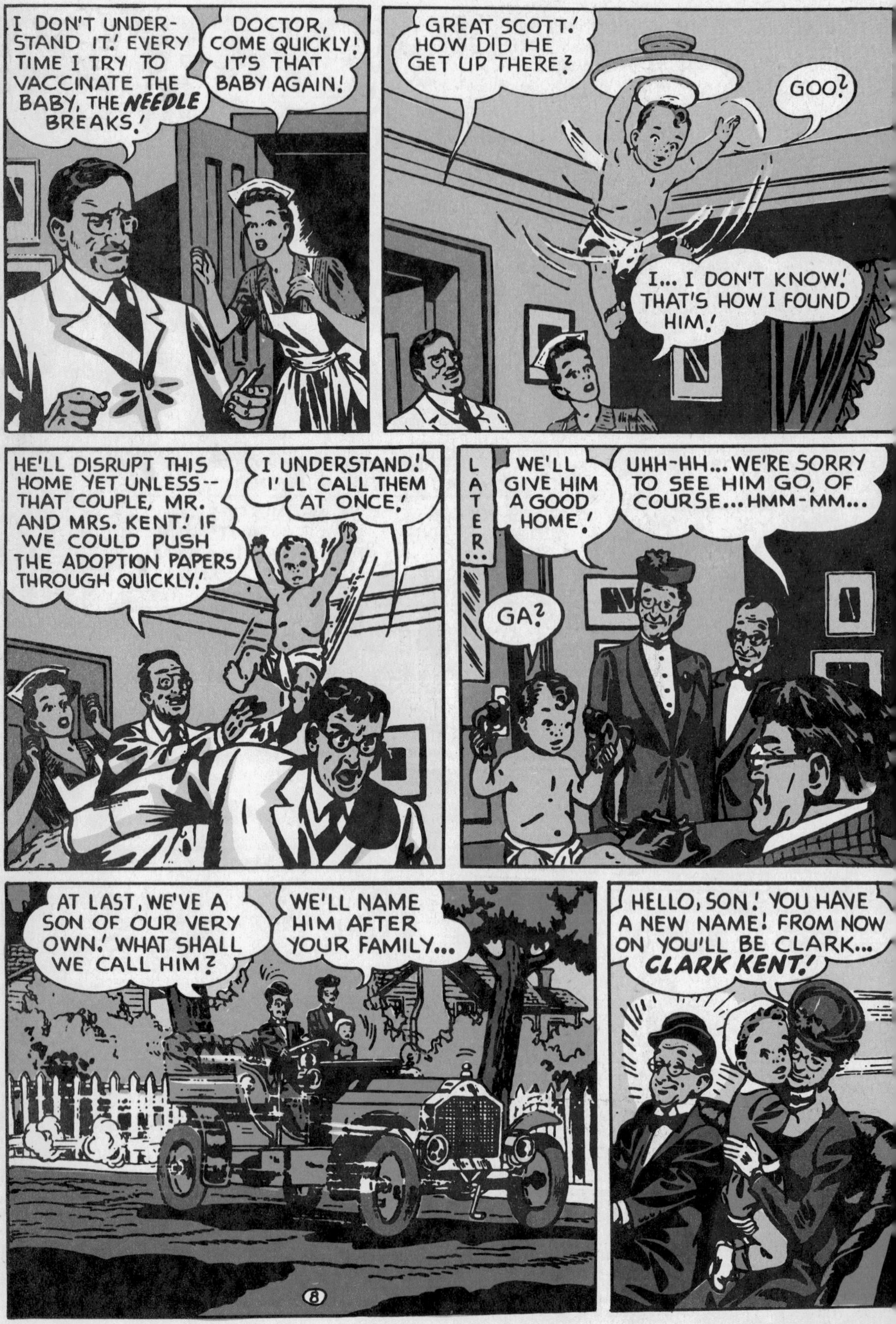
I DON'T UNDERSTAND IT! EVERY TIME I TRY TO VACCINATE THE BABY, THE NEEDLE BREAKS!
DOCTOR, COME QUICKLY! IT'S THAT BABY AGAIN!
GREAT SCOTT! HOW DID HE GET UP THERE?
GOO?
I... I DON'T KNOW! THAT'S HOW I FOUND HIM!
HE'LL DISRUPT THIS HOME YET UNLESS-- THAT COUPLE, MR. AND MRS. KENT! IF WE COULD PUSH THE ADOPTION PAPERS THROUGH QUICKLY!
I UNDERSTAND! I'LL CALL THEM AT ONCE!
LATER...
WE'LL GIVE HIM A GOOD HOME!
UHH-HH... WE'RE SORRY TO SEE HIM GO, OF COURSE... HMM-MM...
GA?
AT LAST, WE'VE A SON OF OUR VERY OWN! WHAT SHALL WE CALL HIM?
WE'LL NAME HIM AFTER YOUR FAMILY...
HELLO, SON! YOU HAVE A NEW NAME! FROM NOW ON YOU'LL BE CLARK... CLARK KENT!
8

YEARS PASSED, AND CERTAIN INCIDENTS MADE THE GROWING BOY REALIZE HE WAS DIFFERENT FROM OTHER YOUNGSTERS.' THERE WAS THE TIME...

LOOK OUT, CLARK.! THAT TRACTOR.! OHHH!

GOOD GOSH.! YOU'RE NOT EVEN HURT.!

BUT LOOK AT THE TRACTOR!

ONCE, WHEN HE WAS LATE FOR SUPPER AND STARTED TO HURRY HOME...

GOLLY! I'M GOING FASTER THAN THE EXPRESS TRAIN.'

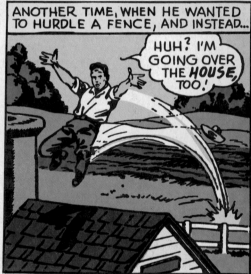

ANOTHER TIME, WHEN HE WANTED TO HURDLE A FENCE, AND INSTEAD...

HUH? I'M GOING OVER THE *HOUSE,* TOO!

...AND THERE WAS THIS INCIDENT...

NOW WHERE DID I PUT MY SPECTACLES ?

THEY'VE FALLEN BEHIND THE CABINET, MOTHER!

WHY, SO THEY ARE! HOW EVER DID YOU KNOW, SON ?

I... I DON'T UNDERSTAND! IT'S AS IF I HAD *X-RAY* EYES.'

HMMM!

⑨

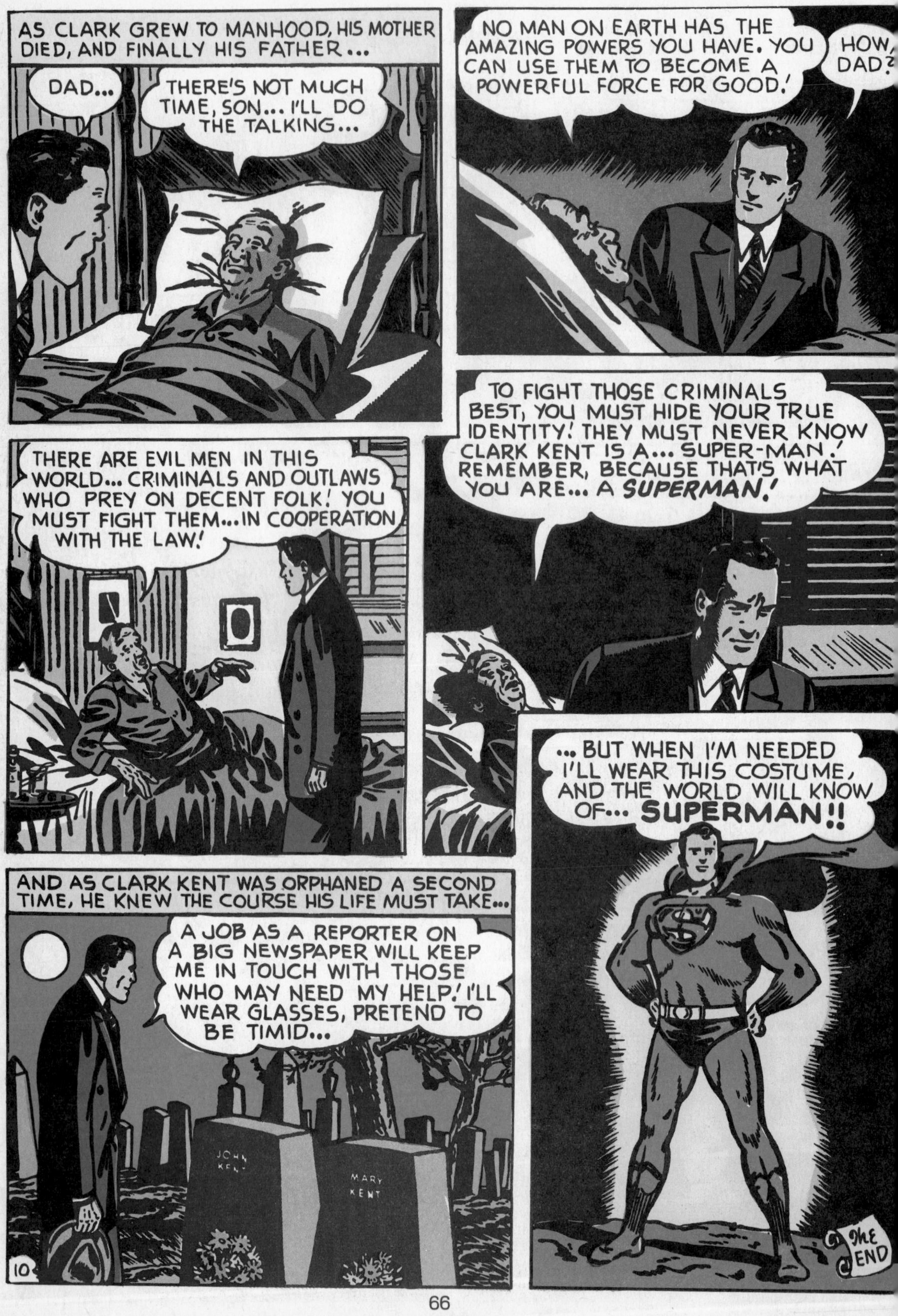
AS CLARK GREW TO MANHOOD, HIS MOTHER DIED, AND FINALLY HIS FATHER...
DAD...
THERE'S NOT MUCH TIME, SON... I'LL DO THE TALKING...
NO MAN ON EARTH HAS THE AMAZING POWERS YOU HAVE. YOU CAN USE THEM TO BECOME A POWERFUL FORCE FOR GOOD!
HOW, DAD?
THERE ARE EVIL MEN IN THIS WORLD... CRIMINALS AND OUTLAWS WHO PREY ON DECENT FOLK! YOU MUST FIGHT THEM...IN COOPERATION WITH THE LAW!
TO FIGHT THOSE CRIMINALS BEST, YOU MUST HIDE YOUR TRUE IDENTITY! THEY MUST NEVER KNOW CLARK KENT IS A... SUPER-MAN! REMEMBER, BECAUSE THAT'S WHAT YOU ARE... A SUPERMAN!
AND AS CLARK KENT WAS ORPHANED A SECOND TIME, HE KNEW THE COURSE HIS LIFE MUST TAKE...
A JOB AS A REPORTER ON A BIG NEWSPAPER WILL KEEP ME IN TOUCH WITH THOSE WHO MAY NEED MY HELP! I'LL WEAR GLASSES, PRETEND TO BE TIMID...
JOHN KENT
MARY KENT
10
... BUT WHEN I'M NEEDED I'LL WEAR THIS COSTUME, AND THE WORLD WILL KNOW OF... SUPERMAN!!
THE END

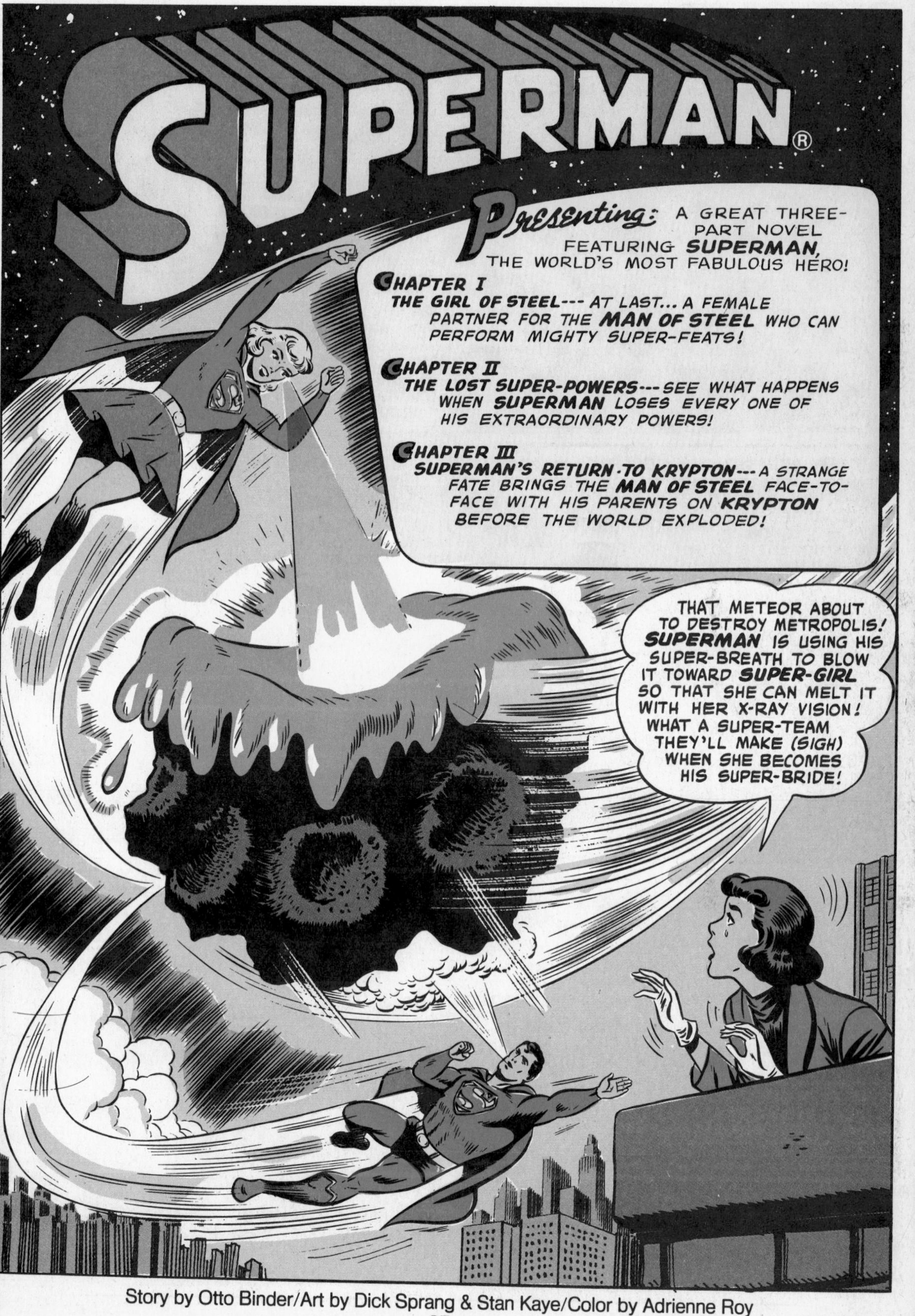
SUPERMAN®
PRESENTING: A GREAT THREE-PART NOVEL FEATURING SUPERMAN, THE WORLD'S MOST FABULOUS HERO!
CHAPTER I
THE GIRL OF STEEL--- AT LAST... A FEMALE PARTNER FOR THE MAN OF STEEL WHO CAN PERFORM MIGHTY SUPER-FEATS!
CHAPTER II
THE LOST SUPER-POWERS--- SEE WHAT HAPPENS WHEN SUPERMAN LOSES EVERY ONE OF HIS EXTRAORDINARY POWERS!
CHAPTER III
SUPERMAN'S RETURN TO KRYPTON--- A STRANGE FATE BRINGS THE MAN OF STEEL FACE-TO-FACE WITH HIS PARENTS ON KRYPTON BEFORE THE WORLD EXPLODED!
THAT METEOR ABOUT TO DESTROY METROPOLIS! SUPERMAN IS USING HIS SUPER-BREATH TO BLOW IT TOWARD SUPER-GIRL SO THAT SHE CAN MELT IT WITH HER X-RAY VISION! WHAT A SUPER-TEAM THEY'LL MAKE (SIGH) WHEN SHE BECOMES HIS SUPER-BRIDE!

Story by Otto Binder/Art by Dick Sprang & Stan Kaye/Color by Adrienne Roy

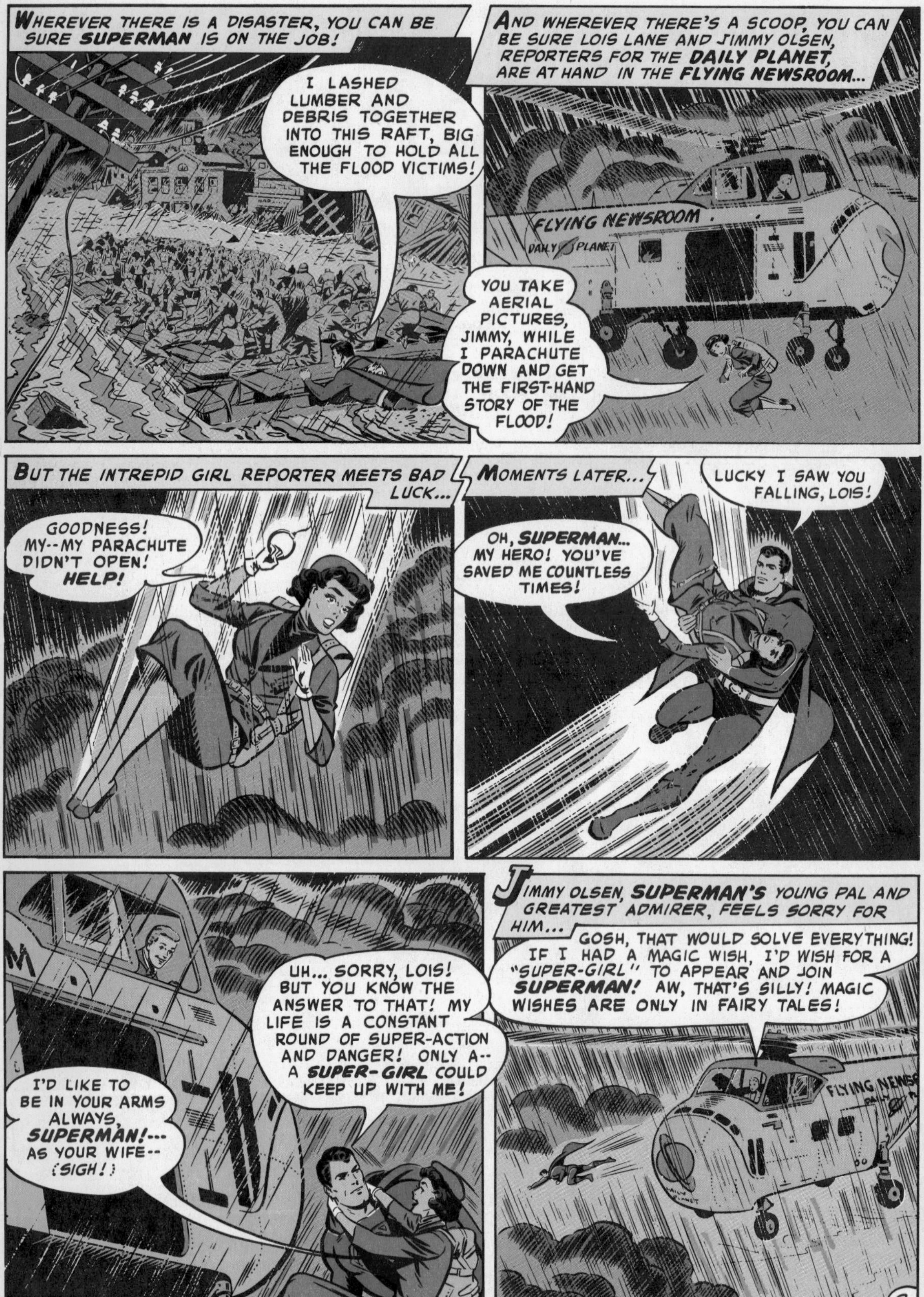
WHEREVER THERE IS A DISASTER, YOU CAN BE SURE SUPERMAN IS ON THE JOB!
I LASHED LUMBER AND DEBRIS TOGETHER INTO THIS RAFT, BIG ENOUGH TO HOLD ALL THE FLOOD VICTIMS!
AND WHEREVER THERE'S A SCOOP, YOU CAN BE SURE LOIS LANE AND JIMMY OLSEN, REPORTERS FOR THE DAILY PLANET, ARE AT HAND IN THE FLYING NEWSROOM...
FLYING NEWSROOM
DAILY PLANET
YOU TAKE AERIAL PICTURES, JIMMY, WHILE I PARACHUTE DOWN AND GET THE FIRST-HAND STORY OF THE FLOOD!
BUT THE INTREPID GIRL REPORTER MEETS BAD LUCK...
GOODNESS! MY--MY PARACHUTE DIDN'T OPEN! HELP!
MOMENTS LATER...
LUCKY I SAW YOU FALLING, LOIS!
OH, SUPERMAN... MY HERO! YOU'VE SAVED ME COUNTLESS TIMES!
I'D LIKE TO BE IN YOUR ARMS ALWAYS, SUPERMAN!--- AS YOUR WIFE-- (SIGH!)
UH... SORRY, LOIS! BUT YOU KNOW THE ANSWER TO THAT! MY LIFE IS A CONSTANT ROUND OF SUPER-ACTION AND DANGER! ONLY A-- A SUPER-GIRL COULD KEEP UP WITH ME!
JIMMY OLSEN, SUPERMAN'S YOUNG PAL AND GREATEST ADMIRER, FEELS SORRY FOR HIM...
GOSH, THAT WOULD SOLVE EVERYTHING! IF I HAD A MAGIC WISH, I'D WISH FOR A "SUPER-GIRL" TO APPEAR AND JOIN SUPERMAN! AW, THAT'S SILLY! MAGIC WISHES ARE ONLY IN FAIRY TALES!
2

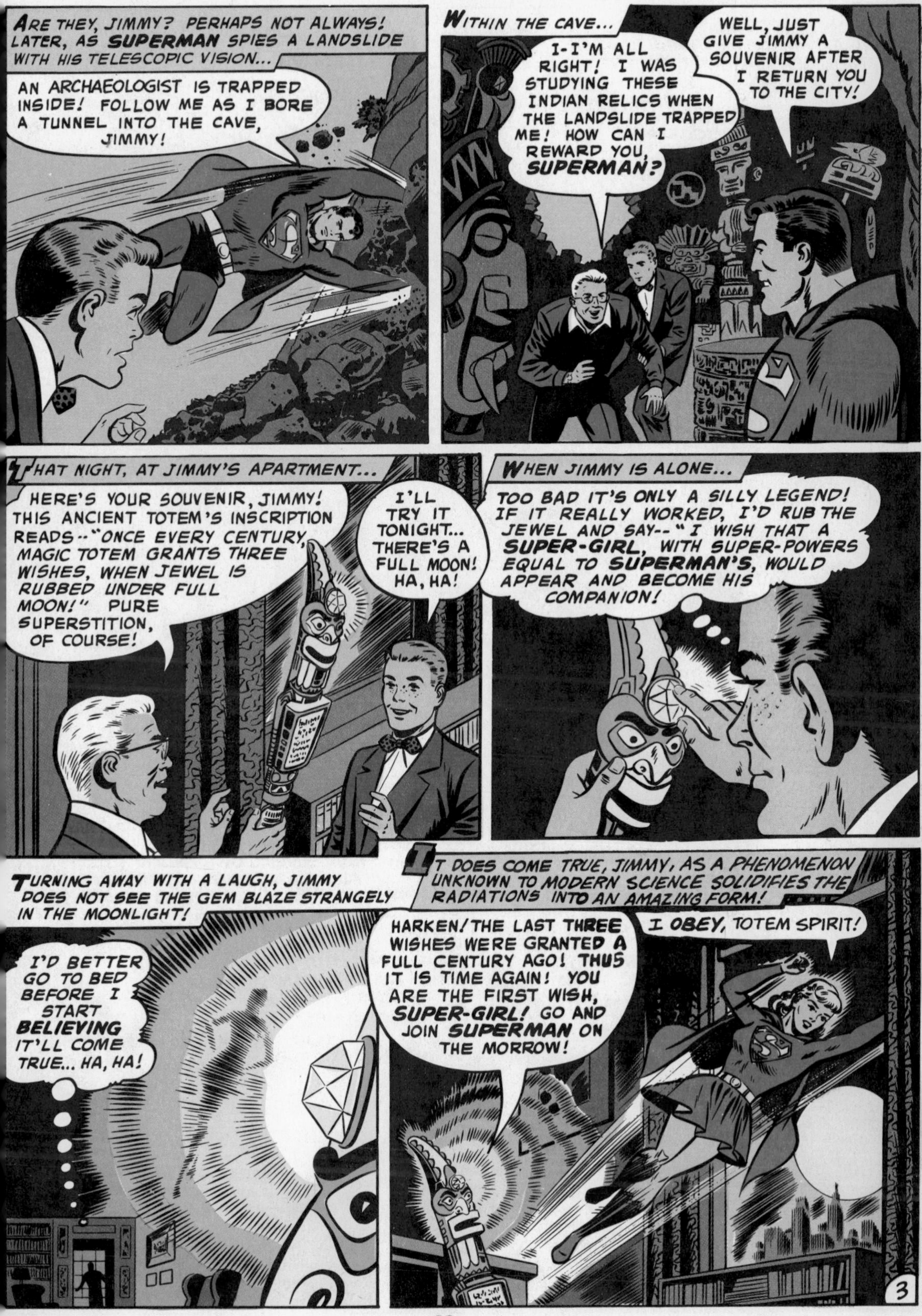

ARE THEY, JIMMY? PERHAPS NOT ALWAYS! LATER, AS SUPERMAN SPIES A LANDSLIDE WITH HIS TELESCOPIC VISION...
AN ARCHAEOLOGIST IS TRAPPED INSIDE! FOLLOW ME AS I BORE A TUNNEL INTO THE CAVE, JIMMY!
WITHIN THE CAVE...
I-I'M ALL RIGHT! I WAS STUDYING THESE INDIAN RELICS WHEN THE LANDSLIDE TRAPPED ME! HOW CAN I REWARD YOU, SUPERMAN?
WELL, JUST GIVE JIMMY A SOUVENIR AFTER I RETURN YOU TO THE CITY!
THAT NIGHT, AT JIMMY'S APARTMENT...
HERE'S YOUR SOUVENIR, JIMMY! THIS ANCIENT TOTEM'S INSCRIPTION READS--"ONCE EVERY CENTURY, MAGIC TOTEM GRANTS THREE WISHES, WHEN JEWEL IS RUBBED UNDER FULL MOON!" PURE SUPERSTITION, OF COURSE!
I'LL TRY IT TONIGHT... THERE'S A FULL MOON! HA, HA!
WHEN JIMMY IS ALONE...
TOO BAD IT'S ONLY A SILLY LEGEND! IF IT REALLY WORKED, I'D RUB THE JEWEL AND SAY--"I WISH THAT A SUPER-GIRL, WITH SUPER-POWERS EQUAL TO SUPERMAN'S, WOULD APPEAR AND BECOME HIS COMPANION!
TURNING AWAY WITH A LAUGH, JIMMY DOES NOT SEE THE GEM BLAZE STRANGELY IN THE MOONLIGHT!
I'D BETTER GO TO BED BEFORE I START BELIEVING IT'LL COME TRUE... HA, HA!
IT DOES COME TRUE, JIMMY, AS A PHENOMENON UNKNOWN TO MODERN SCIENCE SOLIDIFIES THE RADIATIONS INTO AN AMAZING FORM!
HARKEN! THE LAST THREE WISHES WERE GRANTED A FULL CENTURY AGO! THUS IT IS TIME AGAIN! YOU ARE THE FIRST WISH, SUPER-GIRL! GO AND JOIN SUPERMAN ON THE MORROW!
I OBEY, TOTEM SPIRIT!
3

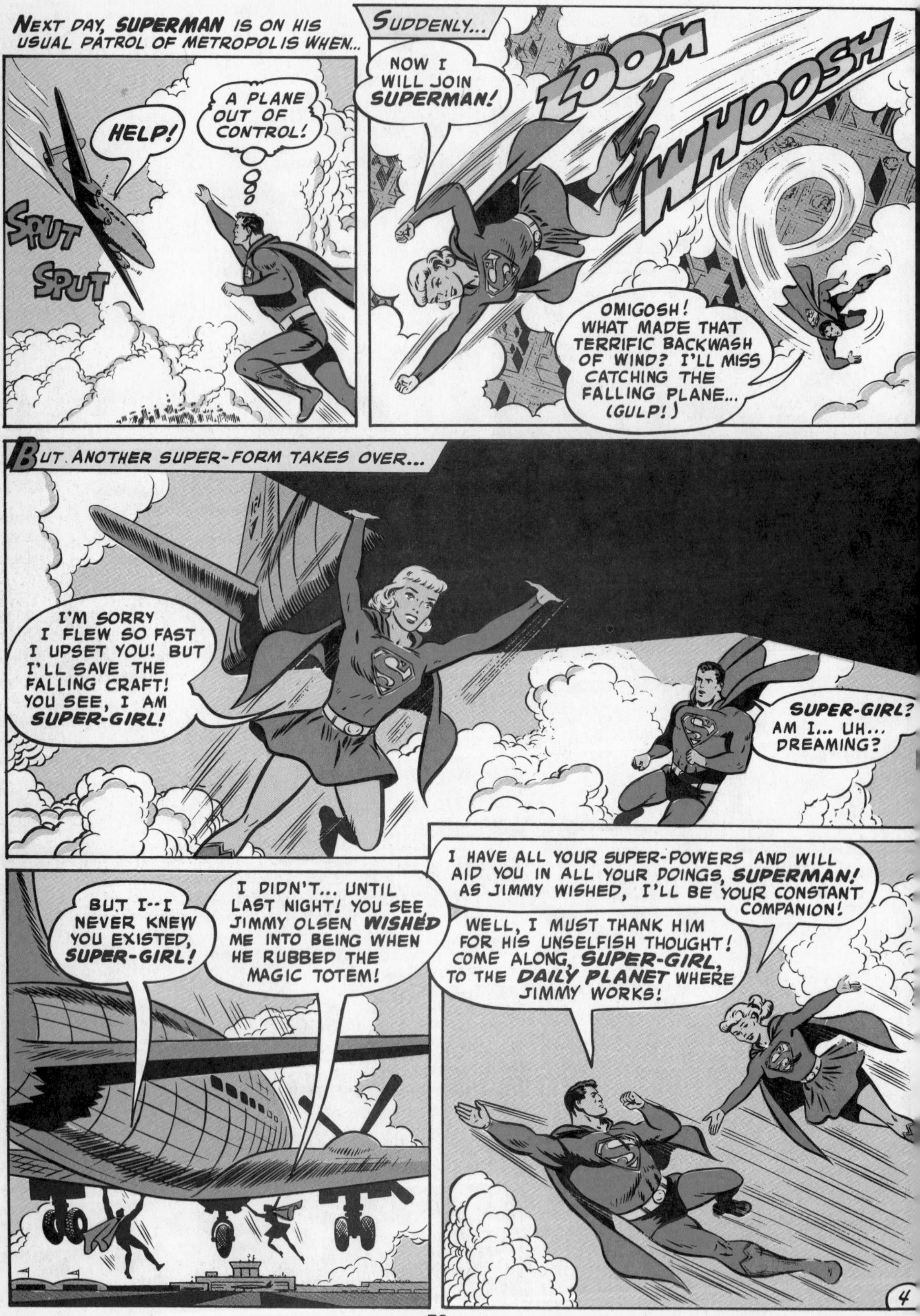
NEXT DAY, SUPERMAN IS ON HIS USUAL PATROL OF METROPOLIS WHEN...
HELP!
A PLANE OUT OF CONTROL!
SPUT
SPUT
SUDDENLY...
NOW I WILL JOIN SUPERMAN!
ZOOM
WHOOSH
OMIGOSH! WHAT MADE THAT TERRIFIC BACKWASH OF WIND? I'LL MISS CATCHING THE FALLING PLANE... (GULP!)
BUT ANOTHER SUPER-FORM TAKES OVER...
I'M SORRY I FLEW SO FAST I UPSET YOU! BUT I'LL SAVE THE FALLING CRAFT! YOU SEE, I AM SUPER-GIRL!
SUPER-GIRL? AM I... UH... DREAMING?
BUT I--I NEVER KNEW YOU EXISTED, SUPER-GIRL!
I DIDN'T... UNTIL LAST NIGHT! YOU SEE, JIMMY OLSEN WISHED ME INTO BEING WHEN HE RUBBED THE MAGIC TOTEM!
I HAVE ALL YOUR SUPER-POWERS AND WILL AID YOU IN ALL YOUR DOINGS, SUPERMAN! AS JIMMY WISHED, I'LL BE YOUR CONSTANT COMPANION!
WELL, I MUST THANK HIM FOR HIS UNSELFISH THOUGHT! COME ALONG, SUPER-GIRL, TO THE DAILY PLANET WHERE JIMMY WORKS!
4

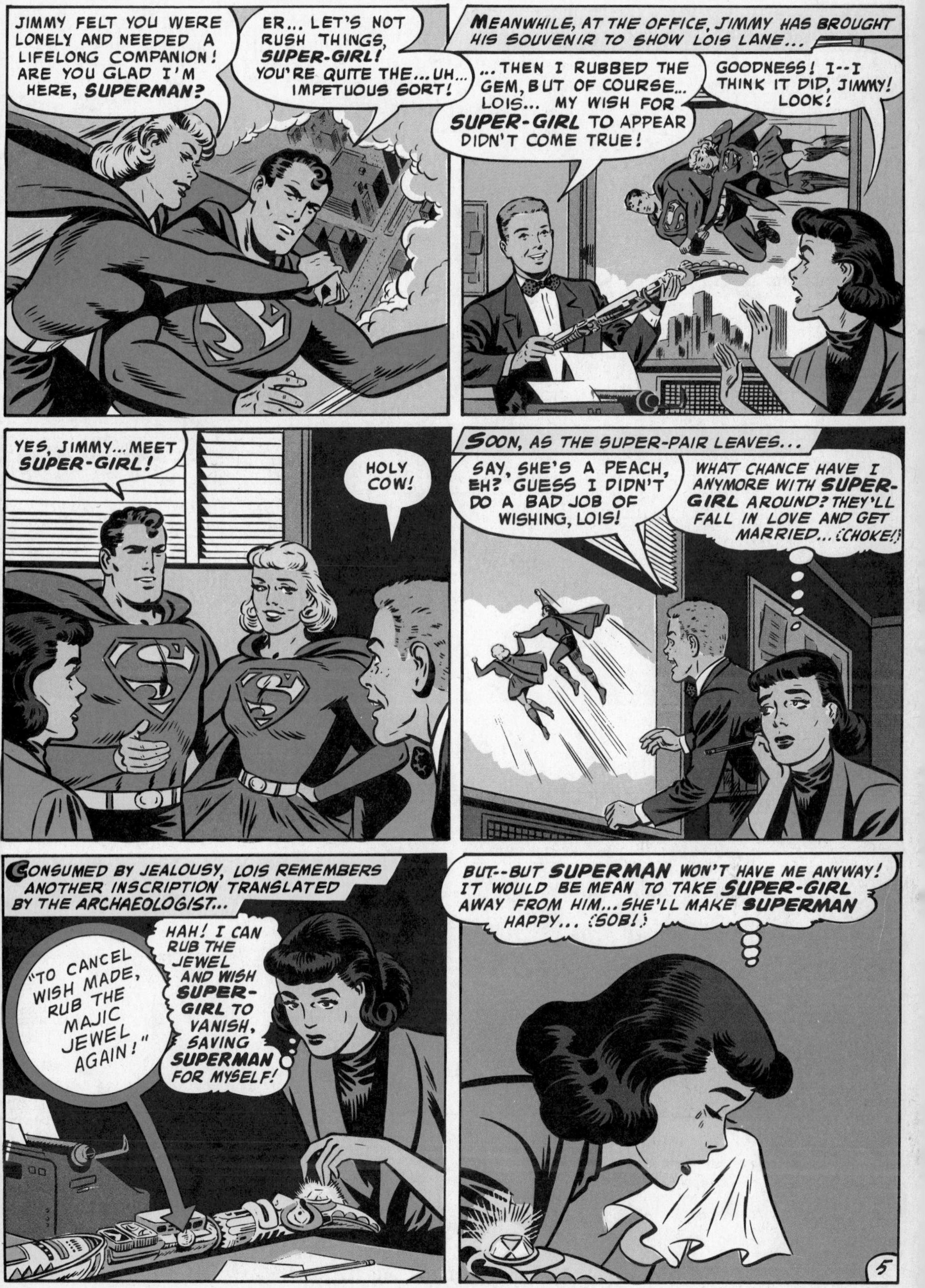
JIMMY FELT YOU WERE LONELY AND NEEDED A LIFELONG COMPANION! ARE YOU GLAD I'M HERE, SUPERMAN?
ER... LET'S NOT RUSH THINGS, SUPER-GIRL! YOU'RE QUITE THE...UH... IMPETUOUS SORT!
MEANWHILE, AT THE OFFICE, JIMMY HAS BROUGHT HIS SOUVENIR TO SHOW LOIS LANE...
...THEN I RUBBED THE GEM, BUT OF COURSE... LOIS... MY WISH FOR SUPER-GIRL TO APPEAR DIDN'T COME TRUE!
GOODNESS! I--I THINK IT DID, JIMMY! LOOK!
YES, JIMMY...MEET SUPER-GIRL!
HOLY COW!
SOON, AS THE SUPER-PAIR LEAVES...
SAY, SHE'S A PEACH, EH? GUESS I DIDN'T DO A BAD JOB OF WISHING, LOIS!
WHAT CHANCE HAVE I ANYMORE WITH SUPER-GIRL AROUND? THEY'LL FALL IN LOVE AND GET MARRIED... (CHOKE!)
CONSUMED BY JEALOUSY, LOIS REMEMBERS ANOTHER INSCRIPTION TRANSLATED BY THE ARCHAEOLOGIST...
"TO CANCEL WISH MADE, RUB THE MAJIC JEWEL AGAIN!"
HAH! I CAN RUB THE JEWEL AND WISH SUPER-GIRL TO VANISH, SAVING SUPERMAN FOR MYSELF!
BUT--BUT SUPERMAN WON'T HAVE ME ANYWAY! IT WOULD BE MEAN TO TAKE SUPER-GIRL AWAY FROM HIM... SHE'LL MAKE SUPERMAN HAPPY... (SOB!)
5

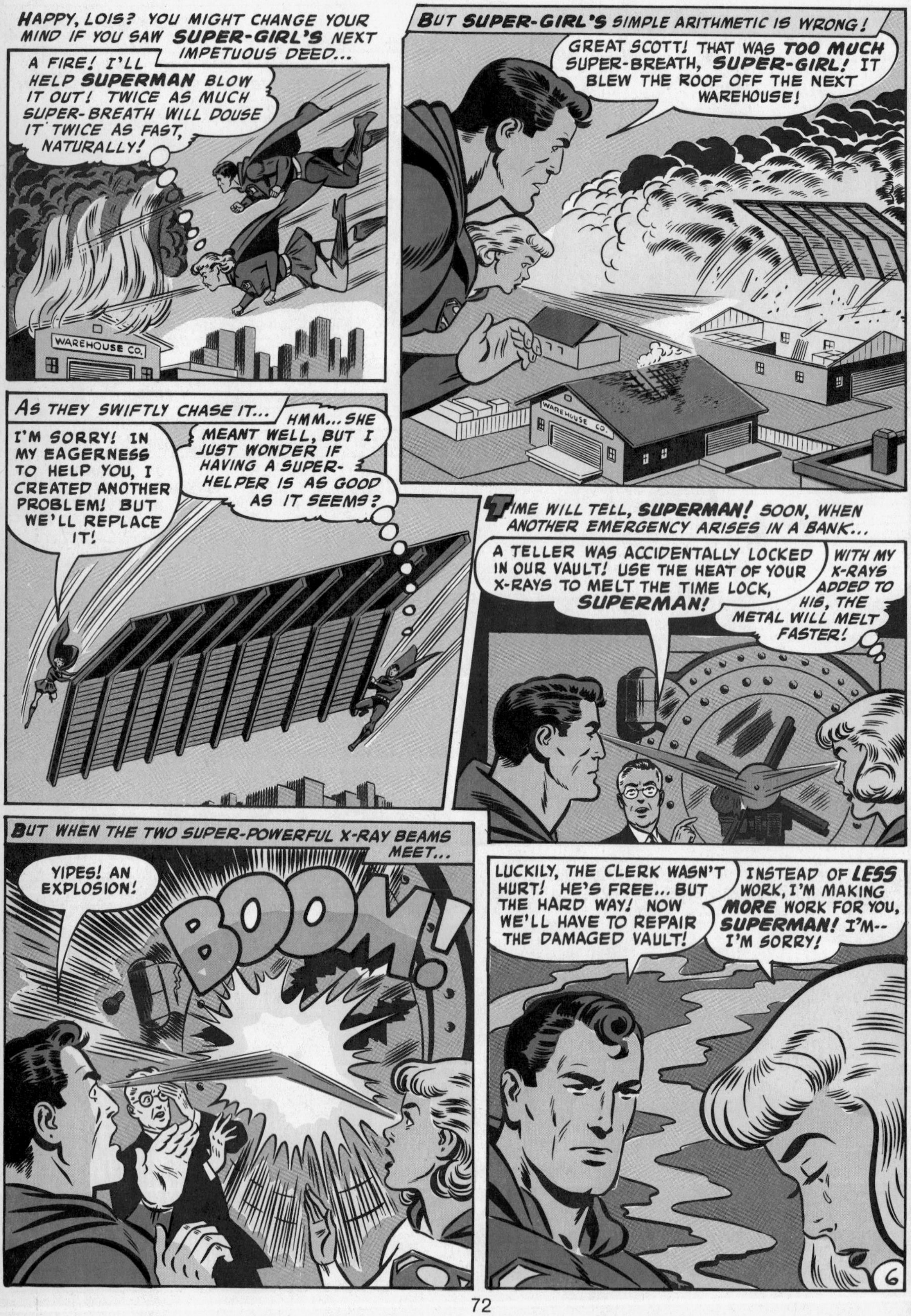
HAPPY, LOIS? YOU MIGHT CHANGE YOUR MIND IF YOU SAW SUPER-GIRL'S NEXT IMPETUOUS DEED...
A FIRE! I'LL HELP SUPERMAN BLOW IT OUT! TWICE AS MUCH SUPER-BREATH WILL DOUSE IT TWICE AS FAST, NATURALLY!
WAREHOUSE CO.
BUT SUPER-GIRL'S SIMPLE ARITHMETIC IS WRONG!
GREAT SCOTT! THAT WAS TOO MUCH SUPER-BREATH, SUPER-GIRL! IT BLEW THE ROOF OFF THE NEXT WAREHOUSE!
WAREHOUSE CO.
AS THEY SWIFTLY CHASE IT...
I'M SORRY! IN MY EAGERNESS TO HELP YOU, I CREATED ANOTHER PROBLEM! BUT WE'LL REPLACE IT!
HMM... SHE MEANT WELL, BUT I JUST WONDER IF HAVING A SUPER-HELPER IS AS GOOD AS IT SEEMS?
TIME WILL TELL, SUPERMAN! SOON, WHEN ANOTHER EMERGENCY ARISES IN A BANK...
A TELLER WAS ACCIDENTALLY LOCKED IN OUR VAULT! USE THE HEAT OF YOUR X-RAYS TO MELT THE TIME LOCK, SUPERMAN!
WITH MY X-RAYS ADDED TO HIS, THE METAL WILL MELT FASTER!
BUT WHEN THE TWO SUPER-POWERFUL X-RAY BEAMS MEET...
YIPES! AN EXPLOSION!
BOOM!
LUCKILY, THE CLERK WASN'T HURT! HE'S FREE... BUT THE HARD WAY! NOW WE'LL HAVE TO REPAIR THE DAMAGED VAULT!
INSTEAD OF LESS WORK, I'M MAKING MORE WORK FOR YOU, SUPERMAN! I'M-- I'M SORRY!
6

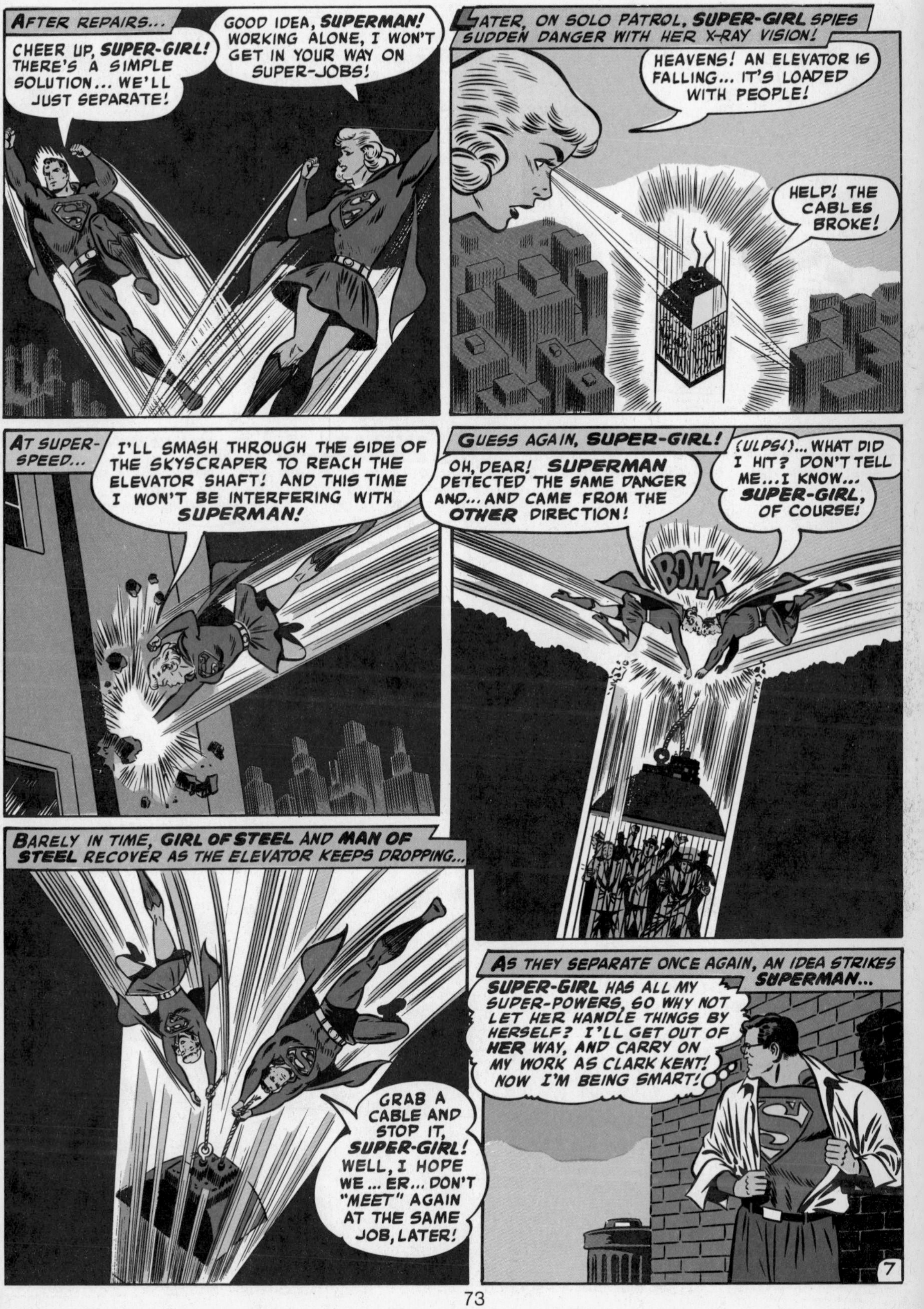
AFTER REPAIRS...
CHEER UP, SUPER-GIRL! THERE'S A SIMPLE SOLUTION... WE'LL JUST SEPARATE!
GOOD IDEA, SUPERMAN! WORKING ALONE, I WON'T GET IN YOUR WAY ON SUPER-JOBS!
LATER, ON SOLO PATROL, SUPER-GIRL SPIES SUDDEN DANGER WITH HER X-RAY VISION!
HEAVENS! AN ELEVATOR IS FALLING... IT'S LOADED WITH PEOPLE!
HELP! THE CABLES BROKE!
AT SUPER-SPEED...
I'LL SMASH THROUGH THE SIDE OF THE SKYSCRAPER TO REACH THE ELEVATOR SHAFT! AND THIS TIME I WON'T BE INTERFERING WITH SUPERMAN!
GUESS AGAIN, SUPER-GIRL!
OH, DEAR! SUPERMAN DETECTED THE SAME DANGER AND... AND CAME FROM THE OTHER DIRECTION!
(ULPS!)... WHAT DID I HIT? DON'T TELL ME... I KNOW... SUPER-GIRL, OF COURSE!
BONK
BARELY IN TIME, GIRL OF STEEL AND MAN OF STEEL RECOVER AS THE ELEVATOR KEEPS DROPPING...
GRAB A CABLE AND STOP IT, SUPER-GIRL! WELL, I HOPE WE... ER... DON'T "MEET" AGAIN AT THE SAME JOB, LATER!
AS THEY SEPARATE ONCE AGAIN, AN IDEA STRIKES SUPERMAN...
SUPER-GIRL HAS ALL MY SUPER-POWERS, SO WHY NOT LET HER HANDLE THINGS BY HERSELF? I'LL GET OUT OF HER WAY, AND CARRY ON MY WORK AS CLARK KENT! NOW I'M BEING SMART!
7

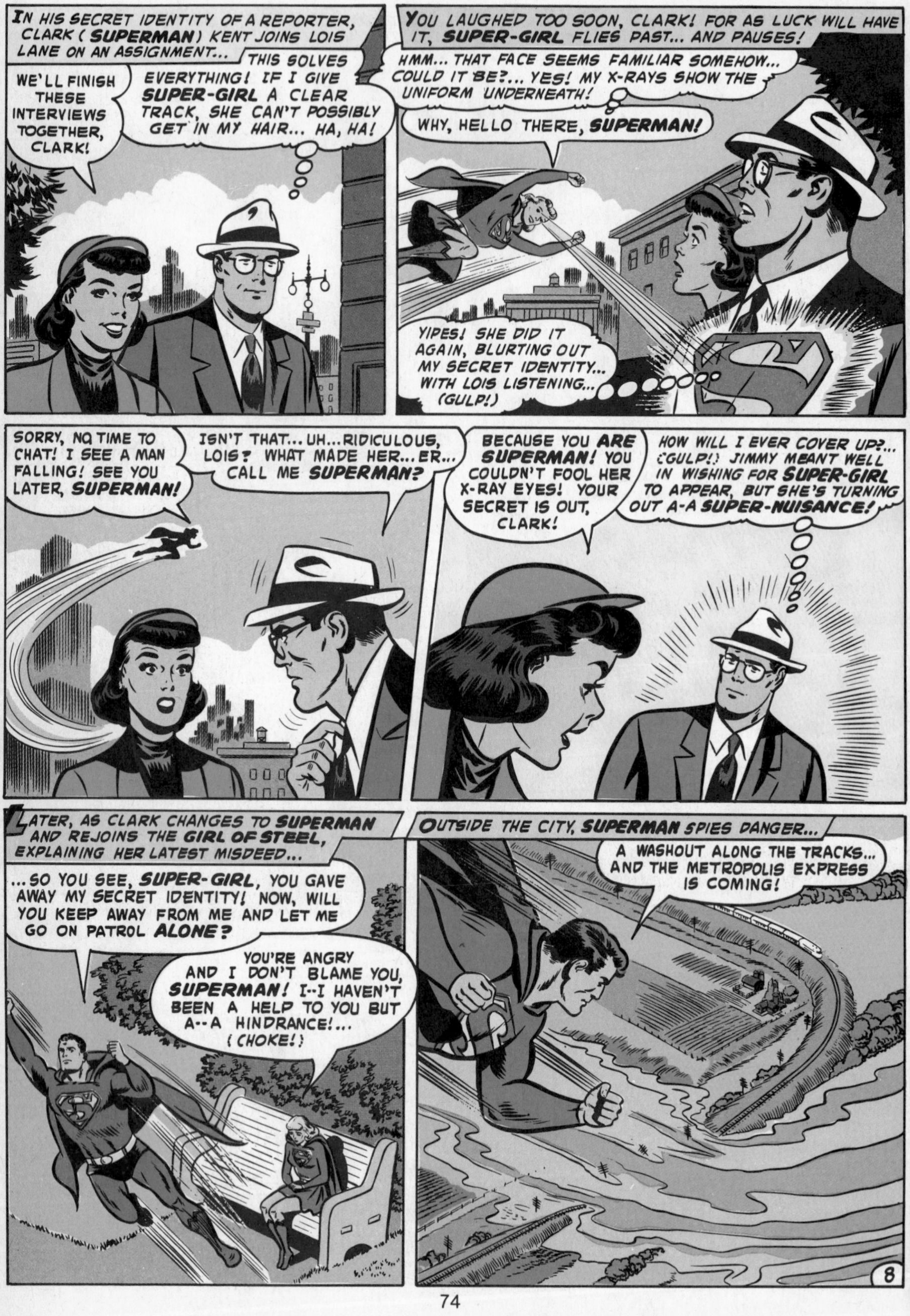
IN HIS SECRET IDENTITY OF A REPORTER, CLARK (SUPERMAN) KENT JOINS LOIS LANE ON AN ASSIGNMENT...
WE'LL FINISH THESE INTERVIEWS TOGETHER, CLARK!
THIS SOLVES EVERYTHING! IF I GIVE SUPER-GIRL A CLEAR TRACK, SHE CAN'T POSSIBLY GET IN MY HAIR... HA, HA!
YOU LAUGHED TOO SOON, CLARK! FOR AS LUCK WILL HAVE IT, SUPER-GIRL FLIES PAST... AND PAUSES!
HMM... THAT FACE SEEMS FAMILIAR SOMEHOW... COULD IT BE?... YES! MY X-RAYS SHOW THE UNIFORM UNDERNEATH!
WHY, HELLO THERE, SUPERMAN!
YIPES! SHE DID IT AGAIN, BLURTING OUT MY SECRET IDENTITY... WITH LOIS LISTENING... (GULP!)
SORRY, NO TIME TO CHAT! I SEE A MAN FALLING! SEE YOU LATER, SUPERMAN!
ISN'T THAT... UH... RIDICULOUS, LOIS? WHAT MADE HER... ER... CALL ME SUPERMAN?
BECAUSE YOU ARE SUPERMAN! YOU COULDN'T FOOL HER X-RAY EYES! YOUR SECRET IS OUT, CLARK!
HOW WILL I EVER COVER UP?... (GULP!) JIMMY MEANT WELL IN WISHING FOR SUPER-GIRL TO APPEAR, BUT SHE'S TURNING OUT A-A SUPER-NUISANCE!
LATER, AS CLARK CHANGES TO SUPERMAN AND REJOINS THE GIRL OF STEEL, EXPLAINING HER LATEST MISDEED...
...SO YOU SEE, SUPER-GIRL, YOU GAVE AWAY MY SECRET IDENTITY! NOW, WILL YOU KEEP AWAY FROM ME AND LET ME GO ON PATROL ALONE?
YOU'RE ANGRY AND I DON'T BLAME YOU, SUPERMAN! I--I HAVEN'T BEEN A HELP TO YOU BUT A--A HINDRANCE!... (CHOKE!)
OUTSIDE THE CITY, SUPERMAN SPIES DANGER...
A WASHOUT ALONG THE TRACKS... AND THE METROPOLIS EXPRESS IS COMING!
8

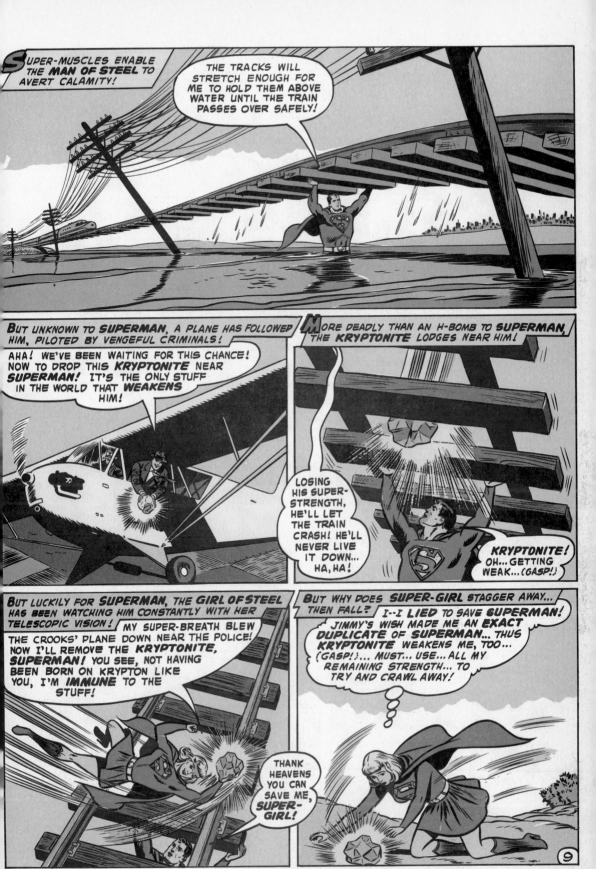

SUPER-MUSCLES ENABLE THE **MAN OF STEEL** TO AVERT CALAMITY!

THE TRACKS WILL STRETCH ENOUGH FOR ME TO HOLD THEM ABOVE WATER UNTIL THE TRAIN PASSES OVER SAFELY!

BUT UNKNOWN TO **SUPERMAN**, A PLANE HAS FOLLOWED HIM, PILOTED BY VENGEFUL CRIMINALS!

AHA! WE'VE BEEN WAITING FOR THIS CHANCE! NOW TO DROP THIS **KRYPTONITE** NEAR **SUPERMAN**! IT'S THE ONLY STUFF IN THE WORLD THAT **WEAKENS** HIM!

MORE DEADLY THAN AN H-BOMB TO **SUPERMAN**, THE **KRYPTONITE** LODGES NEAR HIM!

LOSING HIS SUPER-STRENGTH, HE'LL LET THE TRAIN CRASH! HE'LL NEVER LIVE IT DOWN... HA, HA!

KRYPTONITE! OH... GETTING WEAK... (GASP!)

BUT LUCKILY FOR **SUPERMAN**, THE **GIRL OF STEEL** HAS BEEN WATCHING HIM CONSTANTLY WITH HER TELESCOPIC VISION!

MY SUPER-BREATH BLEW THE CROOKS' PLANE DOWN NEAR THE POLICE! NOW I'LL REMOVE THE **KRYPTONITE**, **SUPERMAN**! YOU SEE, NOT HAVING BEEN BORN ON KRYPTON LIKE YOU, I'M **IMMUNE** TO THE STUFF!

THANK HEAVENS YOU CAN SAVE ME, **SUPER-GIRL**!

BUT WHY DOES **SUPER-GIRL** STAGGER AWAY... THEN FALL?

I--I LIED TO SAVE **SUPERMAN**! JIMMY'S WISH MADE ME AN **EXACT DUPLICATE** OF SUPERMAN... THUS KRYPTONITE WEAKENS ME, TOO... (GASP!)... MUST... USE... ALL MY REMAINING STRENGTH... TO TRY AND CRAWL AWAY!

9

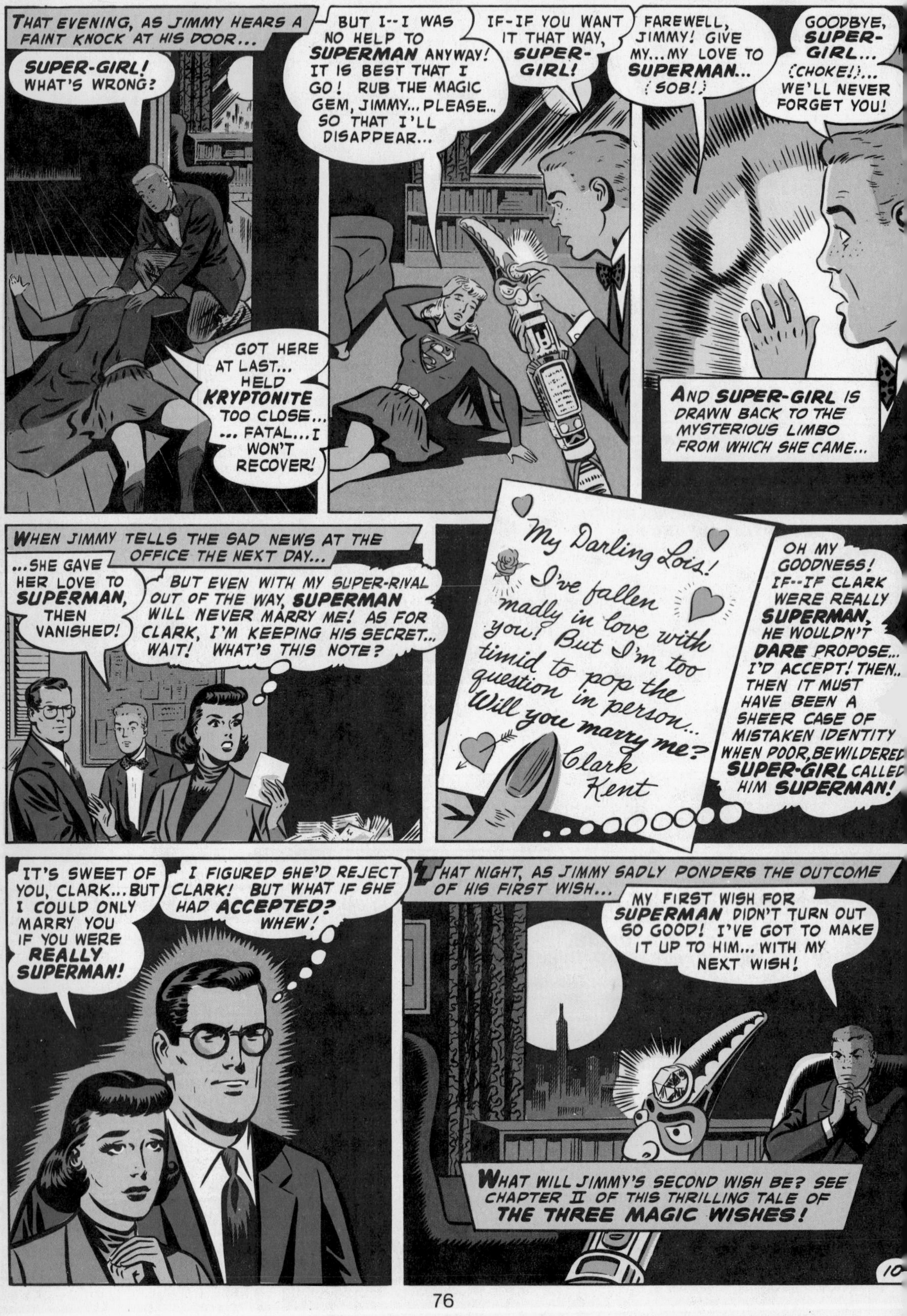
THAT EVENING, AS JIMMY HEARS A FAINT KNOCK AT HIS DOOR...
SUPER-GIRL! WHAT'S WRONG?
GOT HERE AT LAST... HELD KRYPTONITE TOO CLOSE... ...FATAL... I WON'T RECOVER!
BUT I--I WAS NO HELP TO SUPERMAN ANYWAY! IT IS BEST THAT I GO! RUB THE MAGIC GEM, JIMMY... PLEASE.. SO THAT I'LL DISAPPEAR...
IF-IF YOU WANT IT THAT WAY, SUPER-GIRL!
FAREWELL, JIMMY! GIVE MY...MY LOVE TO SUPERMAN... (SOB!)
GOODBYE, SUPER-GIRL... (CHOKE!)... WE'LL NEVER FORGET YOU!
AND SUPER-GIRL IS DRAWN BACK TO THE MYSTERIOUS LIMBO FROM WHICH SHE CAME...
WHEN JIMMY TELLS THE SAD NEWS AT THE OFFICE THE NEXT DAY...
...SHE GAVE HER LOVE TO SUPERMAN, THEN VANISHED!
BUT EVEN WITH MY SUPER-RIVAL OUT OF THE WAY, SUPERMAN WILL NEVER MARRY ME! AS FOR CLARK, I'M KEEPING HIS SECRET... WAIT! WHAT'S THIS NOTE?
My Darling Lois! I've fallen madly in love with you! But I'm too timid to pop the question in person... Will you marry me? Clark Kent
OH MY GOODNESS! IF--IF CLARK WERE REALLY SUPERMAN, HE WOULDN'T DARE PROPOSE... I'D ACCEPT! THEN.. THEN IT MUST HAVE BEEN A SHEER CASE OF MISTAKEN IDENTITY WHEN POOR, BEWILDERED SUPER-GIRL CALLED HIM SUPERMAN!
IT'S SWEET OF YOU, CLARK... BUT I COULD ONLY MARRY YOU IF YOU WERE REALLY SUPERMAN!
I FIGURED SHE'D REJECT CLARK! BUT WHAT IF SHE HAD ACCEPTED? WHEW!
THAT NIGHT, AS JIMMY SADLY PONDERS THE OUTCOME OF HIS FIRST WISH...
MY FIRST WISH FOR SUPERMAN DIDN'T TURN OUT SO GOOD! I'VE GOT TO MAKE IT UP TO HIM... WITH MY NEXT WISH!
WHAT WILL JIMMY'S SECOND WISH BE? SEE CHAPTER II OF THIS THRILLING TALE OF THE THREE MAGIC WISHES!
10

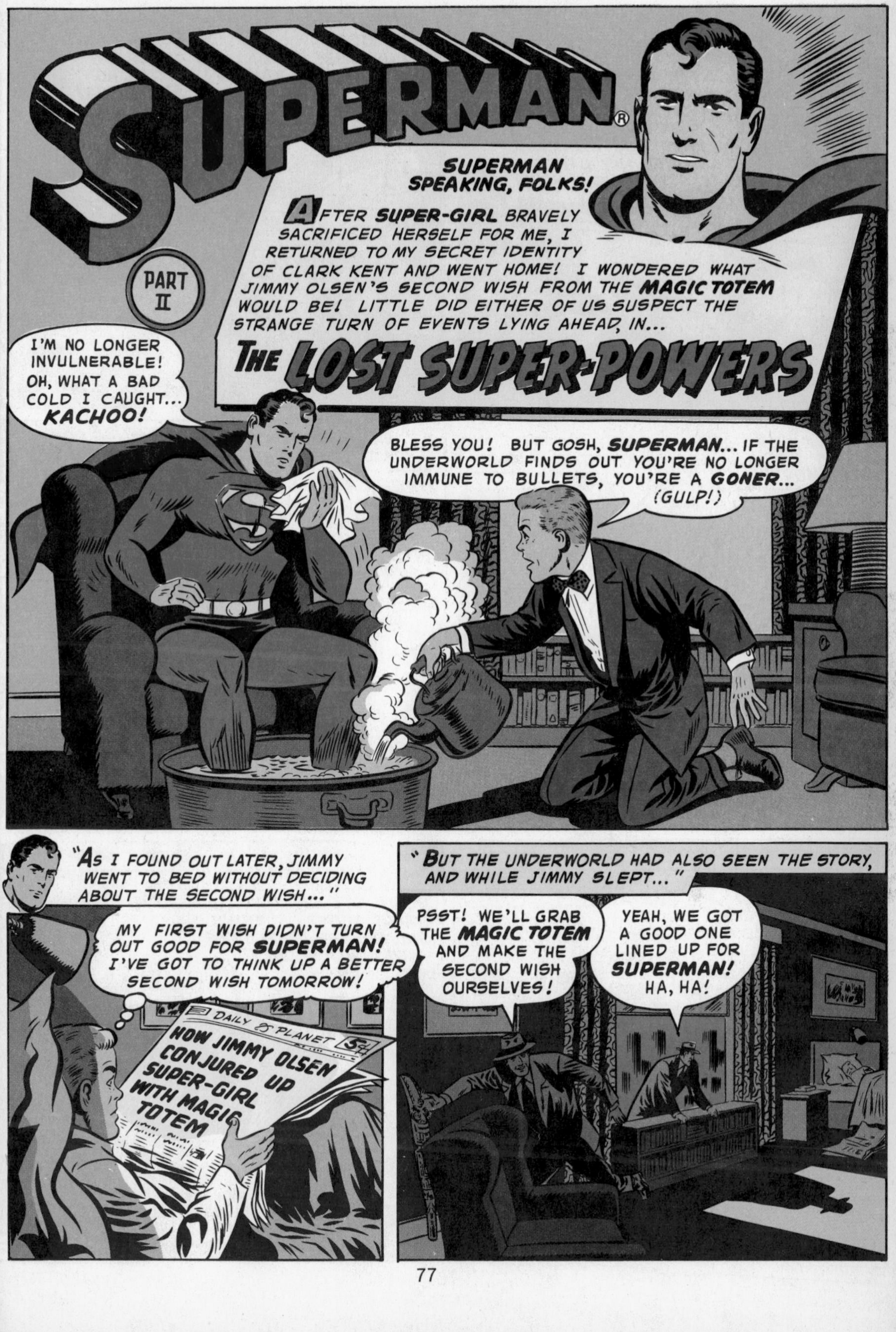
SUPERMAN®
PART II
SUPERMAN SPEAKING, FOLKS!
AFTER SUPER-GIRL BRAVELY SACRIFICED HERSELF FOR ME, I RETURNED TO MY SECRET IDENTITY OF CLARK KENT AND WENT HOME! I WONDERED WHAT JIMMY OLSEN'S SECOND WISH FROM THE MAGIC TOTEM WOULD BE! LITTLE DID EITHER OF US SUSPECT THE STRANGE TURN OF EVENTS LYING AHEAD, IN...
THE LOST SUPER-POWERS
I'M NO LONGER INVULNERABLE! OH, WHAT A BAD COLD I CAUGHT... KACHOO!
BLESS YOU! BUT GOSH, SUPERMAN... IF THE UNDERWORLD FINDS OUT YOU'RE NO LONGER IMMUNE TO BULLETS, YOU'RE A GONER... (GULP!)
"AS I FOUND OUT LATER, JIMMY WENT TO BED WITHOUT DECIDING ABOUT THE SECOND WISH..."
MY FIRST WISH DIDN'T TURN OUT GOOD FOR SUPERMAN! I'VE GOT TO THINK UP A BETTER SECOND WISH TOMORROW!
DAILY PLANET 5¢
HOW JIMMY OLSEN CONJURED UP SUPER-GIRL WITH MAGIC TOTEM
"BUT THE UNDERWORLD HAD ALSO SEEN THE STORY, AND WHILE JIMMY SLEPT..."
PSST! WE'LL GRAB THE MAGIC TOTEM AND MAKE THE SECOND WISH OURSELVES!
YEAH, WE GOT A GOOD ONE LINED UP FOR SUPERMAN! HA, HA!

"LATER, IN THE BACKYARD OF THE GANG'S HIDEOUT..."

I RUB THE MAGIC JEWEL UNDER THE FULL MOON AND... I WISH FOR SUPERMAN TO LOSE ALL HIS SUPER-POWERS!

NOW WE'LL BURY THE MAGIC TOTEM! WITHOUT HIS X-RAY VISION-- SUPERMAN WON'T FIND IT... SO HE CAN'T RUB THE MAGIC JEWEL AND CANCEL THE WISH! HA, HA!

BUT WHAT IF ONLY... ER... GOOD WISHES COME TRUE, NOT BAD ONES? WILL SUPERMAN REALLY LOSE HIS POWERS?

WE'LL MAKE SURE TOMORROW-- BY TAILING SUPERMAN!

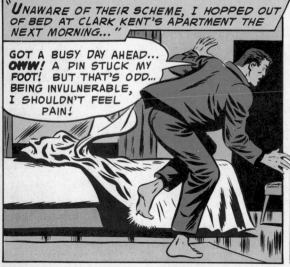

"UNAWARE OF THEIR SCHEME, I HOPPED OUT OF BED AT CLARK KENT'S APARTMENT THE NEXT MORNING..."

GOT A BUSY DAY AHEAD... OWW! A PIN STUCK MY FOOT! BUT THAT'S ODD... BEING INVULNERABLE, I SHOULDN'T FEEL PAIN!

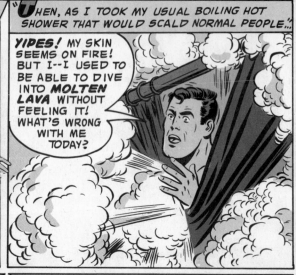

"THEN, AS I TOOK MY USUAL BOILING HOT SHOWER THAT WOULD SCALD NORMAL PEOPLE."

YIPES! MY SKIN SEEMS ON FIRE! BUT I--I USED TO BE ABLE TO DIVE INTO MOLTEN LAVA WITHOUT FEELING IT! WHAT'S WRONG WITH ME TODAY?

"MY BEWILDERMENT GREW DURING MY SETTING-UP EXERCISES."

OOF! I ALWAYS TOSSED THESE AROUND LIKE FEATHERS... BUT NOW I CAN'T BUDGE THEM! WHERE'S MY SUPER-STRENGTH?

1000 lbs

"MOST SHOCKING, WHEN I TRIED TO LEAP FROM THE WINDOW AS USUAL..."

UGH! I-I CAN'T FLY, EITHER! GREAT SCOTT... THERE'S ONLY ONE ANSWER TO ALL THIS... ONE HORRIBLE ANSWER!

CRASH!

2

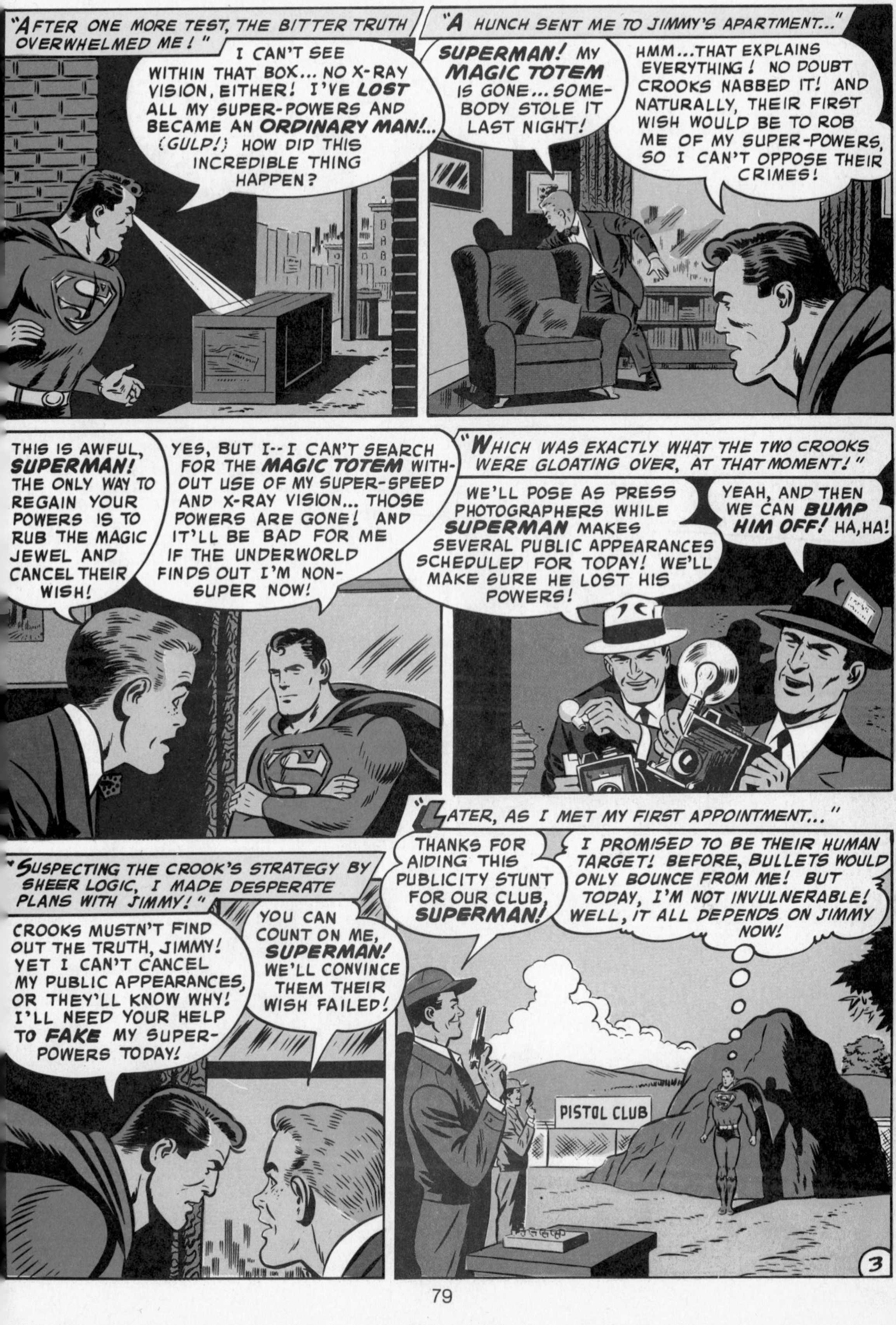
"AFTER ONE MORE TEST, THE BITTER TRUTH OVERWHELMED ME!"
I CAN'T SEE WITHIN THAT BOX... NO X-RAY VISION, EITHER! I'VE LOST ALL MY SUPER-POWERS AND BECAME AN ORDINARY MAN!... (GULP!) HOW DID THIS INCREDIBLE THING HAPPEN?
"A HUNCH SENT ME TO JIMMY'S APARTMENT..."
SUPERMAN! MY MAGIC TOTEM IS GONE... SOMEBODY STOLE IT LAST NIGHT!
HMM...THAT EXPLAINS EVERYTHING! NO DOUBT CROOKS NABBED IT! AND NATURALLY, THEIR FIRST WISH WOULD BE TO ROB ME OF MY SUPER-POWERS, SO I CAN'T OPPOSE THEIR CRIMES!
THIS IS AWFUL, SUPERMAN! THE ONLY WAY TO REGAIN YOUR POWERS IS TO RUB THE MAGIC JEWEL AND CANCEL THEIR WISH!
YES, BUT I-- I CAN'T SEARCH FOR THE MAGIC TOTEM WITHOUT USE OF MY SUPER-SPEED AND X-RAY VISION... THOSE POWERS ARE GONE! AND IT'LL BE BAD FOR ME IF THE UNDERWORLD FINDS OUT I'M NON-SUPER NOW!
"WHICH WAS EXACTLY WHAT THE TWO CROOKS WERE GLOATING OVER, AT THAT MOMENT!"
WE'LL POSE AS PRESS PHOTOGRAPHERS WHILE SUPERMAN MAKES SEVERAL PUBLIC APPEARANCES SCHEDULED FOR TODAY! WE'LL MAKE SURE HE LOST HIS POWERS!
YEAH, AND THEN WE CAN BUMP HIM OFF! HA,HA!
"SUSPECTING THE CROOK'S STRATEGY BY SHEER LOGIC, I MADE DESPERATE PLANS WITH JIMMY!"
CROOKS MUSTN'T FIND OUT THE TRUTH, JIMMY! YET I CAN'T CANCEL MY PUBLIC APPEARANCES, OR THEY'LL KNOW WHY! I'LL NEED YOUR HELP TO FAKE MY SUPER-POWERS TODAY!
YOU CAN COUNT ON ME, SUPERMAN! WE'LL CONVINCE THEM THEIR WISH FAILED!
"LATER, AS I MET MY FIRST APPOINTMENT..."
THANKS FOR AIDING THIS PUBLICITY STUNT FOR OUR CLUB, SUPERMAN!
I PROMISED TO BE THEIR HUMAN TARGET! BEFORE, BULLETS WOULD ONLY BOUNCE FROM ME! BUT TODAY, I'M NOT INVULNERABLE! WELL, IT ALL DEPENDS ON JIMMY NOW!
PISTOL CLUB
3

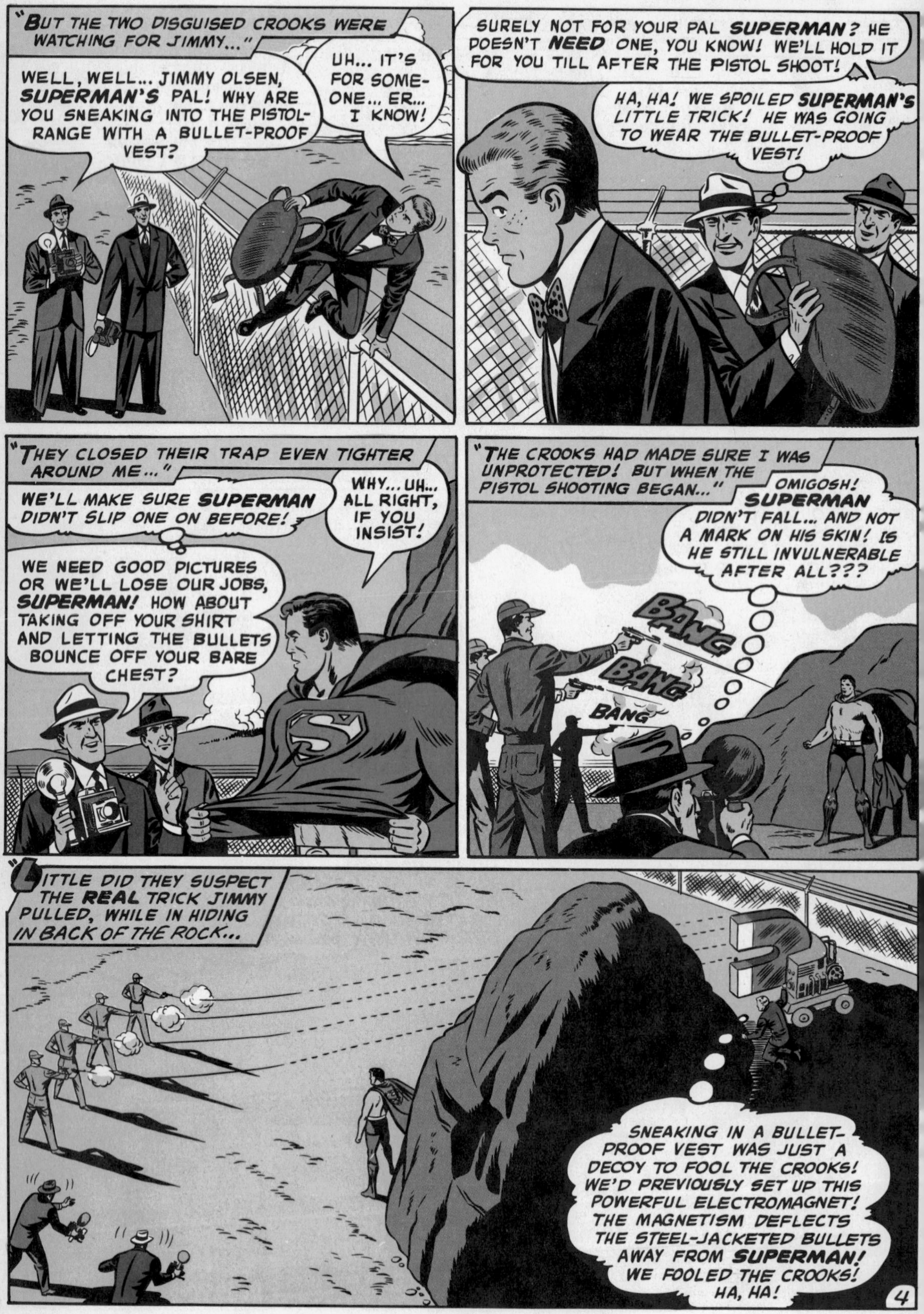

"BUT THE TWO DISGUISED CROOKS WERE WATCHING FOR JIMMY..."
WELL, WELL... JIMMY OLSEN, SUPERMAN'S PAL! WHY ARE YOU SNEAKING INTO THE PISTOL-RANGE WITH A BULLET-PROOF VEST?
UH... IT'S FOR SOME-ONE... ER... I KNOW!
SURELY NOT FOR YOUR PAL SUPERMAN? HE DOESN'T NEED ONE, YOU KNOW! WE'LL HOLD IT FOR YOU TILL AFTER THE PISTOL SHOOT!
HA, HA! WE SPOILED SUPERMAN'S LITTLE TRICK! HE WAS GOING TO WEAR THE BULLET-PROOF VEST!
"THEY CLOSED THEIR TRAP EVEN TIGHTER AROUND ME..."
WE'LL MAKE SURE SUPERMAN DIDN'T SLIP ONE ON BEFORE!
WHY... UH... ALL RIGHT, IF YOU INSIST!
WE NEED GOOD PICTURES OR WE'LL LOSE OUR JOBS, SUPERMAN! HOW ABOUT TAKING OFF YOUR SHIRT AND LETTING THE BULLETS BOUNCE OFF YOUR BARE CHEST?
"THE CROOKS HAD MADE SURE I WAS UNPROTECTED! BUT WHEN THE PISTOL SHOOTING BEGAN..."
OMIGOSH! SUPERMAN DIDN'T FALL... AND NOT A MARK ON HIS SKIN! IS HE STILL INVULNERABLE AFTER ALL???
BANG
BANG
BANG
"LITTLE DID THEY SUSPECT THE REAL TRICK JIMMY PULLED, WHILE IN HIDING IN BACK OF THE ROCK...
SNEAKING IN A BULLET-PROOF VEST WAS JUST A DECOY TO FOOL THE CROOKS! WE'D PREVIOUSLY SET UP THIS POWERFUL ELECTROMAGNET! THE MAGNETISM DEFLECTS THE STEEL-JACKETED BULLETS AWAY FROM SUPERMAN! WE FOOLED THE CROOKS! HA, HA!
4

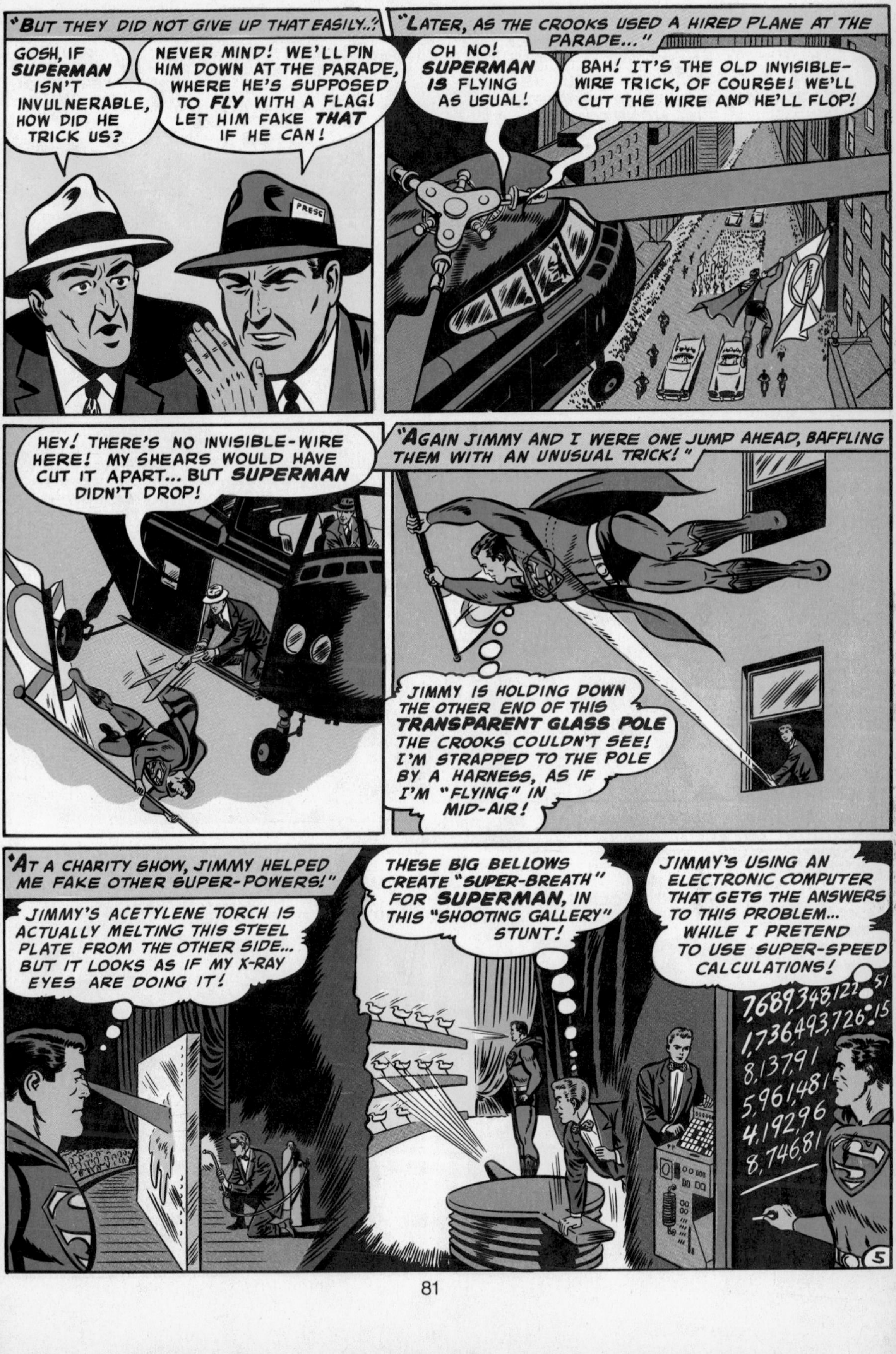
"BUT THEY DID NOT GIVE UP THAT EASILY..!"
GOSH, IF SUPERMAN ISN'T INVULNERABLE, HOW DID HE TRICK US?
NEVER MIND! WE'LL PIN HIM DOWN AT THE PARADE, WHERE HE'S SUPPOSED TO FLY WITH A FLAG! LET HIM FAKE THAT IF HE CAN!
PRESS
"LATER, AS THE CROOKS USED A HIRED PLANE AT THE PARADE..."
OH NO! SUPERMAN IS FLYING AS USUAL!
BAH! IT'S THE OLD INVISIBLE-WIRE TRICK, OF COURSE! WE'LL CUT THE WIRE AND HE'LL FLOP!
HEY! THERE'S NO INVISIBLE-WIRE HERE! MY SHEARS WOULD HAVE CUT IT APART... BUT SUPERMAN DIDN'T DROP!
"AGAIN JIMMY AND I WERE ONE JUMP AHEAD, BAFFLING THEM WITH AN UNUSUAL TRICK!"
JIMMY IS HOLDING DOWN THE OTHER END OF THIS TRANSPARENT GLASS POLE THE CROOKS COULDN'T SEE! I'M STRAPPED TO THE POLE BY A HARNESS, AS IF I'M "FLYING" IN MID-AIR!
"AT A CHARITY SHOW, JIMMY HELPED ME FAKE OTHER SUPER-POWERS!"
JIMMY'S ACETYLENE TORCH IS ACTUALLY MELTING THIS STEEL PLATE FROM THE OTHER SIDE... BUT IT LOOKS AS IF MY X-RAY EYES ARE DOING IT!
THESE BIG BELLOWS CREATE "SUPER-BREATH" FOR SUPERMAN, IN THIS "SHOOTING GALLERY" STUNT!
JIMMY'S USING AN ELECTRONIC COMPUTER THAT GETS THE ANSWERS TO THIS PROBLEM... WHILE I PRETEND TO USE SUPER-SPEED CALCULATIONS!
7,689,348,122 51
1,736,493,726 15
8,137,91
5,961,481
4,192,96
8,746,81
5

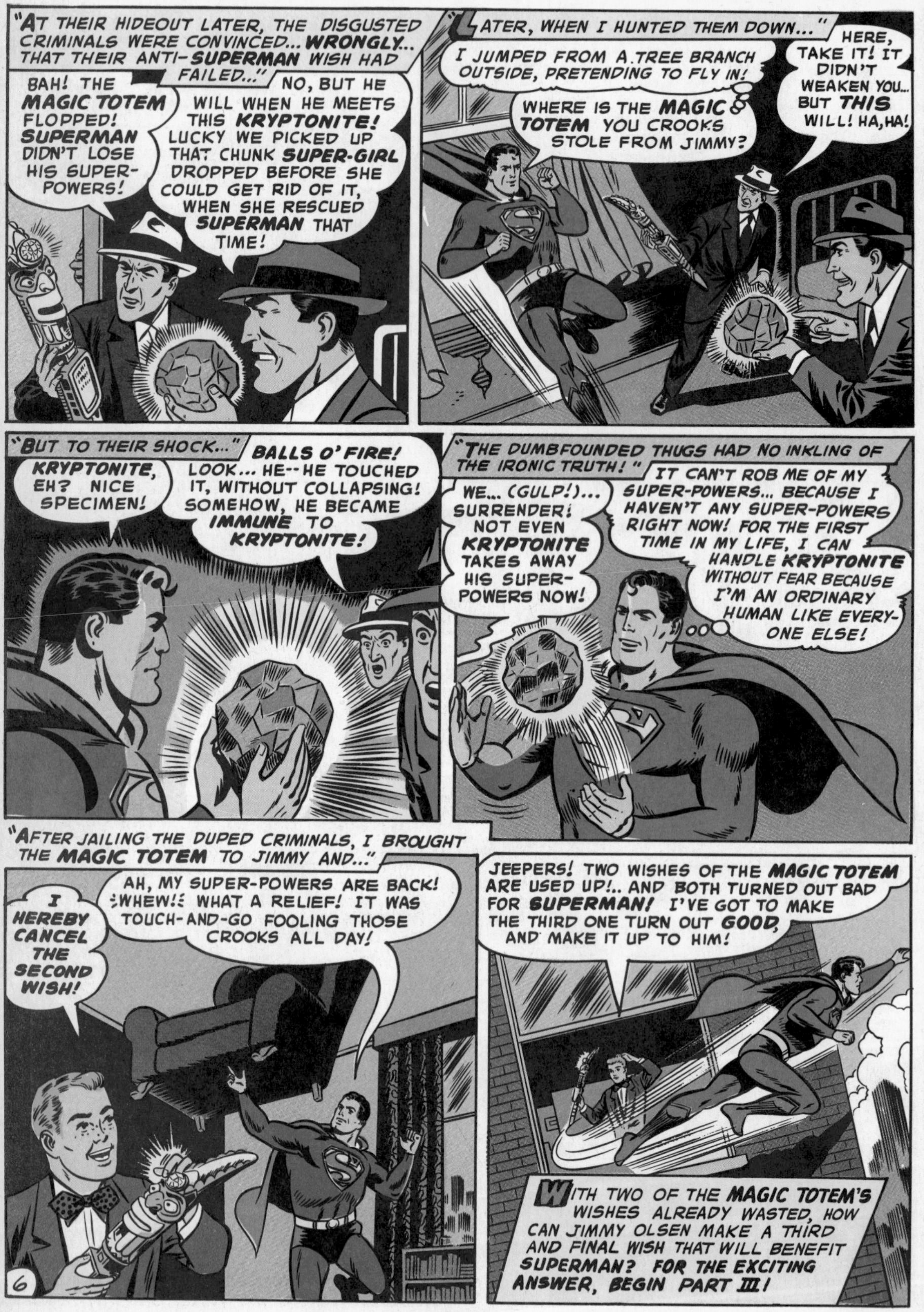
"AT THEIR HIDEOUT LATER, THE DISGUSTED CRIMINALS WERE CONVINCED... WRONGLY... THAT THEIR ANTI-SUPERMAN WISH HAD FAILED..."
BAH! THE MAGIC TOTEM FLOPPED! SUPERMAN DIDN'T LOSE HIS SUPER-POWERS!
NO, BUT HE WILL WHEN HE MEETS THIS KRYPTONITE! LUCKY WE PICKED UP THAT CHUNK SUPER-GIRL DROPPED BEFORE SHE COULD GET RID OF IT, WHEN SHE RESCUED SUPERMAN THAT TIME!
"LATER, WHEN I HUNTED THEM DOWN..."
I JUMPED FROM A TREE BRANCH OUTSIDE, PRETENDING TO FLY IN!
WHERE IS THE MAGIC TOTEM YOU CROOKS STOLE FROM JIMMY?
HERE, TAKE IT! IT DIDN'T WEAKEN YOU... BUT THIS WILL! HA, HA!
"BUT TO THEIR SHOCK..."
KRYPTONITE, EH? NICE SPECIMEN!
BALLS O' FIRE! LOOK... HE--HE TOUCHED IT, WITHOUT COLLAPSING! SOMEHOW, HE BECAME IMMUNE TO KRYPTONITE!
"THE DUMBFOUNDED THUGS HAD NO INKLING OF THE IRONIC TRUTH!"
WE... (GULP!)... SURRENDER! NOT EVEN KRYPTONITE TAKES AWAY HIS SUPER-POWERS NOW!
IT CAN'T ROB ME OF MY SUPER-POWERS... BECAUSE I HAVEN'T ANY SUPER-POWERS RIGHT NOW! FOR THE FIRST TIME IN MY LIFE, I CAN HANDLE KRYPTONITE WITHOUT FEAR BECAUSE I'M AN ORDINARY HUMAN LIKE EVERY-ONE ELSE!
"AFTER JAILING THE DUPED CRIMINALS, I BROUGHT THE MAGIC TOTEM TO JIMMY AND..."
I HEREBY CANCEL THE SECOND WISH!
AH, MY SUPER-POWERS ARE BACK! WHEW! WHAT A RELIEF! IT WAS TOUCH-AND-GO FOOLING THOSE CROOKS ALL DAY!
JEEPERS! TWO WISHES OF THE MAGIC TOTEM ARE USED UP!.. AND BOTH TURNED OUT BAD FOR SUPERMAN! I'VE GOT TO MAKE THE THIRD ONE TURN OUT GOOD, AND MAKE IT UP TO HIM!
WITH TWO OF THE MAGIC TOTEM'S WISHES ALREADY WASTED, HOW CAN JIMMY OLSEN MAKE A THIRD AND FINAL WISH THAT WILL BENEFIT SUPERMAN? FOR THE EXCITING ANSWER, BEGIN PART III!
6

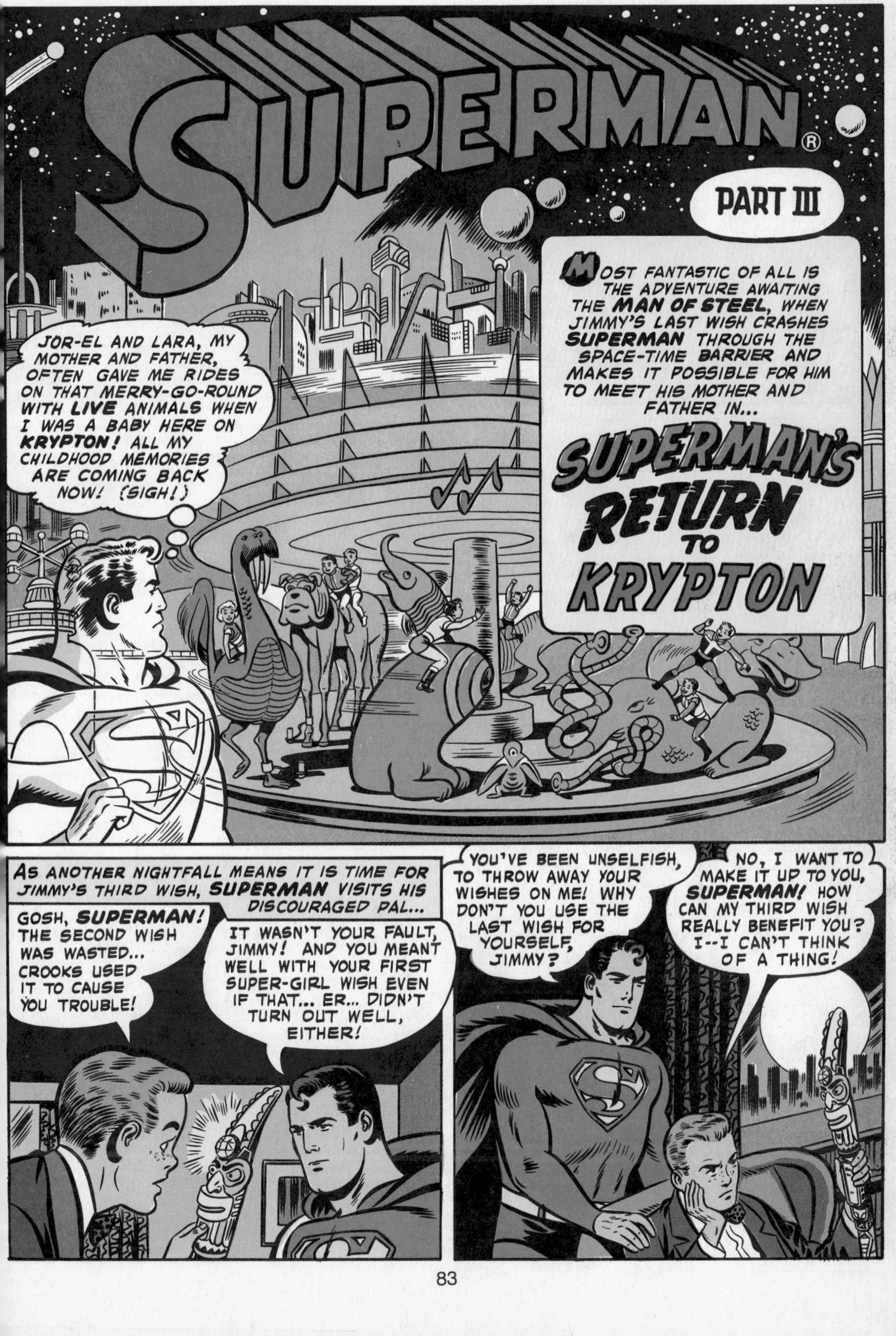
SUPERMAN®
PART III
MOST FANTASTIC OF ALL IS THE ADVENTURE AWAITING THE MAN OF STEEL, WHEN JIMMY'S LAST WISH CRASHES SUPERMAN THROUGH THE SPACE-TIME BARRIER AND MAKES IT POSSIBLE FOR HIM TO MEET HIS MOTHER AND FATHER IN...
SUPERMAN'S RETURN TO KRYPTON
JOR-EL AND LARA, MY MOTHER AND FATHER, OFTEN GAVE ME RIDES ON THAT MERRY-GO-ROUND WITH LIVE ANIMALS WHEN I WAS A BABY HERE ON KRYPTON! ALL MY CHILDHOOD MEMORIES ARE COMING BACK NOW! (SIGH!)
AS ANOTHER NIGHTFALL MEANS IT IS TIME FOR JIMMY'S THIRD WISH, SUPERMAN VISITS HIS DISCOURAGED PAL...
GOSH, SUPERMAN! THE SECOND WISH WAS WASTED... CROOKS USED IT TO CAUSE YOU TROUBLE!
IT WASN'T YOUR FAULT, JIMMY! AND YOU MEANT WELL WITH YOUR FIRST SUPER-GIRL WISH EVEN IF THAT... ER... DIDN'T TURN OUT WELL, EITHER!
YOU'VE BEEN UNSELFISH, TO THROW AWAY YOUR WISHES ON ME! WHY DON'T YOU USE THE LAST WISH FOR YOURSELF, JIMMY?
NO, I WANT TO MAKE IT UP TO YOU, SUPERMAN! HOW CAN MY THIRD WISH REALLY BENEFIT YOU? I--I CAN'T THINK OF A THING!

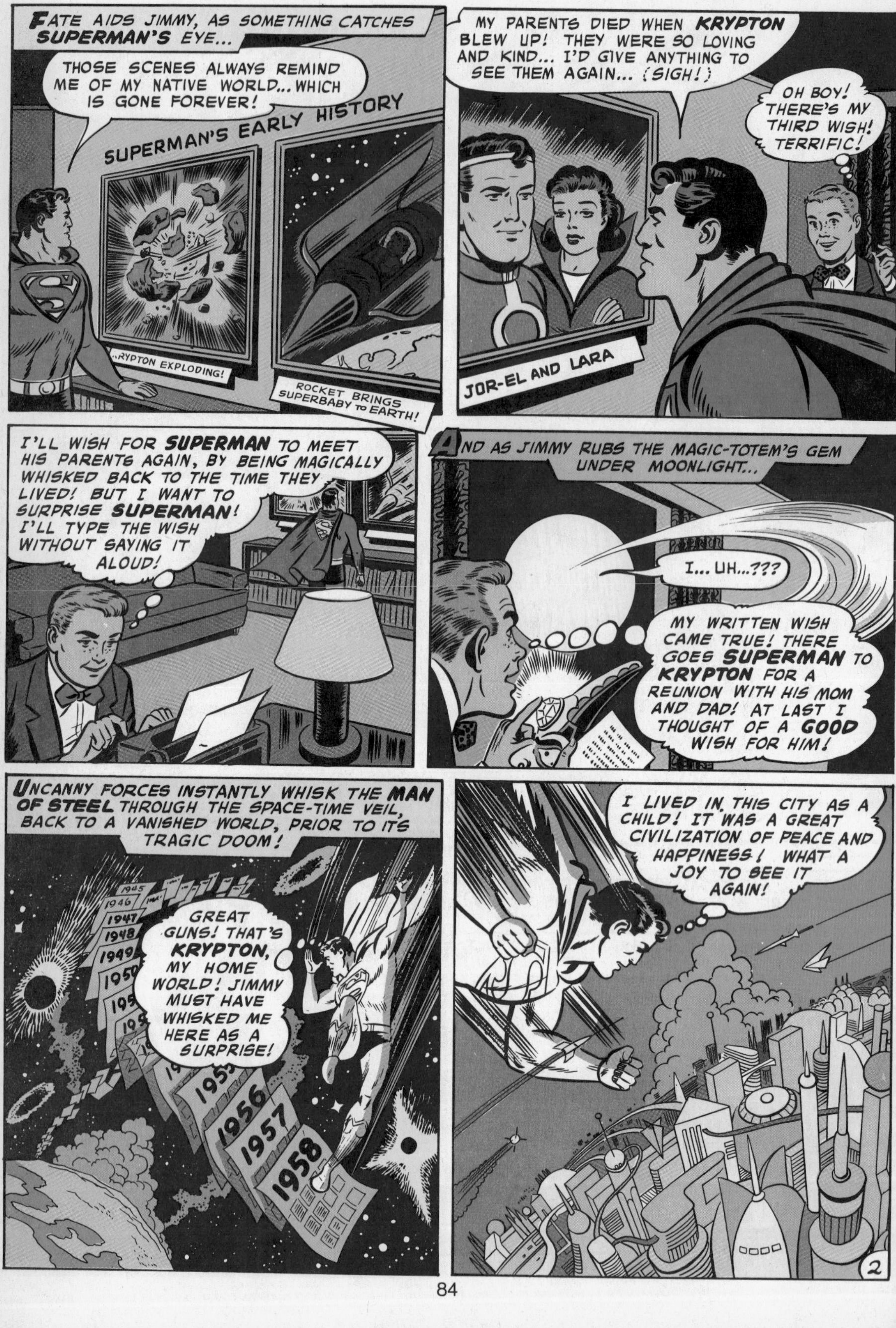
FATE AIDS JIMMY, AS SOMETHING CATCHES SUPERMAN'S EYE...
THOSE SCENES ALWAYS REMIND ME OF MY NATIVE WORLD... WHICH IS GONE FOREVER!
SUPERMAN'S EARLY HISTORY
..RYPTON EXPLODING!
ROCKET BRINGS SUPERBABY TO EARTH!
MY PARENTS DIED WHEN KRYPTON BLEW UP! THEY WERE SO LOVING AND KIND... I'D GIVE ANYTHING TO SEE THEM AGAIN... (SIGH!)
OH BOY! THERE'S MY THIRD WISH! TERRIFIC!
JOR-EL AND LARA
I'LL WISH FOR SUPERMAN TO MEET HIS PARENTS AGAIN, BY BEING MAGICALLY WHISKED BACK TO THE TIME THEY LIVED! BUT I WANT TO SURPRISE SUPERMAN! I'LL TYPE THE WISH WITHOUT SAYING IT ALOUD!
AND AS JIMMY RUBS THE MAGIC-TOTEM'S GEM UNDER MOONLIGHT...
I... UH...???
MY WRITTEN WISH CAME TRUE! THERE GOES SUPERMAN TO KRYPTON FOR A REUNION WITH HIS MOM AND DAD! AT LAST I THOUGHT OF A GOOD WISH FOR HIM!
UNCANNY FORCES INSTANTLY WHISK THE MAN OF STEEL THROUGH THE SPACE-TIME VEIL, BACK TO A VANISHED WORLD, PRIOR TO ITS TRAGIC DOOM!
1945
1946
1947
1948
1949
1950
1955
1956
1957
1958
GREAT GUNS! THAT'S KRYPTON, MY HOME WORLD! JIMMY MUST HAVE WHISKED ME HERE AS A SURPRISE!
I LIVED IN THIS CITY AS A CHILD! IT WAS A GREAT CIVILIZATION OF PEACE AND HAPPINESS! WHAT A JOY TO SEE IT AGAIN!
2

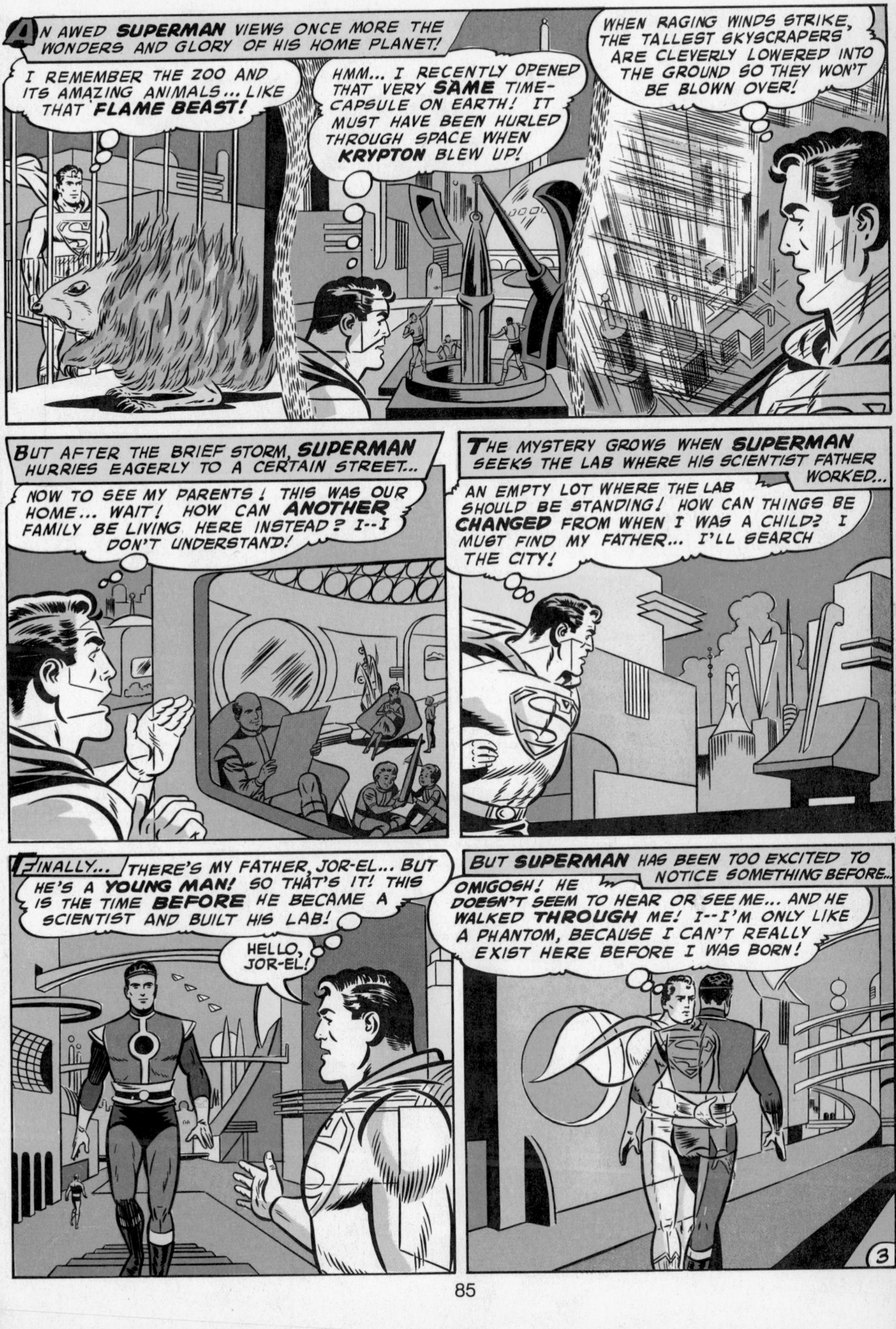
AN AWED SUPERMAN VIEWS ONCE MORE THE WONDERS AND GLORY OF HIS HOME PLANET!
I REMEMBER THE ZOO AND ITS AMAZING ANIMALS... LIKE THAT FLAME BEAST!
HMM... I RECENTLY OPENED THAT VERY SAME TIME-CAPSULE ON EARTH! IT MUST HAVE BEEN HURLED THROUGH SPACE WHEN KRYPTON BLEW UP!
WHEN RAGING WINDS STRIKE, THE TALLEST SKYSCRAPERS ARE CLEVERLY LOWERED INTO THE GROUND SO THEY WON'T BE BLOWN OVER!
BUT AFTER THE BRIEF STORM, SUPERMAN HURRIES EAGERLY TO A CERTAIN STREET...
NOW TO SEE MY PARENTS! THIS WAS OUR HOME... WAIT! HOW CAN ANOTHER FAMILY BE LIVING HERE INSTEAD? I--I DON'T UNDERSTAND!
THE MYSTERY GROWS WHEN SUPERMAN SEEKS THE LAB WHERE HIS SCIENTIST FATHER WORKED...
AN EMPTY LOT WHERE THE LAB SHOULD BE STANDING! HOW CAN THINGS BE CHANGED FROM WHEN I WAS A CHILD? I MUST FIND MY FATHER... I'LL SEARCH THE CITY!
FINALLY...
THERE'S MY FATHER, JOR-EL... BUT HE'S A YOUNG MAN! SO THAT'S IT! THIS IS THE TIME BEFORE HE BECAME A SCIENTIST AND BUILT HIS LAB!
HELLO, JOR-EL!
BUT SUPERMAN HAS BEEN TOO EXCITED TO NOTICE SOMETHING BEFORE...
OMIGOSH! HE DOESN'T SEEM TO HEAR OR SEE ME... AND HE WALKED THROUGH ME! I--I'M ONLY LIKE A PHANTOM, BECAUSE I CAN'T REALLY EXIST HERE BEFORE I WAS BORN!
3

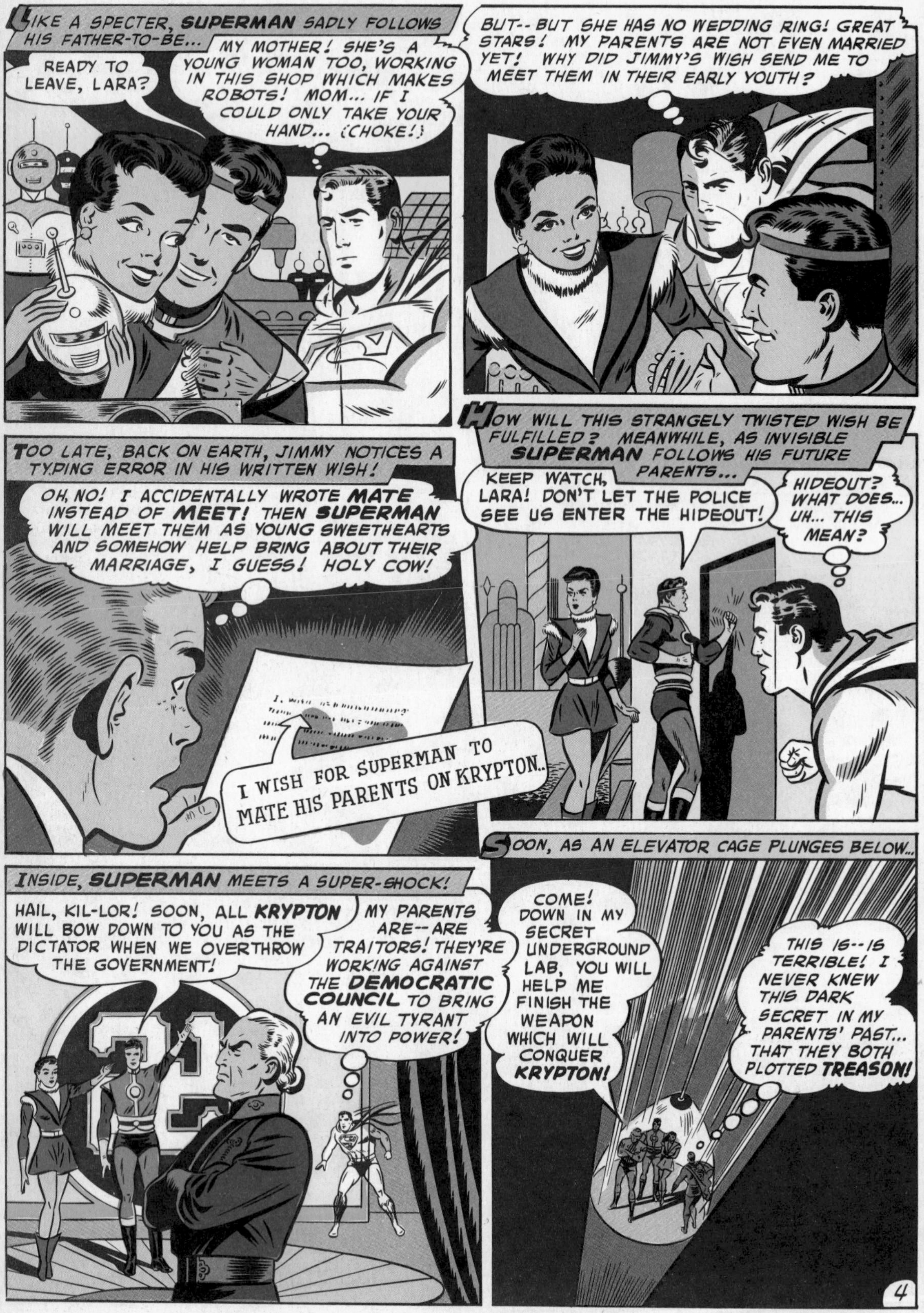
LIKE A SPECTER, SUPERMAN SADLY FOLLOWS HIS FATHER-TO-BE...
READY TO LEAVE, LARA?
MY MOTHER! SHE'S A YOUNG WOMAN TOO, WORKING IN THIS SHOP WHICH MAKES ROBOTS! MOM... IF I COULD ONLY TAKE YOUR HAND... (CHOKE!)
BUT-- BUT SHE HAS NO WEDDING RING! GREAT STARS! MY PARENTS ARE NOT EVEN MARRIED YET! WHY DID JIMMY'S WISH SEND ME TO MEET THEM IN THEIR EARLY YOUTH?
TOO LATE, BACK ON EARTH, JIMMY NOTICES A TYPING ERROR IN HIS WRITTEN WISH!
OH, NO! I ACCIDENTALLY WROTE MATE INSTEAD OF MEET! THEN SUPERMAN WILL MEET THEM AS YOUNG SWEETHEARTS AND SOMEHOW HELP BRING ABOUT THEIR MARRIAGE, I GUESS! HOLY COW!
I WISH FOR SUPERMAN TO MATE HIS PARENTS ON KRYPTON..
HOW WILL THIS STRANGELY TWISTED WISH BE FULFILLED? MEANWHILE, AS INVISIBLE SUPERMAN FOLLOWS HIS FUTURE PARENTS...
KEEP WATCH, LARA! DON'T LET THE POLICE SEE US ENTER THE HIDEOUT!
HIDEOUT? WHAT DOES... UH... THIS MEAN?
INSIDE, SUPERMAN MEETS A SUPER-SHOCK!
HAIL, KIL-LOR! SOON, ALL KRYPTON WILL BOW DOWN TO YOU AS THE DICTATOR WHEN WE OVERTHROW THE GOVERNMENT!
MY PARENTS ARE-- ARE TRAITORS! THEY'RE WORKING AGAINST THE DEMOCRATIC COUNCIL TO BRING AN EVIL TYRANT INTO POWER!
SOON, AS AN ELEVATOR CAGE PLUNGES BELOW...
COME! DOWN IN MY SECRET UNDERGROUND LAB, YOU WILL HELP ME FINISH THE WEAPON WHICH WILL CONQUER KRYPTON!
THIS IS-- IS TERRIBLE! I NEVER KNEW THIS DARK SECRET IN MY PARENTS' PAST... THAT THEY BOTH PLOTTED TREASON!
4

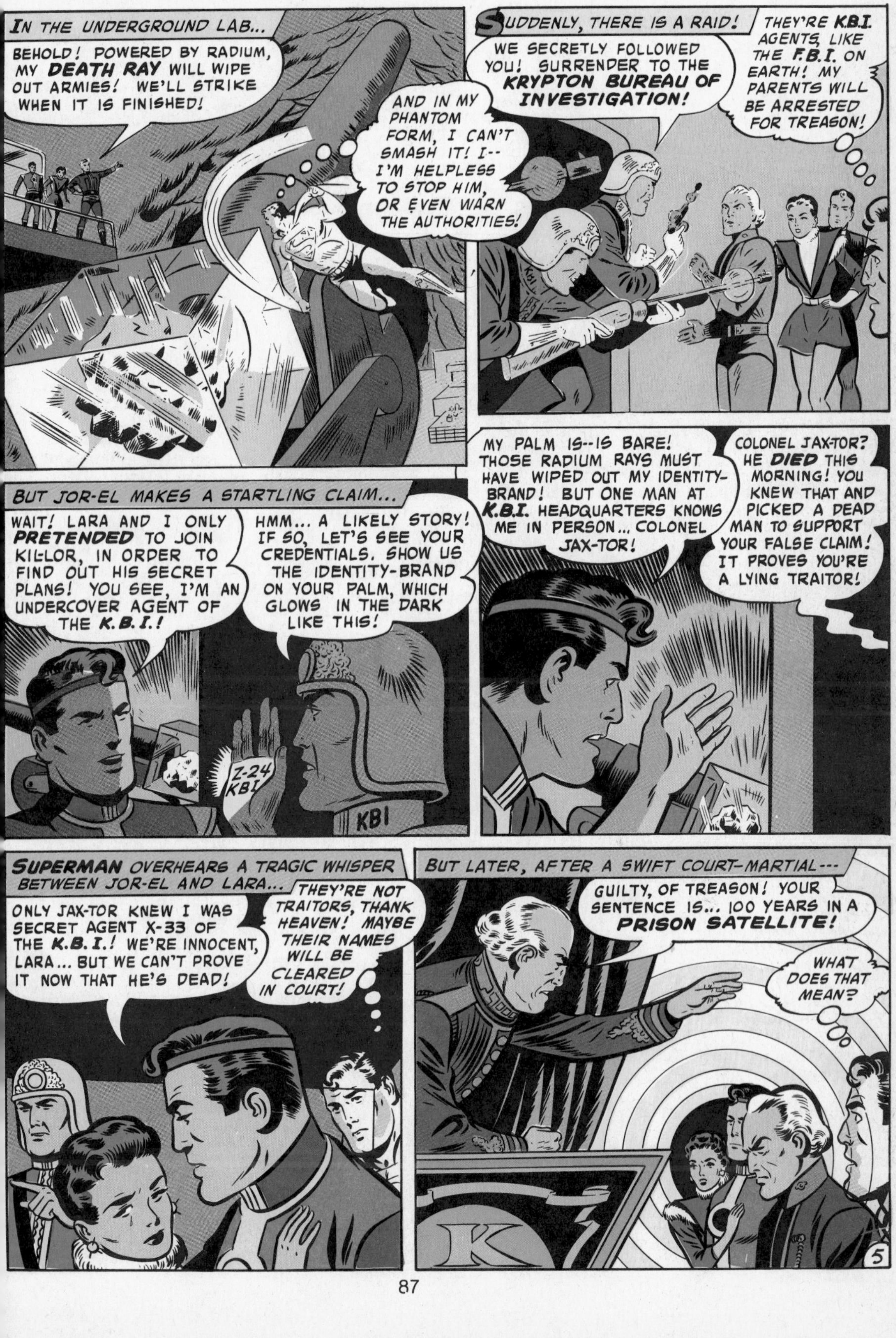

IN THE UNDERGROUND LAB...
BEHOLD! POWERED BY RADIUM, MY DEATH RAY WILL WIPE OUT ARMIES! WE'LL STRIKE WHEN IT IS FINISHED!
AND IN MY PHANTOM FORM, I CAN'T SMASH IT! I-- I'M HELPLESS TO STOP HIM, OR EVEN WARN THE AUTHORITIES!
SUDDENLY, THERE IS A RAID!
WE SECRETLY FOLLOWED YOU! SURRENDER TO THE KRYPTON BUREAU OF INVESTIGATION!
THEY'RE K.B.I. AGENTS, LIKE THE F.B.I. ON EARTH! MY PARENTS WILL BE ARRESTED FOR TREASON!
KBI
BUT JOR-EL MAKES A STARTLING CLAIM...
WAIT! LARA AND I ONLY PRETENDED TO JOIN KIL-LOR, IN ORDER TO FIND OUT HIS SECRET PLANS! YOU SEE, I'M AN UNDERCOVER AGENT OF THE K.B.I.!
HMM... A LIKELY STORY! IF SO, LET'S SEE YOUR CREDENTIALS. SHOW US THE IDENTITY-BRAND ON YOUR PALM, WHICH GLOWS IN THE DARK LIKE THIS!
Z-24 KBI
KBI
MY PALM IS--IS BARE! THOSE RADIUM RAYS MUST HAVE WIPED OUT MY IDENTITY-BRAND! BUT ONE MAN AT K.B.I. HEADQUARTERS KNOWS ME IN PERSON... COLONEL JAX-TOR!
COLONEL JAX-TOR? HE DIED THIS MORNING! YOU KNEW THAT AND PICKED A DEAD MAN TO SUPPORT YOUR FALSE CLAIM! IT PROVES YOU'RE A LYING TRAITOR!
SUPERMAN OVERHEARS A TRAGIC WHISPER BETWEEN JOR-EL AND LARA...
ONLY JAX-TOR KNEW I WAS SECRET AGENT X-33 OF THE K.B.I.! WE'RE INNOCENT, LARA... BUT WE CAN'T PROVE IT NOW THAT HE'S DEAD!
THEY'RE NOT TRAITORS, THANK HEAVEN! MAYBE THEIR NAMES WILL BE CLEARED IN COURT!
BUT LATER, AFTER A SWIFT COURT-MARTIAL---
GUILTY, OF TREASON! YOUR SENTENCE IS... 100 YEARS IN A PRISON SATELLITE!
WHAT DOES THAT MEAN?
K
5

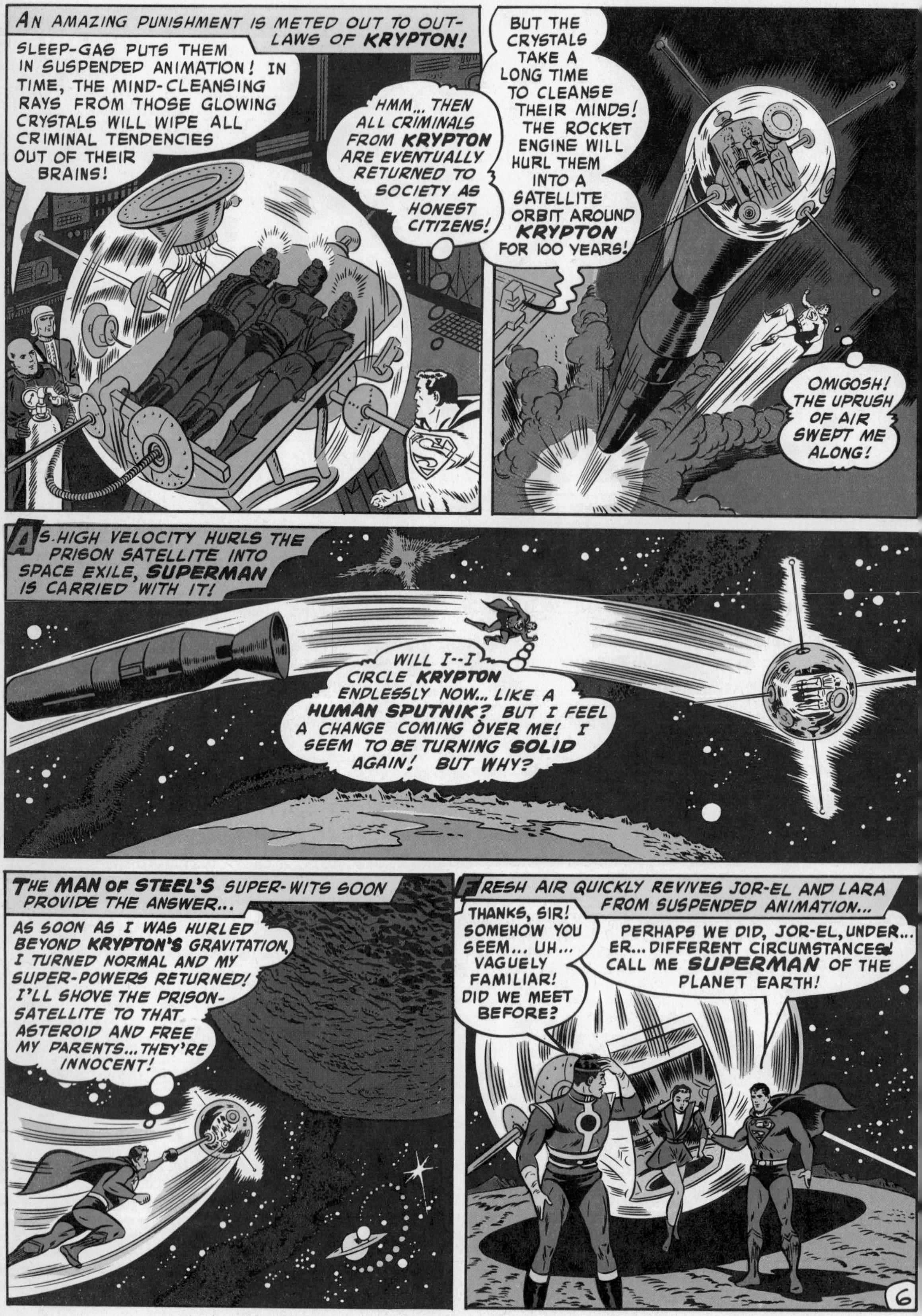

AN AMAZING PUNISHMENT IS METED OUT TO OUT-LAWS OF KRYPTON!
SLEEP-GAS PUTS THEM IN SUSPENDED ANIMATION! IN TIME, THE MIND-CLEANSING RAYS FROM THOSE GLOWING CRYSTALS WILL WIPE ALL CRIMINAL TENDENCIES OUT OF THEIR BRAINS!
HMM... THEN ALL CRIMINALS FROM KRYPTON ARE EVENTUALLY RETURNED TO SOCIETY AS HONEST CITIZENS!
BUT THE CRYSTALS TAKE A LONG TIME TO CLEANSE THEIR MINDS! THE ROCKET ENGINE WILL HURL THEM INTO A SATELLITE ORBIT AROUND KRYPTON FOR 100 YEARS!
OMIGOSH! THE UPRUSH OF AIR SWEPT ME ALONG!
AS HIGH VELOCITY HURLS THE PRISON SATELLITE INTO SPACE EXILE, SUPERMAN IS CARRIED WITH IT!
WILL I--I CIRCLE KRYPTON ENDLESSLY NOW... LIKE A HUMAN SPUTNIK? BUT I FEEL A CHANGE COMING OVER ME! I SEEM TO BE TURNING SOLID AGAIN! BUT WHY?
THE MAN OF STEEL'S SUPER-WITS SOON PROVIDE THE ANSWER...
AS SOON AS I WAS HURLED BEYOND KRYPTON'S GRAVITATION, I TURNED NORMAL AND MY SUPER-POWERS RETURNED! I'LL SHOVE THE PRISON-SATELLITE TO THAT ASTEROID AND FREE MY PARENTS...THEY'RE INNOCENT!
FRESH AIR QUICKLY REVIVES JOR-EL AND LARA FROM SUSPENDED ANIMATION...
THANKS, SIR! SOMEHOW YOU SEEM... UH... VAGUELY FAMILIAR! DID WE MEET BEFORE?
PERHAPS WE DID, JOR-EL, UNDER... ER... DIFFERENT CIRCUMSTANCES! CALL ME SUPERMAN OF THE PLANET EARTH!
6

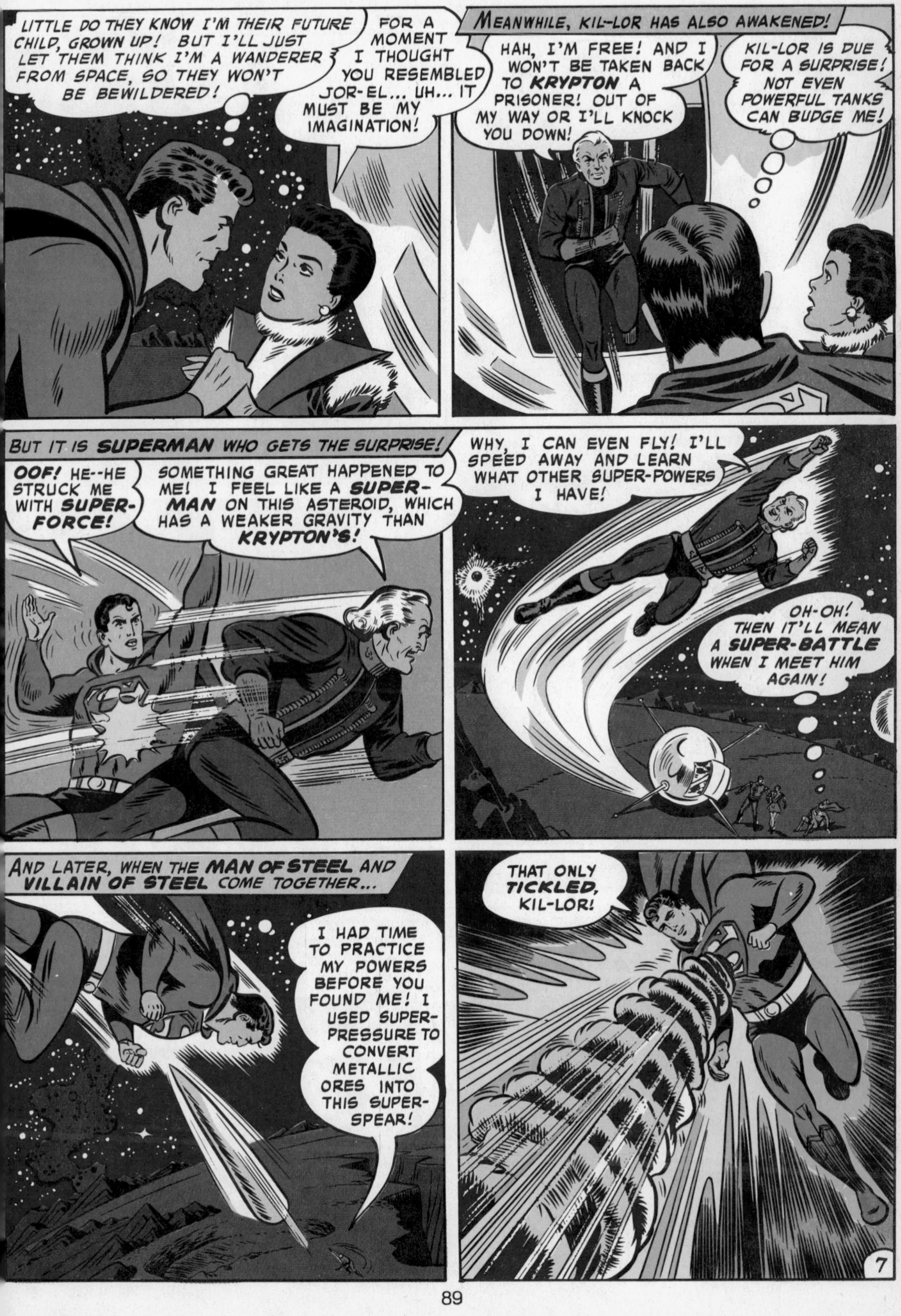
LITTLE DO THEY KNOW I'M THEIR FUTURE CHILD, GROWN UP! BUT I'LL JUST LET THEM THINK I'M A WANDERER FROM SPACE, SO THEY WON'T BE BEWILDERED!
FOR A MOMENT I THOUGHT YOU RESEMBLED JOR-EL... UH... IT MUST BE MY IMAGINATION!
MEANWHILE, KIL-LOR HAS ALSO AWAKENED!
HAH, I'M FREE! AND I WON'T BE TAKEN BACK TO KRYPTON A PRISONER! OUT OF MY WAY OR I'LL KNOCK YOU DOWN!
KIL-LOR IS DUE FOR A SURPRISE! NOT EVEN POWERFUL TANKS CAN BUDGE ME!
BUT IT IS SUPERMAN WHO GETS THE SURPRISE!
OOF! HE--HE STRUCK ME WITH SUPER-FORCE!
SOMETHING GREAT HAPPENED TO ME! I FEEL LIKE A SUPER-MAN ON THIS ASTEROID, WHICH HAS A WEAKER GRAVITY THAN KRYPTON'S!
WHY, I CAN EVEN FLY! I'LL SPEED AWAY AND LEARN WHAT OTHER SUPER-POWERS I HAVE!
OH-OH! THEN IT'LL MEAN A SUPER-BATTLE WHEN I MEET HIM AGAIN!
AND LATER, WHEN THE MAN OF STEEL AND VILLAIN OF STEEL COME TOGETHER...
I HAD TIME TO PRACTICE MY POWERS BEFORE YOU FOUND ME! I USED SUPER-PRESSURE TO CONVERT METALLIC ORES INTO THIS SUPER-SPEAR!
THAT ONLY TICKLED, KIL-LOR!
7

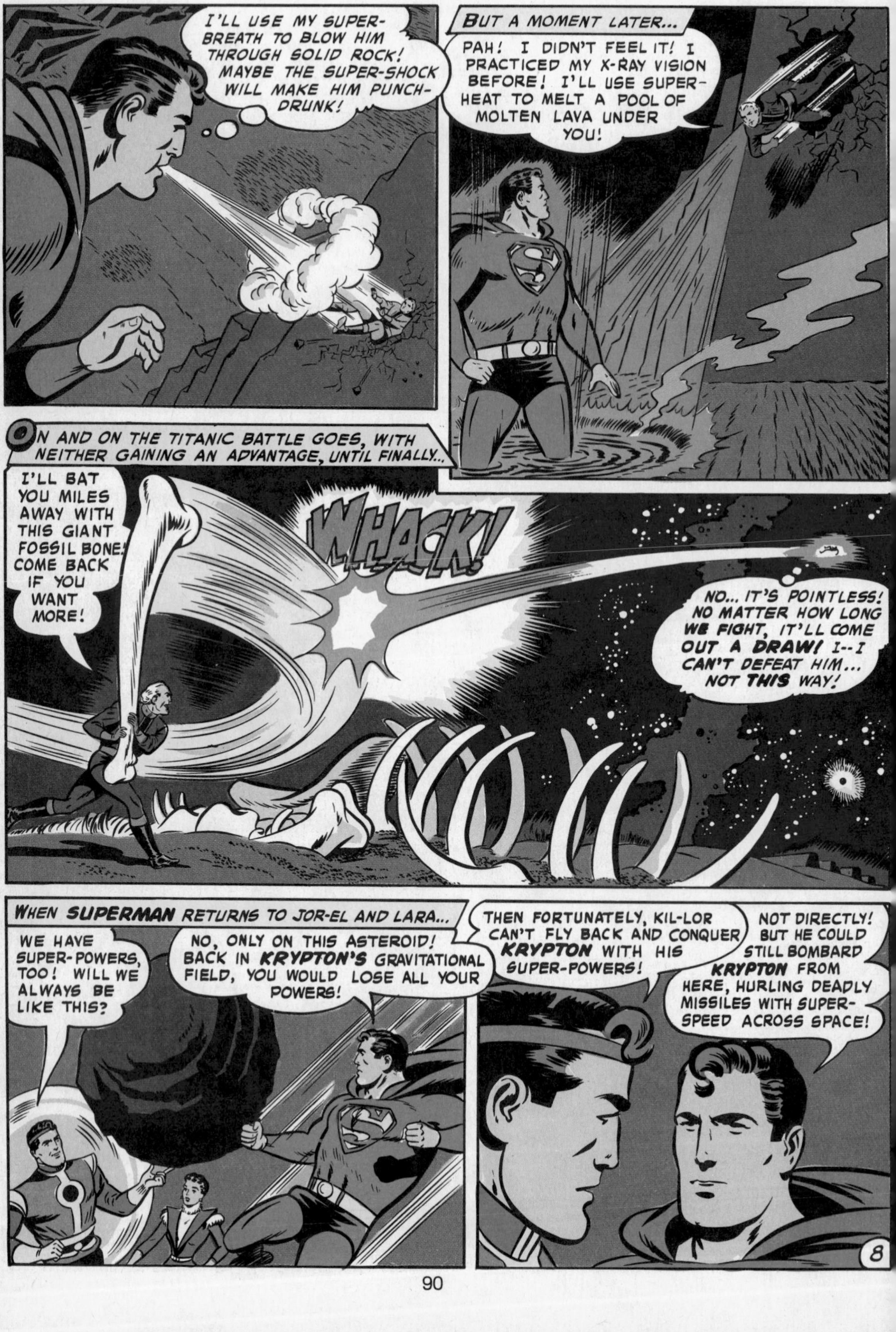

I'LL USE MY SUPER-BREATH TO BLOW HIM THROUGH SOLID ROCK! MAYBE THE SUPER-SHOCK WILL MAKE HIM PUNCH-DRUNK!
BUT A MOMENT LATER...
PAH! I DIDN'T FEEL IT! I PRACTICED MY X-RAY VISION BEFORE! I'LL USE SUPER-HEAT TO MELT A POOL OF MOLTEN LAVA UNDER YOU!
ON AND ON THE TITANIC BATTLE GOES, WITH NEITHER GAINING AN ADVANTAGE, UNTIL FINALLY...
I'LL BAT YOU MILES AWAY WITH THIS GIANT FOSSIL BONE! COME BACK IF YOU WANT MORE!
WHACK!
NO... IT'S POINTLESS! NO MATTER HOW LONG WE FIGHT, IT'LL COME OUT A DRAW! I--I CAN'T DEFEAT HIM... NOT THIS WAY!
WHEN SUPERMAN RETURNS TO JOR-EL AND LARA...
WE HAVE SUPER-POWERS, TOO! WILL WE ALWAYS BE LIKE THIS?
NO, ONLY ON THIS ASTEROID! BACK IN KRYPTON'S GRAVITATIONAL FIELD, YOU WOULD LOSE ALL YOUR POWERS!
THEN FORTUNATELY, KIL-LOR CAN'T FLY BACK AND CONQUER KRYPTON WITH HIS SUPER-POWERS!
NOT DIRECTLY! BUT HE COULD STILL BOMBARD KRYPTON FROM HERE, HURLING DEADLY MISSILES WITH SUPER-SPEED ACROSS SPACE!
8

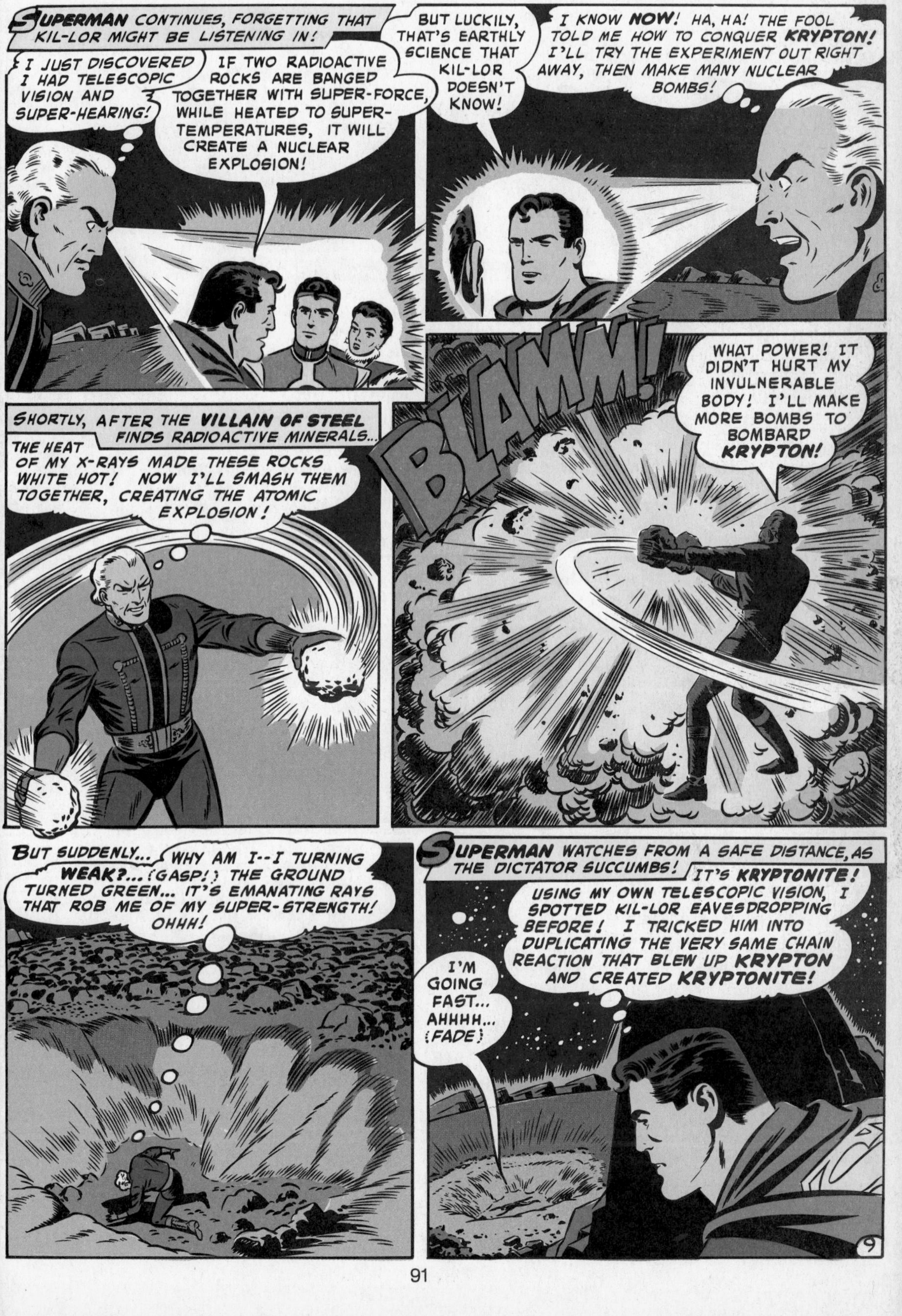
SUPERMAN CONTINUES, FORGETTING THAT KIL-LOR MIGHT BE LISTENING IN!
I JUST DISCOVERED I HAD TELESCOPIC VISION AND SUPER-HEARING!
IF TWO RADIOACTIVE ROCKS ARE BANGED TOGETHER WITH SUPER-FORCE, WHILE HEATED TO SUPER-TEMPERATURES, IT WILL CREATE A NUCLEAR EXPLOSION!
BUT LUCKILY, THAT'S EARTHLY SCIENCE THAT KIL-LOR DOESN'T KNOW!
I KNOW NOW! HA, HA! THE FOOL TOLD ME HOW TO CONQUER KRYPTON! I'LL TRY THE EXPERIMENT OUT RIGHT AWAY, THEN MAKE MANY NUCLEAR BOMBS!
SHORTLY, AFTER THE VILLAIN OF STEEL FINDS RADIOACTIVE MINERALS...
THE HEAT OF MY X-RAYS MADE THESE ROCKS WHITE HOT! NOW I'LL SMASH THEM TOGETHER, CREATING THE ATOMIC EXPLOSION!
BLAMM!
WHAT POWER! IT DIDN'T HURT MY INVULNERABLE BODY! I'LL MAKE MORE BOMBS TO BOMBARD KRYPTON!
BUT SUDDENLY...
WHY AM I--I TURNING WEAK?... (GASP!) THE GROUND TURNED GREEN... IT'S EMANATING RAYS THAT ROB ME OF MY SUPER-STRENGTH! OHHH!
SUPERMAN WATCHES FROM A SAFE DISTANCE, AS THE DICTATOR SUCCUMBS!
IT'S KRYPTONITE! USING MY OWN TELESCOPIC VISION, I SPOTTED KIL-LOR EAVESDROPPING BEFORE! I TRICKED HIM INTO DUPLICATING THE VERY SAME CHAIN REACTION THAT BLEW UP KRYPTON AND CREATED KRYPTONITE!
I'M GOING FAST... AHHHH... (FADE)
9

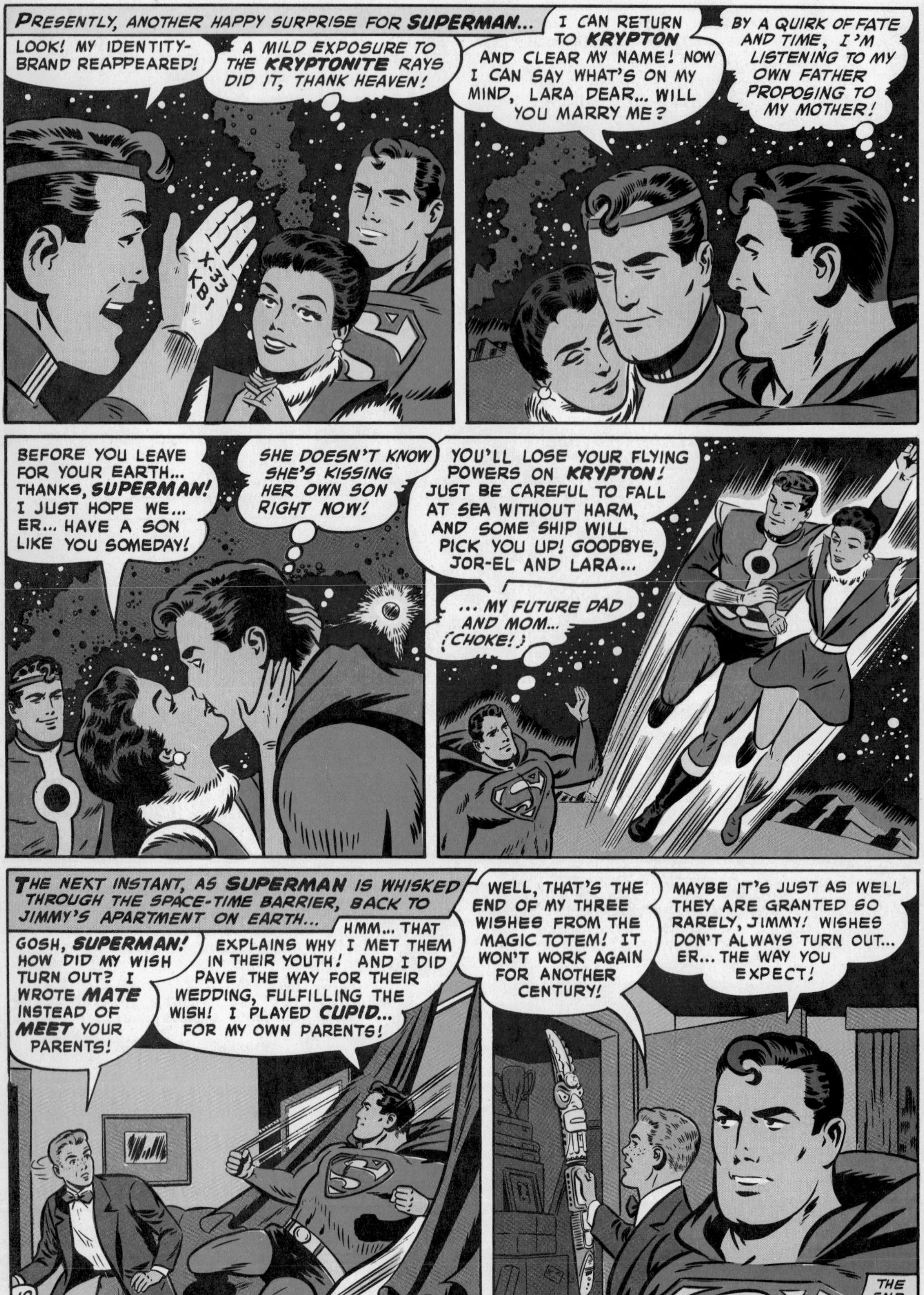

PRESENTLY, ANOTHER HAPPY SURPRISE FOR SUPERMAN...
LOOK! MY IDENTITY-BRAND REAPPEARED!
A MILD EXPOSURE TO THE KRYPTONITE RAYS DID IT, THANK HEAVEN!
X-33 KBI
I CAN RETURN TO KRYPTON AND CLEAR MY NAME! NOW I CAN SAY WHAT'S ON MY MIND, LARA DEAR... WILL YOU MARRY ME?
BY A QUIRK OF FATE AND TIME, I'M LISTENING TO MY OWN FATHER PROPOSING TO MY MOTHER!
BEFORE YOU LEAVE FOR YOUR EARTH... THANKS, SUPERMAN! I JUST HOPE WE... ER... HAVE A SON LIKE YOU SOMEDAY!
SHE DOESN'T KNOW SHE'S KISSING HER OWN SON RIGHT NOW!
YOU'LL LOSE YOUR FLYING POWERS ON KRYPTON! JUST BE CAREFUL TO FALL AT SEA WITHOUT HARM, AND SOME SHIP WILL PICK YOU UP! GOODBYE, JOR-EL AND LARA...
... MY FUTURE DAD AND MOM... (CHOKE!)
THE NEXT INSTANT, AS SUPERMAN IS WHISKED THROUGH THE SPACE-TIME BARRIER, BACK TO JIMMY'S APARTMENT ON EARTH...
GOSH, SUPERMAN! HOW DID MY WISH TURN OUT? I WROTE MATE INSTEAD OF MEET YOUR PARENTS!
HMM... THAT EXPLAINS WHY I MET THEM IN THEIR YOUTH! AND I DID PAVE THE WAY FOR THEIR WEDDING, FULFILLING THE WISH! I PLAYED CUPID... FOR MY OWN PARENTS!
10
WELL, THAT'S THE END OF MY THREE WISHES FROM THE MAGIC TOTEM! IT WON'T WORK AGAIN FOR ANOTHER CENTURY!
MAYBE IT'S JUST AS WELL THEY ARE GRANTED SO RARELY, JIMMY! WISHES DON'T ALWAYS TURN OUT... ER... THE WAY YOU EXPECT!
THE END

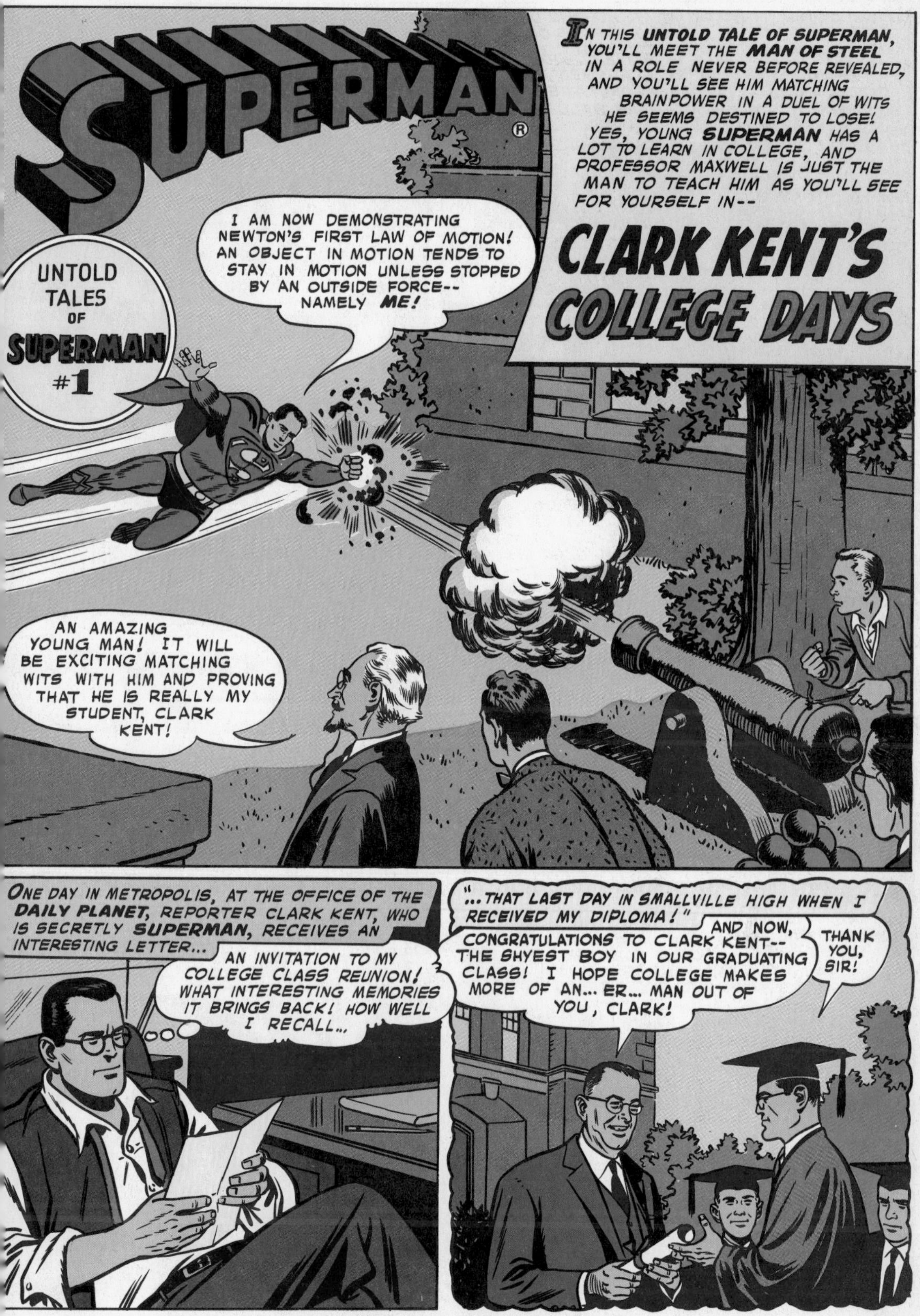
SUPERMAN ®
IN THIS UNTOLD TALE OF SUPERMAN, YOU'LL MEET THE MAN OF STEEL IN A ROLE NEVER BEFORE REVEALED, AND YOU'LL SEE HIM MATCHING BRAINPOWER IN A DUEL OF WITS HE SEEMS DESTINED TO LOSE! YES, YOUNG SUPERMAN HAS A LOT TO LEARN IN COLLEGE, AND PROFESSOR MAXWELL IS JUST THE MAN TO TEACH HIM AS YOU'LL SEE FOR YOURSELF IN--
CLARK KENT'S COLLEGE DAYS
UNTOLD TALES OF SUPERMAN #1
I AM NOW DEMONSTRATING NEWTON'S FIRST LAW OF MOTION! AN OBJECT IN MOTION TENDS TO STAY IN MOTION UNLESS STOPPED BY AN OUTSIDE FORCE-- NAMELY ME!
AN AMAZING YOUNG MAN! IT WILL BE EXCITING MATCHING WITS WITH HIM AND PROVING THAT HE IS REALLY MY STUDENT, CLARK KENT!
ONE DAY IN METROPOLIS, AT THE OFFICE OF THE DAILY PLANET, REPORTER CLARK KENT, WHO IS SECRETLY SUPERMAN, RECEIVES AN INTERESTING LETTER...
AN INVITATION TO MY COLLEGE CLASS REUNION! WHAT INTERESTING MEMORIES IT BRINGS BACK! HOW WELL I RECALL...
"...THAT LAST DAY IN SMALLVILLE HIGH WHEN I RECEIVED MY DIPLOMA!"
AND NOW, CONGRATULATIONS TO CLARK KENT-- THE SHYEST BOY IN OUR GRADUATING CLASS! I HOPE COLLEGE MAKES MORE OF AN... ER... MAN OUT OF YOU, CLARK!
THANK YOU, SIR!

Art by Al Plastino/Color by Helen Vesik

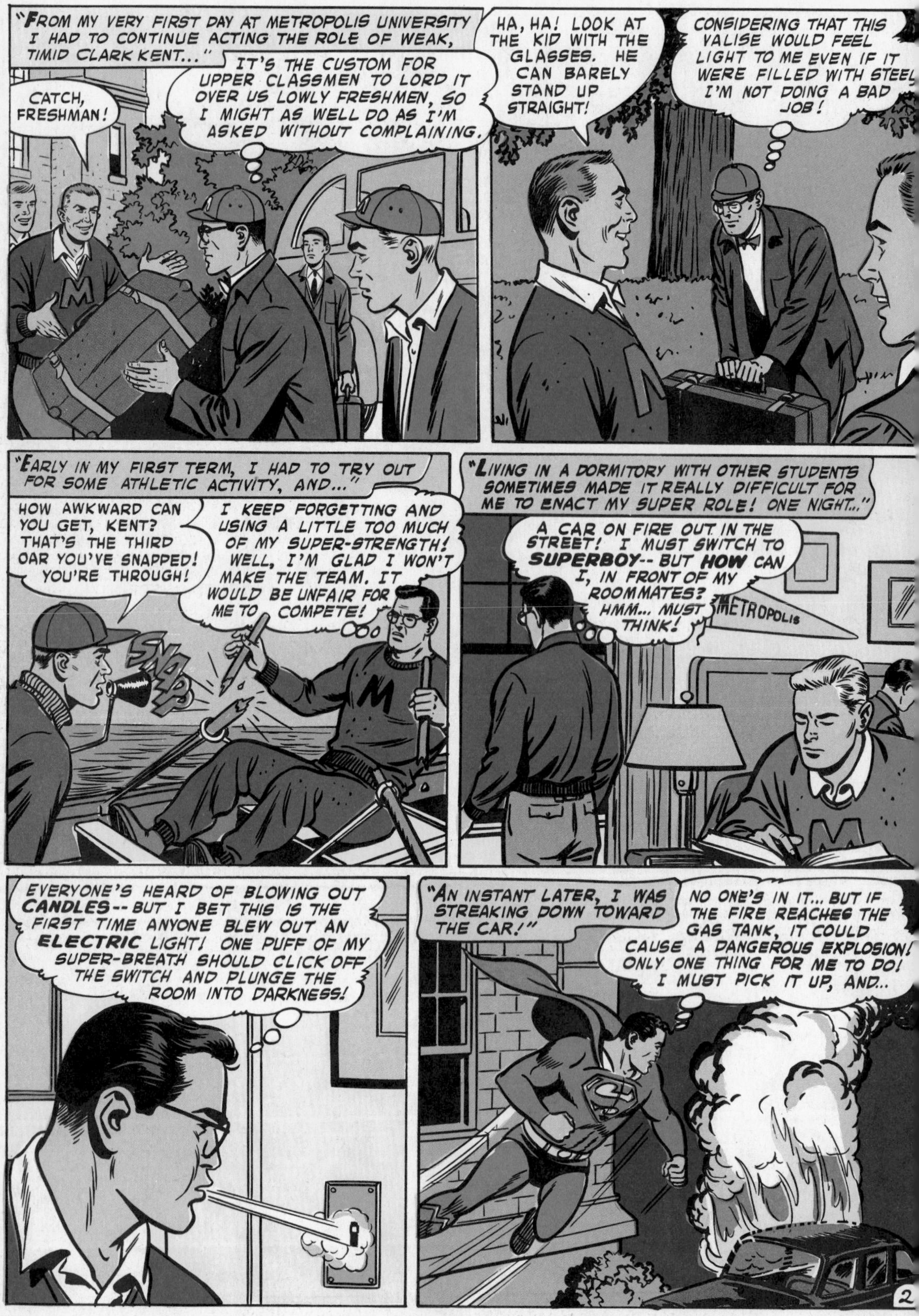
"FROM MY VERY FIRST DAY AT METROPOLIS UNIVERSITY I HAD TO CONTINUE ACTING THE ROLE OF WEAK, TIMID CLARK KENT..."
CATCH, FRESHMAN!
IT'S THE CUSTOM FOR UPPER CLASSMEN TO LORD IT OVER US LOWLY FRESHMEN, SO I MIGHT AS WELL DO AS I'M ASKED WITHOUT COMPLAINING.
HA, HA! LOOK AT THE KID WITH THE GLASSES. HE CAN BARELY STAND UP STRAIGHT!
CONSIDERING THAT THIS VALISE WOULD FEEL LIGHT TO ME EVEN IF IT WERE FILLED WITH STEEL I'M NOT DOING A BAD JOB!
"EARLY IN MY FIRST TERM, I HAD TO TRY OUT FOR SOME ATHLETIC ACTIVITY, AND..."
HOW AWKWARD CAN YOU GET, KENT? THAT'S THE THIRD OAR YOU'VE SNAPPED! YOU'RE THROUGH!
I KEEP FORGETTING AND USING A LITTLE TOO MUCH OF MY SUPER-STRENGTH! WELL, I'M GLAD I WON'T MAKE THE TEAM. IT WOULD BE UNFAIR FOR ME TO COMPETE!
SNAP
"LIVING IN A DORMITORY WITH OTHER STUDENTS SOMETIMES MADE IT REALLY DIFFICULT FOR ME TO ENACT MY SUPER ROLE! ONE NIGHT..."
A CAR ON FIRE OUT IN THE STREET! I MUST SWITCH TO SUPERBOY-- BUT HOW CAN I, IN FRONT OF MY ROOMMATES? HMM... MUST THINK!
METROPOLIS
EVERYONE'S HEARD OF BLOWING OUT CANDLES-- BUT I BET THIS IS THE FIRST TIME ANYONE BLEW OUT AN ELECTRIC LIGHT! ONE PUFF OF MY SUPER-BREATH SHOULD CLICK OFF THE SWITCH AND PLUNGE THE ROOM INTO DARKNESS!
"AN INSTANT LATER, I WAS STREAKING DOWN TOWARD THE CAR!"
NO ONE'S IN IT... BUT IF THE FIRE REACHES THE GAS TANK, IT COULD CAUSE A DANGEROUS EXPLOSION! ONLY ONE THING FOR ME TO DO! I MUST PICK IT UP, AND...
2

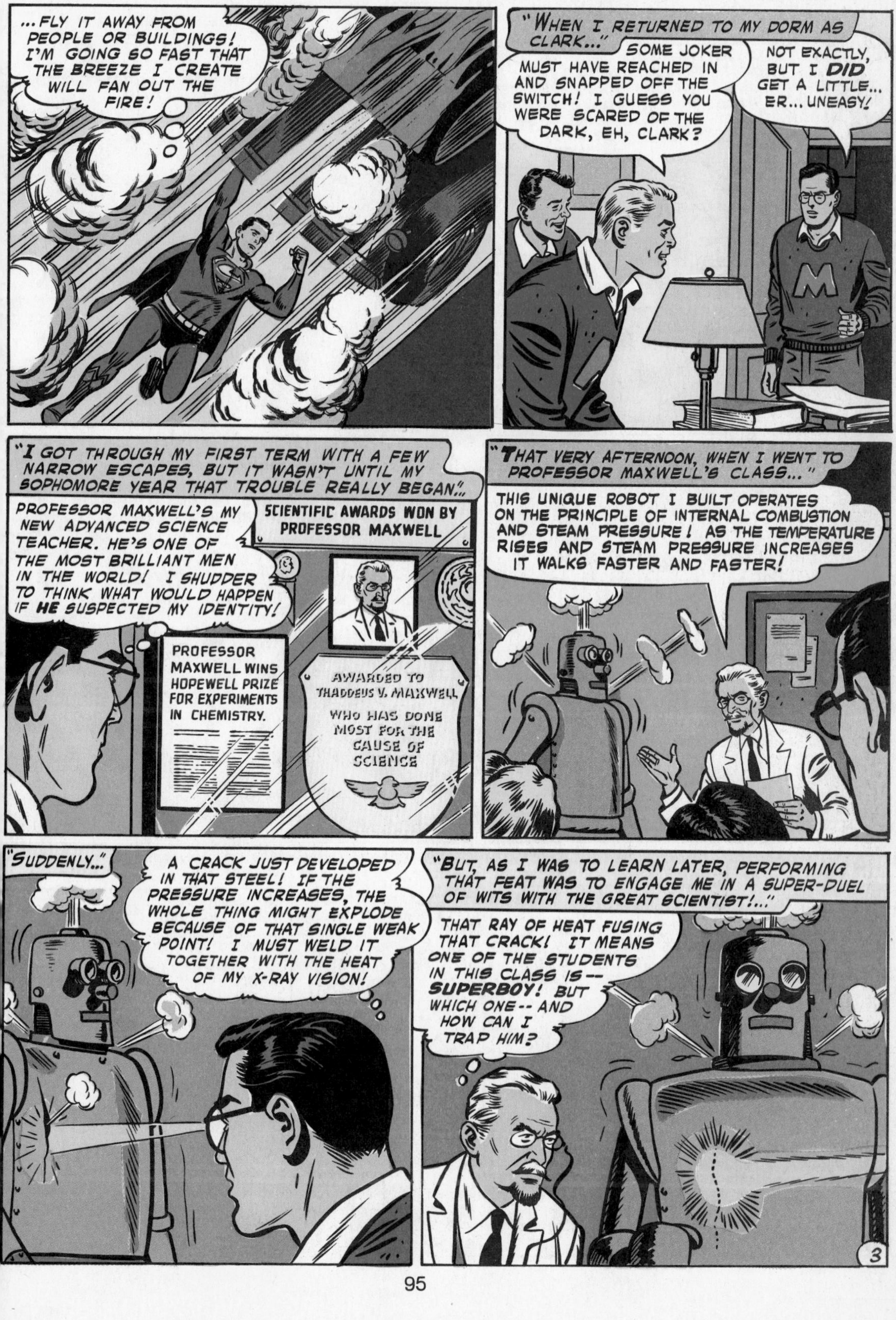
...FLY IT AWAY FROM PEOPLE OR BUILDINGS! I'M GOING SO FAST THAT THE BREEZE I CREATE WILL FAN OUT THE FIRE!
"WHEN I RETURNED TO MY DORM AS CLARK..."
SOME JOKER MUST HAVE REACHED IN AND SNAPPED OFF THE SWITCH! I GUESS YOU WERE SCARED OF THE DARK, EH, CLARK?
NOT EXACTLY, BUT I DID GET A LITTLE... ER... UNEASY!
"I GOT THROUGH MY FIRST TERM WITH A FEW NARROW ESCAPES, BUT IT WASN'T UNTIL MY SOPHOMORE YEAR THAT TROUBLE REALLY BEGAN!..."
PROFESSOR MAXWELL'S MY NEW ADVANCED SCIENCE TEACHER. HE'S ONE OF THE MOST BRILLIANT MEN IN THE WORLD! I SHUDDER TO THINK WHAT WOULD HAPPEN IF HE SUSPECTED MY IDENTITY!
SCIENTIFIC AWARDS WON BY PROFESSOR MAXWELL
PROFESSOR MAXWELL WINS HOPEWELL PRIZE FOR EXPERIMENTS IN CHEMISTRY.
AWARDED TO THADDEUS V. MAXWELL WHO HAS DONE MOST FOR THE CAUSE OF SCIENCE
"THAT VERY AFTERNOON, WHEN I WENT TO PROFESSOR MAXWELL'S CLASS..."
THIS UNIQUE ROBOT I BUILT OPERATES ON THE PRINCIPLE OF INTERNAL COMBUSTION AND STEAM PRESSURE! AS THE TEMPERATURE RISES AND STEAM PRESSURE INCREASES IT WALKS FASTER AND FASTER!
"SUDDENLY..."
A CRACK JUST DEVELOPED IN THAT STEEL! IF THE PRESSURE INCREASES, THE WHOLE THING MIGHT EXPLODE BECAUSE OF THAT SINGLE WEAK POINT! I MUST WELD IT TOGETHER WITH THE HEAT OF MY X-RAY VISION!
"BUT, AS I WAS TO LEARN LATER, PERFORMING THAT FEAT WAS TO ENGAGE ME IN A SUPER-DUEL OF WITS WITH THE GREAT SCIENTIST!..."
THAT RAY OF HEAT FUSING THAT CRACK! IT MEANS ONE OF THE STUDENTS IN THIS CLASS IS -- SUPERBOY! BUT WHICH ONE -- AND HOW CAN I TRAP HIM?
3

"I COULD ALMOST READ THE PROFESSOR'S THOUGHTS AS HE STARED SILENTLY AT THE CLASS..."

NO ONE HAS EVER PENETRATED THE SECRET OF *SUPERBOY'S* IDENTITY, AND I HAVE NEVER FAILED IN AN EXPERIMENT. NOW THAT I AM SURE HE IS A MEMBER OF MY CLASS IT WILL BE INTRIGUING TO SOLVE HIS SECRET-- JUST FOR MY OWN SATISFACTION!

"NEXT DAY IN CLASS, I KNEW I HAD GUESSED WHAT HE WAS THINKING WHEN..."

TODAY WE WILL PERFORM A FEW EXPERIMENTS TO DEMONSTRATE HOW A *LIE DETECTOR* WORKS! *FRED HOLLAND*, PLEASE STEP UP HERE. I SHALL ASK YOU A QUESTION WHICH YOU MAY ANSWER EITHER WITH THE TRUTH OR A FALSEHOOD!

FRED, ARE *YOU* SUPERBOY?

ME, *SUPERBOY?* HA, HA! OF COURSE NOT, PROFESSOR MAXWELL!

AS YOU CAN SEE, THE MACHINE TELLS US FRED DID NOT LIE! IF HE HAD, THE GRAPH WHICH REFLECTS CHANGES IN HEARTBEAT AND BLOOD PRESSURE WOULD NOT BE SO REGULAR.

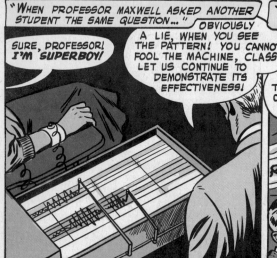

"WHEN PROFESSOR MAXWELL ASKED ANOTHER STUDENT THE SAME QUESTION..."

SURE, PROFESSOR! I'M *SUPERBOY!*

OBVIOUSLY A LIE, WHEN YOU SEE THE PATTERN! YOU CANNOT FOOL THE MACHINE, CLASS! LET US CONTINUE TO DEMONSTRATE ITS EFFECTIVENESS!

"ONE AFTER ANOTHER, EACH MEMBER OF THE CLASS WAS CALLED. AND FINALLY, WHEN IT WAS *MY* TURN..."

TUT-TUT! THE PERIOD ENDED BEFORE YOU HAD *YOUR* CHANCE, KENT! HOWEVER, I'LL GIVE YOU AN OPPORTUNITY AT SOME FUTURE DATE! ANYWAY, WE NOW *KNOW* THAT NO ONE ELSE IN THIS CLASS CAN BE *SUPERBOY*-- EXCEPT YOU! HA, HA-- THAT'S A JOKE!

SAVED BY THE BELL-- SO FAR!

R-R-RIN-N-G

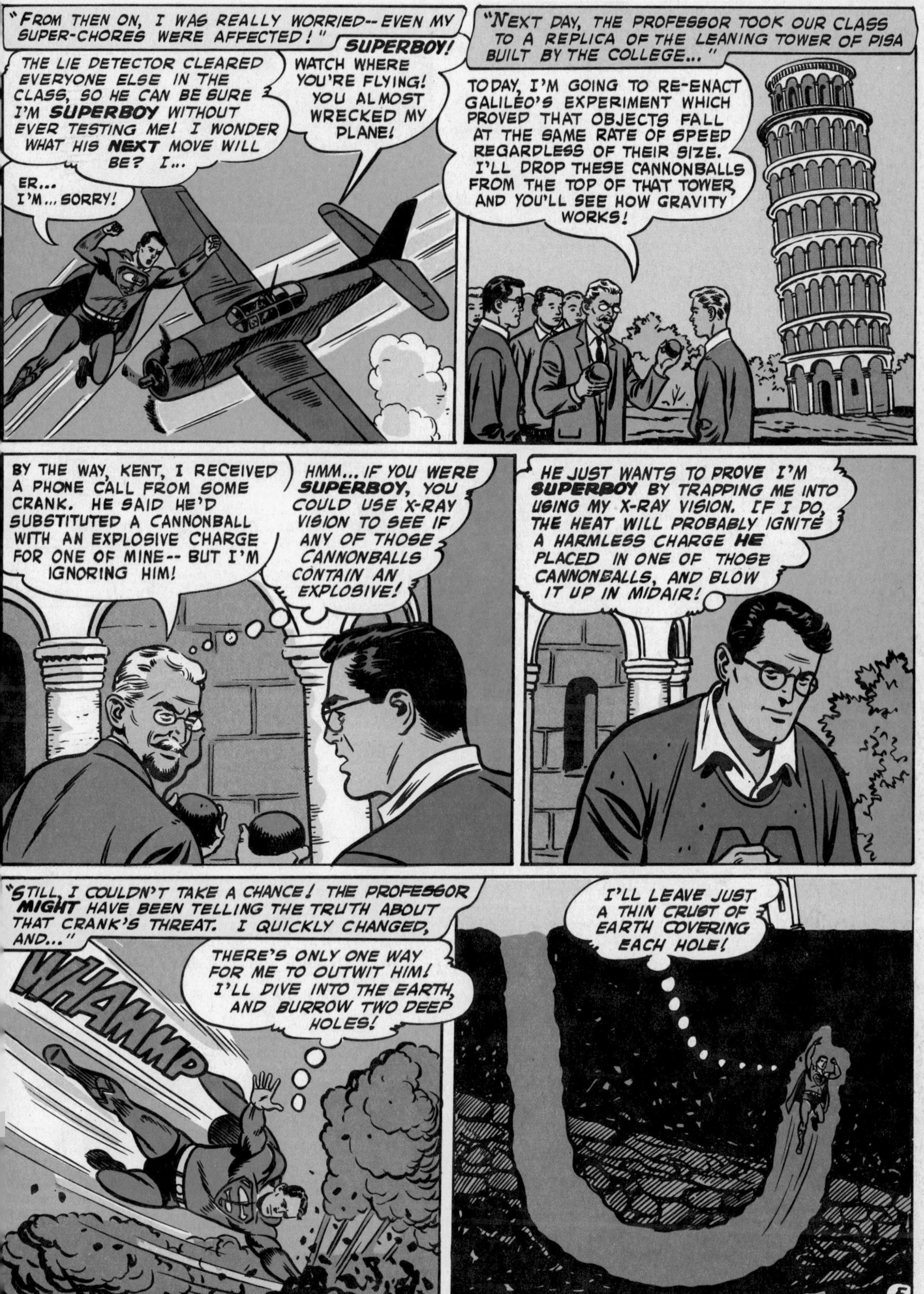
"FROM THEN ON, I WAS REALLY WORRIED-- EVEN MY SUPER-CHORES WERE AFFECTED!"
THE LIE DETECTOR CLEARED EVERYONE ELSE IN THE CLASS, SO HE CAN BE SURE I'M SUPERBOY WITHOUT EVER TESTING ME! I WONDER WHAT HIS NEXT MOVE WILL BE? I...
SUPERBOY! WATCH WHERE YOU'RE FLYING! YOU ALMOST WRECKED MY PLANE!
ER... I'M... SORRY!
"NEXT DAY, THE PROFESSOR TOOK OUR CLASS TO A REPLICA OF THE LEANING TOWER OF PISA BUILT BY THE COLLEGE..."
TODAY, I'M GOING TO RE-ENACT GALILEO'S EXPERIMENT WHICH PROVED THAT OBJECTS FALL AT THE SAME RATE OF SPEED REGARDLESS OF THEIR SIZE. I'LL DROP THESE CANNONBALLS FROM THE TOP OF THAT TOWER, AND YOU'LL SEE HOW GRAVITY WORKS!
BY THE WAY, KENT, I RECEIVED A PHONE CALL FROM SOME CRANK. HE SAID HE'D SUBSTITUTED A CANNONBALL WITH AN EXPLOSIVE CHARGE FOR ONE OF MINE-- BUT I'M IGNORING HIM!
HMM... IF YOU WERE SUPERBOY, YOU COULD USE X-RAY VISION TO SEE IF ANY OF THOSE CANNONBALLS CONTAIN AN EXPLOSIVE!
HE JUST WANTS TO PROVE I'M SUPERBOY BY TRAPPING ME INTO USING MY X-RAY VISION. IF I DO, THE HEAT WILL PROBABLY IGNITE A HARMLESS CHARGE HE PLACED IN ONE OF THOSE CANNONBALLS, AND BLOW IT UP IN MIDAIR!
"STILL, I COULDN'T TAKE A CHANCE! THE PROFESSOR MIGHT HAVE BEEN TELLING THE TRUTH ABOUT THAT CRANK'S THREAT. I QUICKLY CHANGED, AND..."
WHAMMP
THERE'S ONLY ONE WAY FOR ME TO OUTWIT HIM! I'LL DIVE INTO THE EARTH, AND BURROW TWO DEEP HOLES!
I'LL LEAVE JUST A THIN CRUST OF EARTH COVERING EACH HOLE!
5

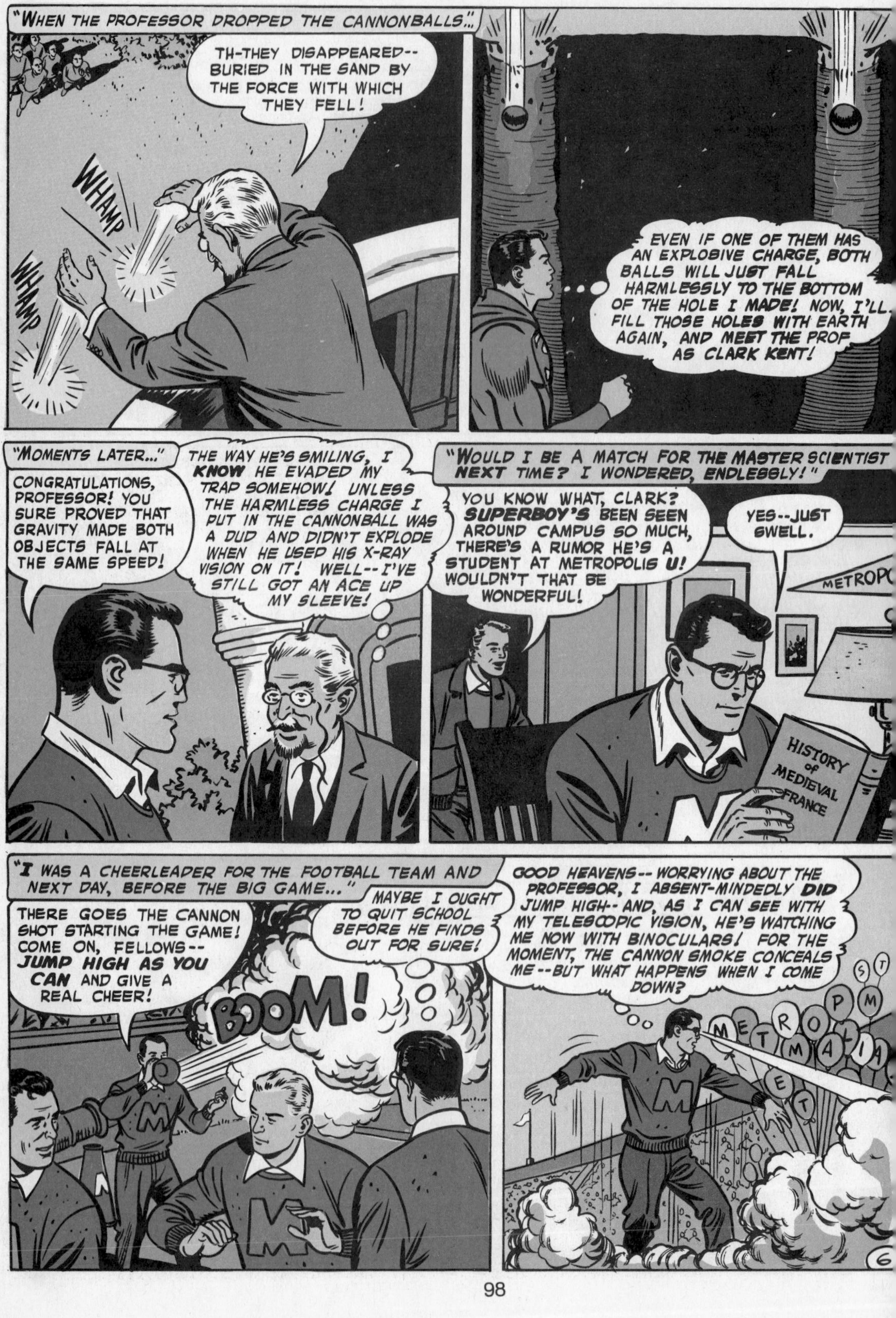
"WHEN THE PROFESSOR DROPPED THE CANNONBALLS..."
TH-THEY DISAPPEARED-- BURIED IN THE SAND BY THE FORCE WITH WHICH THEY FELL!
WHAMP
WHAMP
- EVEN IF ONE OF THEM HAS AN EXPLOSIVE CHARGE, BOTH BALLS WILL JUST FALL HARMLESSLY TO THE BOTTOM OF THE HOLE I MADE! NOW, I'LL FILL THOSE HOLES WITH EARTH AGAIN, AND MEET THE PROF AS CLARK KENT!
"MOMENTS LATER..."
CONGRATULATIONS, PROFESSOR! YOU SURE PROVED THAT GRAVITY MADE BOTH OBJECTS FALL AT THE SAME SPEED!
THE WAY HE'S SMILING, I KNOW HE EVADED MY TRAP SOMEHOW! UNLESS THE HARMLESS CHARGE I PUT IN THE CANNONBALL WAS A DUD AND DIDN'T EXPLODE WHEN HE USED HIS X-RAY VISION ON IT! WELL--I'VE STILL GOT AN ACE UP MY SLEEVE!
"WOULD I BE A MATCH FOR THE MASTER SCIENTIST NEXT TIME? I WONDERED, ENDLESSLY!"
YOU KNOW WHAT, CLARK? SUPERBOY'S BEEN SEEN AROUND CAMPUS SO MUCH, THERE'S A RUMOR HE'S A STUDENT AT METROPOLIS U! WOULDN'T THAT BE WONDERFUL!
YES--JUST SWELL.
METROPO
HISTORY of MEDIEVAL FRANCE
"I WAS A CHEERLEADER FOR THE FOOTBALL TEAM AND NEXT DAY, BEFORE THE BIG GAME..."
THERE GOES THE CANNON SHOT STARTING THE GAME! COME ON, FELLOWS-- JUMP HIGH AS YOU CAN AND GIVE A REAL CHEER!
MAYBE I OUGHT TO QUIT SCHOOL BEFORE HE FINDS OUT FOR SURE!
BOOM!
GOOD HEAVENS-- WORRYING ABOUT THE PROFESSOR, I ABSENT-MINDEDLY DID JUMP HIGH-- AND, AS I CAN SEE WITH MY TELESCOPIC VISION, HE'S WATCHING ME NOW WITH BINOCULARS! FOR THE MOMENT, THE CANNON SMOKE CONCEALS ME--BUT WHAT HAPPENS WHEN I COME DOWN?
6

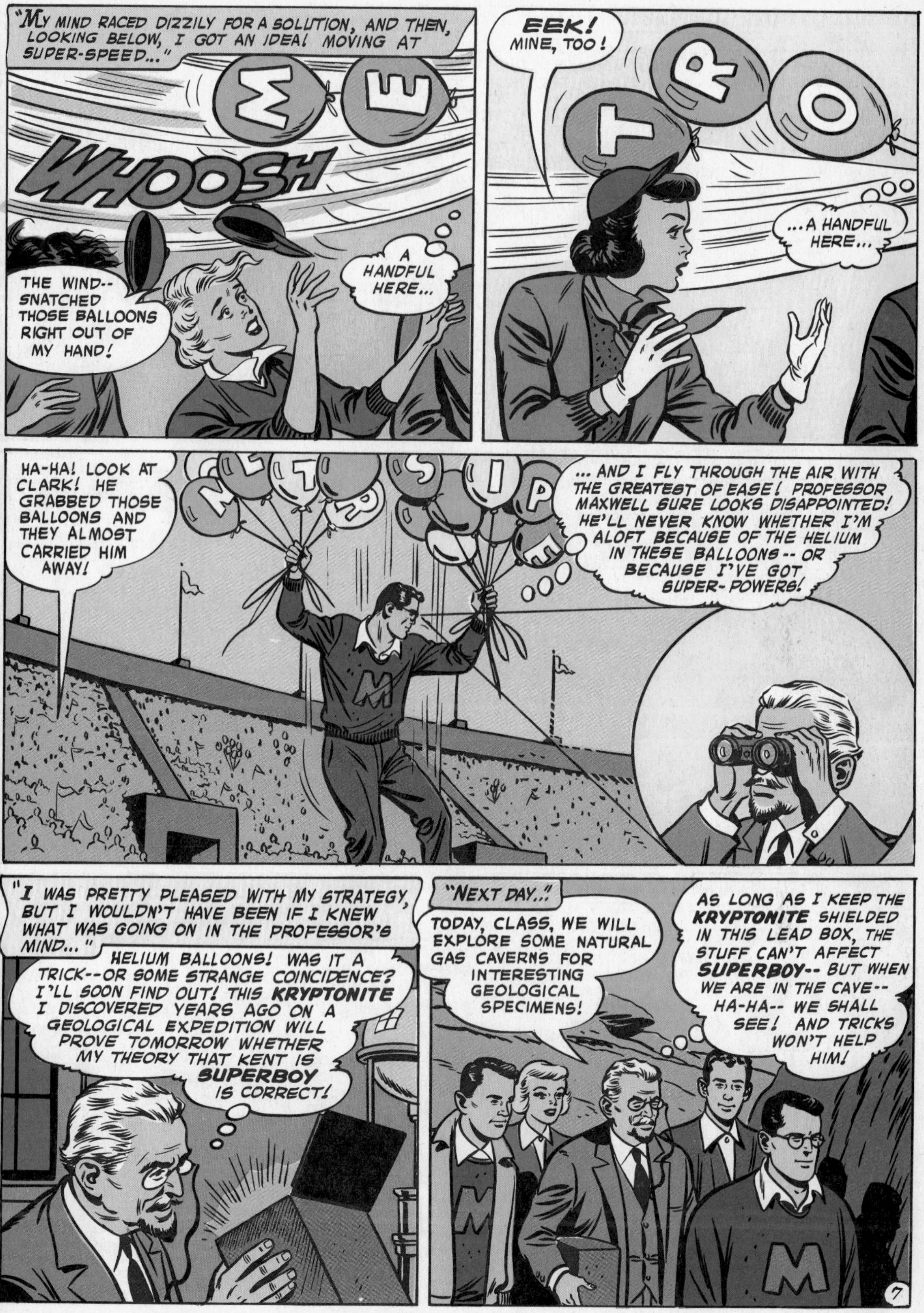
"MY MIND RACED DIZZILY FOR A SOLUTION, AND THEN, LOOKING BELOW, I GOT AN IDEA! MOVING AT SUPER-SPEED..."
M
E
WHOOSH
THE WIND--SNATCHED THOSE BALLOONS RIGHT OUT OF MY HAND!
A HANDFUL HERE...
EEK! MINE, TOO!
T
R
O
...A HANDFUL HERE...
HA-HA! LOOK AT CLARK! HE GRABBED THOSE BALLOONS AND THEY ALMOST CARRIED HIM AWAY!
... AND I FLY THROUGH THE AIR WITH THE GREATEST OF EASE! PROFESSOR MAXWELL SURE LOOKS DISAPPOINTED! HE'LL NEVER KNOW WHETHER I'M ALOFT BECAUSE OF THE HELIUM IN THESE BALLOONS -- OR BECAUSE I'VE GOT SUPER-POWERS!
"I WAS PRETTY PLEASED WITH MY STRATEGY, BUT I WOULDN'T HAVE BEEN IF I KNEW WHAT WAS GOING ON IN THE PROFESSOR'S MIND..."
HELIUM BALLOONS! WAS IT A TRICK--OR SOME STRANGE COINCIDENCE? I'LL SOON FIND OUT! THIS KRYPTONITE I DISCOVERED YEARS AGO ON A GEOLOGICAL EXPEDITION WILL PROVE TOMORROW WHETHER MY THEORY THAT KENT IS SUPERBOY IS CORRECT!
"NEXT DAY..."
TODAY, CLASS, WE WILL EXPLORE SOME NATURAL GAS CAVERNS FOR INTERESTING GEOLOGICAL SPECIMENS!
AS LONG AS I KEEP THE KRYPTONITE SHIELDED IN THIS LEAD BOX, THE STUFF CAN'T AFFECT SUPERBOY-- BUT WHEN WE ARE IN THE CAVE-- HA-HA-- WE SHALL SEE! AND TRICKS WON'T HELP HIM!
7

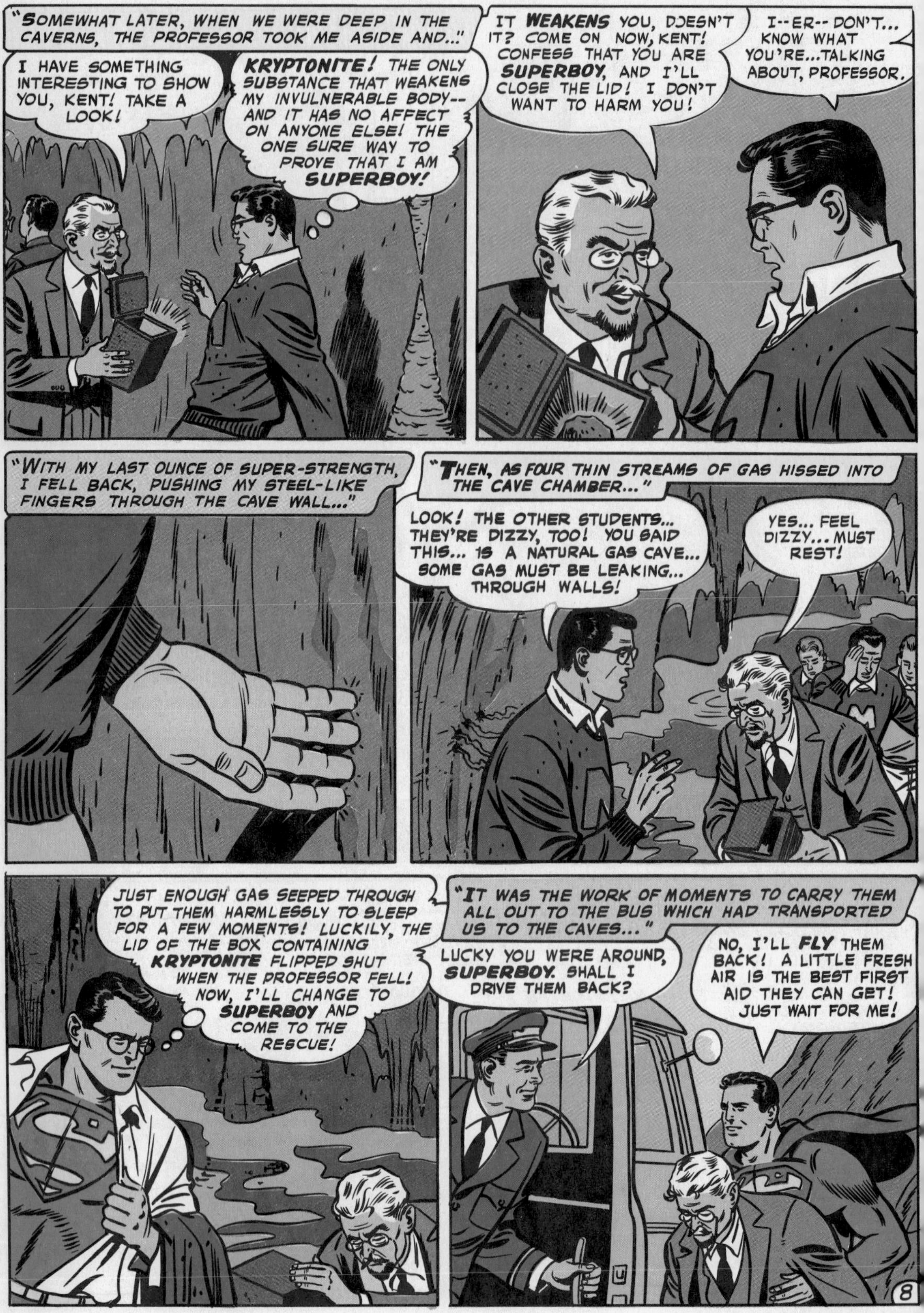
"SOMEWHAT LATER, WHEN WE WERE DEEP IN THE CAVERNS, THE PROFESSOR TOOK ME ASIDE AND..."
I HAVE SOMETHING INTERESTING TO SHOW YOU, KENT! TAKE A LOOK!
KRYPTONITE! THE ONLY SUBSTANCE THAT WEAKENS MY INVULNERABLE BODY-- AND IT HAS NO AFFECT ON ANYONE ELSE! THE ONE SURE WAY TO PROVE THAT I AM SUPERBOY!
IT WEAKENS YOU, DOESN'T IT? COME ON NOW, KENT! CONFESS THAT YOU ARE SUPERBOY, AND I'LL CLOSE THE LID! I DON'T WANT TO HARM YOU!
I--ER-- DON'T... KNOW WHAT YOU'RE...TALKING ABOUT, PROFESSOR.
"WITH MY LAST OUNCE OF SUPER-STRENGTH, I FELL BACK, PUSHING MY STEEL-LIKE FINGERS THROUGH THE CAVE WALL..."
"THEN, AS FOUR THIN STREAMS OF GAS HISSED INTO THE CAVE CHAMBER..."
LOOK! THE OTHER STUDENTS... THEY'RE DIZZY, TOO! YOU SAID THIS... IS A NATURAL GAS CAVE... SOME GAS MUST BE LEAKING... THROUGH WALLS!
YES... FEEL DIZZY... MUST REST!
JUST ENOUGH GAS SEEPED THROUGH TO PUT THEM HARMLESSLY TO SLEEP FOR A FEW MOMENTS! LUCKILY, THE LID OF THE BOX CONTAINING KRYPTONITE FLIPPED SHUT WHEN THE PROFESSOR FELL! NOW, I'LL CHANGE TO SUPERBOY AND COME TO THE RESCUE!
"IT WAS THE WORK OF MOMENTS TO CARRY THEM ALL OUT TO THE BUS WHICH HAD TRANSPORTED US TO THE CAVES..."
LUCKY YOU WERE AROUND, SUPERBOY. SHALL I DRIVE THEM BACK?
NO, I'LL FLY THEM BACK! A LITTLE FRESH AIR IS THE BEST FIRST AID THEY CAN GET! JUST WAIT FOR ME!
8

"THERE WAS ONE MORE CHORE FOR ME TO DO."

THIS SUBTERRANEAN RIVER IS PRACTICALLY BOTTOMLESS! THE PROFESSOR WILL THINK THE *KRYPTONITE* WAS LOST IN THE RESCUE, AND I'LL BE FREE OF *THAT* DANGER FOREVER!

"SO, SOMEWHAT LATER..."

SCHOOL BUS

WHEN I REACH SCHOOL, I'LL GENTLY PLACE THE BUS ON THE GROUND, THEN SNEAK IN AS CLARK AT SUPER-SPEED WHEN THEY ALL GET OFF!

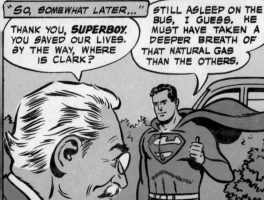

"SO, SOMEWHAT LATER..."

THANK YOU, *SUPERBOY*. YOU SAVED OUR LIVES. BY THE WAY, WHERE IS CLARK?

STILL ASLEEP ON THE BUS, I GUESS. HE MUST HAVE TAKEN A DEEPER BREATH OF THAT NATURAL GAS THAN THE OTHERS.

"SURE ENOUGH, MOMENTS LATER, CLARK *DID* GET OFF"...

HOW DID WE (YAWN) GET HERE?

I'M NOT QUITE SURE, BUT I AM GOING TO FIND OUT! COME TO THE CLASSROOM WITH ME! THERE IS ONE MORE EXPERIMENT I MUST PERFORM!

"WHAT I HAD BEEN DREADING ALL ALONG WAS NOW FACING ME!"

YOU NEVER DID GET *YOUR* CHANCE TO TAKE MY LIE-DETECTOR TEST, KENT. SIT DOWN.

NOW HE'S GOING TO ASK ME IF I'M *SUPERBOY*! IF I TELL A LIE, THE MACHINE'S SENSITIVE APPARATUS WILL SHOW IT, AND IF I TELL THE TRUTH, I AM SUNK!

WELL, CLARK KENT, ARE *YOU* SUPERBOY?

I EXPECTED THIS TEST, AND HID MY COSTUME BEFORE I CHANGED TO CLARK, BUT WHAT CAN I DO NOW? I--I CAN'T TAMPER WITH THE MACHINE-- HE'D SEE THROUGH THAT!

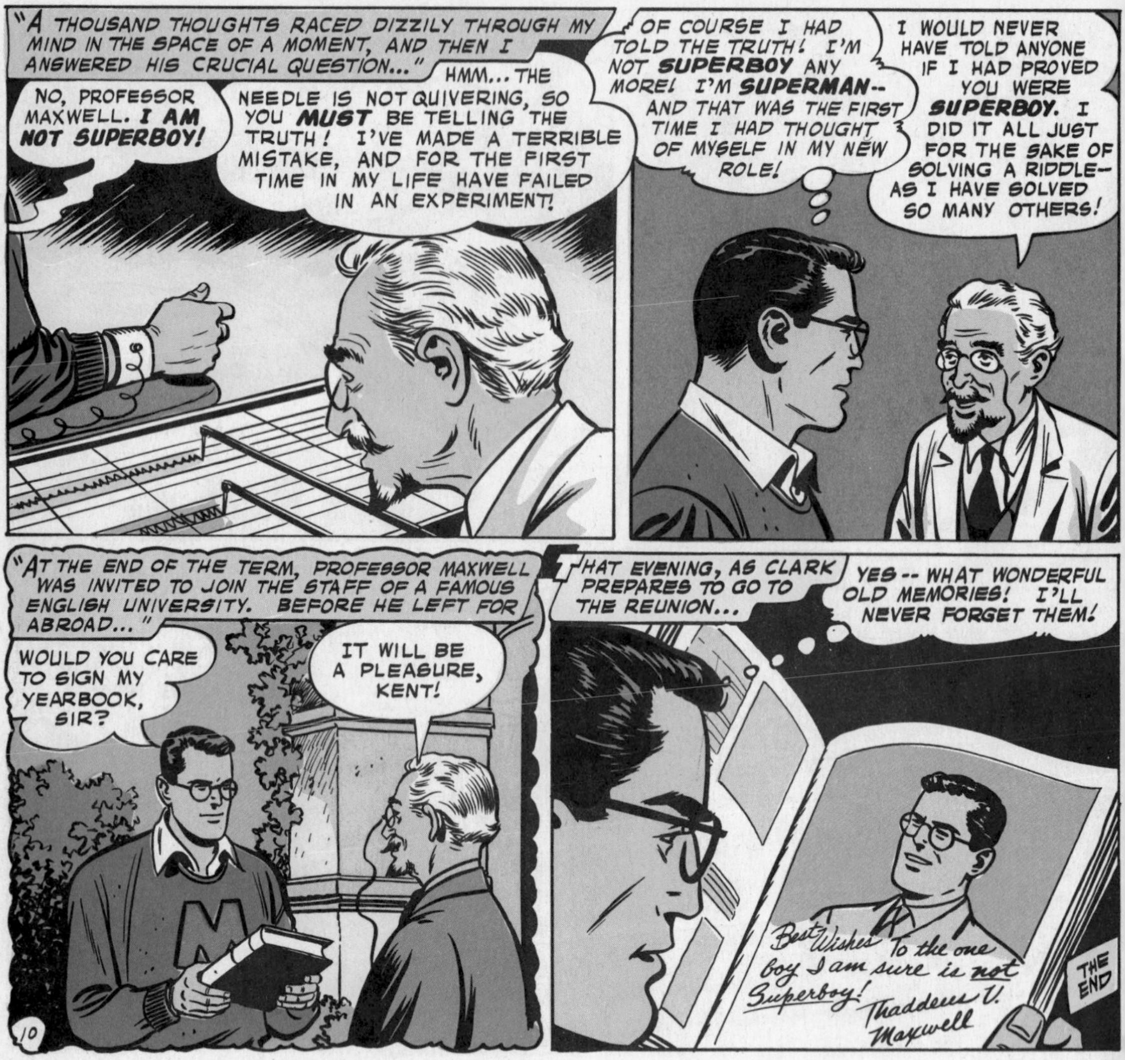
"A THOUSAND THOUGHTS RACED DIZZILY THROUGH MY MIND IN THE SPACE OF A MOMENT, AND THEN I ANSWERED HIS CRUCIAL QUESTION..."
NO, PROFESSOR MAXWELL. I AM NOT SUPERBOY!
HMM... THE NEEDLE IS NOT QUIVERING, SO YOU MUST BE TELLING THE TRUTH! I'VE MADE A TERRIBLE MISTAKE, AND FOR THE FIRST TIME IN MY LIFE HAVE FAILED IN AN EXPERIMENT!
OF COURSE I HAD TOLD THE TRUTH! I'M NOT SUPERBOY ANY MORE! I'M SUPERMAN-- AND THAT WAS THE FIRST TIME I HAD THOUGHT OF MYSELF IN MY NEW ROLE!
I WOULD NEVER HAVE TOLD ANYONE IF I HAD PROVED YOU WERE SUPERBOY. I DID IT ALL JUST FOR THE SAKE OF SOLVING A RIDDLE-- AS I HAVE SOLVED SO MANY OTHERS!
"AT THE END OF THE TERM, PROFESSOR MAXWELL WAS INVITED TO JOIN THE STAFF OF A FAMOUS ENGLISH UNIVERSITY. BEFORE HE LEFT FOR ABROAD..."
WOULD YOU CARE TO SIGN MY YEARBOOK, SIR?
IT WILL BE A PLEASURE, KENT!
M
10
THAT EVENING, AS CLARK PREPARES TO GO TO THE REUNION...
YES -- WHAT WONDERFUL OLD MEMORIES! I'LL NEVER FORGET THEM!
Best Wishes To the one boy I am sure is not Superboy! Thaddeus V. Maxwell
THE END

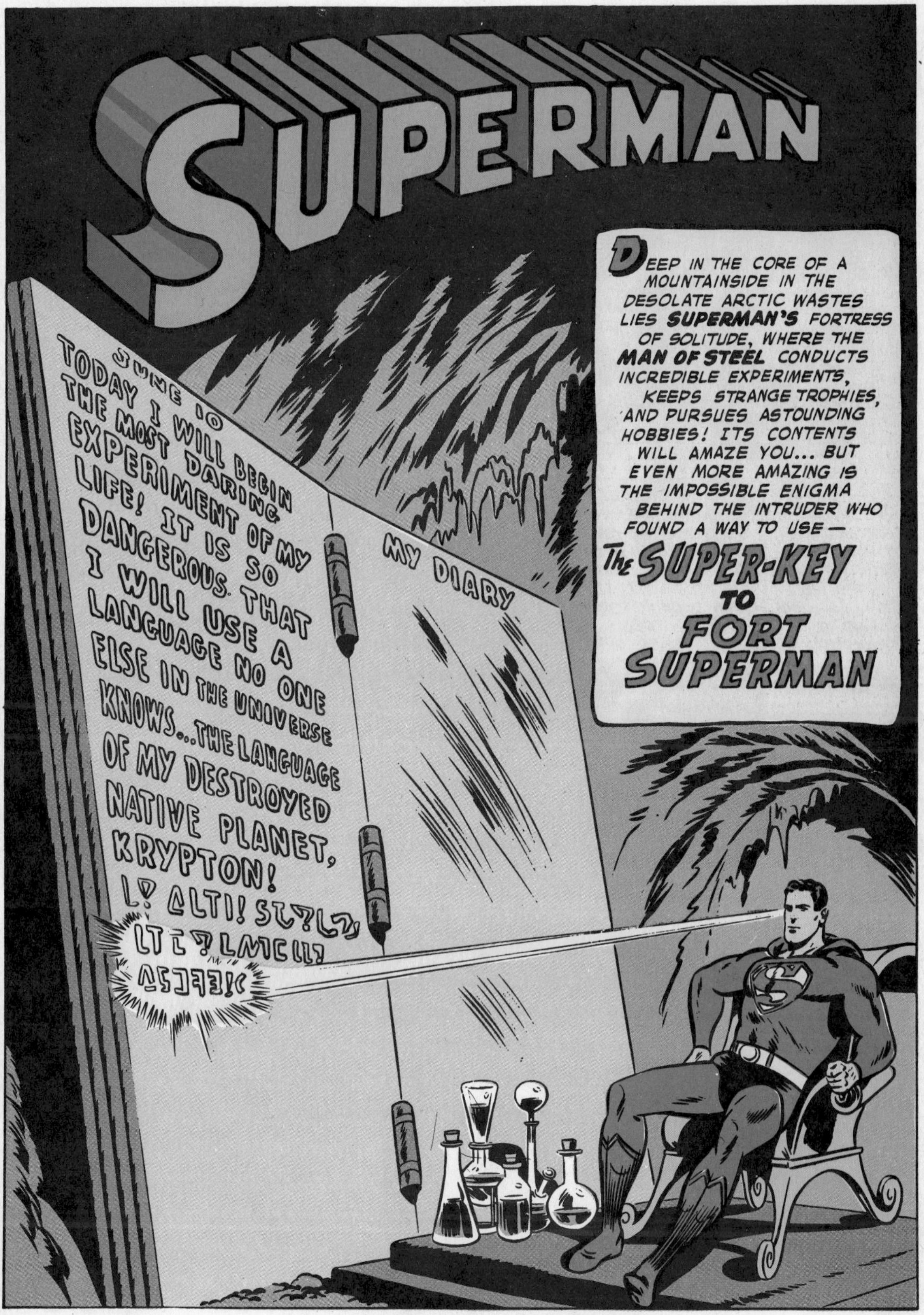
SUPERMAN
DEEP IN THE CORE OF A MOUNTAINSIDE IN THE DESOLATE ARCTIC WASTES LIES SUPERMAN'S FORTRESS OF SOLITUDE, WHERE THE MAN OF STEEL CONDUCTS INCREDIBLE EXPERIMENTS, KEEPS STRANGE TROPHIES, AND PURSUES ASTOUNDING HOBBIES! ITS CONTENTS WILL AMAZE YOU... BUT EVEN MORE AMAZING IS THE IMPOSSIBLE ENIGMA BEHIND THE INTRUDER WHO FOUND A WAY TO USE—
The SUPER-KEY TO FORT SUPERMAN
JUNE 10
TODAY I WILL BEGIN THE MOST DARING EXPERIMENT OF MY LIFE! IT IS SO DANGEROUS THAT I WILL USE A LANGUAGE NO ONE ELSE IN THE UNIVERSE KNOWS...THE LANGUAGE OF MY DESTROYED NATIVE PLANET, KRYPTON!
MY DIARY

Art by Wayne Boring/Color by Carl Gafford

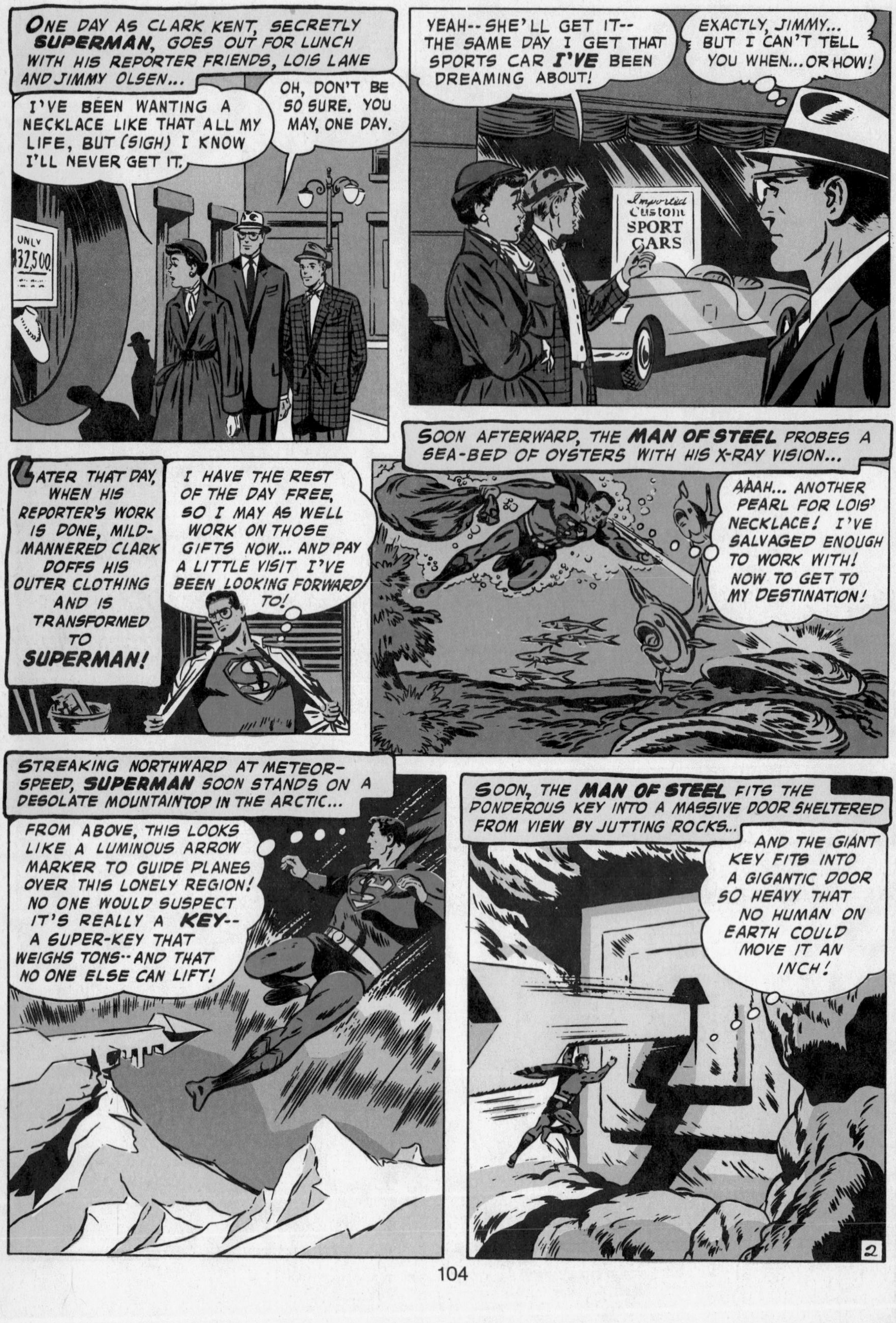
ONE DAY AS CLARK KENT, SECRETLY SUPERMAN, GOES OUT FOR LUNCH WITH HIS REPORTER FRIENDS, LOIS LANE AND JIMMY OLSEN...
I'VE BEEN WANTING A NECKLACE LIKE THAT ALL MY LIFE, BUT (SIGH) I KNOW I'LL NEVER GET IT.
OH, DON'T BE SO SURE. YOU MAY, ONE DAY.
YEAH--SHE'LL GET IT--THE SAME DAY I GET THAT SPORTS CAR I'VE BEEN DREAMING ABOUT!
EXACTLY, JIMMY... BUT I CAN'T TELL YOU WHEN...OR HOW!
Imported Custom SPORT CARS
LATER THAT DAY, WHEN HIS REPORTER'S WORK IS DONE, MILD-MANNERED CLARK DOFFS HIS OUTER CLOTHING AND IS TRANSFORMED TO SUPERMAN!
I HAVE THE REST OF THE DAY FREE, SO I MAY AS WELL WORK ON THOSE GIFTS NOW... AND PAY A LITTLE VISIT I'VE BEEN LOOKING FORWARD TO!
SOON AFTERWARD, THE MAN OF STEEL PROBES A SEA-BED OF OYSTERS WITH HIS X-RAY VISION...
AAAH... ANOTHER PEARL FOR LOIS' NECKLACE! I'VE SALVAGED ENOUGH TO WORK WITH! NOW TO GET TO MY DESTINATION!
STREAKING NORTHWARD AT METEOR-SPEED, SUPERMAN SOON STANDS ON A DESOLATE MOUNTAINTOP IN THE ARCTIC...
FROM ABOVE, THIS LOOKS LIKE A LUMINOUS ARROW MARKER TO GUIDE PLANES OVER THIS LONELY REGION! NO ONE WOULD SUSPECT IT'S REALLY A KEY--A SUPER-KEY THAT WEIGHS TONS--AND THAT NO ONE ELSE CAN LIFT!
SOON, THE MAN OF STEEL FITS THE PONDEROUS KEY INTO A MASSIVE DOOR SHELTERED FROM VIEW BY JUTTING ROCKS...
AND THE GIANT KEY FITS INTO A GIGANTIC DOOR SO HEAVY THAT NO HUMAN ON EARTH COULD MOVE IT AN INCH!
2

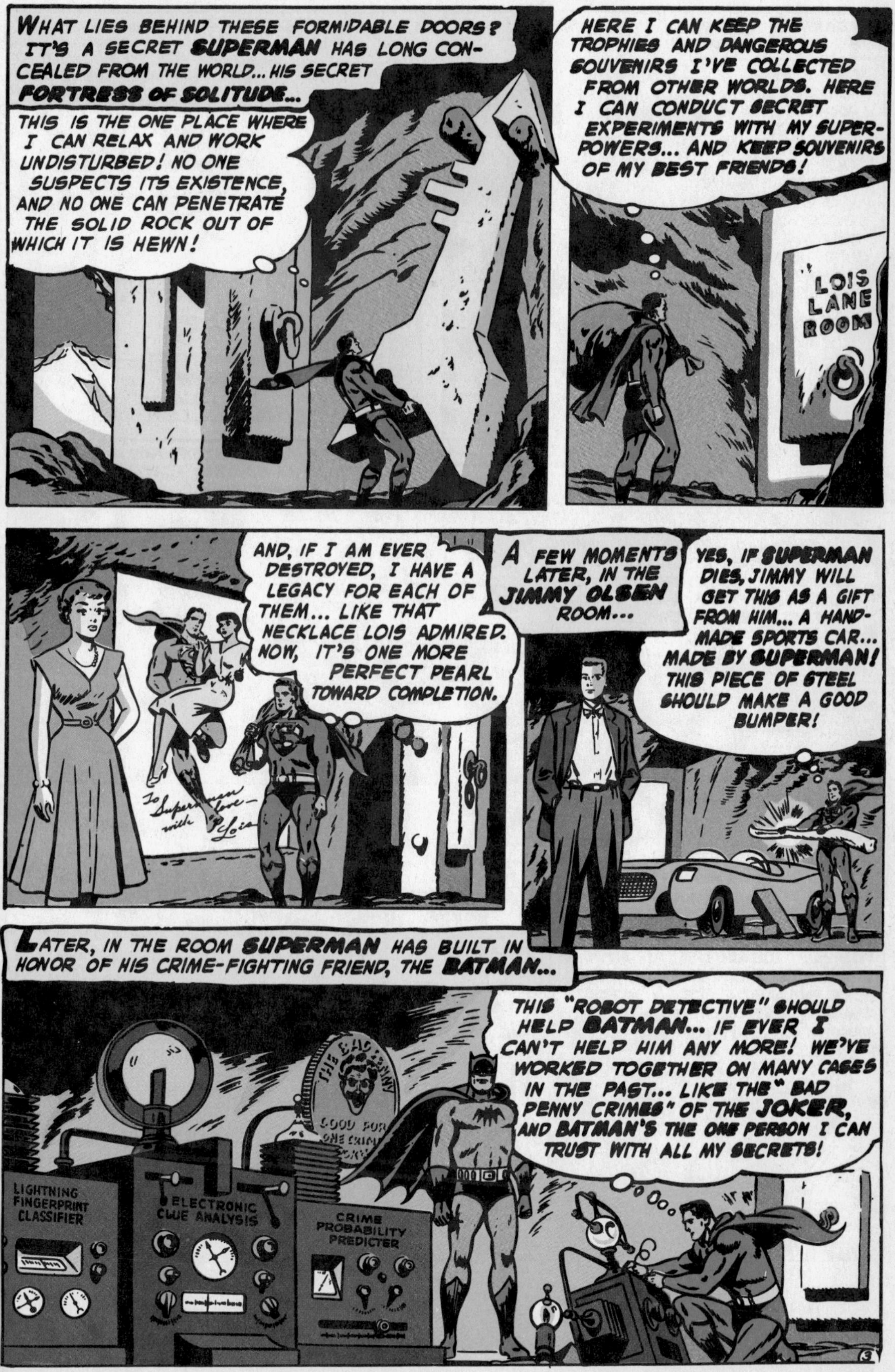
WHAT LIES BEHIND THESE FORMIDABLE DOORS? IT'S A SECRET SUPERMAN HAS LONG CONCEALED FROM THE WORLD... HIS SECRET FORTRESS OF SOLITUDE...
THIS IS THE ONE PLACE WHERE I CAN RELAX AND WORK UNDISTURBED! NO ONE SUSPECTS ITS EXISTENCE, AND NO ONE CAN PENETRATE THE SOLID ROCK OUT OF WHICH IT IS HEWN!
HERE I CAN KEEP THE TROPHIES AND DANGEROUS SOUVENIRS I'VE COLLECTED FROM OTHER WORLDS. HERE I CAN CONDUCT SECRET EXPERIMENTS WITH MY SUPER-POWERS... AND KEEP SOUVENIRS OF MY BEST FRIENDS!
LOIS LANE ROOM
AND, IF I AM EVER DESTROYED, I HAVE A LEGACY FOR EACH OF THEM... LIKE THAT NECKLACE LOIS ADMIRED. NOW, IT'S ONE MORE PERFECT PEARL TOWARD COMPLETION.
To Superman with love— Lois
A FEW MOMENTS LATER, IN THE JIMMY OLSEN ROOM...
YES, IF SUPERMAN DIES, JIMMY WILL GET THIS AS A GIFT FROM HIM... A HAND-MADE SPORTS CAR... MADE BY SUPERMAN! THIS PIECE OF STEEL SHOULD MAKE A GOOD BUMPER!
LATER, IN THE ROOM SUPERMAN HAS BUILT IN HONOR OF HIS CRIME-FIGHTING FRIEND, THE BATMAN...
THIS "ROBOT DETECTIVE" SHOULD HELP BATMAN... IF EVER I CAN'T HELP HIM ANY MORE! WE'VE WORKED TOGETHER ON MANY CASES IN THE PAST... LIKE THE "BAD PENNY CRIMES" OF THE JOKER, AND BATMAN'S THE ONE PERSON I CAN TRUST WITH ALL MY SECRETS!
THE BAD PENNY
GOOD FOR ONE CRIME
LIGHTNING FINGERPRINT CLASSIFIER
ELECTRONIC CLUE ANALYSIS
CRIME PROBABILITY PREDICTER
3

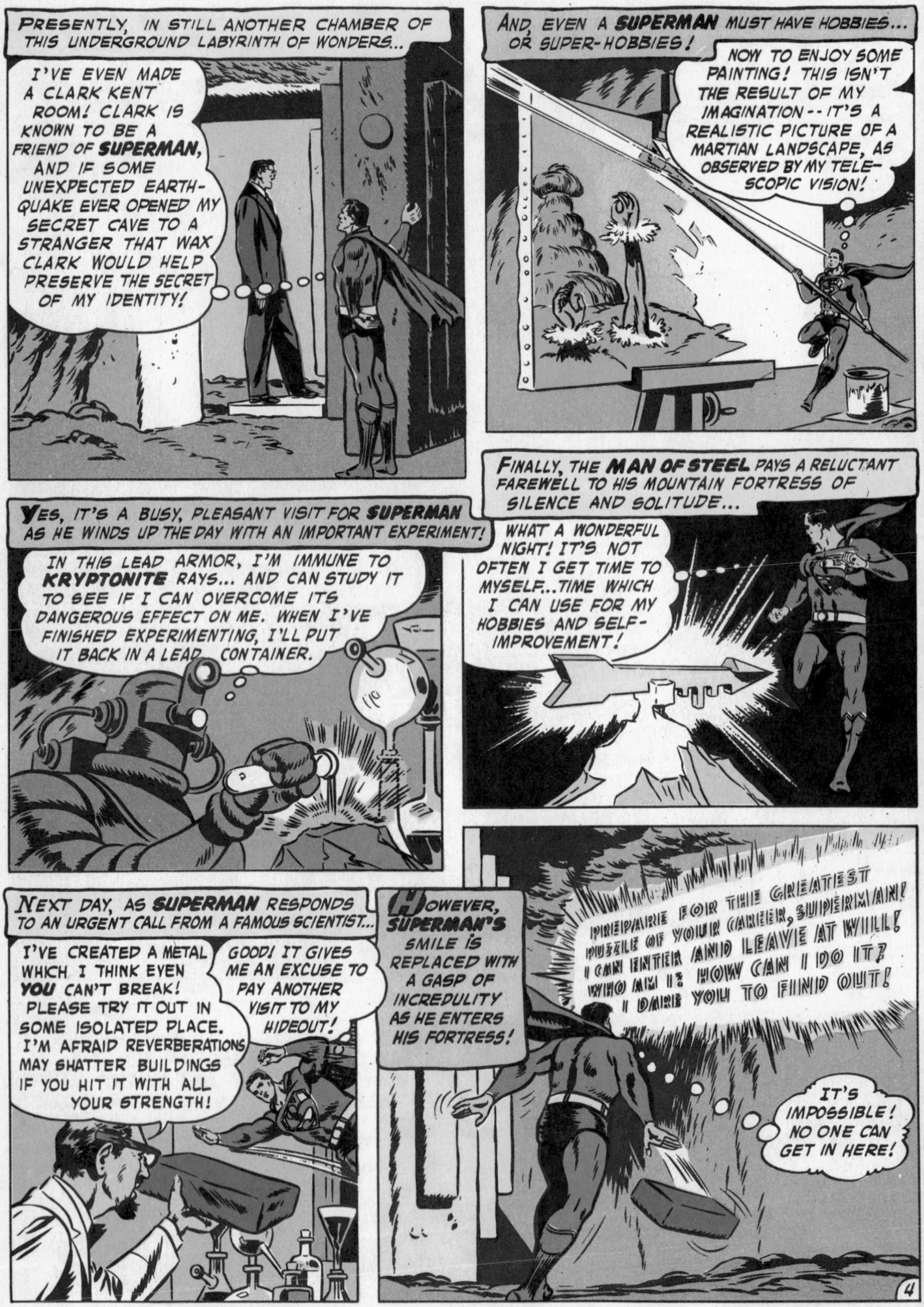

PRESENTLY, IN STILL ANOTHER CHAMBER OF THIS UNDERGROUND LABYRINTH OF WONDERS...
I'VE EVEN MADE A CLARK KENT ROOM! CLARK IS KNOWN TO BE A FRIEND OF SUPERMAN, AND IF SOME UNEXPECTED EARTH-QUAKE EVER OPENED MY SECRET CAVE TO A STRANGER THAT WAX CLARK WOULD HELP PRESERVE THE SECRET OF MY IDENTITY!
AND, EVEN A SUPERMAN MUST HAVE HOBBIES... OR SUPER-HOBBIES!
NOW TO ENJOY SOME PAINTING! THIS ISN'T THE RESULT OF MY IMAGINATION -- IT'S A REALISTIC PICTURE OF A MARTIAN LANDSCAPE, AS OBSERVED BY MY TELE-SCOPIC VISION!
YES, IT'S A BUSY, PLEASANT VISIT FOR SUPERMAN AS HE WINDS UP THE DAY WITH AN IMPORTANT EXPERIMENT!
IN THIS LEAD ARMOR, I'M IMMUNE TO KRYPTONITE RAYS... AND CAN STUDY IT TO SEE IF I CAN OVERCOME ITS DANGEROUS EFFECT ON ME. WHEN I'VE FINISHED EXPERIMENTING, I'LL PUT IT BACK IN A LEAD CONTAINER.
FINALLY, THE MAN OF STEEL PAYS A RELUCTANT FAREWELL TO HIS MOUNTAIN FORTRESS OF SILENCE AND SOLITUDE...
WHAT A WONDERFUL NIGHT! IT'S NOT OFTEN I GET TIME TO MYSELF...TIME WHICH I CAN USE FOR MY HOBBIES AND SELF-IMPROVEMENT!
NEXT DAY, AS SUPERMAN RESPONDS TO AN URGENT CALL FROM A FAMOUS SCIENTIST...
I'VE CREATED A METAL WHICH I THINK EVEN YOU CAN'T BREAK! PLEASE TRY IT OUT IN SOME ISOLATED PLACE. I'M AFRAID REVERBERATIONS MAY SHATTER BUILDINGS IF YOU HIT IT WITH ALL YOUR STRENGTH!
GOOD! IT GIVES ME AN EXCUSE TO PAY ANOTHER VISIT TO MY HIDEOUT!
HOWEVER, SUPERMAN'S SMILE IS REPLACED WITH A GASP OF INCREDULITY AS HE ENTERS HIS FORTRESS!
PREPARE FOR THE GREATEST PUZZLE OF YOUR CAREER, SUPERMAN! I CAN ENTER AND LEAVE AT WILL! WHO AM I? HOW CAN I DO IT? I DARE YOU TO FIND OUT!
IT'S IMPOSSIBLE! NO ONE CAN GET IN HERE!
4

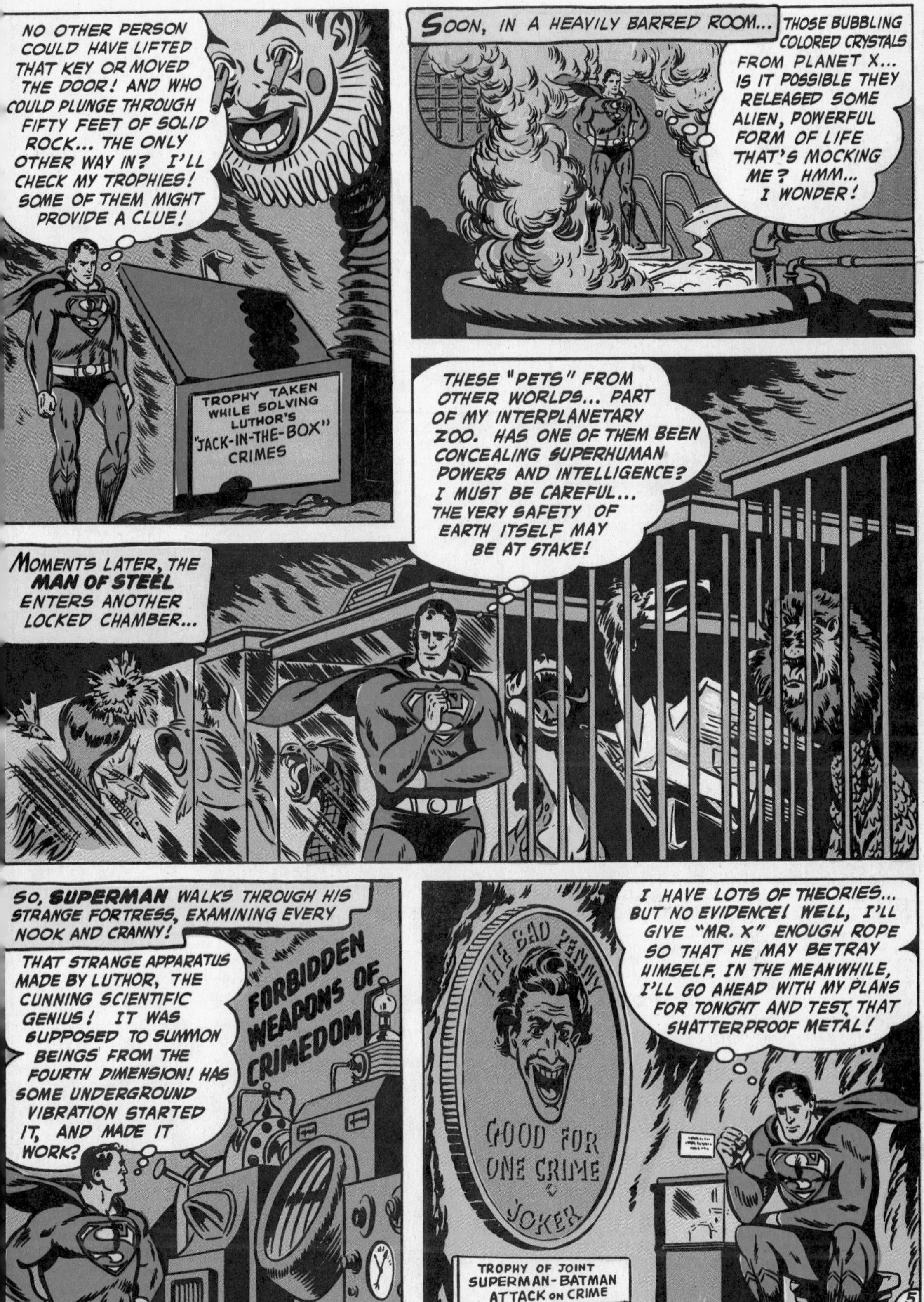
NO OTHER PERSON COULD HAVE LIFTED THAT KEY OR MOVED THE DOOR! AND WHO COULD PLUNGE THROUGH FIFTY FEET OF SOLID ROCK... THE ONLY OTHER WAY IN? I'LL CHECK MY TROPHIES! SOME OF THEM MIGHT PROVIDE A CLUE!
TROPHY TAKEN WHILE SOLVING LUTHOR'S "JACK-IN-THE-BOX" CRIMES
SOON, IN A HEAVILY BARRED ROOM...
THOSE BUBBLING COLORED CRYSTALS FROM PLANET X... IS IT POSSIBLE THEY RELEASED SOME ALIEN, POWERFUL FORM OF LIFE THAT'S MOCKING ME? HMM... I WONDER!
MOMENTS LATER, THE MAN OF STEEL ENTERS ANOTHER LOCKED CHAMBER...
THESE "PETS" FROM OTHER WORLDS... PART OF MY INTERPLANETARY ZOO. HAS ONE OF THEM BEEN CONCEALING SUPERHUMAN POWERS AND INTELLIGENCE? I MUST BE CAREFUL... THE VERY SAFETY OF EARTH ITSELF MAY BE AT STAKE!
SO, SUPERMAN WALKS THROUGH HIS STRANGE FORTRESS, EXAMINING EVERY NOOK AND CRANNY!
THAT STRANGE APPARATUS MADE BY LUTHOR, THE CUNNING SCIENTIFIC GENIUS! IT WAS SUPPOSED TO SUMMON BEINGS FROM THE FOURTH DIMENSION! HAS SOME UNDERGROUND VIBRATION STARTED IT, AND MADE IT WORK?
FORBIDDEN WEAPONS OF CRIMEDOM
I HAVE LOTS OF THEORIES... BUT NO EVIDENCE! WELL, I'LL GIVE "MR. X" ENOUGH ROPE SO THAT HE MAY BETRAY HIMSELF. IN THE MEANWHILE, I'LL GO AHEAD WITH MY PLANS FOR TONIGHT AND TEST THAT SHATTERPROOF METAL!
THE BAD PENNY
GOOD FOR ONE CRIME
JOKER
TROPHY OF JOINT SUPERMAN-BATMAN ATTACK ON CRIME
5

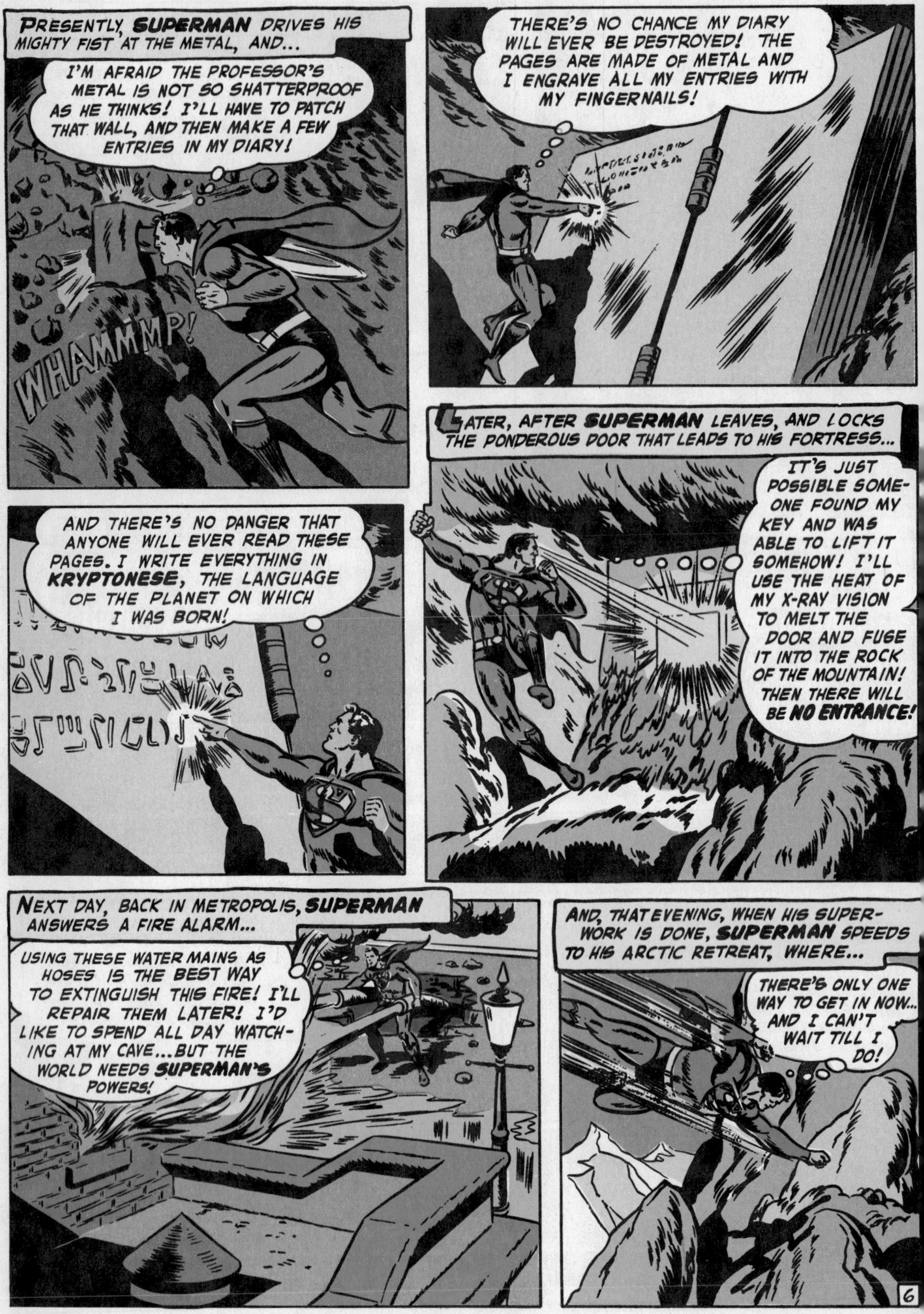
PRESENTLY, SUPERMAN DRIVES HIS MIGHTY FIST AT THE METAL, AND...
I'M AFRAID THE PROFESSOR'S METAL IS NOT SO SHATTERPROOF AS HE THINKS! I'LL HAVE TO PATCH THAT WALL, AND THEN MAKE A FEW ENTRIES IN MY DIARY!
WHAMMMP!
THERE'S NO CHANCE MY DIARY WILL EVER BE DESTROYED! THE PAGES ARE MADE OF METAL AND I ENGRAVE ALL MY ENTRIES WITH MY FINGERNAILS!
AND THERE'S NO DANGER THAT ANYONE WILL EVER READ THESE PAGES. I WRITE EVERYTHING IN KRYPTONESE, THE LANGUAGE OF THE PLANET ON WHICH I WAS BORN!
LATER, AFTER SUPERMAN LEAVES, AND LOCKS THE PONDEROUS DOOR THAT LEADS TO HIS FORTRESS...
IT'S JUST POSSIBLE SOMEONE FOUND MY KEY AND WAS ABLE TO LIFT IT SOMEHOW! I'LL USE THE HEAT OF MY X-RAY VISION TO MELT THE DOOR AND FUSE IT INTO THE ROCK OF THE MOUNTAIN! THEN THERE WILL BE NO ENTRANCE!
NEXT DAY, BACK IN METROPOLIS, SUPERMAN ANSWERS A FIRE ALARM...
USING THESE WATER MAINS AS HOSES IS THE BEST WAY TO EXTINGUISH THIS FIRE! I'LL REPAIR THEM LATER! I'D LIKE TO SPEND ALL DAY WATCHING AT MY CAVE...BUT THE WORLD NEEDS SUPERMAN'S POWERS!
AND, THAT EVENING, WHEN HIS SUPER-WORK IS DONE, SUPERMAN SPEEDS TO HIS ARCTIC RETREAT, WHERE...
THERE'S ONLY ONE WAY TO GET IN NOW... AND I CAN'T WAIT TILL I DO!
6

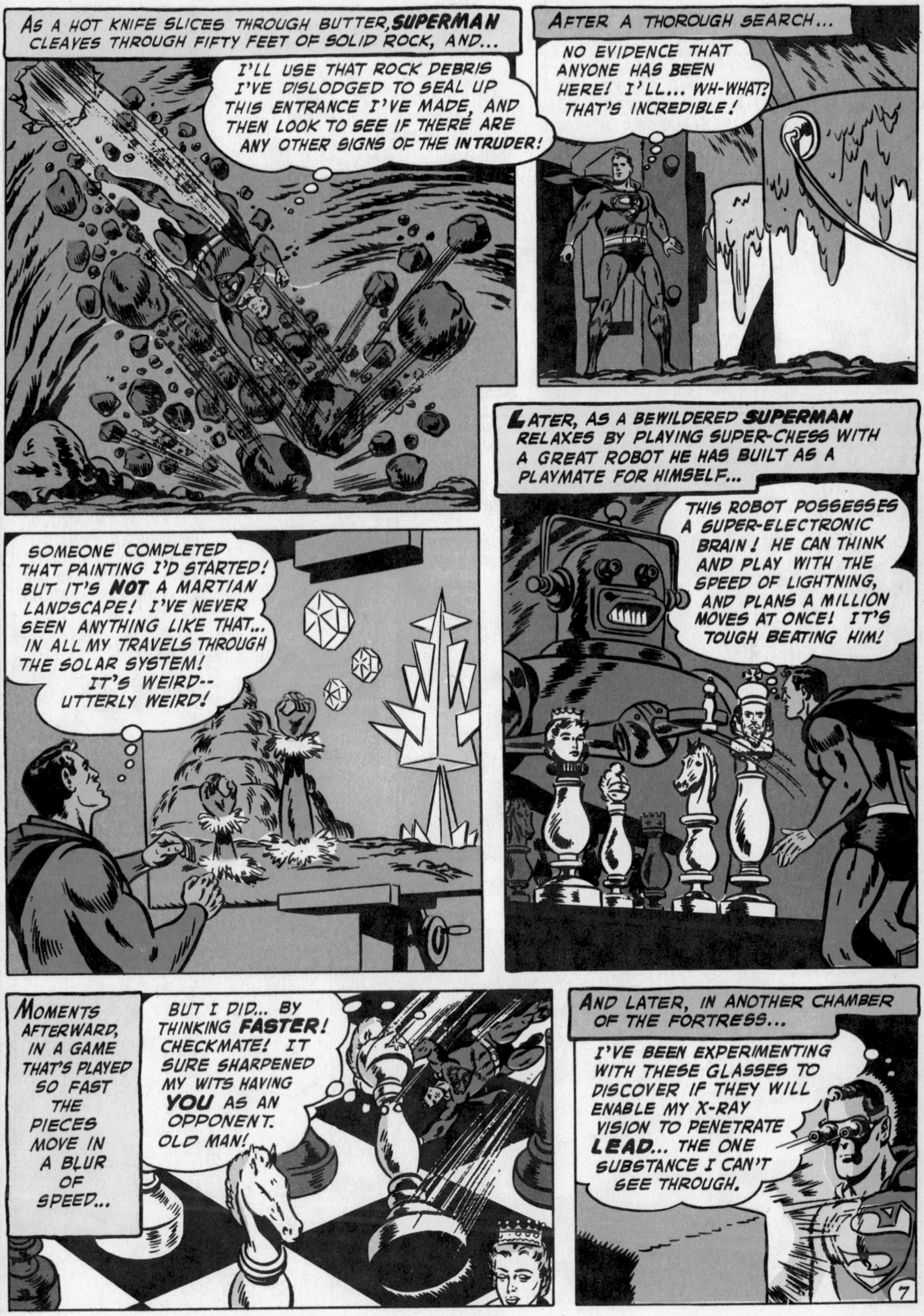
AS A HOT KNIFE SLICES THROUGH BUTTER, SUPERMAN CLEAVES THROUGH FIFTY FEET OF SOLID ROCK, AND...
I'LL USE THAT ROCK DEBRIS I'VE DISLODGED TO SEAL UP THIS ENTRANCE I'VE MADE, AND THEN LOOK TO SEE IF THERE ARE ANY OTHER SIGNS OF THE INTRUDER!
AFTER A THOROUGH SEARCH...
NO EVIDENCE THAT ANYONE HAS BEEN HERE! I'LL... WH-WHAT? THAT'S INCREDIBLE!
SOMEONE COMPLETED THAT PAINTING I'D STARTED! BUT IT'S NOT A MARTIAN LANDSCAPE! I'VE NEVER SEEN ANYTHING LIKE THAT... IN ALL MY TRAVELS THROUGH THE SOLAR SYSTEM! IT'S WEIRD-- UTTERLY WEIRD!
LATER, AS A BEWILDERED SUPERMAN RELAXES BY PLAYING SUPER-CHESS WITH A GREAT ROBOT HE HAS BUILT AS A PLAYMATE FOR HIMSELF...
THIS ROBOT POSSESSES A SUPER-ELECTRONIC BRAIN! HE CAN THINK AND PLAY WITH THE SPEED OF LIGHTNING, AND PLANS A MILLION MOVES AT ONCE! IT'S TOUGH BEATING HIM!
MOMENTS AFTERWARD, IN A GAME THAT'S PLAYED SO FAST THE PIECES MOVE IN A BLUR OF SPEED...
BUT I DID... BY THINKING FASTER! CHECKMATE! IT SURE SHARPENED MY WITS HAVING YOU AS AN OPPONENT, OLD MAN!
AND LATER, IN ANOTHER CHAMBER OF THE FORTRESS...
I'VE BEEN EXPERIMENTING WITH THESE GLASSES TO DISCOVER IF THEY WILL ENABLE MY X-RAY VISION TO PENETRATE LEAD... THE ONE SUBSTANCE I CAN'T SEE THROUGH.
7

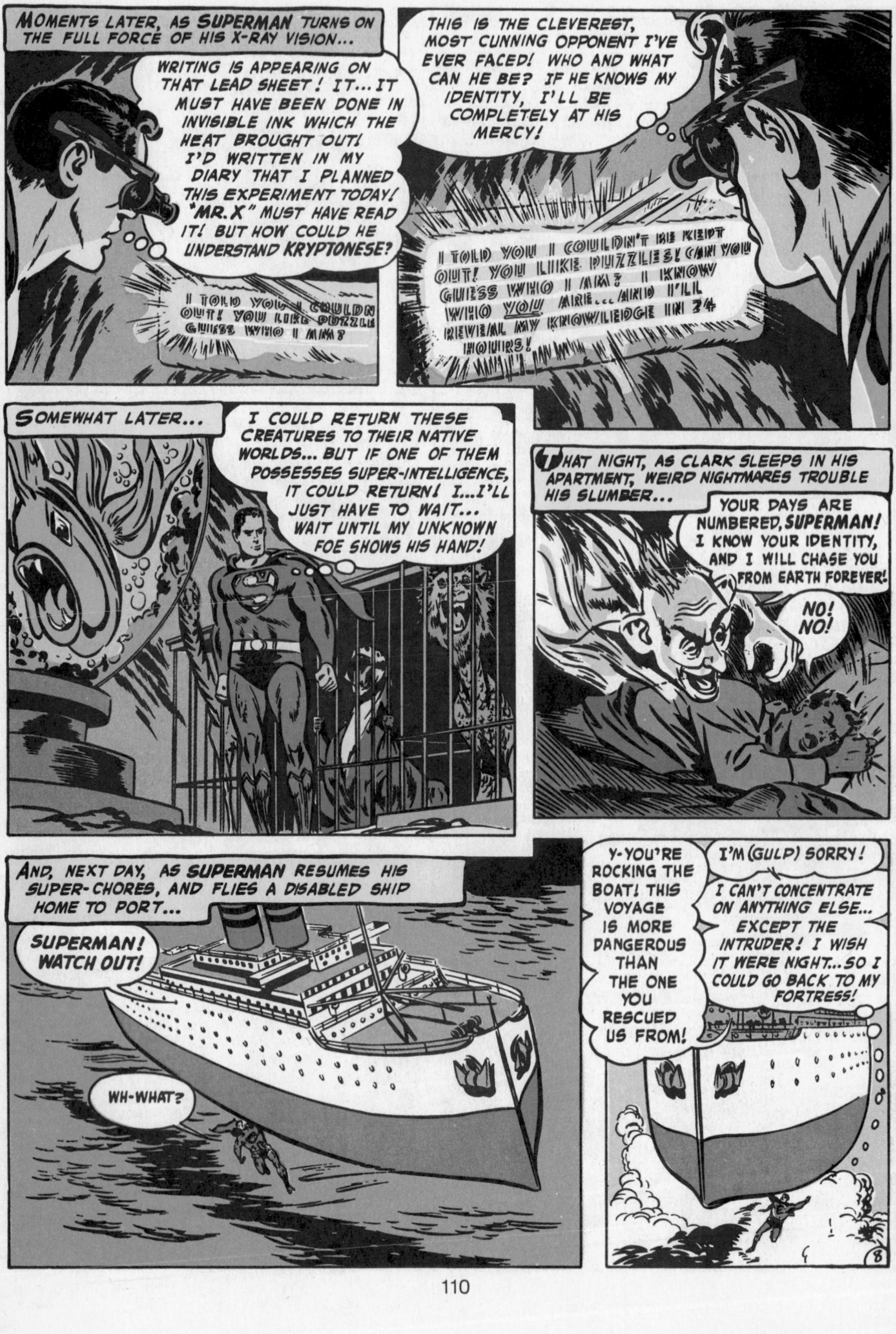
MOMENTS LATER, AS SUPERMAN TURNS ON THE FULL FORCE OF HIS X-RAY VISION...
WRITING IS APPEARING ON THAT LEAD SHEET! IT... IT MUST HAVE BEEN DONE IN INVISIBLE INK WHICH THE HEAT BROUGHT OUT! I'D WRITTEN IN MY DIARY THAT I PLANNED THIS EXPERIMENT TODAY! "MR. X" MUST HAVE READ IT! BUT HOW COULD HE UNDERSTAND KRYPTONESE?
I TOLD YOU I COULDN OUT! YOU LIKE PUZZLE GUESS WHO I AM?
THIS IS THE CLEVEREST, MOST CUNNING OPPONENT I'VE EVER FACED! WHO AND WHAT CAN HE BE? IF HE KNOWS MY IDENTITY, I'LL BE COMPLETELY AT HIS MERCY!
I TOLD YOU I COULDN'T BE KEPT OUT! YOU LIKE PUZZLES! CAN YOU GUESS WHO I AM? I KNOW WHO YOU ARE... AND I'LL REVEAL MY KNOWLEDGE IN 24 HOURS!
SOMEWHAT LATER...
I COULD RETURN THESE CREATURES TO THEIR NATIVE WORLDS... BUT IF ONE OF THEM POSSESSES SUPER-INTELLIGENCE, IT COULD RETURN! I...I'LL JUST HAVE TO WAIT... WAIT UNTIL MY UNKNOWN FOE SHOWS HIS HAND!
THAT NIGHT, AS CLARK SLEEPS IN HIS APARTMENT, WEIRD NIGHTMARES TROUBLE HIS SLUMBER...
YOUR DAYS ARE NUMBERED, SUPERMAN! I KNOW YOUR IDENTITY, AND I WILL CHASE YOU FROM EARTH FOREVER!
NO! NO!
AND, NEXT DAY, AS SUPERMAN RESUMES HIS SUPER-CHORES, AND FLIES A DISABLED SHIP HOME TO PORT...
SUPERMAN! WATCH OUT!
WH-WHAT?
Y-YOU'RE ROCKING THE BOAT! THIS VOYAGE IS MORE DANGEROUS THAN THE ONE YOU RESCUED US FROM!
I'M (GULP) SORRY!
I CAN'T CONCENTRATE ON ANYTHING ELSE... EXCEPT THE INTRUDER! I WISH IT WERE NIGHT... SO I COULD GO BACK TO MY FORTRESS!
8

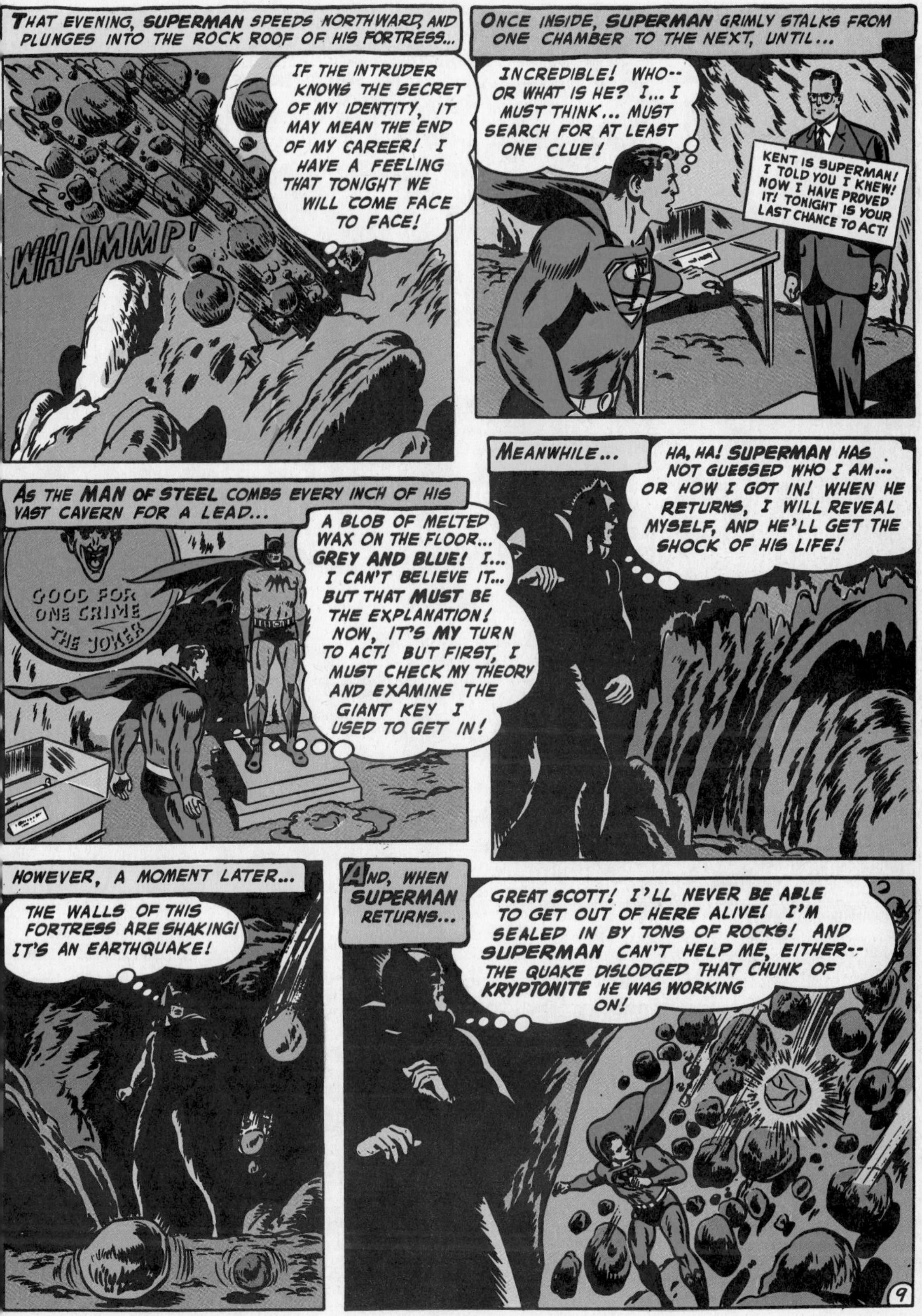

THAT EVENING, SUPERMAN SPEEDS NORTHWARD, AND PLUNGES INTO THE ROCK ROOF OF HIS FORTRESS...
IF THE INTRUDER KNOWS THE SECRET OF MY IDENTITY, IT MAY MEAN THE END OF MY CAREER! I HAVE A FEELING THAT TONIGHT WE WILL COME FACE TO FACE!
WHAMMP!
ONCE INSIDE, SUPERMAN GRIMLY STALKS FROM ONE CHAMBER TO THE NEXT, UNTIL...
INCREDIBLE! WHO-- OR WHAT IS HE? I... I MUST THINK... MUST SEARCH FOR AT LEAST ONE CLUE!
KENT IS SUPERMAN! I TOLD YOU I KNEW! NOW I HAVE PROVED IT! TONIGHT IS YOUR LAST CHANCE TO ACT!
AS THE MAN OF STEEL COMBS EVERY INCH OF HIS VAST CAVERN FOR A LEAD...
GOOD FOR ONE CRIME THE JOKER
A BLOB OF MELTED WAX ON THE FLOOR... GREY AND BLUE! I... I CAN'T BELIEVE IT... BUT THAT MUST BE THE EXPLANATION! NOW, IT'S MY TURN TO ACT! BUT FIRST, I MUST CHECK MY THEORY AND EXAMINE THE GIANT KEY I USED TO GET IN!
MEANWHILE...
HA, HA! SUPERMAN HAS NOT GUESSED WHO I AM... OR HOW I GOT IN! WHEN HE RETURNS, I WILL REVEAL MYSELF, AND HE'LL GET THE SHOCK OF HIS LIFE!
HOWEVER, A MOMENT LATER...
THE WALLS OF THIS FORTRESS ARE SHAKING! IT'S AN EARTHQUAKE!
AND, WHEN SUPERMAN RETURNS...
GREAT SCOTT! I'LL NEVER BE ABLE TO GET OUT OF HERE ALIVE! I'M SEALED IN BY TONS OF ROCKS! AND SUPERMAN CAN'T HELP ME, EITHER-- THE QUAKE DISLODGED THAT CHUNK OF KRYPTONITE HE WAS WORKING ON!
9

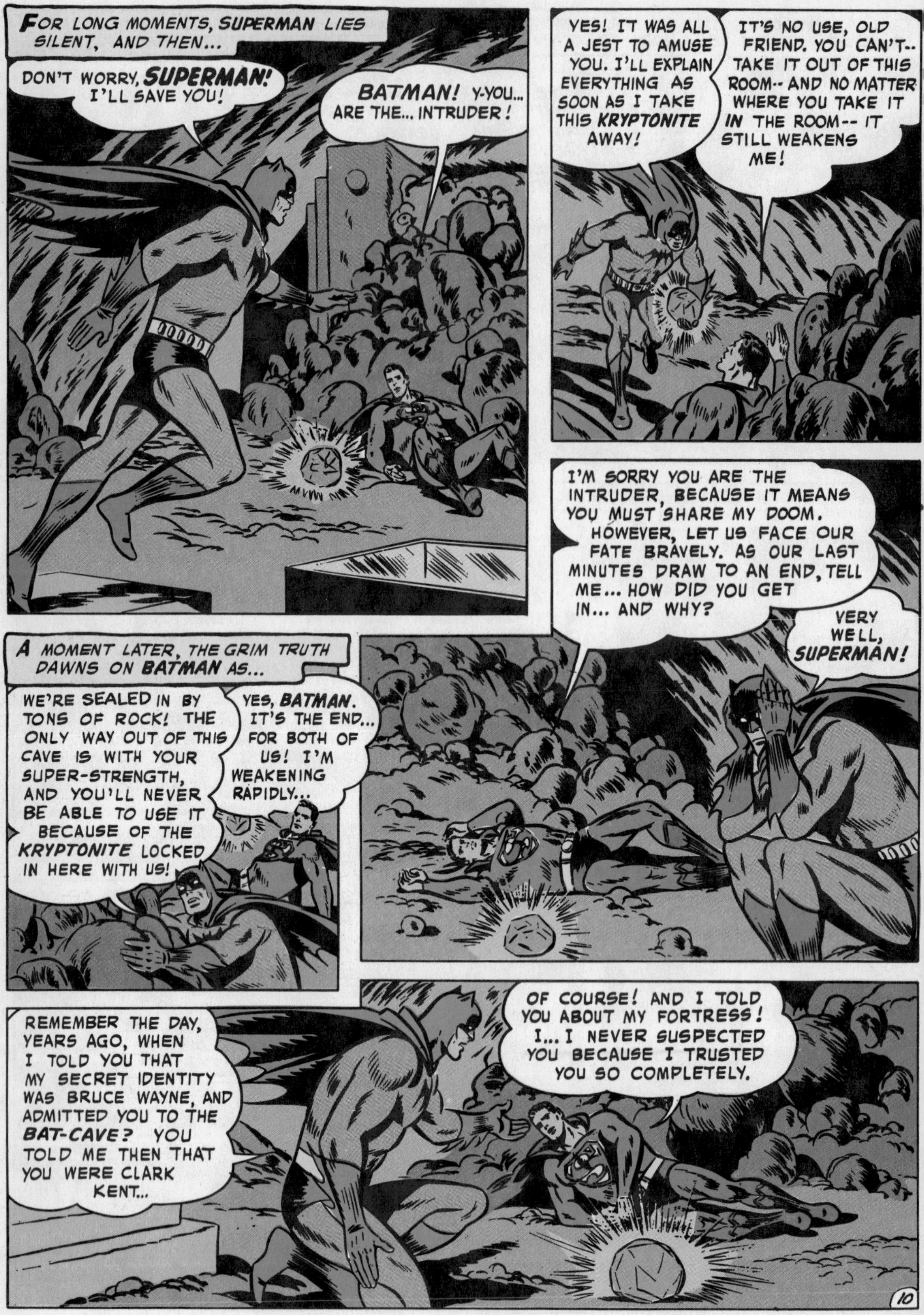
FOR LONG MOMENTS, SUPERMAN LIES SILENT, AND THEN...
DON'T WORRY, SUPERMAN! I'LL SAVE YOU!
BATMAN! Y-YOU... ARE THE... INTRUDER!
YES! IT WAS ALL A JEST TO AMUSE YOU. I'LL EXPLAIN EVERYTHING AS SOON AS I TAKE THIS KRYPTONITE AWAY!
IT'S NO USE, OLD FRIEND. YOU CAN'T-- TAKE IT OUT OF THIS ROOM-- AND NO MATTER WHERE YOU TAKE IT IN THE ROOM-- IT STILL WEAKENS ME!
A MOMENT LATER, THE GRIM TRUTH DAWNS ON BATMAN AS...
WE'RE SEALED IN BY TONS OF ROCK! THE ONLY WAY OUT OF THIS CAVE IS WITH YOUR SUPER-STRENGTH, AND YOU'LL NEVER BE ABLE TO USE IT BECAUSE OF THE KRYPTONITE LOCKED IN HERE WITH US!
YES, BATMAN. IT'S THE END... FOR BOTH OF US! I'M WEAKENING RAPIDLY...
I'M SORRY YOU ARE THE INTRUDER, BECAUSE IT MEANS YOU MUST SHARE MY DOOM. HOWEVER, LET US FACE OUR FATE BRAVELY. AS OUR LAST MINUTES DRAW TO AN END, TELL ME... HOW DID YOU GET IN... AND WHY?
VERY WELL, SUPERMAN!
REMEMBER THE DAY, YEARS AGO, WHEN I TOLD YOU THAT MY SECRET IDENTITY WAS BRUCE WAYNE, AND ADMITTED YOU TO THE BAT-CAVE? YOU TOLD ME THEN THAT YOU WERE CLARK KENT...
OF COURSE! AND I TOLD YOU ABOUT MY FORTRESS! I... I NEVER SUSPECTED YOU BECAUSE I TRUSTED YOU SO COMPLETELY.
10

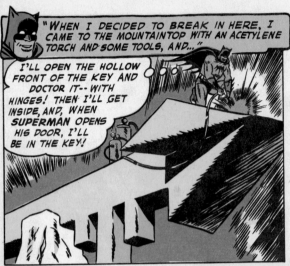

"WHEN I DECIDED TO BREAK IN HERE, I CAME TO THE MOUNTAINTOP WITH AN ACETYLENE TORCH AND SOME TOOLS, AND..."

I'LL OPEN THE HOLLOW FRONT OF THE KEY AND DOCTOR IT-- WITH HINGES! THEN I'LL GET INSIDE, AND, WHEN SUPERMAN OPENS HIS DOOR, I'LL BE IN THE KEY!

"MY PLAN WORKED PERFECTLY!"

I KNOW SUPERMAN WILL COME AGAIN TOMORROW IN TIME TO DISCOVER THERE'S BEEN AN INTRUDER, BECAUSE I ARRANGED WITH PROFESSOR WELKINS TO GIVE HIM SOME METAL THAT COULD ONLY BE TESTED IN HIS FORT!

"WHILE YOU WERE BUSY, I SLIPPED OUT OF THE KEY AND HID. THEN, WHEN YOU LEFT..."

I KNEW THIS "BAD PENNY" WAS ONE OF SUPERMAN'S TROPHIES... SINCE WE WORKED ON THE CASE TOGETHER! AND, AS IT'S MADE OF LEAD WHICH HIS X-RAY VISION CAN'T PIERCE, ITS INTERIOR WILL BE A PERFECT HIDING PLACE! WHAT A PUZZLE I'LL GIVE HIM!

THE BAD PENNY

"EARLIER TONIGHT I MELTED DOWN THE WAX FIGURE OF ME IN THE "BATMAN" ROOM" WITH A FLARE FROM MY UTILITY BELT..."

IF HE DOESN'T GUESS THE SOLUTION TONIGHT, I'LL LEAP DOWN, SURPRISE HIM, AND TELL HIM!

I NEVER GUESSED WE'D SHARE OUR DOOM INSTEAD OF... WH-WHAT? Y-YOU'RE LAUGHING!

S-SORRY (HA-HA) BATMAN! I CAN'T CONTROL MYSELF ANY LONGER. YOU SEE, SINCE YOU TRICKED ME, I DECIDED IT WAS ONLY FAIR FOR ME TO TRICK YOU!

SUDDENLY, THE MAN OF STEEL LEAPS UP, AND...

THAT KRYPTONITE IS PHONY AND THE 'QUAKE WAS CAUSED BY VIBRATIONS FROM A SUPER-CLAP OF MY HANDS. THE REST OF THE FORT IS STILL UNHARMED!

WHEW! YOU CERTAINLY FOOLED ME--AS MUCH AS I FOOLED YOU! BUT HOW DID YOU GUESS I WAS THE INTRUDER?

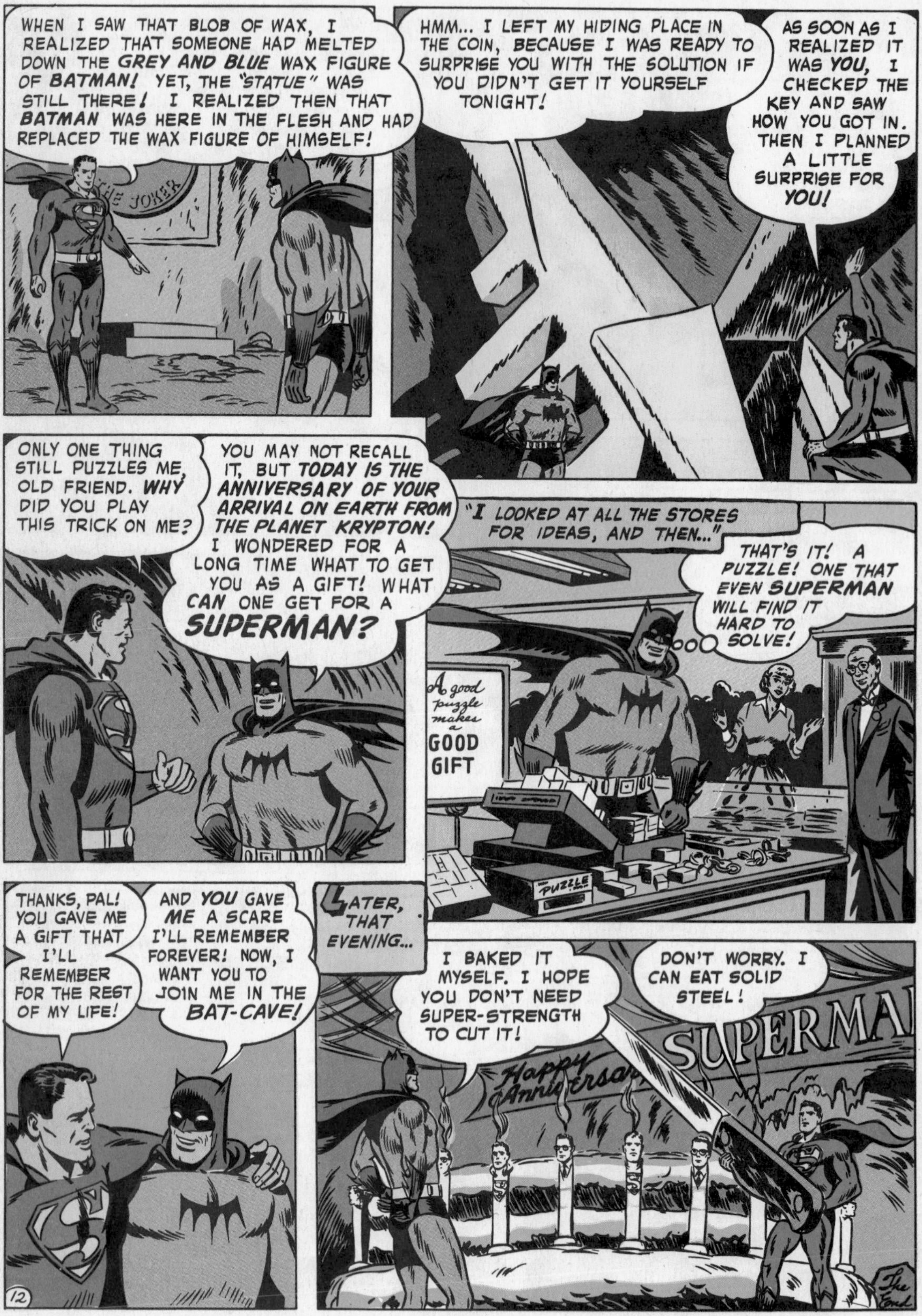
WHEN I SAW THAT BLOB OF WAX, I REALIZED THAT SOMEONE HAD MELTED DOWN THE GREY AND BLUE WAX FIGURE OF BATMAN! YET, THE "STATUE" WAS STILL THERE! I REALIZED THEN THAT BATMAN WAS HERE IN THE FLESH AND HAD REPLACED THE WAX FIGURE OF HIMSELF!
THE JOKER
HMM... I LEFT MY HIDING PLACE IN THE COIN, BECAUSE I WAS READY TO SURPRISE YOU WITH THE SOLUTION IF YOU DIDN'T GET IT YOURSELF TONIGHT!
AS SOON AS I REALIZED IT WAS YOU, I CHECKED THE KEY AND SAW HOW YOU GOT IN. THEN I PLANNED A LITTLE SURPRISE FOR YOU!
ONLY ONE THING STILL PUZZLES ME, OLD FRIEND. WHY DID YOU PLAY THIS TRICK ON ME?
YOU MAY NOT RECALL IT, BUT TODAY IS THE ANNIVERSARY OF YOUR ARRIVAL ON EARTH FROM THE PLANET KRYPTON! I WONDERED FOR A LONG TIME WHAT TO GET YOU AS A GIFT! WHAT CAN ONE GET FOR A SUPERMAN?
"I LOOKED AT ALL THE STORES FOR IDEAS, AND THEN..."
THAT'S IT! A PUZZLE! ONE THAT EVEN SUPERMAN WILL FIND IT HARD TO SOLVE!
A good puzzle makes a GOOD GIFT
PUZZLE
THANKS, PAL! YOU GAVE ME A GIFT THAT I'LL REMEMBER FOR THE REST OF MY LIFE!
AND YOU GAVE ME A SCARE I'LL REMEMBER FOREVER! NOW, I WANT YOU TO JOIN ME IN THE BAT-CAVE!
12
LATER, THAT EVENING...
I BAKED IT MYSELF. I HOPE YOU DON'T NEED SUPER-STRENGTH TO CUT IT!
DON'T WORRY. I CAN EAT SOLID STEEL!
Happy
The End

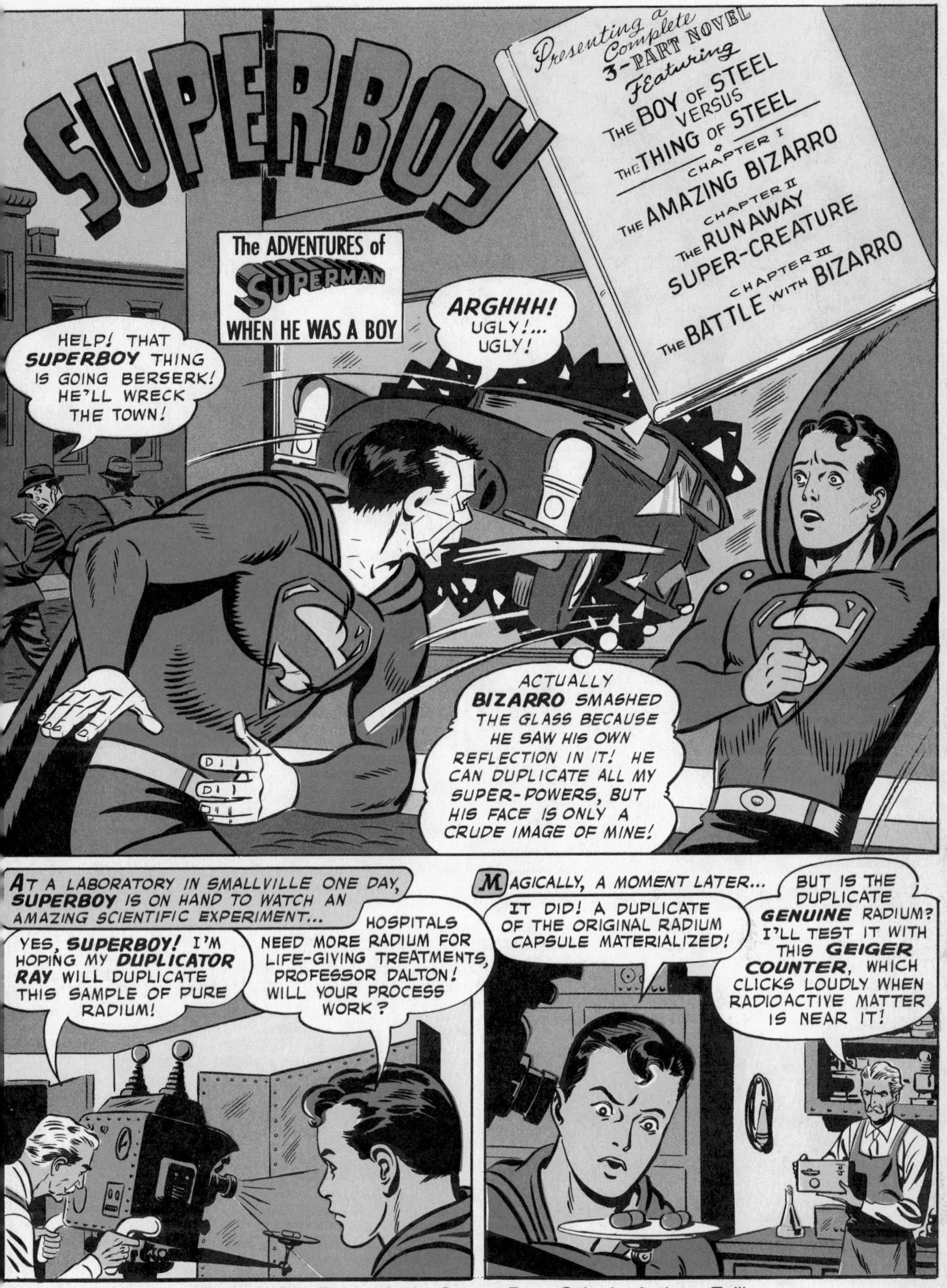
SUPERBOY
The ADVENTURES of SUPERMAN WHEN HE WAS A BOY
Presenting a Complete 3-PART NOVEL Featuring THE BOY OF STEEL VERSUS THE THING OF STEEL
CHAPTER I THE AMAZING BIZARRO
CHAPTER II THE RUNAWAY SUPER-CREATURE
CHAPTER III THE BATTLE WITH BIZARRO
HELP! THAT SUPERBOY THING IS GOING BERSERK! HE'LL WRECK THE TOWN!
ARGHHH! UGLY!... UGLY!
ACTUALLY BIZARRO SMASHED THE GLASS BECAUSE HE SAW HIS OWN REFLECTION IN IT! HE CAN DUPLICATE ALL MY SUPER-POWERS, BUT HIS FACE IS ONLY A CRUDE IMAGE OF MINE!
AT A LABORATORY IN SMALLVILLE ONE DAY, SUPERBOY IS ON HAND TO WATCH AN AMAZING SCIENTIFIC EXPERIMENT...
YES, SUPERBOY! I'M HOPING MY DUPLICATOR RAY WILL DUPLICATE THIS SAMPLE OF PURE RADIUM!
HOSPITALS NEED MORE RADIUM FOR LIFE-GIVING TREATMENTS, PROFESSOR DALTON! WILL YOUR PROCESS WORK?
MAGICALLY, A MOMENT LATER...
IT DID! A DUPLICATE OF THE ORIGINAL RADIUM CAPSULE MATERIALIZED!
BUT IS THE DUPLICATE GENUINE RADIUM? I'LL TEST IT WITH THIS GEIGER COUNTER, WHICH CLICKS LOUDLY WHEN RADIOACTIVE MATTER IS NEAR IT!

Story by Otto Binder/Art by George Papp/Color by Anthony Tollin

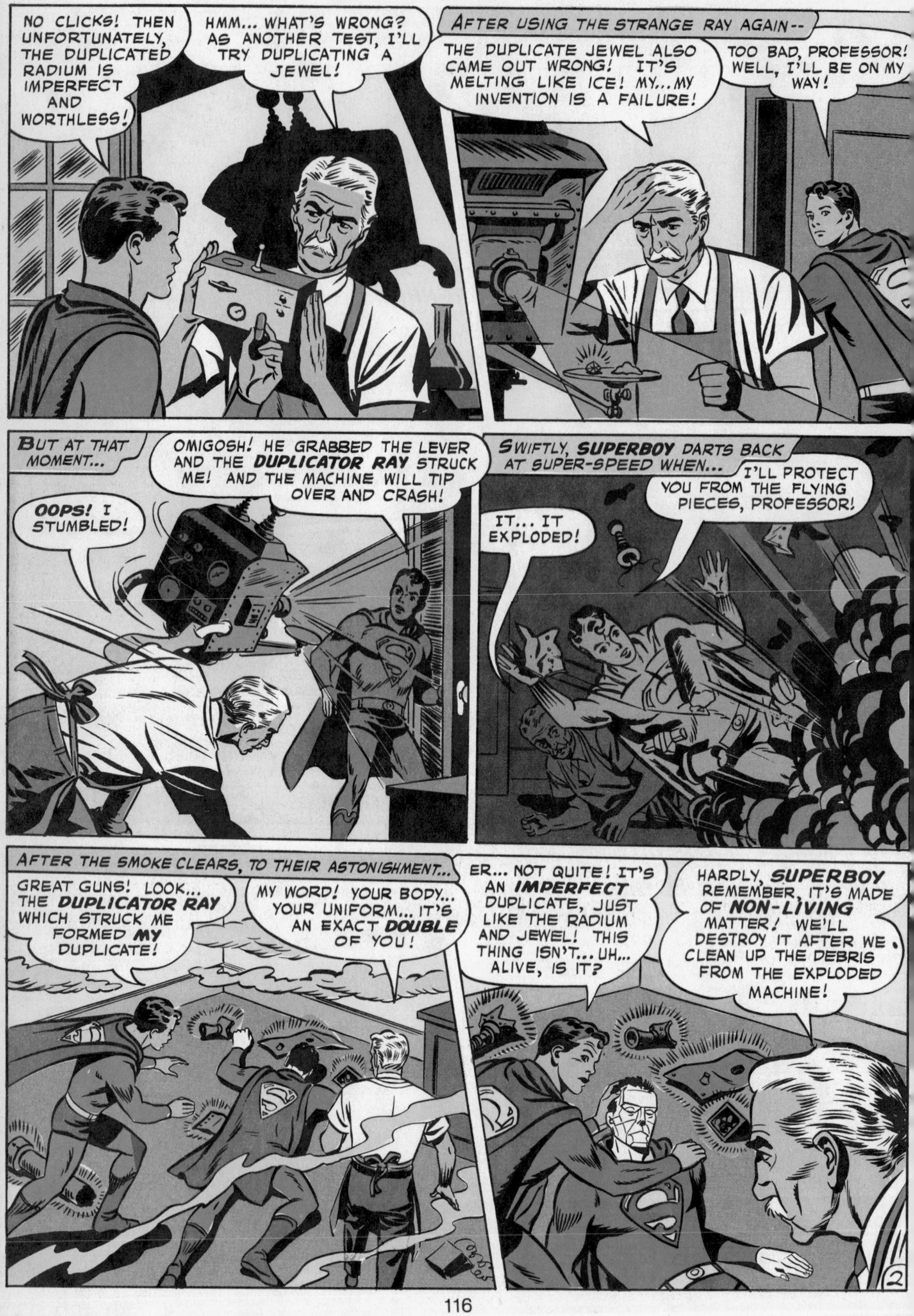
NO CLICKS! THEN UNFORTUNATELY, THE DUPLICATED RADIUM IS IMPERFECT AND WORTHLESS!
HMM... WHAT'S WRONG? AS ANOTHER TEST, I'LL TRY DUPLICATING A JEWEL!
AFTER USING THE STRANGE RAY AGAIN--
THE DUPLICATE JEWEL ALSO CAME OUT WRONG! IT'S MELTING LIKE ICE! MY... MY INVENTION IS A FAILURE!
TOO BAD, PROFESSOR! WELL, I'LL BE ON MY WAY!
BUT AT THAT MOMENT...
OOPS! I STUMBLED!
OMIGOSH! HE GRABBED THE LEVER AND THE DUPLICATOR RAY STRUCK ME! AND THE MACHINE WILL TIP OVER AND CRASH!
SWIFTLY, SUPERBOY DARTS BACK AT SUPER-SPEED WHEN...
IT... IT EXPLODED!
I'LL PROTECT YOU FROM THE FLYING PIECES, PROFESSOR!
AFTER THE SMOKE CLEARS, TO THEIR ASTONISHMENT...
GREAT GUNS! LOOK... THE DUPLICATOR RAY WHICH STRUCK ME FORMED MY DUPLICATE!
MY WORD! YOUR BODY... YOUR UNIFORM... IT'S AN EXACT DOUBLE OF YOU!
ER... NOT QUITE! IT'S AN IMPERFECT DUPLICATE, JUST LIKE THE RADIUM AND JEWEL! THIS THING ISN'T... UH... ALIVE, IS IT?
HARDLY, SUPERBOY. REMEMBER, IT'S MADE OF NON-LIVING MATTER! WE'LL DESTROY IT AFTER WE CLEAN UP THE DEBRIS FROM THE EXPLODED MACHINE!
2

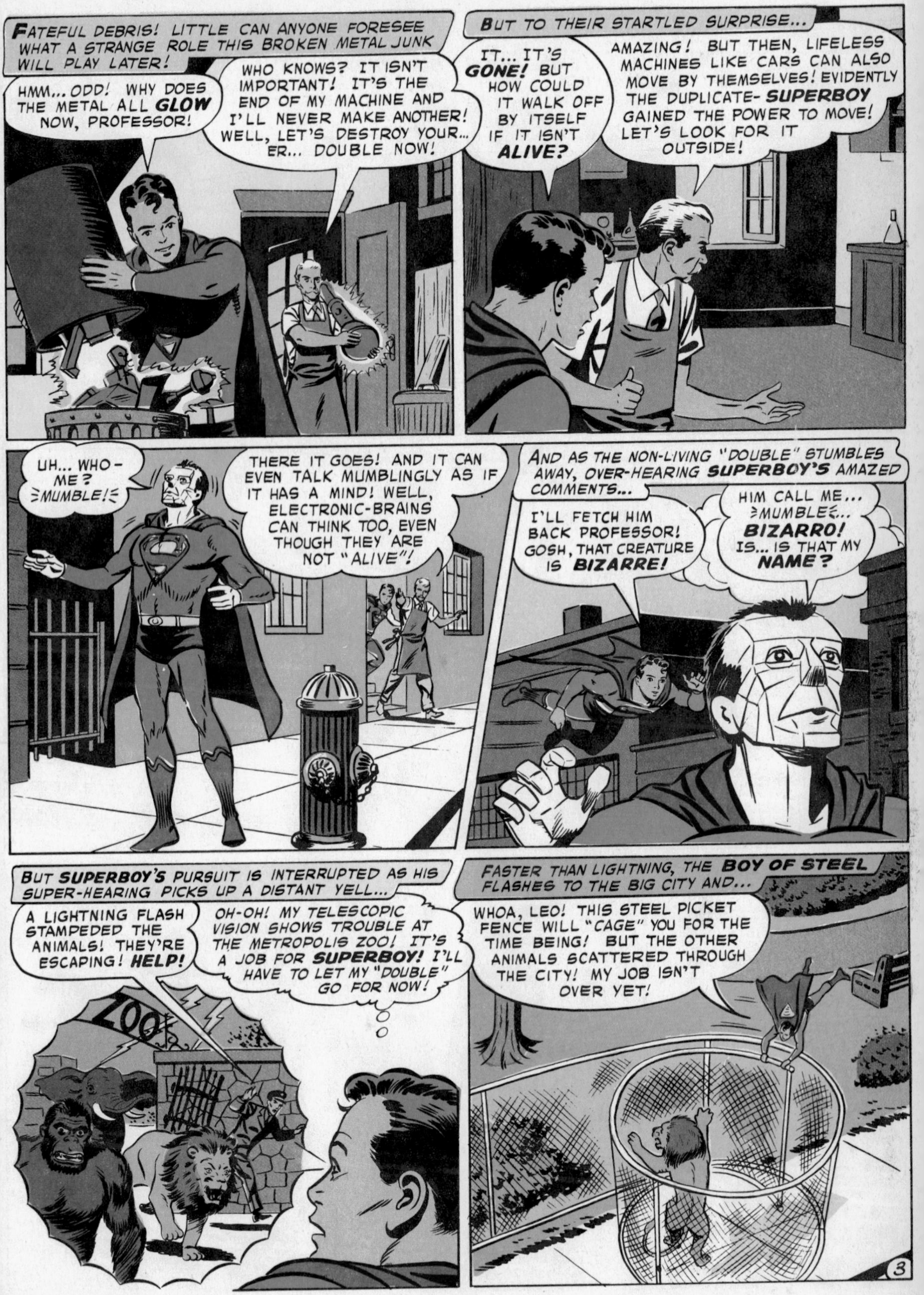
FATEFUL DEBRIS! LITTLE CAN ANYONE FORESEE WHAT A STRANGE ROLE THIS BROKEN METAL JUNK WILL PLAY LATER!
HMM... ODD! WHY DOES THE METAL ALL GLOW NOW, PROFESSOR!
WHO KNOWS? IT ISN'T IMPORTANT! IT'S THE END OF MY MACHINE AND I'LL NEVER MAKE ANOTHER! WELL, LET'S DESTROY YOUR... ER... DOUBLE NOW!
BUT TO THEIR STARTLED SURPRISE...
IT... IT'S GONE! BUT HOW COULD IT WALK OFF BY ITSELF IF IT ISN'T ALIVE?
AMAZING! BUT THEN, LIFELESS MACHINES LIKE CARS CAN ALSO MOVE BY THEMSELVES! EVIDENTLY THE DUPLICATE-SUPERBOY GAINED THE POWER TO MOVE! LET'S LOOK FOR IT OUTSIDE!
UH... WHO-ME? MUMBLE!
THERE IT GOES! AND IT CAN EVEN TALK MUMBLINGLY AS IF IT HAS A MIND! WELL, ELECTRONIC-BRAINS CAN THINK TOO, EVEN THOUGH THEY ARE NOT "ALIVE"!
AND AS THE NON-LIVING "DOUBLE" STUMBLES AWAY, OVER-HEARING SUPERBOY'S AMAZED COMMENTS...
I'LL FETCH HIM BACK PROFESSOR! GOSH, THAT CREATURE IS BIZARRE!
HIM CALL ME... MUMBLE... BIZARRO! IS... IS THAT MY NAME?
BUT SUPERBOY'S PURSUIT IS INTERRUPTED AS HIS SUPER-HEARING PICKS UP A DISTANT YELL...
A LIGHTNING FLASH STAMPEDED THE ANIMALS! THEY'RE ESCAPING! HELP!
OH-OH! MY TELESCOPIC VISION SHOWS TROUBLE AT THE METROPOLIS ZOO! IT'S A JOB FOR SUPERBOY! I'LL HAVE TO LET MY "DOUBLE" GO FOR NOW!
ZOO
FASTER THAN LIGHTNING, THE BOY OF STEEL FLASHES TO THE BIG CITY AND...
WHOA, LEO! THIS STEEL PICKET FENCE WILL "CAGE" YOU FOR THE TIME BEING! BUT THE OTHER ANIMALS SCATTERED THROUGH THE CITY! MY JOB ISN'T OVER YET!
3

MEANWHILE, AS BIZARRO, THE ARTIFICIAL SUPERBOY, WANDERS ON THROUGH SMALLVILLE...
ME LOOK AROUND TOWN! WANT TO MAKE FRIENDS WITH PEOPLE!
WHY, HELLO THERE, SUPERBOY! IT'S NICE TO MEET YOU!
U.S. MAIL
ONE HOUR PARKING P.D.
BUT AT A CLOSER LOOK...
EEK! THAT CAN'T BE SUPERBOY! IT... IT'S SOME KIND OF MONSTER DRESSED LIKE HIM! HELP... RUN!
WAIT! BIZARRO NOT HARM YOU! WHY YOU SCARED OF ME???
WHEN BIZARRO SEES HIS OWN REFLECTION IN A PLATE-GLASS WINDOW...
OHHH! THAT FACE-- IT UGLY...UGLY!
SOON, ALARMINGLY...
ME DESTROY UGLY FACE! ARGHHH!
LOOK! THAT CREATURE HAS SUPER-STRENGTH LIKE SUPERBOY! IT HEAVED A PARKED CAR THROUGH THE GLASS! IT'S DANGEROUS! WE NEED SUPERBOY... WHERE IS HE?
BUT SUPERBOY IS STILL BUSY IN METROPOLIS, AND FINALLY, A POSSE IS FORMED AND LED BY PROFESSOR DALTON HIMSELF...
I FEEL RESPONSIBLE FOR THAT CREATURE'S EXISTENCE! IT'S NOT ALIVE! IT'S NOT EVEN A MONSTER! IT'S JUST A... A THING! OPEN FIRE, MEN! THE WAY HE SMASHES THINGS PROVES HE'S DANGEROUS!
BUT LOOK... BULLETS ONLY BOUNCE! HE'S INVULNERABLE, LIKE SUPERBOY!
WHY THEY HUNT ME? ME NOT BAD! WHY THEY HATE ME?... CHOKE!
4

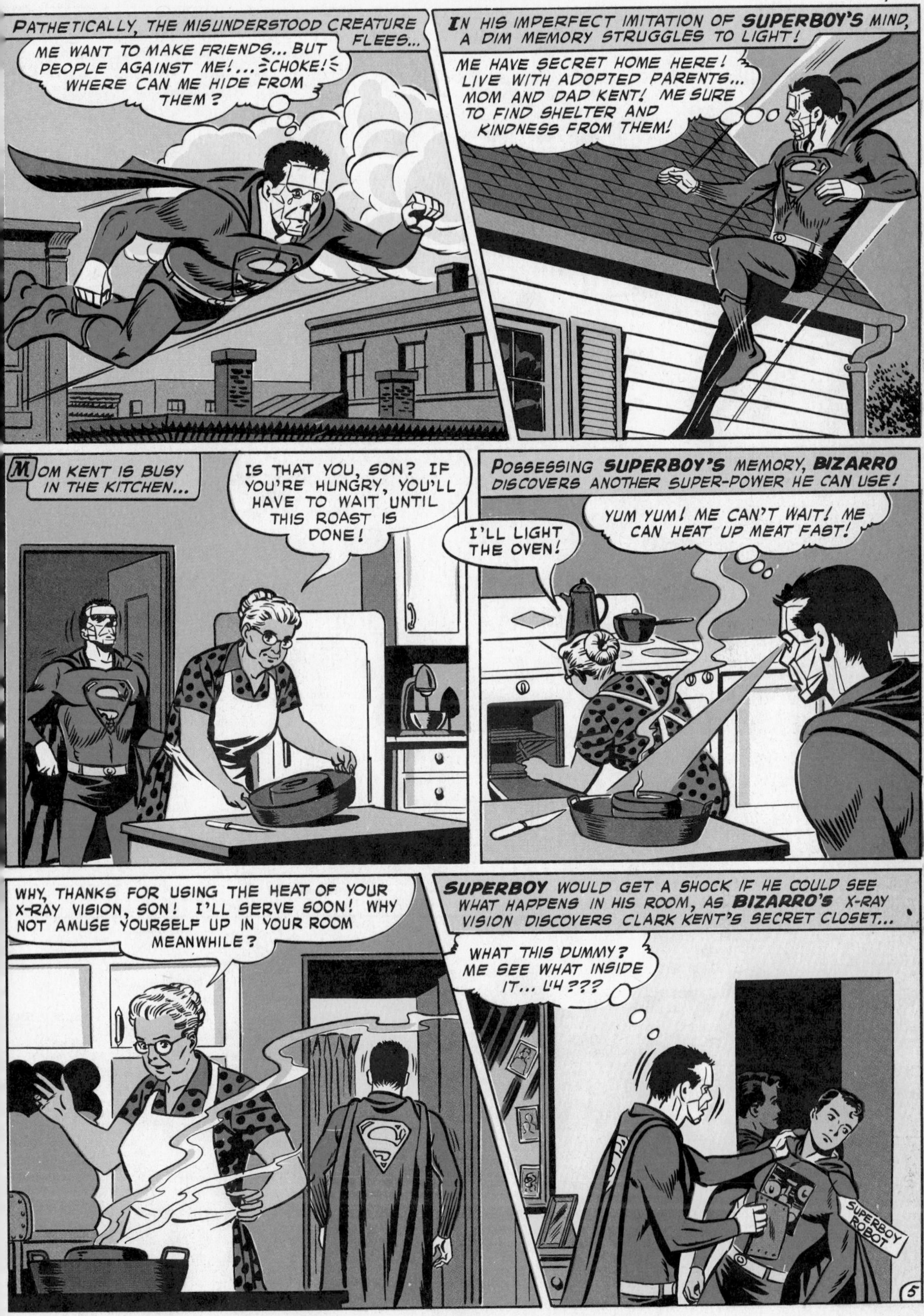
PATHETICALLY, THE MISUNDERSTOOD CREATURE FLEES...
ME WANT TO MAKE FRIENDS... BUT PEOPLE AGAINST ME!... CHOKE! WHERE CAN ME HIDE FROM THEM?
IN HIS IMPERFECT IMITATION OF SUPERBOY'S MIND, A DIM MEMORY STRUGGLES TO LIGHT!
ME HAVE SECRET HOME HERE! LIVE WITH ADOPTED PARENTS... MOM AND DAD KENT! ME SURE TO FIND SHELTER AND KINDNESS FROM THEM!
MOM KENT IS BUSY IN THE KITCHEN...
IS THAT YOU, SON? IF YOU'RE HUNGRY, YOU'LL HAVE TO WAIT UNTIL THIS ROAST IS DONE!
POSSESSING SUPERBOY'S MEMORY, BIZARRO DISCOVERS ANOTHER SUPER-POWER HE CAN USE!
I'LL LIGHT THE OVEN!
YUM YUM! ME CAN'T WAIT! ME CAN HEAT UP MEAT FAST!
WHY, THANKS FOR USING THE HEAT OF YOUR X-RAY VISION, SON! I'LL SERVE SOON! WHY NOT AMUSE YOURSELF UP IN YOUR ROOM MEANWHILE?
SUPERBOY WOULD GET A SHOCK IF HE COULD SEE WHAT HAPPENS IN HIS ROOM, AS BIZARRO'S X-RAY VISION DISCOVERS CLARK KENT'S SECRET CLOSET...
WHAT THIS DUMMY? ME SEE WHAT INSIDE IT... UH???
SUPERBOY ROBOT
5

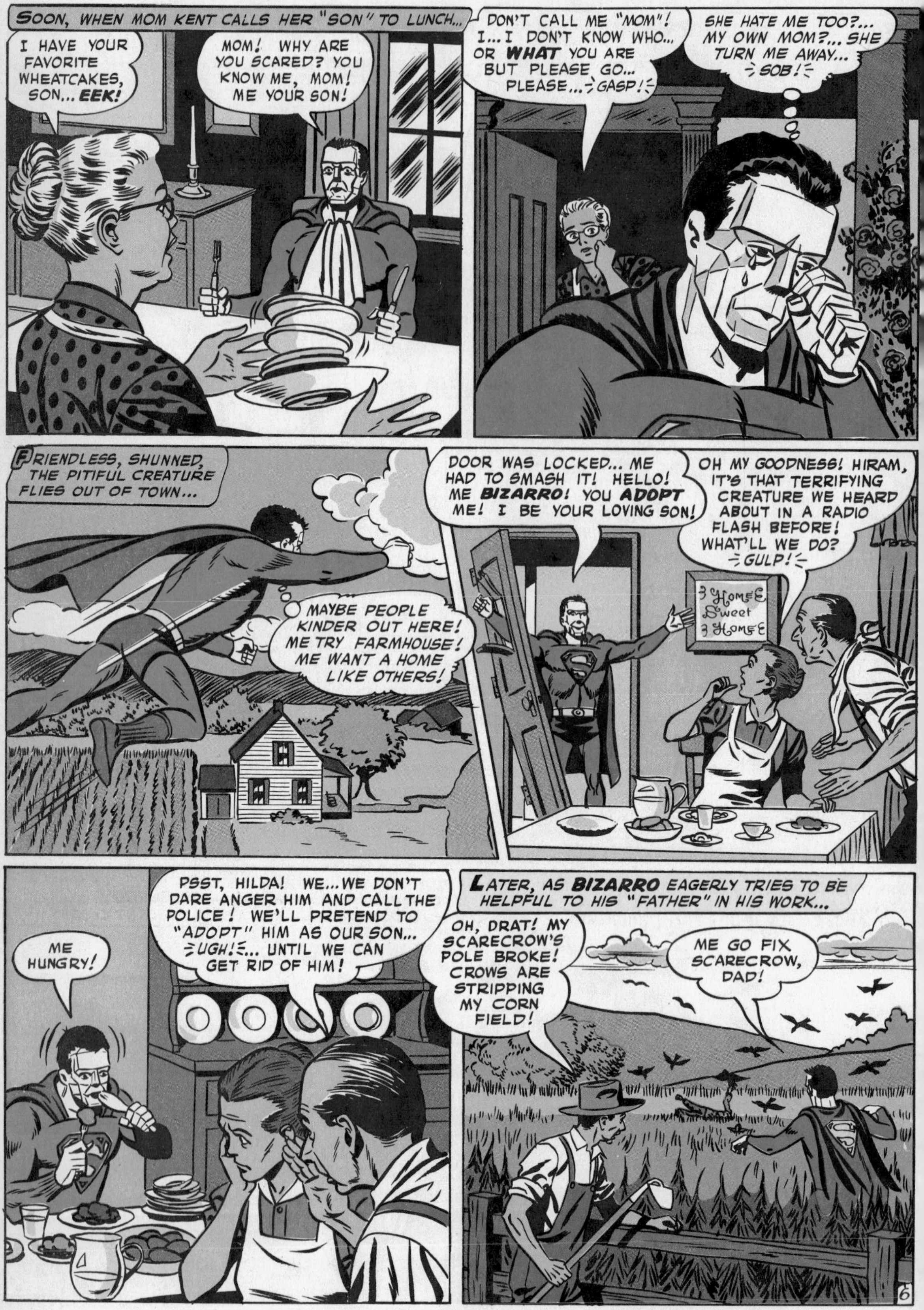
SOON, WHEN MOM KENT CALLS HER "SON" TO LUNCH...
I HAVE YOUR FAVORITE WHEATCAKES, SON... EEK!
MOM! WHY ARE YOU SCARED? YOU KNOW ME, MOM! ME YOUR SON!
DON'T CALL ME "MOM"! I...I DON'T KNOW WHO... OR WHAT YOU ARE BUT PLEASE GO... PLEASE... GASP!
SHE HATE ME TOO?... MY OWN MOM?... SHE TURN ME AWAY... SOB!
FRIENDLESS, SHUNNED, THE PITIFUL CREATURE FLIES OUT OF TOWN...
MAYBE PEOPLE KINDER OUT HERE! ME TRY FARMHOUSE! ME WANT A HOME LIKE OTHERS!
DOOR WAS LOCKED... ME HAD TO SMASH IT! HELLO! ME BIZARRO! YOU ADOPT ME! I BE YOUR LOVING SON!
OH MY GOODNESS! HIRAM, IT'S THAT TERRIFYING CREATURE WE HEARD ABOUT IN A RADIO FLASH BEFORE! WHAT'LL WE DO? GULP!
HOME SWEET HOME
ME HUNGRY!
PSST, HILDA! WE...WE DON'T DARE ANGER HIM AND CALL THE POLICE! WE'LL PRETEND TO "ADOPT" HIM AS OUR SON... UGH!... UNTIL WE CAN GET RID OF HIM!
LATER, AS BIZARRO EAGERLY TRIES TO BE HELPFUL TO HIS "FATHER" IN HIS WORK...
OH, DRAT! MY SCARECROW'S POLE BROKE! CROWS ARE STRIPPING MY CORN FIELD!
ME GO FIX SCARECROW, DAD!
6

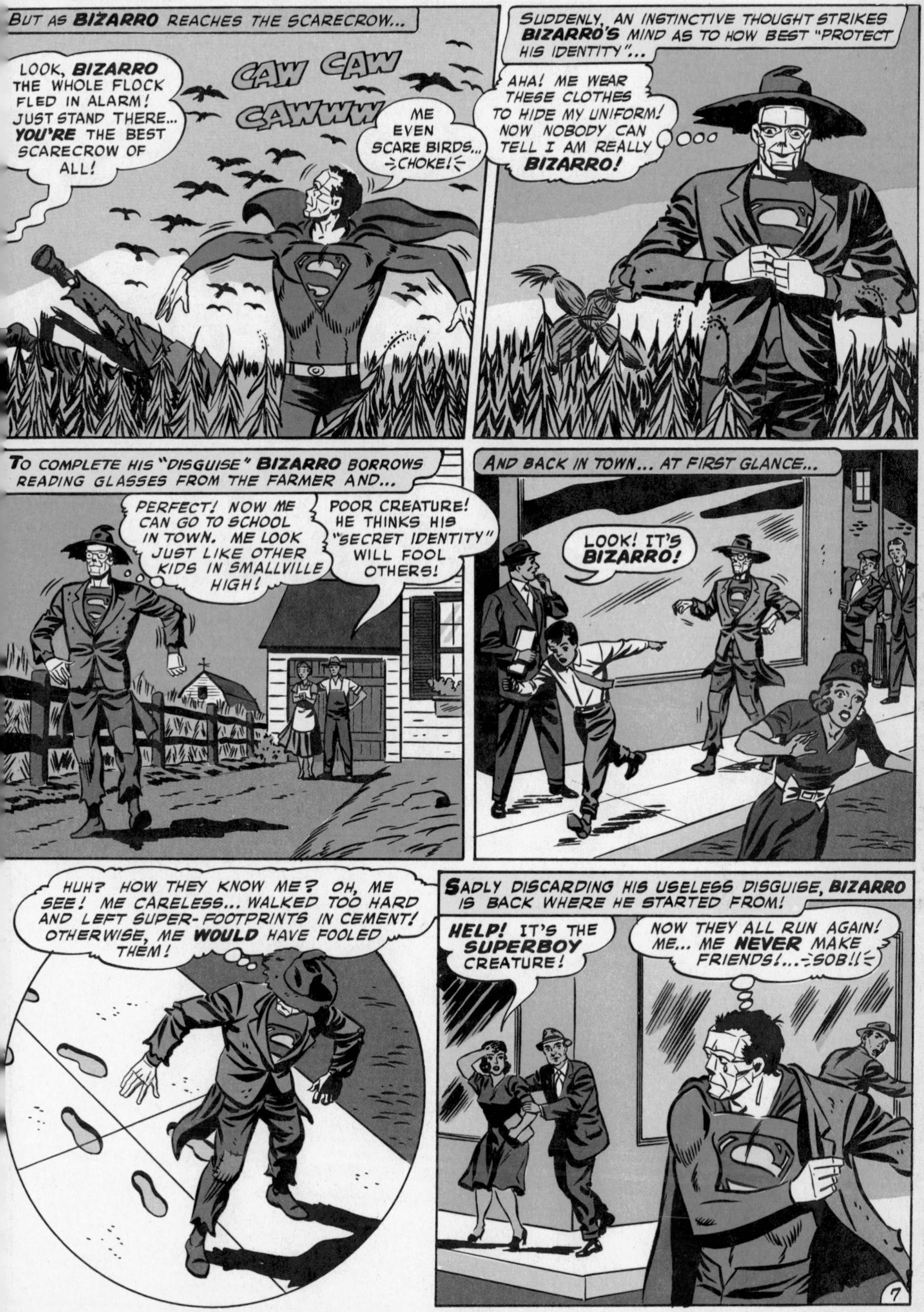

BUT AS BIZARRO REACHES THE SCARECROW...
LOOK, BIZARRO THE WHOLE FLOCK FLED IN ALARM! JUST STAND THERE... YOU'RE THE BEST SCARECROW OF ALL!
CAW CAW
CAWWW
ME EVEN SCARE BIRDS... CHOKE!
SUDDENLY, AN INSTINCTIVE THOUGHT STRIKES BIZARRO'S MIND AS TO HOW BEST "PROTECT HIS IDENTITY"...
AHA! ME WEAR THESE CLOTHES TO HIDE MY UNIFORM! NOW NOBODY CAN TELL I AM REALLY BIZARRO!
TO COMPLETE HIS "DISGUISE" BIZARRO BORROWS READING GLASSES FROM THE FARMER AND...
PERFECT! NOW ME CAN GO TO SCHOOL IN TOWN. ME LOOK JUST LIKE OTHER KIDS IN SMALLVILLE HIGH!
POOR CREATURE! HE THINKS HIS "SECRET IDENTITY" WILL FOOL OTHERS!
AND BACK IN TOWN... AT FIRST GLANCE...
LOOK! IT'S BIZARRO!
HUH? HOW THEY KNOW ME? OH, ME SEE! ME CARELESS... WALKED TOO HARD AND LEFT SUPER-FOOTPRINTS IN CEMENT! OTHERWISE, ME WOULD HAVE FOOLED THEM!
SADLY DISCARDING HIS USELESS DISGUISE, BIZARRO IS BACK WHERE HE STARTED FROM!
HELP! IT'S THE SUPERBOY CREATURE!
NOW THEY ALL RUN AGAIN! ME... ME NEVER MAKE FRIENDS!... SOB!!
7

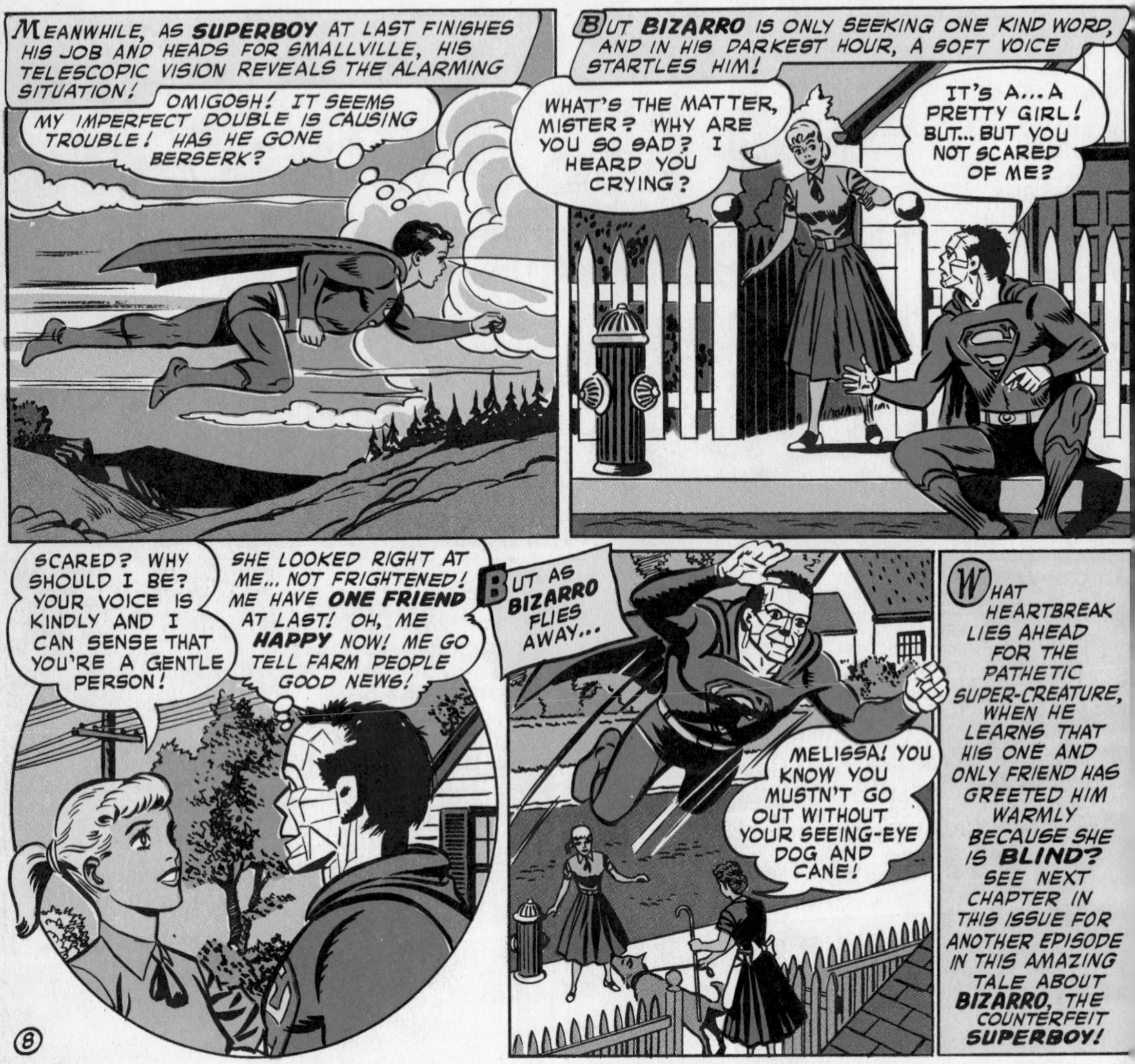
MEANWHILE, AS SUPERBOY AT LAST FINISHES HIS JOB AND HEADS FOR SMALLVILLE, HIS TELESCOPIC VISION REVEALS THE ALARMING SITUATION!
OMIGOSH! IT SEEMS MY IMPERFECT DOUBLE IS CAUSING TROUBLE! HAS HE GONE BERSERK?
BUT BIZARRO IS ONLY SEEKING ONE KIND WORD, AND IN HIS DARKEST HOUR, A SOFT VOICE STARTLES HIM!
WHAT'S THE MATTER, MISTER? WHY ARE YOU SO SAD? I HEARD YOU CRYING?
IT'S A...A PRETTY GIRL! BUT... BUT YOU NOT SCARED OF ME?
SCARED? WHY SHOULD I BE? YOUR VOICE IS KINDLY AND I CAN SENSE THAT YOU'RE A GENTLE PERSON!
SHE LOOKED RIGHT AT ME... NOT FRIGHTENED! ME HAVE ONE FRIEND AT LAST! OH, ME HAPPY NOW! ME GO TELL FARM PEOPLE GOOD NEWS!
8
BUT AS BIZARRO FLIES AWAY...
MELISSA! YOU KNOW YOU MUSTN'T GO OUT WITHOUT YOUR SEEING-EYE DOG AND CANE!
WHAT HEARTBREAK LIES AHEAD FOR THE PATHETIC SUPER-CREATURE, WHEN HE LEARNS THAT HIS ONE AND ONLY FRIEND HAS GREETED HIM WARMLY BECAUSE SHE IS BLIND? SEE NEXT CHAPTER IN THIS ISSUE FOR ANOTHER EPISODE IN THIS AMAZING TALE ABOUT BIZARRO, THE COUNTERFEIT SUPERBOY!

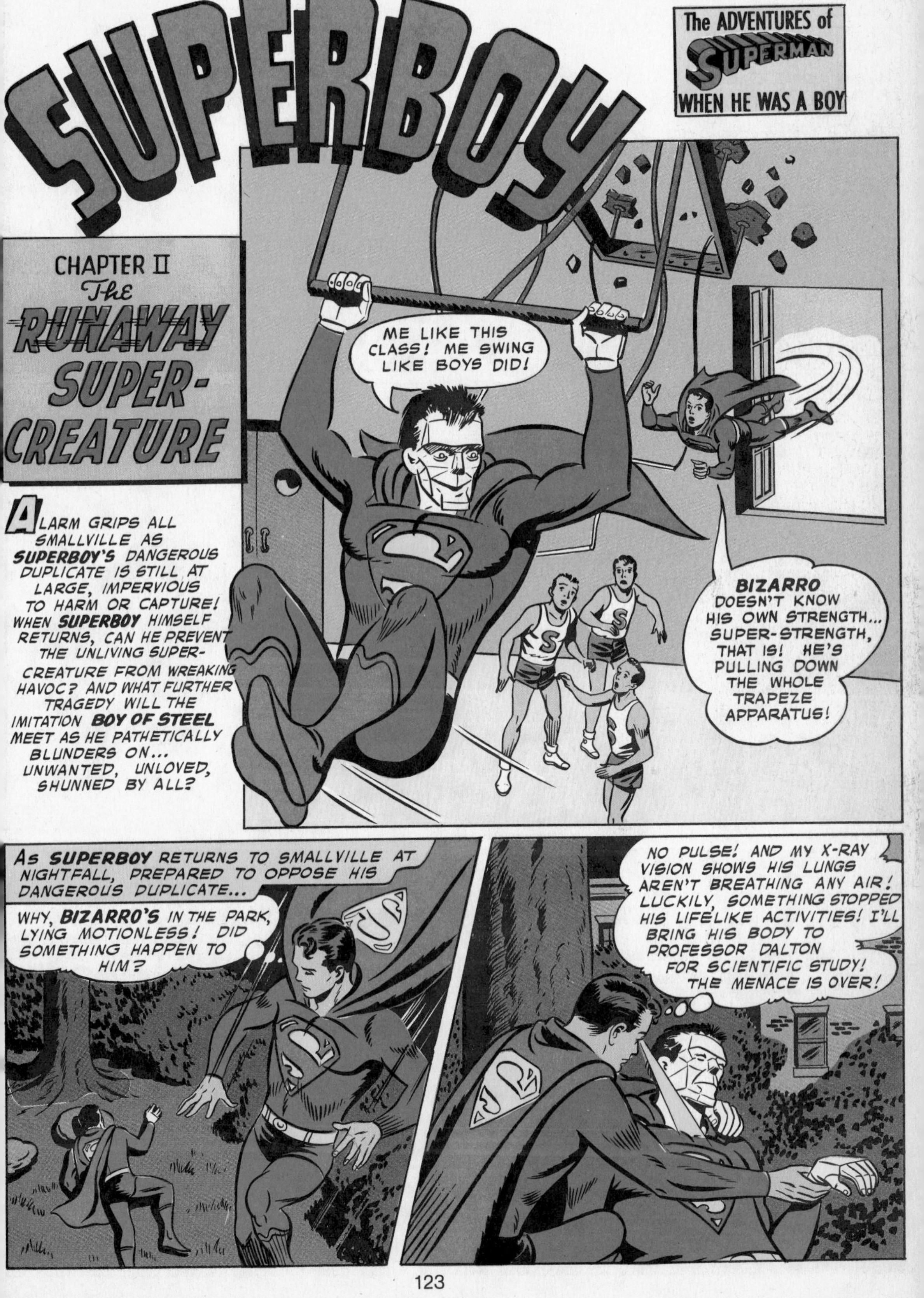
SUPERBOY
The ADVENTURES of SUPERMAN WHEN HE WAS A BOY
CHAPTER II The RUNAWAY SUPER-CREATURE
ALARM GRIPS ALL SMALLVILLE AS SUPERBOY'S DANGEROUS DUPLICATE IS STILL AT LARGE, IMPERVIOUS TO HARM OR CAPTURE! WHEN SUPERBOY HIMSELF RETURNS, CAN HE PREVENT THE UNLIVING SUPER-CREATURE FROM WREAKING HAVOC? AND WHAT FURTHER TRAGEDY WILL THE IMITATION BOY OF STEEL MEET AS HE PATHETICALLY BLUNDERS ON... UNWANTED, UNLOVED, SHUNNED BY ALL?
ME LIKE THIS CLASS! ME SWING LIKE BOYS DID!
BIZARRO DOESN'T KNOW HIS OWN STRENGTH... SUPER-STRENGTH, THAT IS! HE'S PULLING DOWN THE WHOLE TRAPEZE APPARATUS!
AS SUPERBOY RETURNS TO SMALLVILLE AT NIGHTFALL, PREPARED TO OPPOSE HIS DANGEROUS DUPLICATE...
WHY, BIZARRO'S IN THE PARK, LYING MOTIONLESS! DID SOMETHING HAPPEN TO HIM?
NO PULSE! AND MY X-RAY VISION SHOWS HIS LUNGS AREN'T BREATHING ANY AIR! LUCKILY, SOMETHING STOPPED HIS LIFELIKE ACTIVITIES! I'LL BRING HIS BODY TO PROFESSOR DALTON FOR SCIENTIFIC STUDY! THE MENACE IS OVER!

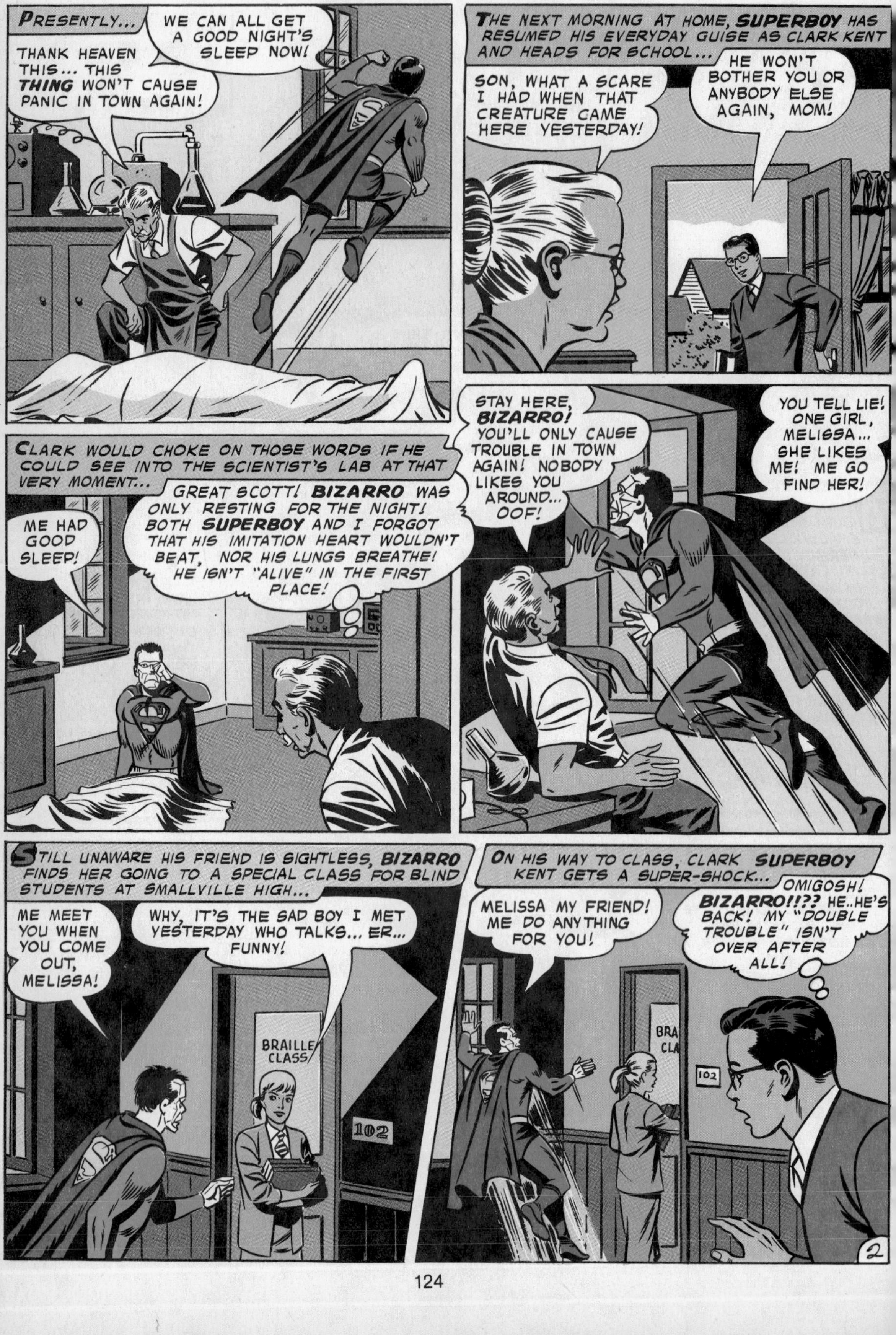
PRESENTLY...
THANK HEAVEN THIS... THIS THING WON'T CAUSE PANIC IN TOWN AGAIN!
WE CAN ALL GET A GOOD NIGHT'S SLEEP NOW!
THE NEXT MORNING AT HOME, SUPERBOY HAS RESUMED HIS EVERYDAY GUISE AS CLARK KENT AND HEADS FOR SCHOOL...
SON, WHAT A SCARE I HAD WHEN THAT CREATURE CAME HERE YESTERDAY!
HE WON'T BOTHER YOU OR ANYBODY ELSE AGAIN, MOM!
CLARK WOULD CHOKE ON THOSE WORDS IF HE COULD SEE INTO THE SCIENTIST'S LAB AT THAT VERY MOMENT...
ME HAD GOOD SLEEP!
GREAT SCOTT! BIZARRO WAS ONLY RESTING FOR THE NIGHT! BOTH SUPERBOY AND I FORGOT THAT HIS IMITATION HEART WOULDN'T BEAT, NOR HIS LUNGS BREATHE! HE ISN'T "ALIVE" IN THE FIRST PLACE!
STAY HERE, BIZARRO! YOU'LL ONLY CAUSE TROUBLE IN TOWN AGAIN! NOBODY LIKES YOU AROUND... OOF!
YOU TELL LIE! ONE GIRL, MELISSA... SHE LIKES ME! ME GO FIND HER!
STILL UNAWARE HIS FRIEND IS SIGHTLESS, BIZARRO FINDS HER GOING TO A SPECIAL CLASS FOR BLIND STUDENTS AT SMALLVILLE HIGH...
ME MEET YOU WHEN YOU COME OUT, MELISSA!
WHY, IT'S THE SAD BOY I MET YESTERDAY WHO TALKS... ER... FUNNY!
BRAILLE CLASS
102
ON HIS WAY TO CLASS, CLARK SUPERBOY KENT GETS A SUPER-SHOCK...
MELISSA MY FRIEND! ME DO ANYTHING FOR YOU!
OMIGOSH! BIZARRO!!?? HE..HE'S BACK! MY "DOUBLE TROUBLE" ISN'T OVER AFTER ALL!
102
2

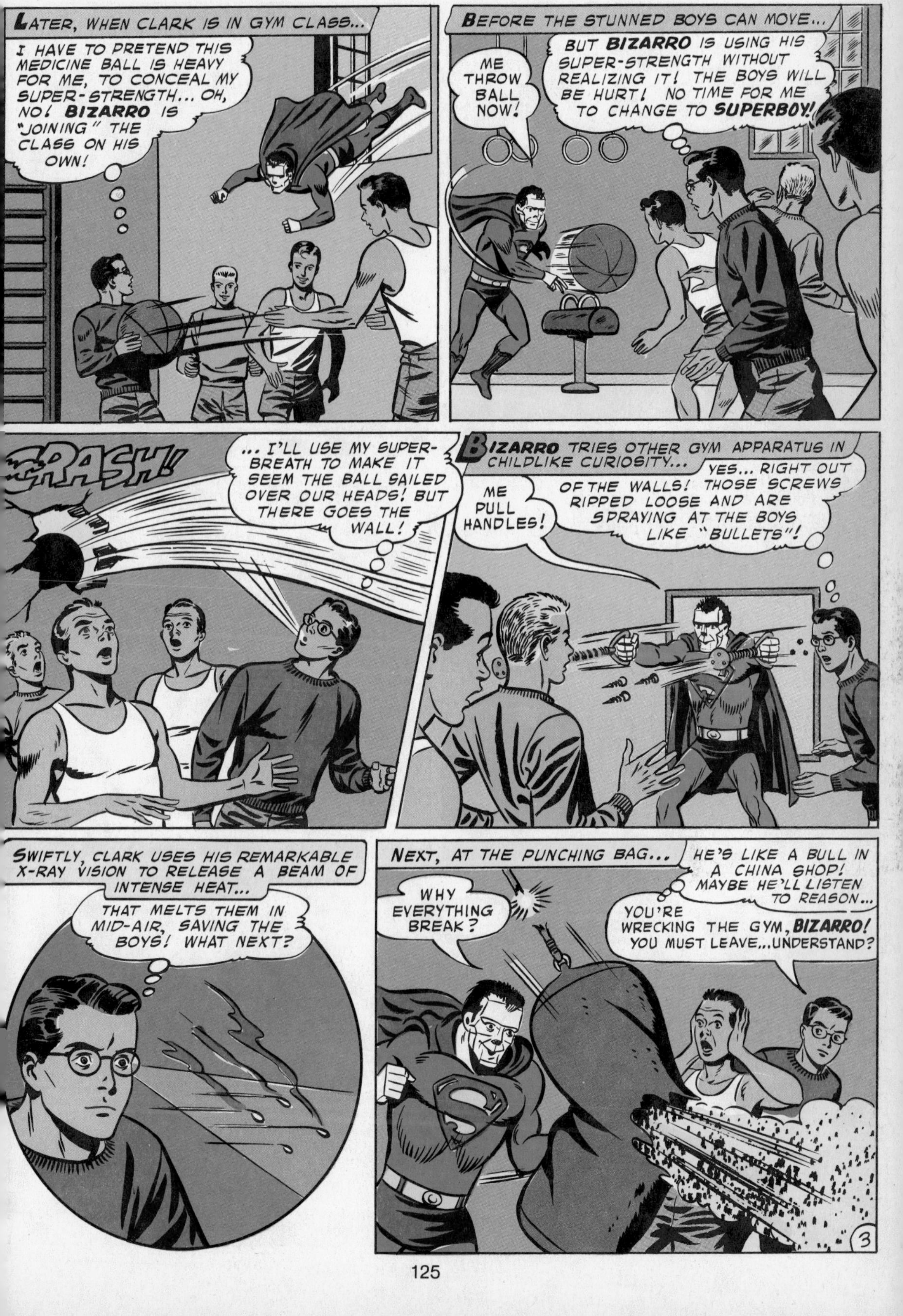
LATER, WHEN CLARK IS IN GYM CLASS...
I HAVE TO PRETEND THIS MEDICINE BALL IS HEAVY FOR ME, TO CONCEAL MY SUPER-STRENGTH... OH, NO! BIZARRO IS "JOINING" THE CLASS ON HIS OWN!
BEFORE THE STUNNED BOYS CAN MOVE...
ME THROW BALL NOW!
BUT BIZARRO IS USING HIS SUPER-STRENGTH WITHOUT REALIZING IT! THE BOYS WILL BE HURT! NO TIME FOR ME TO CHANGE TO SUPERBOY!
CRASH!
... I'LL USE MY SUPER-BREATH TO MAKE IT SEEM THE BALL SAILED OVER OUR HEADS! BUT THERE GOES THE WALL!
BIZARRO TRIES OTHER GYM APPARATUS IN CHILDLIKE CURIOSITY...
ME PULL HANDLES!
YES... RIGHT OUT OF THE WALLS! THOSE SCREWS RIPPED LOOSE AND ARE SPRAYING AT THE BOYS LIKE "BULLETS"!
SWIFTLY, CLARK USES HIS REMARKABLE X-RAY VISION TO RELEASE A BEAM OF INTENSE HEAT...
THAT MELTS THEM IN MID-AIR, SAVING THE BOYS! WHAT NEXT?
NEXT, AT THE PUNCHING BAG...
WHY EVERYTHING BREAK?
HE'S LIKE A BULL IN A CHINA SHOP! MAYBE HE'LL LISTEN TO REASON...
YOU'RE WRECKING THE GYM, BIZARRO! YOU MUST LEAVE...UNDERSTAND?
3

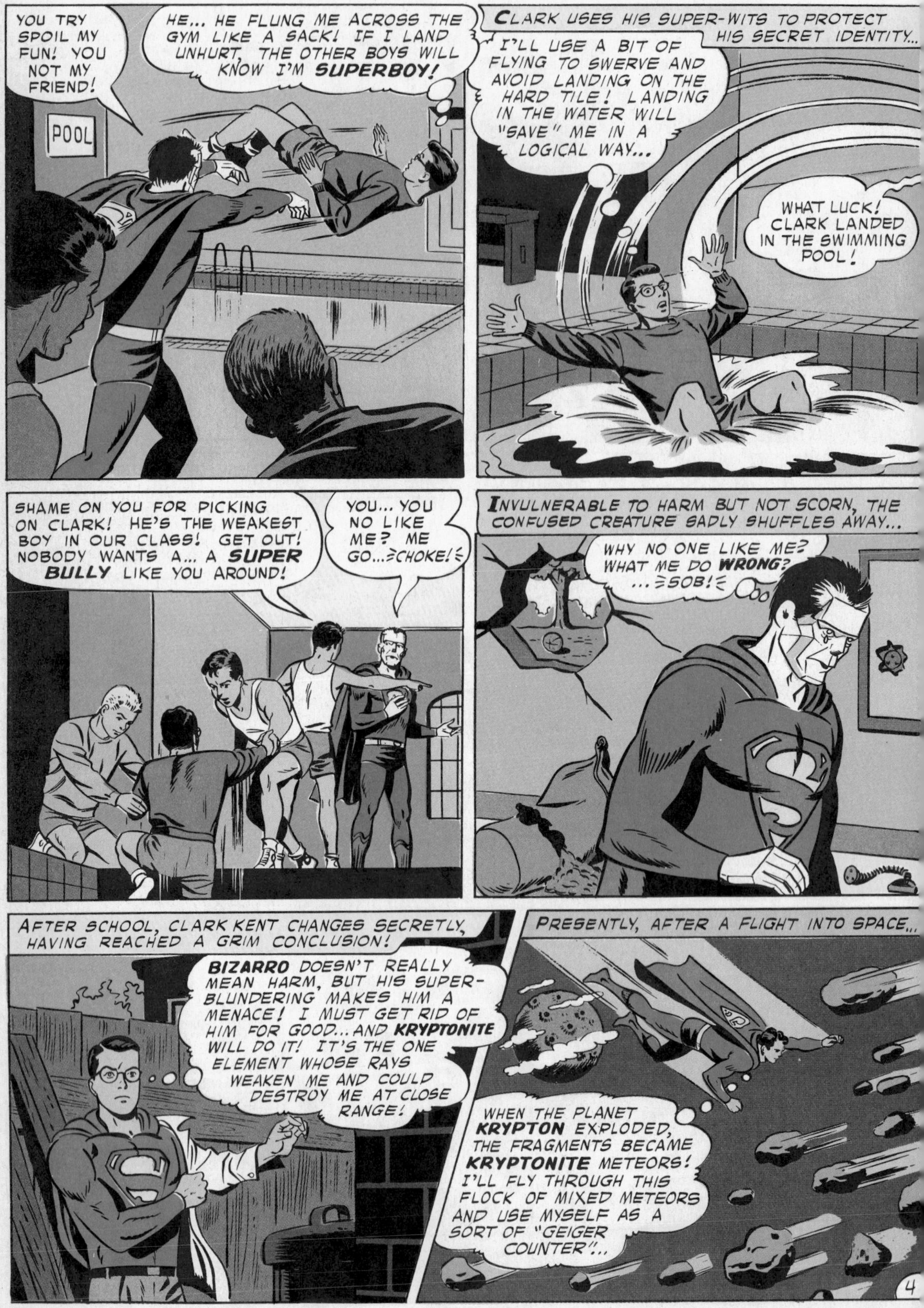
YOU TRY SPOIL MY FUN! YOU NOT MY FRIEND!
HE... HE FLUNG ME ACROSS THE GYM LIKE A SACK! IF I LAND UNHURT, THE OTHER BOYS WILL KNOW I'M SUPERBOY!
POOL
CLARK USES HIS SUPER-WITS TO PROTECT HIS SECRET IDENTITY...
I'LL USE A BIT OF FLYING TO SWERVE AND AVOID LANDING ON THE HARD TILE! LANDING IN THE WATER WILL "SAVE" ME IN A LOGICAL WAY...
WHAT LUCK! CLARK LANDED IN THE SWIMMING POOL!
SHAME ON YOU FOR PICKING ON CLARK! HE'S THE WEAKEST BOY IN OUR CLASS! GET OUT! NOBODY WANTS A... A SUPER BULLY LIKE YOU AROUND!
YOU... YOU NO LIKE ME? ME GO... CHOKE!
INVULNERABLE TO HARM BUT NOT SCORN, THE CONFUSED CREATURE SADLY SHUFFLES AWAY...
WHY NO ONE LIKE ME? WHAT ME DO WRONG? ...SOB!
AFTER SCHOOL, CLARK KENT CHANGES SECRETLY, HAVING REACHED A GRIM CONCLUSION!
BIZARRO DOESN'T REALLY MEAN HARM, BUT HIS SUPER-BLUNDERING MAKES HIM A MENACE! I MUST GET RID OF HIM FOR GOOD... AND KRYPTONITE WILL DO IT! IT'S THE ONE ELEMENT WHOSE RAYS WEAKEN ME AND COULD DESTROY ME AT CLOSE RANGE!
PRESENTLY, AFTER A FLIGHT INTO SPACE...
WHEN THE PLANET KRYPTON EXPLODED, THE FRAGMENTS BECAME KRYPTONITE METEORS! I'LL FLY THROUGH THIS FLOCK OF MIXED METEORS AND USE MYSELF AS A SORT OF "GEIGER COUNTER"...
4

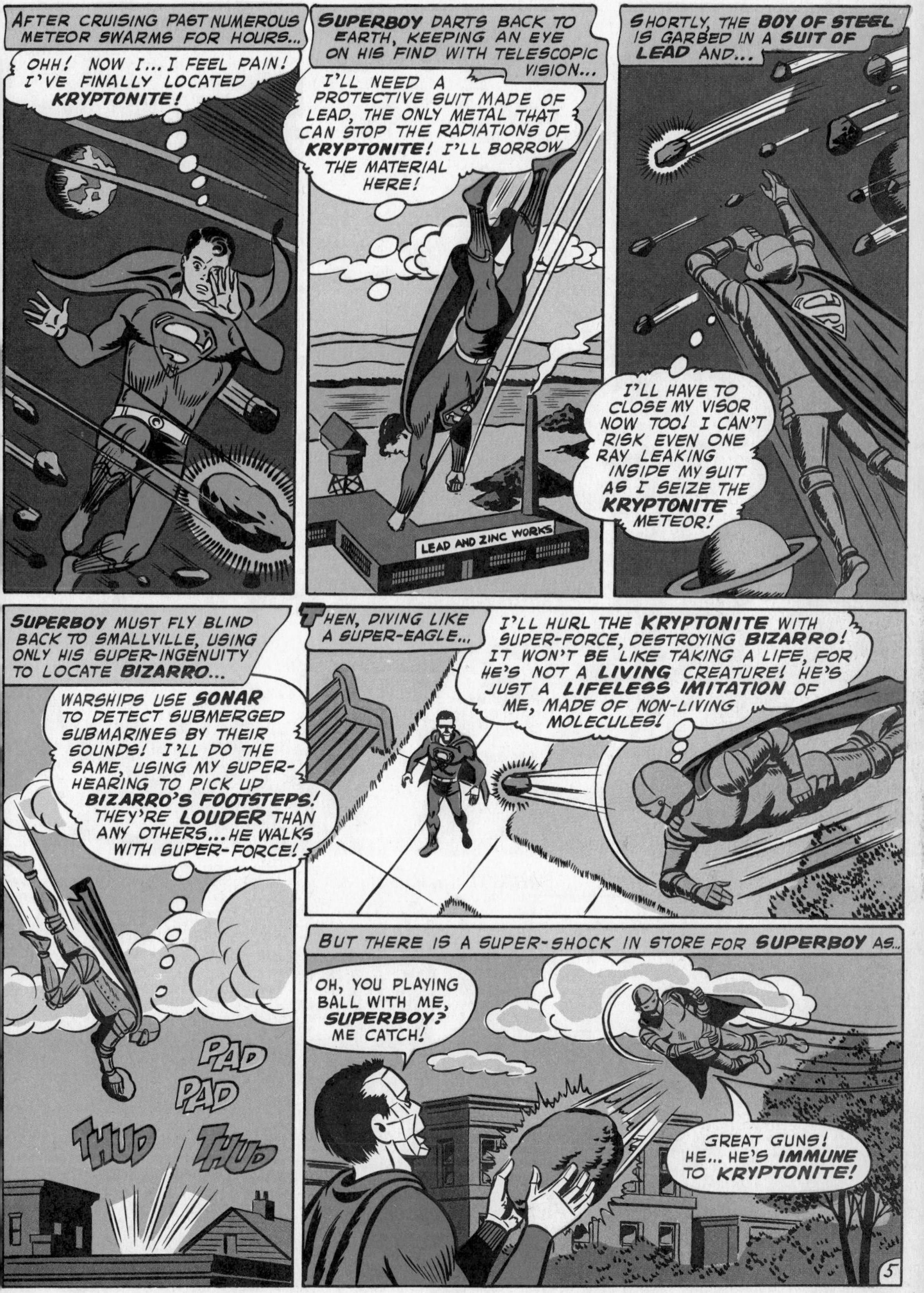
AFTER CRUISING PAST NUMEROUS METEOR SWARMS FOR HOURS...
OHH! NOW I... I FEEL PAIN! I'VE FINALLY LOCATED KRYPTONITE!
SUPERBOY DARTS BACK TO EARTH, KEEPING AN EYE ON HIS FIND WITH TELESCOPIC VISION...
I'LL NEED A PROTECTIVE SUIT MADE OF LEAD, THE ONLY METAL THAT CAN STOP THE RADIATIONS OF KRYPTONITE! I'LL BORROW THE MATERIAL HERE!
LEAD AND ZINC WORKS
SHORTLY, THE BOY OF STEEL IS GARBED IN A SUIT OF LEAD AND...
I'LL HAVE TO CLOSE MY VISOR NOW TOO! I CAN'T RISK EVEN ONE RAY LEAKING INSIDE MY SUIT AS I SEIZE THE KRYPTONITE METEOR!
SUPERBOY MUST FLY BLIND BACK TO SMALLVILLE, USING ONLY HIS SUPER-INGENUITY TO LOCATE BIZARRO...
WARSHIPS USE SONAR TO DETECT SUBMERGED SUBMARINES BY THEIR SOUNDS! I'LL DO THE SAME, USING MY SUPER-HEARING TO PICK UP BIZARRO'S FOOTSTEPS! THEY'RE LOUDER THAN ANY OTHERS... HE WALKS WITH SUPER-FORCE!
PAD
PAD
THUD
THUD
THEN, DIVING LIKE A SUPER-EAGLE...
I'LL HURL THE KRYPTONITE WITH SUPER-FORCE, DESTROYING BIZARRO! IT WON'T BE LIKE TAKING A LIFE, FOR HE'S NOT A LIVING CREATURE! HE'S JUST A LIFELESS IMITATION OF ME, MADE OF NON-LIVING MOLECULES!
BUT THERE IS A SUPER-SHOCK IN STORE FOR SUPERBOY AS...
OH, YOU PLAYING BALL WITH ME, SUPERBOY? ME CATCH!
GREAT GUNS! HE... HE'S IMMUNE TO KRYPTONITE!
5

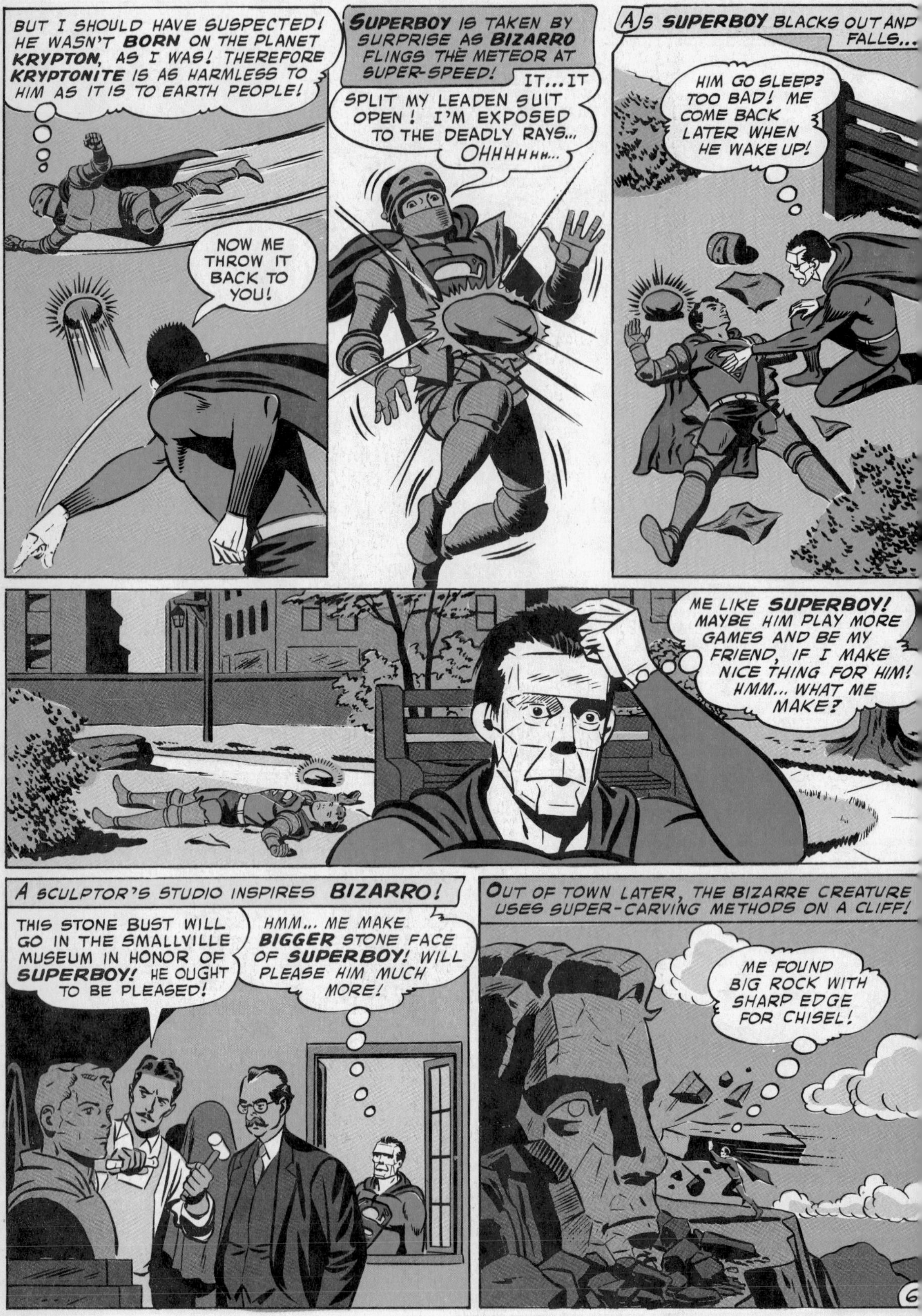
BUT I SHOULD HAVE SUSPECTED! HE WASN'T BORN ON THE PLANET KRYPTON, AS I WAS! THEREFORE KRYPTONITE IS AS HARMLESS TO HIM AS IT IS TO EARTH PEOPLE!
NOW ME THROW IT BACK TO YOU!
SUPERBOY IS TAKEN BY SURPRISE AS BIZARRO FLINGS THE METEOR AT SUPER-SPEED!
IT...IT SPLIT MY LEADEN SUIT OPEN! I'M EXPOSED TO THE DEADLY RAYS... OHHHHHH...
AS SUPERBOY BLACKS OUT AND FALLS...
HIM GO SLEEP? TOO BAD! ME COME BACK LATER WHEN HE WAKE UP!
ME LIKE SUPERBOY! MAYBE HIM PLAY MORE GAMES AND BE MY FRIEND, IF I MAKE NICE THING FOR HIM! HMM... WHAT ME MAKE?
A SCULPTOR'S STUDIO INSPIRES BIZARRO!
THIS STONE BUST WILL GO IN THE SMALLVILLE MUSEUM IN HONOR OF SUPERBOY! HE OUGHT TO BE PLEASED!
HMM... ME MAKE BIGGER STONE FACE OF SUPERBOY! WILL PLEASE HIM MUCH MORE!
OUT OF TOWN LATER, THE BIZARRE CREATURE USES SUPER-CARVING METHODS ON A CLIFF!
ME FOUND BIG ROCK WITH SHARP EDGE FOR CHISEL!
6

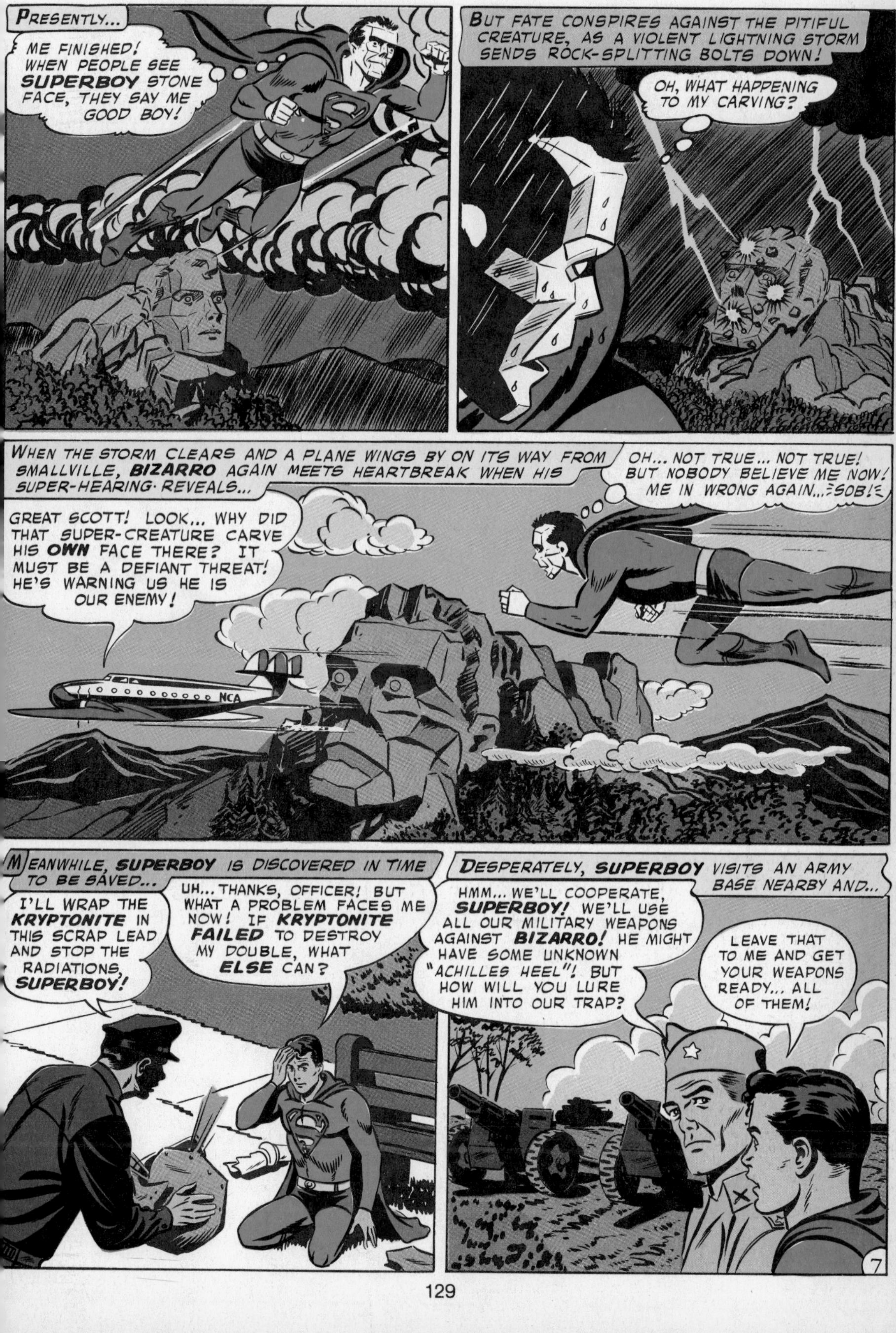
PRESENTLY...
ME FINISHED! WHEN PEOPLE SEE SUPERBOY STONE FACE, THEY SAY ME GOOD BOY!
BUT FATE CONSPIRES AGAINST THE PITIFUL CREATURE, AS A VIOLENT LIGHTNING STORM SENDS ROCK-SPLITTING BOLTS DOWN!
OH, WHAT HAPPENING TO MY CARVING?
WHEN THE STORM CLEARS AND A PLANE WINGS BY ON ITS WAY FROM SMALLVILLE, BIZARRO AGAIN MEETS HEARTBREAK WHEN HIS SUPER-HEARING REVEALS...
GREAT SCOTT! LOOK... WHY DID THAT SUPER-CREATURE CARVE HIS OWN FACE THERE? IT MUST BE A DEFIANT THREAT! HE'S WARNING US HE IS OUR ENEMY!
OH... NOT TRUE... NOT TRUE! BUT NOBODY BELIEVE ME NOW! ME IN WRONG AGAIN... SOB!
NCA
MEANWHILE, SUPERBOY IS DISCOVERED IN TIME TO BE SAVED...
I'LL WRAP THE KRYPTONITE IN THIS SCRAP LEAD AND STOP THE RADIATIONS, SUPERBOY!
UH... THANKS, OFFICER! BUT WHAT A PROBLEM FACES ME NOW! IF KRYPTONITE FAILED TO DESTROY MY DOUBLE, WHAT ELSE CAN?
DESPERATELY, SUPERBOY VISITS AN ARMY BASE NEARBY AND...
HMM... WE'LL COOPERATE, SUPERBOY! WE'LL USE ALL OUR MILITARY WEAPONS AGAINST BIZARRO! HE MIGHT HAVE SOME UNKNOWN "ACHILLES HEEL"! BUT HOW WILL YOU LURE HIM INTO OUR TRAP?
LEAVE THAT TO ME AND GET YOUR WEAPONS READY... ALL OF THEM!
7

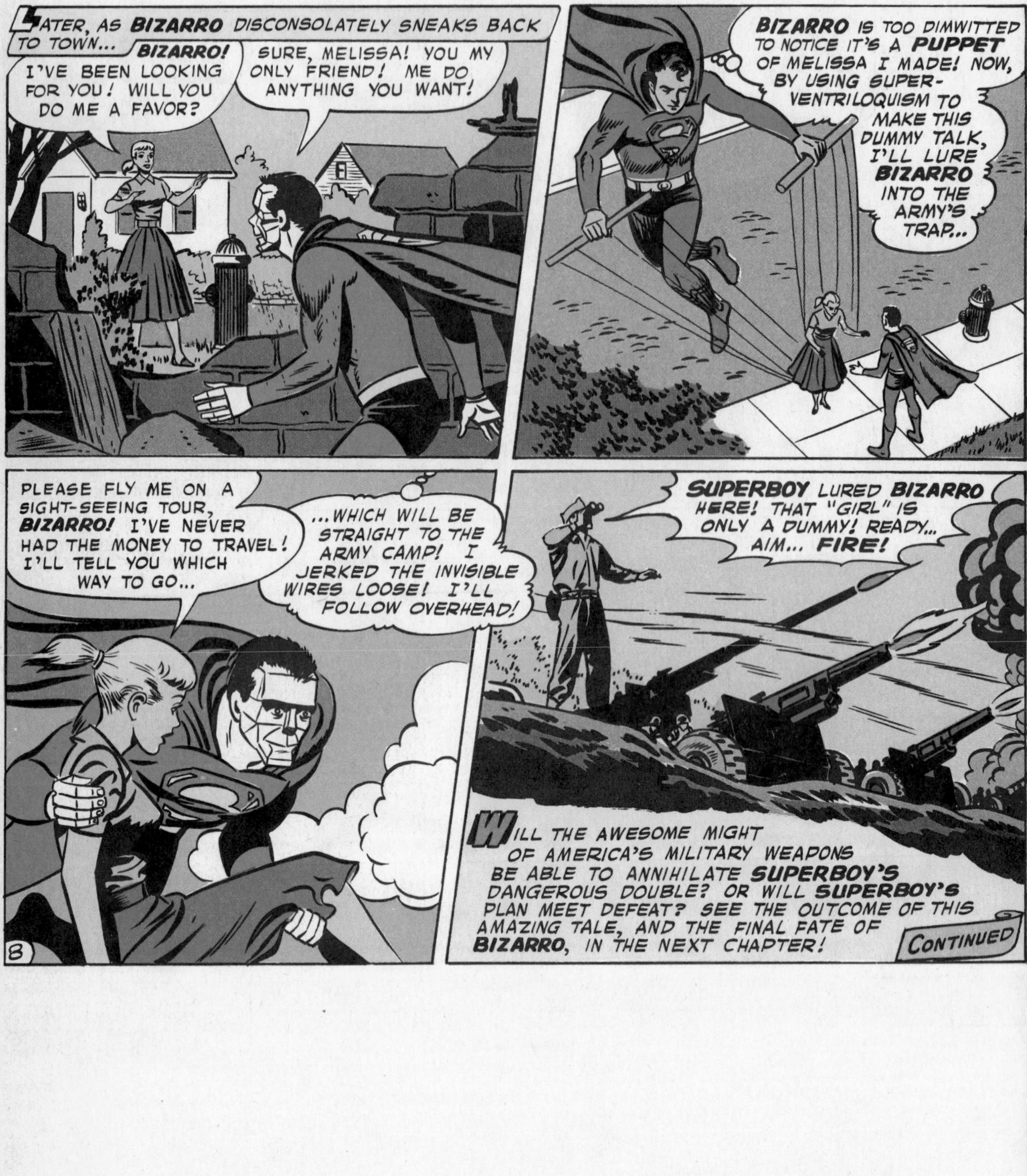
LATER, AS BIZARRO DISCONSOLATELY SNEAKS BACK TO TOWN...
BIZARRO! I'VE BEEN LOOKING FOR YOU! WILL YOU DO ME A FAVOR?
SURE, MELISSA! YOU MY ONLY FRIEND! ME DO ANYTHING YOU WANT!
BIZARRO IS TOO DIMWITTED TO NOTICE IT'S A PUPPET OF MELISSA I MADE! NOW, BY USING SUPER-VENTRILOQUISM TO MAKE THIS DUMMY TALK, I'LL LURE BIZARRO INTO THE ARMY'S TRAP...
PLEASE FLY ME ON A SIGHT-SEEING TOUR, BIZARRO! I'VE NEVER HAD THE MONEY TO TRAVEL! I'LL TELL YOU WHICH WAY TO GO...
...WHICH WILL BE STRAIGHT TO THE ARMY CAMP! I JERKED THE INVISIBLE WIRES LOOSE! I'LL FOLLOW OVERHEAD!
8
SUPERBOY LURED BIZARRO HERE! THAT "GIRL" IS ONLY A DUMMY! READY... AIM... FIRE!
WILL THE AWESOME MIGHT OF AMERICA'S MILITARY WEAPONS BE ABLE TO ANNIHILATE SUPERBOY'S DANGEROUS DOUBLE? OR WILL SUPERBOY'S PLAN MEET DEFEAT? SEE THE OUTCOME OF THIS AMAZING TALE, AND THE FINAL FATE OF BIZARRO, IN THE NEXT CHAPTER!
CONTINUED

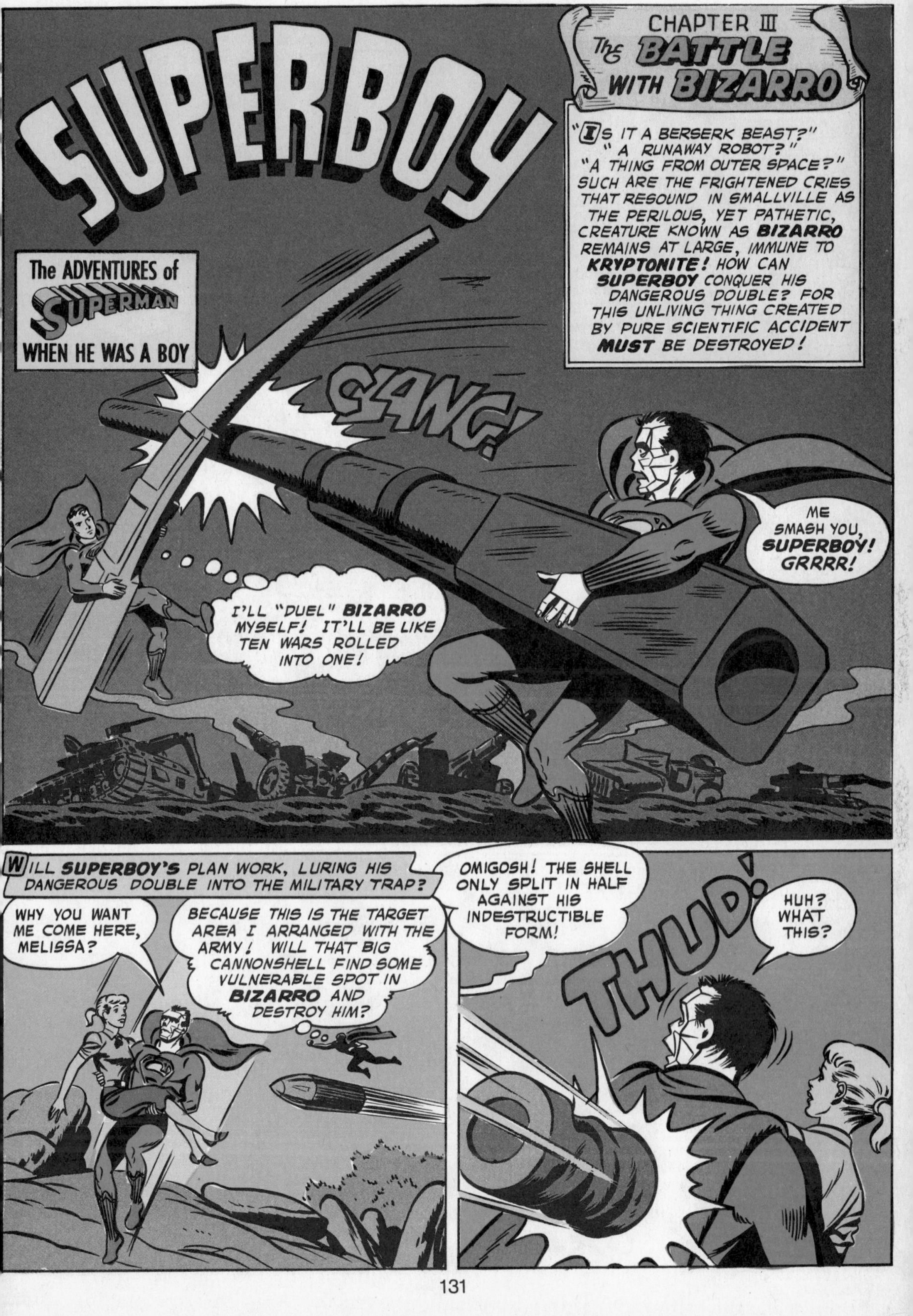
SUPERBOY
The ADVENTURES of SUPERMAN WHEN HE WAS A BOY
CHAPTER III
The BATTLE WITH BIZARRO
"IS IT A BERSERK BEAST?" "A RUNAWAY ROBOT?" "A THING FROM OUTER SPACE?" SUCH ARE THE FRIGHTENED CRIES THAT RESOUND IN SMALLVILLE AS THE PERILOUS, YET PATHETIC, CREATURE KNOWN AS BIZARRO REMAINS AT LARGE, IMMUNE TO KRYPTONITE! HOW CAN SUPERBOY CONQUER HIS DANGEROUS DOUBLE? FOR THIS UNLIVING THING CREATED BY PURE SCIENTIFIC ACCIDENT MUST BE DESTROYED!
CLANG!
ME SMASH YOU, SUPERBOY! GRRRR!
I'LL "DUEL" BIZARRO MYSELF! IT'LL BE LIKE TEN WARS ROLLED INTO ONE!
WILL SUPERBOY'S PLAN WORK, LURING HIS DANGEROUS DOUBLE INTO THE MILITARY TRAP?
WHY YOU WANT ME COME HERE, MELISSA?
BECAUSE THIS IS THE TARGET AREA I ARRANGED WITH THE ARMY! WILL THAT BIG CANNONSHELL FIND SOME VULNERABLE SPOT IN BIZARRO AND DESTROY HIM?
OMIGOSH! THE SHELL ONLY SPLIT IN HALF AGAINST HIS INDESTRUCTIBLE FORM!
THUD!
HUH? WHAT THIS?

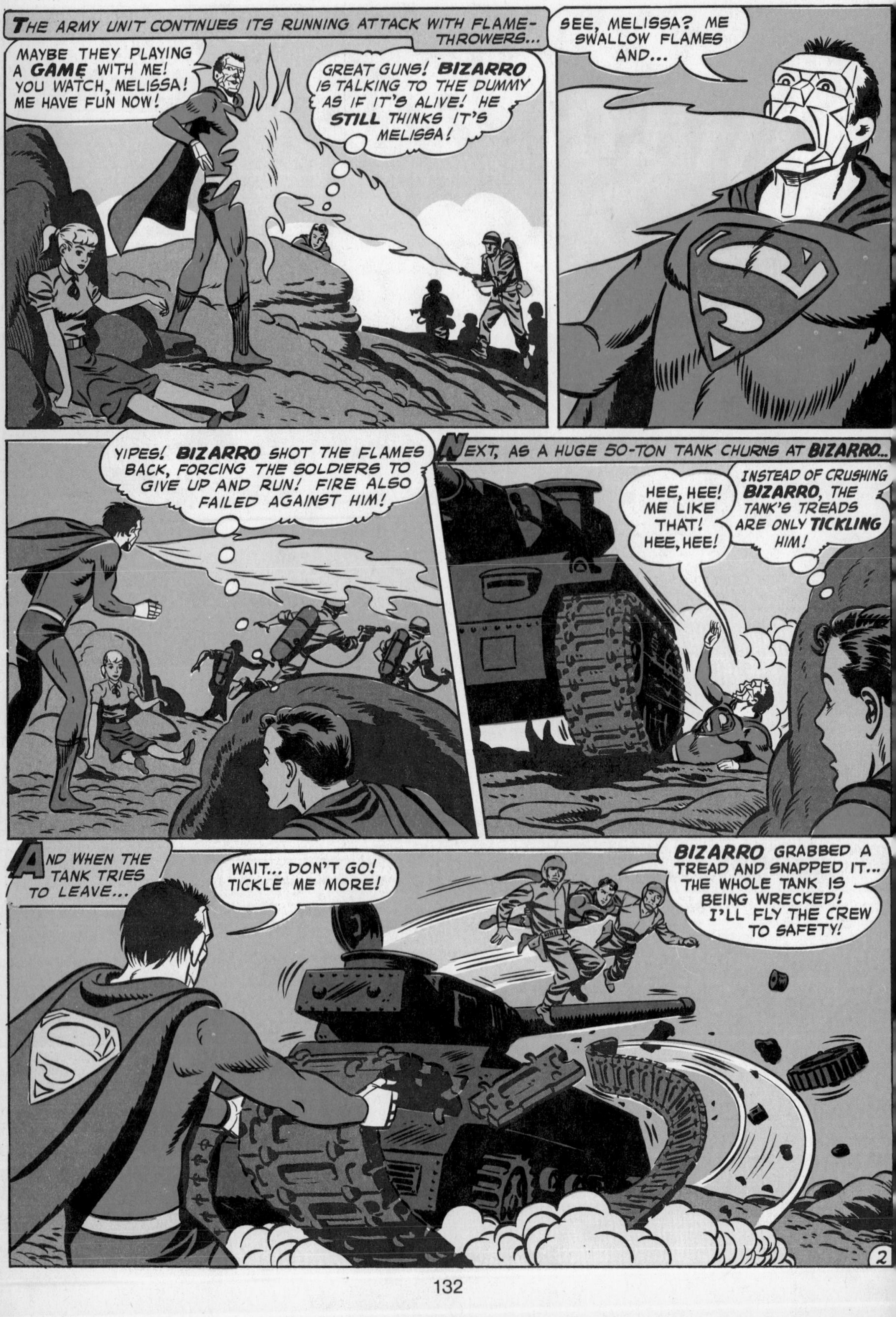

THE ARMY UNIT CONTINUES ITS RUNNING ATTACK WITH FLAME-THROWERS...
MAYBE THEY PLAYING A GAME WITH ME! YOU WATCH, MELISSA! ME HAVE FUN NOW!
GREAT GUNS! BIZARRO IS TALKING TO THE DUMMY AS IF IT'S ALIVE! HE STILL THINKS IT'S MELISSA!
SEE, MELISSA? ME SWALLOW FLAMES AND...
YIPES! BIZARRO SHOT THE FLAMES BACK, FORCING THE SOLDIERS TO GIVE UP AND RUN! FIRE ALSO FAILED AGAINST HIM!
NEXT, AS A HUGE 50-TON TANK CHURNS AT BIZARRO...
HEE, HEE! ME LIKE THAT! HEE, HEE!
INSTEAD OF CRUSHING BIZARRO, THE TANK'S TREADS ARE ONLY TICKLING HIM!
AND WHEN THE TANK TRIES TO LEAVE...
WAIT... DON'T GO! TICKLE ME MORE!
BIZARRO GRABBED A TREAD AND SNAPPED IT... THE WHOLE TANK IS BEING WRECKED! I'LL FLY THE CREW TO SAFETY!
2

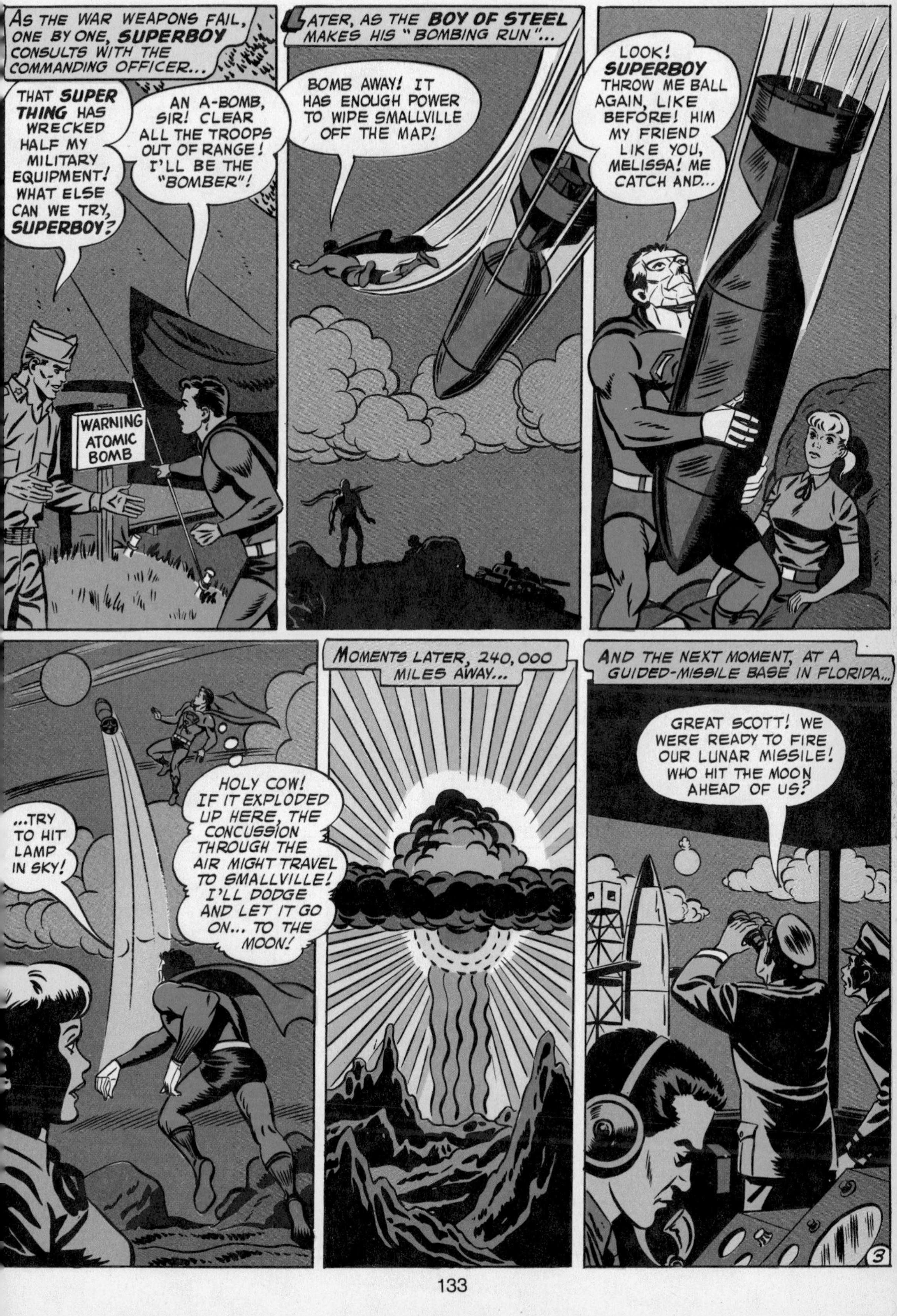
AS THE WAR WEAPONS FAIL, ONE BY ONE, SUPERBOY CONSULTS WITH THE COMMANDING OFFICER...
THAT SUPER THING HAS WRECKED HALF MY MILITARY EQUIPMENT! WHAT ELSE CAN WE TRY, SUPERBOY?
AN A-BOMB, SIR! CLEAR ALL THE TROOPS OUT OF RANGE! I'LL BE THE "BOMBER"!
WARNING ATOMIC BOMB
LATER, AS THE BOY OF STEEL MAKES HIS "BOMBING RUN"...
BOMB AWAY! IT HAS ENOUGH POWER TO WIPE SMALLVILLE OFF THE MAP!
LOOK! SUPERBOY THROW ME BALL AGAIN, LIKE BEFORE! HIM MY FRIEND LIKE YOU, MELISSA! ME CATCH AND...
...TRY TO HIT LAMP IN SKY!
HOLY COW! IF IT EXPLODED UP HERE, THE CONCUSSION THROUGH THE AIR MIGHT TRAVEL TO SMALLVILLE! I'LL DODGE AND LET IT GO ON... TO THE MOON!
MOMENTS LATER, 240,000 MILES AWAY...
AND THE NEXT MOMENT, AT A GUIDED-MISSILE BASE IN FLORIDA...
GREAT SCOTT! WE WERE READY TO FIRE OUR LUNAR MISSILE! WHO HIT THE MOON AHEAD OF US?
3

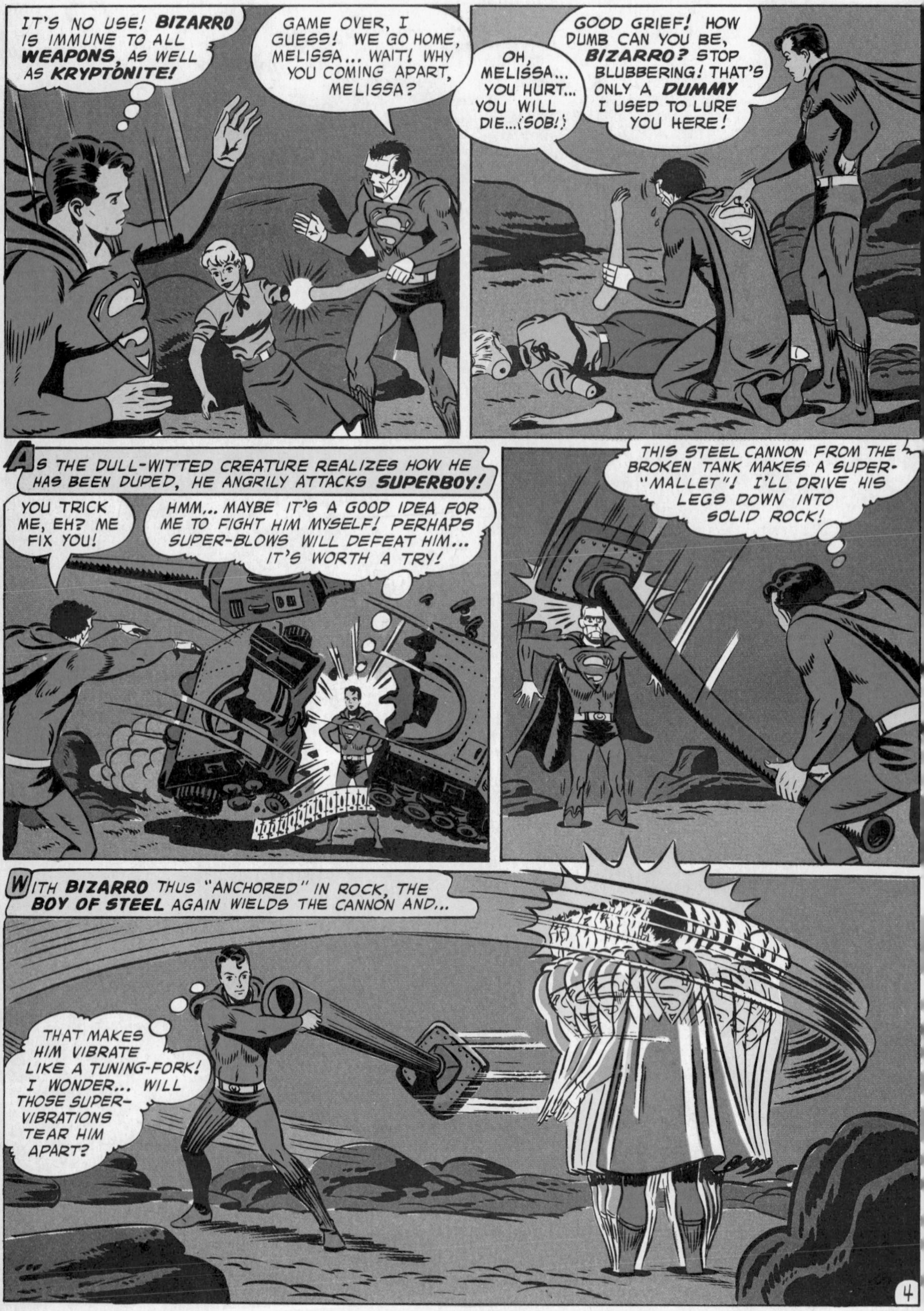
IT'S NO USE! BIZARRO IS IMMUNE TO ALL WEAPONS, AS WELL AS KRYPTONITE!
GAME OVER, I GUESS! WE GO HOME, MELISSA... WAIT! WHY YOU COMING APART, MELISSA?
OH, MELISSA... YOU HURT... YOU WILL DIE...(SOB!)
GOOD GRIEF! HOW DUMB CAN YOU BE, BIZARRO? STOP BLUBBERING! THAT'S ONLY A DUMMY I USED TO LURE YOU HERE!
AS THE DULL-WITTED CREATURE REALIZES HOW HE HAS BEEN DUPED, HE ANGRILY ATTACKS SUPERBOY!
YOU TRICK ME, EH? ME FIX YOU!
HMM... MAYBE IT'S A GOOD IDEA FOR ME TO FIGHT HIM MYSELF! PERHAPS SUPER-BLOWS WILL DEFEAT HIM... IT'S WORTH A TRY!
THIS STEEL CANNON FROM THE BROKEN TANK MAKES A SUPER-"MALLET"! I'LL DRIVE HIS LEGS DOWN INTO SOLID ROCK!
WITH BIZARRO THUS "ANCHORED" IN ROCK, THE BOY OF STEEL AGAIN WIELDS THE CANNON AND...
THAT MAKES HIM VIBRATE LIKE A TUNING-FORK! I WONDER... WILL THOSE SUPER-VIBRATIONS TEAR HIM APART?
4

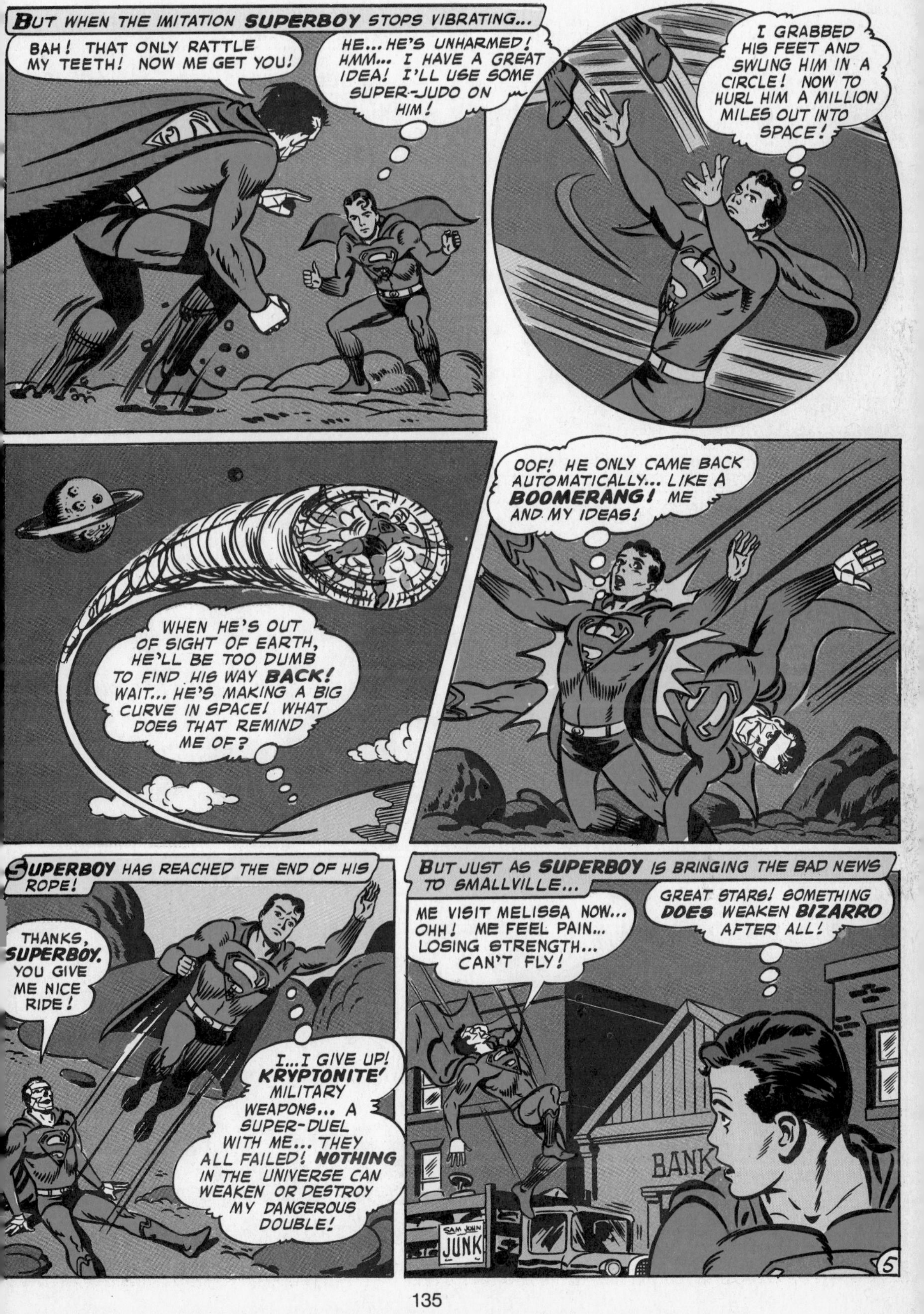
BUT WHEN THE IMITATION SUPERBOY STOPS VIBRATING...
BAH! THAT ONLY RATTLE MY TEETH! NOW ME GET YOU!
HE... HE'S UNHARMED! HMM... I HAVE A GREAT IDEA! I'LL USE SOME SUPER-JUDO ON HIM!
I GRABBED HIS FEET AND SWUNG HIM IN A CIRCLE! NOW TO HURL HIM A MILLION MILES OUT INTO SPACE!
WHEN HE'S OUT OF SIGHT OF EARTH, HE'LL BE TOO DUMB TO FIND HIS WAY BACK! WAIT... HE'S MAKING A BIG CURVE IN SPACE! WHAT DOES THAT REMIND ME OF?
OOF! HE ONLY CAME BACK AUTOMATICALLY... LIKE A BOOMERANG! ME AND MY IDEAS!
SUPERBOY HAS REACHED THE END OF HIS ROPE!
THANKS, SUPERBOY. YOU GIVE ME NICE RIDE!
I...I GIVE UP! KRYPTONITE' MILITARY WEAPONS... A SUPER-DUEL WITH ME... THEY ALL FAILED! NOTHING IN THE UNIVERSE CAN WEAKEN OR DESTROY MY DANGEROUS DOUBLE!
BUT JUST AS SUPERBOY IS BRINGING THE BAD NEWS TO SMALLVILLE...
ME VISIT MELISSA NOW... OHH! ME FEEL PAIN... LOSING STRENGTH... CAN'T FLY!
GREAT STARS! SOMETHING DOES WEAKEN BIZARRO AFTER ALL!
BANK
SAM JOHN
JUNK
5

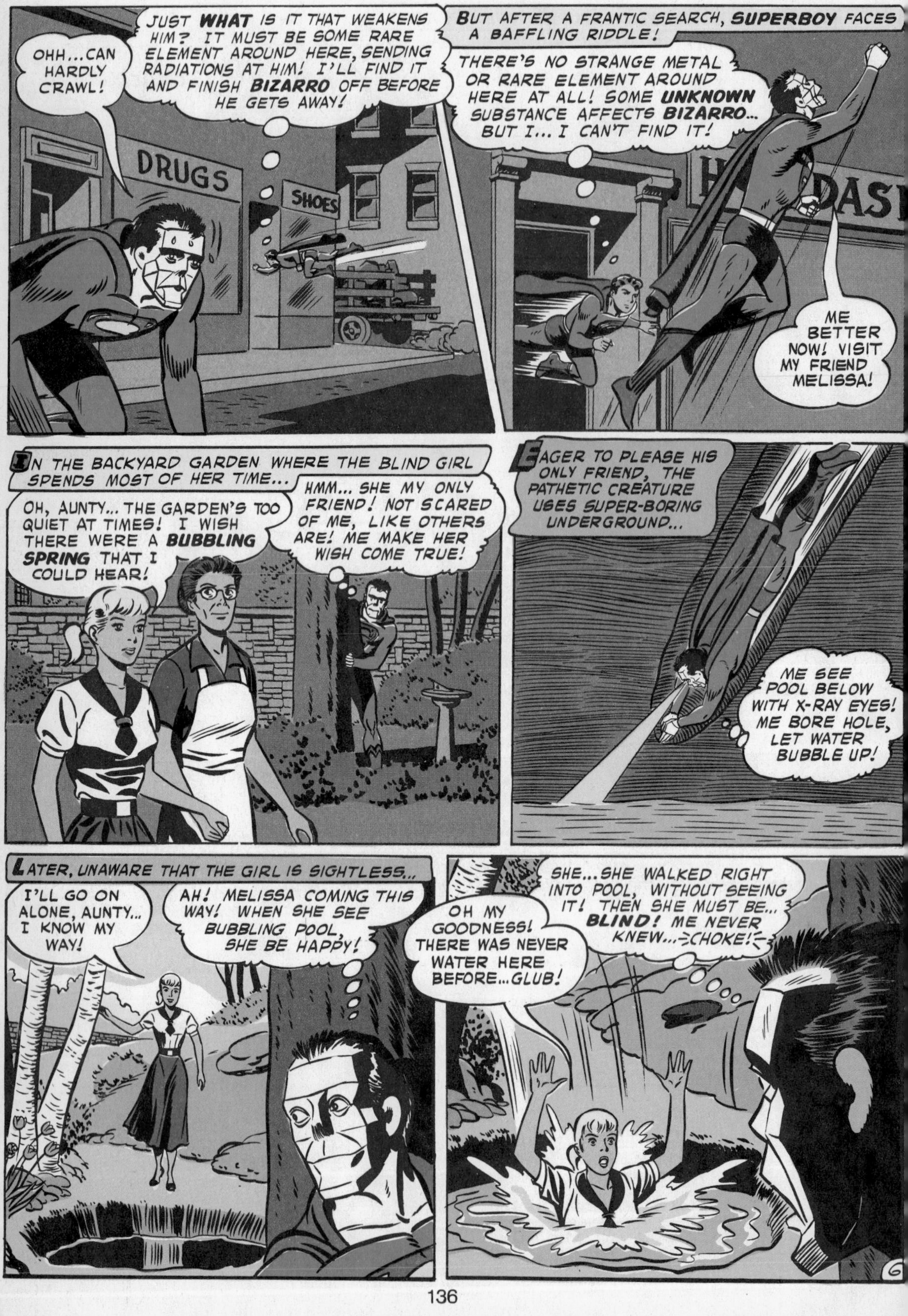
OHH...CAN HARDLY CRAWL!
JUST WHAT IS IT THAT WEAKENS HIM? IT MUST BE SOME RARE ELEMENT AROUND HERE, SENDING RADIATIONS AT HIM! I'LL FIND IT AND FINISH BIZARRO OFF BEFORE HE GETS AWAY!
DRUGS
SHOES
BUT AFTER A FRANTIC SEARCH, SUPERBOY FACES A BAFFLING RIDDLE!
THERE'S NO STRANGE METAL OR RARE ELEMENT AROUND HERE AT ALL! SOME UNKNOWN SUBSTANCE AFFECTS BIZARRO... BUT I... I CAN'T FIND IT!
ME BETTER NOW! VISIT MY FRIEND MELISSA!
IN THE BACKYARD GARDEN WHERE THE BLIND GIRL SPENDS MOST OF HER TIME...
OH, AUNTY... THE GARDEN'S TOO QUIET AT TIMES! I WISH THERE WERE A BUBBLING SPRING THAT I COULD HEAR!
HMM... SHE MY ONLY FRIEND! NOT SCARED OF ME, LIKE OTHERS ARE! ME MAKE HER WISH COME TRUE!
EAGER TO PLEASE HIS ONLY FRIEND, THE PATHETIC CREATURE USES SUPER-BORING UNDERGROUND...
ME SEE POOL BELOW WITH X-RAY EYES! ME BORE HOLE, LET WATER BUBBLE UP!
LATER, UNAWARE THAT THE GIRL IS SIGHTLESS...
I'LL GO ON ALONE, AUNTY... I KNOW MY WAY!
AH! MELISSA COMING THIS WAY! WHEN SHE SEE BUBBLING POOL, SHE BE HAPPY!
OH MY GOODNESS! THERE WAS NEVER WATER HERE BEFORE...GLUB!
SHE...SHE WALKED RIGHT INTO POOL, WITHOUT SEEING IT! THEN SHE MUST BE... BLIND! ME NEVER KNEW...CHOKE!
6

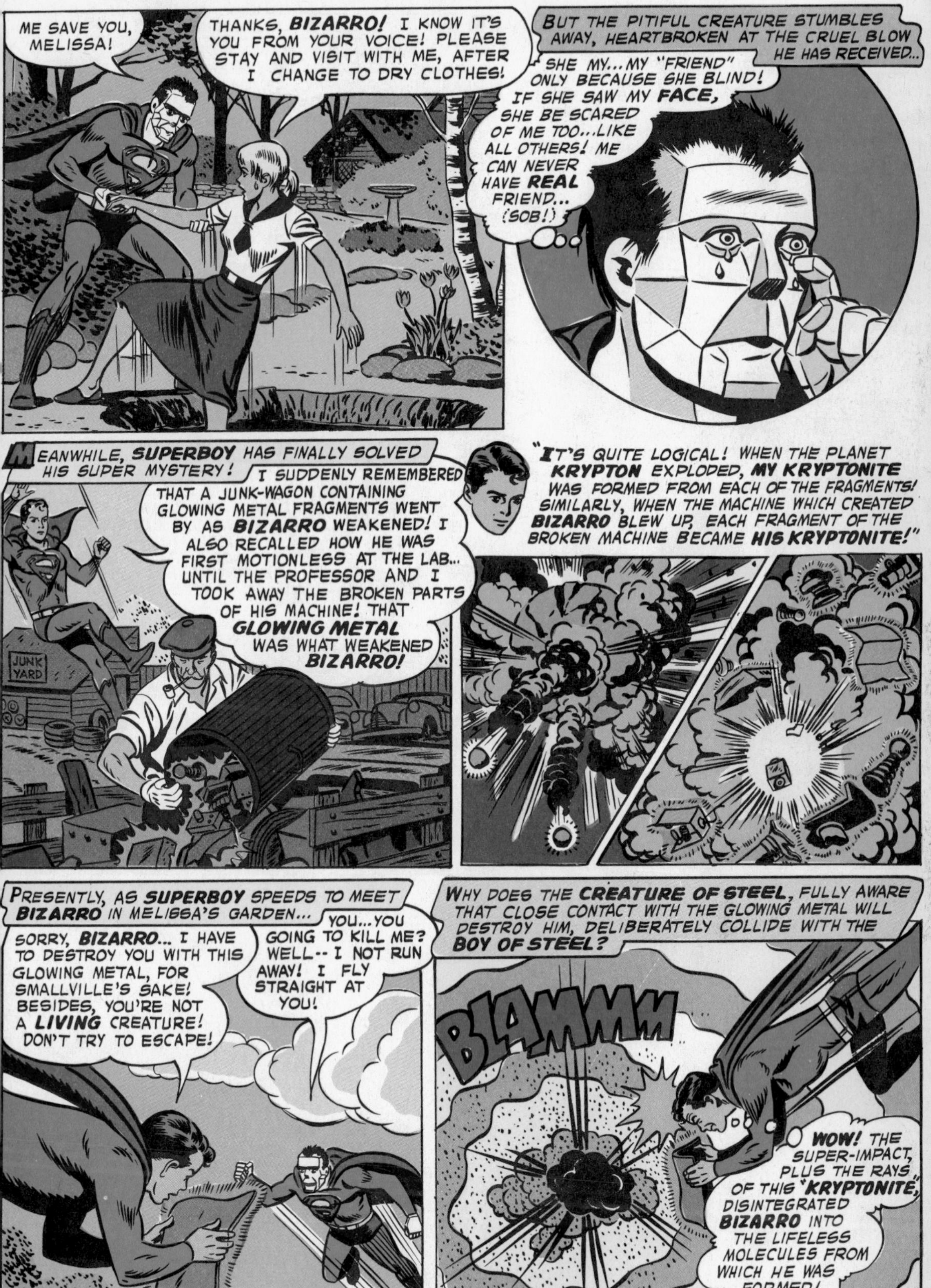
ME SAVE YOU, MELISSA!
THANKS, BIZARRO! I KNOW IT'S YOU FROM YOUR VOICE! PLEASE STAY AND VISIT WITH ME, AFTER I CHANGE TO DRY CLOTHES!
BUT THE PITIFUL CREATURE STUMBLES AWAY, HEARTBROKEN AT THE CRUEL BLOW HE HAS RECEIVED...
SHE MY... MY "FRIEND" ONLY BECAUSE SHE BLIND! IF SHE SAW MY FACE, SHE BE SCARED OF ME TOO...LIKE ALL OTHERS! ME CAN NEVER HAVE REAL FRIEND... (SOB!)
MEANWHILE, SUPERBOY HAS FINALLY SOLVED HIS SUPER MYSTERY!
I SUDDENLY REMEMBERED THAT A JUNK-WAGON CONTAINING GLOWING METAL FRAGMENTS WENT BY AS BIZARRO WEAKENED! I ALSO RECALLED HOW HE WAS FIRST MOTIONLESS AT THE LAB... UNTIL THE PROFESSOR AND I TOOK AWAY THE BROKEN PARTS OF HIS MACHINE! THAT GLOWING METAL WAS WHAT WEAKENED BIZARRO!
JUNK YARD
"IT'S QUITE LOGICAL! WHEN THE PLANET KRYPTON EXPLODED, MY KRYPTONITE WAS FORMED FROM EACH OF THE FRAGMENTS! SIMILARLY, WHEN THE MACHINE WHICH CREATED BIZARRO BLEW UP, EACH FRAGMENT OF THE BROKEN MACHINE BECAME HIS KRYPTONITE!"
PRESENTLY, AS SUPERBOY SPEEDS TO MEET BIZARRO IN MELISSA'S GARDEN...
SORRY, BIZARRO... I HAVE TO DESTROY YOU WITH THIS GLOWING METAL, FOR SMALLVILLE'S SAKE! BESIDES, YOU'RE NOT A LIVING CREATURE! DON'T TRY TO ESCAPE!
YOU...YOU GOING TO KILL ME? WELL-- I NOT RUN AWAY! I FLY STRAIGHT AT YOU!
WHY DOES THE CREATURE OF STEEL, FULLY AWARE THAT CLOSE CONTACT WITH THE GLOWING METAL WILL DESTROY HIM, DELIBERATELY COLLIDE WITH THE BOY OF STEEL?
BLAMMM
WOW! THE SUPER-IMPACT, PLUS THE RAYS OF THIS "KRYPTONITE," DISINTEGRATED BIZARRO INTO THE LIFELESS MOLECULES FROM WHICH HE WAS FORMED!
7

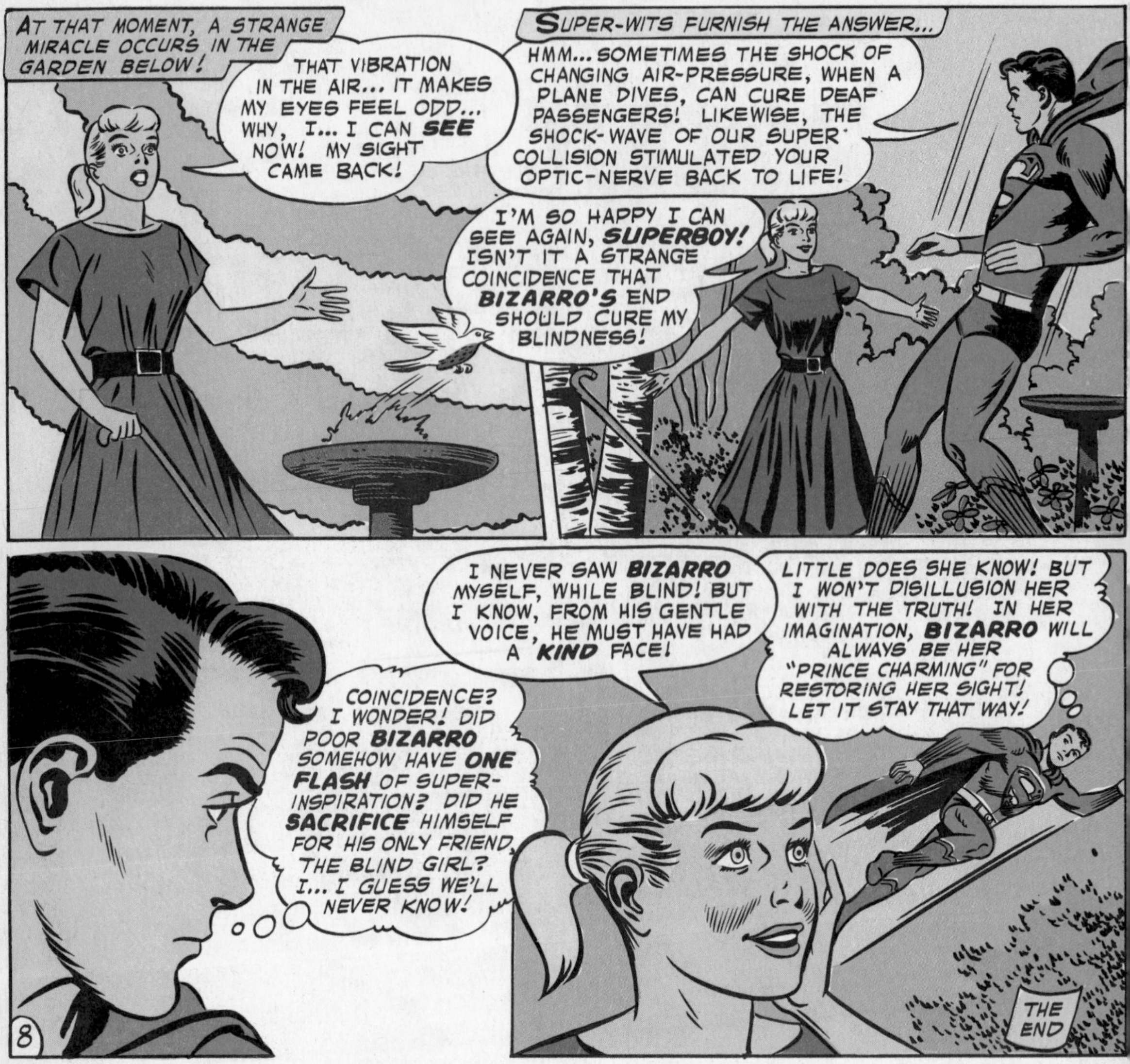
AT THAT MOMENT, A STRANGE MIRACLE OCCURS IN THE GARDEN BELOW!
THAT VIBRATION IN THE AIR... IT MAKES MY EYES FEEL ODD... WHY, I... I CAN SEE NOW! MY SIGHT CAME BACK!
SUPER-WITS FURNISH THE ANSWER...
HMM... SOMETIMES THE SHOCK OF CHANGING AIR-PRESSURE, WHEN A PLANE DIVES, CAN CURE DEAF PASSENGERS! LIKEWISE, THE SHOCK-WAVE OF OUR SUPER COLLISION STIMULATED YOUR OPTIC-NERVE BACK TO LIFE!
I'M SO HAPPY I CAN SEE AGAIN, SUPERBOY! ISN'T IT A STRANGE COINCIDENCE THAT BIZARRO'S END SHOULD CURE MY BLINDNESS!
COINCIDENCE? I WONDER! DID POOR BIZARRO SOMEHOW HAVE ONE FLASH OF SUPER-INSPIRATION? DID HE SACRIFICE HIMSELF FOR HIS ONLY FRIEND, THE BLIND GIRL? I... I GUESS WE'LL NEVER KNOW!
8
I NEVER SAW BIZARRO MYSELF, WHILE BLIND! BUT I KNOW, FROM HIS GENTLE VOICE, HE MUST HAVE HAD A KIND FACE!
LITTLE DOES SHE KNOW! BUT I WON'T DISILLUSION HER WITH THE TRUTH! IN HER IMAGINATION, BIZARRO WILL ALWAYS BE HER "PRINCE CHARMING" FOR RESTORING HER SIGHT! LET IT STAY THAT WAY!
THE END

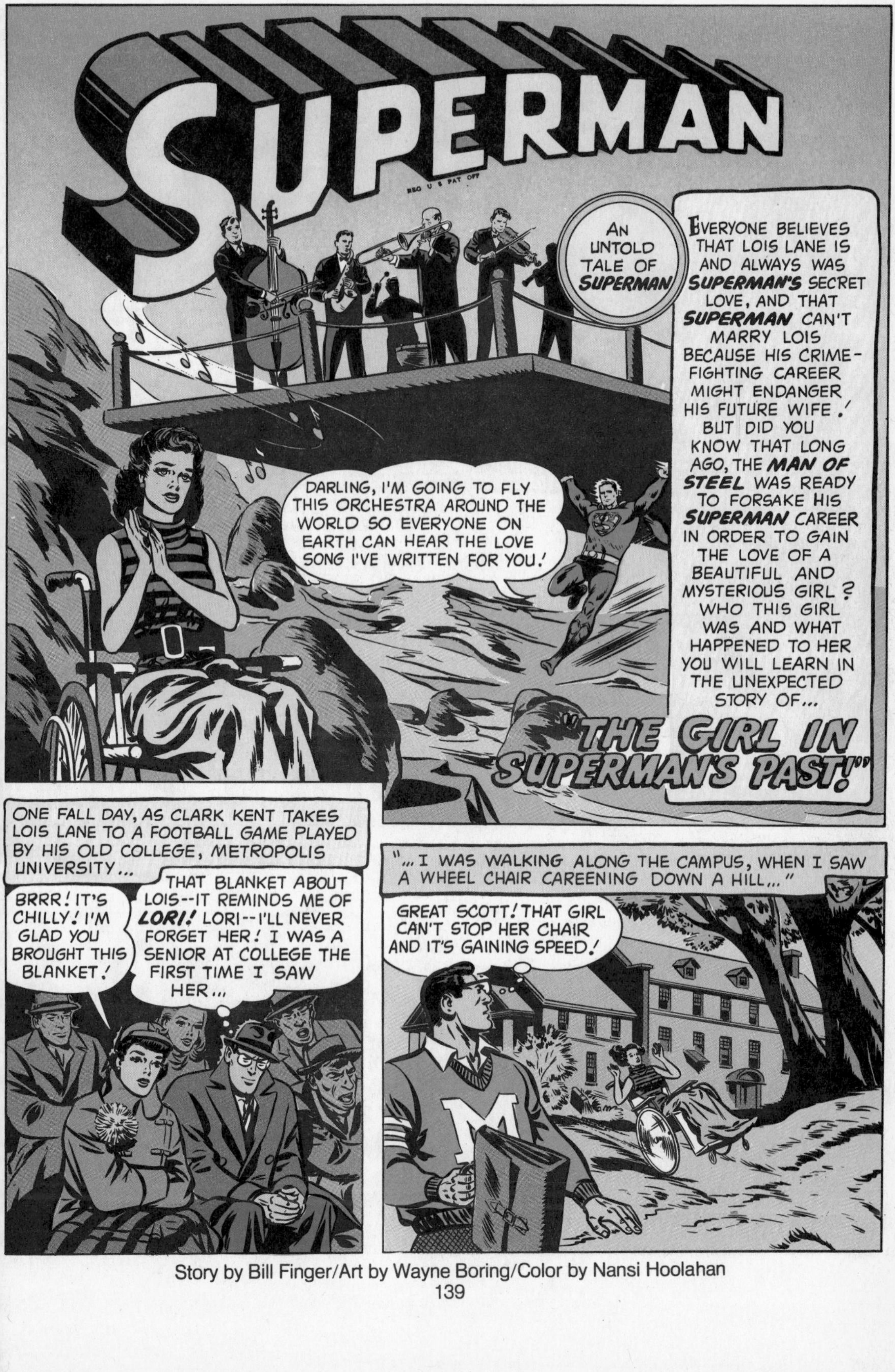
SUPERMAN
REG U S PAT OFF
AN UNTOLD TALE OF SUPERMAN
EVERYONE BELIEVES THAT LOIS LANE IS AND ALWAYS WAS SUPERMAN'S SECRET LOVE, AND THAT SUPERMAN CAN'T MARRY LOIS BECAUSE HIS CRIME-FIGHTING CAREER MIGHT ENDANGER HIS FUTURE WIFE.! BUT DID YOU KNOW THAT LONG AGO, THE MAN OF STEEL WAS READY TO FORSAKE HIS SUPERMAN CAREER IN ORDER TO GAIN THE LOVE OF A BEAUTIFUL AND MYSTERIOUS GIRL? WHO THIS GIRL WAS AND WHAT HAPPENED TO HER YOU WILL LEARN IN THE UNEXPECTED STORY OF...
DARLING, I'M GOING TO FLY THIS ORCHESTRA AROUND THE WORLD SO EVERYONE ON EARTH CAN HEAR THE LOVE SONG I'VE WRITTEN FOR YOU.!
"THE GIRL IN SUPERMAN'S PAST!"
ONE FALL DAY, AS CLARK KENT TAKES LOIS LANE TO A FOOTBALL GAME PLAYED BY HIS OLD COLLEGE, METROPOLIS UNIVERSITY...
BRRR! IT'S CHILLY! I'M GLAD YOU BROUGHT THIS BLANKET!
THAT BLANKET ABOUT LOIS--IT REMINDS ME OF LORI! LORI--I'LL NEVER FORGET HER! I WAS A SENIOR AT COLLEGE THE FIRST TIME I SAW HER...
"...I WAS WALKING ALONG THE CAMPUS, WHEN I SAW A WHEEL CHAIR CAREENING DOWN A HILL..."
GREAT SCOTT! THAT GIRL CAN'T STOP HER CHAIR AND IT'S GAINING SPEED!

Story by Bill Finger/Art by Wayne Boring/Color by Nansi Hoolahan

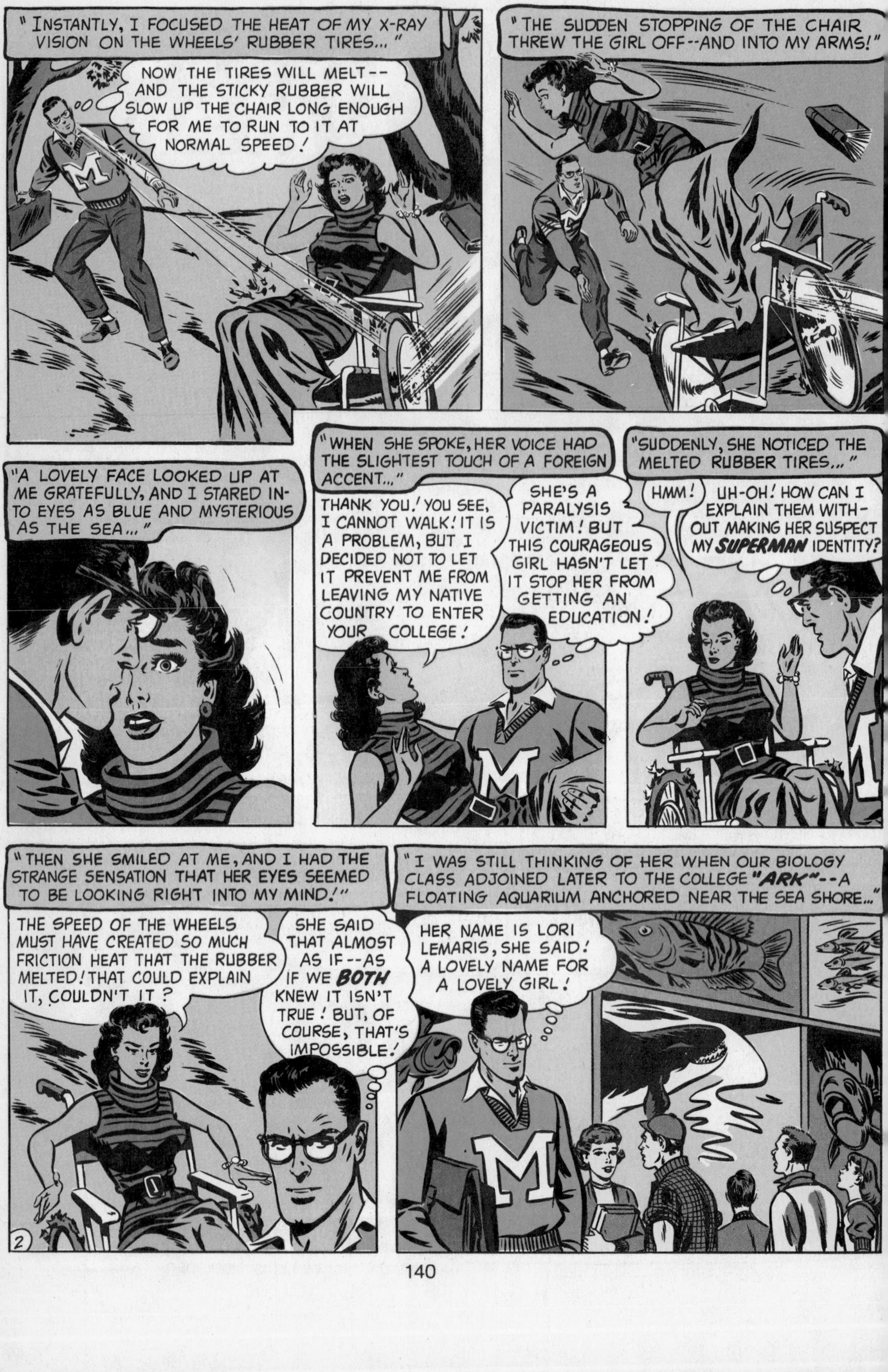

"INSTANTLY, I FOCUSED THE HEAT OF MY X-RAY VISION ON THE WHEELS' RUBBER TIRES..."
NOW THE TIRES WILL MELT--AND THE STICKY RUBBER WILL SLOW UP THE CHAIR LONG ENOUGH FOR ME TO RUN TO IT AT NORMAL SPEED!
"THE SUDDEN STOPPING OF THE CHAIR THREW THE GIRL OFF--AND INTO MY ARMS!"
"A LOVELY FACE LOOKED UP AT ME GRATEFULLY, AND I STARED INTO EYES AS BLUE AND MYSTERIOUS AS THE SEA..."
"WHEN SHE SPOKE, HER VOICE HAD THE SLIGHTEST TOUCH OF A FOREIGN ACCENT..."
THANK YOU! YOU SEE, I CANNOT WALK! IT IS A PROBLEM, BUT I DECIDED NOT TO LET IT PREVENT ME FROM LEAVING MY NATIVE COUNTRY TO ENTER YOUR COLLEGE!
SHE'S A PARALYSIS VICTIM! BUT THIS COURAGEOUS GIRL HASN'T LET IT STOP HER FROM GETTING AN EDUCATION!
"SUDDENLY, SHE NOTICED THE MELTED RUBBER TIRES..."
HMM!
UH-OH! HOW CAN I EXPLAIN THEM WITHOUT MAKING HER SUSPECT MY SUPERMAN IDENTITY?
"THEN SHE SMILED AT ME, AND I HAD THE STRANGE SENSATION THAT HER EYES SEEMED TO BE LOOKING RIGHT INTO MY MIND!"
THE SPEED OF THE WHEELS MUST HAVE CREATED SO MUCH FRICTION HEAT THAT THE RUBBER MELTED! THAT COULD EXPLAIN IT, COULDN'T IT?
SHE SAID THAT ALMOST AS IF--AS IF WE BOTH KNEW IT ISN'T TRUE! BUT, OF COURSE, THAT'S IMPOSSIBLE!
2
"I WAS STILL THINKING OF HER WHEN OUR BIOLOGY CLASS ADJOINED LATER TO THE COLLEGE "ARK"--A FLOATING AQUARIUM ANCHORED NEAR THE SEA SHORE..."
HER NAME IS LORI LEMARIS, SHE SAID! A LOVELY NAME FOR A LOVELY GIRL!

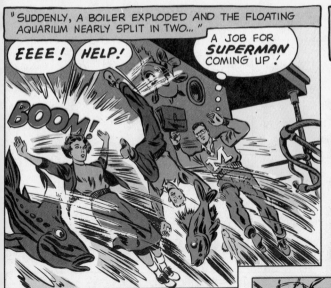

"SUDDENLY, A BOILER EXPLODED AND THE FLOATING AQUARIUM NEARLY SPLIT IN TWO..."

EEEE! HELP!

A JOB FOR *SUPERMAN* COMING UP!

BOOM!

"EVERYONE JUMPED INTO THE WATER AND SWAM TO SHORE A FEW YARDS AWAY--SO I WAS UNOBSERVED AS I DIVED TO AN UNDERWATER CAVERN..."

I'M GLAD I MADE A HABIT OF CARRYING MY SUPER-COSTUME IN MY SCHOOL BRIEFCASE!

"THEN I BECAME AN UNDERWATER "COWBOY", HERDING TOGETHER ALL THE FISH THAT HAD ESCAPED FROM THE AQUARIUM..."

GIT ALONG, LITTLE DOGIE!

NOW I'LL WEAVE THESE LONG STRANDS OF SEA WEED INTO A NET "CAGE" ABOUT THE SPECIMENS UNTIL THE AQUARIUM IS REPAIRED AND READY TO STOCK THEM AGAIN!

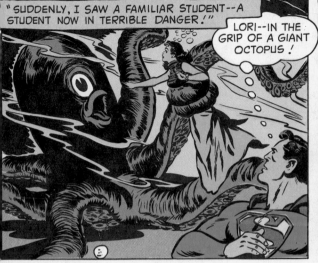

"SUDDENLY, I SAW A FAMILIAR STUDENT--A STUDENT NOW IN TERRIBLE DANGER!"

LORI--IN THE GRIP OF A GIANT OCTOPUS!

"EVEN AS I SHOT FORWARD, I WAS AMAZED TO SEE THAT LORI WAS NOT FRIGHTENED, BUT CALMLY REGARDING THE CREATURE..."

HER LIPS ARE MOVING! IF I DIDN'T KNOW BETTER, I'D ALMOST BELIEVE SHE WAS TALKING TO THE OCTOPUS!

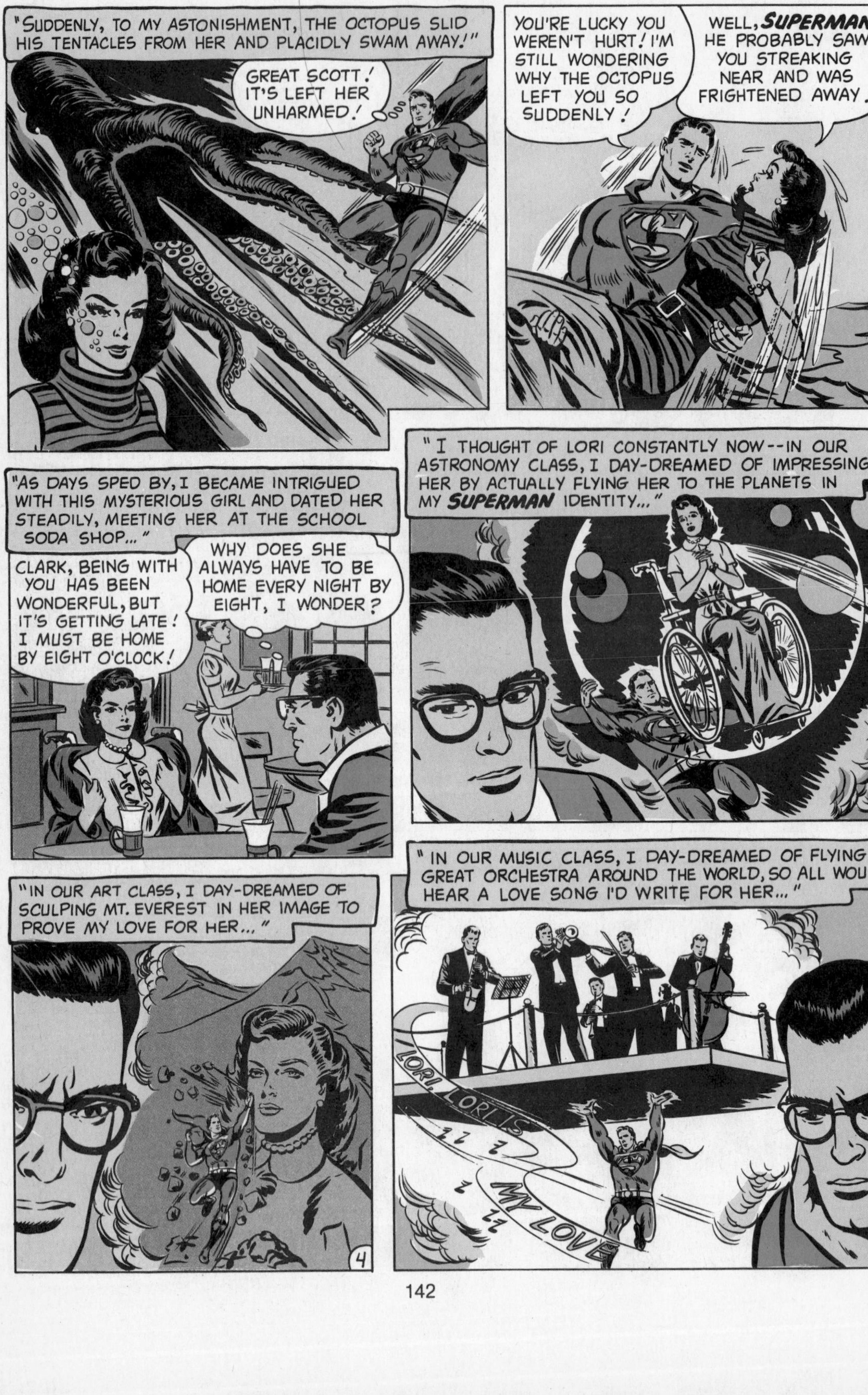

"SUDDENLY, TO MY ASTONISHMENT, THE OCTOPUS SLID HIS TENTACLES FROM HER AND PLACIDLY SWAM AWAY!"
GREAT SCOTT! IT'S LEFT HER UNHARMED!
YOU'RE LUCKY YOU WEREN'T HURT! I'M STILL WONDERING WHY THE OCTOPUS LEFT YOU SO SUDDENLY!
WELL, SUPERMAN... HE PROBABLY SAW YOU STREAKING NEAR AND WAS FRIGHTENED AWAY!
"AS DAYS SPED BY, I BECAME INTRIGUED WITH THIS MYSTERIOUS GIRL AND DATED HER STEADILY, MEETING HER AT THE SCHOOL SODA SHOP..."
CLARK, BEING WITH YOU HAS BEEN WONDERFUL, BUT IT'S GETTING LATE! I MUST BE HOME BY EIGHT O'CLOCK!
WHY DOES SHE ALWAYS HAVE TO BE HOME EVERY NIGHT BY EIGHT, I WONDER?
"I THOUGHT OF LORI CONSTANTLY NOW--IN OUR ASTRONOMY CLASS, I DAY-DREAMED OF IMPRESSING HER BY ACTUALLY FLYING HER TO THE PLANETS IN MY SUPERMAN IDENTITY..."
"IN OUR ART CLASS, I DAY-DREAMED OF SCULPING MT. EVEREST IN HER IMAGE TO PROVE MY LOVE FOR HER..."
4
"IN OUR MUSIC CLASS, I DAY-DREAMED OF FLYING A GREAT ORCHESTRA AROUND THE WORLD, SO ALL WOULD HEAR A LOVE SONG I'D WRITE FOR HER..."
LORI LORI IS MY LOVE

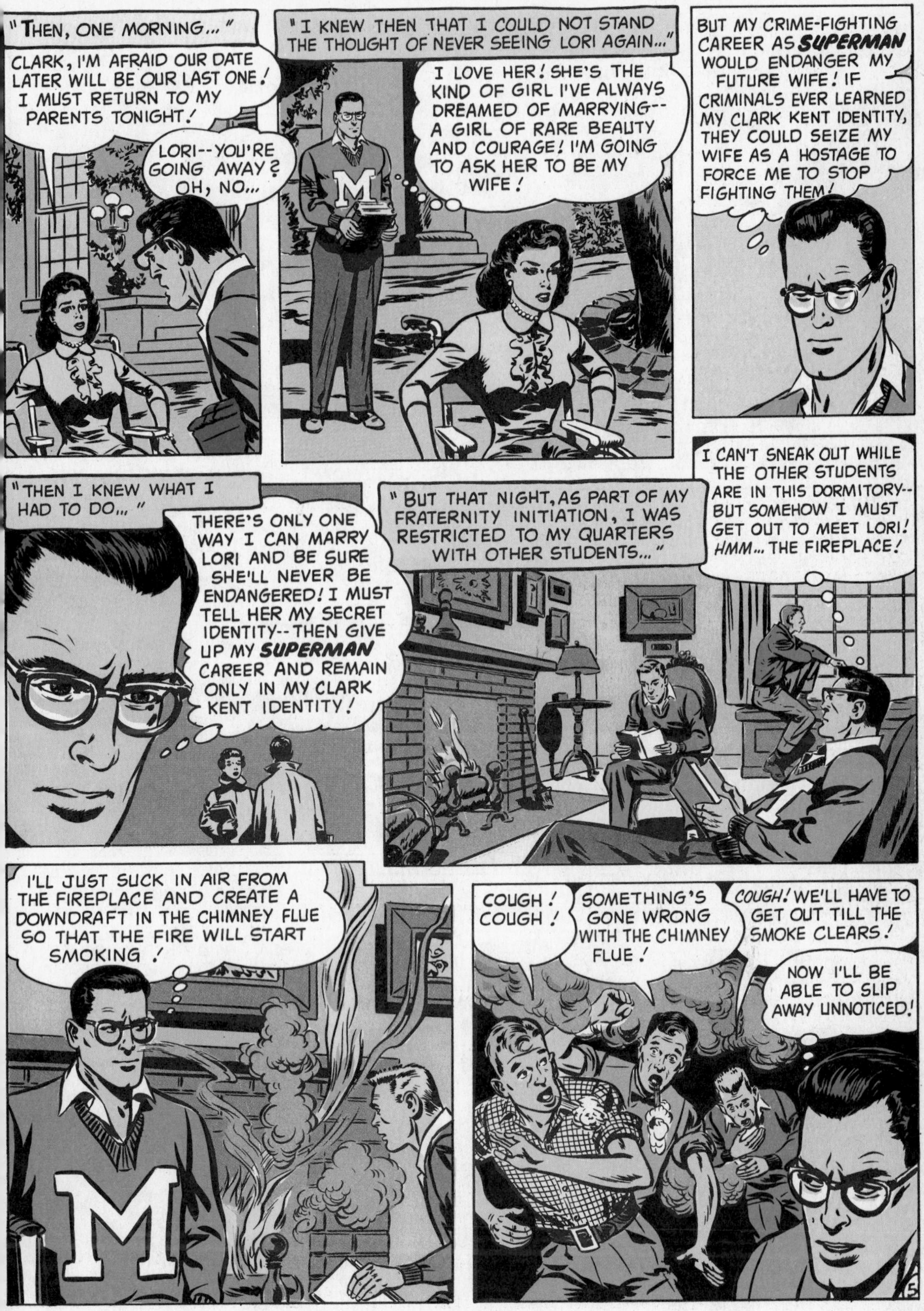
"THEN, ONE MORNING..."
CLARK, I'M AFRAID OUR DATE LATER WILL BE OUR LAST ONE! I MUST RETURN TO MY PARENTS TONIGHT!
LORI--YOU'RE GOING AWAY? OH, NO...
"I KNEW THEN THAT I COULD NOT STAND THE THOUGHT OF NEVER SEEING LORI AGAIN..."
I LOVE HER! SHE'S THE KIND OF GIRL I'VE ALWAYS DREAMED OF MARRYING-- A GIRL OF RARE BEAUTY AND COURAGE! I'M GOING TO ASK HER TO BE MY WIFE!
BUT MY CRIME-FIGHTING CAREER AS SUPERMAN WOULD ENDANGER MY FUTURE WIFE! IF CRIMINALS EVER LEARNED MY CLARK KENT IDENTITY, THEY COULD SEIZE MY WIFE AS A HOSTAGE TO FORCE ME TO STOP FIGHTING THEM!
"THEN I KNEW WHAT I HAD TO DO..."
THERE'S ONLY ONE WAY I CAN MARRY LORI AND BE SURE SHE'LL NEVER BE ENDANGERED! I MUST TELL HER MY SECRET IDENTITY-- THEN GIVE UP MY SUPERMAN CAREER AND REMAIN ONLY IN MY CLARK KENT IDENTITY!
"BUT THAT NIGHT, AS PART OF MY FRATERNITY INITIATION, I WAS RESTRICTED TO MY QUARTERS WITH OTHER STUDENTS..."
I CAN'T SNEAK OUT WHILE THE OTHER STUDENTS ARE IN THIS DORMITORY-- BUT SOMEHOW I MUST GET OUT TO MEET LORI! HMM... THE FIREPLACE!
I'LL JUST SUCK IN AIR FROM THE FIREPLACE AND CREATE A DOWNDRAFT IN THE CHIMNEY FLUE SO THAT THE FIRE WILL START SMOKING!
COUGH! COUGH!
SOMETHING'S GONE WRONG WITH THE CHIMNEY FLUE!
COUGH! WE'LL HAVE TO GET OUT TILL THE SMOKE CLEARS!
NOW I'LL BE ABLE TO SLIP AWAY UNNOTICED!
5

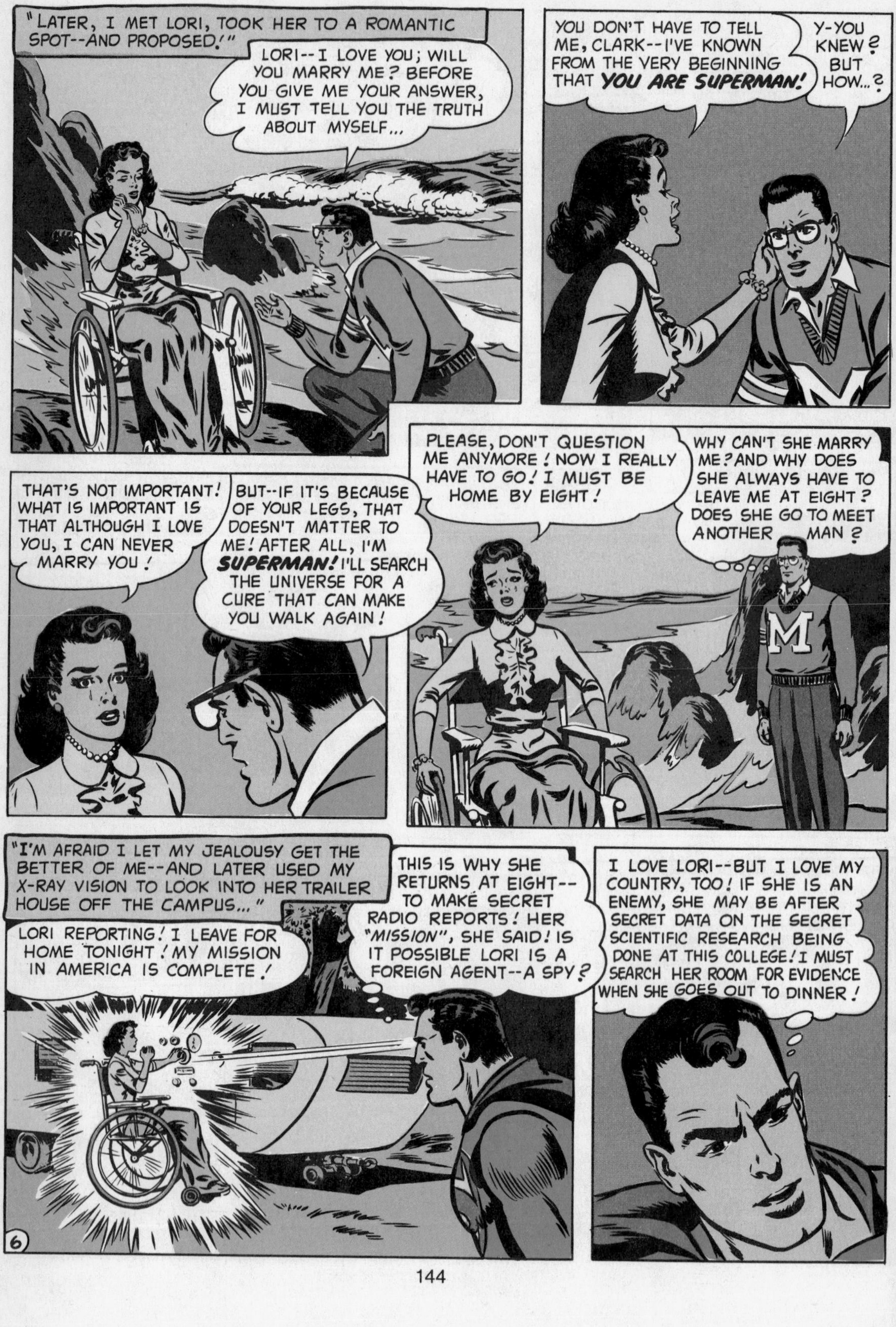
"LATER, I MET LORI, TOOK HER TO A ROMANTIC SPOT--AND PROPOSED!"
LORI--I LOVE YOU; WILL YOU MARRY ME? BEFORE YOU GIVE ME YOUR ANSWER, I MUST TELL YOU THE TRUTH ABOUT MYSELF...
YOU DON'T HAVE TO TELL ME, CLARK--I'VE KNOWN FROM THE VERY BEGINNING THAT YOU ARE SUPERMAN!
Y-YOU KNEW? BUT HOW...?
THAT'S NOT IMPORTANT! WHAT IS IMPORTANT IS THAT ALTHOUGH I LOVE YOU, I CAN NEVER MARRY YOU!
BUT--IF IT'S BECAUSE OF YOUR LEGS, THAT DOESN'T MATTER TO ME! AFTER ALL, I'M SUPERMAN! I'LL SEARCH THE UNIVERSE FOR A CURE THAT CAN MAKE YOU WALK AGAIN!
PLEASE, DON'T QUESTION ME ANYMORE! NOW I REALLY HAVE TO GO! I MUST BE HOME BY EIGHT!
WHY CAN'T SHE MARRY ME? AND WHY DOES SHE ALWAYS HAVE TO LEAVE ME AT EIGHT? DOES SHE GO TO MEET ANOTHER MAN?
"I'M AFRAID I LET MY JEALOUSY GET THE BETTER OF ME--AND LATER USED MY X-RAY VISION TO LOOK INTO HER TRAILER HOUSE OFF THE CAMPUS..."
LORI REPORTING! I LEAVE FOR HOME TONIGHT! MY MISSION IN AMERICA IS COMPLETE!
THIS IS WHY SHE RETURNS AT EIGHT--TO MAKE SECRET RADIO REPORTS! HER "MISSION", SHE SAID! IS IT POSSIBLE LORI IS A FOREIGN AGENT--A SPY?
LORI--
6
I LOVE LORI--BUT I LOVE MY COUNTRY, TOO! IF SHE IS AN ENEMY, SHE MAY BE AFTER SECRET DATA ON THE SECRET SCIENTIFIC RESEARCH BEING DONE AT THIS COLLEGE! I MUST SEARCH HER ROOM FOR EVIDENCE WHEN SHE GOES OUT TO DINNER!

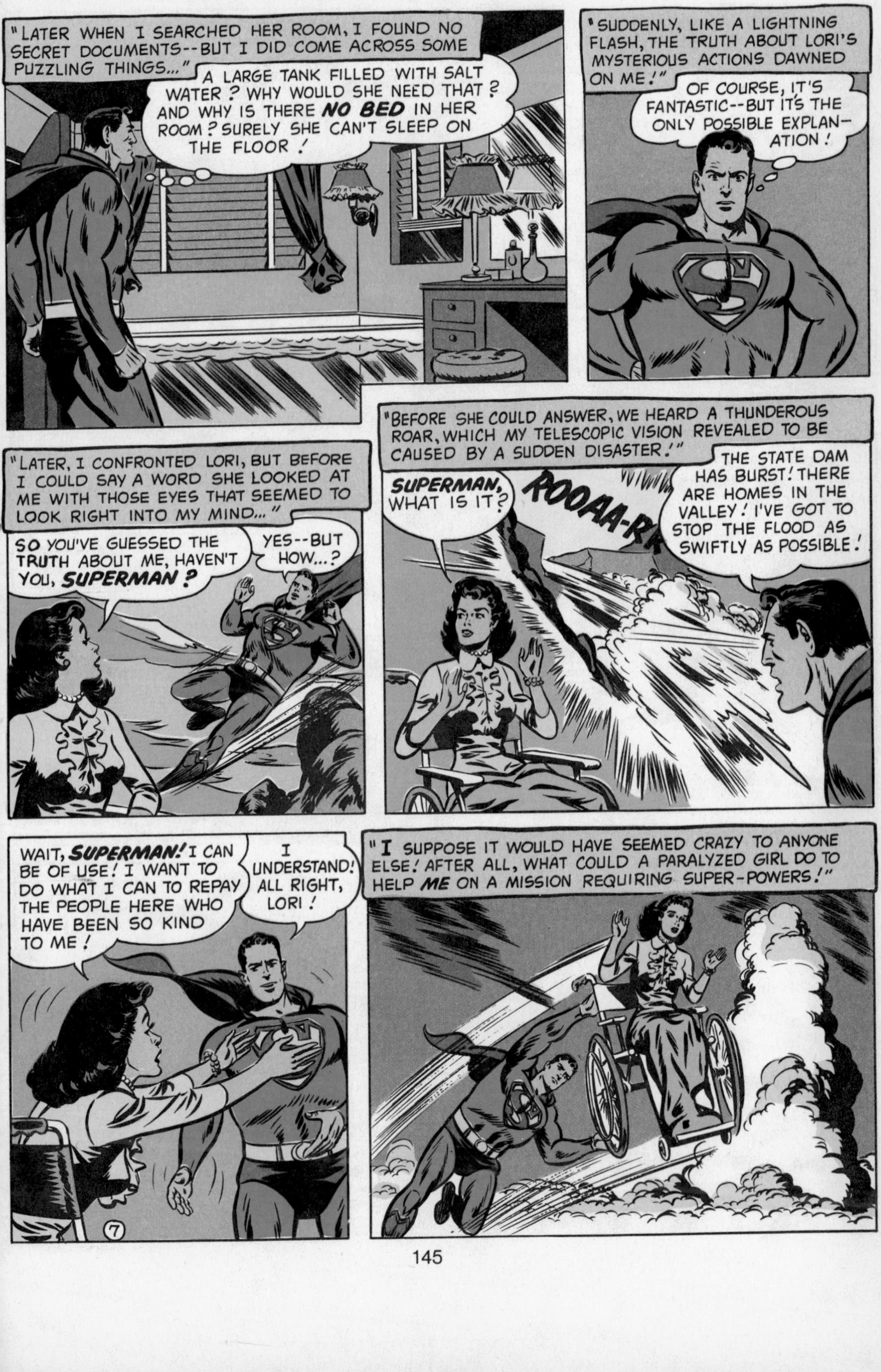
"LATER WHEN I SEARCHED HER ROOM, I FOUND NO SECRET DOCUMENTS--BUT I DID COME ACROSS SOME PUZZLING THINGS..."
A LARGE TANK FILLED WITH SALT WATER? WHY WOULD SHE NEED THAT? AND WHY IS THERE NO BED IN HER ROOM? SURELY SHE CAN'T SLEEP ON THE FLOOR!
"SUDDENLY, LIKE A LIGHTNING FLASH, THE TRUTH ABOUT LORI'S MYSTERIOUS ACTIONS DAWNED ON ME!"
OF COURSE, IT'S FANTASTIC--BUT IT'S THE ONLY POSSIBLE EXPLANATION!
"LATER, I CONFRONTED LORI, BUT BEFORE I COULD SAY A WORD SHE LOOKED AT ME WITH THOSE EYES THAT SEEMED TO LOOK RIGHT INTO MY MIND..."
SO YOU'VE GUESSED THE TRUTH ABOUT ME, HAVEN'T YOU, SUPERMAN?
YES--BUT HOW...?
"BEFORE SHE COULD ANSWER, WE HEARD A THUNDEROUS ROAR, WHICH MY TELESCOPIC VISION REVEALED TO BE CAUSED BY A SUDDEN DISASTER!"
SUPERMAN, WHAT IS IT?
ROOAAA-RR
THE STATE DAM HAS BURST! THERE ARE HOMES IN THE VALLEY! I'VE GOT TO STOP THE FLOOD AS SWIFTLY AS POSSIBLE!
WAIT, SUPERMAN! I CAN BE OF USE! I WANT TO DO WHAT I CAN TO REPAY THE PEOPLE HERE WHO HAVE BEEN SO KIND TO ME!
I UNDERSTAND! ALL RIGHT, LORI!
7
"I SUPPOSE IT WOULD HAVE SEEMED CRAZY TO ANYONE ELSE! AFTER ALL, WHAT COULD A PARALYZED GIRL DO TO HELP ME ON A MISSION REQUIRING SUPER-POWERS!"

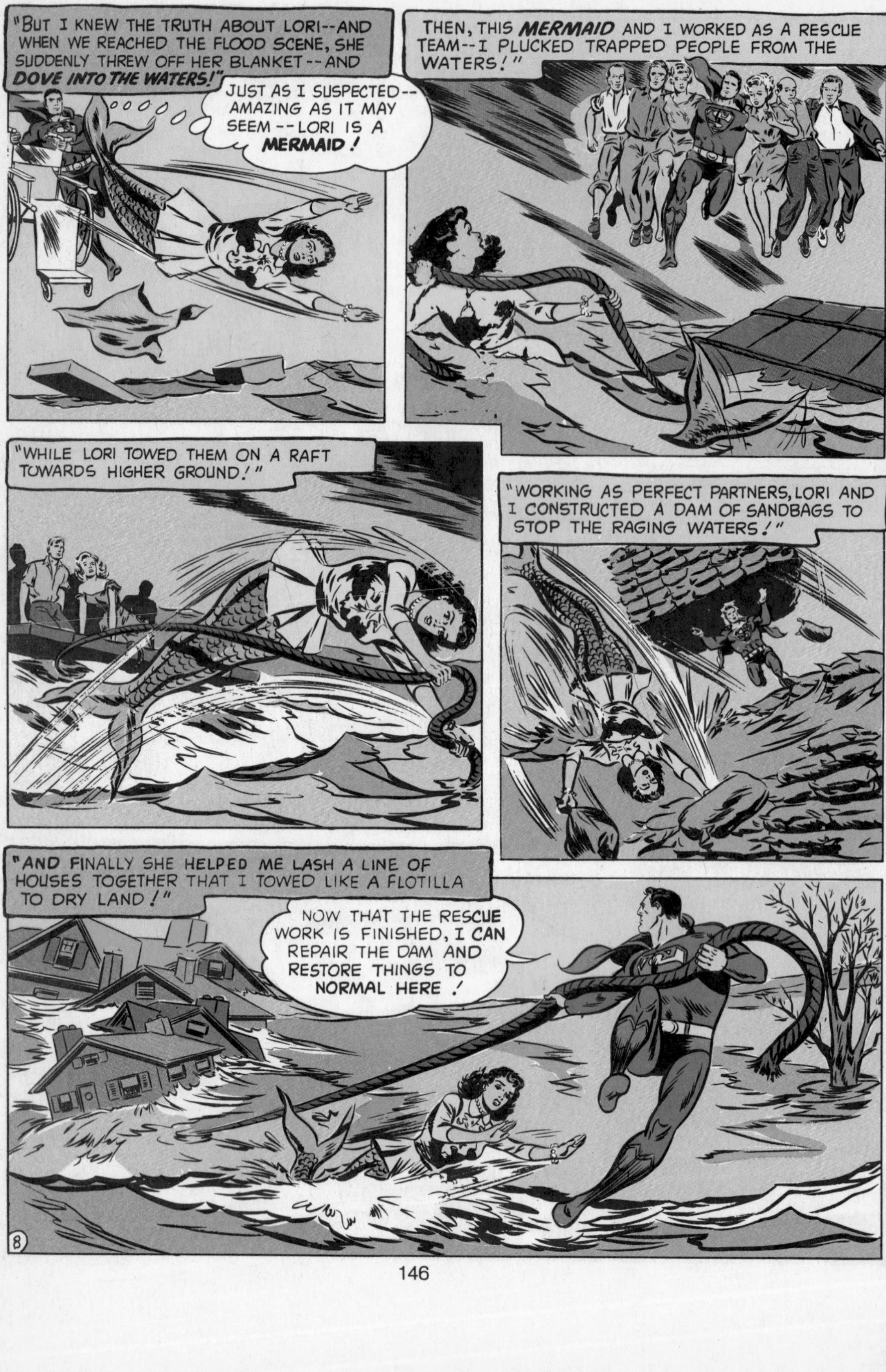
"BUT I KNEW THE TRUTH ABOUT LORI--AND WHEN WE REACHED THE FLOOD SCENE, SHE SUDDENLY THREW OFF HER BLANKET--AND DOVE INTO THE WATERS!"
JUST AS I SUSPECTED--AMAZING AS IT MAY SEEM--LORI IS A MERMAID!
THEN, THIS MERMAID AND I WORKED AS A RESCUE TEAM--I PLUCKED TRAPPED PEOPLE FROM THE WATERS!"
"WHILE LORI TOWED THEM ON A RAFT TOWARDS HIGHER GROUND!"
"WORKING AS PERFECT PARTNERS, LORI AND I CONSTRUCTED A DAM OF SANDBAGS TO STOP THE RAGING WATERS!"
"AND FINALLY SHE HELPED ME LASH A LINE OF HOUSES TOGETHER THAT I TOWED LIKE A FLOTILLA TO DRY LAND!"
NOW THAT THE RESCUE WORK IS FINISHED, I CAN REPAIR THE DAM AND RESTORE THINGS TO NORMAL HERE!
8

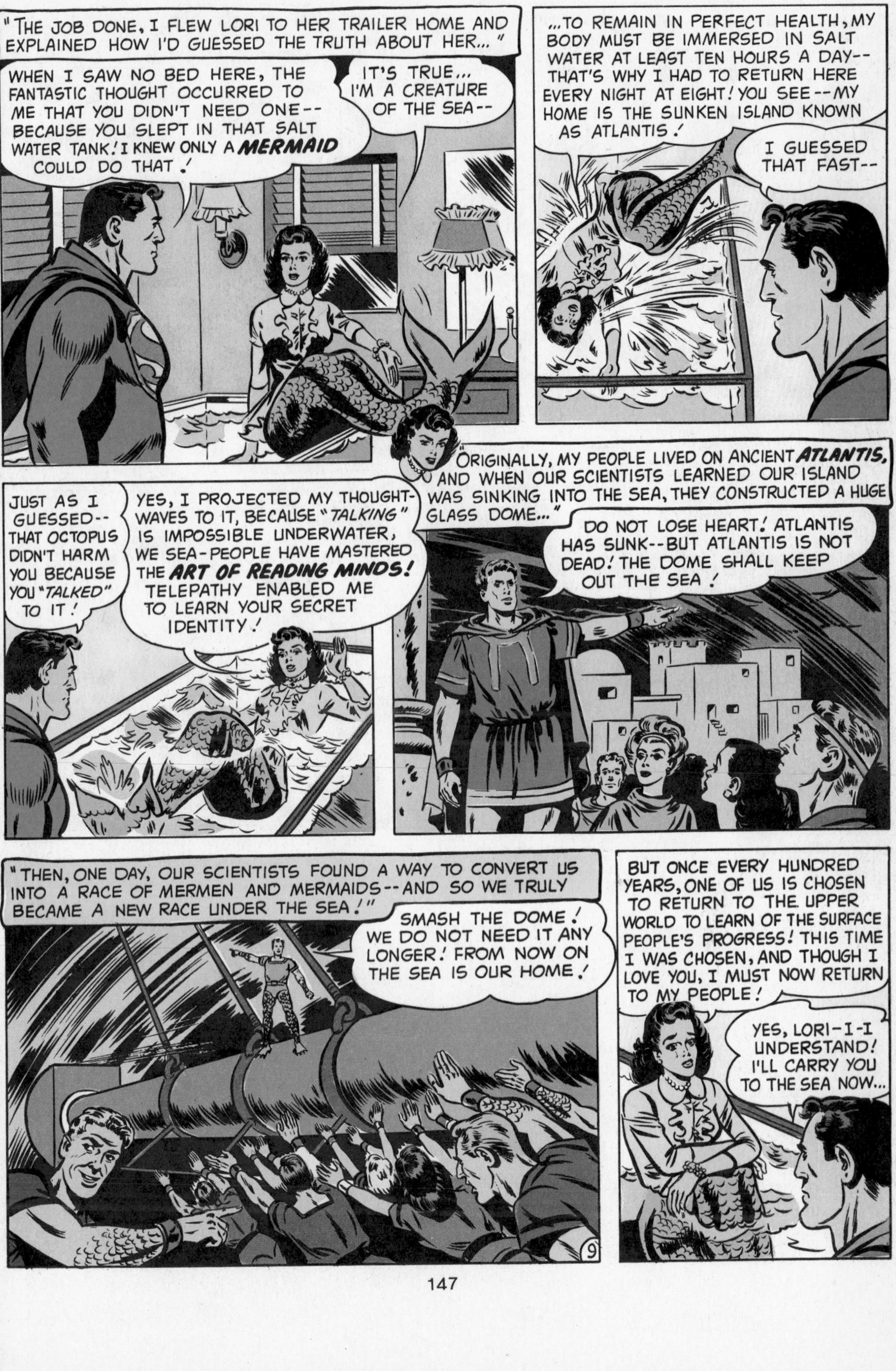
"THE JOB DONE, I FLEW LORI TO HER TRAILER HOME AND EXPLAINED HOW I'D GUESSED THE TRUTH ABOUT HER... "
WHEN I SAW NO BED HERE, THE FANTASTIC THOUGHT OCCURRED TO ME THAT YOU DIDN'T NEED ONE-- BECAUSE YOU SLEPT IN THAT SALT WATER TANK! I KNEW ONLY A MERMAID COULD DO THAT!
IT'S TRUE... I'M A CREATURE OF THE SEA--
...TO REMAIN IN PERFECT HEALTH, MY BODY MUST BE IMMERSED IN SALT WATER AT LEAST TEN HOURS A DAY-- THAT'S WHY I HAD TO RETURN HERE EVERY NIGHT AT EIGHT! YOU SEE--MY HOME IS THE SUNKEN ISLAND KNOWN AS ATLANTIS!
I GUESSED THAT FAST--
JUST AS I GUESSED-- THAT OCTOPUS DIDN'T HARM YOU BECAUSE YOU "TALKED" TO IT!
YES, I PROJECTED MY THOUGHT-WAVES TO IT, BECAUSE "TALKING" IS IMPOSSIBLE UNDERWATER, WE SEA-PEOPLE HAVE MASTERED THE ART OF READING MINDS! TELEPATHY ENABLED ME TO LEARN YOUR SECRET IDENTITY!
"ORIGINALLY, MY PEOPLE LIVED ON ANCIENT ATLANTIS, AND WHEN OUR SCIENTISTS LEARNED OUR ISLAND WAS SINKING INTO THE SEA, THEY CONSTRUCTED A HUGE GLASS DOME..."
DO NOT LOSE HEART! ATLANTIS HAS SUNK--BUT ATLANTIS IS NOT DEAD! THE DOME SHALL KEEP OUT THE SEA!
"THEN, ONE DAY, OUR SCIENTISTS FOUND A WAY TO CONVERT US INTO A RACE OF MERMEN AND MERMAIDS--AND SO WE TRULY BECAME A NEW RACE UNDER THE SEA!"
SMASH THE DOME! WE DO NOT NEED IT ANY LONGER! FROM NOW ON THE SEA IS OUR HOME!
9
BUT ONCE EVERY HUNDRED YEARS, ONE OF US IS CHOSEN TO RETURN TO THE UPPER WORLD TO LEARN OF THE SURFACE PEOPLE'S PROGRESS! THIS TIME I WAS CHOSEN, AND THOUGH I LOVE YOU, I MUST NOW RETURN TO MY PEOPLE!
YES, LORI-I-I UNDERSTAND! I'LL CARRY YOU TO THE SEA NOW...

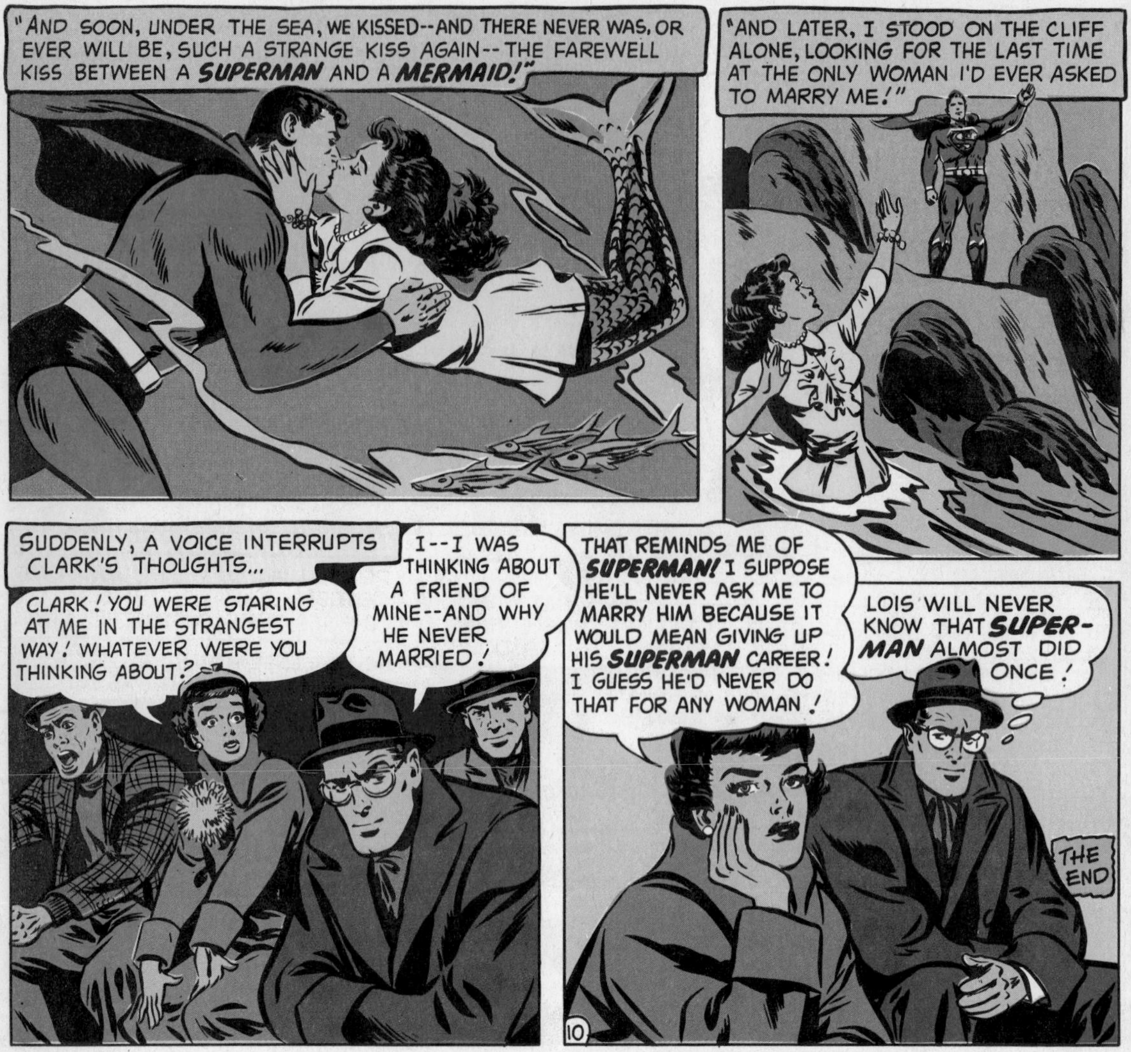
"AND SOON, UNDER THE SEA, WE KISSED--AND THERE NEVER WAS, OR EVER WILL BE, SUCH A STRANGE KISS AGAIN--THE FAREWELL KISS BETWEEN A SUPERMAN AND A MERMAID!"
"AND LATER, I STOOD ON THE CLIFF ALONE, LOOKING FOR THE LAST TIME AT THE ONLY WOMAN I'D EVER ASKED TO MARRY ME!"
SUDDENLY, A VOICE INTERRUPTS CLARK'S THOUGHTS...
CLARK! YOU WERE STARING AT ME IN THE STRANGEST WAY! WHATEVER WERE YOU THINKING ABOUT?
I--I WAS THINKING ABOUT A FRIEND OF MINE--AND WHY HE NEVER MARRIED!
THAT REMINDS ME OF SUPERMAN! I SUPPOSE HE'LL NEVER ASK ME TO MARRY HIM BECAUSE IT WOULD MEAN GIVING UP HIS SUPERMAN CAREER! I GUESS HE'D NEVER DO THAT FOR ANY WOMAN!
LOIS WILL NEVER KNOW THAT SUPER-MAN ALMOST DID ONCE!
THE END
10

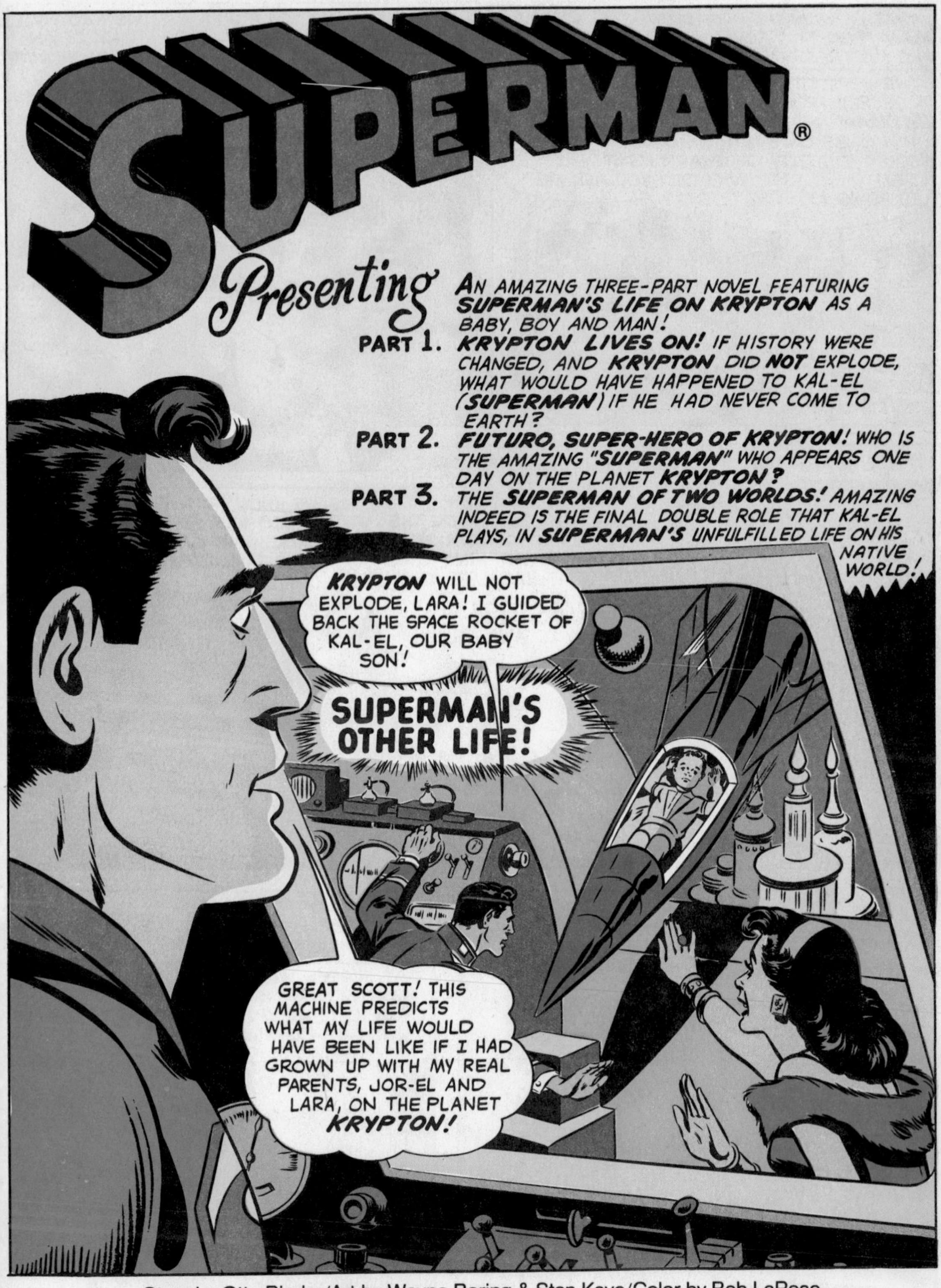
SUPERMAN®
Presenting
AN AMAZING THREE-PART NOVEL FEATURING SUPERMAN'S LIFE ON KRYPTON AS A BABY, BOY AND MAN!
PART 1. KRYPTON LIVES ON! IF HISTORY WERE CHANGED, AND KRYPTON DID NOT EXPLODE, WHAT WOULD HAVE HAPPENED TO KAL-EL (SUPERMAN) IF HE HAD NEVER COME TO EARTH?
PART 2. FUTURO, SUPER-HERO OF KRYPTON! WHO IS THE AMAZING "SUPERMAN" WHO APPEARS ONE DAY ON THE PLANET KRYPTON?
PART 3. THE SUPERMAN OF TWO WORLDS! AMAZING INDEED IS THE FINAL DOUBLE ROLE THAT KAL-EL PLAYS, IN SUPERMAN'S UNFULFILLED LIFE ON HIS NATIVE WORLD!
KRYPTON WILL NOT EXPLODE, LARA! I GUIDED BACK THE SPACE ROCKET OF KAL-EL, OUR BABY SON!
SUPERMAN'S OTHER LIFE!
GREAT SCOTT! THIS MACHINE PREDICTS WHAT MY LIFE WOULD HAVE BEEN LIKE IF I HAD GROWN UP WITH MY REAL PARENTS, JOR-EL AND LARA, ON THE PLANET KRYPTON!

Story by Otto Binder/Art by Wayne Boring & Stan Kaye/Color by Bob LeRose

SOMEWHERE IN THE ARCTIC ONE DAY, *SUPER-MAN* FLIES TWO FAMOUS FRIENDS OF HIS TO THE *FORTRESS OF SOLITUDE*...

I'VE KEPT THE LOCATION OF MY *FORTRESS* A SECRET FROM EVERYONE... EXCEPT YOU, *BATMAN* AND *ROBIN!* YOU ARE ALSO THE ONLY ONES ON EARTH WHO KNOW MY SECRET IDENTITY OF CLARK KENT! BUT TELL ME... JUST WHY DID YOU ASK ME TO BRING YOU HERE TODAY?

WE WANT TO GIVE YOU A GIFT FOR SAVING US FROM THAT CRIME-TRAP LAST WEEK IN GOTHAM CITY! BUT YOU ALREADY HAVE *EVERY-THING* UNDER THE SUN IN YOUR COLLECTION!

WE HAD TO THINK OF AN *EXTRAORDINARY* GIFT! HERE, *SUPERMAN!*

AFTER *SUPERMAN* OPENS IT...

BUT...ER...THESE ARE ONLY COPIES OF PHOTOS OF LIFE ON *KRYPTON,* MY HOME WORLD! I MADE THE ORIGINALS BY OVERTAKING AND PHOTOGRAPHING LIGHT RAYS THAT HAD LEFT *KRYPTON* BEFORE IT EXPLODED! I MYSELF DONATED THE PHOTOS TO A MUSEUM!

JOR-EL AND LARA

KAL-EL

KRYPTONOPOLIS

KRYPTON BEAST

YES, WE KNOW! BUT FEED THESE PHOTOS INTO YOUR *SUPER UNIVAC* AS FACTORS, SO WE CAN LEARN HOW IT SOLVES THIS *SUPER* PROBLEM!

WHAT WOULD *SUPERMAN'S* OTHER LIFE HAVE BEEN, IF *KRYPTON* HAD *NOT* EXPLODED?

GREAT SCOTT! I...UH...NEVER THOUGHT OF FINDING THAT OUT MYSELF! WILL I BE *GLAD* OR *SORRY* AT SEEING MY *MIGHT-HAVE-BEEN* LIFE ON *KRYPTON?*

UNFIT FOR LIFE

SOLAR SYSTEM OF KRYPTON, THREE MILLION LIGHT YEARS FROM

2

CURIOUS, *SUPERMAN* PRESSES THE BUTTON WHICH STARTS THE PREDICTIONS OF THE SUPER-ANALYZING MACHINE!

THAT SCREEN WILL SHOW US THE SCENES AND ALSO TRANSLATE *KRYPTONESE* INTO EARTH LANGUAGE!

THIS IS YOUR LIFE, *SUPERMAN...* YOUR *OTHER* LIFE...IF *KRYPTON* HAD *NOT* MET DOOM!

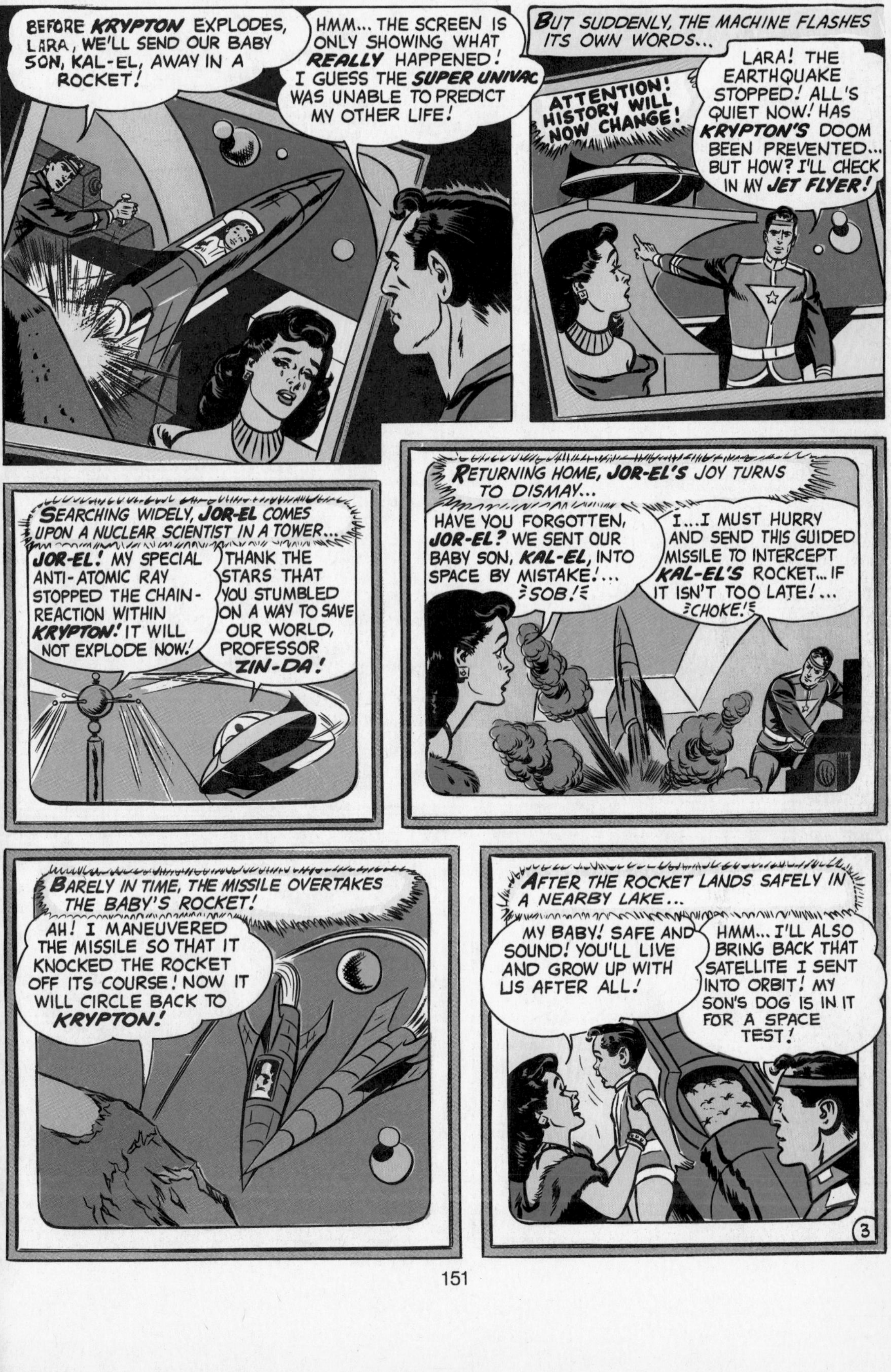

BEFORE KRYPTON EXPLODES, LARA, WE'LL SEND OUR BABY SON, KAL-EL, AWAY IN A ROCKET!
HMM... THE SCREEN IS ONLY SHOWING WHAT REALLY HAPPENED! I GUESS THE SUPER UNIVAC WAS UNABLE TO PREDICT MY OTHER LIFE!
BUT SUDDENLY, THE MACHINE FLASHES ITS OWN WORDS...
ATTENTION! HISTORY WILL NOW CHANGE!
LARA! THE EARTHQUAKE STOPPED! ALL'S QUIET NOW! HAS KRYPTON'S DOOM BEEN PREVENTED... BUT HOW? I'LL CHECK IN MY JET FLYER!
SEARCHING WIDELY, JOR-EL COMES UPON A NUCLEAR SCIENTIST IN A TOWER...
JOR-EL! MY SPECIAL ANTI-ATOMIC RAY STOPPED THE CHAIN-REACTION WITHIN KRYPTON! IT WILL NOT EXPLODE NOW!
THANK THE STARS THAT YOU STUMBLED ON A WAY TO SAVE OUR WORLD, PROFESSOR ZIN-DA!
RETURNING HOME, JOR-EL'S JOY TURNS TO DISMAY...
HAVE YOU FORGOTTEN, JOR-EL? WE SENT OUR BABY SON, KAL-EL, INTO SPACE BY MISTAKE!... SOB!
I...I MUST HURRY AND SEND THIS GUIDED MISSILE TO INTERCEPT KAL-EL'S ROCKET... IF IT ISN'T TOO LATE!... CHOKE!
BARELY IN TIME, THE MISSILE OVERTAKES THE BABY'S ROCKET!
AH! I MANEUVERED THE MISSILE SO THAT IT KNOCKED THE ROCKET OFF ITS COURSE! NOW IT WILL CIRCLE BACK TO KRYPTON!
AFTER THE ROCKET LANDS SAFELY IN A NEARBY LAKE...
MY BABY! SAFE AND SOUND! YOU'LL LIVE AND GROW UP WITH US AFTER ALL!
HMM... I'LL ALSO BRING BACK THAT SATELLITE I SENT INTO ORBIT! MY SON'S DOG IS IN IT FOR A SPACE TEST!
3

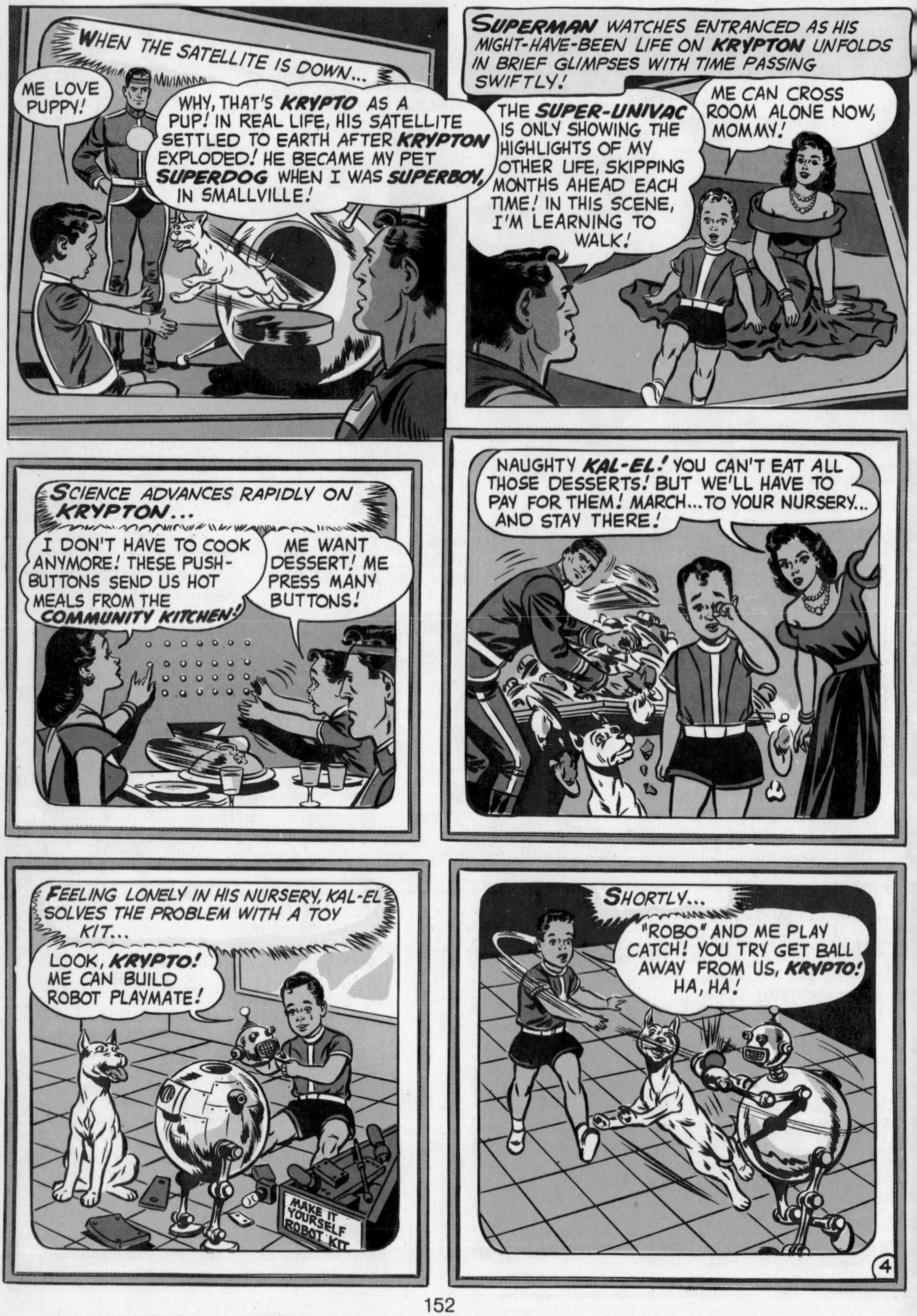
WHEN THE SATELLITE IS DOWN...
ME LOVE PUPPY!
WHY, THAT'S KRYPTO AS A PUP! IN REAL LIFE, HIS SATELLITE SETTLED TO EARTH AFTER KRYPTON EXPLODED! HE BECAME MY PET SUPERDOG WHEN I WAS SUPERBOY, IN SMALLVILLE!
SUPERMAN WATCHES ENTRANCED AS HIS MIGHT-HAVE-BEEN LIFE ON KRYPTON UNFOLDS IN BRIEF GLIMPSES WITH TIME PASSING SWIFTLY!
THE SUPER-UNIVAC IS ONLY SHOWING THE HIGHLIGHTS OF MY OTHER LIFE, SKIPPING MONTHS AHEAD EACH TIME! IN THIS SCENE, I'M LEARNING TO WALK!
ME CAN CROSS ROOM ALONE NOW, MOMMY!
SCIENCE ADVANCES RAPIDLY ON KRYPTON...
I DON'T HAVE TO COOK ANYMORE! THESE PUSH-BUTTONS SEND US HOT MEALS FROM THE COMMUNITY KITCHEN!
ME WANT DESSERT! ME PRESS MANY BUTTONS!
NAUGHTY KAL-EL! YOU CAN'T EAT ALL THOSE DESSERTS! BUT WE'LL HAVE TO PAY FOR THEM! MARCH...TO YOUR NURSERY... AND STAY THERE!
FEELING LONELY IN HIS NURSERY, KAL-EL SOLVES THE PROBLEM WITH A TOY KIT...
LOOK, KRYPTO! ME CAN BUILD ROBOT PLAYMATE!
MAKE IT YOURSELF ROBOT KIT
SHORTLY...
"ROBO" AND ME PLAY CATCH! YOU TRY GET BALL AWAY FROM US, KRYPTO! HA, HA!
4

OH...LOOK OUT, *KRYPTO!* YOU BUMPED LEVER TO FULL POWER! ME WONDER...UH...WHAT HAPPEN NOW?

ROBOT THROW BALL TOO HARD! ME CAN'T CATCH IT...*OWWW!*

AND I GET A BLACK EYE! I'M *NOT INVULNERABLE* ON *KRYPTON!* I ONLY GAINED MY SUPER-POWERS UNDER EARTH'S LESSER GRAVITY CONDITIONS!

MY HAIR COULD BE TRIMMED THERE, TOO! IT CAN'T BE CUT OR GROW HERE IN EARTH'S ATMOSPHERE!

YOU MUST LOOK YOUR BEST, KAL-EL! IT'S YOUR FIRST DAY OF SCHOOL!

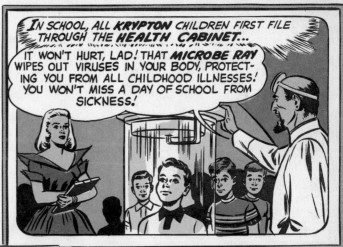

IN SCHOOL, ALL KRYPTON CHILDREN FIRST FILE THROUGH THE HEALTH CABINET...

IT WON'T HURT, LAD! THAT *MICROBE RAY* WIPES OUT VIRUSES IN YOUR BODY, PROTECTING YOU FROM ALL CHILDHOOD ILLNESSES! YOU WON'T MISS A DAY OF SCHOOL FROM SICKNESS!

IN CLASS, LESSONS ARE TAUGHT WITH THE SWIFTNESS OF THOUGHT...

YOUR TELEPATHY HELMETS ARE ALL PLUGGED IN, PUPILS! I'LL TRANSMIT ALL EARLY *KRYPTON* HISTORY IN ONE HOUR BY THOUGHT-WAVES! SPOKEN WORDS WOULD TAKE A WEEK!

WHEN HE IS OLD ENOUGH, KAL-EL JOINS THE KRYPTON YOUTH SCOUTS...

BOYS! TO WIN THE *SUPREME MERIT* BADGE, EACH OF YOU MUST PERFORM A GOOD DEED...BUT ON *ANOTHER WORLD!* YOU WILL USE THAT SPACE TELESCOPE AND LONG-RANGE POWER-RAYS!

5

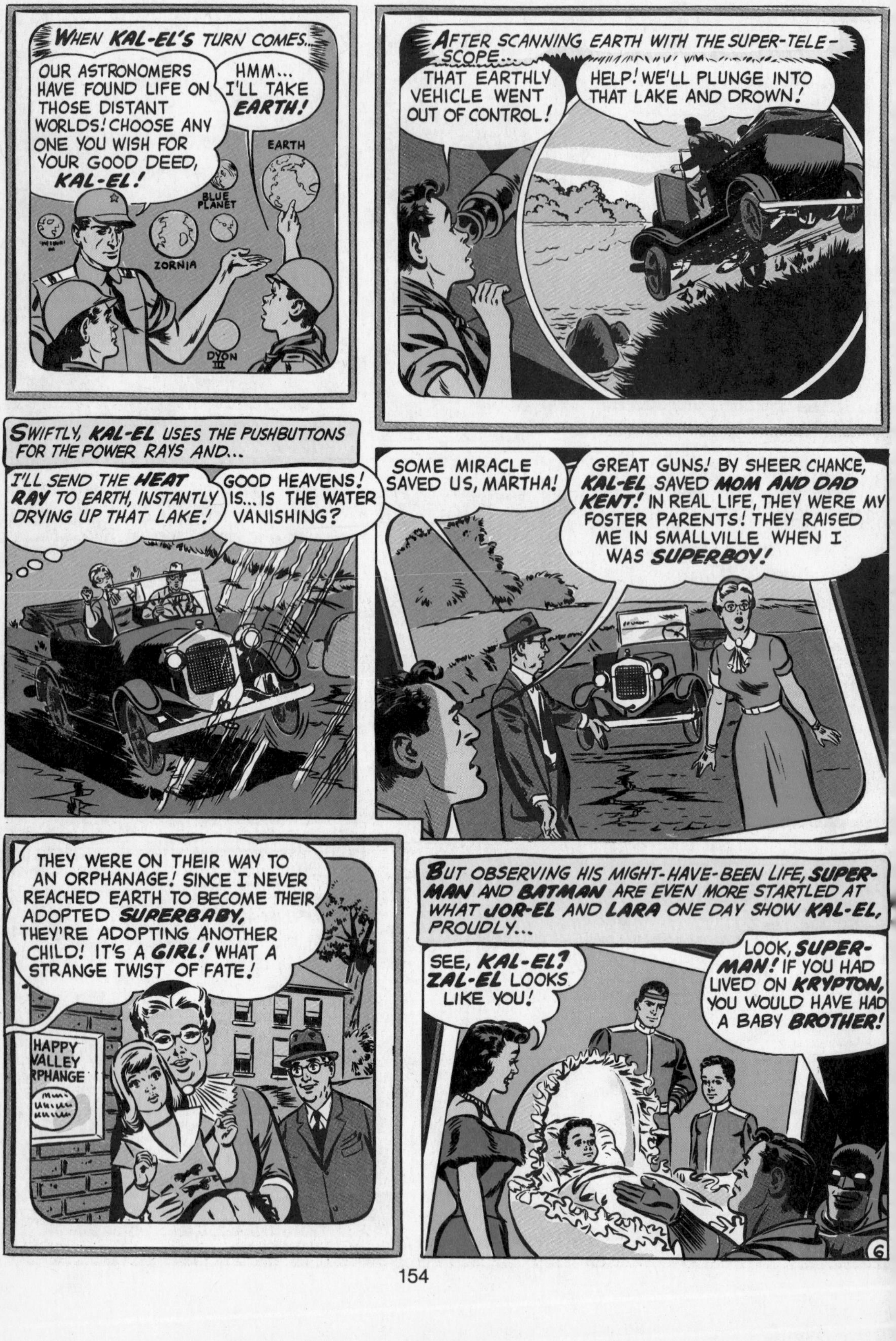
WHEN KAL-EL'S TURN COMES...
OUR ASTRONOMERS HAVE FOUND LIFE ON THOSE DISTANT WORLDS! CHOOSE ANY ONE YOU WISH FOR YOUR GOOD DEED, KAL-EL!
HMM... I'LL TAKE EARTH!
EARTH
BLUE PLANET
ZORNIA
DYON III
AFTER SCANNING EARTH WITH THE SUPER-TELE-SCOPE...
THAT EARTHLY VEHICLE WENT OUT OF CONTROL!
HELP! WE'LL PLUNGE INTO THAT LAKE AND DROWN!
SWIFTLY, KAL-EL USES THE PUSHBUTTONS FOR THE POWER RAYS AND...
I'LL SEND THE HEAT RAY TO EARTH, INSTANTLY DRYING UP THAT LAKE!
GOOD HEAVENS! IS... IS THE WATER VANISHING?
SOME MIRACLE SAVED US, MARTHA!
GREAT GUNS! BY SHEER CHANCE, KAL-EL SAVED MOM AND DAD KENT! IN REAL LIFE, THEY WERE MY FOSTER PARENTS! THEY RAISED ME IN SMALLVILLE WHEN I WAS SUPERBOY!
THEY WERE ON THEIR WAY TO AN ORPHANAGE! SINCE I NEVER REACHED EARTH TO BECOME THEIR ADOPTED SUPERBABY, THEY'RE ADOPTING ANOTHER CHILD! IT'S A GIRL! WHAT A STRANGE TWIST OF FATE!
HAPPY VALLEY RPHANGE
BUT OBSERVING HIS MIGHT-HAVE-BEEN LIFE, SUPERMAN AND BATMAN ARE EVEN MORE STARTLED AT WHAT JOR-EL AND LARA ONE DAY SHOW KAL-EL, PROUDLY...
SEE, KAL-EL? ZAL-EL LOOKS LIKE YOU!
LOOK, SUPERMAN! IF YOU HAD LIVED ON KRYPTON, YOU WOULD HAVE HAD A BABY BROTHER!
6

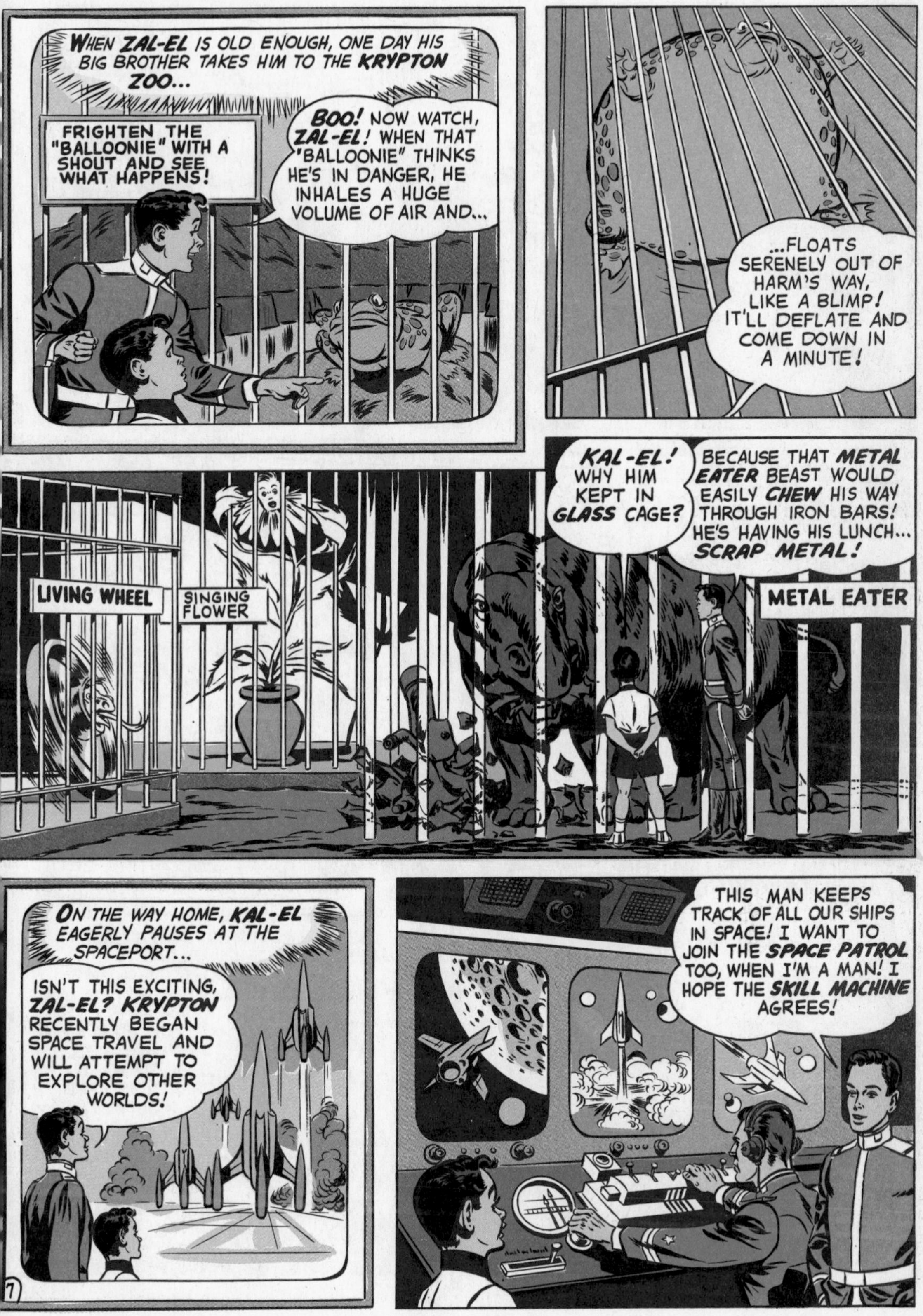

WHEN ZAL-EL IS OLD ENOUGH, ONE DAY HIS BIG BROTHER TAKES HIM TO THE KRYPTON ZOO...
FRIGHTEN THE "BALLOONIE" WITH A SHOUT AND SEE WHAT HAPPENS!
BOO! NOW WATCH, ZAL-EL! WHEN THAT "BALLOONIE" THINKS HE'S IN DANGER, HE INHALES A HUGE VOLUME OF AIR AND...
...FLOATS SERENELY OUT OF HARM'S WAY, LIKE A BLIMP! IT'LL DEFLATE AND COME DOWN IN A MINUTE!
KAL-EL! WHY HIM KEPT IN GLASS CAGE?
BECAUSE THAT METAL EATER BEAST WOULD EASILY CHEW HIS WAY THROUGH IRON BARS! HE'S HAVING HIS LUNCH... SCRAP METAL!
LIVING WHEEL
SINGING FLOWER
METAL EATER
ON THE WAY HOME, KAL-EL EAGERLY PAUSES AT THE SPACEPORT...
ISN'T THIS EXCITING, ZAL-EL? KRYPTON RECENTLY BEGAN SPACE TRAVEL AND WILL ATTEMPT TO EXPLORE OTHER WORLDS!
7
THIS MAN KEEPS TRACK OF ALL OUR SHIPS IN SPACE! I WANT TO JOIN THE SPACE PATROL TOO, WHEN I'M A MAN! I HOPE THE SKILL MACHINE AGREES!

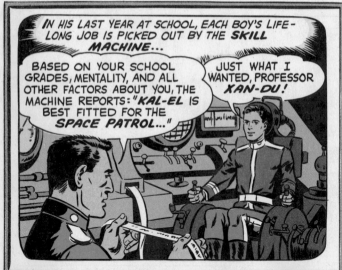

IN HIS LAST YEAR AT SCHOOL, EACH BOY'S LIFE-LONG JOB IS PICKED OUT BY THE *SKILL MACHINE*...

BASED ON YOUR SCHOOL GRADES, MENTALITY, AND ALL OTHER FACTORS ABOUT YOU, THE MACHINE REPORTS: "KAL-EL IS BEST FITTED FOR THE *SPACE PATROL*..."

JUST WHAT I WANTED, PROFESSOR *XAN-DU!*

YOU DIDN'T LET ME FINISH! IT ENDS SAYING: "...AS A *DIS-PATCHER!*"

BUT...BUT THE DISPATCHER *NEVER* LEAVES *KRYPTON!* I WANT TO BE A *SPACEMAN!* THE MACHINE MUST BE *WRONG!*

THE MACHINE IS *NEVER* WRONG, LAD! ITS VERDICT IS THE LAW, ACCORDING TO THE *KRYPTON* COUNCIL! COME AND WATCH MY NEW LABORATORY EXPERIMENT! IT WILL HELP YOU FORGET ABOUT THE MACHINE!

I INVENTED THIS *SUPER-STATIC RAY* AFTER SCHOOL HOURS! I'M HOPING IT WILL INCREASE THE SIZE OF TEST ANIMALS! WATCH CLOSELY, *KAL-EL*...

MOMENTS LATER...

LOOK, *XAN-DU!* THE RABBIT CHANGED COMPLETELY... INTO A BIRD!

GREAT STARS! I... ER...NEVER EXPECTED MY *STATIC RAY* TO DO THAT! I'LL TRY IT AGAIN WITH ANOTHER *GUINEA-PIG!*

THIS TIME, EVEN MORE ASTOUNDINGLY...

WHY, THE ANIMAL TURNED INTO *GLASS!* MY *STATIC RAY* IS COMPLETELY UNPREDICTABLE! IT DOES FREAKISH THINGS TO LIVING CREATURES!

TOO BAD, *XAN-DU!* WELL, I'LL GO HOME OR I'LL BE LATE FOR SUPPER!

8

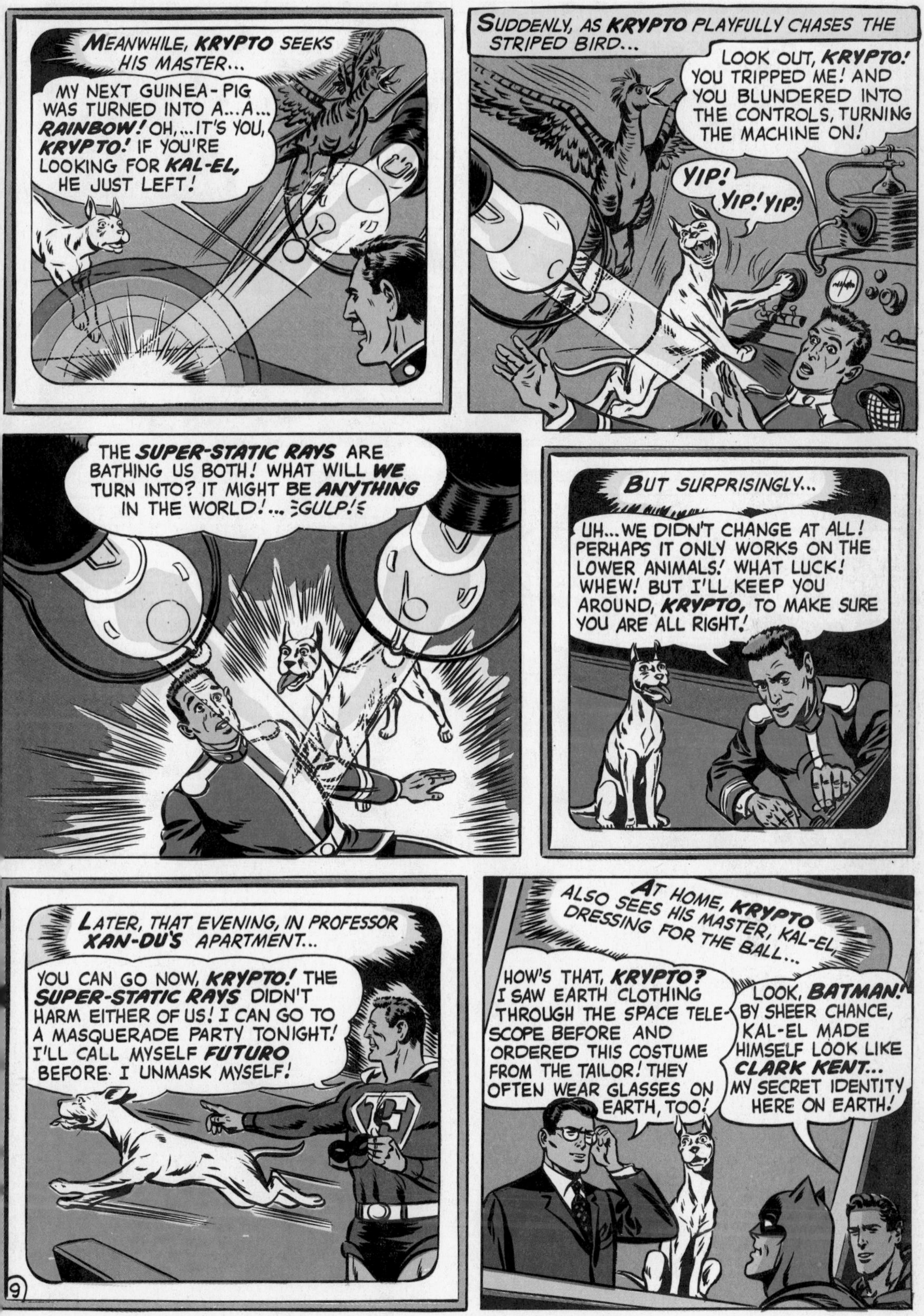
MEANWHILE, KRYPTO SEEKS HIS MASTER...
MY NEXT GUINEA-PIG WAS TURNED INTO A...A... RAINBOW! OH,...IT'S YOU, KRYPTO! IF YOU'RE LOOKING FOR KAL-EL, HE JUST LEFT!
SUDDENLY, AS KRYPTO PLAYFULLY CHASES THE STRIPED BIRD...
LOOK OUT, KRYPTO! YOU TRIPPED ME! AND YOU BLUNDERED INTO THE CONTROLS, TURNING THE MACHINE ON!
YIP!
YIP! YIP!
THE SUPER-STATIC RAYS ARE BATHING US BOTH! WHAT WILL WE TURN INTO? IT MIGHT BE ANYTHING IN THE WORLD!... GULP!
BUT SURPRISINGLY...
UH...WE DIDN'T CHANGE AT ALL! PERHAPS IT ONLY WORKS ON THE LOWER ANIMALS! WHAT LUCK! WHEW! BUT I'LL KEEP YOU AROUND, KRYPTO, TO MAKE SURE YOU ARE ALL RIGHT!
LATER, THAT EVENING, IN PROFESSOR XAN-DU'S APARTMENT...
YOU CAN GO NOW, KRYPTO! THE SUPER-STATIC RAYS DIDN'T HARM EITHER OF US! I CAN GO TO A MASQUERADE PARTY TONIGHT! I'LL CALL MYSELF FUTURO BEFORE I UNMASK MYSELF!
9
AT HOME, KRYPTO ALSO SEES HIS MASTER, KAL-EL, DRESSING FOR THE BALL...
HOW'S THAT, KRYPTO? I SAW EARTH CLOTHING THROUGH THE SPACE TELE-SCOPE BEFORE AND ORDERED THIS COSTUME FROM THE TAILOR! THEY OFTEN WEAR GLASSES ON EARTH, TOO!
LOOK, BATMAN! BY SHEER CHANCE, KAL-EL MADE HIMSELF LOOK LIKE CLARK KENT... MY SECRET IDENTITY HERE ON EARTH!

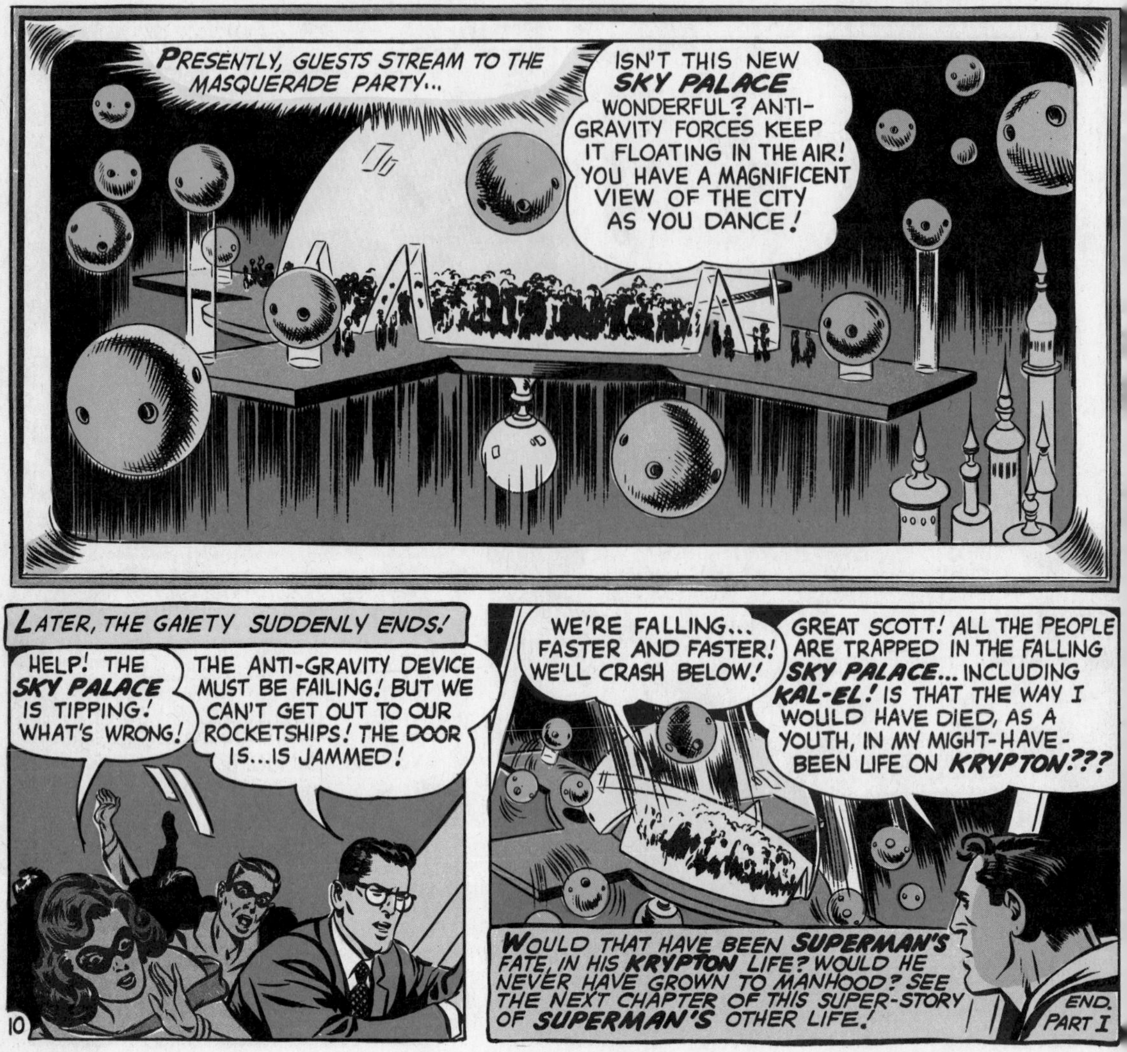
PRESENTLY, GUESTS STREAM TO THE MASQUERADE PARTY...
ISN'T THIS NEW SKY PALACE WONDERFUL? ANTI-GRAVITY FORCES KEEP IT FLOATING IN THE AIR! YOU HAVE A MAGNIFICENT VIEW OF THE CITY AS YOU DANCE!
LATER, THE GAIETY SUDDENLY ENDS!
HELP! THE SKY PALACE IS TIPPING! WHAT'S WRONG!
THE ANTI-GRAVITY DEVICE MUST BE FAILING! BUT WE CAN'T GET OUT TO OUR ROCKETSHIPS! THE DOOR IS...IS JAMMED!
10
WE'RE FALLING... FASTER AND FASTER! WE'LL CRASH BELOW!
GREAT SCOTT! ALL THE PEOPLE ARE TRAPPED IN THE FALLING SKY PALACE... INCLUDING KAL-EL! IS THAT THE WAY I WOULD HAVE DIED, AS A YOUTH, IN MY MIGHT-HAVE-BEEN LIFE ON KRYPTON???
WOULD THAT HAVE BEEN SUPERMAN'S FATE, IN HIS KRYPTON LIFE? WOULD HE NEVER HAVE GROWN TO MANHOOD? SEE THE NEXT CHAPTER OF THIS SUPER-STORY OF SUPERMAN'S OTHER LIFE!
END. PART I

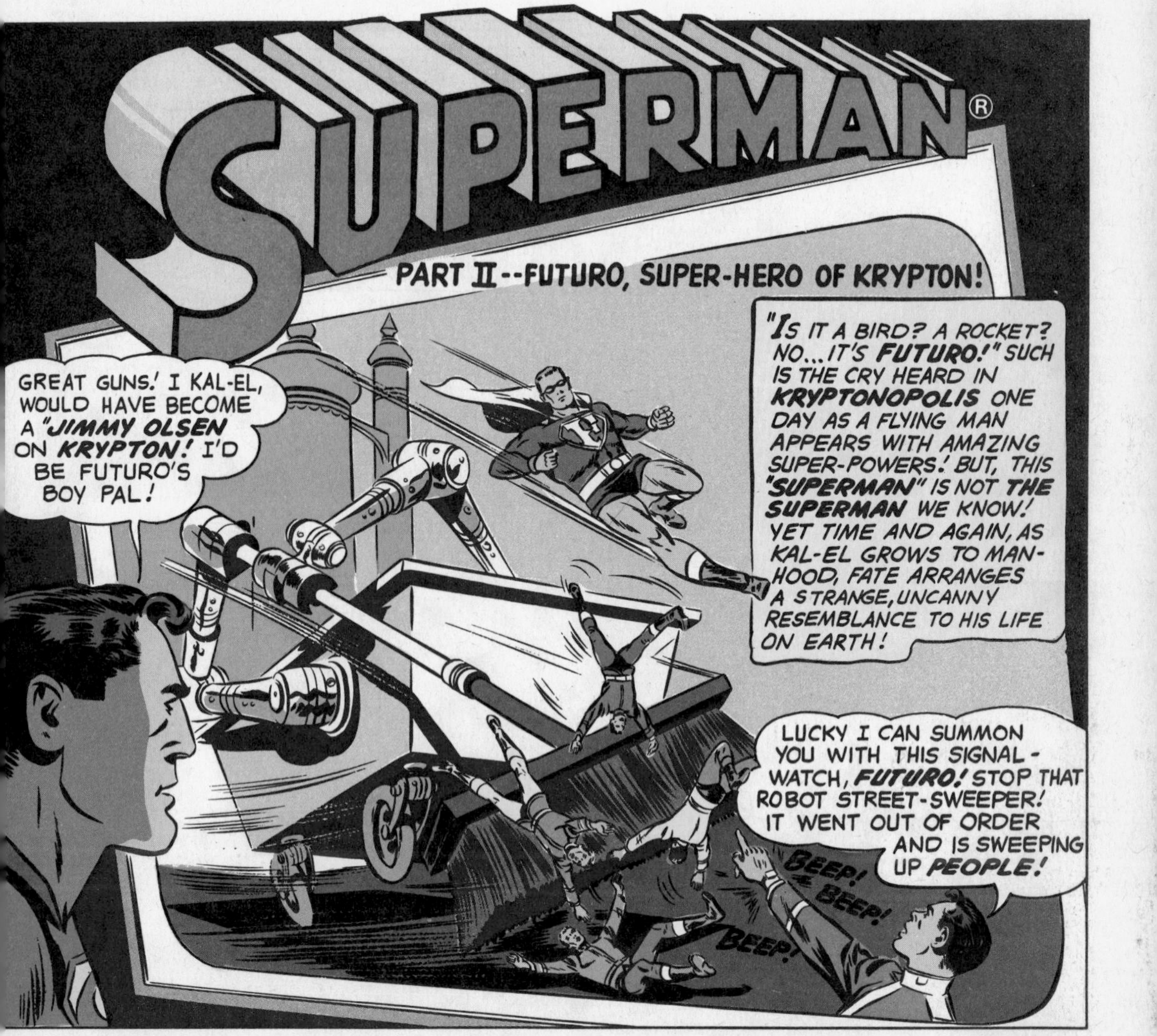
SUPERMAN®
PART II--FUTURO, SUPER-HERO OF KRYPTON!
"IS IT A BIRD? A ROCKET? NO...IT'S FUTURO!" SUCH IS THE CRY HEARD IN KRYPTONOPOLIS ONE DAY AS A FLYING MAN APPEARS WITH AMAZING SUPER-POWERS! BUT, THIS "SUPERMAN" IS NOT THE SUPERMAN WE KNOW! YET TIME AND AGAIN, AS KAL-EL GROWS TO MANHOOD, FATE ARRANGES A STRANGE, UNCANNY RESEMBLANCE TO HIS LIFE ON EARTH!
GREAT GUNS! I KAL-EL, WOULD HAVE BECOME A "JIMMY OLSEN ON KRYPTON! I'D BE FUTURO'S BOY PAL!
LUCKY I CAN SUMMON YOU WITH THIS SIGNAL-WATCH, FUTURO! STOP THAT ROBOT STREET-SWEEPER! IT WENT OUT OF ORDER AND IS SWEEPING UP PEOPLE!
BEEP! BEEP! BEEP!

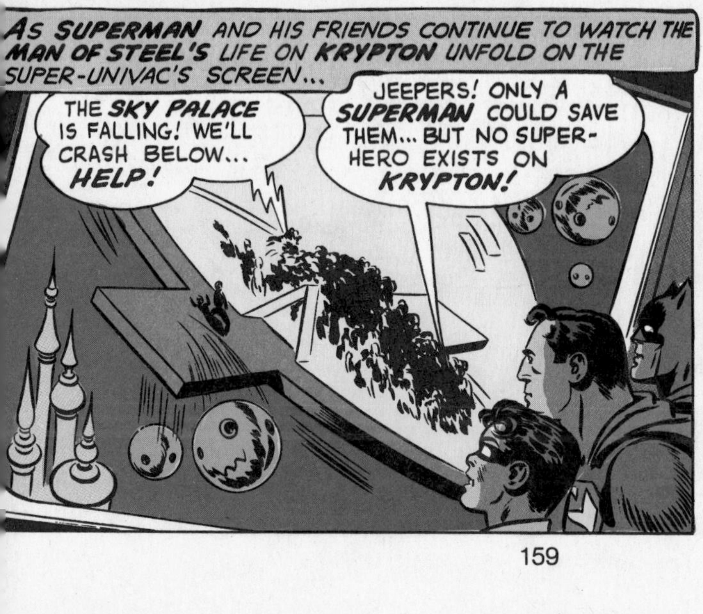
AS SUPERMAN AND HIS FRIENDS CONTINUE TO WATCH THE MAN OF STEEL'S LIFE ON KRYPTON UNFOLD ON THE SUPER-UNIVAC'S SCREEN...
THE SKY PALACE IS FALLING! WE'LL CRASH BELOW... HELP!
JEEPERS! ONLY A SUPERMAN COULD SAVE THEM... BUT NO SUPER-HERO EXISTS ON KRYPTON!

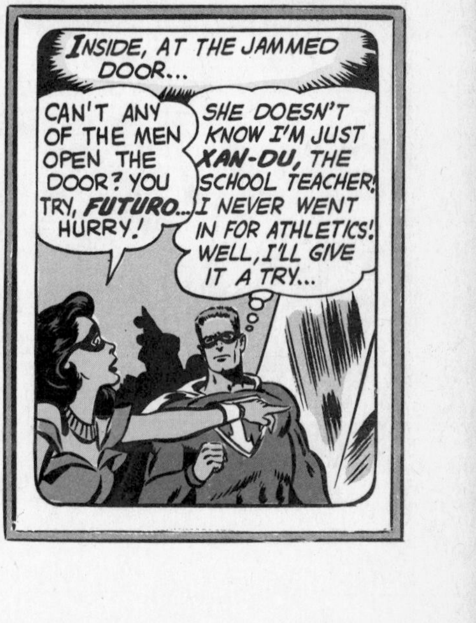
INSIDE, AT THE JAMMED DOOR...
CAN'T ANY OF THE MEN OPEN THE DOOR? YOU TRY, FUTURO... HURRY!
SHE DOESN'T KNOW I'M JUST XAN-DU, THE SCHOOL TEACHER! I NEVER WENT IN FOR ATHLETICS! WELL, I'LL GIVE IT A TRY...

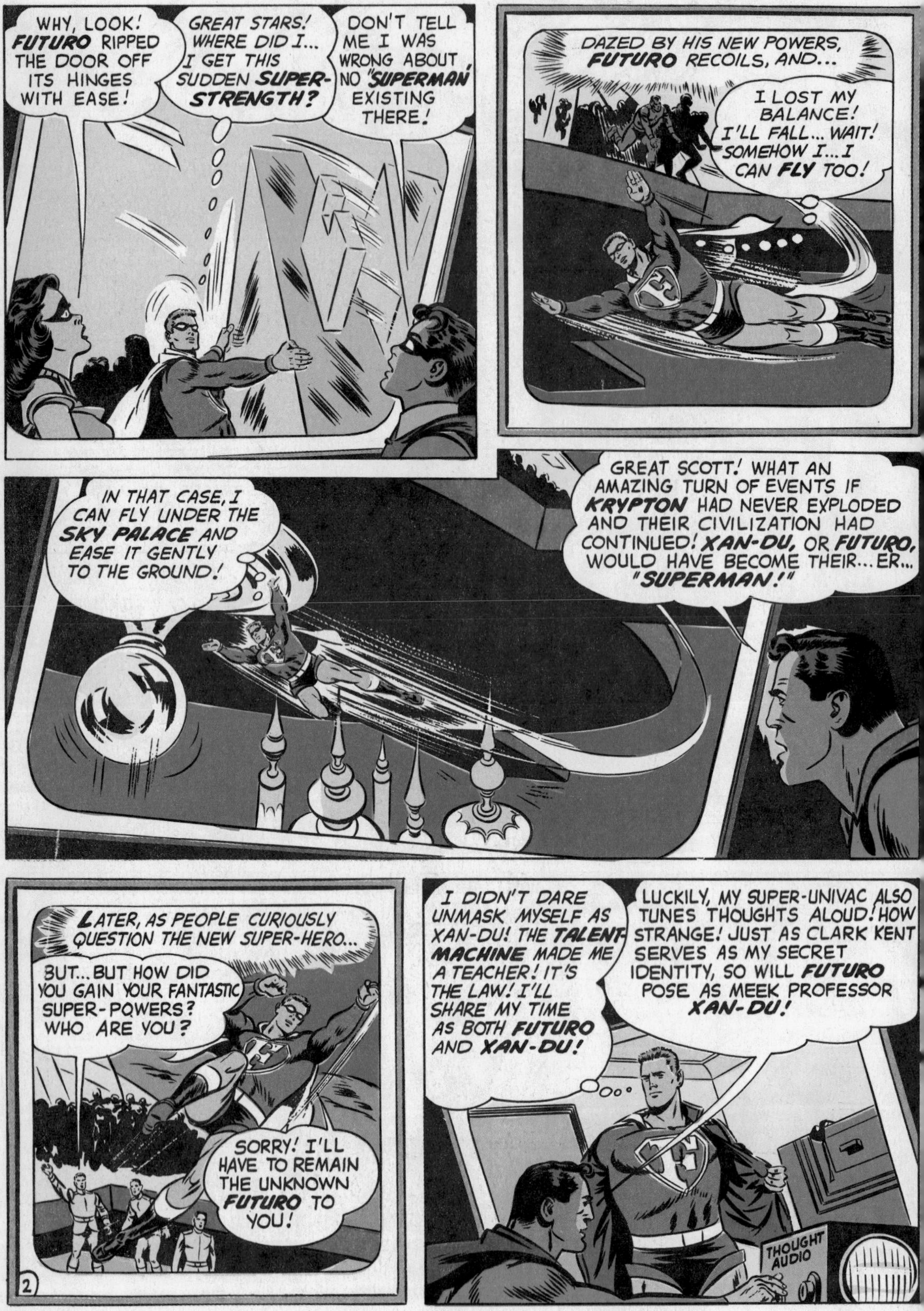

WHY, LOOK! FUTURO RIPPED THE DOOR OFF ITS HINGES WITH EASE!
GREAT STARS! WHERE DID I... I GET THIS SUDDEN SUPER-STRENGTH?
DON'T TELL ME I WAS WRONG ABOUT NO "SUPERMAN" EXISTING THERE!
DAZED BY HIS NEW POWERS, FUTURO RECOILS, AND...
I LOST MY BALANCE! I'LL FALL... WAIT! SOMEHOW I...I CAN FLY TOO!
IN THAT CASE, I CAN FLY UNDER THE SKY PALACE AND EASE IT GENTLY TO THE GROUND!
GREAT SCOTT! WHAT AN AMAZING TURN OF EVENTS IF KRYPTON HAD NEVER EXPLODED AND THEIR CIVILIZATION HAD CONTINUED! XAN-DU, OR FUTURO, WOULD HAVE BECOME THEIR...ER... "SUPERMAN!"
LATER, AS PEOPLE CURIOUSLY QUESTION THE NEW SUPER-HERO...
BUT...BUT HOW DID YOU GAIN YOUR FANTASTIC SUPER-POWERS? WHO ARE YOU?
SORRY! I'LL HAVE TO REMAIN THE UNKNOWN FUTURO TO YOU!
2
I DIDN'T DARE UNMASK MYSELF AS XAN-DU! THE TALENT-MACHINE MADE ME A TEACHER! IT'S THE LAW! I'LL SHARE MY TIME AS BOTH FUTURO AND XAN-DU!
LUCKILY, MY SUPER-UNIVAC ALSO TUNES THOUGHTS ALOUD! HOW STRANGE! JUST AS CLARK KENT SERVES AS MY SECRET IDENTITY, SO WILL FUTURO POSE AS MEEK PROFESSOR XAN-DU!
THOUGHT AUDIO

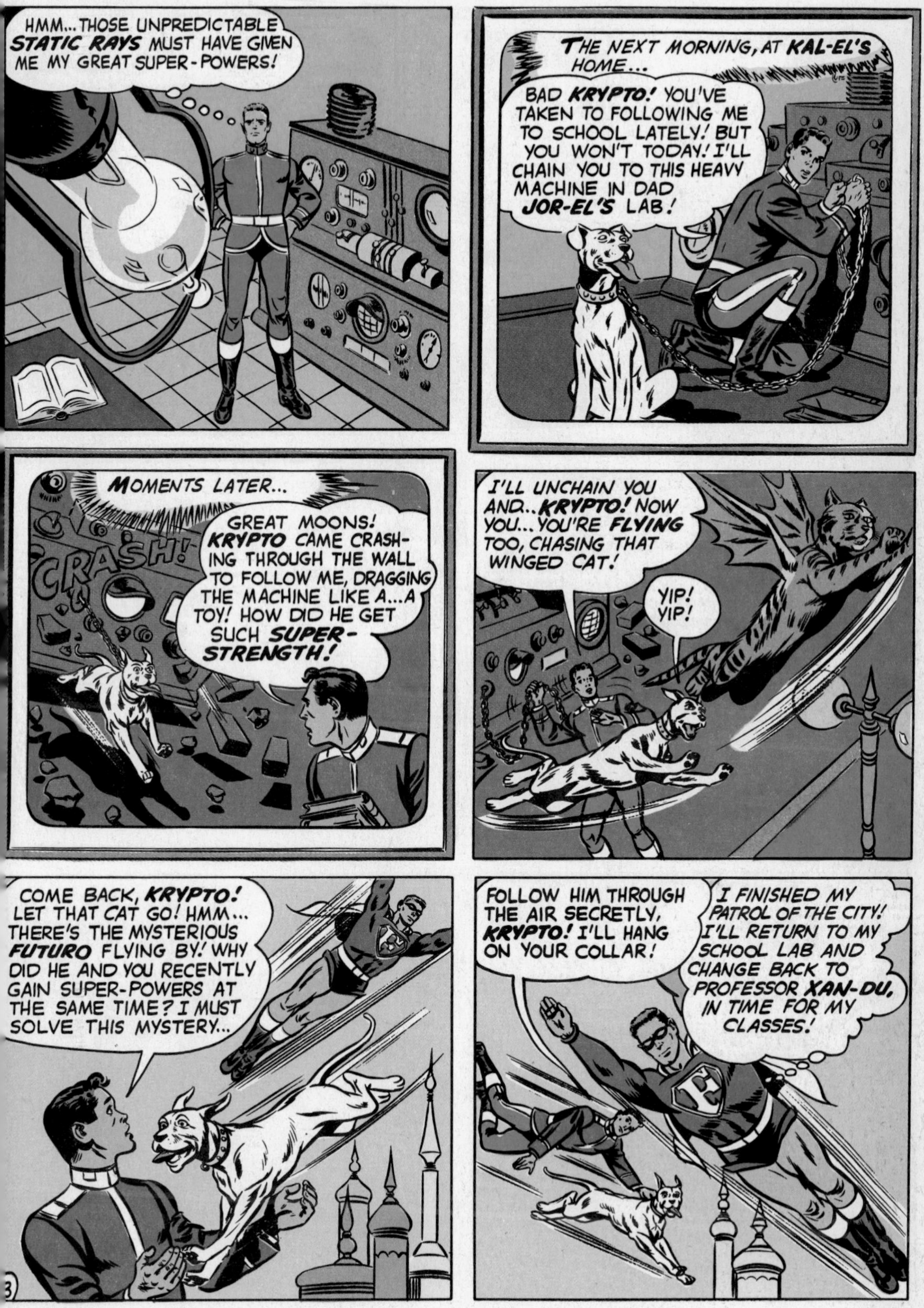
HMM...THOSE UNPREDICTABLE STATIC RAYS MUST HAVE GIVEN ME MY GREAT SUPER-POWERS!
THE NEXT MORNING, AT KAL-EL'S HOME...
BAD KRYPTO! YOU'VE TAKEN TO FOLLOWING ME TO SCHOOL LATELY! BUT YOU WON'T TODAY! I'LL CHAIN YOU TO THIS HEAVY MACHINE IN DAD JOR-EL'S LAB!
MOMENTS LATER...
CRASH!
GREAT MOONS! KRYPTO CAME CRASHING THROUGH THE WALL TO FOLLOW ME, DRAGGING THE MACHINE LIKE A...A TOY! HOW DID HE GET SUCH SUPER-STRENGTH!
I'LL UNCHAIN YOU AND...KRYPTO! NOW YOU...YOU'RE FLYING TOO, CHASING THAT WINGED CAT!
YIP! YIP!
COME BACK, KRYPTO! LET THAT CAT GO! HMM... THERE'S THE MYSTERIOUS FUTURO FLYING BY! WHY DID HE AND YOU RECENTLY GAIN SUPER-POWERS AT THE SAME TIME? I MUST SOLVE THIS MYSTERY...
FOLLOW HIM THROUGH THE AIR SECRETLY, KRYPTO! I'LL HANG ON YOUR COLLAR!
I FINISHED MY PATROL OF THE CITY! I'LL RETURN TO MY SCHOOL LAB AND CHANGE BACK TO PROFESSOR XAN-DU, IN TIME FOR MY CLASSES!

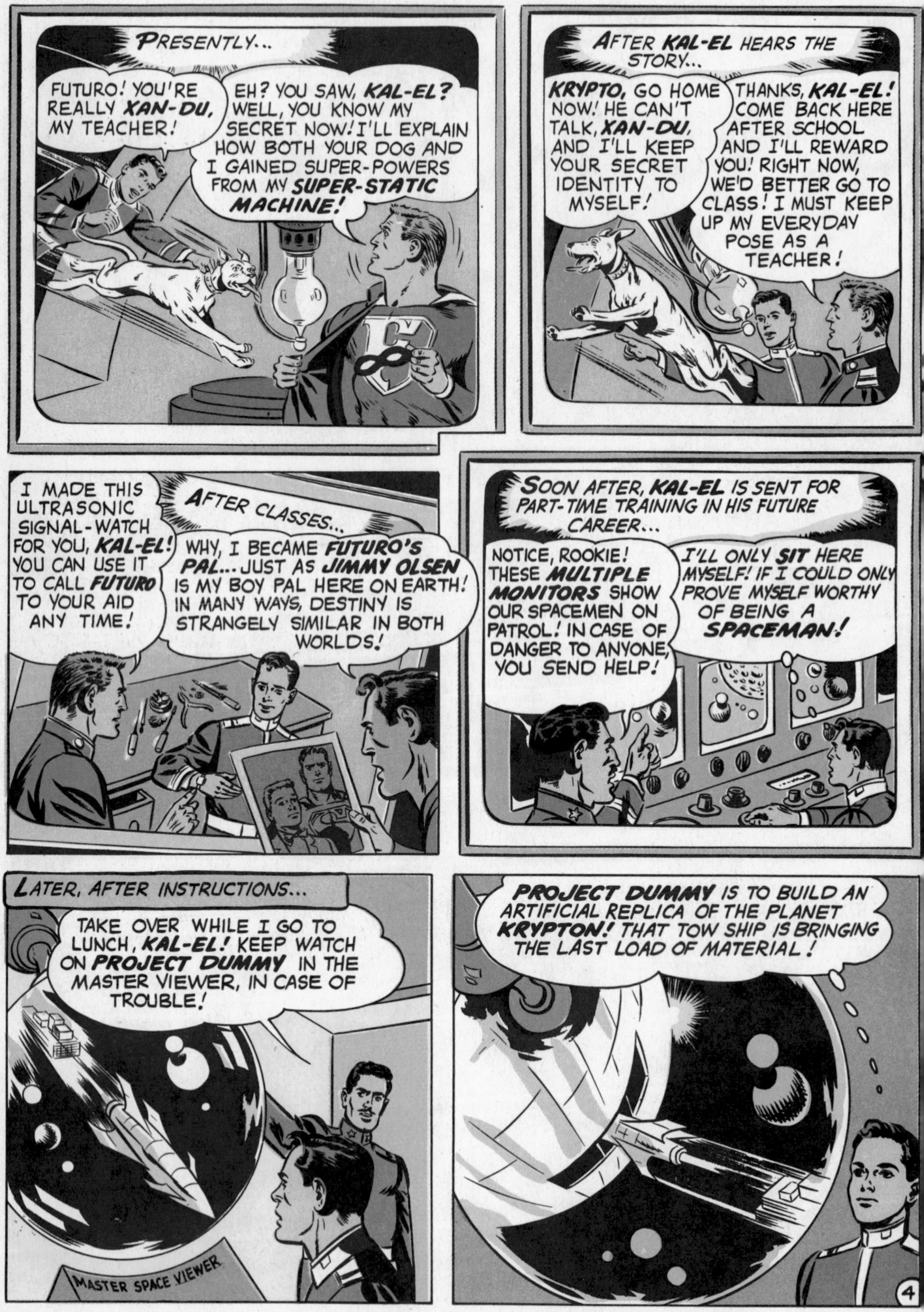
PRESENTLY...
FUTURO! YOU'RE REALLY XAN-DU, MY TEACHER!
EH? YOU SAW, KAL-EL? WELL, YOU KNOW MY SECRET NOW! I'LL EXPLAIN HOW BOTH YOUR DOG AND I GAINED SUPER-POWERS FROM MY SUPER-STATIC MACHINE!
AFTER KAL-EL HEARS THE STORY...
KRYPTO, GO HOME NOW! HE CAN'T TALK, XAN-DU, AND I'LL KEEP YOUR SECRET IDENTITY TO MYSELF!
THANKS, KAL-EL! COME BACK HERE AFTER SCHOOL AND I'LL REWARD YOU! RIGHT NOW, WE'D BETTER GO TO CLASS! I MUST KEEP UP MY EVERYDAY POSE AS A TEACHER!
AFTER CLASSES...
I MADE THIS ULTRASONIC SIGNAL-WATCH FOR YOU, KAL-EL! YOU CAN USE IT TO CALL FUTURO TO YOUR AID ANY TIME!
WHY, I BECAME FUTURO'S PAL... JUST AS JIMMY OLSEN IS MY BOY PAL HERE ON EARTH! IN MANY WAYS, DESTINY IS STRANGELY SIMILAR IN BOTH WORLDS!
SOON AFTER, KAL-EL IS SENT FOR PART-TIME TRAINING IN HIS FUTURE CAREER...
NOTICE, ROOKIE! THESE MULTIPLE MONITORS SHOW OUR SPACEMEN ON PATROL! IN CASE OF DANGER TO ANYONE, YOU SEND HELP!
I'LL ONLY SIT HERE MYSELF! IF I COULD ONLY PROVE MYSELF WORTHY OF BEING A SPACEMAN!
LATER, AFTER INSTRUCTIONS...
TAKE OVER WHILE I GO TO LUNCH, KAL-EL! KEEP WATCH ON PROJECT DUMMY IN THE MASTER VIEWER, IN CASE OF TROUBLE!
MASTER SPACE VIEWER
PROJECT DUMMY IS TO BUILD AN ARTIFICIAL REPLICA OF THE PLANET KRYPTON! THAT TOW SHIP IS BRINGING THE LAST LOAD OF MATERIAL!
4

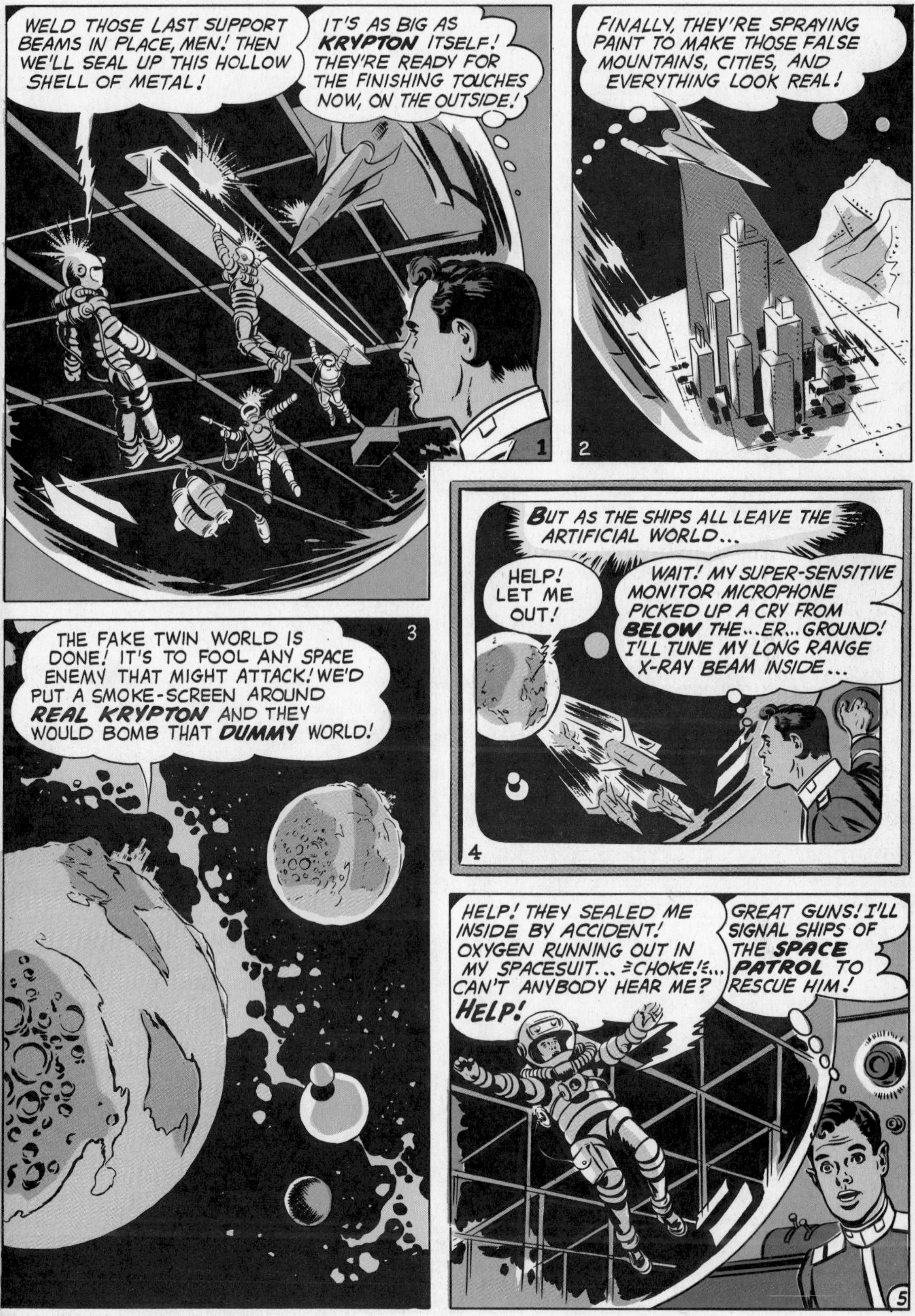
WELD THOSE LAST SUPPORT BEAMS IN PLACE, MEN! THEN WE'LL SEAL UP THIS HOLLOW SHELL OF METAL!
IT'S AS BIG AS KRYPTON ITSELF! THEY'RE READY FOR THE FINISHING TOUCHES NOW, ON THE OUTSIDE!
1
FINALLY, THEY'RE SPRAYING PAINT TO MAKE THOSE FALSE MOUNTAINS, CITIES, AND EVERYTHING LOOK REAL!
2
THE FAKE TWIN WORLD IS DONE! IT'S TO FOOL ANY SPACE ENEMY THAT MIGHT ATTACK! WE'D PUT A SMOKE-SCREEN AROUND REAL KRYPTON AND THEY WOULD BOMB THAT DUMMY WORLD!
3
BUT AS THE SHIPS ALL LEAVE THE ARTIFICIAL WORLD...
HELP! LET ME OUT!
WAIT! MY SUPER-SENSITIVE MONITOR MICROPHONE PICKED UP A CRY FROM BELOW THE...ER...GROUND! I'LL TUNE MY LONG RANGE X-RAY BEAM INSIDE...
4
HELP! THEY SEALED ME INSIDE BY ACCIDENT! OXYGEN RUNNING OUT IN MY SPACESUIT... ≡CHOKE!≡... CAN'T ANYBODY HEAR ME? HELP!
GREAT GUNS! I'LL SIGNAL SHIPS OF THE SPACE PATROL TO RESCUE HIM!
5

BUT WHEN THE *SPACE PATROL'S* WARSHIPS ARRIVE...

OUR BIGGEST BOMBS AND BLAST-RAYS CAN'T EVEN SCRATCH THAT METAL SHELL! IT WAS MADE SUPER-HARD SO THAT AN ATTACKING SPACE ENEMY WOULD WASTE ALL ITS AMMUNITION!

IS...IS THAT POOR FELLOW DOOMED?

WAIT! *FUTURO* HAS SUPER-POWERS! HE COULD SMASH THROUGH ANYTHING! I'LL USE MY SIGNAL-WATCH!

JUST LIKE *JIMMY OLSEN* CALLS ME FOR SUPER-JOBS!

ZEEP! ZEEP! ZEEP!

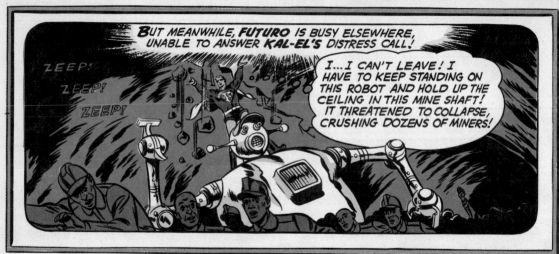

BUT MEANWHILE, *FUTURO* IS BUSY ELSEWHERE, UNABLE TO ANSWER *KAL-EL'S* DISTRESS CALL!

ZEEP! ZEEP! ZEEP!

I...I CAN'T LEAVE! I HAVE TO KEEP STANDING ON THIS ROBOT AND HOLD UP THE CEILING IN THIS MINE SHAFT! IT THREATENED TO COLLAPSE, CRUSHING DOZENS OF MINERS!

WHEN *FUTURO* FAILS TO APPEAR...

I HAVE AN IDEA! LUCKILY, ALL PATROL SHIPS ARE RUN BY PUSH-BUTTONS AND AUTOMATIC PILOTS! I'LL STOP OFF AT THE ZOO FIRST FOR A CERTAIN ANIMAL!

SPACE PATROL

THEN, AFTER A TOP-SPEED TRIP TO THE DUMMY WORLD...

I TOOK ALONG THE *METAL-EATER!* NOW THAT THE SLEEP-GAS I GAVE HIM WORE OFF, HE'S EATING A HOLE THROUGH THE METAL SHELL! I'LL GO IN AND BRING OUT THE TRAPPED SPACEMAN!

6

164

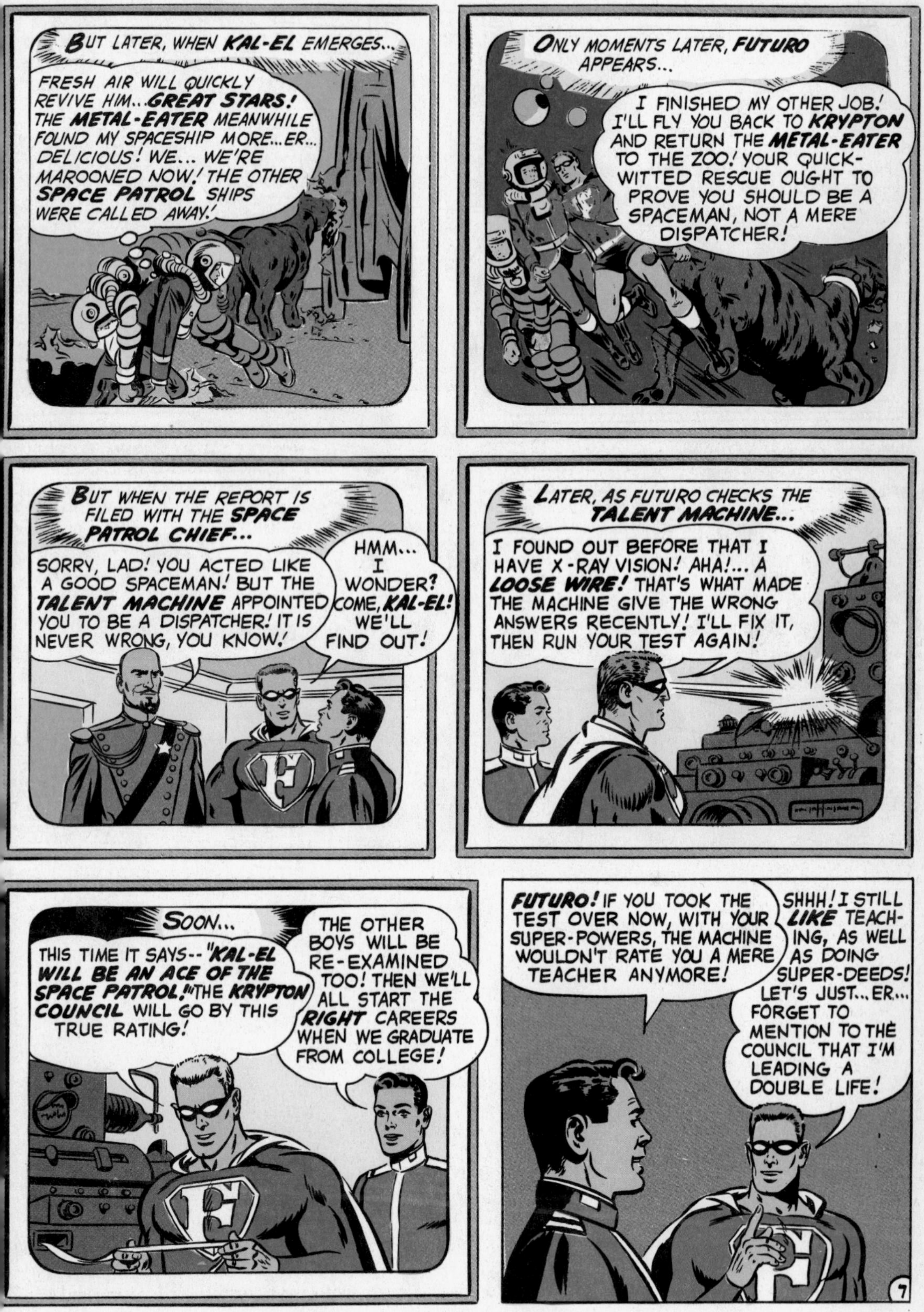
BUT LATER, WHEN KAL-EL EMERGES...
FRESH AIR WILL QUICKLY REVIVE HIM...GREAT STARS! THE METAL-EATER MEANWHILE FOUND MY SPACESHIP MORE...ER... DELICIOUS! WE... WE'RE MAROONED NOW! THE OTHER SPACE PATROL SHIPS WERE CALLED AWAY!
ONLY MOMENTS LATER, FUTURO APPEARS...
I FINISHED MY OTHER JOB! I'LL FLY YOU BACK TO KRYPTON AND RETURN THE METAL-EATER TO THE ZOO! YOUR QUICK-WITTED RESCUE OUGHT TO PROVE YOU SHOULD BE A SPACEMAN, NOT A MERE DISPATCHER!
BUT WHEN THE REPORT IS FILED WITH THE SPACE PATROL CHIEF...
SORRY, LAD! YOU ACTED LIKE A GOOD SPACEMAN! BUT THE TALENT MACHINE APPOINTED YOU TO BE A DISPATCHER! IT IS NEVER WRONG, YOU KNOW!
HMM... I WONDER? COME, KAL-EL! WE'LL FIND OUT!
LATER, AS FUTURO CHECKS THE TALENT MACHINE...
I FOUND OUT BEFORE THAT I HAVE X-RAY VISION! AHA!... A LOOSE WIRE! THAT'S WHAT MADE THE MACHINE GIVE THE WRONG ANSWERS RECENTLY! I'LL FIX IT, THEN RUN YOUR TEST AGAIN!
SOON...
THIS TIME IT SAYS--"KAL-EL WILL BE AN ACE OF THE SPACE PATROL!" THE KRYPTON COUNCIL WILL GO BY THIS TRUE RATING!
THE OTHER BOYS WILL BE RE-EXAMINED TOO! THEN WE'LL ALL START THE RIGHT CAREERS WHEN WE GRADUATE FROM COLLEGE!
FUTURO! IF YOU TOOK THE TEST OVER NOW, WITH YOUR SUPER-POWERS, THE MACHINE WOULDN'T RATE YOU A MERE TEACHER ANYMORE!
SHHH! I STILL LIKE TEACHING, AS WELL AS DOING SUPER-DEEDS! LET'S JUST...ER... FORGET TO MENTION TO THE COUNCIL THAT I'M LEADING A DOUBLE LIFE!
7

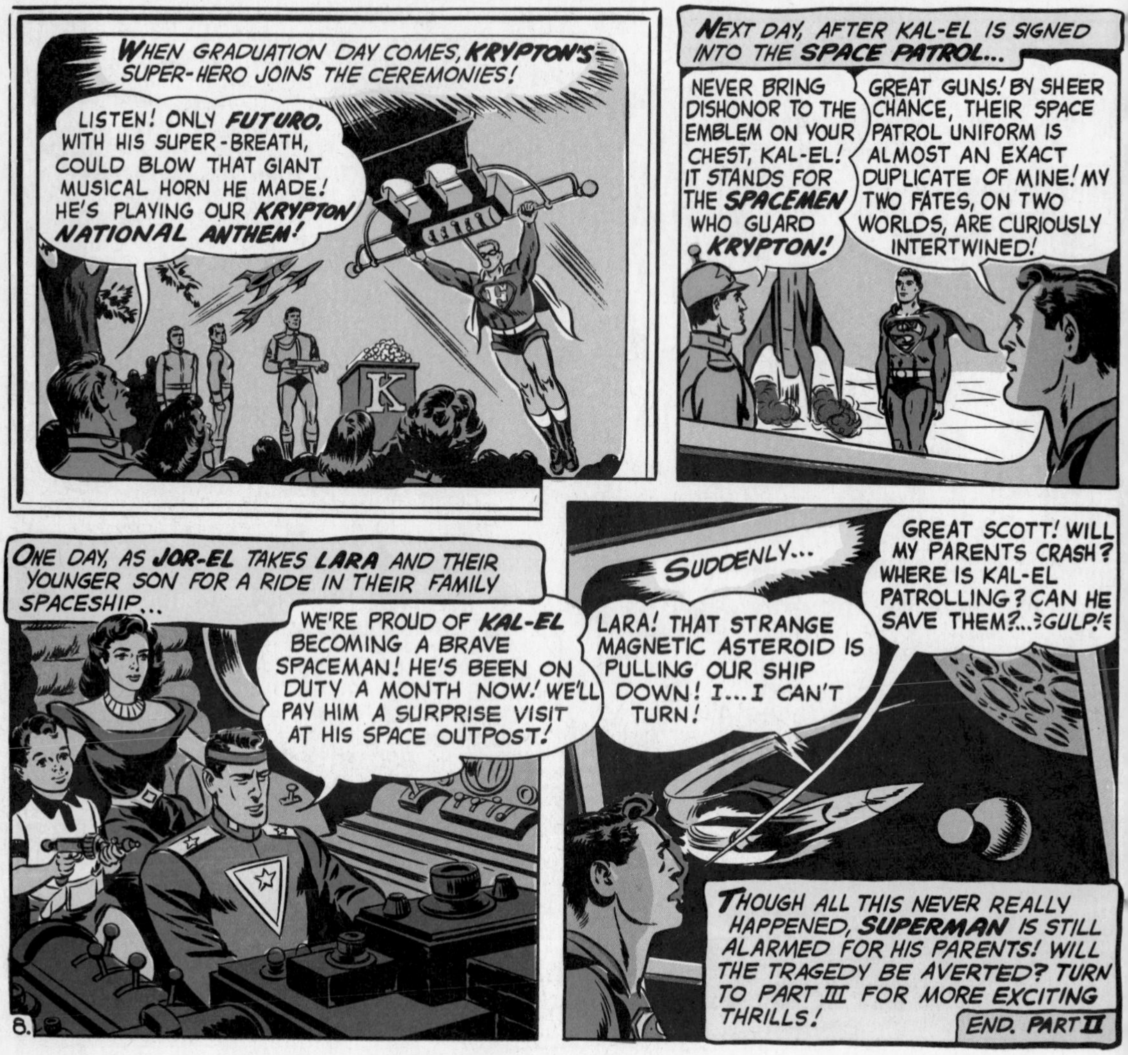
WHEN GRADUATION DAY COMES, KRYPTON'S SUPER-HERO JOINS THE CEREMONIES!
LISTEN! ONLY FUTURO, WITH HIS SUPER-BREATH, COULD BLOW THAT GIANT MUSICAL HORN HE MADE! HE'S PLAYING OUR KRYPTON NATIONAL ANTHEM!
NEXT DAY, AFTER KAL-EL IS SIGNED INTO THE SPACE PATROL...
NEVER BRING DISHONOR TO THE EMBLEM ON YOUR CHEST, KAL-EL! IT STANDS FOR THE SPACEMEN WHO GUARD KRYPTON!
GREAT GUNS! BY SHEER CHANCE, THEIR SPACE PATROL UNIFORM IS ALMOST AN EXACT DUPLICATE OF MINE! MY TWO FATES, ON TWO WORLDS, ARE CURIOUSLY INTERTWINED!
ONE DAY, AS JOR-EL TAKES LARA AND THEIR YOUNGER SON FOR A RIDE IN THEIR FAMILY SPACESHIP...
WE'RE PROUD OF KAL-EL BECOMING A BRAVE SPACEMAN! HE'S BEEN ON DUTY A MONTH NOW! WE'LL PAY HIM A SURPRISE VISIT AT HIS SPACE OUTPOST!
8.
SUDDENLY...
LARA! THAT STRANGE MAGNETIC ASTEROID IS PULLING OUR SHIP DOWN! I...I CAN'T TURN!
GREAT SCOTT! WILL MY PARENTS CRASH? WHERE IS KAL-EL PATROLLING? CAN HE SAVE THEM?...GULP!
THOUGH ALL THIS NEVER REALLY HAPPENED, SUPERMAN IS STILL ALARMED FOR HIS PARENTS! WILL THE TRAGEDY BE AVERTED? TURN TO PART III FOR MORE EXCITING THRILLS!
END. PART II

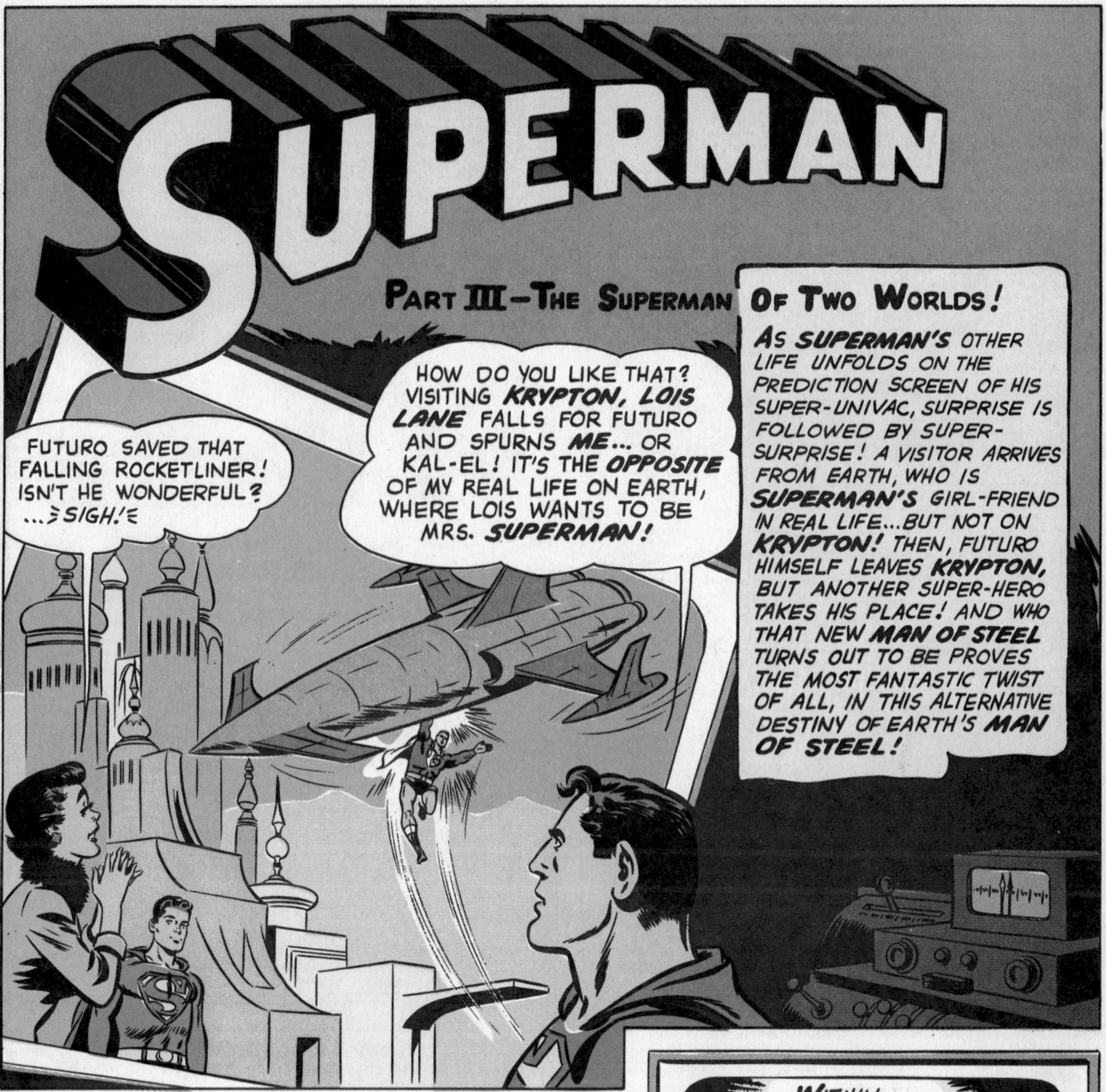
SUPERMAN
PART III—THE SUPERMAN OF TWO WORLDS!
AS SUPERMAN'S OTHER LIFE UNFOLDS ON THE PREDICTION SCREEN OF HIS SUPER-UNIVAC, SURPRISE IS FOLLOWED BY SUPER-SURPRISE! A VISITOR ARRIVES FROM EARTH, WHO IS SUPERMAN'S GIRL-FRIEND IN REAL LIFE...BUT NOT ON KRYPTON! THEN, FUTURO HIMSELF LEAVES KRYPTON, BUT ANOTHER SUPER-HERO TAKES HIS PLACE! AND WHO THAT NEW MAN OF STEEL TURNS OUT TO BE PROVES THE MOST FANTASTIC TWIST OF ALL, IN THIS ALTERNATIVE DESTINY OF EARTH'S MAN OF STEEL!
FUTURO SAVED THAT FALLING ROCKETLINER! ISN'T HE WONDERFUL? ...SIGH!
HOW DO YOU LIKE THAT? VISITING KRYPTON, LOIS LANE FALLS FOR FUTURO AND SPURNS ME... OR KAL-EL! IT'S THE OPPOSITE OF MY REAL LIFE ON EARTH, WHERE LOIS WANTS TO BE MRS. SUPERMAN!

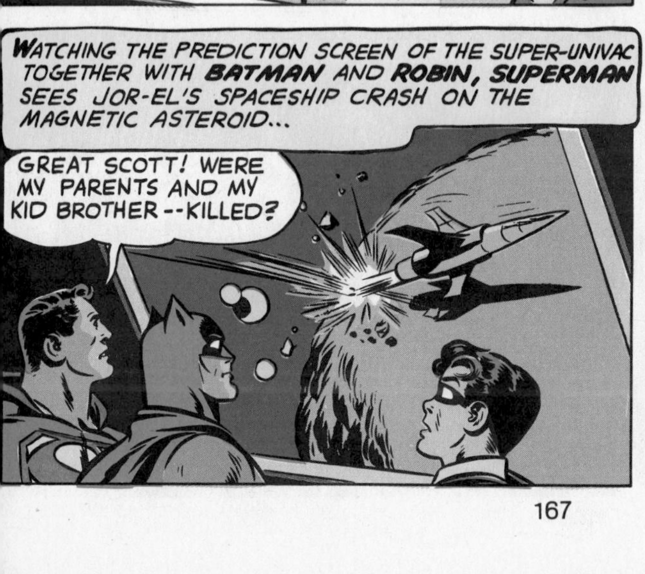
WATCHING THE PREDICTION SCREEN OF THE SUPER-UNIVAC TOGETHER WITH BATMAN AND ROBIN, SUPERMAN SEES JOR-EL'S SPACESHIP CRASH ON THE MAGNETIC ASTEROID...
GREAT SCOTT! WERE MY PARENTS AND MY KID BROTHER--KILLED?

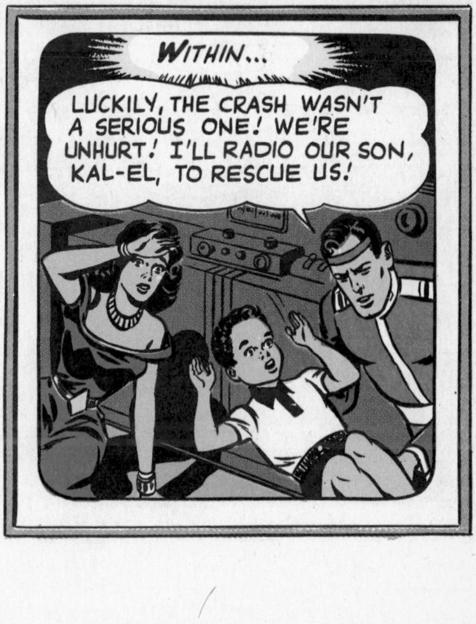
WITHIN...
LUCKILY, THE CRASH WASN'T A SERIOUS ONE! WE'RE UNHURT! I'LL RADIO OUR SON, KAL-EL, TO RESCUE US!

ELSEWHERE, AS SPACEMAN KAL-EL PICKS UP THE DISTRESS CALL...

I'LL RUSH THERE RIGHT AWAY, DAD JOR-EL, AND PICK YOU UP!

BUT HURRY, SON! MY... MY INSTRUMENTS SHOW THIS ASTEROID HAS A SOLID CORE OF *URANIUM!* THE JOLT OF OUR CRASHING SHIP STARTED A *CHAIN-REACTION!* HURRY, SON... OR IT MAY BE TOO LATE!

IT *IS* TOO LATE WHEN KAL-EL SPEEDS TO THE SCENE!

THE CHAIN-REACTION CAUSED AN ATOMIC EXPLOSION! GOODBYE, SON...

JOR-EL!... LARA!... ZAL-EL!... THEIR LIVES WERE SNUFFED OUT BEFORE MY EYES! ≥SOB!≤

FOR A MOMENT, *SUPERMAN* IS OVERCOME WITH SORROW, THOUGH THIS TRAGEDY NEVER REALLY HAPPENED...

IN THIS OTHER LIFE OF MINE, MY PARENTS ESCAPED THE DOOM OF *KRYPTON* EXPLODING... ONLY TO MEET THE *SAME* END ON AN EXPLODING ASTEROID! SO IN *EITHER* LIFE, I... I WAS DESTINED TO BE AN *ORPHAN!*

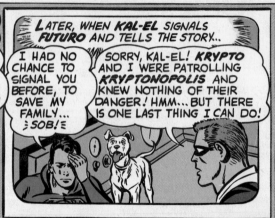

LATER, WHEN *KAL-EL* SIGNALS *FUTURO* AND TELLS THE STORY...

I HAD NO CHANCE TO SIGNAL YOU BEFORE, TO SAVE MY FAMILY... ≥SOB!≤

SORRY, KAL-EL! *KRYPTO* AND I WERE PATROLLING *KRYPTONOPOLIS* AND KNEW NOTHING OF THEIR DANGER! HMM... BUT THERE IS ONE LAST THING I CAN DO!

FUTURO LEAVES THE SHIP, AND...

THAT GIANT METEOR IS ALL THAT'S LEFT OF THE EXPLODED ASTEROID! I'LL USE THE HEAT OF MY X-RAY VISION TO MELT FACES IN THE STONE!

IT'S LIKE THE *MOUNT RUSHMORE MEMORIAL* HERE ON EARTH! *FUTURO* MADE A *SPACE MEMORIAL* IN HONOR OF KAL-EL'S FAMILY! ≥CHOKE!≤

IN MEMORY OF KAL-EL LARA AND ZAL-EL

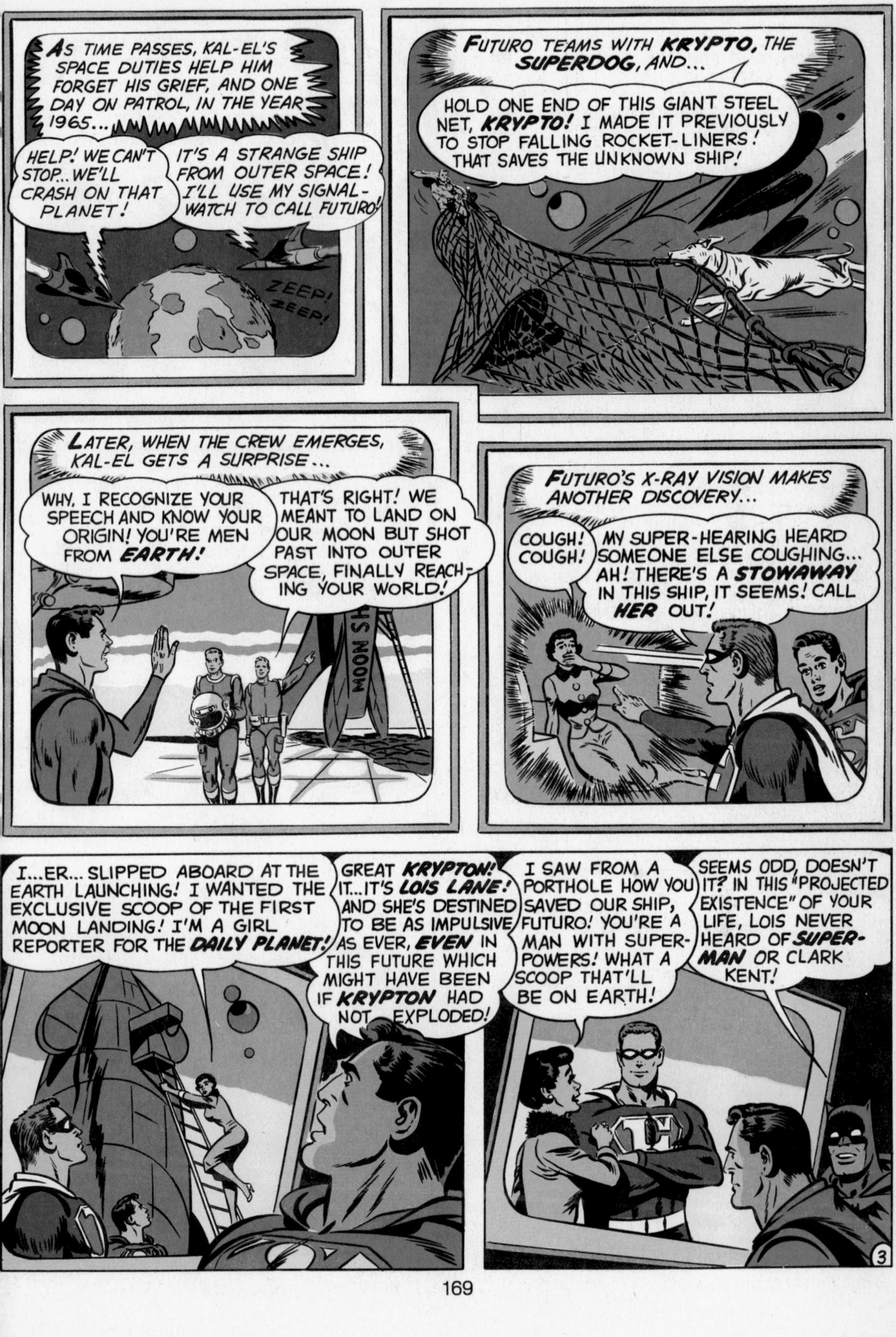
AS TIME PASSES, KAL-EL'S SPACE DUTIES HELP HIM FORGET HIS GRIEF, AND ONE DAY ON PATROL, IN THE YEAR 1965...
HELP! WE CAN'T STOP... WE'LL CRASH ON THAT PLANET!
IT'S A STRANGE SHIP FROM OUTER SPACE! I'LL USE MY SIGNAL-WATCH TO CALL FUTURO!
ZEEP! ZEEP!
FUTURO TEAMS WITH KRYPTO, THE SUPERDOG, AND...
HOLD ONE END OF THIS GIANT STEEL NET, KRYPTO! I MADE IT PREVIOUSLY TO STOP FALLING ROCKET-LINERS! THAT SAVES THE UNKNOWN SHIP!
LATER, WHEN THE CREW EMERGES, KAL-EL GETS A SURPRISE...
WHY, I RECOGNIZE YOUR SPEECH AND KNOW YOUR ORIGIN! YOU'RE MEN FROM EARTH!
THAT'S RIGHT! WE MEANT TO LAND ON OUR MOON BUT SHOT PAST INTO OUTER SPACE, FINALLY REACHING YOUR WORLD!
FUTURO'S X-RAY VISION MAKES ANOTHER DISCOVERY...
COUGH! COUGH!
MY SUPER-HEARING HEARD SOMEONE ELSE COUGHING... AH! THERE'S A STOWAWAY IN THIS SHIP, IT SEEMS! CALL HER OUT!
I...ER... SLIPPED ABOARD AT THE EARTH LAUNCHING! I WANTED THE EXCLUSIVE SCOOP OF THE FIRST MOON LANDING! I'M A GIRL REPORTER FOR THE DAILY PLANET!
GREAT KRYPTON! IT...IT'S LOIS LANE! AND SHE'S DESTINED TO BE AS IMPULSIVE AS EVER, EVEN IN THIS FUTURE WHICH MIGHT HAVE BEEN IF KRYPTON HAD NOT EXPLODED!
I SAW FROM A PORTHOLE HOW YOU SAVED OUR SHIP, FUTURO! YOU'RE A MAN WITH SUPER-POWERS! WHAT A SCOOP THAT'LL BE ON EARTH!
SEEMS ODD, DOESN'T IT? IN THIS "PROJECTED EXISTENCE" OF YOUR LIFE, LOIS NEVER HEARD OF SUPERMAN OR CLARK KENT!
3

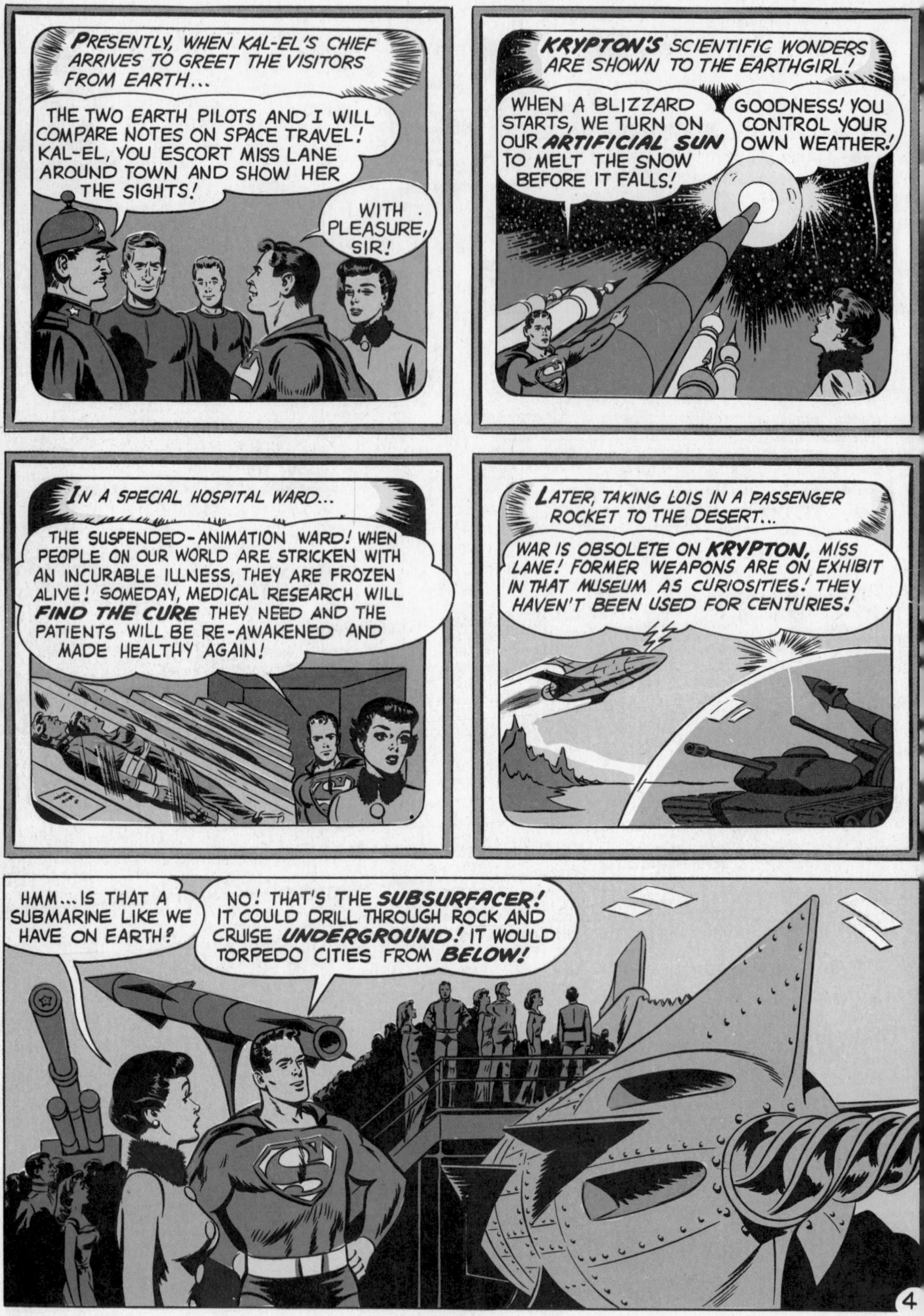
PRESENTLY, WHEN KAL-EL'S CHIEF ARRIVES TO GREET THE VISITORS FROM EARTH...
THE TWO EARTH PILOTS AND I WILL COMPARE NOTES ON SPACE TRAVEL! KAL-EL, YOU ESCORT MISS LANE AROUND TOWN AND SHOW HER THE SIGHTS!
WITH PLEASURE, SIR!
KRYPTON'S SCIENTIFIC WONDERS ARE SHOWN TO THE EARTHGIRL!
WHEN A BLIZZARD STARTS, WE TURN ON OUR ARTIFICIAL SUN TO MELT THE SNOW BEFORE IT FALLS!
GOODNESS! YOU CONTROL YOUR OWN WEATHER!
IN A SPECIAL HOSPITAL WARD...
THE SUSPENDED-ANIMATION WARD! WHEN PEOPLE ON OUR WORLD ARE STRICKEN WITH AN INCURABLE ILLNESS, THEY ARE FROZEN ALIVE! SOMEDAY, MEDICAL RESEARCH WILL FIND THE CURE THEY NEED AND THE PATIENTS WILL BE RE-AWAKENED AND MADE HEALTHY AGAIN!
LATER, TAKING LOIS IN A PASSENGER ROCKET TO THE DESERT...
WAR IS OBSOLETE ON KRYPTON, MISS LANE! FORMER WEAPONS ARE ON EXHIBIT IN THAT MUSEUM AS CURIOSITIES! THEY HAVEN'T BEEN USED FOR CENTURIES!
HMM... IS THAT A SUBMARINE LIKE WE HAVE ON EARTH?
NO! THAT'S THE SUBSURFACER! IT COULD DRILL THROUGH ROCK AND CRUISE UNDERGROUND! IT WOULD TORPEDO CITIES FROM BELOW!
4

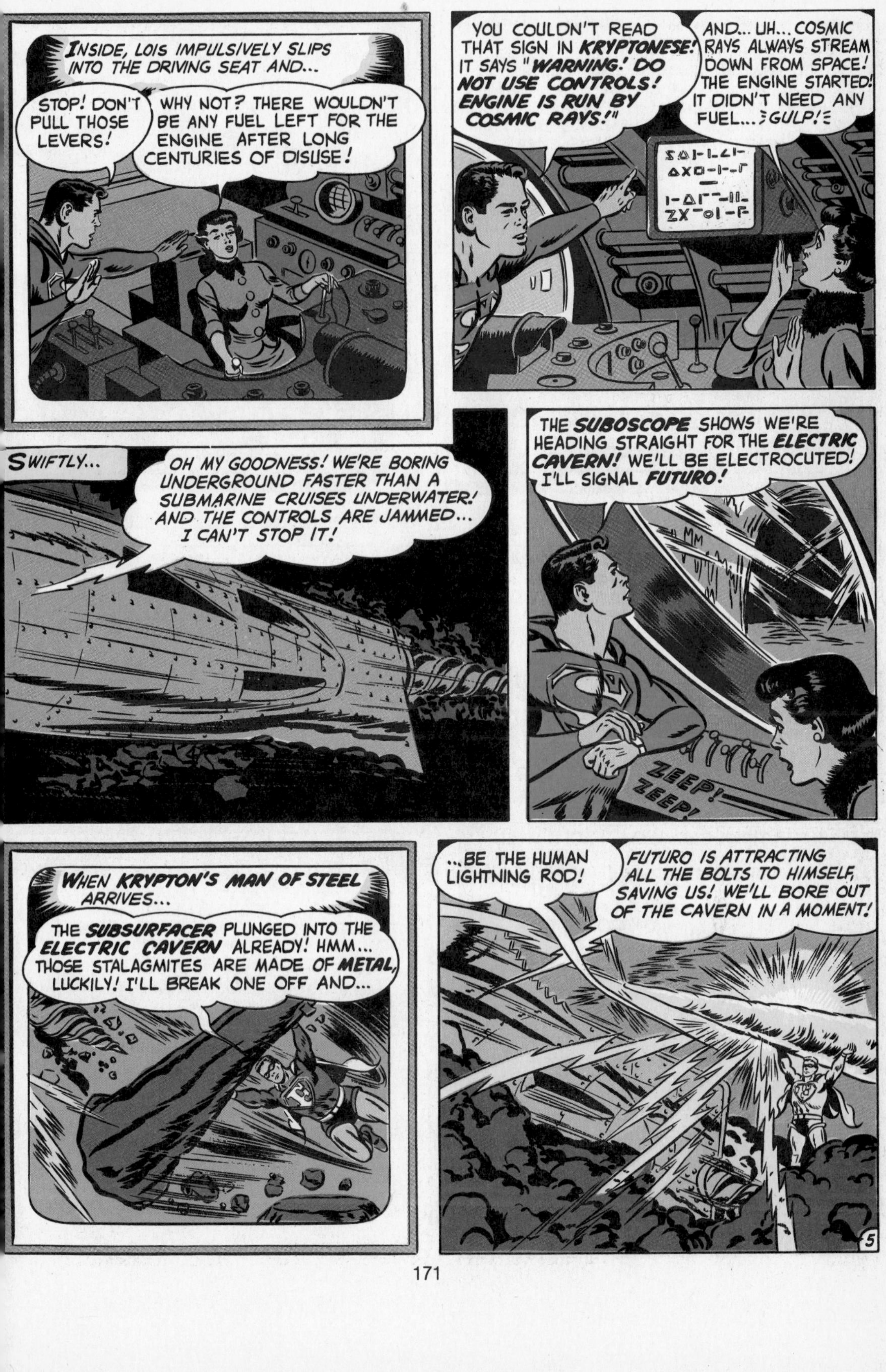
INSIDE, LOIS IMPULSIVELY SLIPS INTO THE DRIVING SEAT AND...
STOP! DON'T PULL THOSE LEVERS!
WHY NOT? THERE WOULDN'T BE ANY FUEL LEFT FOR THE ENGINE AFTER LONG CENTURIES OF DISUSE!
YOU COULDN'T READ THAT SIGN IN KRYPTONESE! IT SAYS "WARNING! DO NOT USE CONTROLS! ENGINE IS RUN BY COSMIC RAYS!"
AND... UH... COSMIC RAYS ALWAYS STREAM DOWN FROM SPACE! THE ENGINE STARTED! IT DIDN'T NEED ANY FUEL... GULP!
SWIFTLY...
OH MY GOODNESS! WE'RE BORING UNDERGROUND FASTER THAN A SUBMARINE CRUISES UNDERWATER! AND THE CONTROLS ARE JAMMED... I CAN'T STOP IT!
THE SUBOSCOPE SHOWS WE'RE HEADING STRAIGHT FOR THE ELECTRIC CAVERN! WE'LL BE ELECTROCUTED! I'LL SIGNAL FUTURO!
ZEEP! ZEEP!
WHEN KRYPTON'S MAN OF STEEL ARRIVES...
THE SUBSURFACER PLUNGED INTO THE ELECTRIC CAVERN ALREADY! HMM... THOSE STALAGMITES ARE MADE OF METAL, LUCKILY! I'LL BREAK ONE OFF AND...
...BE THE HUMAN LIGHTNING ROD!
FUTURO IS ATTRACTING ALL THE BOLTS TO HIMSELF, SAVING US! WE'LL BORE OUT OF THE CAVERN IN A MOMENT!
5

AFTER KAL-EL MANAGES TO TURN THE CRAFT UPWARD TO THE SURFACE...

BUT THE CORKSCREW IS STILL WHIRLING! I'LL LET IT HIT MY INVULNERABLE BODY AND BURST APART! THIS DANGEROUS CRAFT SHOULD BE DESTROYED ANYWAY!

WHEN LOIS AND KAL-EL COME OUT...

YOU'RE SO WONDERFUL, FUTURO! WHOEVER BECOMES MRS. FUTURO WOULD BE THE LUCKIEST GIRL ALIVE!...*SIGH!*

SAME OLD LOIS, EH, SUPERMAN? SHE FELL FOR YOU ON EARTH...AND SHE'S FALLING FOR THAT OTHER "SUPERMAN" ON KRYPTON!

BUT LOOK! THERE'S A NEW TWIST! SUPERMAN NEVER FELL FOR LOIS...BUT FUTURO DID!

I...ER...LIKED YOU AT FIRST SIGHT, EARTHGIRL! I...UH...WELL, WHY WASTE TIME? WILL YOU MARRY ME?

OH, YES...YES, FUTURO DARLING! BUT I WANT TO HAVE A HOME ON MY OWN WORLD, NOT HERE!

HMM...I WOULD STILL HAVE SUPER-POWERS ON EARTH, SO WE'LL SETTLE DOWN THERE! ANYTHING TO MAKE YOU HAPPY, MY DEAR!

BUT...BUT FUTURO! IF YOU MOVE TO EARTH, YOU'LL BE LEAVING YOUR OWN NATIVE WORLD WITHOUT A SUPER-HERO!

NO, KAL-EL! COME WITH ME TO MY LAB!

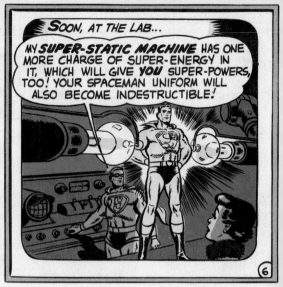

SOON, AT THE LAB...

MY SUPER-STATIC MACHINE HAS ONE MORE CHARGE OF SUPER-ENERGY IN IT, WHICH WILL GIVE YOU SUPER-POWERS, TOO! YOUR SPACEMAN UNIFORM WILL ALSO BECOME INDESTRUCTIBLE!

6

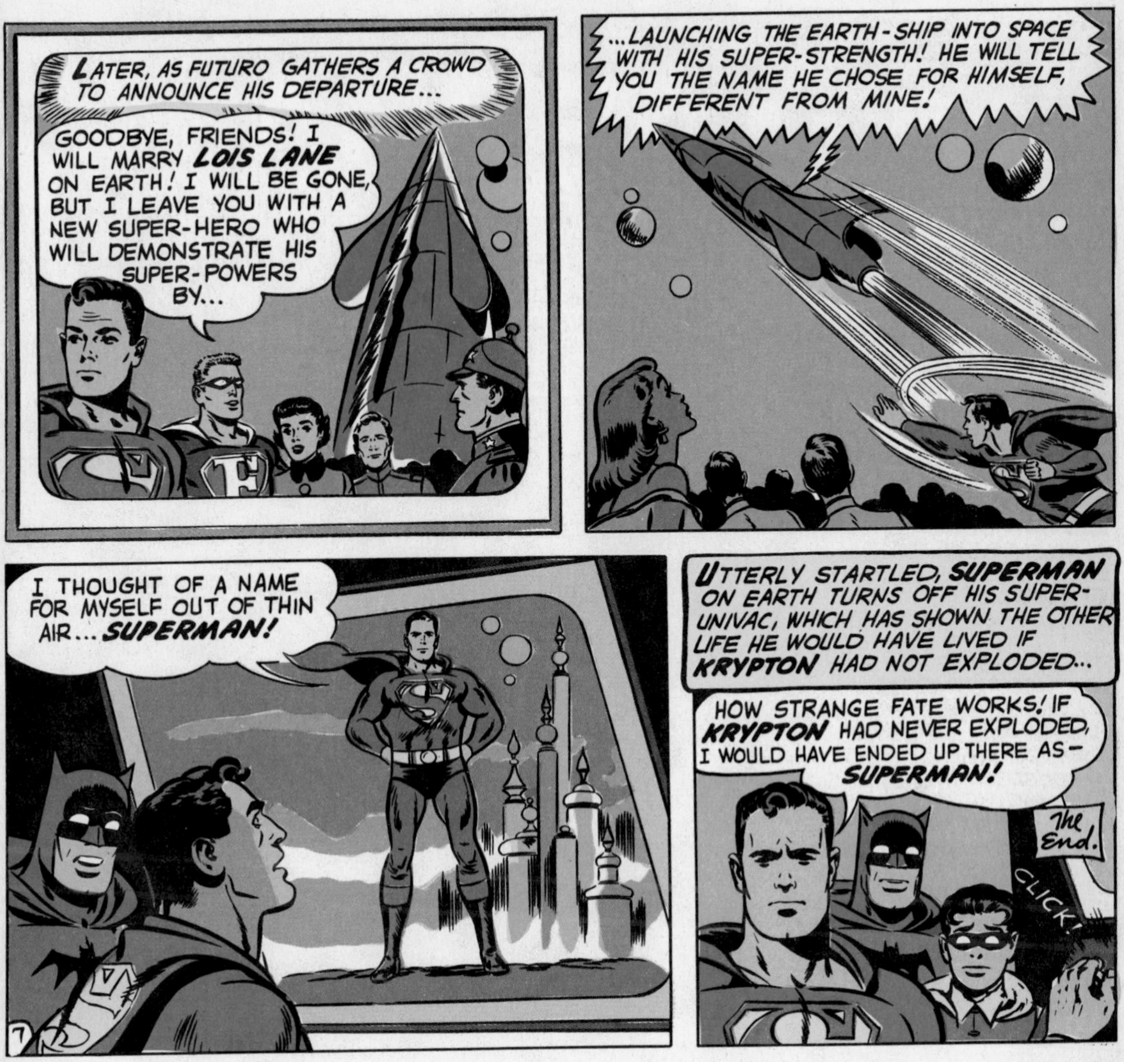
LATER, AS FUTURO GATHERS A CROWD TO ANNOUNCE HIS DEPARTURE...
GOODBYE, FRIENDS! I WILL MARRY LOIS LANE ON EARTH! I WILL BE GONE, BUT I LEAVE YOU WITH A NEW SUPER-HERO WHO WILL DEMONSTRATE HIS SUPER-POWERS BY...
...LAUNCHING THE EARTH-SHIP INTO SPACE WITH HIS SUPER-STRENGTH! HE WILL TELL YOU THE NAME HE CHOSE FOR HIMSELF, DIFFERENT FROM MINE!
I THOUGHT OF A NAME FOR MYSELF OUT OF THIN AIR... SUPERMAN!
7
UTTERLY STARTLED, SUPERMAN ON EARTH TURNS OFF HIS SUPER-UNIVAC, WHICH HAS SHOWN THE OTHER LIFE HE WOULD HAVE LIVED IF KRYPTON HAD NOT EXPLODED...
HOW STRANGE FATE WORKS! IF KRYPTON HAD NEVER EXPLODED, I WOULD HAVE ENDED UP THERE AS—SUPERMAN!
The End.
CLICK!

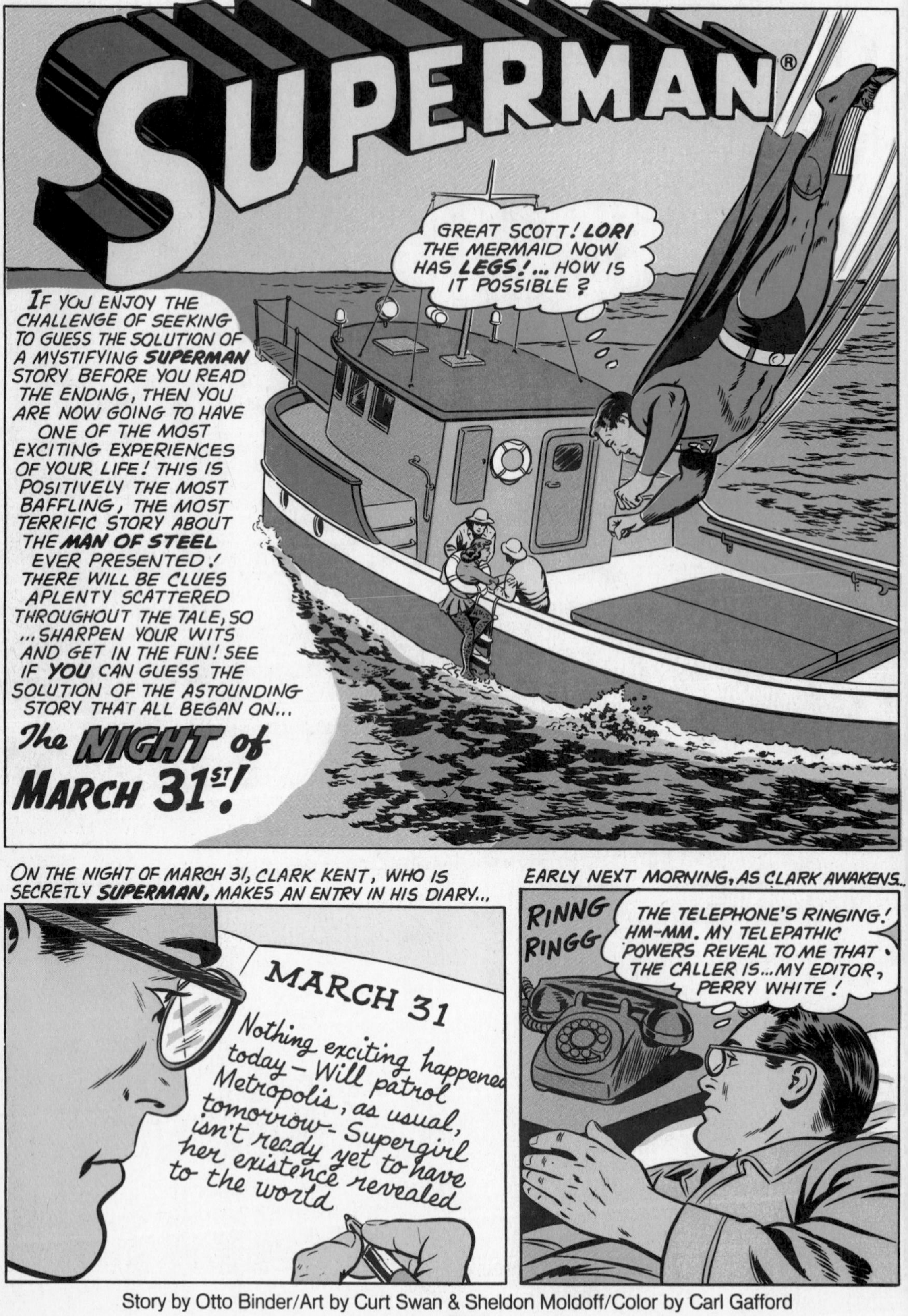
SUPERMAN®
GREAT SCOTT! LORI THE MERMAID NOW HAS LEGS!... HOW IS IT POSSIBLE?
IF YOU ENJOY THE CHALLENGE OF SEEKING TO GUESS THE SOLUTION OF A MYSTIFYING SUPERMAN STORY BEFORE YOU READ THE ENDING, THEN YOU ARE NOW GOING TO HAVE ONE OF THE MOST EXCITING EXPERIENCES OF YOUR LIFE! THIS IS POSITIVELY THE MOST BAFFLING, THE MOST TERRIFIC STORY ABOUT THE MAN OF STEEL EVER PRESENTED! THERE WILL BE CLUES APLENTY SCATTERED THROUGHOUT THE TALE, SO ...SHARPEN YOUR WITS AND GET IN THE FUN! SEE IF YOU CAN GUESS THE SOLUTION OF THE ASTOUNDING STORY THAT ALL BEGAN ON...
The NIGHT of MARCH 31ST!
ON THE NIGHT OF MARCH 31, CLARK KENT, WHO IS SECRETLY SUPERMAN, MAKES AN ENTRY IN HIS DIARY...
MARCH 31
Nothing exciting happened today - Will patrol Metropolis, as usual, tomorrow - Supergirl isn't ready yet to have her existence revealed to the world
EARLY NEXT MORNING, AS CLARK AWAKENS...
RINNG RINGG
THE TELEPHONE'S RINGING! HM-MM. MY TELEPATHIC POWERS REVEAL TO ME THAT THE CALLER IS...MY EDITOR, PERRY WHITE!

Story by Otto Binder/Art by Curt Swan & Sheldon Moldoff/Color by Carl Gafford

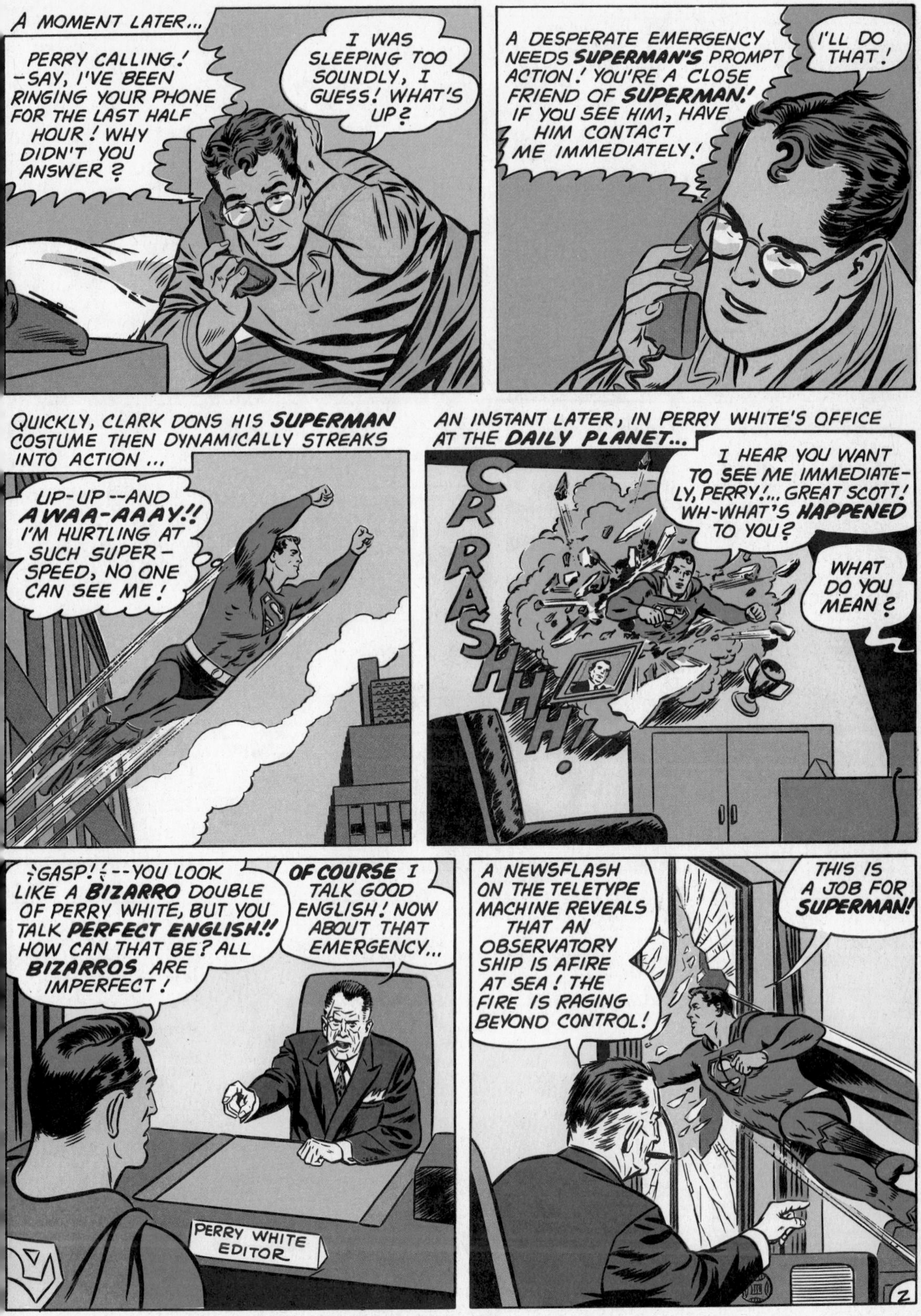
A MOMENT LATER...
PERRY CALLING! -SAY, I'VE BEEN RINGING YOUR PHONE FOR THE LAST HALF HOUR! WHY DIDN'T YOU ANSWER?
I WAS SLEEPING TOO SOUNDLY, I GUESS! WHAT'S UP?
A DESPERATE EMERGENCY NEEDS SUPERMAN'S PROMPT ACTION! YOU'RE A CLOSE FRIEND OF SUPERMAN! IF YOU SEE HIM, HAVE HIM CONTACT ME IMMEDIATELY!
I'LL DO THAT!
QUICKLY, CLARK DONS HIS SUPERMAN COSTUME THEN DYNAMICALLY STREAKS INTO ACTION...
UP-UP--AND AWAA-AAAY!! I'M HURTLING AT SUCH SUPER-SPEED, NO ONE CAN SEE ME!
AN INSTANT LATER, IN PERRY WHITE'S OFFICE AT THE DAILY PLANET...
CRASHHH!
I HEAR YOU WANT TO SEE ME IMMEDIATE-LY, PERRY!... GREAT SCOTT! WH-WHAT'S HAPPENED TO YOU?
WHAT DO YOU MEAN?
GASP! --YOU LOOK LIKE A BIZARRO DOUBLE OF PERRY WHITE, BUT YOU TALK PERFECT ENGLISH!! HOW CAN THAT BE? ALL BIZARROS ARE IMPERFECT!
OF COURSE I TALK GOOD ENGLISH! NOW ABOUT THAT EMERGENCY...
PERRY WHITE
EDITOR
A NEWSFLASH ON THE TELETYPE MACHINE REVEALS THAT AN OBSERVATORY SHIP IS AFIRE AT SEA! THE FIRE IS RAGING BEYOND CONTROL!
THIS IS A JOB FOR SUPERMAN!
2

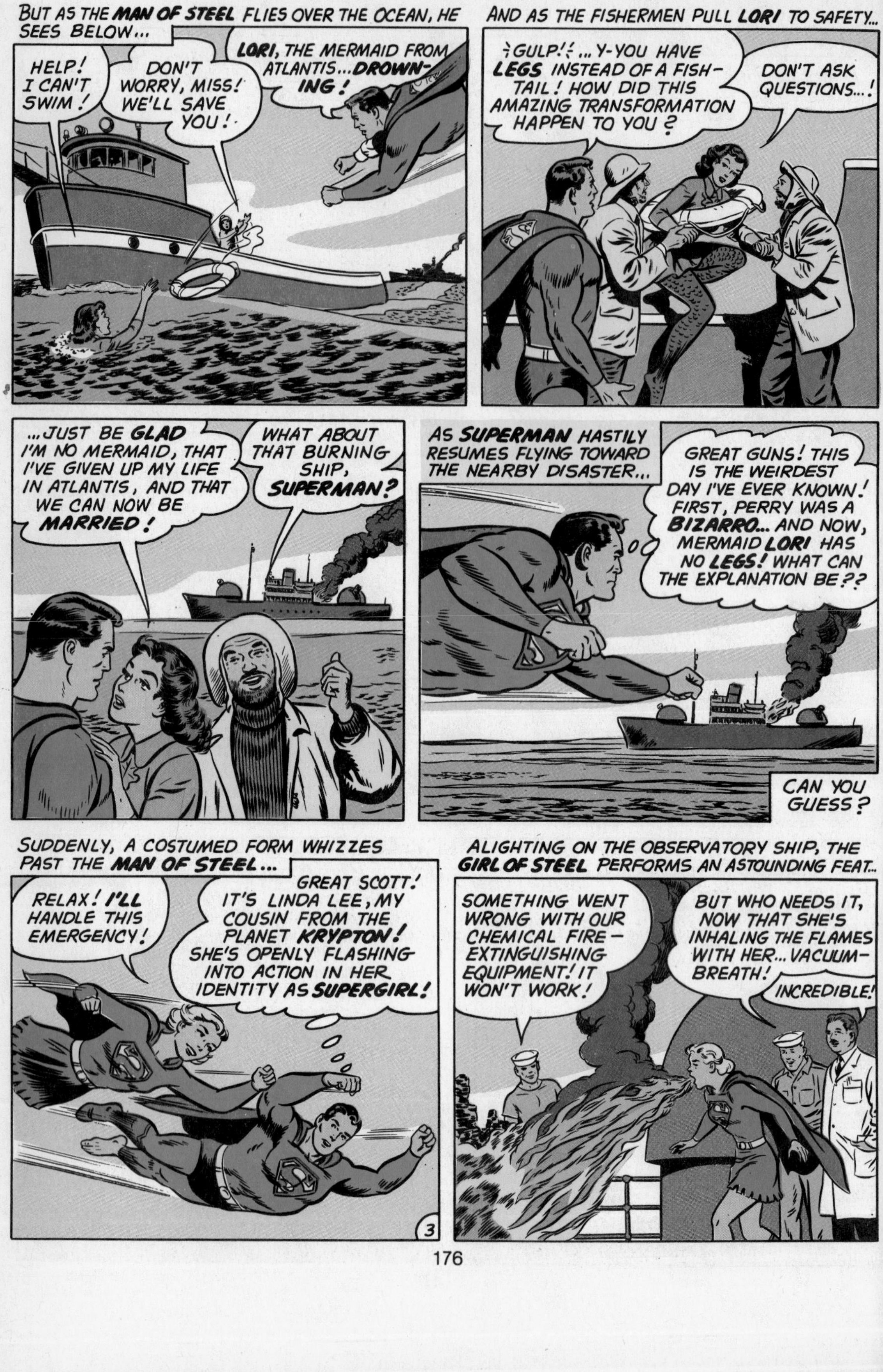
BUT AS THE MAN OF STEEL FLIES OVER THE OCEAN, HE SEES BELOW...
HELP! I CAN'T SWIM!
DON'T WORRY, MISS! WE'LL SAVE YOU!
LORI, THE MERMAID FROM ATLANTIS... DROWNING!
AND AS THE FISHERMEN PULL LORI TO SAFETY...
GULP! ... Y-YOU HAVE LEGS INSTEAD OF A FISH-TAIL! HOW DID THIS AMAZING TRANSFORMATION HAPPEN TO YOU?
DON'T ASK QUESTIONS...!
...JUST BE GLAD I'M NO MERMAID, THAT I'VE GIVEN UP MY LIFE IN ATLANTIS, AND THAT WE CAN NOW BE MARRIED!
WHAT ABOUT THAT BURNING SHIP, SUPERMAN?
AS SUPERMAN HASTILY RESUMES FLYING TOWARD THE NEARBY DISASTER...
GREAT GUNS! THIS IS THE WEIRDEST DAY I'VE EVER KNOWN! FIRST, PERRY WAS A BIZARRO... AND NOW, MERMAID LORI HAS NO LEGS! WHAT CAN THE EXPLANATION BE??
CAN YOU GUESS?
SUDDENLY, A COSTUMED FORM WHIZZES PAST THE MAN OF STEEL...
RELAX! I'LL HANDLE THIS EMERGENCY!
GREAT SCOTT! IT'S LINDA LEE, MY COUSIN FROM THE PLANET KRYPTON! SHE'S OPENLY FLASHING INTO ACTION IN HER IDENTITY AS SUPERGIRL!
3
ALIGHTING ON THE OBSERVATORY SHIP, THE GIRL OF STEEL PERFORMS AN ASTOUNDING FEAT...
SOMETHING WENT WRONG WITH OUR CHEMICAL FIRE-EXTINGUISHING EQUIPMENT! IT WON'T WORK!
BUT WHO NEEDS IT, NOW THAT SHE'S INHALING THE FLAMES WITH HER... VACUUM-BREATH!
INCREDIBLE!

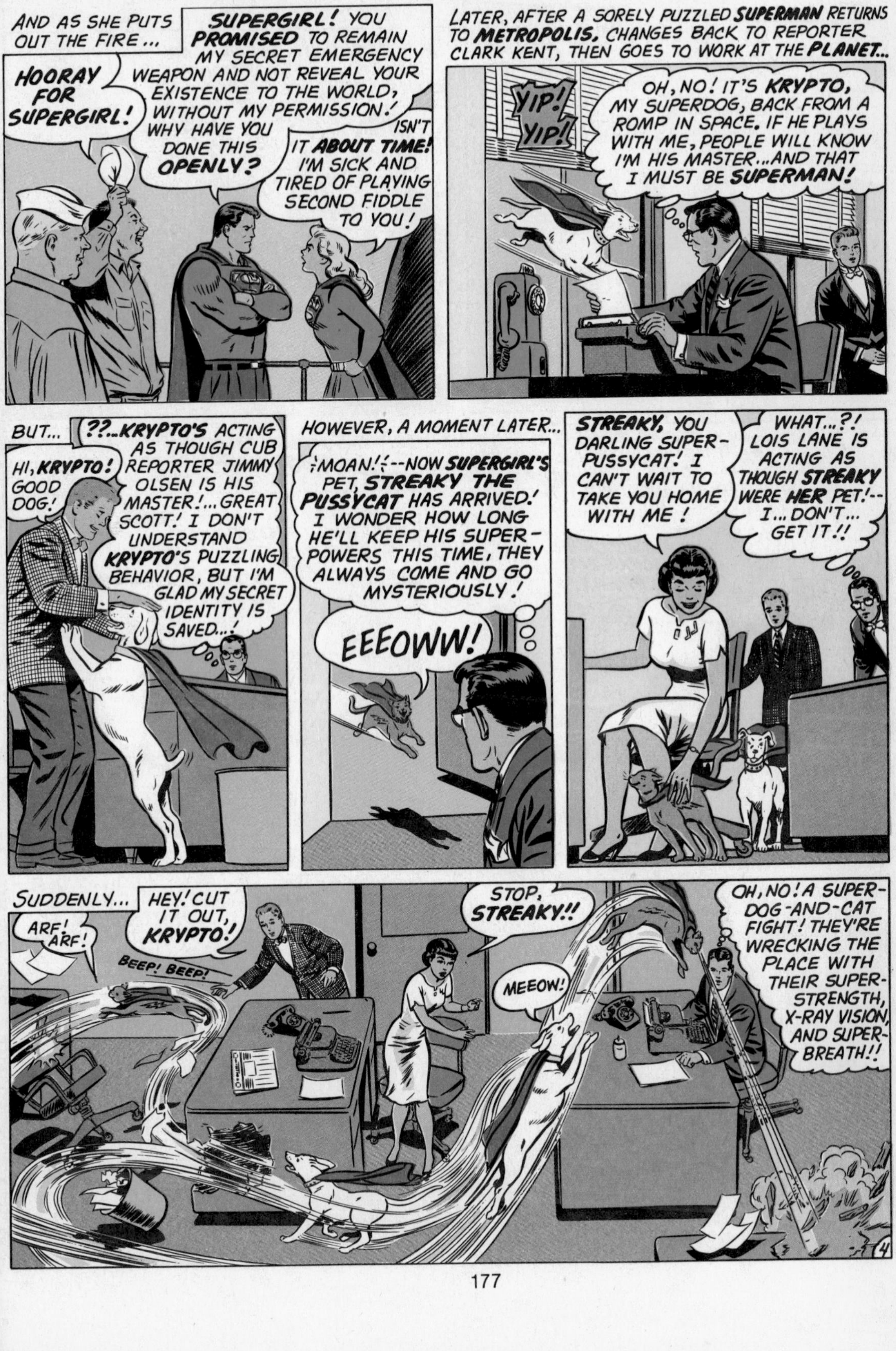
AND AS SHE PUTS OUT THE FIRE...
HOORAY FOR SUPERGIRL!
SUPERGIRL! YOU PROMISED TO REMAIN MY SECRET EMERGENCY WEAPON AND NOT REVEAL YOUR EXISTENCE TO THE WORLD, WITHOUT MY PERMISSION! WHY HAVE YOU DONE THIS OPENLY?
ISN'T IT ABOUT TIME! I'M SICK AND TIRED OF PLAYING SECOND FIDDLE TO YOU!
LATER, AFTER A SORELY PUZZLED SUPERMAN RETURNS TO METROPOLIS, CHANGES BACK TO REPORTER CLARK KENT, THEN GOES TO WORK AT THE PLANET...
YIP! YIP!
OH, NO! IT'S KRYPTO, MY SUPERDOG, BACK FROM A ROMP IN SPACE. IF HE PLAYS WITH ME, PEOPLE WILL KNOW I'M HIS MASTER...AND THAT I MUST BE SUPERMAN!
BUT...
HI, KRYPTO! GOOD DOG!
??..KRYPTO'S ACTING AS THOUGH CUB REPORTER JIMMY OLSEN IS HIS MASTER!...GREAT SCOTT! I DON'T UNDERSTAND KRYPTO'S PUZZLING BEHAVIOR, BUT I'M GLAD MY SECRET IDENTITY IS SAVED...!
HOWEVER, A MOMENT LATER...
-MOAN!- --NOW SUPERGIRL'S PET, STREAKY THE PUSSYCAT HAS ARRIVED! I WONDER HOW LONG HE'LL KEEP HIS SUPER-POWERS THIS TIME, THEY ALWAYS COME AND GO MYSTERIOUSLY!
EEEOWW!
STREAKY, YOU DARLING SUPER-PUSSYCAT! I CAN'T WAIT TO TAKE YOU HOME WITH ME!
WHAT...?! LOIS LANE IS ACTING AS THOUGH STREAKY WERE HER PET!-- I...DON'T... GET IT!!
SUDDENLY...
ARF! ARF!
HEY! CUT IT OUT, KRYPTO!
BEEP! BEEP!
STOP, STREAKY!!
MEEOW!
OH, NO! A SUPER-DOG-AND-CAT FIGHT! THEY'RE WRECKING THE PLACE WITH THEIR SUPER-STRENGTH, X-RAY VISION, AND SUPER-BREATH!!
4

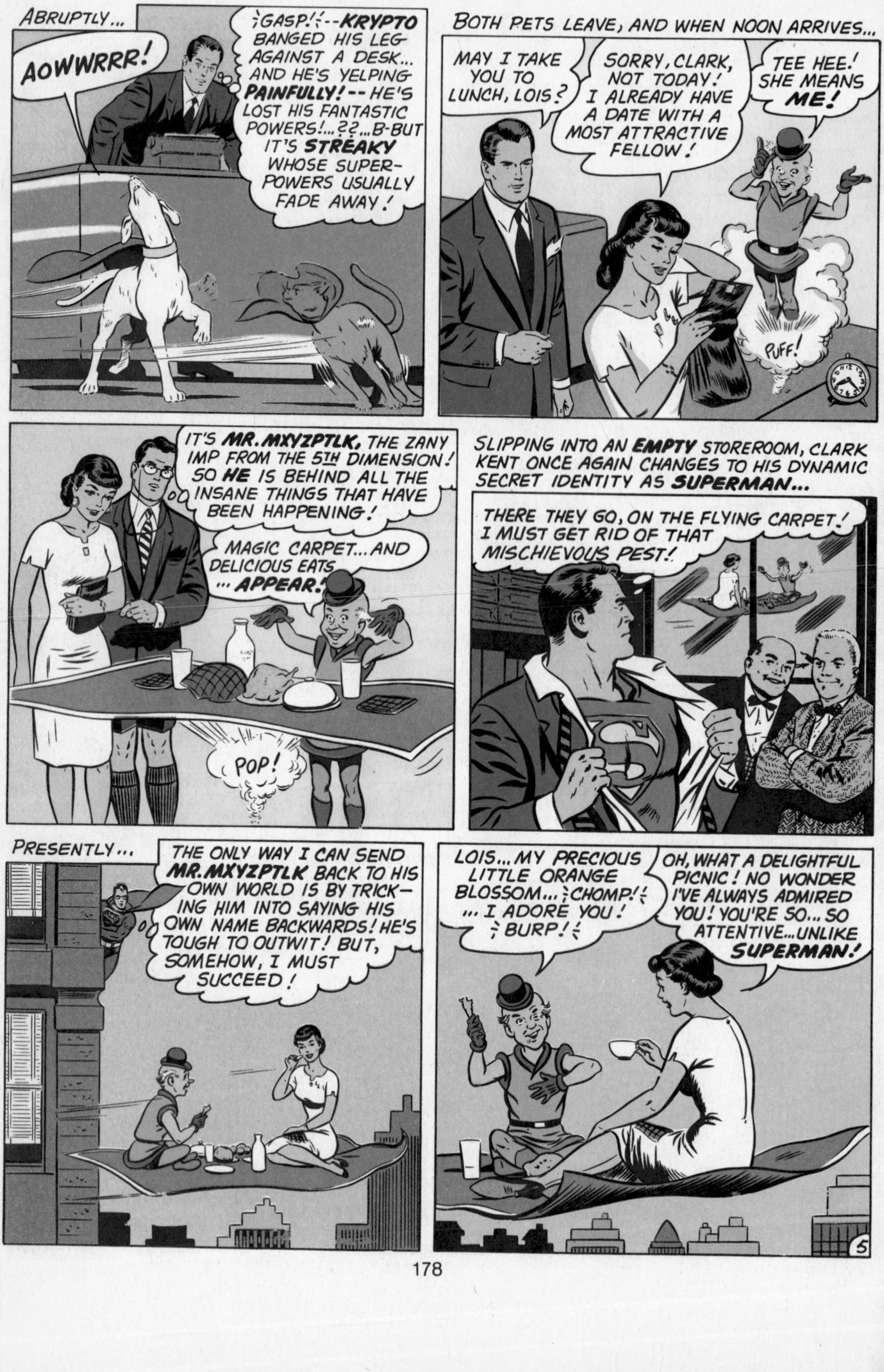
ABRUPTLY...
AOWWRRR!
¡GASP!¡--KRYPTO BANGED HIS LEG AGAINST A DESK... AND HE'S YELPING PAINFULLY!--HE'S LOST HIS FANTASTIC POWERS!...??...B-BUT IT'S STREAKY WHOSE SUPER-POWERS USUALLY FADE AWAY!
BOTH PETS LEAVE, AND WHEN NOON ARRIVES...
MAY I TAKE YOU TO LUNCH, LOIS?
SORRY, CLARK, NOT TODAY! I ALREADY HAVE A DATE WITH A MOST ATTRACTIVE FELLOW!
TEE HEE! SHE MEANS ME!
PUFF!
IT'S MR. MXYZPTLK, THE ZANY IMP FROM THE 5TH DIMENSION! SO HE IS BEHIND ALL THE INSANE THINGS THAT HAVE BEEN HAPPENING!
MAGIC CARPET...AND DELICIOUS EATS ...APPEAR!
POP!
SLIPPING INTO AN EMPTY STOREROOM, CLARK KENT ONCE AGAIN CHANGES TO HIS DYNAMIC SECRET IDENTITY AS SUPERMAN...
THERE THEY GO, ON THE FLYING CARPET! I MUST GET RID OF THAT MISCHIEVOUS PEST!
PRESENTLY...
THE ONLY WAY I CAN SEND MR. MXYZPTLK BACK TO HIS OWN WORLD IS BY TRICKING HIM INTO SAYING HIS OWN NAME BACKWARDS! HE'S TOUGH TO OUTWIT! BUT, SOMEHOW, I MUST SUCCEED!
LOIS...MY PRECIOUS LITTLE ORANGE BLOSSOM...¡CHOMP!¡ ...I ADORE YOU! ¡BURP!¡
OH, WHAT A DELIGHTFUL PICNIC! NO WONDER I'VE ALWAYS ADMIRED YOU! YOU'RE SO...SO ATTENTIVE...UNLIKE SUPERMAN!
5

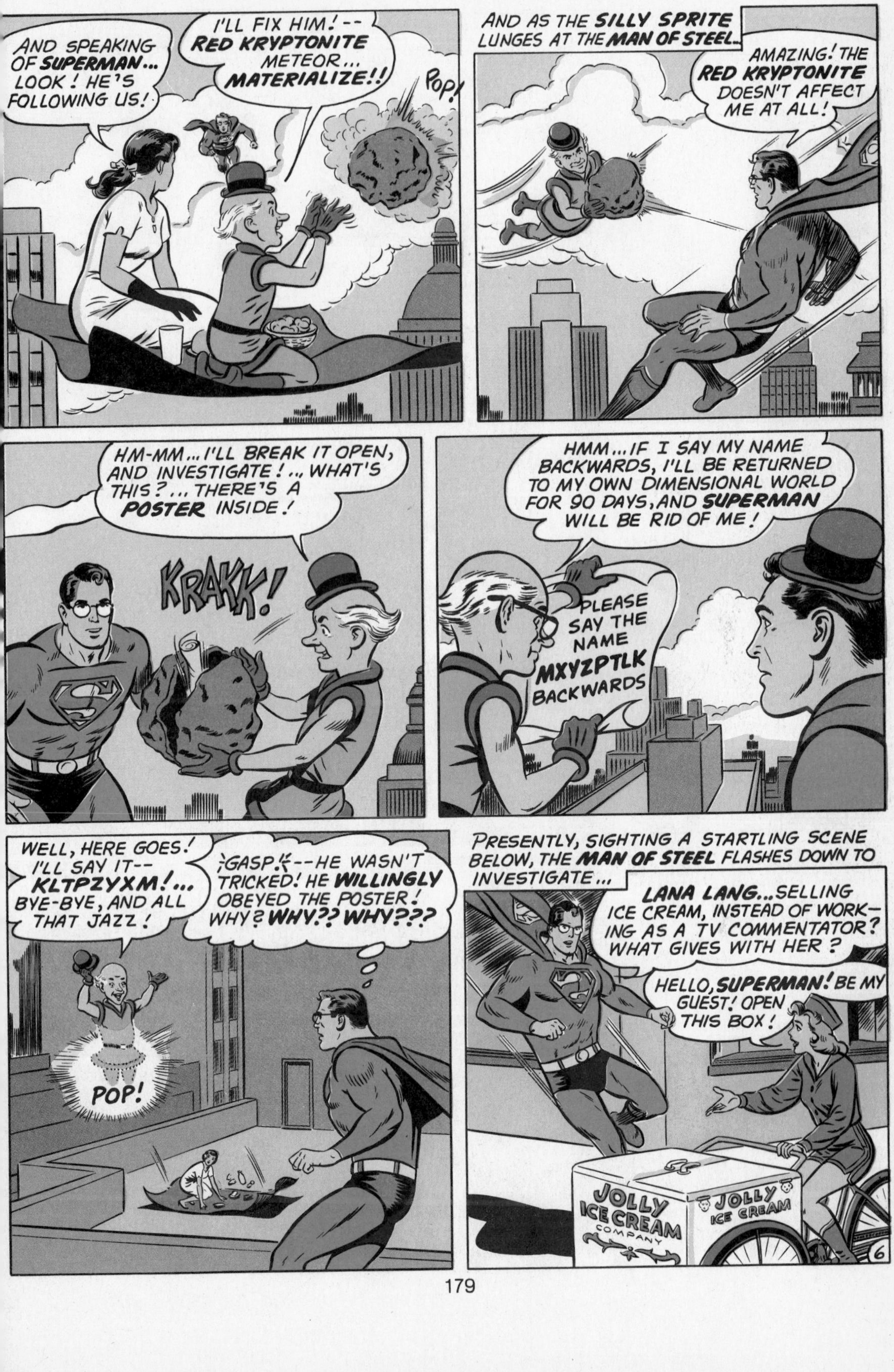
AND SPEAKING OF SUPERMAN... LOOK! HE'S FOLLOWING US!
I'LL FIX HIM! -- RED KRYPTONITE METEOR... MATERIALIZE!!
POP!
AND AS THE SILLY SPRITE LUNGES AT THE MAN OF STEEL...
AMAZING! THE RED KRYPTONITE DOESN'T AFFECT ME AT ALL!
HM-MM... I'LL BREAK IT OPEN, AND INVESTIGATE! ... WHAT'S THIS? ... THERE'S A POSTER INSIDE!
KRAKK!
HMM... IF I SAY MY NAME BACKWARDS, I'LL BE RETURNED TO MY OWN DIMENSIONAL WORLD FOR 90 DAYS, AND SUPERMAN WILL BE RID OF ME!
PLEASE SAY THE NAME MXYZPTLK BACKWARDS
WELL, HERE GOES! I'LL SAY IT-- KLTPZYXM!... BYE-BYE, AND ALL THAT JAZZ!
¡GASP!-- HE WASN'T TRICKED! HE WILLINGLY OBEYED THE POSTER! WHY? WHY?? WHY???
POP!
PRESENTLY, SIGHTING A STARTLING SCENE BELOW, THE MAN OF STEEL FLASHES DOWN TO INVESTIGATE...
LANA LANG... SELLING ICE CREAM, INSTEAD OF WORKING AS A TV COMMENTATOR? WHAT GIVES WITH HER?
HELLO, SUPERMAN! BE MY GUEST! OPEN THIS BOX!
JOLLY ICE CREAM COMPANY
JOLLY ICE CREAM
6

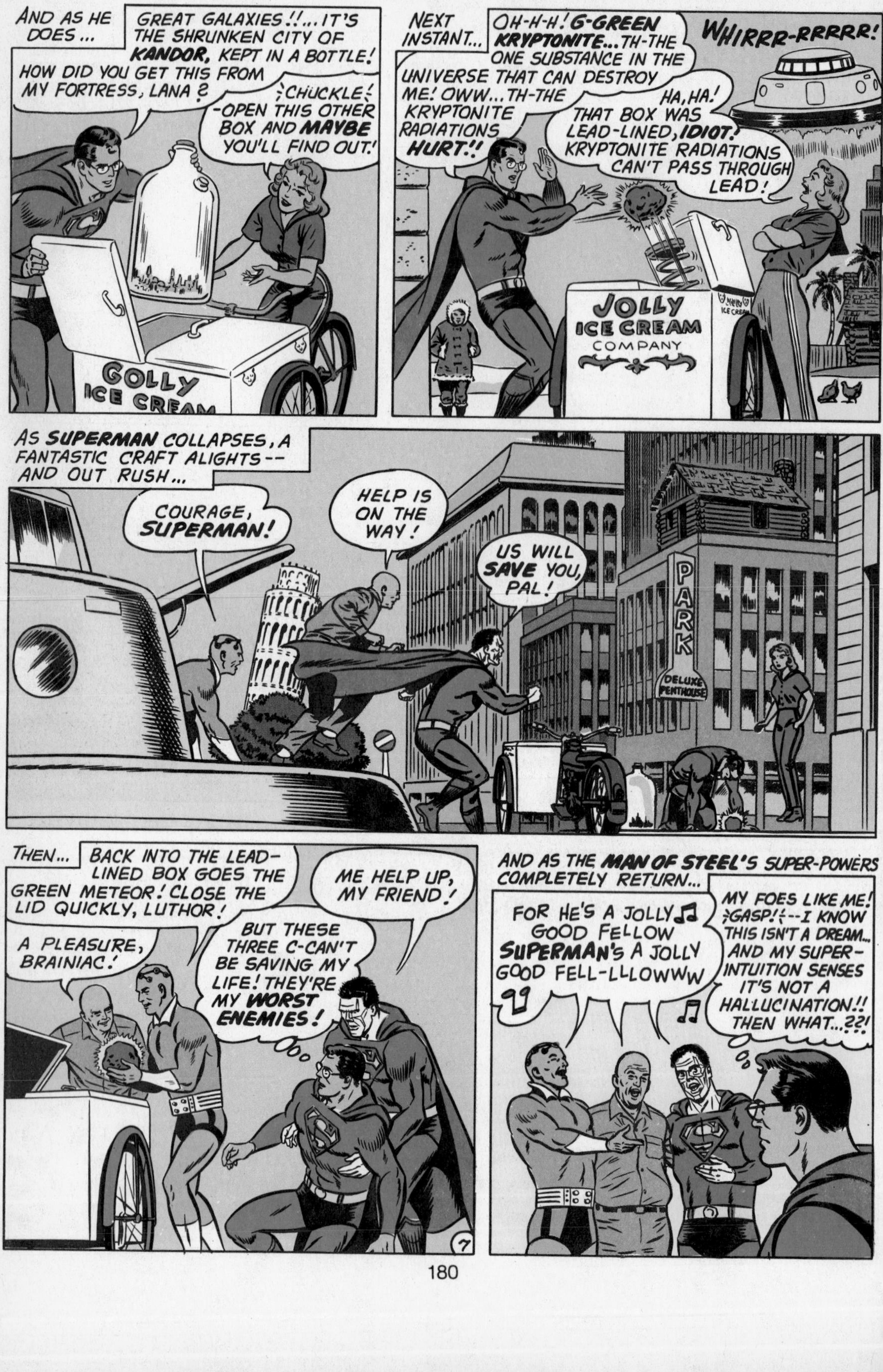
AND AS HE DOES...
GREAT GALAXIES!!... IT'S THE SHRUNKEN CITY OF KANDOR, KEPT IN A BOTTLE! HOW DID YOU GET THIS FROM MY FORTRESS, LANA?
CHUCKLE-OPEN THIS OTHER BOX AND MAYBE YOU'LL FIND OUT!
GOLLY ICE CREAM
NEXT INSTANT...
OH-H-H! G-GREEN KRYPTONITE...TH-THE ONE SUBSTANCE IN THE UNIVERSE THAT CAN DESTROY ME! OWW...TH-THE KRYPTONITE RADIATIONS HURT!!
WHIRRR-RRRRR!
HA, HA! THAT BOX WAS LEAD-LINED, IDIOT! KRYPTONITE RADIATIONS CAN'T PASS THROUGH LEAD!
JOLLY ICE CREAM COMPANY
AS SUPERMAN COLLAPSES, A FANTASTIC CRAFT ALIGHTS--AND OUT RUSH...
COURAGE, SUPERMAN!
HELP IS ON THE WAY!
US WILL SAVE YOU, PAL!
PARK
DELUXE PENTHOUSE
THEN...
BACK INTO THE LEAD-LINED BOX GOES THE GREEN METEOR! CLOSE THE LID QUICKLY, LUTHOR!
A PLEASURE, BRAINIAC!
ME HELP UP, MY FRIEND!
BUT THESE THREE C-CAN'T BE SAVING MY LIFE! THEY'RE MY WORST ENEMIES!
7
AND AS THE MAN OF STEEL'S SUPER-POWERS COMPLETELY RETURN...
FOR HE'S A JOLLY GOOD FELLOW SUPERMAN'S A JOLLY GOOD FELL-LLLOWWW
MY FOES LIKE ME! *GASP!*--I KNOW THIS ISN'T A DREAM... AND MY SUPER-INTUITION SENSES IT'S NOT A HALLUCINATION!! THEN WHAT...??!

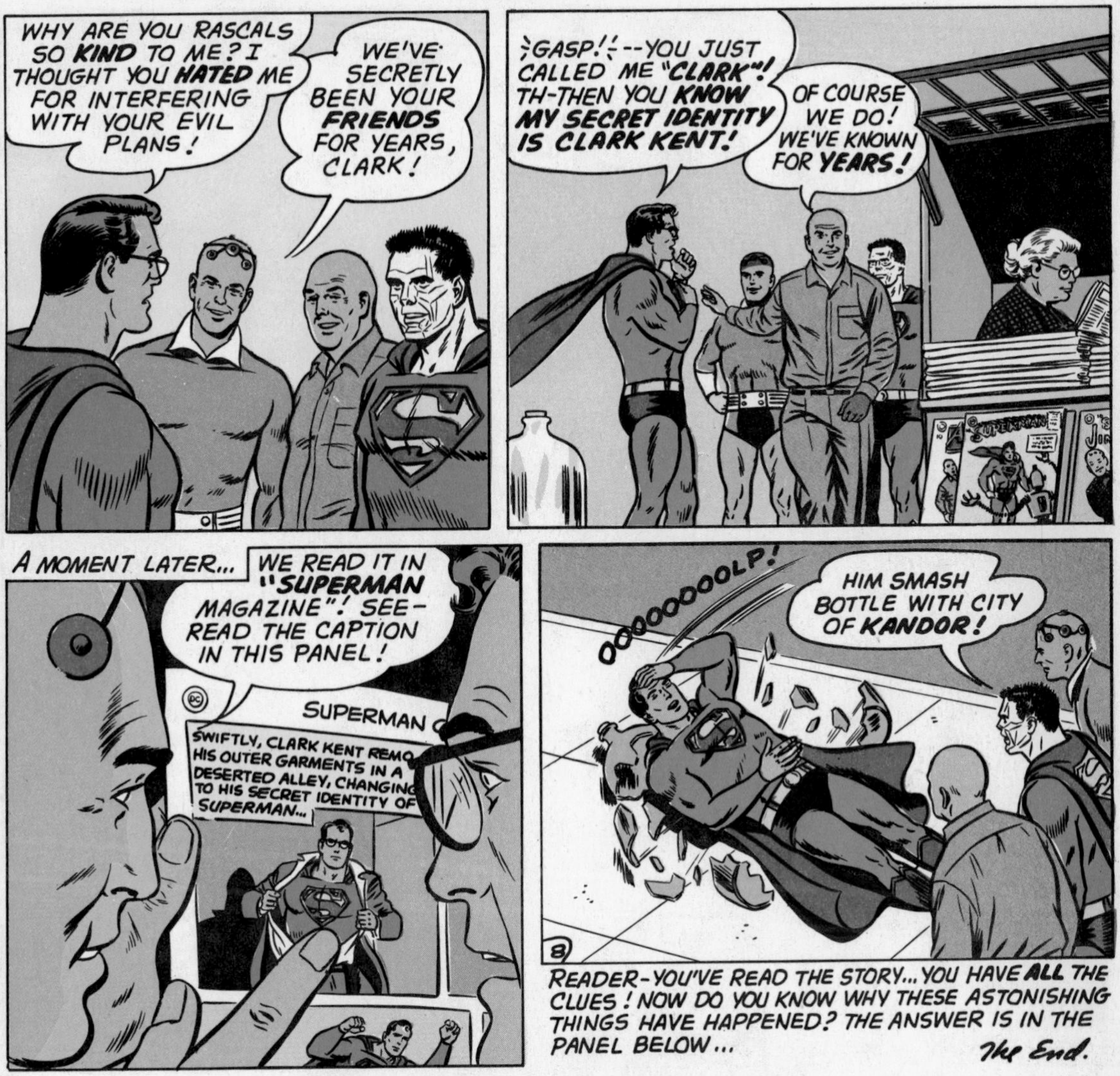
WHY ARE YOU RASCALS SO KIND TO ME? I THOUGHT YOU HATED ME FOR INTERFERING WITH YOUR EVIL PLANS!
WE'VE SECRETLY BEEN YOUR FRIENDS FOR YEARS, CLARK!
GASP! --YOU JUST CALLED ME "CLARK"! TH-THEN YOU KNOW MY SECRET IDENTITY IS CLARK KENT!
OF COURSE WE DO! WE'VE KNOWN FOR YEARS!
A MOMENT LATER...
WE READ IT IN "SUPERMAN MAGAZINE"! SEE--READ THE CAPTION IN THIS PANEL!
SUPERMAN
SWIFTLY, CLARK KENT REMO
HIS OUTER GARMENTS IN A
DESERTED ALLEY, CHANGING
TO HIS SECRET IDENTITY OF
SUPERMAN...
OOOOOOOOOLP!
HIM SMASH BOTTLE WITH CITY OF KANDOR!
8
READER--YOU'VE READ THE STORY... YOU HAVE ALL THE CLUES! NOW DO YOU KNOW WHY THESE ASTONISHING THINGS HAVE HAPPENED? THE ANSWER IS IN THE PANEL BELOW...
The End.

THE GREAT BOO-BOO CONTEST

Our older readers may recall having read this issue's Hall of Fame Classic, "The Night of March 31st." But how many of you, reading it for the first time, guessed what it was all about? The story began on the "Night of March 31st," of course—but all the action took place the next day—April 1st, or April Fool's Day! In fact, this was the story on which our "Great Boo-Boo Contest" was based a few years ago. We received over 30,000 letters pointing out the goofs in the story. Here are a few of the hundreds they spotted:

On page 1, Superman is wearing a boot on one foot and a shoe and sock on the other. As Clark Kent, he wears his glasses to bed—and has telepathic powers. On page 2, panel 1, the phone cord is missing; in panel 3, Superman wears no cape; he is wantonly destructive, needlessly bursting through a wall and a window; Perry White is a Bizarro. On page 3, Lori the Mermaid has legs instead of a fish tail; in panel 1, Superman has one white shirt sleeve; there's a pay phone on Clark's desk; in panel 4, Jimmy wears formal clothes to work; in panel 5, Krypto has a short tail.

On page 4, Clark's glasses are missing—except for one panel, in which he wears a pince-nez and Bermuda shorts; Lois' hair changes from short to long and back again; she's going to lunch when the clock says 8:22; Krypto feels pain; and Clark switches to Superman in front of witnesses.

On page 5, Superman wears Clark's glasses; Lois has a pony tail and gloves in one panel; she tries to kill Superman, while his enemies come to his rescue; the Leaning Tower of Pisa is in Metropolis; a "deluxe penthouse" is a log cabin; and the last panel shows Lana standing in mid-air. On the final page, Ma Kent is selling Superman comic books in Metropolis; and Superman's enemies learn his identity from reading these mags.

Now look the story over carefully and see how many more of our deliberate boners you can spot.

—Ed.

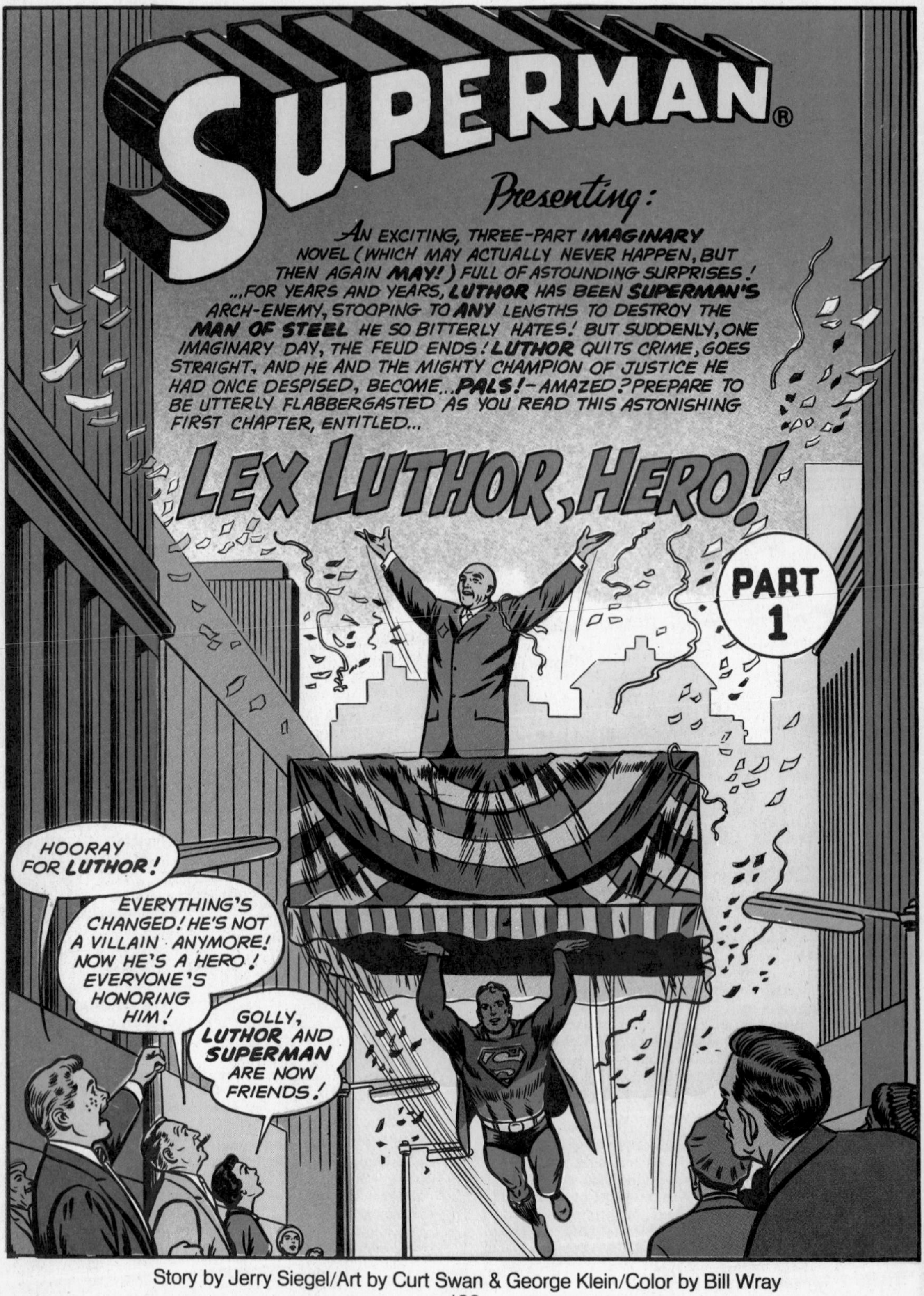
SUPERMAN®
Presenting:
AN EXCITING, THREE-PART IMAGINARY NOVEL (WHICH MAY ACTUALLY NEVER HAPPEN, BUT THEN AGAIN MAY!) FULL OF ASTOUNDING SURPRISES! ...FOR YEARS AND YEARS, LUTHOR HAS BEEN SUPERMAN'S ARCH-ENEMY, STOOPING TO ANY LENGTHS TO DESTROY THE MAN OF STEEL HE SO BITTERLY HATES! BUT SUDDENLY, ONE IMAGINARY DAY, THE FEUD ENDS! LUTHOR QUITS CRIME, GOES STRAIGHT, AND HE AND THE MIGHTY CHAMPION OF JUSTICE HE HAD ONCE DESPISED, BECOME...PALS!—AMAZED? PREPARE TO BE UTTERLY FLABBERGASTED AS YOU READ THIS ASTONISHING FIRST CHAPTER, ENTITLED...
LEX LUTHOR, HERO!
PART 1
HOORAY FOR LUTHOR!
EVERYTHING'S CHANGED! HE'S NOT A VILLAIN ANYMORE! NOW HE'S A HERO! EVERYONE'S HONORING HIM!
GOLLY, LUTHOR AND SUPERMAN ARE NOW FRIENDS!

Story by Jerry Siegel/Art by Curt Swan & George Klein/Color by Bill Wray

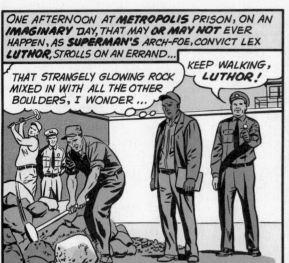

ONE AFTERNOON AT **METROPOLIS** PRISON, ON AN **IMAGINARY** DAY, THAT MAY **OR MAY NOT** EVER HAPPEN, AS **SUPERMAN'S** ARCH-FOE, CONVICT LEX **LUTHOR**, STROLLS ON AN ERRAND...

THAT STRANGELY GLOWING ROCK MIXED IN WITH ALL THE OTHER BOULDERS, I WONDER...

KEEP WALKING, **LUTHOR!**

SUDDENLY...

YOU'VE GOT A BIG MOUTH, SYKES! I THINK I'LL SHUT IT!

HOLY CATS! **LUTHOR** SOCKED A GUARD! THEY'LL THROW THE BOOK AT HIM!

YOU'LL LOSE YOUR SOFT JOB IN THE PRISON LIBRARY FOR THIS, **LUTHOR!**

IT WAS WORTH IT! PUT ME TO WORK ON THE ROCK-PILE, FOR ALL I CARE!

WHICH IS EXACTLY WHAT I **WANT!** THAT'S WHY I **REALLY** HIT HIM!

NEXT DAY...

SATISFIED, CON?

YOU BET! NOW I CAN SECRETLY EXAMINE THIS GLOWING ROCK!

HMMM — JUST AS I SUSPECTED! THIS IS NO ORDINARY ROCK! ITS PITTED SURFACE REVEALS IT'S A METEOR FROM OUTER SPACE! I'LL SLIP A HANDFUL OF THE CRUSHED STUFF INTO MY **POCKET**, UNSEEN!

THAT NIGHT, IN THE RENEGADE SCIENTIST'S CELL...

THE METEOR GRANULES EMANATE A TWINKLING, MULTI-COLORED BRILLIANCE IN THE DARK, AND FEEL **WARM** TO THE TOUCH! I'VE A STRONG HUNCH THIS IS **ELEMENT "Z"**...!!

2

"ELEMENT Z" IS A MYSTERIOUS CHEMICAL SUBSTANCE WHICH I'VE LONG-BELIEVED EXISTED ELSEWHERE IN THE UNIVERSE! -- IF "ELEMENT Z" HAS NOW REACHED EARTH, THEN I'M ON THE THRESHOLD OF A TREMENDOUS DISCOVERY...!

NEXT MORNING, IN THE WARDEN'S OFFICE...

LUTHOR, YOU'RE OUT OF YOUR MIND, TO MAKE SUCH A REQUEST!

ALL I ASK, SIR, IS ...LET ME USE THE PRISON HOSPITAL'S LABORATORY FACILITIES FOR 24 HOURS!

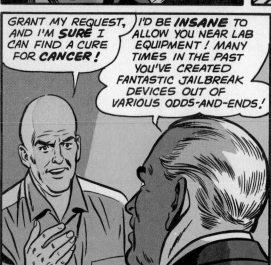

GRANT MY REQUEST, AND I'M SURE I CAN FIND A CURE FOR CANCER!

I'D BE INSANE TO ALLOW YOU NEAR LAB EQUIPMENT! MANY TIMES IN THE PAST YOU'VE CREATED FANTASTIC JAILBREAK DEVICES OUT OF VARIOUS ODDS-AND-ENDS!

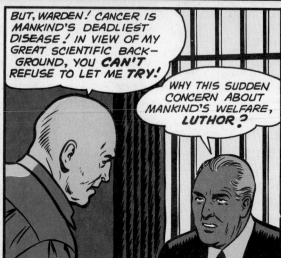

BUT, WARDEN! CANCER IS MANKIND'S DEADLIEST DISEASE! IN VIEW OF MY GREAT SCIENTIFIC BACK-GROUND, YOU CAN'T REFUSE TO LET ME TRY!

WHY THIS SUDDEN CONCERN ABOUT MANKIND'S WELFARE, LUTHOR?

ALL YOUR LIFE YOU'VE TRIED TO CRUSH AND RULE MANKIND WITH ONE MAD INVENTION AFTER ANOTHER! YOU'D HAVE SUCCEEDED, TOO, EXCEPT FOR SUPERMAN!

THAT'S WHY THIS EXPERIMENT MEANS SO MUCH TO ME!

Regards from Superman

I REALIZE AT LAST HOW WRONG I'VE BEEN TO USE MY GREAT BRAIN TO FIGHT, RATHER THAN AID, MANKIND! PLEASE GIVE ME THIS CHANCE TO ATONE...!

OKAY! 24 HOURS! -- BUT YOU'LL BE CLOSELY GUARDED EVERY SECOND!

3

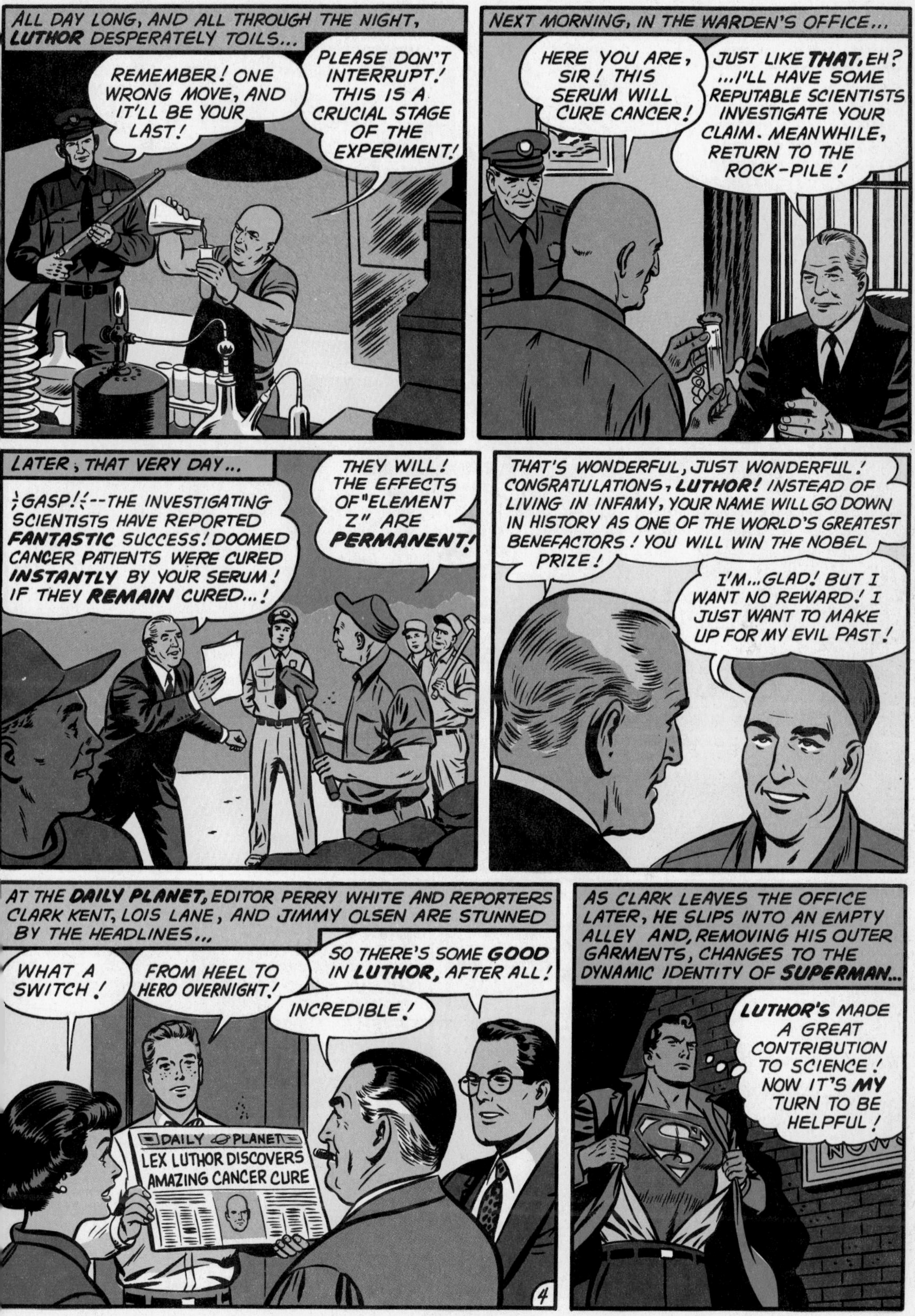
ALL DAY LONG, AND ALL THROUGH THE NIGHT, LUTHOR DESPERATELY TOILS...
REMEMBER! ONE WRONG MOVE, AND IT'LL BE YOUR LAST!
PLEASE DON'T INTERRUPT! THIS IS A CRUCIAL STAGE OF THE EXPERIMENT!
NEXT MORNING, IN THE WARDEN'S OFFICE...
HERE YOU ARE, SIR! THIS SERUM WILL CURE CANCER!
JUST LIKE THAT, EH? ...I'LL HAVE SOME REPUTABLE SCIENTISTS INVESTIGATE YOUR CLAIM. MEANWHILE, RETURN TO THE ROCK-PILE!
LATER, THAT VERY DAY...
GASP! --THE INVESTIGATING SCIENTISTS HAVE REPORTED FANTASTIC SUCCESS! DOOMED CANCER PATIENTS WERE CURED INSTANTLY BY YOUR SERUM! IF THEY REMAIN CURED...!
THEY WILL! THE EFFECTS OF "ELEMENT Z" ARE PERMANENT!
THAT'S WONDERFUL, JUST WONDERFUL! CONGRATULATIONS, LUTHOR! INSTEAD OF LIVING IN INFAMY, YOUR NAME WILL GO DOWN IN HISTORY AS ONE OF THE WORLD'S GREATEST BENEFACTORS! YOU WILL WIN THE NOBEL PRIZE!
I'M...GLAD! BUT I WANT NO REWARD! I JUST WANT TO MAKE UP FOR MY EVIL PAST!
AT THE DAILY PLANET, EDITOR PERRY WHITE AND REPORTERS CLARK KENT, LOIS LANE, AND JIMMY OLSEN ARE STUNNED BY THE HEADLINES...
WHAT A SWITCH!
FROM HEEL TO HERO OVERNIGHT!
SO THERE'S SOME GOOD IN LUTHOR, AFTER ALL!
INCREDIBLE!
DAILY PLANET
LEX LUTHOR DISCOVERS AMAZING CANCER CURE
4
AS CLARK LEAVES THE OFFICE LATER, HE SLIPS INTO AN EMPTY ALLEY AND, REMOVING HIS OUTER GARMENTS, CHANGES TO THE DYNAMIC IDENTITY OF SUPERMAN...
LUTHOR'S MADE A GREAT CONTRIBUTION TO SCIENCE! NOW IT'S MY TURN TO BE HELPFUL!

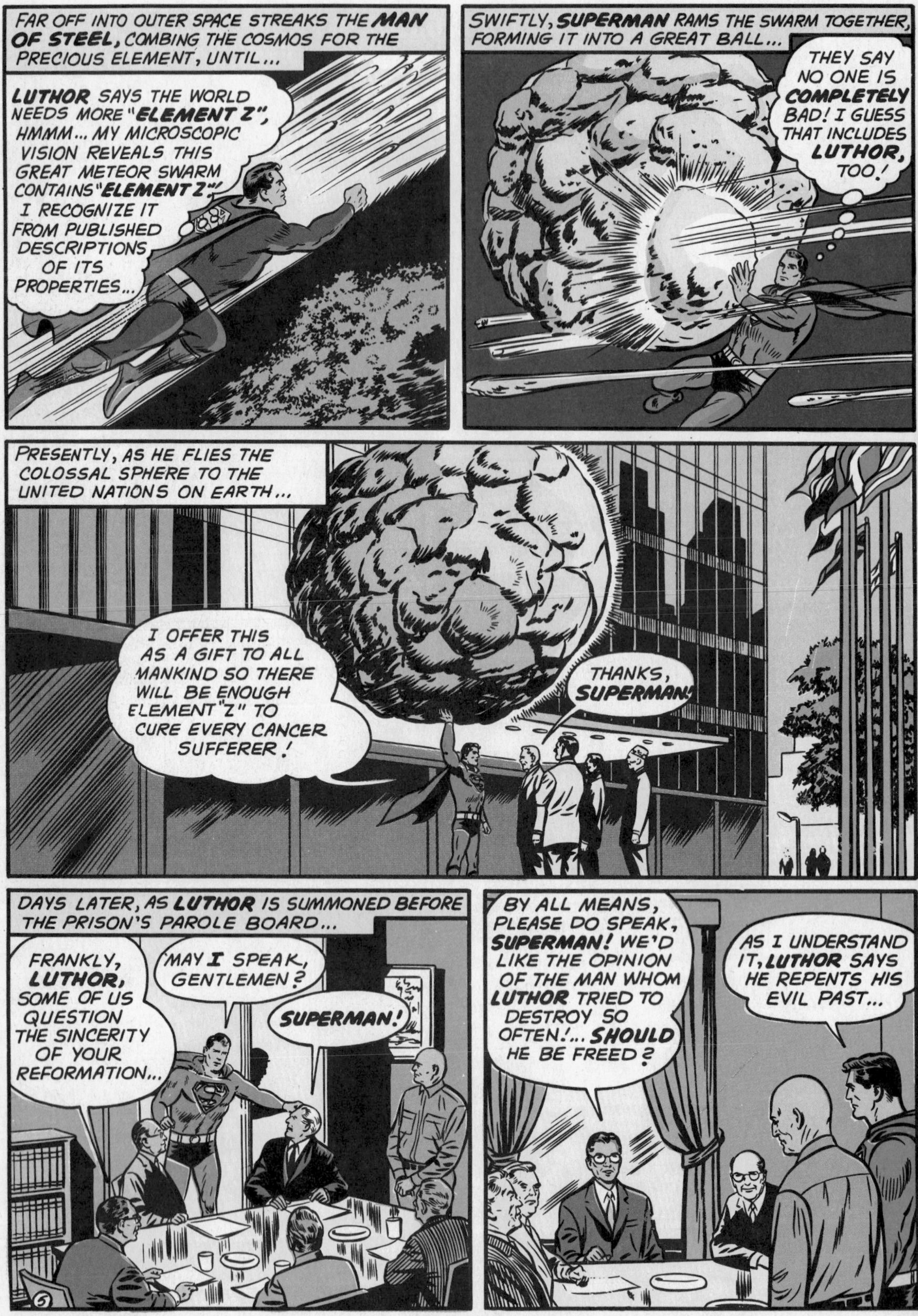
FAR OFF INTO OUTER SPACE STREAKS THE MAN OF STEEL, COMBING THE COSMOS FOR THE PRECIOUS ELEMENT, UNTIL...
LUTHOR SAYS THE WORLD NEEDS MORE "ELEMENT Z", HMMM... MY MICROSCOPIC VISION REVEALS THIS GREAT METEOR SWARM CONTAINS "ELEMENT Z"! I RECOGNIZE IT FROM PUBLISHED DESCRIPTIONS OF ITS PROPERTIES...
SWIFTLY, SUPERMAN RAMS THE SWARM TOGETHER, FORMING IT INTO A GREAT BALL...
THEY SAY NO ONE IS COMPLETELY BAD! I GUESS THAT INCLUDES LUTHOR, TOO!
PRESENTLY, AS HE FLIES THE COLOSSAL SPHERE TO THE UNITED NATIONS ON EARTH...
I OFFER THIS AS A GIFT TO ALL MANKIND SO THERE WILL BE ENOUGH ELEMENT "Z" TO CURE EVERY CANCER SUFFERER!
THANKS, SUPERMAN!
DAYS LATER, AS LUTHOR IS SUMMONED BEFORE THE PRISON'S PAROLE BOARD...
FRANKLY, LUTHOR, SOME OF US QUESTION THE SINCERITY OF YOUR REFORMATION...
MAY I SPEAK, GENTLEMEN?
SUPERMAN!
5
BY ALL MEANS, PLEASE DO SPEAK, SUPERMAN! WE'D LIKE THE OPINION OF THE MAN WHOM LUTHOR TRIED TO DESTROY SO OFTEN!... SHOULD HE BE FREED?
AS I UNDERSTAND IT, LUTHOR SAYS HE REPENTS HIS EVIL PAST...

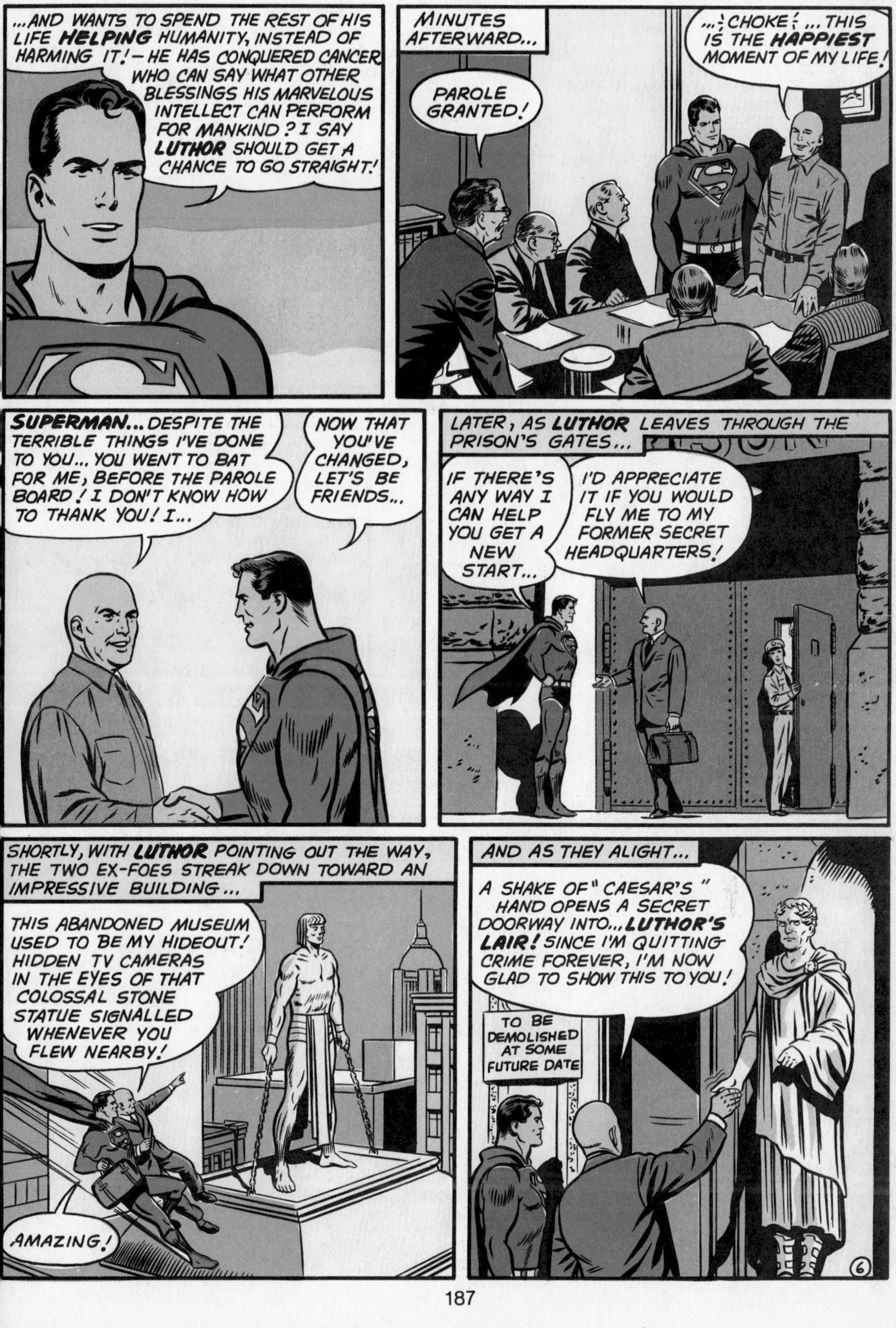
...AND WANTS TO SPEND THE REST OF HIS LIFE HELPING HUMANITY, INSTEAD OF HARMING IT! — HE HAS CONQUERED CANCER WHO CAN SAY WHAT OTHER BLESSINGS HIS MARVELOUS INTELLECT CAN PERFORM FOR MANKIND? I SAY LUTHOR SHOULD GET A CHANCE TO GO STRAIGHT!
MINUTES AFTERWARD...
PAROLE GRANTED!
...CHOKE ... THIS IS THE HAPPIEST MOMENT OF MY LIFE!
SUPERMAN... DESPITE THE TERRIBLE THINGS I'VE DONE TO YOU... YOU WENT TO BAT FOR ME, BEFORE THE PAROLE BOARD! I DON'T KNOW HOW TO THANK YOU! I...
NOW THAT YOU'VE CHANGED, LET'S BE FRIENDS...
LATER, AS LUTHOR LEAVES THROUGH THE PRISON'S GATES...
IF THERE'S ANY WAY I CAN HELP YOU GET A NEW START...
I'D APPRECIATE IT IF YOU WOULD FLY ME TO MY FORMER SECRET HEADQUARTERS!
SHORTLY, WITH LUTHOR POINTING OUT THE WAY, THE TWO EX-FOES STREAK DOWN TOWARD AN IMPRESSIVE BUILDING...
THIS ABANDONED MUSEUM USED TO BE MY HIDEOUT! HIDDEN TV CAMERAS IN THE EYES OF THAT COLOSSAL STONE STATUE SIGNALLED WHENEVER YOU FLEW NEARBY!
AMAZING!
AND AS THEY ALIGHT...
A SHAKE OF "CAESAR'S" HAND OPENS A SECRET DOORWAY INTO... LUTHOR'S LAIR! SINCE I'M QUITTING CRIME FOREVER, I'M NOW GLAD TO SHOW THIS TO YOU!
TO BE DEMOLISHED AT SOME FUTURE DATE
6

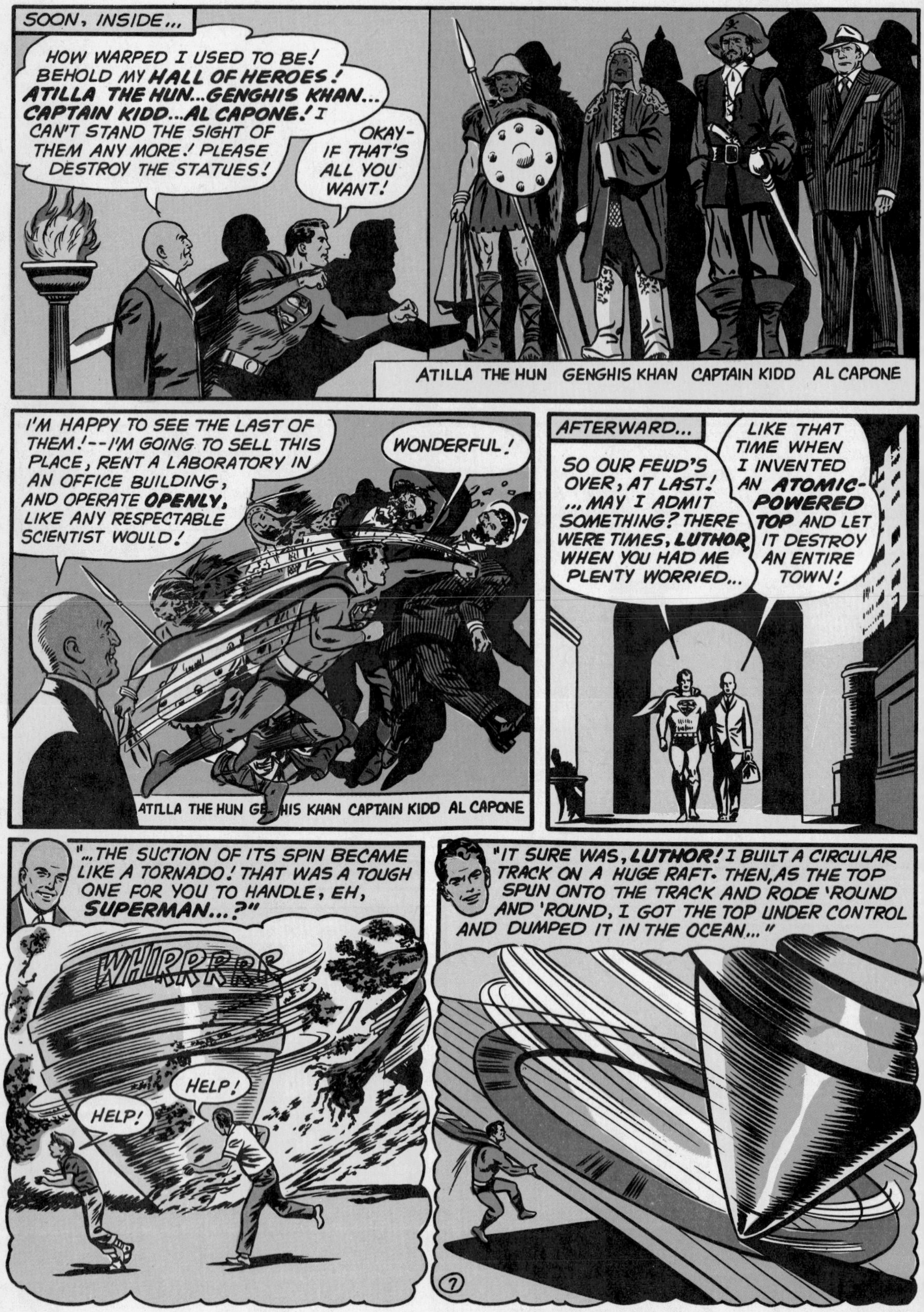
SOON, INSIDE...
HOW WARPED I USED TO BE! BEHOLD MY HALL OF HEROES! ATILLA THE HUN...GENGHIS KHAN... CAPTAIN KIDD...AL CAPONE! I CAN'T STAND THE SIGHT OF THEM ANY MORE! PLEASE DESTROY THE STATUES!
OKAY- IF THAT'S ALL YOU WANT!
ATILLA THE HUN GENGHIS KHAN CAPTAIN KIDD AL CAPONE
I'M HAPPY TO SEE THE LAST OF THEM!--I'M GOING TO SELL THIS PLACE, RENT A LABORATORY IN AN OFFICE BUILDING, AND OPERATE OPENLY, LIKE ANY RESPECTABLE SCIENTIST WOULD!
WONDERFUL!
ATILLA THE HUN GE HIS KHAN CAPTAIN KIDD AL CAPONE
AFTERWARD...
SO OUR FEUD'S OVER, AT LAST! ...MAY I ADMIT SOMETHING? THERE WERE TIMES, LUTHOR, WHEN YOU HAD ME PLENTY WORRIED...
LIKE THAT TIME WHEN I INVENTED AN ATOMIC-POWERED TOP AND LET IT DESTROY AN ENTIRE TOWN!
"...THE SUCTION OF ITS SPIN BECAME LIKE A TORNADO! THAT WAS A TOUGH ONE FOR YOU TO HANDLE, EH, SUPERMAN...?"
WHIRRRRR
HELP!
HELP!
"IT SURE WAS, LUTHOR! I BUILT A CIRCULAR TRACK ON A HUGE RAFT. THEN, AS THE TOP SPUN ONTO THE TRACK AND RODE 'ROUND AND 'ROUND, I GOT THE TOP UNDER CONTROL AND DUMPED IT IN THE OCEAN..."
7

"AND I'LL NEVER FORGET HOW YOU ONCE DISGUISED YOURSELF AS A PROFESSOR AND FOCUSED A *DUPLICATOR RAY* ON ME AND FORMED AN IMPERFECT DOUBLE OF MYSELF... *BIZARRO!* YOU CAN'T IMAGINE ALL THE PROBLEMS THAT *IDIOT OF STEEL* HAS GIVEN ME SINCE THEN..."

EARLY ONE AFTERNOON, AFTER *LUTHOR* DISPOSES OF HIS MUSEUM HIDEOUT, AND RENTS A LAB IN AN OFFICE BUILDING...

MY NEXT GOAL, GENTLEMEN OF THE PRESS? I'M GOING TO FIND A CURE FOR... HEART DISEASE!

WONDERFUL! HOW FORTUNATE FOR HUMANITY THAT YOU'VE GIVEN UP CRIME IN ORDER TO MAKE IMPORTANT DISCOVERIES!

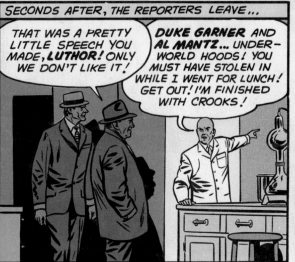

SECONDS AFTER, THE REPORTERS LEAVE...

THAT WAS A PRETTY LITTLE SPEECH YOU MADE, *LUTHOR!* ONLY WE DON'T LIKE IT!

DUKE GARNER AND *AL MANTZ*... UNDERWORLD HOODS! YOU MUST HAVE STOLEN IN WHILE I WENT FOR LUNCH! GET OUT! I'M FINISHED WITH CROOKS!

BUT WE'RE NOT FINISHED WITH YOU!... TELL HIM, AL!

EITHER YOU KILL *SUPERMAN*, OR WE *KILL YOU!*... WHO'S GONNA DIE, GENIUS? *YOU*...OR *SUPERMAN?!!*

END, PART I

WHAT WILL *LUTHOR* DECIDE? TURN TO THE NEXT CHAPTER! (8)

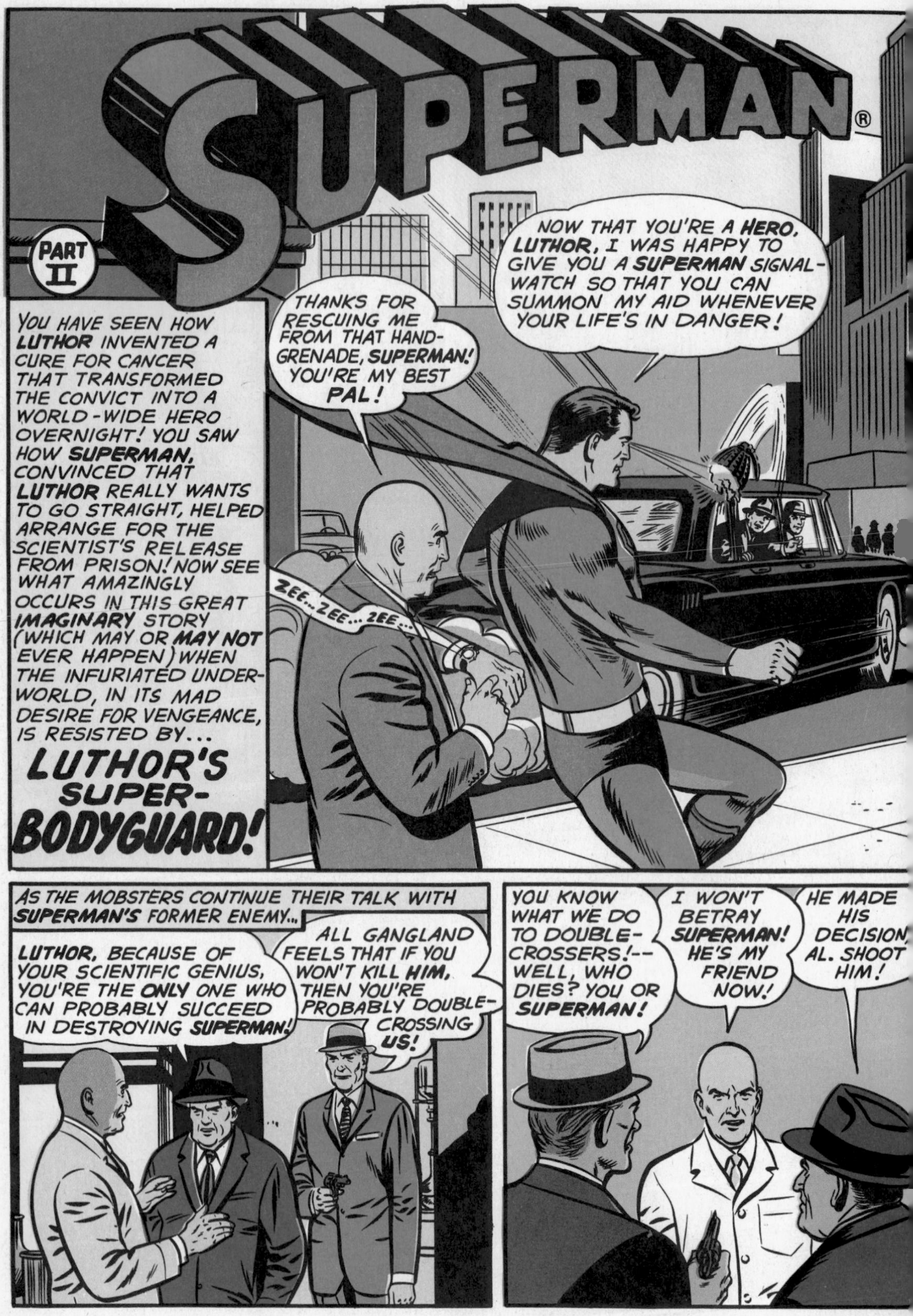
SUPERMAN®
PART II
YOU HAVE SEEN HOW LUTHOR INVENTED A CURE FOR CANCER THAT TRANSFORMED THE CONVICT INTO A WORLD-WIDE HERO OVERNIGHT! YOU SAW HOW SUPERMAN, CONVINCED THAT LUTHOR REALLY WANTS TO GO STRAIGHT, HELPED ARRANGE FOR THE SCIENTIST'S RELEASE FROM PRISON! NOW SEE WHAT AMAZINGLY OCCURS IN THIS GREAT IMAGINARY STORY (WHICH MAY OR MAY NOT EVER HAPPEN) WHEN THE INFURIATED UNDERWORLD, IN ITS MAD DESIRE FOR VENGEANCE, IS RESISTED BY...
LUTHOR'S SUPER-BODYGUARD!
THANKS FOR RESCUING ME FROM THAT HAND-GRENADE, SUPERMAN! YOU'RE MY BEST PAL!
NOW THAT YOU'RE A HERO, LUTHOR, I WAS HAPPY TO GIVE YOU A SUPERMAN SIGNAL-WATCH SO THAT YOU CAN SUMMON MY AID WHENEVER YOUR LIFE'S IN DANGER!
ZEE...ZEE...ZEE...
AS THE MOBSTERS CONTINUE THEIR TALK WITH SUPERMAN'S FORMER ENEMY...
LUTHOR, BECAUSE OF YOUR SCIENTIFIC GENIUS, YOU'RE THE ONLY ONE WHO CAN PROBABLY SUCCEED IN DESTROYING SUPERMAN!
ALL GANGLAND FEELS THAT IF YOU WON'T KILL HIM, THEN YOU'RE PROBABLY DOUBLE-CROSSING US!
YOU KNOW WHAT WE DO TO DOUBLE-CROSSERS!-- WELL, WHO DIES? YOU OR SUPERMAN!
I WON'T BETRAY SUPERMAN! HE'S MY FRIEND NOW!
HE MADE HIS DECISION, AL. SHOOT HIM!

BUT AS THE TRIGGER-MAN FIRES...

YOU'RE WASTING THOSE BULLETS!

BANG! BANG!

SUPERMAN! FOR THE FIRST TIME IN MY LIFE, I'M *GLAD* TO SEE BULLETS BOUNCING OFF YOU!

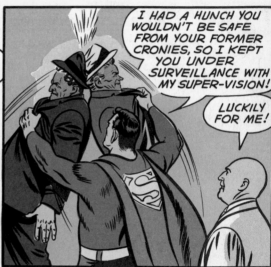

I HAD A HUNCH YOU WOULDN'T BE SAFE FROM YOUR FORMER CRONIES, SO I KEPT YOU UNDER SURVEILLANCE WITH MY SUPER-VISION!

LUCKILY FOR ME!

SUPERMAN REMOVES AN OBJECT FROM HIS CAPE'S SECRET POUCH, THEN...

PROBABLY, THERE WILL BE OTHER ATTEMPTS BY THE UNDERWORLD TO DESTROY YOU! THAT'S WHY I MADE THIS SIGNAL-WATCH! PLEASE ACCEPT IT! IT'S LIKE JIMMY OLSEN'S WATCH, BUT OPERATES ON A DIFFERENT ULTRASONIC FREQUENCY...

WHENEVER YOU'RE IN DANGER, PRESS THE BUTTON ON THE WATCH! I'LL FLASH TO YOUR RESCUE, IN RESPONSE TO THE ULTRASONIC DISTRESS-SIGNAL!

THANK YOU, SUPERMAN! YOU'RE... A WONDERFUL FRIEND!

SHORTLY, AT A MEETING OF GANGLAND BIG-SHOTS...

WE'LL KEEP ON TRYING TO RUB OUT *LUTHOR*, UNTIL WE *SUCCEED!*

RIGHT! HE RATTED OUT ON HIS PROMISE TO DESTROY *SUPERMAN!* FOR THAT, HE'LL DIE!

AGAIN, THE UNDERWORLD STRIKES...

HERE'S A PRESENT, LUTHOR!

A HAND-GRENADE! I MUST PRESS THE BUTTON ON MY *SUPERMAN* SIGNAL-WATCH, IMMEDIATELY!

ZEE-ZEE-ZEE

2

191

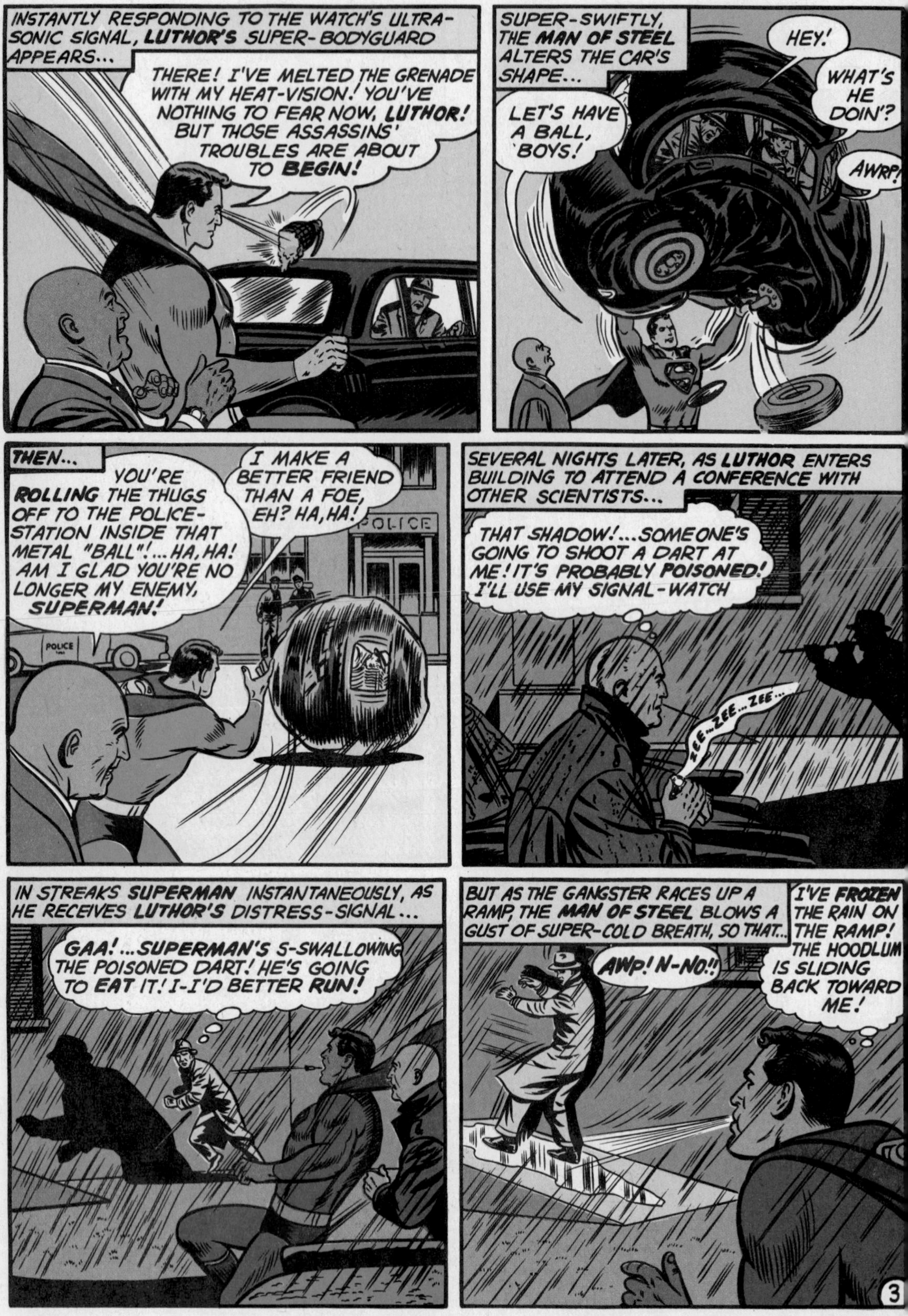
INSTANTLY RESPONDING TO THE WATCH'S ULTRA-SONIC SIGNAL, LUTHOR'S SUPER-BODYGUARD APPEARS...
THERE! I'VE MELTED THE GRENADE WITH MY HEAT-VISION! YOU'VE NOTHING TO FEAR NOW, LUTHOR! BUT THOSE ASSASSINS' TROUBLES ARE ABOUT TO BEGIN!
SUPER-SWIFTLY, THE MAN OF STEEL ALTERS THE CAR'S SHAPE...
HEY!
WHAT'S HE DOIN'?
LET'S HAVE A BALL, BOYS!
AWRP!
THEN...
YOU'RE ROLLING THE THUGS OFF TO THE POLICE-STATION INSIDE THAT METAL "BALL"!... HA, HA! AM I GLAD YOU'RE NO LONGER MY ENEMY, SUPERMAN!
I MAKE A BETTER FRIEND THAN A FOE, EH? HA, HA!
POLICE
POLICE
SEVERAL NIGHTS LATER, AS LUTHOR ENTERS BUILDING TO ATTEND A CONFERENCE WITH OTHER SCIENTISTS...
THAT SHADOW!...SOMEONE'S GOING TO SHOOT A DART AT ME! IT'S PROBABLY POISONED! I'LL USE MY SIGNAL-WATCH
ZEE...ZEE...ZEE...
IN STREAKS SUPERMAN INSTANTANEOUSLY, AS HE RECEIVES LUTHOR'S DISTRESS-SIGNAL...
GAA!...SUPERMAN'S S-SWALLOWING THE POISONED DART! HE'S GOING TO EAT IT! I-I'D BETTER RUN!
BUT AS THE GANGSTER RACES UP A RAMP, THE MAN OF STEEL BLOWS A GUST OF SUPER-COLD BREATH, SO THAT...
I'VE FROZEN THE RAIN ON THE RAMP! THE HOODLUM IS SLIDING BACK TOWARD ME!
AWP! N-NO!!
3

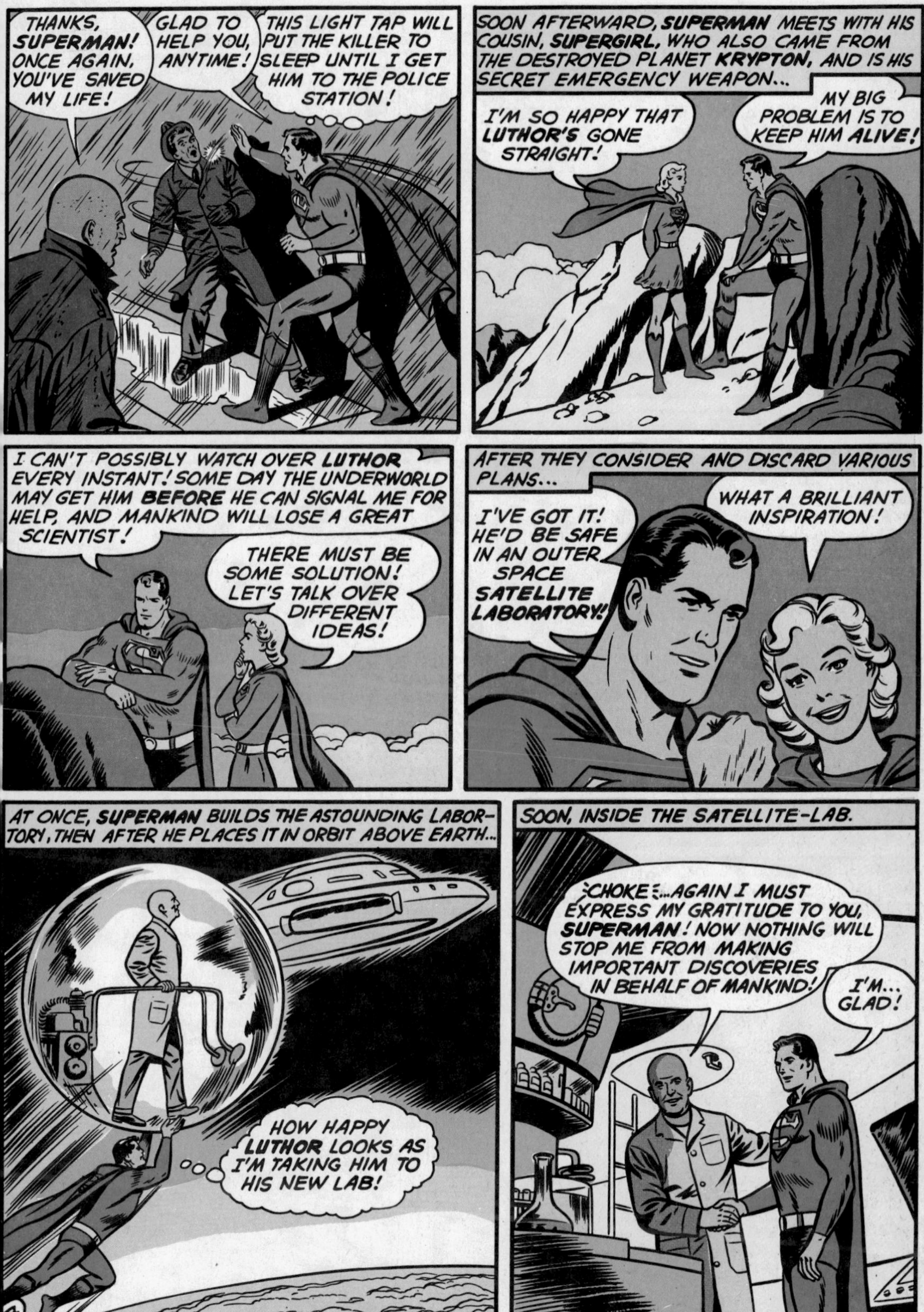
THANKS, SUPERMAN! ONCE AGAIN, YOU'VE SAVED MY LIFE!
GLAD TO HELP YOU, ANYTIME!
THIS LIGHT TAP WILL PUT THE KILLER TO SLEEP UNTIL I GET HIM TO THE POLICE STATION!
SOON AFTERWARD, SUPERMAN MEETS WITH HIS COUSIN, SUPERGIRL, WHO ALSO CAME FROM THE DESTROYED PLANET KRYPTON, AND IS HIS SECRET EMERGENCY WEAPON...
I'M SO HAPPY THAT LUTHOR'S GONE STRAIGHT!
MY BIG PROBLEM IS TO KEEP HIM ALIVE!
I CAN'T POSSIBLY WATCH OVER LUTHOR EVERY INSTANT! SOME DAY THE UNDERWORLD MAY GET HIM BEFORE HE CAN SIGNAL ME FOR HELP, AND MANKIND WILL LOSE A GREAT SCIENTIST!
THERE MUST BE SOME SOLUTION! LET'S TALK OVER DIFFERENT IDEAS!
AFTER THEY CONSIDER AND DISCARD VARIOUS PLANS...
I'VE GOT IT! HE'D BE SAFE IN AN OUTER SPACE SATELLITE LABORATORY!
WHAT A BRILLIANT INSPIRATION!
AT ONCE, SUPERMAN BUILDS THE ASTOUNDING LABORTORY, THEN AFTER HE PLACES IT IN ORBIT ABOVE EARTH...
HOW HAPPY LUTHOR LOOKS AS I'M TAKING HIM TO HIS NEW LAB!
4
SOON, INSIDE THE SATELLITE-LAB.
:CHOKE:...AGAIN I MUST EXPRESS MY GRATITUDE TO YOU, SUPERMAN! NOW NOTHING WILL STOP ME FROM MAKING IMPORTANT DISCOVERIES IN BEHALF OF MANKIND!
I'M... GLAD!

PRESENTLY, INFURIATED UNDERWORLD CHIEFS HOLD A WAR COUNCIL...

SATELLITE OR NO SATELLITE, WE CAN STILL KILL LUTHOR, BUT IT'LL COST A FORTUNE!

PRICE IS NO OBJECT! KILL HIM!

WEEKS LATER, AS SUPERMAN FLIES ALONG ON PATROL...

GREAT SCOTT! MY TELESCOPIC SIGHT REVEALS AN INCREDIBLE THREAT TO LUTHOR'S LIFE!

UP INTO OUTER SPACE DESPERATELY FLASHES THE MAN OF STEEL...

THAT MISSILE-BOMB WILL EXPLODE LUTHOR'S LABORATORY, UNLESS I DESTROY THE MISSILE FIRST!

DELIBERATELY, SUPERMAN MEETS THE MISSILE IN A HEAD-ON COLLISION...

JUST IN TIME!... I'M UNHARMED! HMM... GANGLAND MAY HAVE MANY SUCH MISSILE-LAUNCHING BASES! I MUST DO SOMETHING TO PERMANENTLY CANCEL OUT THE MISSILE-THREAT!

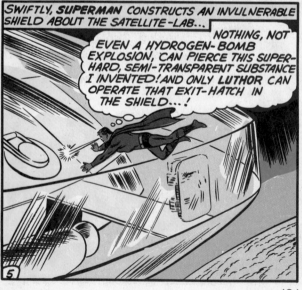

SWIFTLY, SUPERMAN CONSTRUCTS AN INVULNERABLE SHIELD ABOUT THE SATELLITE-LAB...

NOTHING, NOT EVEN A HYDROGEN-BOMB EXPLOSION, CAN PIERCE THIS SUPER-HARD, SEMI-TRANSPARENT SUBSTANCE I INVENTED! AND ONLY LUTHOR CAN OPERATE THAT EXIT-HATCH IN THE SHIELD...!

SHORTLY, IN THE SATELLITE LAB...

THE SIGNAL-WATCH'S ULTRASONIC WAVES CAN'T TRAVEL THROUGH OUTER SPACE! IF YOU EVER URGENTLY NEED ME, FIRE THIS JET-ROCKET, WHICH RESEMBLES YOU, INTO EARTH'S UPPER ATMOSPHERE!

I'LL DO THAT!

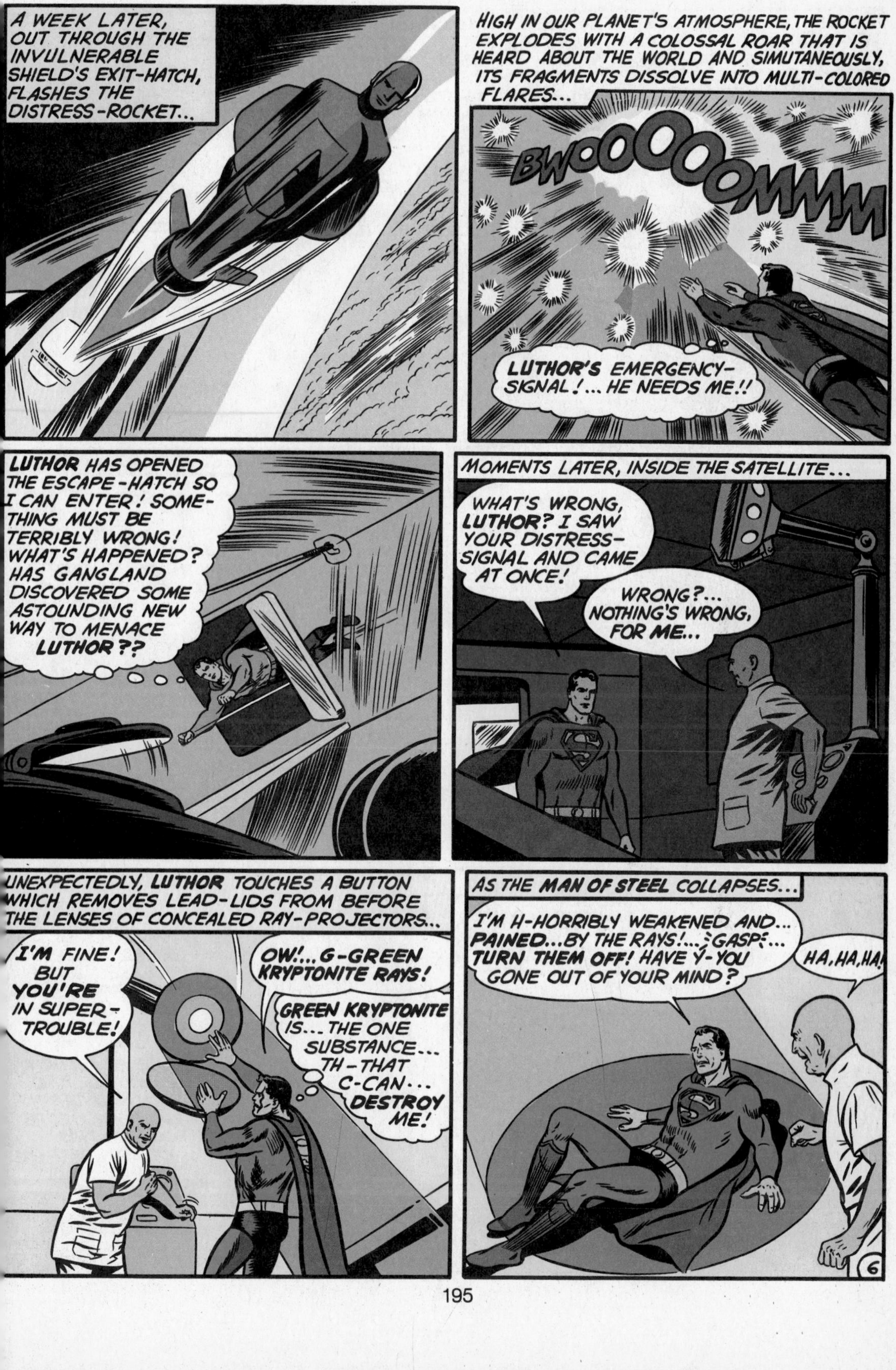

A WEEK LATER, OUT THROUGH THE INVULNERABLE SHIELD'S EXIT-HATCH, FLASHES THE DISTRESS-ROCKET...
HIGH IN OUR PLANET'S ATMOSPHERE, THE ROCKET EXPLODES WITH A COLOSSAL ROAR THAT IS HEARD ABOUT THE WORLD AND SIMUTANEOUSLY, ITS FRAGMENTS DISSOLVE INTO MULTI-COLORED FLARES...
BWOOOOOOMMMM
LUTHOR'S EMERGENCY-SIGNAL!... HE NEEDS ME.!!
LUTHOR HAS OPENED THE ESCAPE-HATCH SO I CAN ENTER! SOMETHING MUST BE TERRIBLY WRONG! WHAT'S HAPPENED? HAS GANGLAND DISCOVERED SOME ASTOUNDING NEW WAY TO MENACE LUTHOR??
MOMENTS LATER, INSIDE THE SATELLITE...
WHAT'S WRONG, LUTHOR? I SAW YOUR DISTRESS-SIGNAL AND CAME AT ONCE!
WRONG?... NOTHING'S WRONG, FOR ME...
UNEXPECTEDLY, LUTHOR TOUCHES A BUTTON WHICH REMOVES LEAD-LIDS FROM BEFORE THE LENSES OF CONCEALED RAY-PROJECTORS...
I'M FINE! BUT YOU'RE IN SUPER-TROUBLE!
OW!... G-GREEN KRYPTONITE RAYS!
GREEN KRYPTONITE IS... THE ONE SUBSTANCE... TH-THAT C-CAN... DESTROY ME!
AS THE MAN OF STEEL COLLAPSES...
I'M H-HORRIBLY WEAKENED AND... PAINED... BY THE RAYS!... ;GASP;... TURN THEM OFF! HAVE Y-YOU GONE OUT OF YOUR MIND?
HA, HA, HA!
6

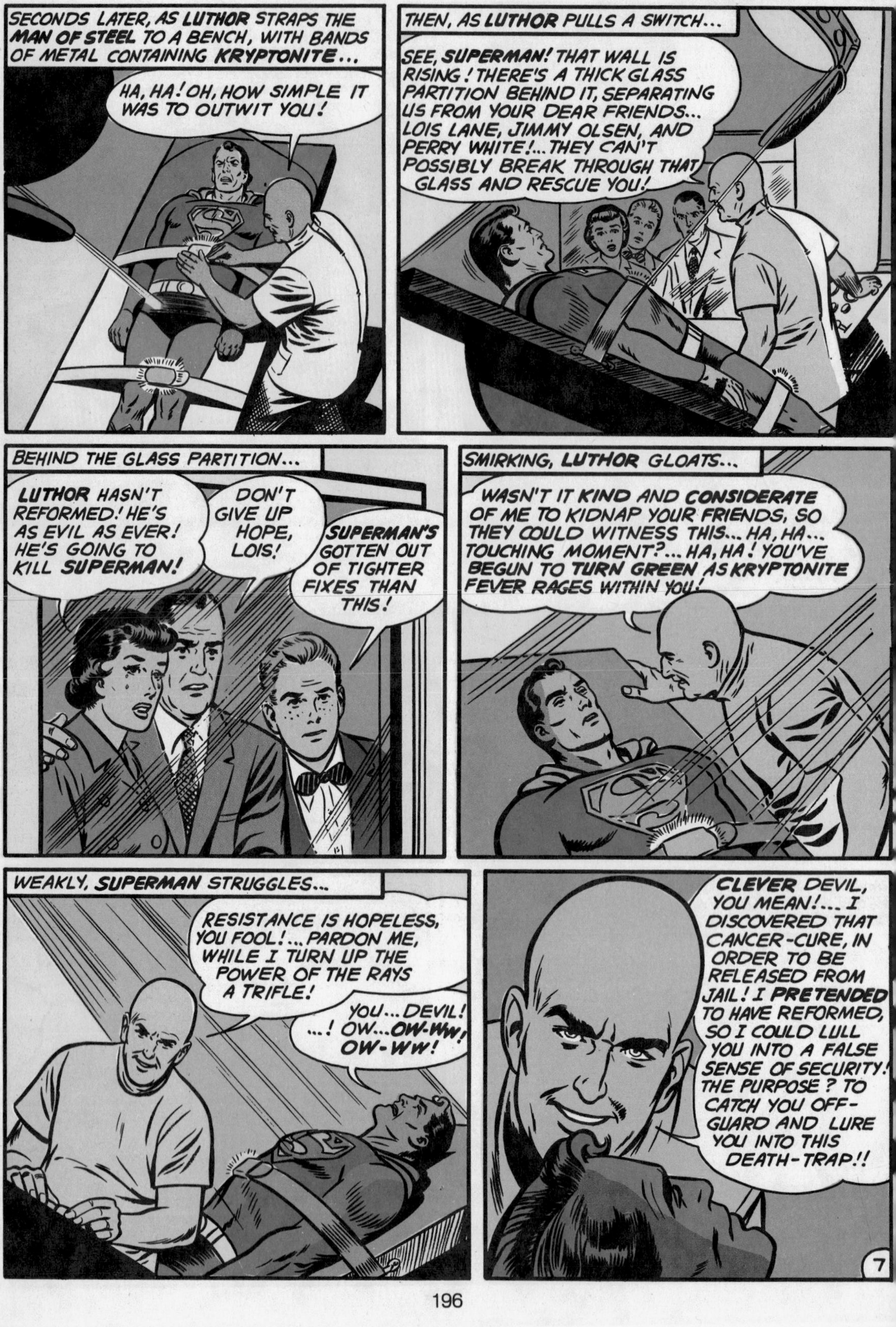
SECONDS LATER, AS LUTHOR STRAPS THE MAN OF STEEL TO A BENCH, WITH BANDS OF METAL CONTAINING KRYPTONITE...
HA, HA! OH, HOW SIMPLE IT WAS TO OUTWIT YOU!
THEN, AS LUTHOR PULLS A SWITCH...
SEE, SUPERMAN! THAT WALL IS RISING! THERE'S A THICK GLASS PARTITION BEHIND IT, SEPARATING US FROM YOUR DEAR FRIENDS... LOIS LANE, JIMMY OLSEN, AND PERRY WHITE!... THEY CAN'T POSSIBLY BREAK THROUGH THAT GLASS AND RESCUE YOU!
BEHIND THE GLASS PARTITION...
LUTHOR HASN'T REFORMED! HE'S AS EVIL AS EVER! HE'S GOING TO KILL SUPERMAN!
DON'T GIVE UP HOPE, LOIS!
SUPERMAN'S GOTTEN OUT OF TIGHTER FIXES THAN THIS!
SMIRKING, LUTHOR GLOATS...
WASN'T IT KIND AND CONSIDERATE OF ME TO KIDNAP YOUR FRIENDS, SO THEY COULD WITNESS THIS... HA, HA... TOUCHING MOMENT?... HA, HA! YOU'VE BEGUN TO TURN GREEN AS KRYPTONITE FEVER RAGES WITHIN YOU!
WEAKLY, SUPERMAN STRUGGLES...
RESISTANCE IS HOPELESS, YOU FOOL!... PARDON ME, WHILE I TURN UP THE POWER OF THE RAYS A TRIFLE!
YOU... DEVIL! ...! OW... OW-WW! OW-WW!
CLEVER DEVIL, YOU MEAN!... I DISCOVERED THAT CANCER-CURE, IN ORDER TO BE RELEASED FROM JAIL! I PRETENDED TO HAVE REFORMED, SO I COULD LULL YOU INTO A FALSE SENSE OF SECURITY! THE PURPOSE? TO CATCH YOU OFF-GUARD AND LURE YOU INTO THIS DEATH-TRAP!!
7

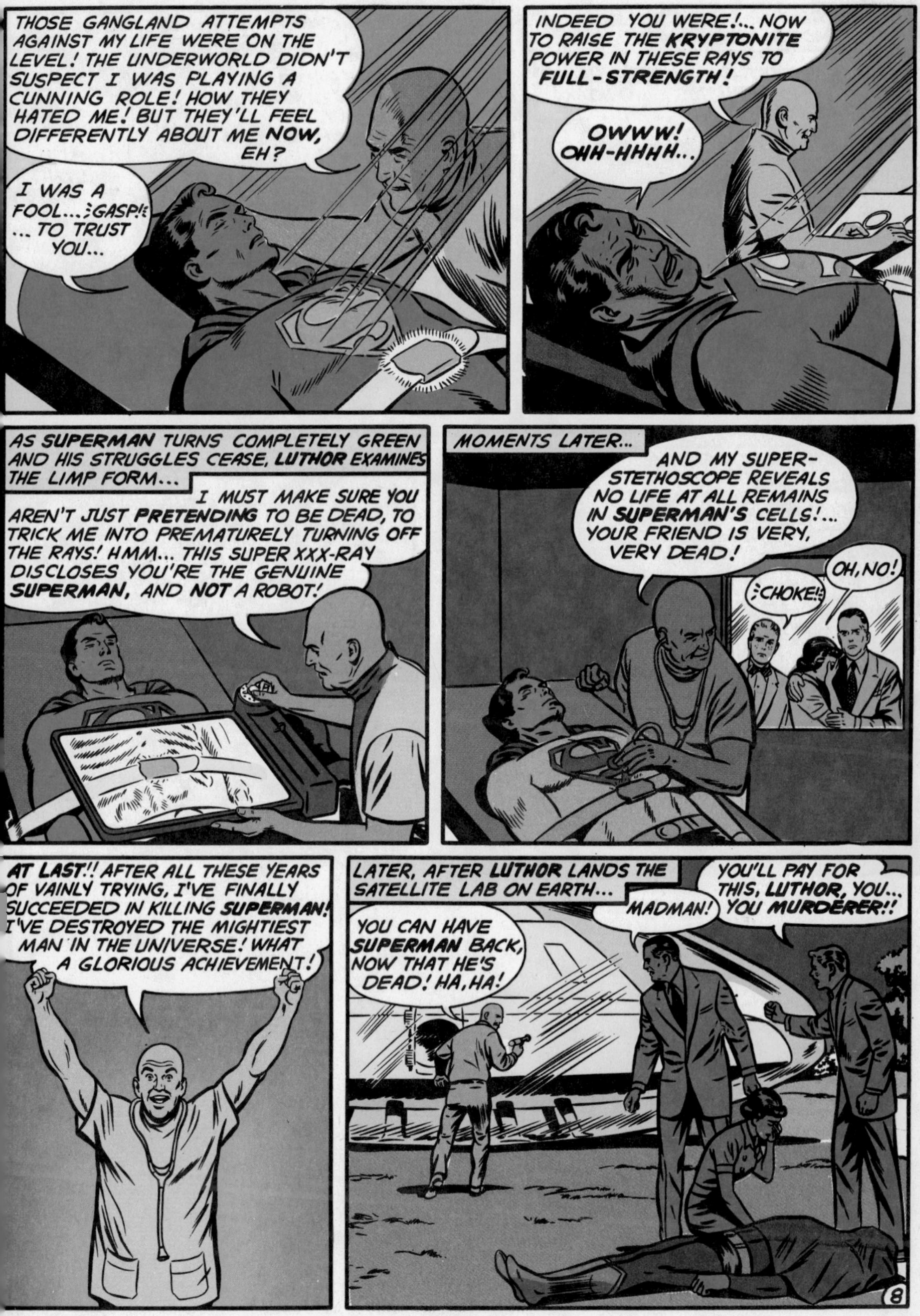
THOSE GANGLAND ATTEMPTS AGAINST MY LIFE WERE ON THE LEVEL! THE UNDERWORLD DIDN'T SUSPECT I WAS PLAYING A CUNNING ROLE! HOW THEY HATED ME! BUT THEY'LL FEEL DIFFERENTLY ABOUT ME NOW, EH?
I WAS A FOOL... ¿GASP!¿ ... TO TRUST YOU...
INDEED YOU WERE!... NOW TO RAISE THE KRYPTONITE POWER IN THESE RAYS TO FULL-STRENGTH!
OWWW! OHH-HHHH...
AS SUPERMAN TURNS COMPLETELY GREEN AND HIS STRUGGLES CEASE, LUTHOR EXAMINES THE LIMP FORM...
I MUST MAKE SURE YOU AREN'T JUST PRETENDING TO BE DEAD, TO TRICK ME INTO PREMATURELY TURNING OFF THE RAYS! HMM... THIS SUPER XXX-RAY DISCLOSES YOU'RE THE GENUINE SUPERMAN, AND NOT A ROBOT!
MOMENTS LATER...
AND MY SUPER-STETHOSCOPE REVEALS NO LIFE AT ALL REMAINS IN SUPERMAN'S CELLS!... YOUR FRIEND IS VERY, VERY DEAD!
OH, NO!
¿CHOKE!¿
AT LAST!! AFTER ALL THESE YEARS OF VAINLY TRYING, I'VE FINALLY SUCCEEDED IN KILLING SUPERMAN! I'VE DESTROYED THE MIGHTIEST MAN IN THE UNIVERSE! WHAT A GLORIOUS ACHIEVEMENT!
LATER, AFTER LUTHOR LANDS THE SATELLITE LAB ON EARTH...
YOU CAN HAVE SUPERMAN BACK, NOW THAT HE'S DEAD! HA, HA!
MADMAN!
YOU'LL PAY FOR THIS, LUTHOR, YOU... YOU MURDERER!!
8

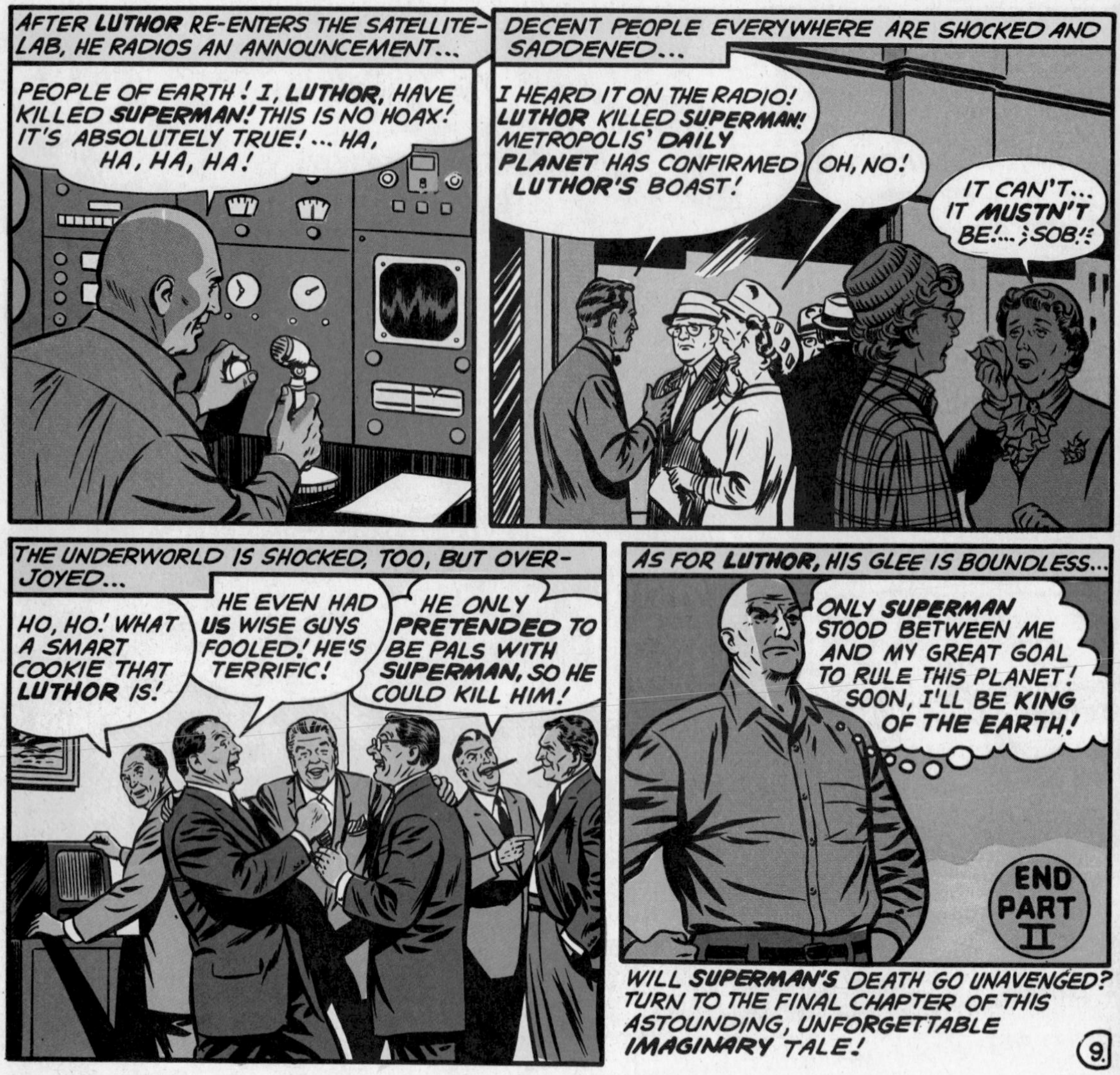
AFTER LUTHOR RE-ENTERS THE SATELLITE-LAB, HE RADIOS AN ANNOUNCEMENT...
PEOPLE OF EARTH! I, LUTHOR, HAVE KILLED SUPERMAN! THIS IS NO HOAX! IT'S ABSOLUTELY TRUE! ... HA, HA, HA, HA!
DECENT PEOPLE EVERYWHERE ARE SHOCKED AND SADDENED...
I HEARD IT ON THE RADIO! LUTHOR KILLED SUPERMAN! METROPOLIS' DAILY PLANET HAS CONFIRMED LUTHOR'S BOAST!
OH, NO!
IT CAN'T... IT MUSTN'T BE!... ¿SOB!¿
THE UNDERWORLD IS SHOCKED, TOO, BUT OVER-JOYED...
HO, HO! WHAT A SMART COOKIE THAT LUTHOR IS!
HE EVEN HAD US WISE GUYS FOOLED! HE'S TERRIFIC!
HE ONLY PRETENDED TO BE PALS WITH SUPERMAN, SO HE COULD KILL HIM!
AS FOR LUTHOR, HIS GLEE IS BOUNDLESS...
ONLY SUPERMAN STOOD BETWEEN ME AND MY GREAT GOAL TO RULE THIS PLANET! SOON, I'LL BE KING OF THE EARTH!
END PART II
WILL SUPERMAN'S DEATH GO UNAVENGED? TURN TO THE FINAL CHAPTER OF THIS ASTOUNDING, UNFORGETTABLE IMAGINARY TALE!
9

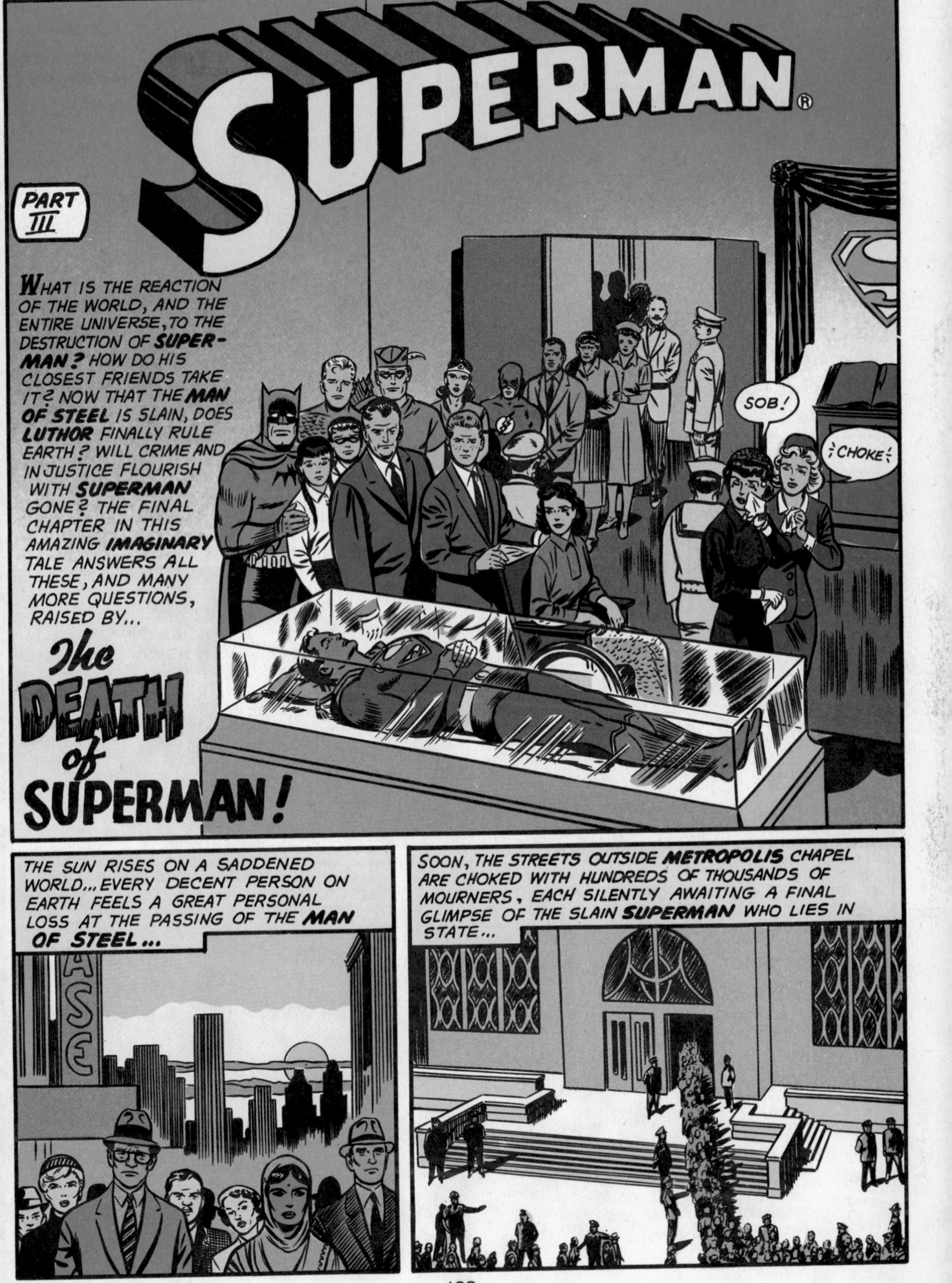
SUPERMAN®
PART III
WHAT IS THE REACTION OF THE WORLD, AND THE ENTIRE UNIVERSE, TO THE DESTRUCTION OF SUPERMAN? HOW DO HIS CLOSEST FRIENDS TAKE IT? NOW THAT THE MAN OF STEEL IS SLAIN, DOES LUTHOR FINALLY RULE EARTH? WILL CRIME AND INJUSTICE FLOURISH WITH SUPERMAN GONE? THE FINAL CHAPTER IN THIS AMAZING IMAGINARY TALE ANSWERS ALL THESE, AND MANY MORE QUESTIONS, RAISED BY...
The DEATH of SUPERMAN!
SOB!
CHOKE
THE SUN RISES ON A SADDENED WORLD... EVERY DECENT PERSON ON EARTH FEELS A GREAT PERSONAL LOSS AT THE PASSING OF THE MAN OF STEEL...
ASE
SOON, THE STREETS OUTSIDE METROPOLIS CHAPEL ARE CHOKED WITH HUNDREDS OF THOUSANDS OF MOURNERS, EACH SILENTLY AWAITING A FINAL GLIMPSE OF THE SLAIN SUPERMAN WHO LIES IN STATE...

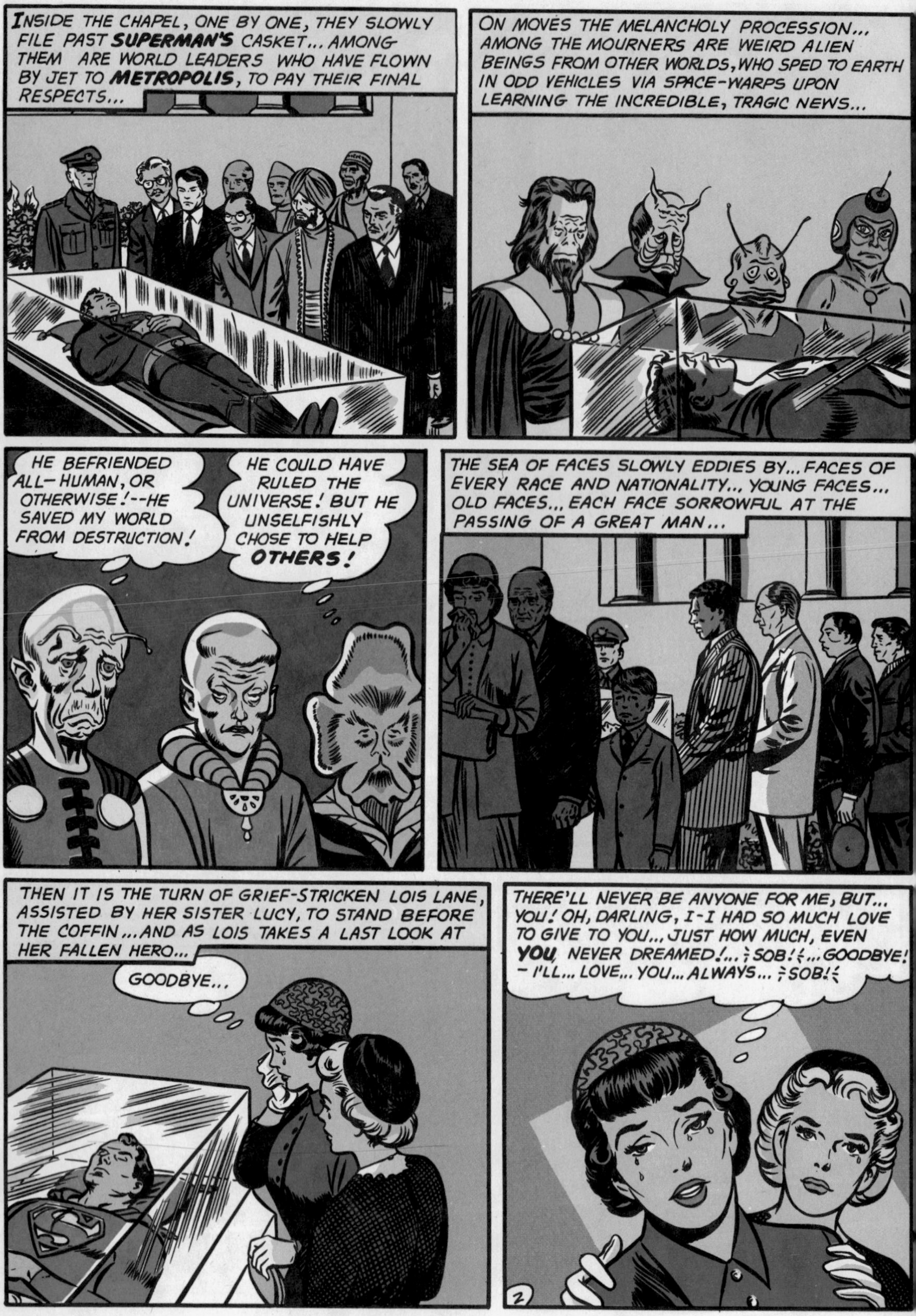
INSIDE THE CHAPEL, ONE BY ONE, THEY SLOWLY FILE PAST SUPERMAN'S CASKET... AMONG THEM ARE WORLD LEADERS WHO HAVE FLOWN BY JET TO METROPOLIS, TO PAY THEIR FINAL RESPECTS...
ON MOVES THE MELANCHOLY PROCESSION... AMONG THE MOURNERS ARE WEIRD ALIEN BEINGS FROM OTHER WORLDS, WHO SPED TO EARTH IN ODD VEHICLES VIA SPACE-WARPS UPON LEARNING THE INCREDIBLE, TRAGIC NEWS...
HE BEFRIENDED ALL-HUMAN, OR OTHERWISE!--HE SAVED MY WORLD FROM DESTRUCTION!
HE COULD HAVE RULED THE UNIVERSE! BUT HE UNSELFISHLY CHOSE TO HELP OTHERS!
THE SEA OF FACES SLOWLY EDDIES BY... FACES OF EVERY RACE AND NATIONALITY... YOUNG FACES... OLD FACES... EACH FACE SORROWFUL AT THE PASSING OF A GREAT MAN...
THEN IT IS THE TURN OF GRIEF-STRICKEN LOIS LANE, ASSISTED BY HER SISTER LUCY, TO STAND BEFORE THE COFFIN... AND AS LOIS TAKES A LAST LOOK AT HER FALLEN HERO...
GOODBYE...
THERE'LL NEVER BE ANYONE FOR ME, BUT... YOU! OH, DARLING, I-I HAD SO MUCH LOVE TO GIVE TO YOU... JUST HOW MUCH, EVEN YOU NEVER DREAMED!... ;SOB!;... GOODBYE! - I'LL... LOVE... YOU... ALWAYS... ;SOB!;
2

NEXT, **SUPERMAN'S** FRIENDS, JIMMY OLSEN, PERRY WHITE...AND MERMAID **LORI LEMARIS** FROM **ATLANTIS**... TAKE LAST, LINGERING LOOKS...

> ⸮CHOKE⸝ ... SO LONG, PAL! NO ONE EVER HAD A TRUER BUDDY THAN YOU!

> I'LL... MISS YOU...

> I'LL NEVER FORGET YOU!

AFTER THEM COMES LANA LANG...

> IT SEEMS LIKE ONLY YESTERDAY THAT I WAS YOUR CHILDHOOD FRIEND IN SMALLVILLE! FIRST, I WAS AN AWFUL PEST, THEN I GOT A CRUSH ON YOU. WHEN I GREW UP, THE CRUSH RIPENED INTO LOVE! NOW YOU'RE... GONE! FAREWELL...⸮CHOKE⸝

THEN THE **MAN OF STEEL'S** FAITHFUL PET **KRYPTO** PASSES THE COFFIN...

> I WILL NEVER KNOW ANOTHER MASTER LIKE YOU! ⸮CHOKE⸝ — GOODBYE! — WHEN I THINK OF ALL THE ADVENTURES WE HAD TOGETHER...

ON MOVE THE FACES, ONE AFTER ANOTHER... THEN, BEFORE THE SLAIN **MAN OF STEEL**, APPEARS THE TEAR-STAINED FEATURES OF A TEEN-AGED GIRL WHOM NO ONE SUSPECTS IS HIS **SUPERGIRL** COUSIN LINDA, FROM **KRYPTON**...

> TOGETHER, WE EXPLORED THE UNIVERSE... BUT EVEN INFINITY WASN'T AS BIG AS YOUR...⸮CHOKE⸝ ...GALLANT, NOBLE HEART...

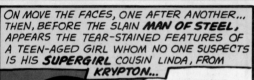

AND NOW, THERE FILES PAST -- **THE LEGION OF SUPER-HEROES** FROM THE DISTANT FUTURE...!

> WE SALUTE YOU IN DEATH AS WE HONORED YOU IN LIFE, COMRADE!

> OF ALL THE SUPER-HEROES, YOU WERE THE **GREATEST!!**

THOUSANDS OF MILES AWAY, IN **SUPERMAN'S** ARCTIC **FORTRESS OF SOLITUDE**, THE **SUPERMAN** ROBOTS, TOO, PAY THEIR FINAL RESPECTS TO THEIR SLAIN MASTER...

> THERE'S NOT A ONE OF US WHO WOULDN'T HAVE DIED GLADLY, IN HIS PLACE!

AND INSIDE THE MINIATURE BOTTLE-CITY OF **KANDOR**, IN THE FORTRESS, **VAN-ZEE** AND **SYLVIA** JOIN MILLIONS OF OTHER KANDORIANS IN AN IMPRESSIVE TRIBUTE...

> WHY ARE THEY LOWERING THE KRYPTONIAN FLAG, MOMMY?

> A GREAT MAN HAS DIED --⸮CHOKE⸝ — **SUPERMAN** WILL NEVER VISIT US... AGAIN...⸮SOB!⸝

3

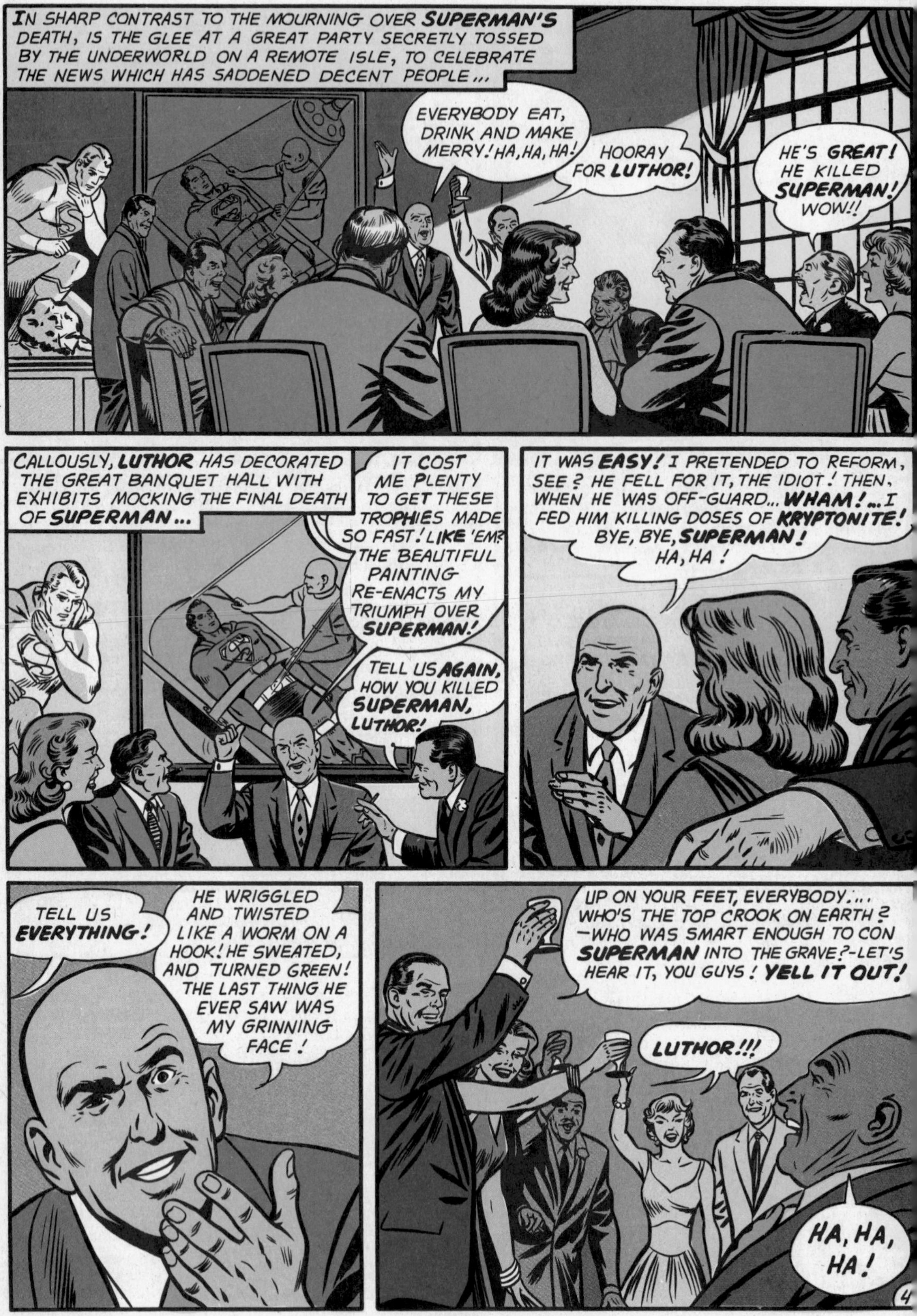
IN SHARP CONTRAST TO THE MOURNING OVER SUPERMAN'S DEATH, IS THE GLEE AT A GREAT PARTY SECRETLY TOSSED BY THE UNDERWORLD ON A REMOTE ISLE, TO CELEBRATE THE NEWS WHICH HAS SADDENED DECENT PEOPLE...
EVERYBODY EAT, DRINK AND MAKE MERRY! HA, HA, HA!
HOORAY FOR LUTHOR!
HE'S GREAT! HE KILLED SUPERMAN! WOW!!
CALLOUSLY, LUTHOR HAS DECORATED THE GREAT BANQUET HALL WITH EXHIBITS MOCKING THE FINAL DEATH OF SUPERMAN...
IT COST ME PLENTY TO GET THESE TROPHIES MADE SO FAST! LIKE 'EM? THE BEAUTIFUL PAINTING RE-ENACTS MY TRIUMPH OVER SUPERMAN!
TELL US AGAIN, HOW YOU KILLED SUPERMAN, LUTHOR!
IT WAS EASY! I PRETENDED TO REFORM, SEE? HE FELL FOR IT, THE IDIOT! THEN, WHEN HE WAS OFF-GUARD... WHAM!...I FED HIM KILLING DOSES OF KRYPTONITE! BYE, BYE, SUPERMAN! HA, HA!
TELL US EVERYTHING!
HE WRIGGLED AND TWISTED LIKE A WORM ON A HOOK! HE SWEATED, AND TURNED GREEN! THE LAST THING HE EVER SAW WAS MY GRINNING FACE!
UP ON YOUR FEET, EVERYBODY!... WHO'S THE TOP CROOK ON EARTH? —WHO WAS SMART ENOUGH TO CON SUPERMAN INTO THE GRAVE?—LET'S HEAR IT, YOU GUYS! YELL IT OUT!
LUTHOR!!!
HA, HA, HA!
4

SUDDENLY, THE MERRIMENT CHOKES IN THE MOBSTERS' THROATS AS, ASTOUNDINGLY...

GAAA! IT'S... SUPERMAN!

AWRP!... S-SUPERMAN'S ALIVE!

HE CAN'T BE! I KILLED HIM! I'M POSITIVE OF IT!

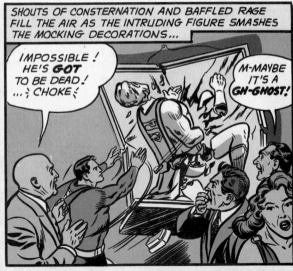

SHOUTS OF CONSTERNATION AND BAFFLED RAGE FILL THE AIR AS THE INTRUDING FIGURE SMASHES THE MOCKING DECORATIONS...

IMPOSSIBLE! HE'S GOT TO BE DEAD! ...₹ CHOKE ₹

M-MAYBE IT'S A GH-GHOST!

TO THE ASTONISHMENT OF THE CRINGING GANG-STERS, THE SUPER-POWERFUL FORM FLEXES MIGHTY MUSCLES, THEN...

A DISGUISE IS FLYING OFF! IT AIN'T SUPERMAN! IT'S...

...A GIRL WITH S-SUPER-POWERS!

AND NOW THE FLABBERGASTED UNDERWORLD LEARNS...

MY NAME IS... SUPERGIRL! I'M SUPERMAN'S COUSIN FROM KRYPTON! I'VE BEEN HIS SECRET EMERGENCY WEAPON FOR YEARS!... LUTHOR, IN THE NAME OF PLANET KRYPTON, I ARREST YOU FOR MURDER!

YOU CAN STOP WASTING BULLETS! I HAVE ALL OF SUPERMAN'S ASTONISHING POWERS! — GANGDOM MAY HAVE SUCCEEDED IN TREACHEROUSLY KILLING SUPERMAN, BUT I'M GOING TO CARRY ON HIS GREAT WORK!

SOON, IN A KANDORIAN COURTROOM, AFTER SUPERGIRL TRANSPORTS LUTHOR, AND PROSECUTION WITNESSES, INTO THE MINIATURE CITY, VIA A TRANSFER-RAY...

LEX LUTHOR, YOU KILLED A KRYPTONIAN, AND SO YOU WILL BE TRIED BY KRYPTONIANS!

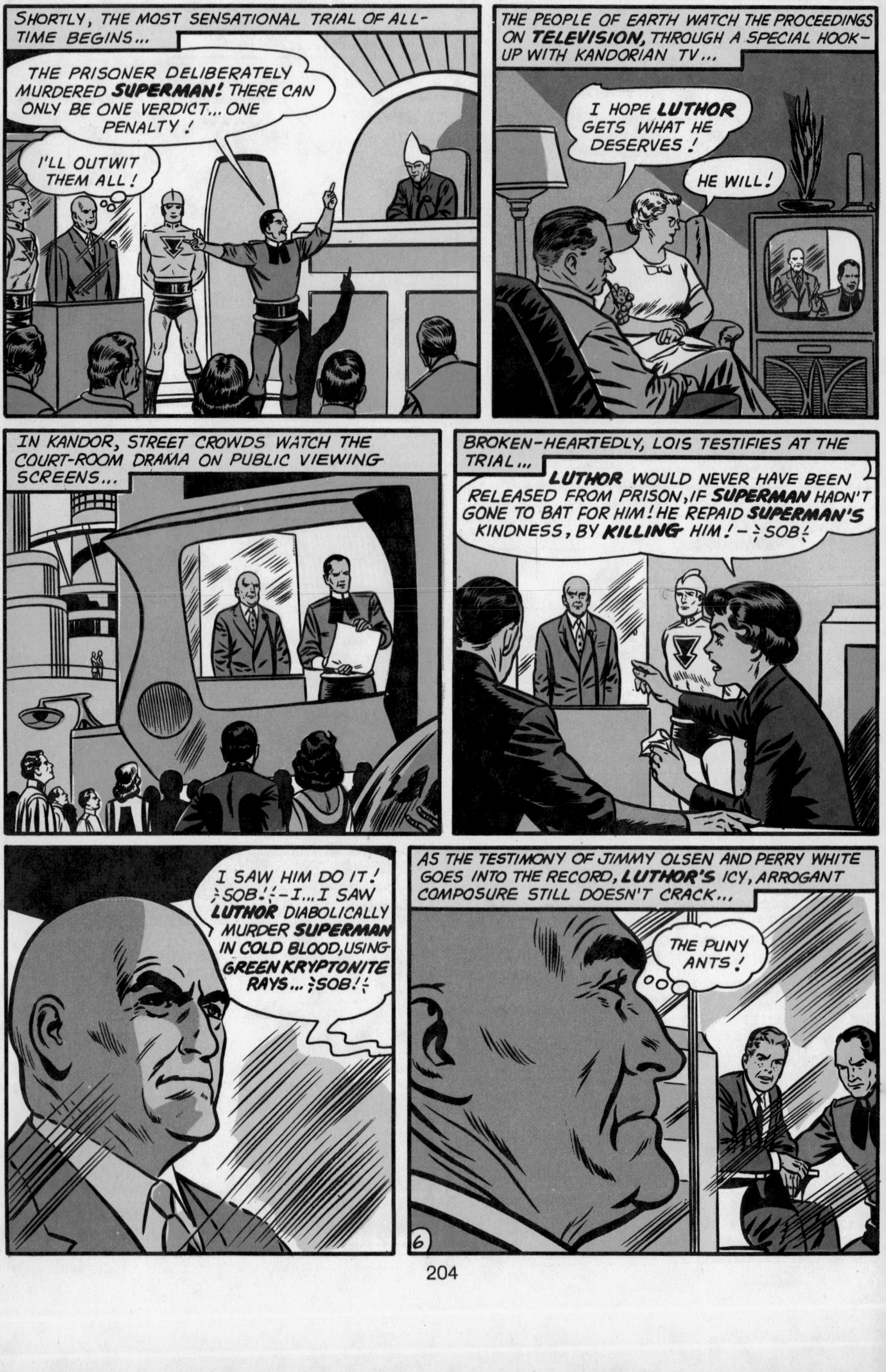
SHORTLY, THE MOST SENSATIONAL TRIAL OF ALL-TIME BEGINS...
THE PRISONER DELIBERATELY MURDERED SUPERMAN! THERE CAN ONLY BE ONE VERDICT... ONE PENALTY!
I'LL OUTWIT THEM ALL!
THE PEOPLE OF EARTH WATCH THE PROCEEDINGS ON TELEVISION, THROUGH A SPECIAL HOOK-UP WITH KANDORIAN TV...
I HOPE LUTHOR GETS WHAT HE DESERVES!
HE WILL!
IN KANDOR, STREET CROWDS WATCH THE COURT-ROOM DRAMA ON PUBLIC VIEWING-SCREENS...
BROKEN-HEARTEDLY, LOIS TESTIFIES AT THE TRIAL...
LUTHOR WOULD NEVER HAVE BEEN RELEASED FROM PRISON, IF SUPERMAN HADN'T GONE TO BAT FOR HIM! HE REPAID SUPERMAN'S KINDNESS, BY KILLING HIM! -SOB!
I SAW HIM DO IT! SOB! -I...I SAW LUTHOR DIABOLICALLY MURDER SUPERMAN IN COLD BLOOD, USING GREEN KRYPTONITE RAYS... SOB!
6
AS THE TESTIMONY OF JIMMY OLSEN AND PERRY WHITE GOES INTO THE RECORD, LUTHOR'S ICY, ARROGANT COMPOSURE STILL DOESN'T CRACK...
THE PUNY ANTS!

THEY AREN'T DEALING WITH AN ORDINARY HOOD! THEY'RE UP AGAINST A CRIMINAL MASTERMIND! I'LL WRIGGLE OUT OF PAYING THE PENALTY, WITH THE HIDDEN ACE I'VE GOT UP MY SLEEVE!

WHEN IT IS LUTHOR'S TURN TO TESTIFY...

I'M... GUILTY!

BUT I WON'T PAY FOR MY CRIME!

GUILTY? THEN THERE CAN BE BUT ONE PUNISHMENT... THE PRISONER WILL BE SENT INTO THE PHANTOM ZONE, AT ONCE!

AS THE PHANTOM ZONE RAY IS BROUGHT INTO COURT, LUTHOR PLAYS HIS ACE...

PUNISHING ME WON'T BRING SUPERMAN BACK! LET'S COMPROMISE! LET ME GO, AND I'LL BUILD A RAY THAT'LL ENLARGE KANDOR...

...BACK TO THE NORMAL SIZE IT WAS BEFORE SPACE VILLAIN BRAINIAC SHRANK YOUR CITY WITH A REDUCING-RAY! YOU WON'T HAVE TO LIVE IN A BOTTLE ANYMORE! IS IT DEAL?

NATURALLY, THEY WON'T REFUSE! BEING MADE NORMAL-SIZED AGAIN HAS BEEN THEIR GREATEST DESIRE!

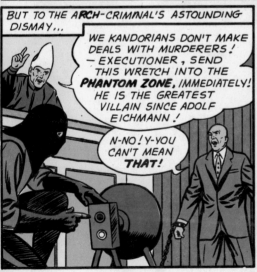

BUT TO THE ARCH-CRIMINAL'S ASTOUNDING DISMAY...

WE KANDORIANS DON'T MAKE DEALS WITH MURDERERS! — EXECUTIONER, SEND THIS WRETCH INTO THE PHANTOM ZONE, IMMEDIATELY! HE IS THE GREATEST VILLAIN SINCE ADOLF EICHMANN!

N-NO! Y-YOU CAN'T MEAN THAT!

AN INSTANT LATER, AFTER THE RAY'S BLACK BUTTON IS PUSHED...

JUSTICE HAS BEEN DONE! BECAUSE OF HIS CRIME, LUTHOR WILL REMAIN A PHANTOM FOR ALL ETERNITY! NEVER AGAIN WILL HE HARM THE WORLD OF MEN!

7

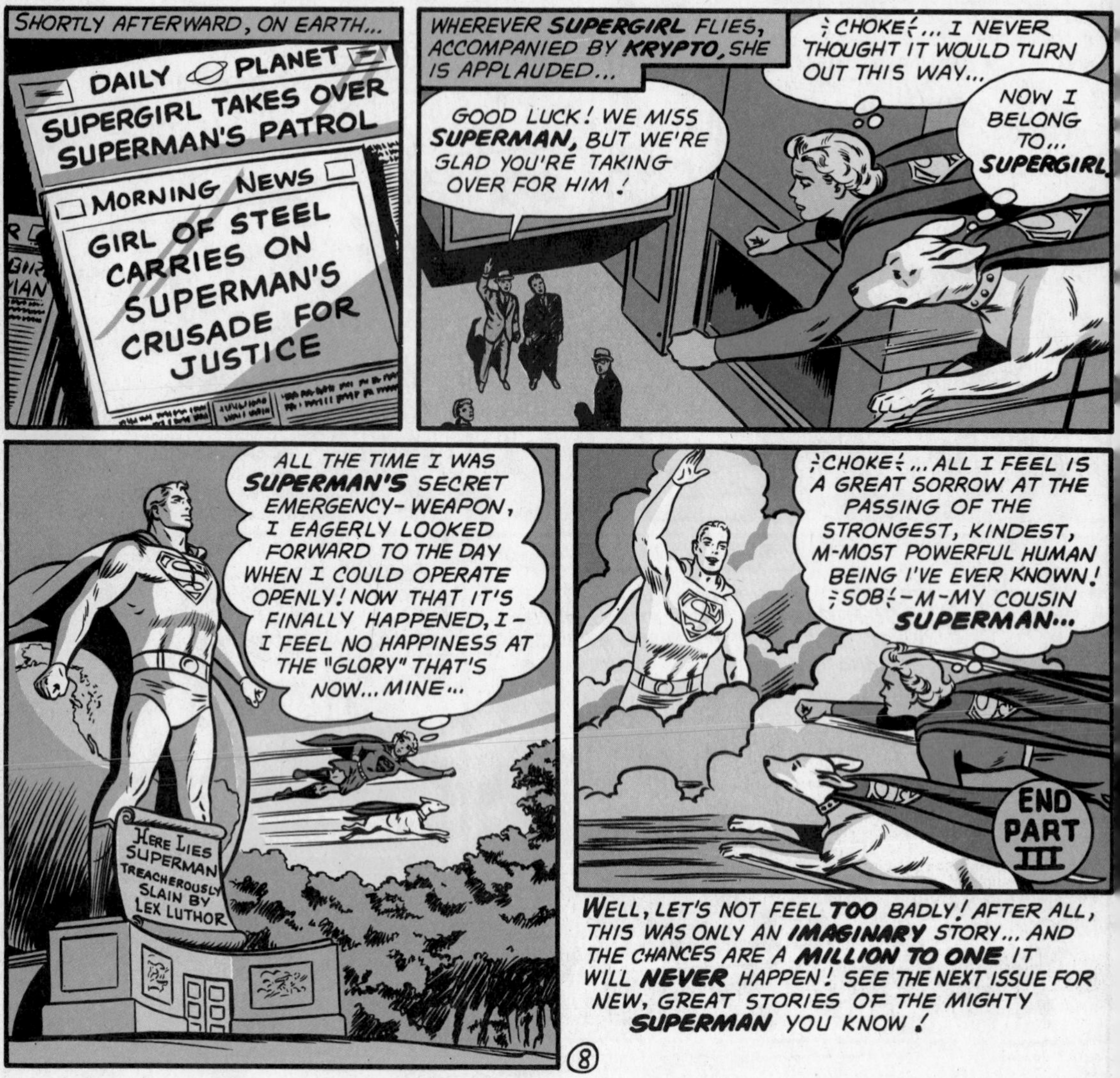
SHORTLY AFTERWARD, ON EARTH...
DAILY PLANET
SUPERGIRL TAKES OVER SUPERMAN'S PATROL
MORNING NEWS
GIRL OF STEEL CARRIES ON SUPERMAN'S CRUSADE FOR JUSTICE
WHEREVER SUPERGIRL FLIES, ACCOMPANIED BY KRYPTO, SHE IS APPLAUDED...
GOOD LUCK! WE MISS SUPERMAN, BUT WE'RE GLAD YOU'RE TAKING OVER FOR HIM!
CHOKE ... I NEVER THOUGHT IT WOULD TURN OUT THIS WAY...
NOW I BELONG TO... SUPERGIRL
ALL THE TIME I WAS SUPERMAN'S SECRET EMERGENCY-WEAPON, I EAGERLY LOOKED FORWARD TO THE DAY WHEN I COULD OPERATE OPENLY! NOW THAT IT'S FINALLY HAPPENED, I-I FEEL NO HAPPINESS AT THE "GLORY" THAT'S NOW... MINE...
HERE LIES SUPERMAN TREACHEROUSLY SLAIN BY LEX LUTHOR
CHOKE ... ALL I FEEL IS A GREAT SORROW AT THE PASSING OF THE STRONGEST, KINDEST, M-MOST POWERFUL HUMAN BEING I'VE EVER KNOWN! SOB -M-MY COUSIN SUPERMAN...
END PART III
WELL, LET'S NOT FEEL TOO BADLY! AFTER ALL, THIS WAS ONLY AN IMAGINARY STORY... AND THE CHANCES ARE A MILLION TO ONE IT WILL NEVER HAPPEN! SEE THE NEXT ISSUE FOR NEW, GREAT STORIES OF THE MIGHTY SUPERMAN YOU KNOW!
8

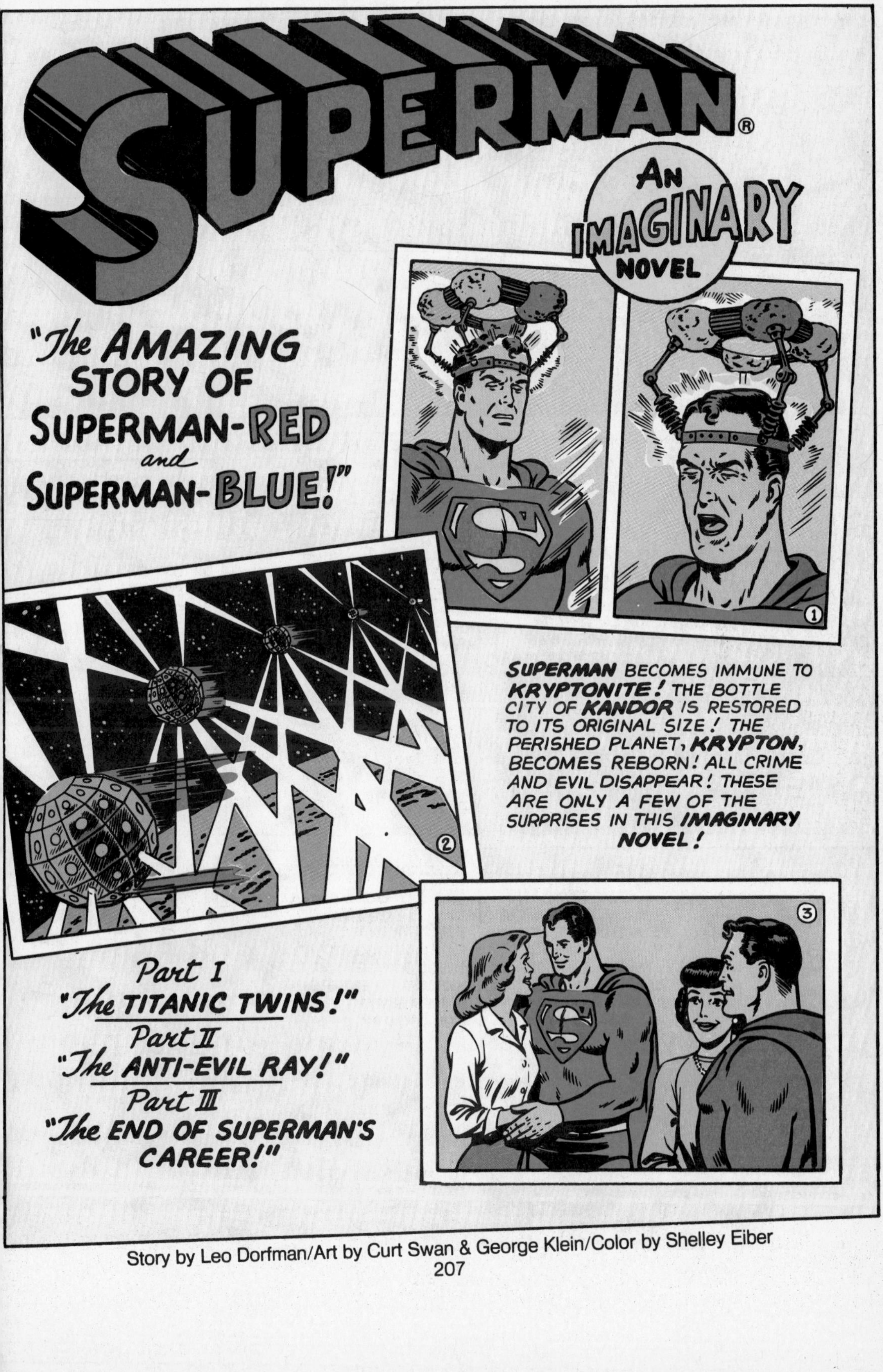
SUPERMAN®
AN IMAGINARY NOVEL
"The AMAZING STORY OF SUPERMAN-RED and SUPERMAN-BLUE!"
SUPERMAN BECOMES IMMUNE TO KRYPTONITE! THE BOTTLE CITY OF KANDOR IS RESTORED TO ITS ORIGINAL SIZE! THE PERISHED PLANET, KRYPTON, BECOMES REBORN! ALL CRIME AND EVIL DISAPPEAR! THESE ARE ONLY A FEW OF THE SURPRISES IN THIS IMAGINARY NOVEL!
Part I
"The TITANIC TWINS!"
Part II
"The ANTI-EVIL RAY!"
Part III
"The END OF SUPERMAN'S CAREER!"

Story by Leo Dorfman/Art by Curt Swan & George Klein/Color by Shelley Eiber

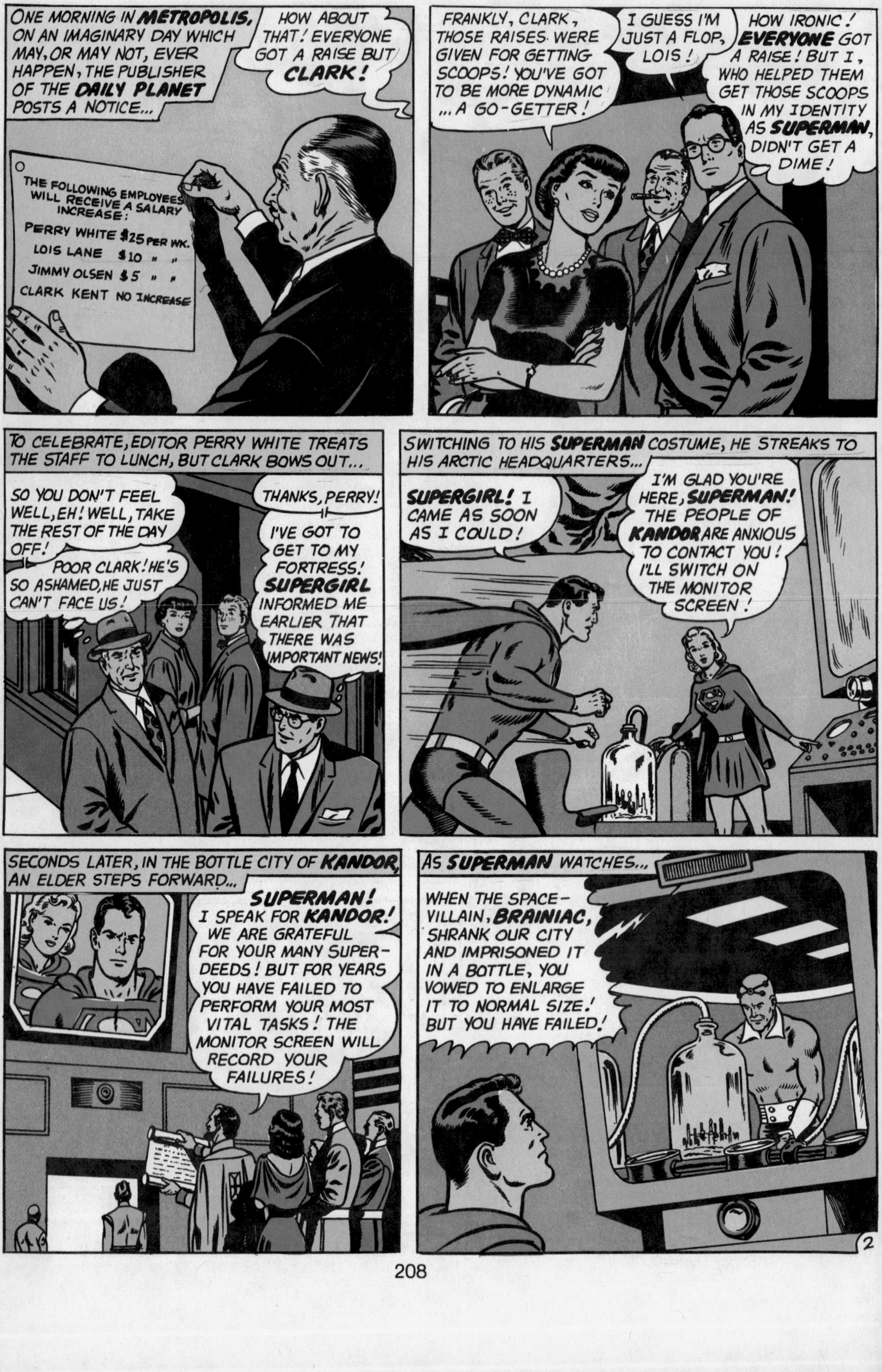
ONE MORNING IN METROPOLIS, ON AN IMAGINARY DAY WHICH MAY, OR MAY NOT, EVER HAPPEN, THE PUBLISHER OF THE DAILY PLANET POSTS A NOTICE...
HOW ABOUT THAT! EVERYONE GOT A RAISE BUT CLARK!
THE FOLLOWING EMPLOYEES WILL RECEIVE A SALARY INCREASE:
PERRY WHITE $25 PER WK.
LOIS LANE $10 " "
JIMMY OLSEN $5 " "
CLARK KENT NO INCREASE
FRANKLY, CLARK, THOSE RAISES WERE GIVEN FOR GETTING SCOOPS! YOU'VE GOT TO BE MORE DYNAMIC ...A GO-GETTER!
I GUESS I'M JUST A FLOP, LOIS!
HOW IRONIC! EVERYONE GOT A RAISE! BUT I, WHO HELPED THEM GET THOSE SCOOPS IN MY IDENTITY AS SUPERMAN, DIDN'T GET A DIME!
TO CELEBRATE, EDITOR PERRY WHITE TREATS THE STAFF TO LUNCH, BUT CLARK BOWS OUT...
SO YOU DON'T FEEL WELL, EH! WELL, TAKE THE REST OF THE DAY OFF!
POOR CLARK! HE'S SO ASHAMED, HE JUST CAN'T FACE US!
THANKS, PERRY!
I'VE GOT TO GET TO MY FORTRESS! SUPERGIRL INFORMED ME EARLIER THAT THERE WAS IMPORTANT NEWS!
SWITCHING TO HIS SUPERMAN COSTUME, HE STREAKS TO HIS ARCTIC HEADQUARTERS...
SUPERGIRL! I CAME AS SOON AS I COULD!
I'M GLAD YOU'RE HERE, SUPERMAN! THE PEOPLE OF KANDOR ARE ANXIOUS TO CONTACT YOU! I'LL SWITCH ON THE MONITOR SCREEN!
SECONDS LATER, IN THE BOTTLE CITY OF KANDOR, AN ELDER STEPS FORWARD...
SUPERMAN! I SPEAK FOR KANDOR! WE ARE GRATEFUL FOR YOUR MANY SUPER-DEEDS! BUT FOR YEARS YOU HAVE FAILED TO PERFORM YOUR MOST VITAL TASKS! THE MONITOR SCREEN WILL RECORD YOUR FAILURES!
AS SUPERMAN WATCHES...
WHEN THE SPACE-VILLAIN, BRAINIAC, SHRANK OUR CITY AND IMPRISONED IT IN A BOTTLE, YOU VOWED TO ENLARGE IT TO NORMAL SIZE! BUT YOU HAVE FAILED!
2

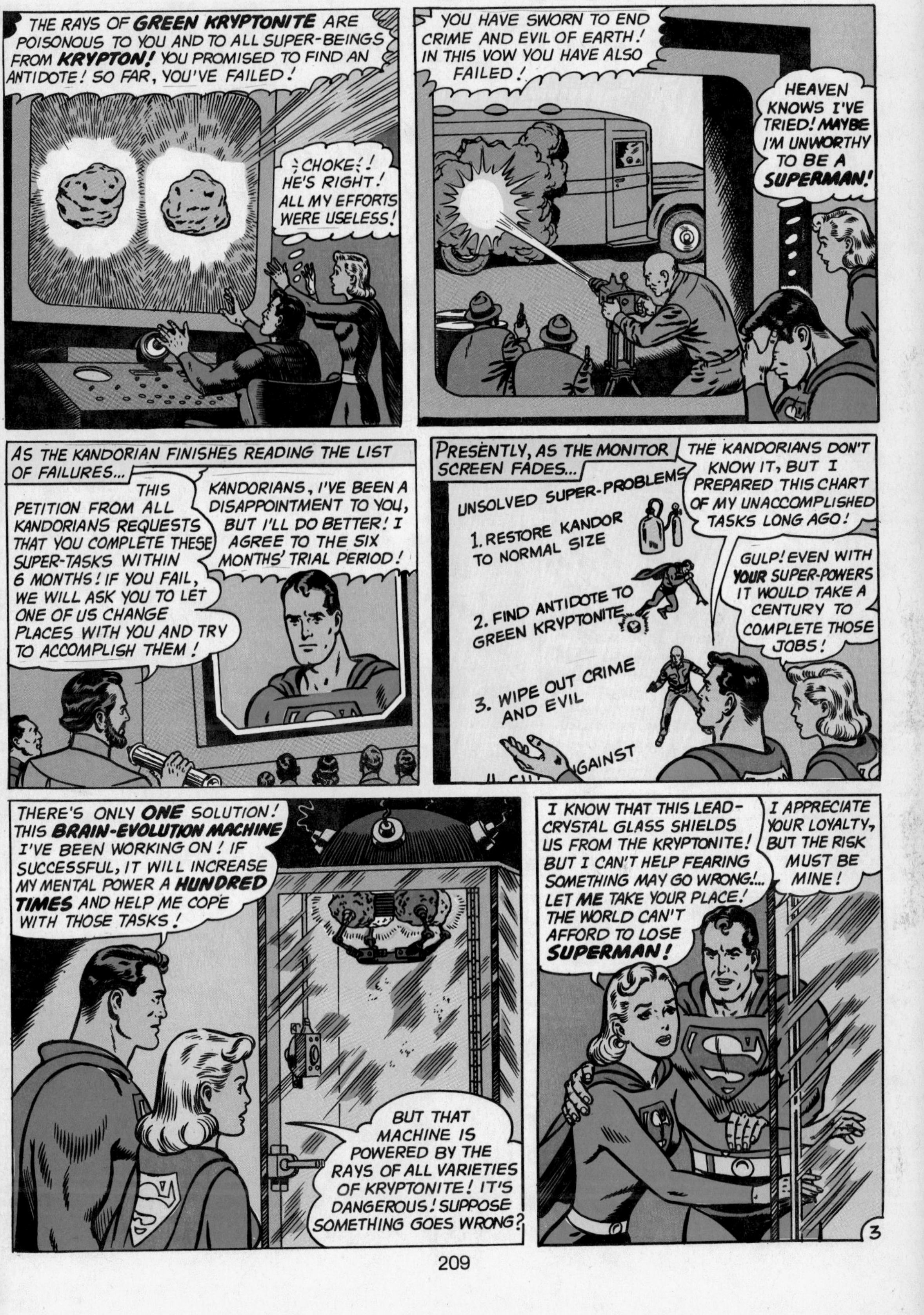
THE RAYS OF GREEN KRYPTONITE ARE POISONOUS TO YOU AND TO ALL SUPER-BEINGS FROM KRYPTON! YOU PROMISED TO FIND AN ANTIDOTE! SO FAR, YOU'VE FAILED!
CHOKE! HE'S RIGHT! ALL MY EFFORTS WERE USELESS!
YOU HAVE SWORN TO END CRIME AND EVIL OF EARTH! IN THIS VOW YOU HAVE ALSO FAILED!
HEAVEN KNOWS I'VE TRIED! MAYBE I'M UNWORTHY TO BE A SUPERMAN!
AS THE KANDORIAN FINISHES READING THE LIST OF FAILURES...
THIS PETITION FROM ALL KANDORIANS REQUESTS THAT YOU COMPLETE THESE SUPER-TASKS WITHIN 6 MONTHS! IF YOU FAIL, WE WILL ASK YOU TO LET ONE OF US CHANGE PLACES WITH YOU AND TRY TO ACCOMPLISH THEM!
KANDORIANS, I'VE BEEN A DISAPPOINTMENT TO YOU, BUT I'LL DO BETTER! I AGREE TO THE SIX MONTHS' TRIAL PERIOD!
PRESENTLY, AS THE MONITOR SCREEN FADES...
UNSOLVED SUPER-PROBLEMS
1. RESTORE KANDOR TO NORMAL SIZE
2. FIND ANTIDOTE TO GREEN KRYPTONITE
3. WIPE OUT CRIME AND EVIL
GAINST
THE KANDORIANS DON'T KNOW IT, BUT I PREPARED THIS CHART OF MY UNACCOMPLISHED TASKS LONG AGO!
GULP! EVEN WITH YOUR SUPER-POWERS IT WOULD TAKE A CENTURY TO COMPLETE THOSE JOBS!
THERE'S ONLY ONE SOLUTION! THIS BRAIN-EVOLUTION MACHINE I'VE BEEN WORKING ON! IF SUCCESSFUL, IT WILL INCREASE MY MENTAL POWER A HUNDRED TIMES AND HELP ME COPE WITH THOSE TASKS!
BUT THAT MACHINE IS POWERED BY THE RAYS OF ALL VARIETIES OF KRYPTONITE! IT'S DANGEROUS! SUPPOSE SOMETHING GOES WRONG?
I KNOW THAT THIS LEAD-CRYSTAL GLASS SHIELDS US FROM THE KRYPTONITE! BUT I CAN'T HELP FEARING SOMETHING MAY GO WRONG!... LET ME TAKE YOUR PLACE! THE WORLD CAN'T AFFORD TO LOSE SUPERMAN!
I APPRECIATE YOUR LOYALTY, BUT THE RISK MUST BE MINE!
3

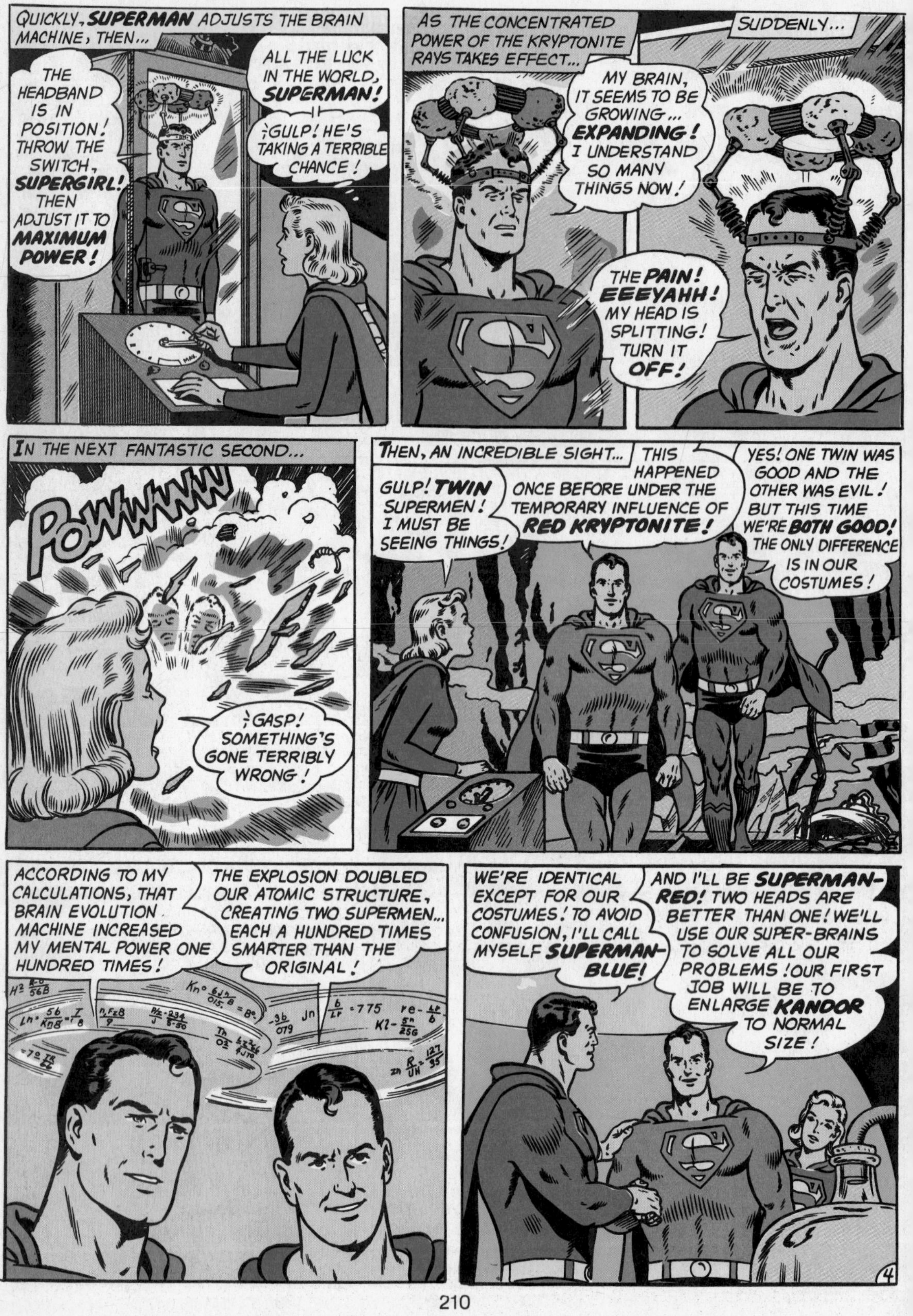
QUICKLY, SUPERMAN ADJUSTS THE BRAIN MACHINE, THEN...
THE HEADBAND IS IN POSITION! THROW THE SWITCH, SUPERGIRL! THEN ADJUST IT TO MAXIMUM POWER!
ALL THE LUCK IN THE WORLD, SUPERMAN!
¡GULP! HE'S TAKING A TERRIBLE CHANCE!
AS THE CONCENTRATED POWER OF THE KRYPTONITE RAYS TAKES EFFECT...
MY BRAIN, IT SEEMS TO BE GROWING... EXPANDING! I UNDERSTAND SO MANY THINGS NOW!
SUDDENLY...
THE PAIN! EEEYAHH! MY HEAD IS SPLITTING! TURN IT OFF!
IN THE NEXT FANTASTIC SECOND...
POWWWW
¡GASP! SOMETHING'S GONE TERRIBLY WRONG!
THEN, AN INCREDIBLE SIGHT...
GULP! TWIN SUPERMEN! I MUST BE SEEING THINGS!
THIS HAPPENED ONCE BEFORE UNDER THE TEMPORARY INFLUENCE OF RED KRYPTONITE!
YES! ONE TWIN WAS GOOD AND THE OTHER WAS EVIL! BUT THIS TIME WE'RE BOTH GOOD! THE ONLY DIFFERENCE IS IN OUR COSTUMES!
ACCORDING TO MY CALCULATIONS, THAT BRAIN EVOLUTION MACHINE INCREASED MY MENTAL POWER ONE HUNDRED TIMES!
THE EXPLOSION DOUBLED OUR ATOMIC STRUCTURE, CREATING TWO SUPERMEN... EACH A HUNDRED TIMES SMARTER THAN THE ORIGINAL!
WE'RE IDENTICAL EXCEPT FOR OUR COSTUMES! TO AVOID CONFUSION, I'LL CALL MYSELF SUPERMAN-BLUE!
AND I'LL BE SUPERMAN-RED! TWO HEADS ARE BETTER THAN ONE! WE'LL USE OUR SUPER-BRAINS TO SOLVE ALL OUR PROBLEMS! OUR FIRST JOB WILL BE TO ENLARGE KANDOR TO NORMAL SIZE!
4

AT SUPER-SPEED, THE TWO SUPERMEN PUT THEIR MAGNIFICENT MENTAL POWERS INTO ACTION...

CHAMBER

TRIGGER MECH.

RELAY.

I GOT *BRAINIAC'S* ENLARGING RAY GUN FROM THE FORTRESS MUSEUM! I'VE NEVER BEEN ABLE TO REPAIR ITS DAMAGED CIRCUITS BEFORE! IT'S CHILD PLAY NOW! BUT WE'LL NEED A RAY-FORCE PELLET TO OPERATE IT!

IT'S SIMPLE, *SUPERMAN-RED!* USING YOUR DRAWINGS, I CAN CALCULATE HOW TO CREATE THE CONCENTRATED FORCE-PELLET THAT *BRAINIAC* USED!

PRESENTLY, THE PEOPLE OF *KANDOR* RECEIVE STARTLING NEWS...

KANDORIANS! WITH OUR MULTIPLE BRAIN-POWER, WE'VE REPAIRED *BRAINIAC'S* EXPANDING RAY GUN! WE CAN RESTORE *KANDOR* TO NORMAL AND ALSO RECREATE THE PLANET *KRYPTON!* GET READY FOR A TRIP INTO OUTER SPACE!

¡CHOKE!¿ *KANDOR* ENLARGED! OUR MOTHER PLANET *KRYPTON* RESTORED TO EXISTENCE! I CAN'T BELIEVE IT!

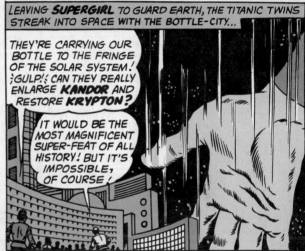

LEAVING *SUPERGIRL* TO GUARD EARTH, THE TITANIC TWINS STREAK INTO SPACE WITH THE BOTTLE-CITY...

THEY'RE CARRYING OUR BOTTLE TO THE FRINGE OF THE SOLAR SYSTEM! ¿GULP!¿ CAN THEY REALLY ENLARGE *KANDOR* AND RESTORE *KRYPTON?*

IT WOULD BE THE MOST MAGNIFICENT SUPER-FEAT OF ALL HISTORY! BUT IT'S IMPOSSIBLE, OF COURSE!

IN THE METEOR BELT, THE TWO SUPERMEN SEARCH FOR FRAGMENTS OF A MYSTERIOUS ELEMENT UNKNOWN ON EARTH, THEN...

THESE FRAGMENTS ARE MADE OF *HYPER-MAGNETON!* WHEN WE HURL THEM TOGETHER, THEY WILL FUSE INTO A PLANETOID WITH STRANGE MAGNETIC POWERS!

PRESENTLY... IF OUR THEORIES ARE CORRECT, THE STRANGE MAGNETIC BEAMS OF THAT PLANETOID WILL SCATTER THROUGH THE UNIVERSE AND ATTRACT EVERY PIECE OF KRYPTONITE BACK TO THIS SPOT!

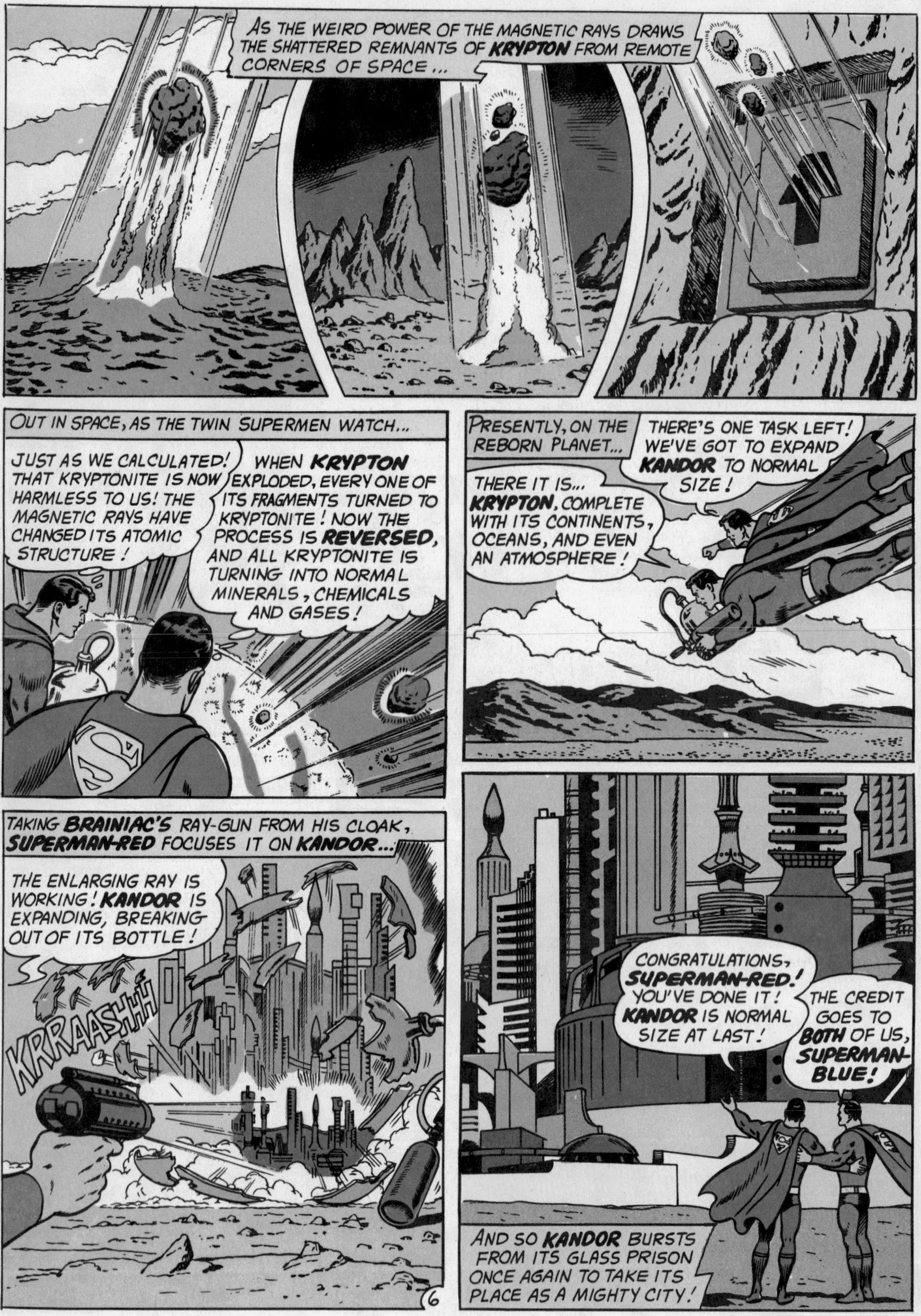
AS THE WEIRD POWER OF THE MAGNETIC RAYS DRAWS THE SHATTERED REMNANTS OF KRYPTON FROM REMOTE CORNERS OF SPACE...
OUT IN SPACE, AS THE TWIN SUPERMEN WATCH...
JUST AS WE CALCULATED! THAT KRYPTONITE IS NOW HARMLESS TO US! THE MAGNETIC RAYS HAVE CHANGED ITS ATOMIC STRUCTURE!
WHEN KRYPTON EXPLODED, EVERY ONE OF ITS FRAGMENTS TURNED TO KRYPTONITE! NOW THE PROCESS IS REVERSED, AND ALL KRYPTONITE IS TURNING INTO NORMAL MINERALS, CHEMICALS AND GASES!
PRESENTLY, ON THE REBORN PLANET...
THERE'S ONE TASK LEFT! WE'VE GOT TO EXPAND KANDOR TO NORMAL SIZE!
THERE IT IS... KRYPTON, COMPLETE WITH ITS CONTINENTS, OCEANS, AND EVEN AN ATMOSPHERE!
TAKING BRAINIAC'S RAY-GUN FROM HIS CLOAK, SUPERMAN-RED FOCUSES IT ON KANDOR...
THE ENLARGING RAY IS WORKING! KANDOR IS EXPANDING, BREAKING OUT OF ITS BOTTLE!
KRRAASHHH
6
CONGRATULATIONS, SUPERMAN-RED! YOU'VE DONE IT! KANDOR IS NORMAL SIZE AT LAST!
THE CREDIT GOES TO BOTH OF US, SUPERMAN-BLUE!
AND SO KANDOR BURSTS FROM ITS GLASS PRISON ONCE AGAIN TO TAKE ITS PLACE AS A MIGHTY CITY!

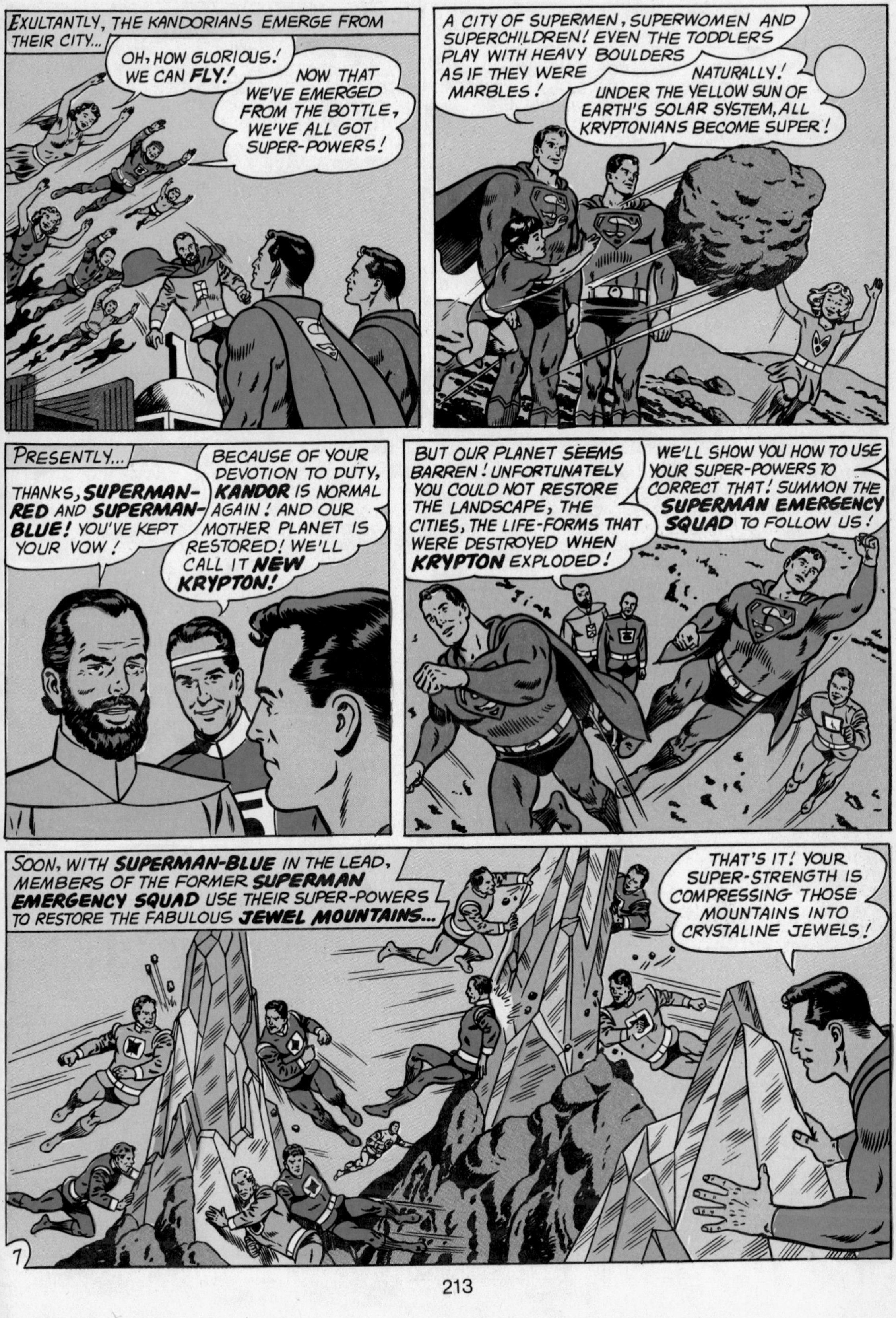
EXULTANTLY, THE KANDORIANS EMERGE FROM THEIR CITY...
OH, HOW GLORIOUS! WE CAN FLY!
NOW THAT WE'VE EMERGED FROM THE BOTTLE, WE'VE ALL GOT SUPER-POWERS!
A CITY OF SUPERMEN, SUPERWOMEN AND SUPERCHILDREN! EVEN THE TODDLERS PLAY WITH HEAVY BOULDERS AS IF THEY WERE MARBLES!
NATURALLY! UNDER THE YELLOW SUN OF EARTH'S SOLAR SYSTEM, ALL KRYPTONIANS BECOME SUPER!
PRESENTLY...
THANKS, SUPERMAN-RED AND SUPERMAN-BLUE! YOU'VE KEPT YOUR VOW!
BECAUSE OF YOUR DEVOTION TO DUTY, KANDOR IS NORMAL AGAIN! AND OUR MOTHER PLANET IS RESTORED! WE'LL CALL IT NEW KRYPTON!
BUT OUR PLANET SEEMS BARREN! UNFORTUNATELY YOU COULD NOT RESTORE THE LANDSCAPE, THE CITIES, THE LIFE-FORMS THAT WERE DESTROYED WHEN KRYPTON EXPLODED!
WE'LL SHOW YOU HOW TO USE YOUR SUPER-POWERS TO CORRECT THAT! SUMMON THE SUPERMAN EMERGENCY SQUAD TO FOLLOW US!
SOON, WITH SUPERMAN-BLUE IN THE LEAD, MEMBERS OF THE FORMER SUPERMAN EMERGENCY SQUAD USE THEIR SUPER-POWERS TO RESTORE THE FABULOUS JEWEL MOUNTAINS...
THAT'S IT! YOUR SUPER-STRENGTH IS COMPRESSING THOSE MOUNTAINS INTO CRYSTALINE JEWELS!
7

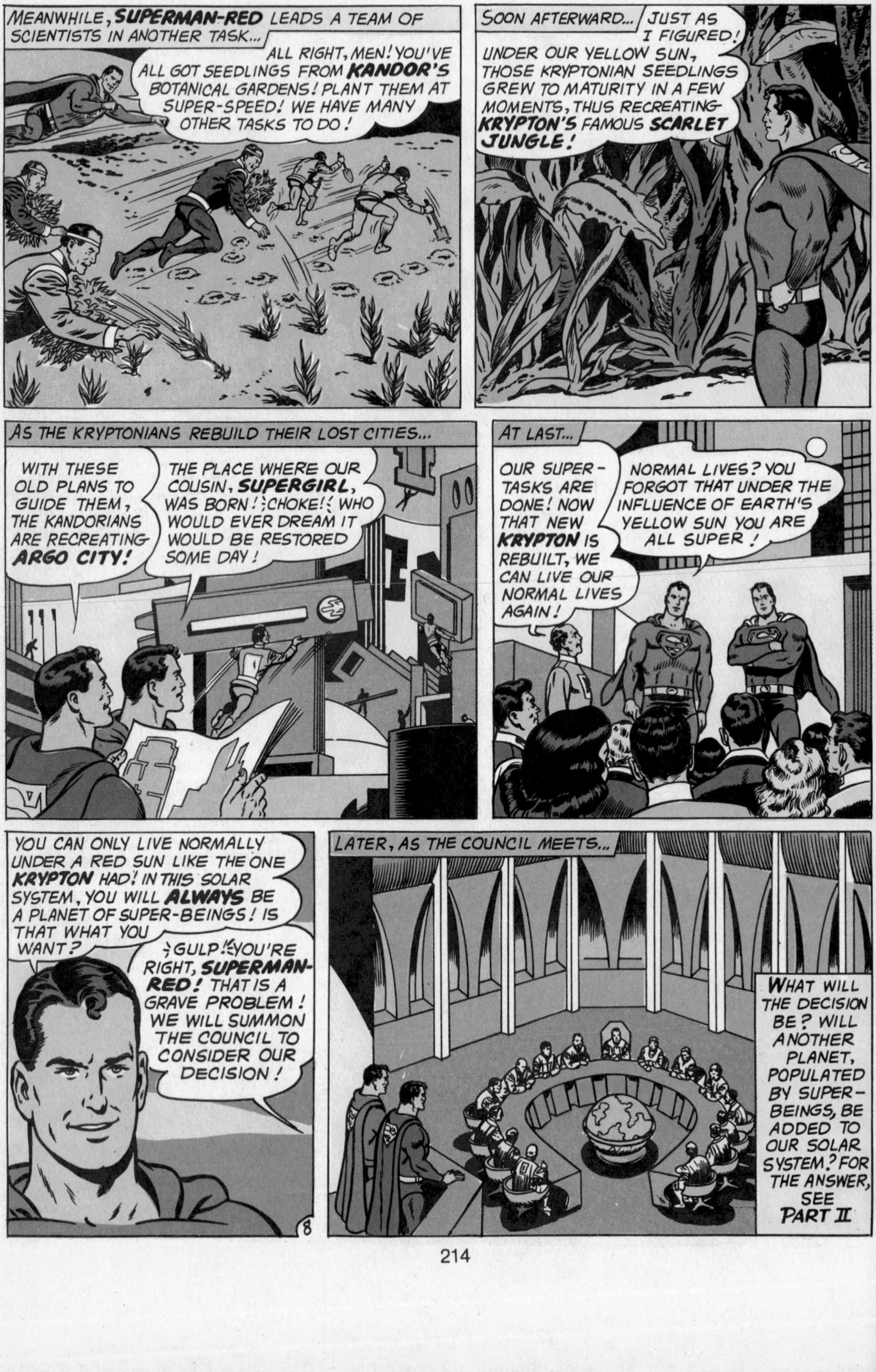
MEANWHILE, SUPERMAN-RED LEADS A TEAM OF SCIENTISTS IN ANOTHER TASK...
ALL RIGHT, MEN! YOU'VE ALL GOT SEEDLINGS FROM KANDOR'S BOTANICAL GARDENS! PLANT THEM AT SUPER-SPEED! WE HAVE MANY OTHER TASKS TO DO!
SOON AFTERWARD...
JUST AS I FIGURED! UNDER OUR YELLOW SUN, THOSE KRYPTONIAN SEEDLINGS GREW TO MATURITY IN A FEW MOMENTS, THUS RECREATING KRYPTON'S FAMOUS SCARLET JUNGLE!
AS THE KRYPTONIANS REBUILD THEIR LOST CITIES...
WITH THESE OLD PLANS TO GUIDE THEM, THE KANDORIANS ARE RECREATING ARGO CITY!
THE PLACE WHERE OUR COUSIN, SUPERGIRL, WAS BORN! ;CHOKE!; WHO WOULD EVER DREAM IT WOULD BE RESTORED SOME DAY!
AT LAST...
OUR SUPER-TASKS ARE DONE! NOW THAT NEW KRYPTON IS REBUILT, WE CAN LIVE OUR NORMAL LIVES AGAIN!
NORMAL LIVES? YOU FORGOT THAT UNDER THE INFLUENCE OF EARTH'S YELLOW SUN YOU ARE ALL SUPER!
YOU CAN ONLY LIVE NORMALLY UNDER A RED SUN LIKE THE ONE KRYPTON HAD! IN THIS SOLAR SYSTEM, YOU WILL ALWAYS BE A PLANET OF SUPER-BEINGS! IS THAT WHAT YOU WANT?
;GULP!; YOU'RE RIGHT, SUPERMAN-RED! THAT IS A GRAVE PROBLEM! WE WILL SUMMON THE COUNCIL TO CONSIDER OUR DECISION!
8
LATER, AS THE COUNCIL MEETS...
WHAT WILL THE DECISION BE? WILL ANOTHER PLANET, POPULATED BY SUPER-BEINGS, BE ADDED TO OUR SOLAR SYSTEM? FOR THE ANSWER, SEE PART II

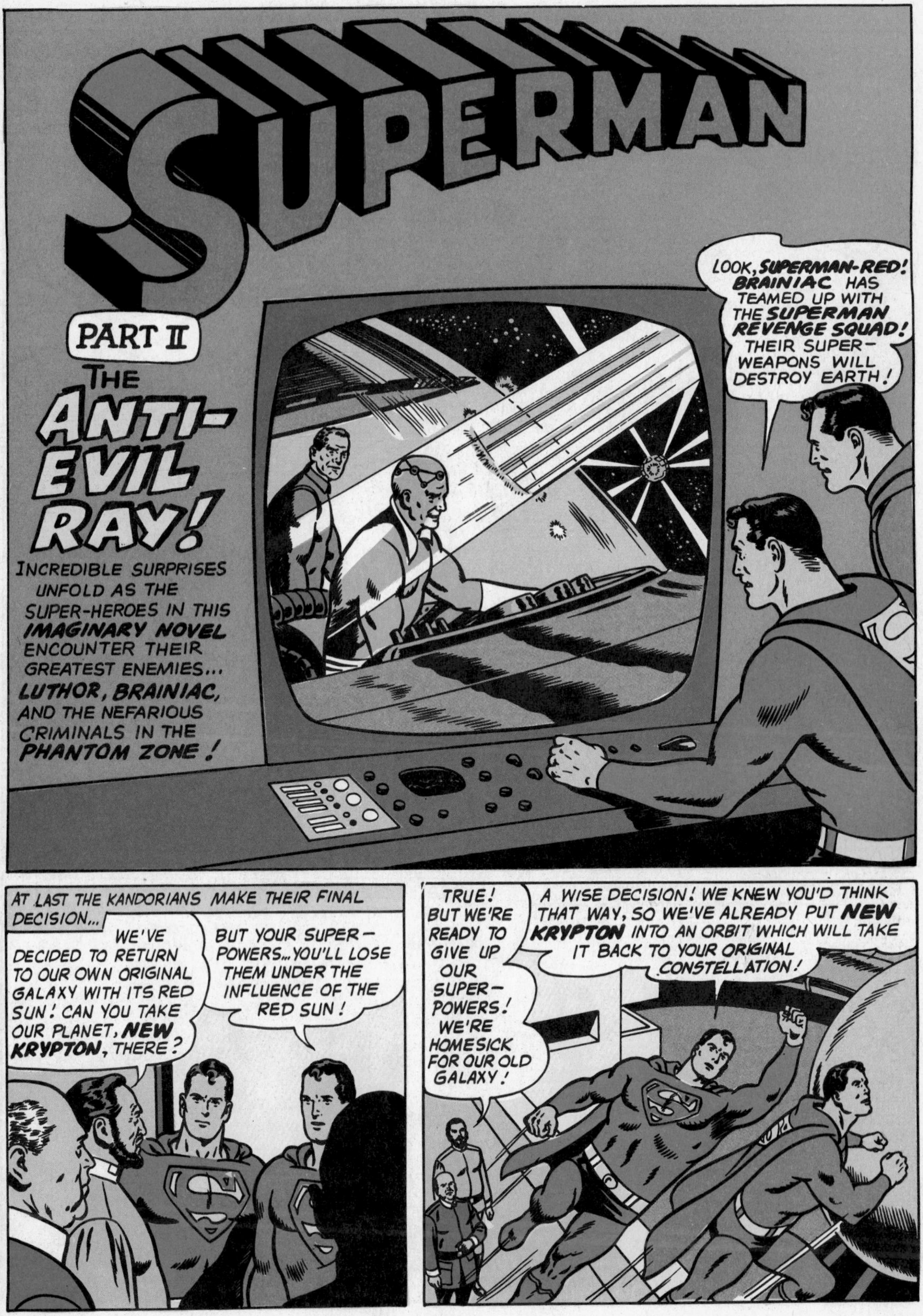
SUPERMAN
PART II
THE ANTI-EVIL RAY!
INCREDIBLE SURPRISES UNFOLD AS THE SUPER-HEROES IN THIS IMAGINARY NOVEL ENCOUNTER THEIR GREATEST ENEMIES... LUTHOR, BRAINIAC, AND THE NEFARIOUS CRIMINALS IN THE PHANTOM ZONE!
LOOK, SUPERMAN-RED! BRAINIAC HAS TEAMED UP WITH THE SUPERMAN REVENGE SQUAD! THEIR SUPER-WEAPONS WILL DESTROY EARTH!
AT LAST THE KANDORIANS MAKE THEIR FINAL DECISION...
WE'VE DECIDED TO RETURN TO OUR OWN ORIGINAL GALAXY WITH ITS RED SUN! CAN YOU TAKE OUR PLANET, NEW KRYPTON, THERE?
BUT YOUR SUPER-POWERS...YOU'LL LOSE THEM UNDER THE INFLUENCE OF THE RED SUN!
TRUE! BUT WE'RE READY TO GIVE UP OUR SUPER-POWERS! WE'RE HOMESICK FOR OUR OLD GALAXY!
A WISE DECISION! WE KNEW YOU'D THINK THAT WAY, SO WE'VE ALREADY PUT NEW KRYPTON INTO AN ORBIT WHICH WILL TAKE IT BACK TO YOUR ORIGINAL CONSTELLATION!

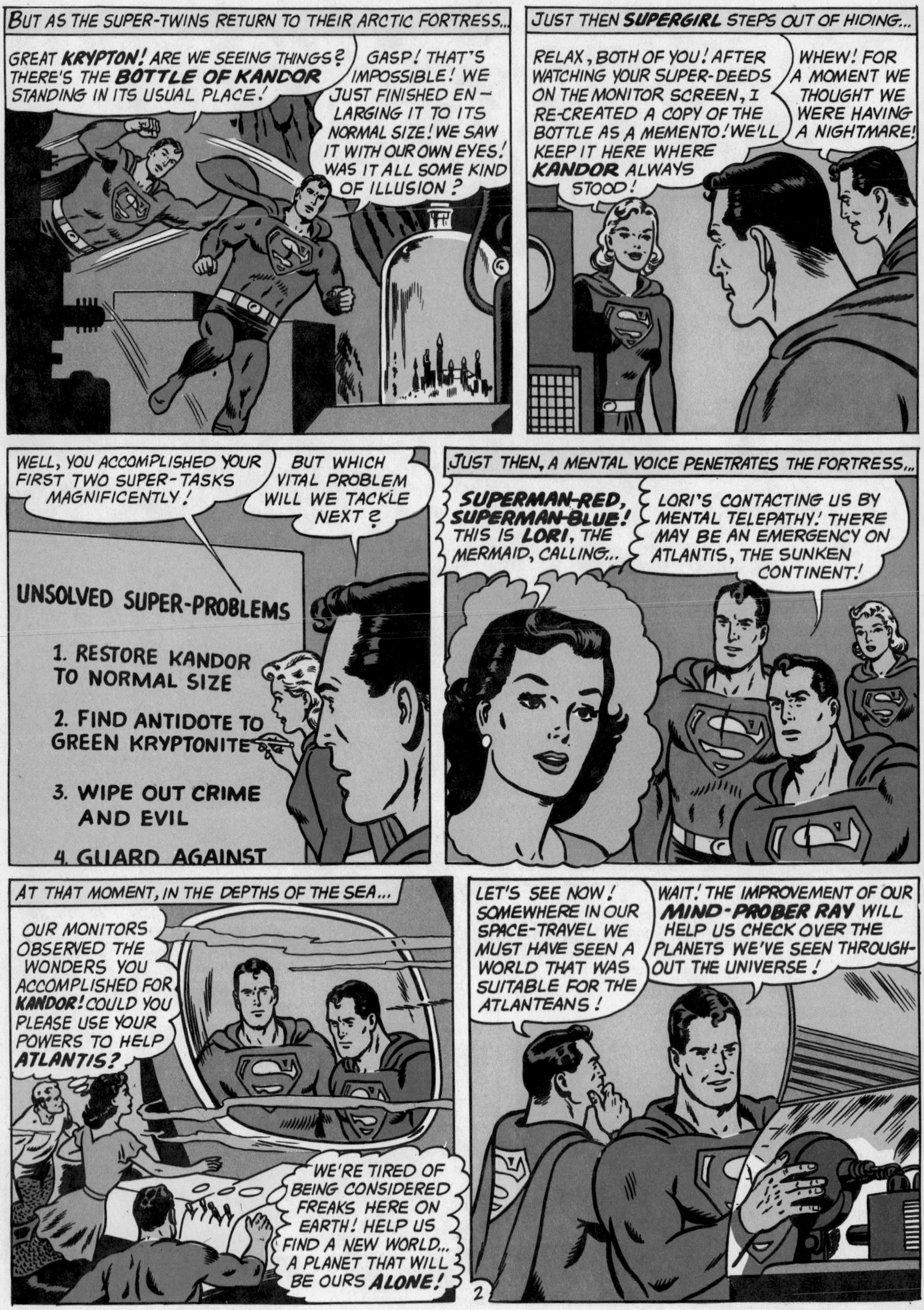
BUT AS THE SUPER-TWINS RETURN TO THEIR ARCTIC FORTRESS...
GREAT KRYPTON! ARE WE SEEING THINGS? THERE'S THE BOTTLE OF KANDOR STANDING IN ITS USUAL PLACE!
GASP! THAT'S IMPOSSIBLE! WE JUST FINISHED EN-LARGING IT TO ITS NORMAL SIZE! WE SAW IT WITH OUR OWN EYES! WAS IT ALL SOME KIND OF ILLUSION?
JUST THEN SUPERGIRL STEPS OUT OF HIDING...
RELAX, BOTH OF YOU! AFTER WATCHING YOUR SUPER-DEEDS ON THE MONITOR SCREEN, I RE-CREATED A COPY OF THE BOTTLE AS A MEMENTO! WE'LL KEEP IT HERE WHERE KANDOR ALWAYS STOOD!
WHEW! FOR A MOMENT WE THOUGHT WE WERE HAVING A NIGHTMARE!
WELL, YOU ACCOMPLISHED YOUR FIRST TWO SUPER-TASKS MAGNIFICENTLY!
BUT WHICH VITAL PROBLEM WILL WE TACKLE NEXT?
UNSOLVED SUPER-PROBLEMS
1. RESTORE KANDOR TO NORMAL SIZE
2. FIND ANTIDOTE TO GREEN KRYPTONITE
3. WIPE OUT CRIME AND EVIL
4. GUARD AGAINST
JUST THEN, A MENTAL VOICE PENETRATES THE FORTRESS...
SUPERMAN-RED, SUPERMAN-BLUE! THIS IS LORI, THE MERMAID, CALLING...
LORI'S CONTACTING US BY MENTAL TELEPATHY! THERE MAY BE AN EMERGENCY ON ATLANTIS, THE SUNKEN CONTINENT!
AT THAT MOMENT, IN THE DEPTHS OF THE SEA...
OUR MONITORS OBSERVED THE WONDERS YOU ACCOMPLISHED FOR KANDOR! COULD YOU PLEASE USE YOUR POWERS TO HELP ATLANTIS?
WE'RE TIRED OF BEING CONSIDERED FREAKS HERE ON EARTH! HELP US FIND A NEW WORLD... A PLANET THAT WILL BE OURS ALONE!
2
LET'S SEE NOW! SOMEWHERE IN OUR SPACE-TRAVEL WE MUST HAVE SEEN A WORLD THAT WAS SUITABLE FOR THE ATLANTEANS!
WAIT! THE IMPROVEMENT OF OUR MIND-PROBER RAY WILL HELP US CHECK OVER THE PLANETS WE'VE SEEN THROUGH-OUT THE UNIVERSE!

AS THE WEIRD MACHINE IS SWITCHED ON...

BY FOCUSING ITS BEAM ON OUR BRAINS, THE RAY PRODUCES A PICTURE OF OUR MEMORIES ON THAT SCREEN! CONCENTRATE ON ALL THE PLANETS WE'VE EVER SEEN!

I'M WITH YOU, *RED!*

THEN, SUDDENLY...

IT'S FANTASTIC! YOU'RE BOTH CONCENTRATING ON THE SAME PLANET, THE *MEMORIAL WORLD OF KRYPTON* WHICH I ONCE HELPED YOU BUILD!

THAT PLANET IS EXACTLY WHAT WE'RE LOOKING FOR, *SUPERGIRL!*

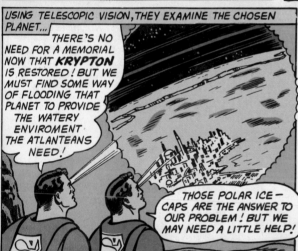

USING TELESCOPIC VISION, THEY EXAMINE THE CHOSEN PLANET...

THERE'S NO NEED FOR A MEMORIAL NOW THAT *KRYPTON* IS RESTORED! BUT WE MUST FIND SOME WAY OF FLOODING THAT PLANET TO PROVIDE THE WATERY ENVIRONMENT THE ATLANTEANS NEED!

THOSE POLAR ICE-CAPS ARE THE ANSWER TO OUR PROBLEM! BUT WE MAY NEED A LITTLE HELP!

WHISTLING A SUPERSONIC SIGNAL, THE SUPER-DUO SUMMONS *KRYPTO*, THE SUPER-DOG, AND...

KRYPTO! WE HATE TO BREAK UP YOUR FUN!

...BUT WE'VE GOT AN IMPORTANT JOB FOR YOU!

ARRFFF! TWIN-SUPERMEN! I DON'T KNOW HOW IT HAPPENED, BUT THEY BOTH SOUND EXACTLY LIKE MY OLD MASTER, SO I GUESS I'D BETTER OBEY!

PRESENTLY, AS THE FANTASTIC PLAN IS PUT INTO OPERATION...

REMEMBER! WE *ALL* FOCUS OUR HEAT VISION ON THE POLAR ICE-CAPS OF THE *MEMORIAL PLANET!*

KRYPTO AND I WILL CONCENTRATE ON THE NORTH POLE! YOU AND *SUPERGIRL* TAKE THE SOUTH... POUR IT ON!

ACROSS THE GULF OF SPACE, THE SEARING BLAST OF THEIR COMBINED HEAT-VISION BEGINS TO MELT THE GLACIAL ICE...

SSSSSSS! KRAKKK!

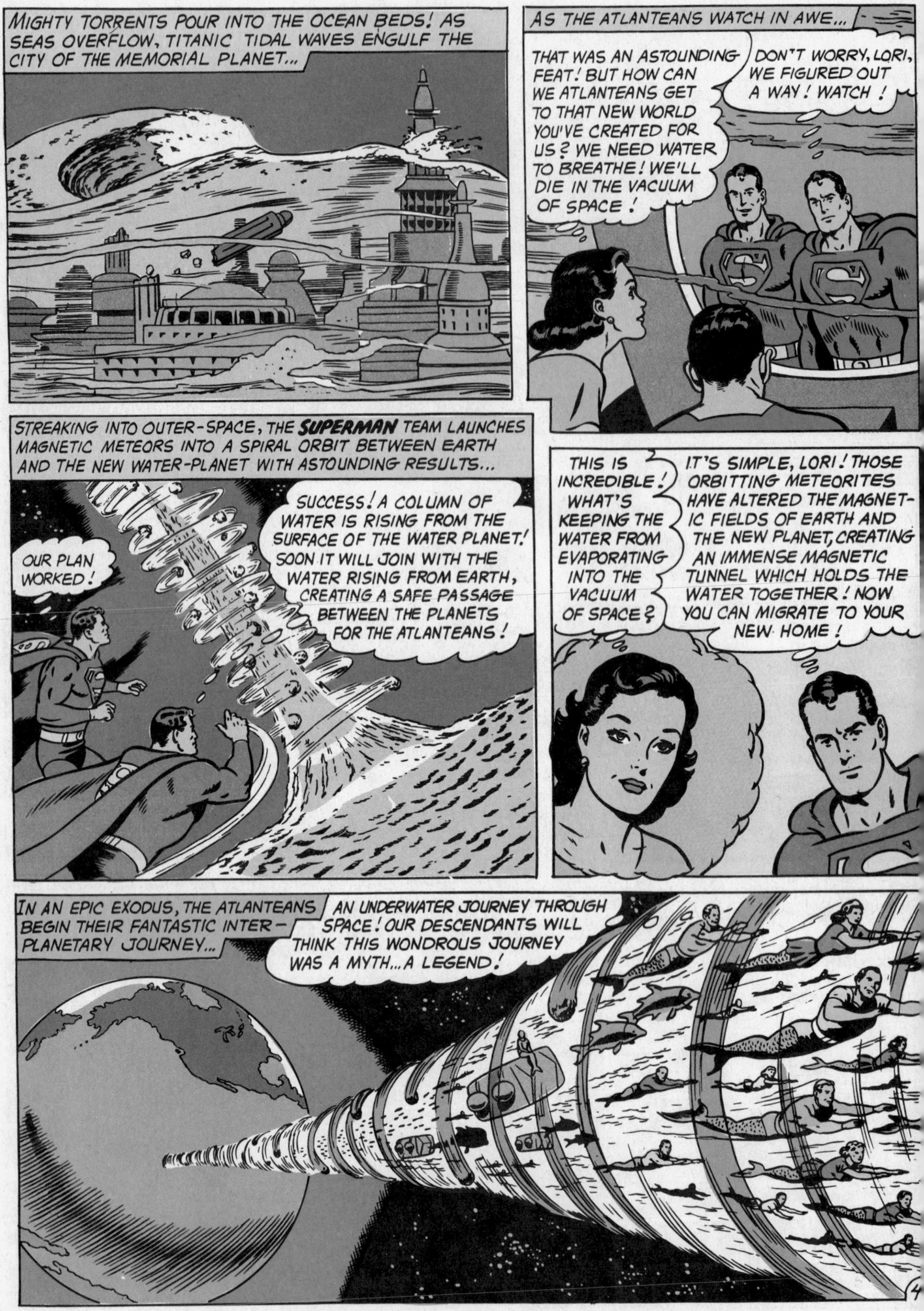
MIGHTY TORRENTS POUR INTO THE OCEAN BEDS! AS SEAS OVERFLOW, TITANIC TIDAL WAVES ENGULF THE CITY OF THE MEMORIAL PLANET...
AS THE ATLANTEANS WATCH IN AWE...
THAT WAS AN ASTOUNDING FEAT! BUT HOW CAN WE ATLANTEANS GET TO THAT NEW WORLD YOU'VE CREATED FOR US? WE NEED WATER TO BREATHE! WE'LL DIE IN THE VACUUM OF SPACE!
DON'T WORRY, LORI, WE FIGURED OUT A WAY! WATCH!
STREAKING INTO OUTER-SPACE, THE SUPERMAN TEAM LAUNCHES MAGNETIC METEORS INTO A SPIRAL ORBIT BETWEEN EARTH AND THE NEW WATER-PLANET WITH ASTOUNDING RESULTS...
OUR PLAN WORKED!
SUCCESS! A COLUMN OF WATER IS RISING FROM THE SURFACE OF THE WATER PLANET! SOON IT WILL JOIN WITH THE WATER RISING FROM EARTH, CREATING A SAFE PASSAGE BETWEEN THE PLANETS FOR THE ATLANTEANS!
THIS IS INCREDIBLE! WHAT'S KEEPING THE WATER FROM EVAPORATING INTO THE VACUUM OF SPACE?
IT'S SIMPLE, LORI! THOSE ORBITTING METEORITES HAVE ALTERED THE MAGNETIC FIELDS OF EARTH AND THE NEW PLANET, CREATING AN IMMENSE MAGNETIC TUNNEL WHICH HOLDS THE WATER TOGETHER! NOW YOU CAN MIGRATE TO YOUR NEW HOME!
IN AN EPIC EXODUS, THE ATLANTEANS BEGIN THEIR FANTASTIC INTER-PLANETARY JOURNEY...
AN UNDERWATER JOURNEY THROUGH SPACE! OUR DESCENDANTS WILL THINK THIS WONDROUS JOURNEY WAS A MYTH...A LEGEND!

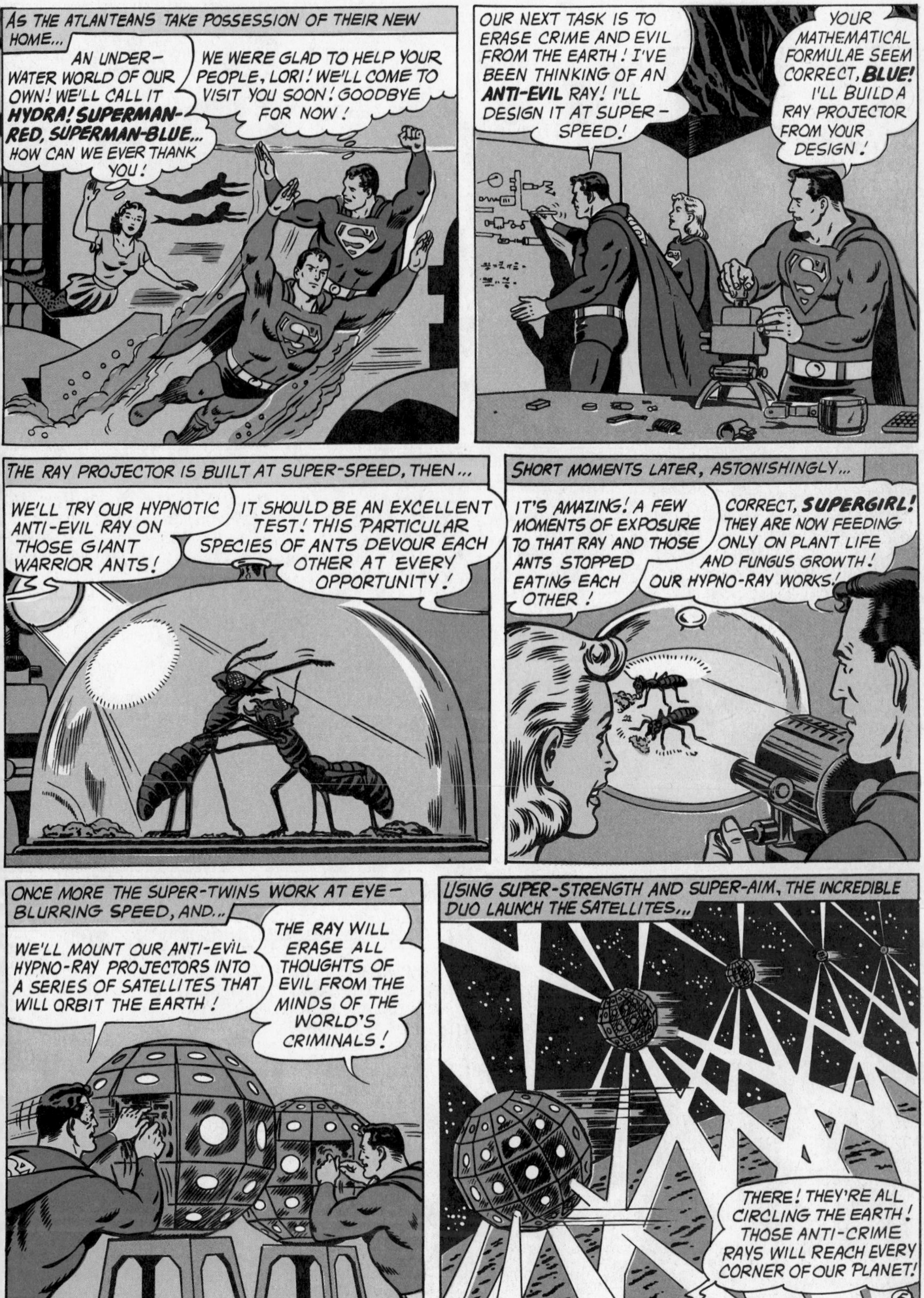
AS THE ATLANTEANS TAKE POSSESSION OF THEIR NEW HOME...
AN UNDER-WATER WORLD OF OUR OWN! WE'LL CALL IT HYDRA! SUPERMAN-RED, SUPERMAN-BLUE... HOW CAN WE EVER THANK YOU!
WE WERE GLAD TO HELP YOUR PEOPLE, LORI! WE'LL COME TO VISIT YOU SOON! GOODBYE FOR NOW!
OUR NEXT TASK IS TO ERASE CRIME AND EVIL FROM THE EARTH! I'VE BEEN THINKING OF AN ANTI-EVIL RAY! I'LL DESIGN IT AT SUPER-SPEED!
YOUR MATHEMATICAL FORMULAE SEEM CORRECT, BLUE! I'LL BUILD A RAY PROJECTOR FROM YOUR DESIGN!
THE RAY PROJECTOR IS BUILT AT SUPER-SPEED, THEN...
WE'LL TRY OUR HYPNOTIC ANTI-EVIL RAY ON THOSE GIANT WARRIOR ANTS!
IT SHOULD BE AN EXCELLENT TEST! THIS PARTICULAR SPECIES OF ANTS DEVOUR EACH OTHER AT EVERY OPPORTUNITY!
SHORT MOMENTS LATER, ASTONISHINGLY...
IT'S AMAZING! A FEW MOMENTS OF EXPOSURE TO THAT RAY AND THOSE ANTS STOPPED EATING EACH OTHER!
CORRECT, SUPERGIRL! THEY ARE NOW FEEDING ONLY ON PLANT LIFE AND FUNGUS GROWTH! OUR HYPNO-RAY WORKS!
ONCE MORE THE SUPER-TWINS WORK AT EYE-BLURRING SPEED, AND...
WE'LL MOUNT OUR ANTI-EVIL HYPNO-RAY PROJECTORS INTO A SERIES OF SATELLITES THAT WILL ORBIT THE EARTH!
THE RAY WILL ERASE ALL THOUGHTS OF EVIL FROM THE MINDS OF THE WORLD'S CRIMINALS!
USING SUPER-STRENGTH AND SUPER-AIM, THE INCREDIBLE DUO LAUNCH THE SATELLITES...
THERE! THEY'RE ALL CIRCLING THE EARTH! THOSE ANTI-CRIME RAYS WILL REACH EVERY CORNER OF OUR PLANET!
5

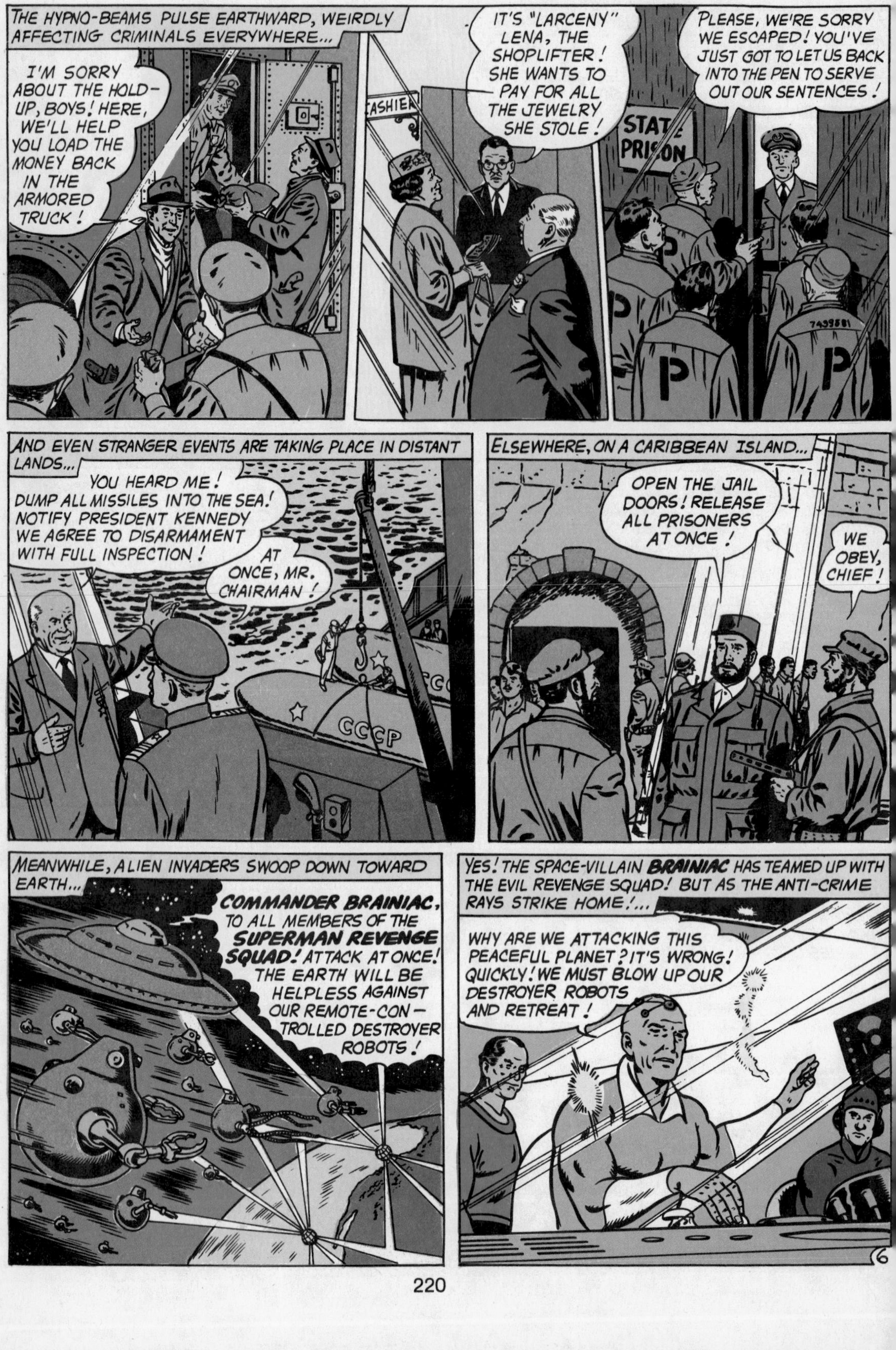
THE HYPNO-BEAMS PULSE EARTHWARD, WEIRDLY AFFECTING CRIMINALS EVERYWHERE...
I'M SORRY ABOUT THE HOLD-UP, BOYS! HERE, WE'LL HELP YOU LOAD THE MONEY BACK IN THE ARMORED TRUCK!
IT'S "LARCENY" LENA, THE SHOPLIFTER! SHE WANTS TO PAY FOR ALL THE JEWELRY SHE STOLE!
PLEASE, WE'RE SORRY WE ESCAPED! YOU'VE JUST GOT TO LET US BACK INTO THE PEN TO SERVE OUT OUR SENTENCES!
STATE PRISON
AND EVEN STRANGER EVENTS ARE TAKING PLACE IN DISTANT LANDS...
YOU HEARD ME! DUMP ALL MISSILES INTO THE SEA! NOTIFY PRESIDENT KENNEDY WE AGREE TO DISARMAMENT WITH FULL INSPECTION!
AT ONCE, MR. CHAIRMAN!
CCCP
ELSEWHERE, ON A CARIBBEAN ISLAND...
OPEN THE JAIL DOORS! RELEASE ALL PRISONERS AT ONCE!
WE OBEY, CHIEF!
MEANWHILE, ALIEN INVADERS SWOOP DOWN TOWARD EARTH...
COMMANDER BRAINIAC, TO ALL MEMBERS OF THE SUPERMAN REVENGE SQUAD! ATTACK AT ONCE! THE EARTH WILL BE HELPLESS AGAINST OUR REMOTE-CONTROLLED DESTROYER ROBOTS!
YES! THE SPACE-VILLAIN BRAINIAC HAS TEAMED UP WITH THE EVIL REVENGE SQUAD! BUT AS THE ANTI-CRIME RAYS STRIKE HOME!...
WHY ARE WE ATTACKING THIS PEACEFUL PLANET? IT'S WRONG! QUICKLY! WE MUST BLOW UP OUR DESTROYER ROBOTS AND RETREAT!
6

I THOUGHT WE'D HAVE TO TACKLE THOSE INVADERS! BUT THOSE ANTI-CRIME HYPNO-RAYS DID THE JOB FOR US!

RIGHT! THEY'RE HEADING BACK TOWARD THEIR OWN GALAXY!

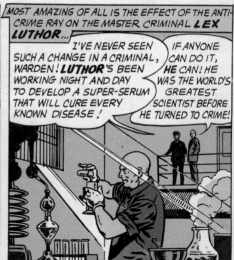

MOST AMAZING OF ALL IS THE EFFECT OF THE ANTI-CRIME RAY ON THE MASTER CRIMINAL LEX LUTHOR...

I'VE NEVER SEEN SUCH A CHANGE IN A CRIMINAL, WARDEN! LUTHOR'S BEEN WORKING NIGHT AND DAY TO DEVELOP A SUPER-SERUM THAT WILL CURE EVERY KNOWN DISEASE!

IF ANYONE CAN DO IT, HE CAN! HE WAS THE WORLD'S GREATEST SCIENTIST BEFORE HE TURNED TO CRIME!

THE NEXT DAY, AS THE SUPERMEN ARE SUMMONED TO METROPOLIS PRISON...

THIS SERUM WILL REPAY ALL THE EVIL I'VE EVER DONE! JUST SCATTER IT IN THE WORLD'S DRINKING WATER, AND IN TWO DAYS IT WILL WIPE ALL DISEASE FROM THE EARTH!

I'VE ANALYZED THIS FLUID WITH MY MICROSCOPIC VISION! IT'S THE MOST EFFECTIVE ANTIBIOTIC EVER INVENTED! WE'LL TRY IT AT ONCE!

SHORTLY, THE TWIN SUPERMEN SPRAY THE SERUM OVER THE EARTH...

A FEW DROPS SHOULD BE ENOUGH TO AFFECT THE ENTIRE MISSISSIPPI VALLEY!

THERE! THIS SHOULD TAKE CARE OF THE AMAZON AREA!

AS THE SERUM TAKES MIRACULOUS EFFECT...

IT'S A MIRACLE! ONE DRINK OF WATER AND MY SIGHT RETURNED!

HELP THE BLIND

IT'S UNCANNY! EVERY HELPLESS CRIPPLE HAS SUDDENLY BEGUN TO WALK AGAIN!

AND IN LUTHOR'S CELL...

LOOK! THE SERUM IS WORKING ON ME, TOO! I'M NO LONGER BALD!

7

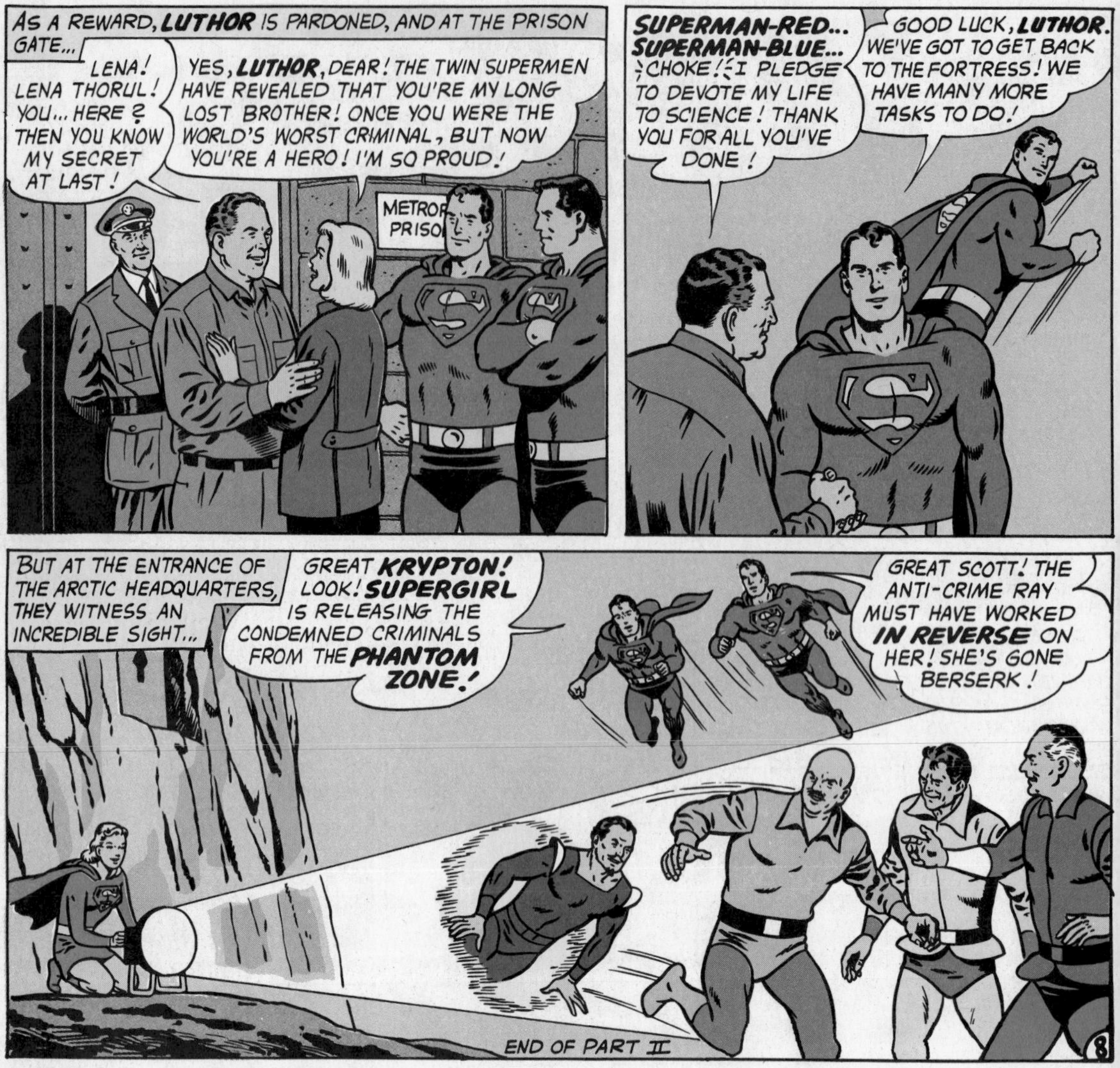
AS A REWARD, **LUTHOR** IS PARDONED, AND AT THE PRISON GATE...
LENA! LENA THORUL! YOU... HERE? THEN YOU KNOW MY SECRET AT LAST!
YES, **LUTHOR**, DEAR! THE TWIN SUPERMEN HAVE REVEALED THAT YOU'RE MY LONG LOST BROTHER! ONCE YOU WERE THE WORLD'S WORST CRIMINAL, BUT NOW YOU'RE A HERO! I'M SO PROUD!
METRO PRISO
SUPERMAN-RED... SUPERMAN-BLUE... -CHOKE!- I PLEDGE TO DEVOTE MY LIFE TO SCIENCE! THANK YOU FOR ALL YOU'VE DONE!
GOOD LUCK, **LUTHOR**. WE'VE GOT TO GET BACK TO THE FORTRESS! WE HAVE MANY MORE TASKS TO DO!
BUT AT THE ENTRANCE OF THE ARCTIC HEADQUARTERS, THEY WITNESS AN INCREDIBLE SIGHT...
GREAT **KRYPTON!** LOOK! **SUPERGIRL** IS RELEASING THE CONDEMNED CRIMINALS FROM THE **PHANTOM ZONE!**
GREAT SCOTT! THE ANTI-CRIME RAY MUST HAVE WORKED **IN REVERSE** ON HER! SHE'S GONE BERSERK!
END OF PART II
8

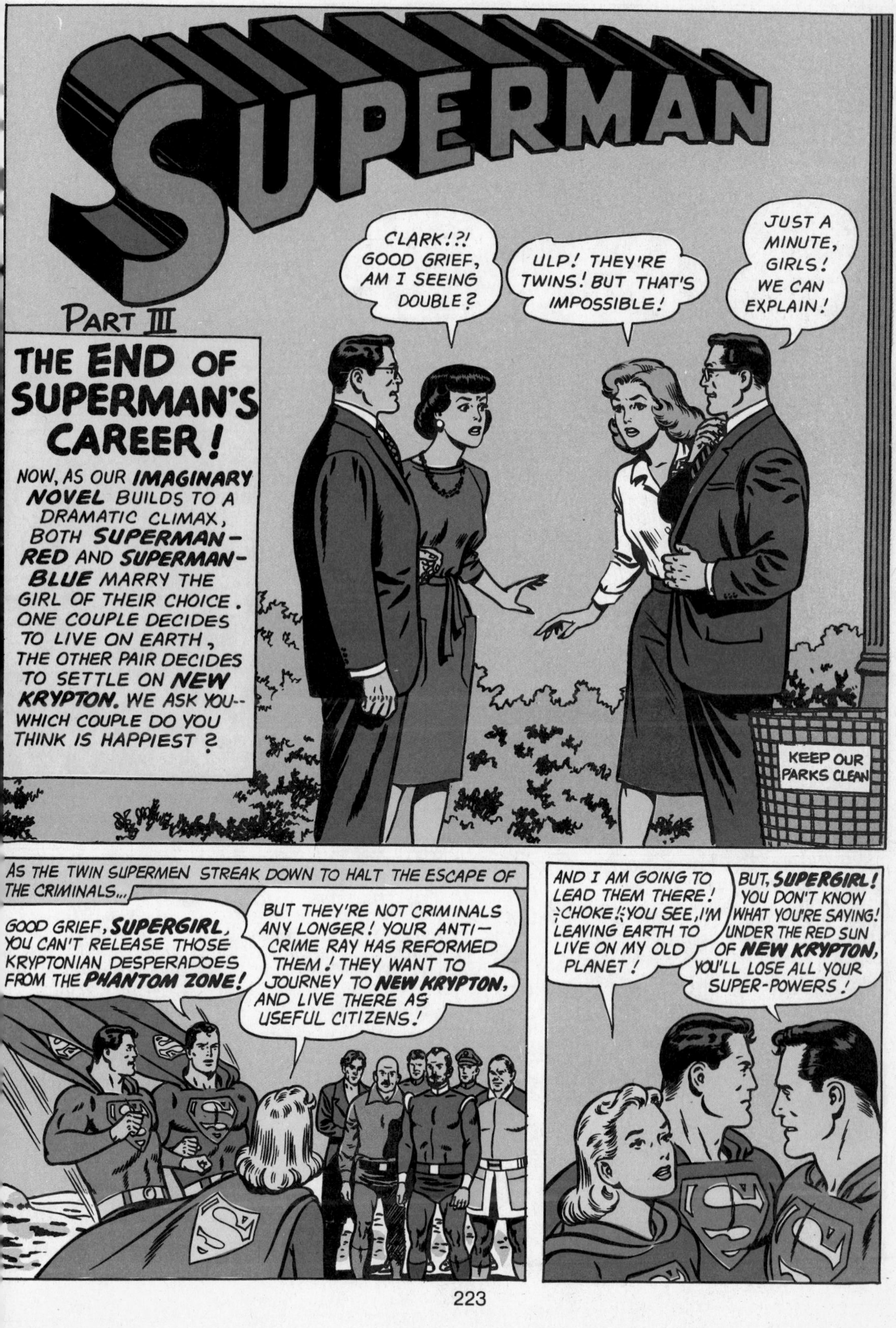
SUPERMAN
PART III
THE END OF SUPERMAN'S CAREER!
NOW, AS OUR IMAGINARY NOVEL BUILDS TO A DRAMATIC CLIMAX, BOTH SUPERMAN-RED AND SUPERMAN-BLUE MARRY THE GIRL OF THEIR CHOICE. ONE COUPLE DECIDES TO LIVE ON EARTH, THE OTHER PAIR DECIDES TO SETTLE ON NEW KRYPTON. WE ASK YOU-- WHICH COUPLE DO YOU THINK IS HAPPIEST?
CLARK!?! GOOD GRIEF, AM I SEEING DOUBLE?
ULP! THEY'RE TWINS! BUT THAT'S IMPOSSIBLE!
JUST A MINUTE, GIRLS! WE CAN EXPLAIN!
KEEP OUR PARKS CLEAN
AS THE TWIN SUPERMEN STREAK DOWN TO HALT THE ESCAPE OF THE CRIMINALS...
GOOD GRIEF, SUPERGIRL, YOU CAN'T RELEASE THOSE KRYPTONIAN DESPERADOES FROM THE PHANTOM ZONE!
BUT THEY'RE NOT CRIMINALS ANY LONGER! YOUR ANTI-CRIME RAY HAS REFORMED THEM! THEY WANT TO JOURNEY TO NEW KRYPTON, AND LIVE THERE AS USEFUL CITIZENS!
AND I AM GOING TO LEAD THEM THERE! *CHOKE!* YOU SEE, I'M LEAVING EARTH TO LIVE ON MY OLD PLANET!
BUT, SUPERGIRL! YOU DON'T KNOW WHAT YOU'RE SAYING! UNDER THE RED SUN OF NEW KRYPTON, YOU'LL LOSE ALL YOUR SUPER-POWERS!

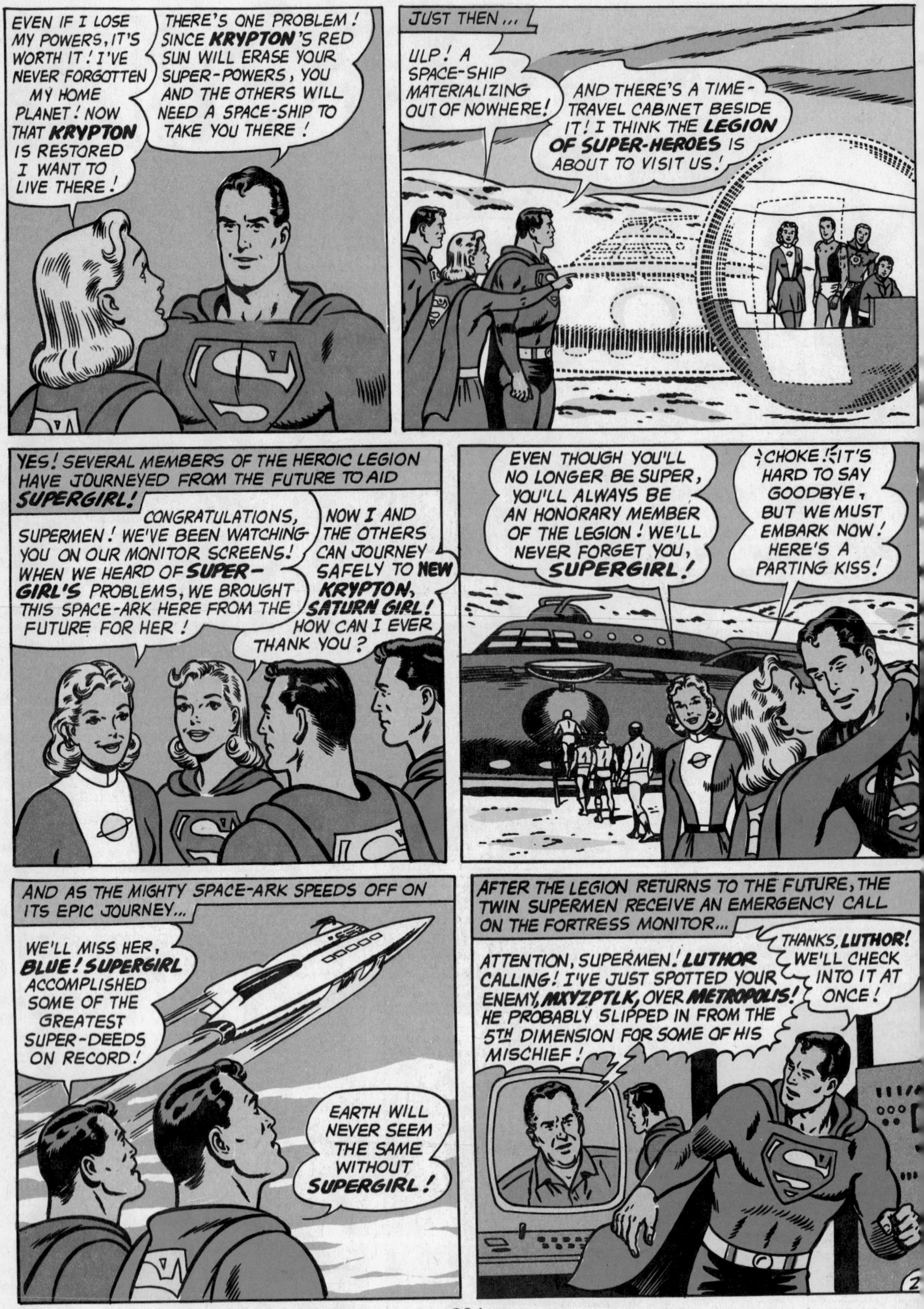
EVEN IF I LOSE MY POWERS, IT'S WORTH IT! I'VE NEVER FORGOTTEN MY HOME PLANET! NOW THAT KRYPTON IS RESTORED I WANT TO LIVE THERE!
THERE'S ONE PROBLEM! SINCE KRYPTON'S RED SUN WILL ERASE YOUR SUPER-POWERS, YOU AND THE OTHERS WILL NEED A SPACE-SHIP TO TAKE YOU THERE!
JUST THEN...
ULP! A SPACE-SHIP MATERIALIZING OUT OF NOWHERE!
AND THERE'S A TIME-TRAVEL CABINET BESIDE IT! I THINK THE LEGION OF SUPER-HEROES IS ABOUT TO VISIT US!
YES! SEVERAL MEMBERS OF THE HEROIC LEGION HAVE JOURNEYED FROM THE FUTURE TO AID SUPERGIRL!
CONGRATULATIONS, SUPERMEN! WE'VE BEEN WATCHING YOU ON OUR MONITOR SCREENS! WHEN WE HEARD OF SUPERGIRL'S PROBLEMS, WE BROUGHT THIS SPACE-ARK HERE FROM THE FUTURE FOR HER!
NOW I AND THE OTHERS CAN JOURNEY SAFELY TO NEW KRYPTON, SATURN GIRL! HOW CAN I EVER THANK YOU?
EVEN THOUGH YOU'LL NO LONGER BE SUPER, YOU'LL ALWAYS BE AN HONORARY MEMBER OF THE LEGION! WE'LL NEVER FORGET YOU, SUPERGIRL!
CHOKE! IT'S HARD TO SAY GOODBYE, BUT WE MUST EMBARK NOW! HERE'S A PARTING KISS!
AND AS THE MIGHTY SPACE-ARK SPEEDS OFF ON ITS EPIC JOURNEY...
WE'LL MISS HER, BLUE! SUPERGIRL ACCOMPLISHED SOME OF THE GREATEST SUPER-DEEDS ON RECORD!
EARTH WILL NEVER SEEM THE SAME WITHOUT SUPERGIRL!
AFTER THE LEGION RETURNS TO THE FUTURE, THE TWIN SUPERMEN RECEIVE AN EMERGENCY CALL ON THE FORTRESS MONITOR...
ATTENTION, SUPERMEN! LUTHOR CALLING! I'VE JUST SPOTTED YOUR ENEMY, MXYZPTLK, OVER METROPOLIS! HE PROBABLY SLIPPED IN FROM THE 5TH DIMENSION FOR SOME OF HIS MISCHIEF!
THANKS, LUTHOR! WE'LL CHECK INTO IT AT ONCE!

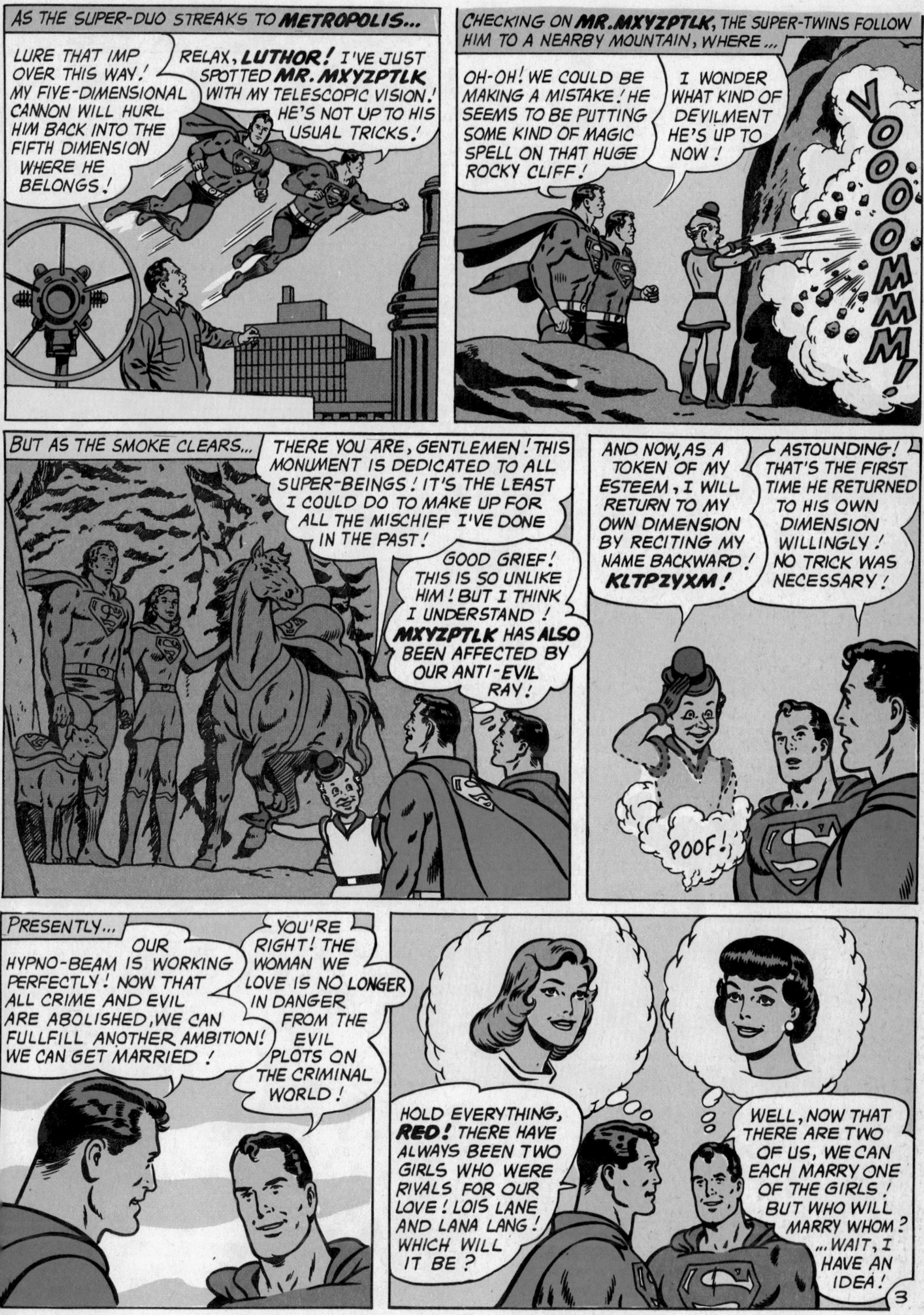
AS THE SUPER-DUO STREAKS TO METROPOLIS...
LURE THAT IMP OVER THIS WAY! MY FIVE-DIMENSIONAL CANNON WILL HURL HIM BACK INTO THE FIFTH DIMENSION WHERE HE BELONGS!
RELAX, LUTHOR! I'VE JUST SPOTTED MR. MXYZPTLK WITH MY TELESCOPIC VISION! HE'S NOT UP TO HIS USUAL TRICKS!
CHECKING ON MR. MXYZPTLK, THE SUPER-TWINS FOLLOW HIM TO A NEARBY MOUNTAIN, WHERE...
OH-OH! WE COULD BE MAKING A MISTAKE! HE SEEMS TO BE PUTTING SOME KIND OF MAGIC SPELL ON THAT HUGE ROCKY CLIFF!
I WONDER WHAT KIND OF DEVILMENT HE'S UP TO NOW!
VOOOOMMM!
BUT AS THE SMOKE CLEARS...
THERE YOU ARE, GENTLEMEN! THIS MONUMENT IS DEDICATED TO ALL SUPER-BEINGS! IT'S THE LEAST I COULD DO TO MAKE UP FOR ALL THE MISCHIEF I'VE DONE IN THE PAST!
GOOD GRIEF! THIS IS SO UNLIKE HIM! BUT I THINK I UNDERSTAND! MXYZPTLK HAS ALSO BEEN AFFECTED BY OUR ANTI-EVIL RAY!
AND NOW, AS A TOKEN OF MY ESTEEM, I WILL RETURN TO MY OWN DIMENSION BY RECITING MY NAME BACKWARD! KLTPZYXM!
ASTOUNDING! THAT'S THE FIRST TIME HE RETURNED TO HIS OWN DIMENSION WILLINGLY! NO TRICK WAS NECESSARY!
POOF!
PRESENTLY...
OUR HYPNO-BEAM IS WORKING PERFECTLY! NOW THAT ALL CRIME AND EVIL ARE ABOLISHED, WE CAN FULLFILL ANOTHER AMBITION! WE CAN GET MARRIED!
YOU'RE RIGHT! THE WOMAN WE LOVE IS NO LONGER IN DANGER FROM THE EVIL PLOTS ON THE CRIMINAL WORLD!
HOLD EVERYTHING, RED! THERE HAVE ALWAYS BEEN TWO GIRLS WHO WERE RIVALS FOR OUR LOVE! LOIS LANE AND LANA LANG! WHICH WILL IT BE?
WELL, NOW THAT THERE ARE TWO OF US, WE CAN EACH MARRY ONE OF THE GIRLS! BUT WHO WILL MARRY WHOM? ...WAIT, I HAVE AN IDEA!
3

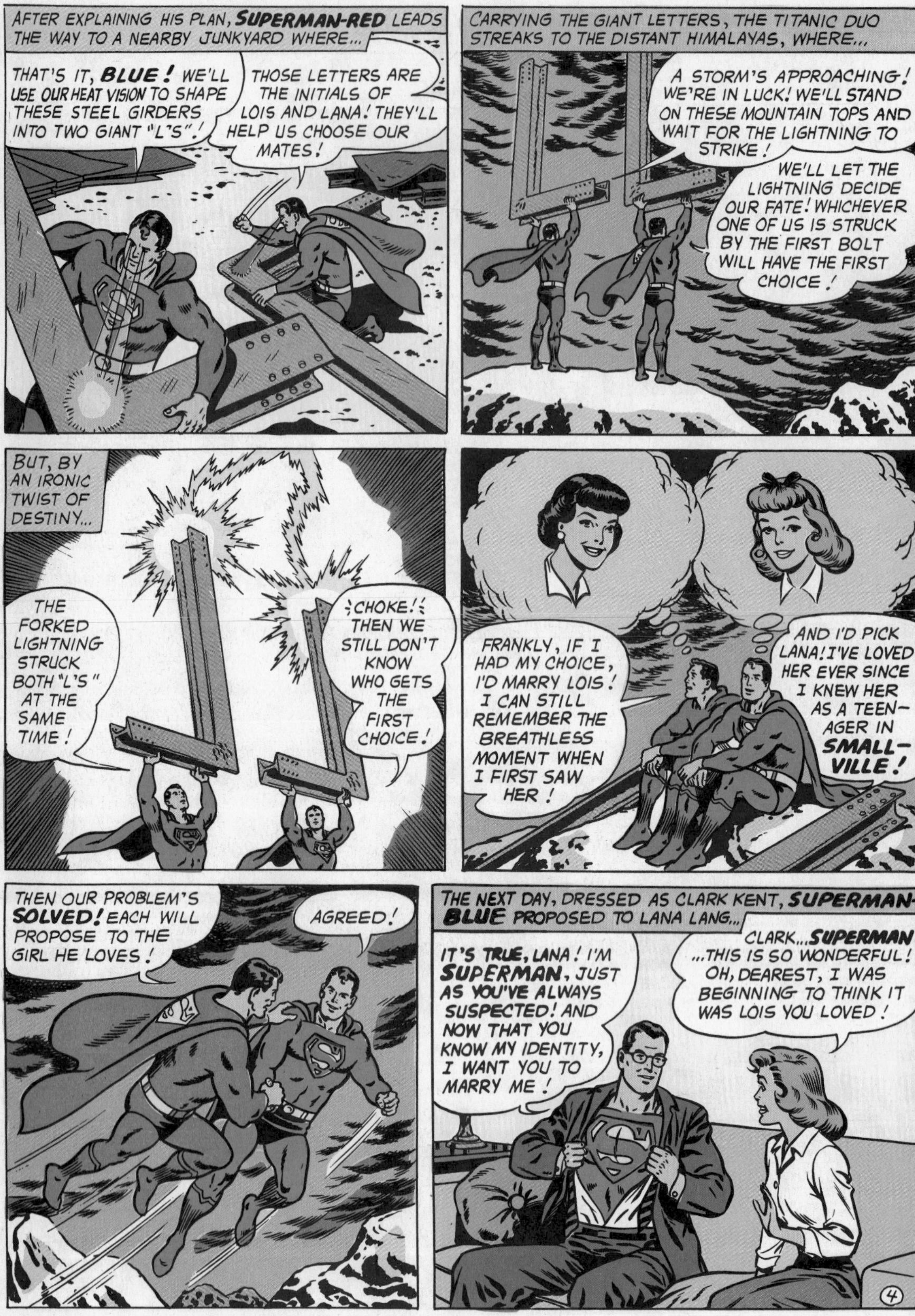
AFTER EXPLAINING HIS PLAN, SUPERMAN-RED LEADS THE WAY TO A NEARBY JUNKYARD WHERE...
THAT'S IT, BLUE! WE'LL USE OUR HEAT VISION TO SHAPE THESE STEEL GIRDERS INTO TWO GIANT "L'S"!
THOSE LETTERS ARE THE INITIALS OF LOIS AND LANA! THEY'LL HELP US CHOOSE OUR MATES!
CARRYING THE GIANT LETTERS, THE TITANIC DUO STREAKS TO THE DISTANT HIMALAYAS, WHERE...
A STORM'S APPROACHING! WE'RE IN LUCK! WE'LL STAND ON THESE MOUNTAIN TOPS AND WAIT FOR THE LIGHTNING TO STRIKE!
WE'LL LET THE LIGHTNING DECIDE OUR FATE! WHICHEVER ONE OF US IS STRUCK BY THE FIRST BOLT WILL HAVE THE FIRST CHOICE!
BUT, BY AN IRONIC TWIST OF DESTINY...
THE FORKED LIGHTNING STRUCK BOTH "L'S" AT THE SAME TIME!
CHOKE! THEN WE STILL DON'T KNOW WHO GETS THE FIRST CHOICE!
FRANKLY, IF I HAD MY CHOICE, I'D MARRY LOIS! I CAN STILL REMEMBER THE BREATHLESS MOMENT WHEN I FIRST SAW HER!
AND I'D PICK LANA! I'VE LOVED HER EVER SINCE I KNEW HER AS A TEEN-AGER IN SMALLVILLE!
THEN OUR PROBLEM'S SOLVED! EACH WILL PROPOSE TO THE GIRL HE LOVES!
AGREED!
THE NEXT DAY, DRESSED AS CLARK KENT, SUPERMAN-BLUE PROPOSED TO LANA LANG...
IT'S TRUE, LANA! I'M SUPERMAN, JUST AS YOU'VE ALWAYS SUSPECTED! AND NOW THAT YOU KNOW MY IDENTITY, I WANT YOU TO MARRY ME!
CLARK...SUPERMAN ...THIS IS SO WONDERFUL! OH, DEAREST, I WAS BEGINNING TO THINK IT WAS LOIS YOU LOVED!
4

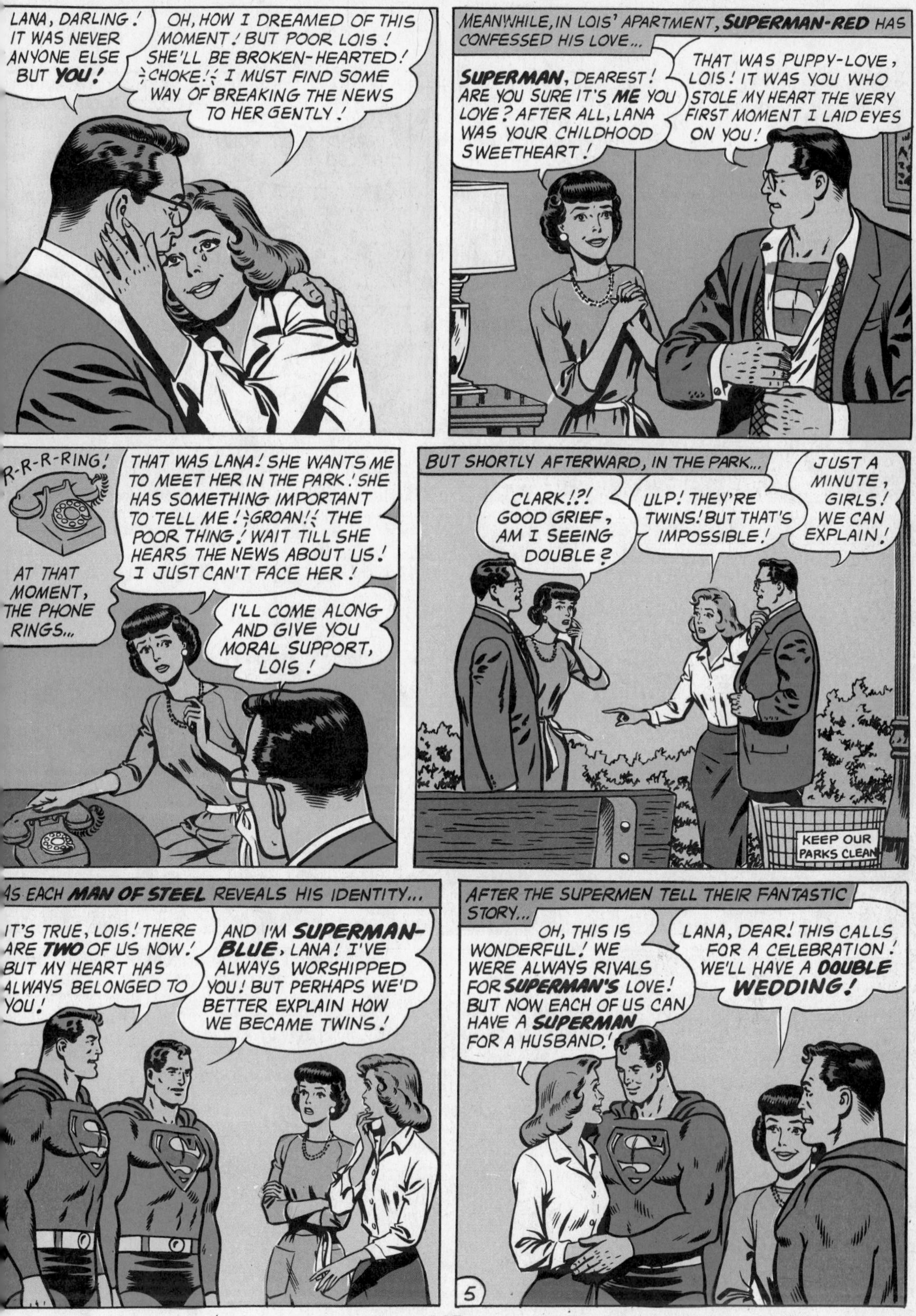
LANA, DARLING! IT WAS NEVER ANYONE ELSE BUT YOU!
OH, HOW I DREAMED OF THIS MOMENT! BUT POOR LOIS! SHE'LL BE BROKEN-HEARTED! CHOKE! I MUST FIND SOME WAY OF BREAKING THE NEWS TO HER GENTLY!
MEANWHILE, IN LOIS' APARTMENT, SUPERMAN-RED HAS CONFESSED HIS LOVE...
SUPERMAN, DEAREST! ARE YOU SURE IT'S ME YOU LOVE? AFTER ALL, LANA WAS YOUR CHILDHOOD SWEETHEART!
THAT WAS PUPPY-LOVE, LOIS! IT WAS YOU WHO STOLE MY HEART THE VERY FIRST MOMENT I LAID EYES ON YOU!
R-R-R-RING!
AT THAT MOMENT, THE PHONE RINGS...
THAT WAS LANA! SHE WANTS ME TO MEET HER IN THE PARK! SHE HAS SOMETHING IMPORTANT TO TELL ME! GROAN! THE POOR THING! WAIT TILL SHE HEARS THE NEWS ABOUT US! I JUST CAN'T FACE HER!
I'LL COME ALONG AND GIVE YOU MORAL SUPPORT, LOIS!
BUT SHORTLY AFTERWARD, IN THE PARK...
CLARK!?! GOOD GRIEF, AM I SEEING DOUBLE?
ULP! THEY'RE TWINS! BUT THAT'S IMPOSSIBLE!
JUST A MINUTE, GIRLS! WE CAN EXPLAIN!
KEEP OUR PARKS CLEAN
AS EACH MAN OF STEEL REVEALS HIS IDENTITY...
IT'S TRUE, LOIS! THERE ARE TWO OF US NOW! BUT MY HEART HAS ALWAYS BELONGED TO YOU!
AND I'M SUPERMAN-BLUE, LANA! I'VE ALWAYS WORSHIPPED YOU! BUT PERHAPS WE'D BETTER EXPLAIN HOW WE BECAME TWINS!
AFTER THE SUPERMEN TELL THEIR FANTASTIC STORY...
OH, THIS IS WONDERFUL! WE WERE ALWAYS RIVALS FOR SUPERMAN'S LOVE! BUT NOW EACH OF US CAN HAVE A SUPERMAN FOR A HUSBAND!
LANA, DEAR! THIS CALLS FOR A CELEBRATION! WE'LL HAVE A DOUBLE WEDDING!
5

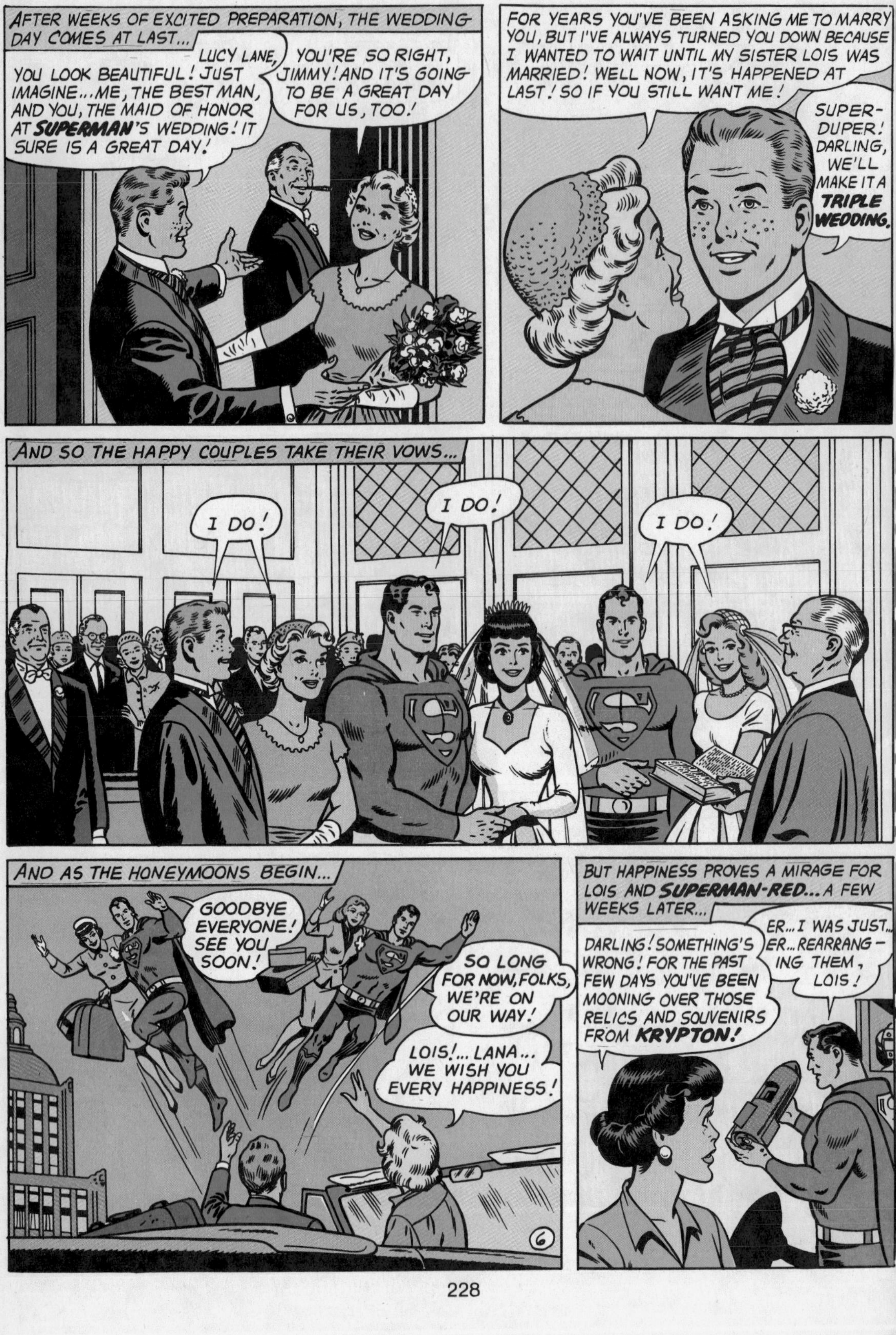

AFTER WEEKS OF EXCITED PREPARATION, THE WEDDING DAY COMES AT LAST...
LUCY LANE, YOU LOOK BEAUTIFUL! JUST IMAGINE...ME, THE BEST MAN, AND YOU, THE MAID OF HONOR AT SUPERMAN'S WEDDING! IT SURE IS A GREAT DAY!
YOU'RE SO RIGHT, JIMMY! AND IT'S GOING TO BE A GREAT DAY FOR US, TOO!
FOR YEARS YOU'VE BEEN ASKING ME TO MARRY YOU, BUT I'VE ALWAYS TURNED YOU DOWN BECAUSE I WANTED TO WAIT UNTIL MY SISTER LOIS WAS MARRIED! WELL NOW, IT'S HAPPENED AT LAST! SO IF YOU STILL WANT ME!
SUPER-DUPER! DARLING, WE'LL MAKE IT A TRIPLE WEDDING.
AND SO THE HAPPY COUPLES TAKE THEIR VOWS...
I DO!
I DO!
I DO!
AND AS THE HONEYMOONS BEGIN...
GOODBYE EVERYONE! SEE YOU SOON!
SO LONG FOR NOW, FOLKS, WE'RE ON OUR WAY!
LOIS!... LANA... WE WISH YOU EVERY HAPPINESS!
6
BUT HAPPINESS PROVES A MIRAGE FOR LOIS AND SUPERMAN-RED... A FEW WEEKS LATER...
DARLING! SOMETHING'S WRONG! FOR THE PAST FEW DAYS YOU'VE BEEN MOONING OVER THOSE RELICS AND SOUVENIRS FROM KRYPTON!
ER... I WAS JUST... ER... REARRANGING THEM, LOIS!

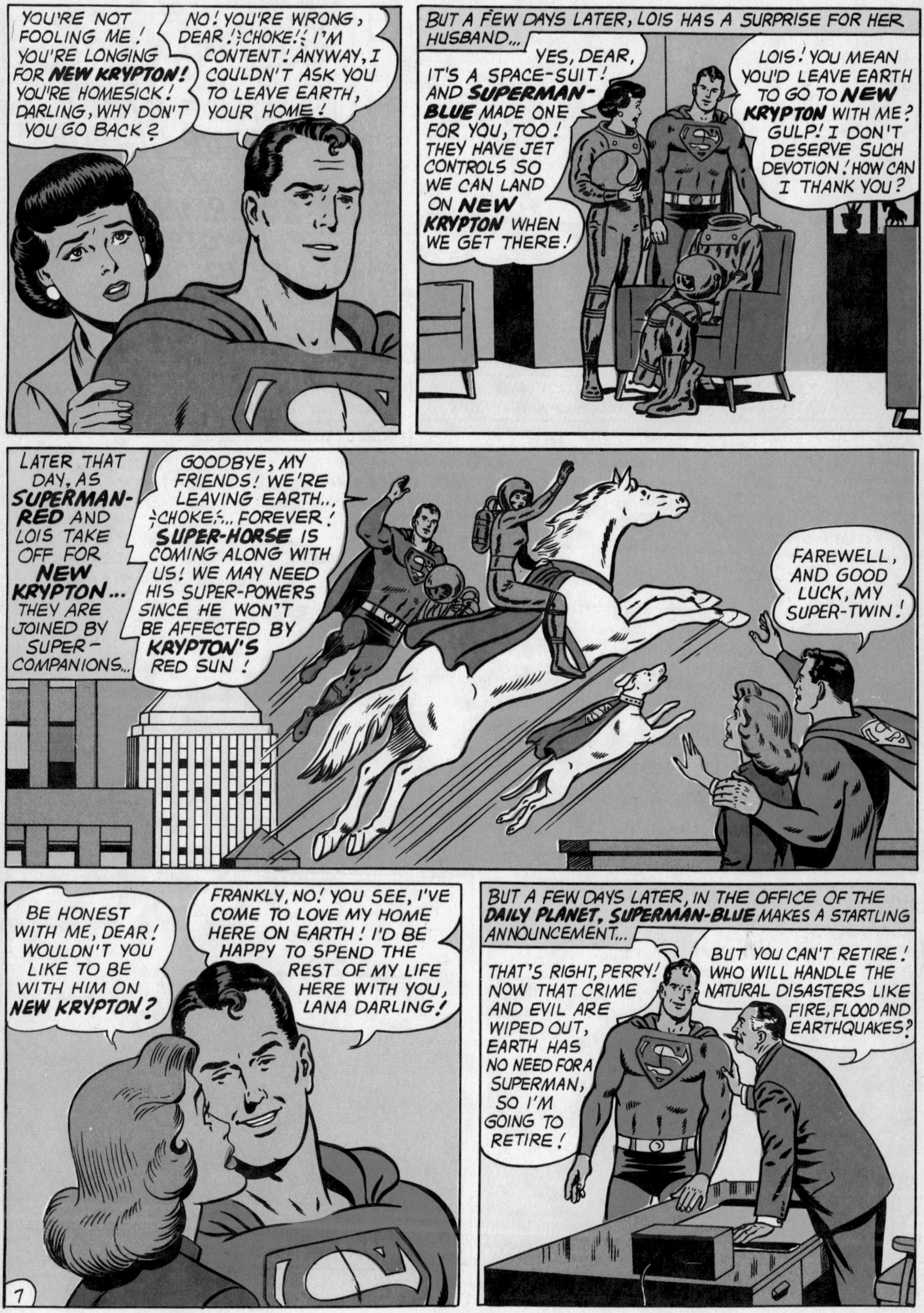
YOU'RE NOT FOOLING ME! YOU'RE LONGING FOR NEW KRYPTON! YOU'RE HOMESICK! DARLING, WHY DON'T YOU GO BACK?
NO! YOU'RE WRONG, DEAR! CHOKE! I'M CONTENT! ANYWAY, I COULDN'T ASK YOU TO LEAVE EARTH, YOUR HOME!
BUT A FEW DAYS LATER, LOIS HAS A SURPRISE FOR HER HUSBAND...
YES, DEAR, IT'S A SPACE-SUIT! AND SUPERMAN-BLUE MADE ONE FOR YOU, TOO! THEY HAVE JET CONTROLS SO WE CAN LAND ON NEW KRYPTON WHEN WE GET THERE!
LOIS! YOU MEAN YOU'D LEAVE EARTH TO GO TO NEW KRYPTON WITH ME? GULP! I DON'T DESERVE SUCH DEVOTION! HOW CAN I THANK YOU?
LATER THAT DAY, AS SUPERMAN-RED AND LOIS TAKE OFF FOR NEW KRYPTON... THEY ARE JOINED BY SUPER-COMPANIONS...
GOODBYE, MY FRIENDS! WE'RE LEAVING EARTH... CHOKE... FOREVER! SUPER-HORSE IS COMING ALONG WITH US! WE MAY NEED HIS SUPER-POWERS SINCE HE WON'T BE AFFECTED BY KRYPTON'S RED SUN!
FAREWELL, AND GOOD LUCK, MY SUPER-TWIN!
BE HONEST WITH ME, DEAR! WOULDN'T YOU LIKE TO BE WITH HIM ON NEW KRYPTON?
FRANKLY, NO! YOU SEE, I'VE COME TO LOVE MY HOME HERE ON EARTH! I'D BE HAPPY TO SPEND THE REST OF MY LIFE HERE WITH YOU, LANA DARLING!
7
BUT A FEW DAYS LATER, IN THE OFFICE OF THE DAILY PLANET, SUPERMAN-BLUE MAKES A STARTLING ANNOUNCEMENT...
THAT'S RIGHT, PERRY! NOW THAT CRIME AND EVIL ARE WIPED OUT, EARTH HAS NO NEED FOR A SUPERMAN, SO I'M GOING TO RETIRE!
BUT YOU CAN'T RETIRE! WHO WILL HANDLE THE NATURAL DISASTERS LIKE FIRE, FLOOD AND EARTHQUAKES?

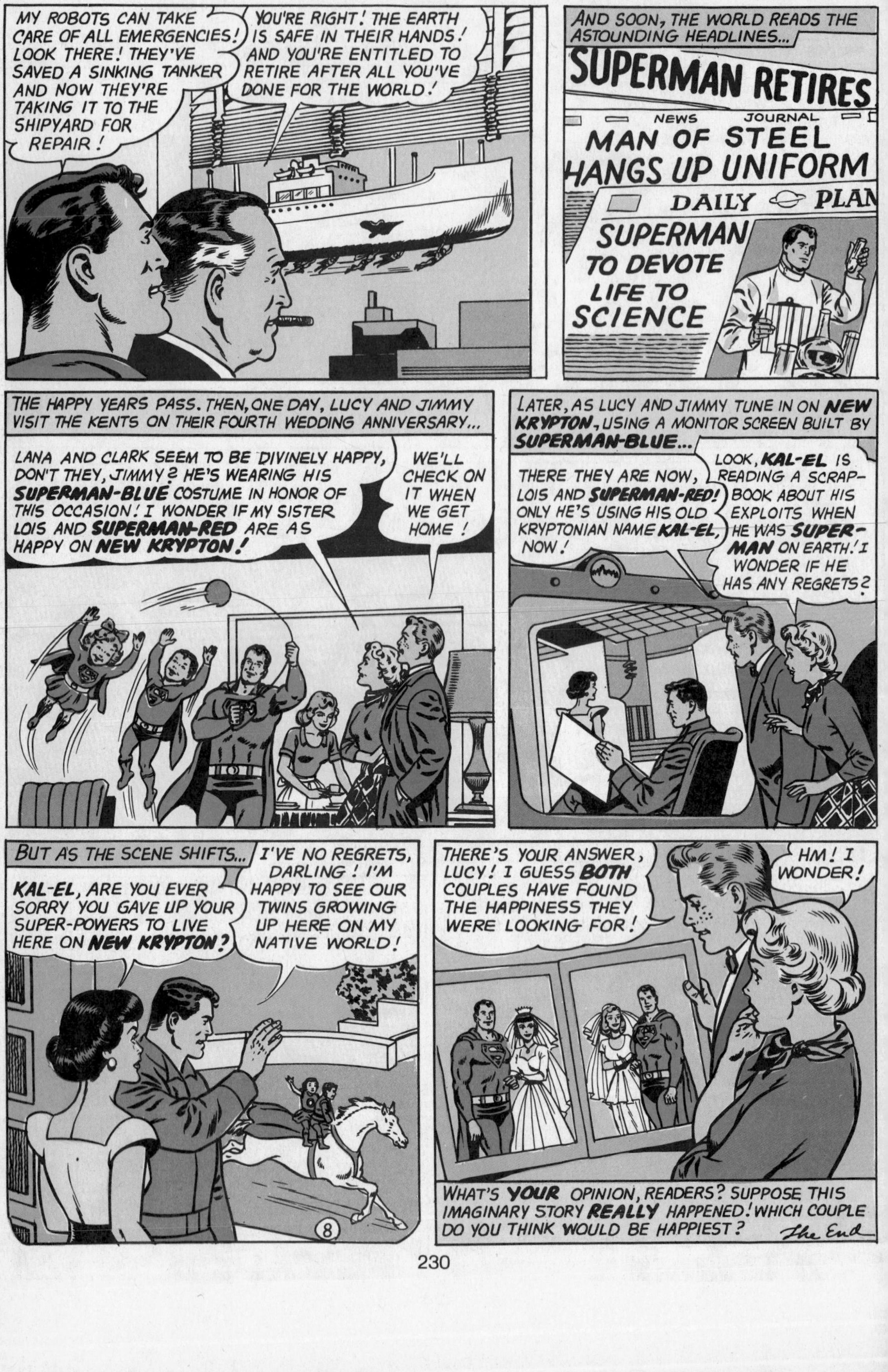
MY ROBOTS CAN TAKE CARE OF ALL EMERGENCIES! LOOK THERE! THEY'VE SAVED A SINKING TANKER AND NOW THEY'RE TAKING IT TO THE SHIPYARD FOR REPAIR!
YOU'RE RIGHT! THE EARTH IS SAFE IN THEIR HANDS! AND YOU'RE ENTITLED TO RETIRE AFTER ALL YOU'VE DONE FOR THE WORLD!
AND SOON, THE WORLD READS THE ASTOUNDING HEADLINES...
SUPERMAN RETIRES
NEWS JOURNAL
MAN OF STEEL HANGS UP UNIFORM
DAILY PLAN
SUPERMAN TO DEVOTE LIFE TO SCIENCE
THE HAPPY YEARS PASS. THEN, ONE DAY, LUCY AND JIMMY VISIT THE KENTS ON THEIR FOURTH WEDDING ANNIVERSARY...
LANA AND CLARK SEEM TO BE DIVINELY HAPPY, DON'T THEY, JIMMY? HE'S WEARING HIS SUPERMAN-BLUE COSTUME IN HONOR OF THIS OCCASION! I WONDER IF MY SISTER LOIS AND SUPERMAN-RED ARE AS HAPPY ON NEW KRYPTON!
WE'LL CHECK ON IT WHEN WE GET HOME!
LATER, AS LUCY AND JIMMY TUNE IN ON NEW KRYPTON, USING A MONITOR SCREEN BUILT BY SUPERMAN-BLUE...
THERE THEY ARE NOW, LOIS AND SUPERMAN-RED! ONLY HE'S USING HIS OLD KRYPTONIAN NAME KAL-EL, NOW!
LOOK, KAL-EL IS READING A SCRAP-BOOK ABOUT HIS EXPLOITS WHEN HE WAS SUPER-MAN ON EARTH! I WONDER IF HE HAS ANY REGRETS?
BUT AS THE SCENE SHIFTS...
KAL-EL, ARE YOU EVER SORRY YOU GAVE UP YOUR SUPER-POWERS TO LIVE HERE ON NEW KRYPTON?
I'VE NO REGRETS, DARLING! I'M HAPPY TO SEE OUR TWINS GROWING UP HERE ON MY NATIVE WORLD!
8
THERE'S YOUR ANSWER, LUCY! I GUESS BOTH COUPLES HAVE FOUND THE HAPPINESS THEY WERE LOOKING FOR!
HM! I WONDER!
WHAT'S YOUR OPINION, READERS? SUPPOSE THIS IMAGINARY STORY REALLY HAPPENED! WHICH COUPLE DO YOU THINK WOULD BE HAPPIEST?
The End

LISTEN TO THE NIGHT--YOU MAY HEAR SOUNDS HEARD BY FEW MEN... WATCH FOR THE LIGHT--YOU'LL SEE IT, IF YOU'RE SHARP, AND THEN...
SCRRREEEEEERRREEEEE
HOLD YOUR EARS--IT MUST BE COMING THROUGH-- FROM THERE TO HERE-- ON A TRIP WITH A INFINITE VIEW...
RRREEEEEEEEEEE
WHAT IS IT? WHO'S IN IT? WELL THEY'RE BOTH NEW TO THIS AGE... STAND BACK FOR THE ANSWERS-- THEY'RE ON THE NEXT PAGE--
EEEEEEEE
X-100
1

Color by Jerry Serpe

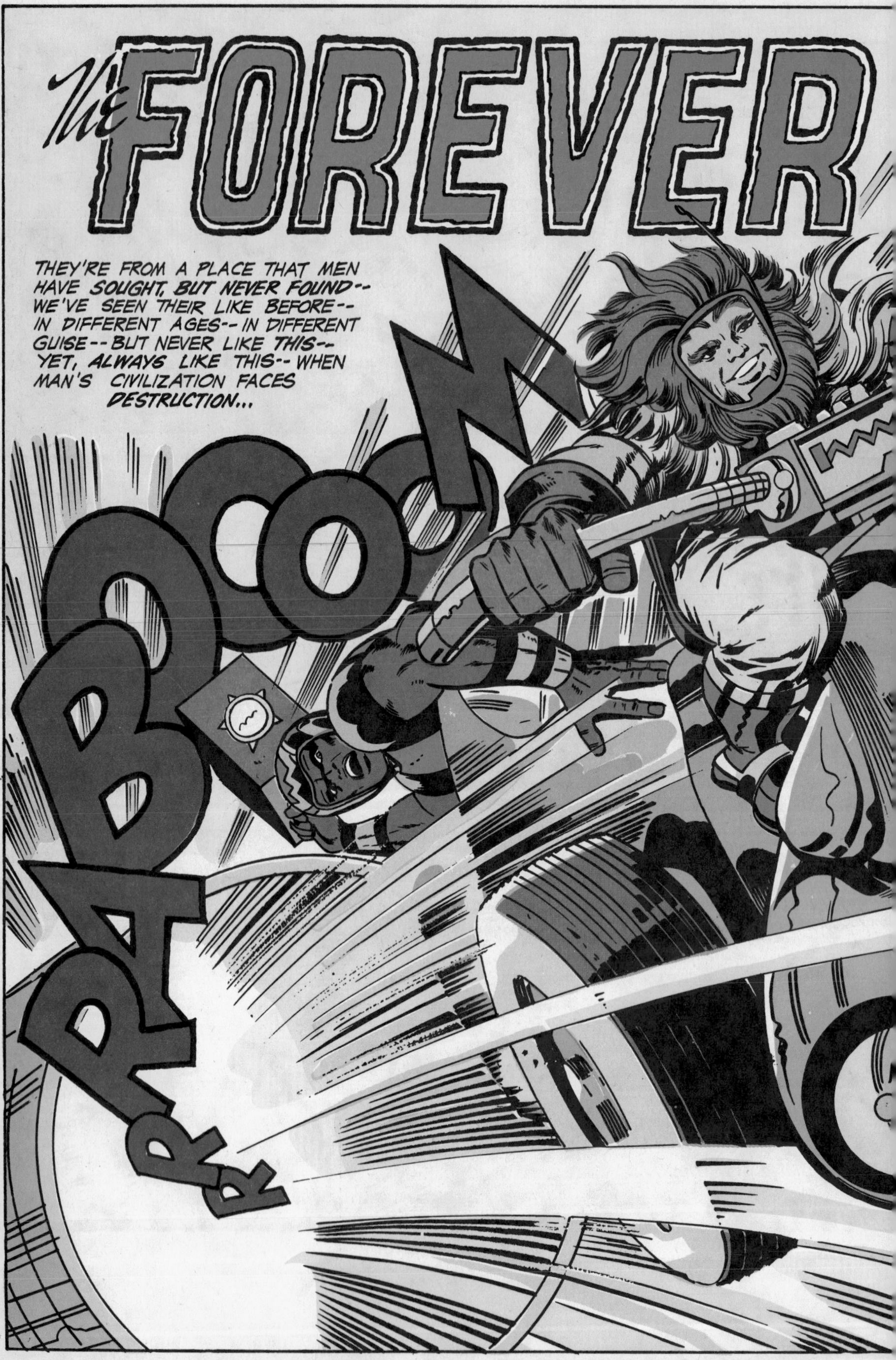
The FOREVER
THEY'RE FROM A PLACE THAT MEN HAVE SOUGHT, BUT NEVER FOUND-- WE'VE SEEN THEIR LIKE BEFORE-- IN DIFFERENT AGES-- IN DIFFERENT GUISE-- BUT NEVER LIKE THIS-- YET, ALWAYS LIKE THIS-- WHEN MAN'S CIVILIZATION FACES DESTRUCTION...
RABOOOM

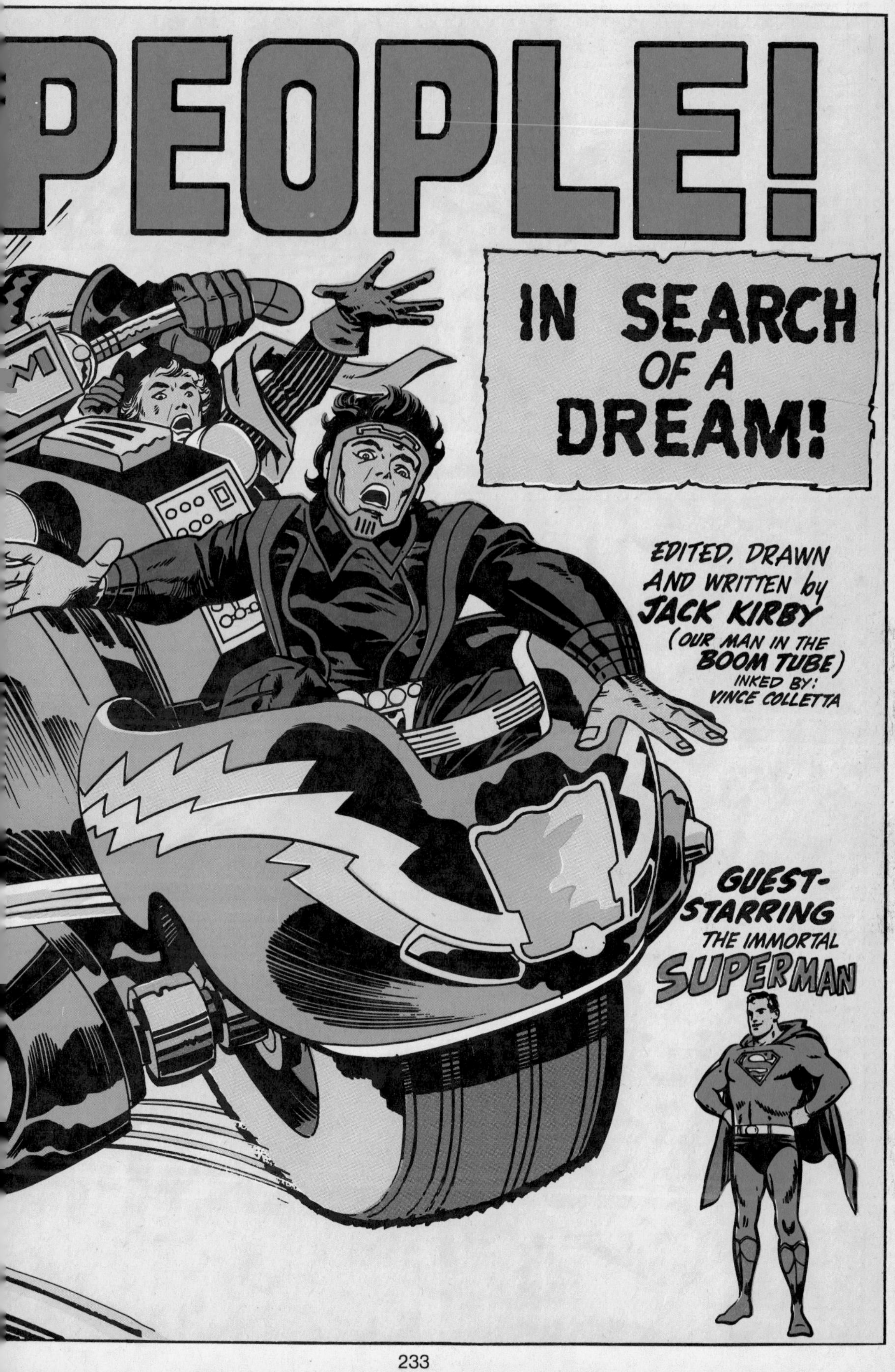
PEOPLE!
IN SEARCH OF A DREAM!
EDITED, DRAWN AND WRITTEN by JACK KIRBY (OUR MAN IN THE BOOM TUBE)
INKED BY: VINCE COLLETTA
GUEST-STARRING THE IMMORTAL SUPERMAN

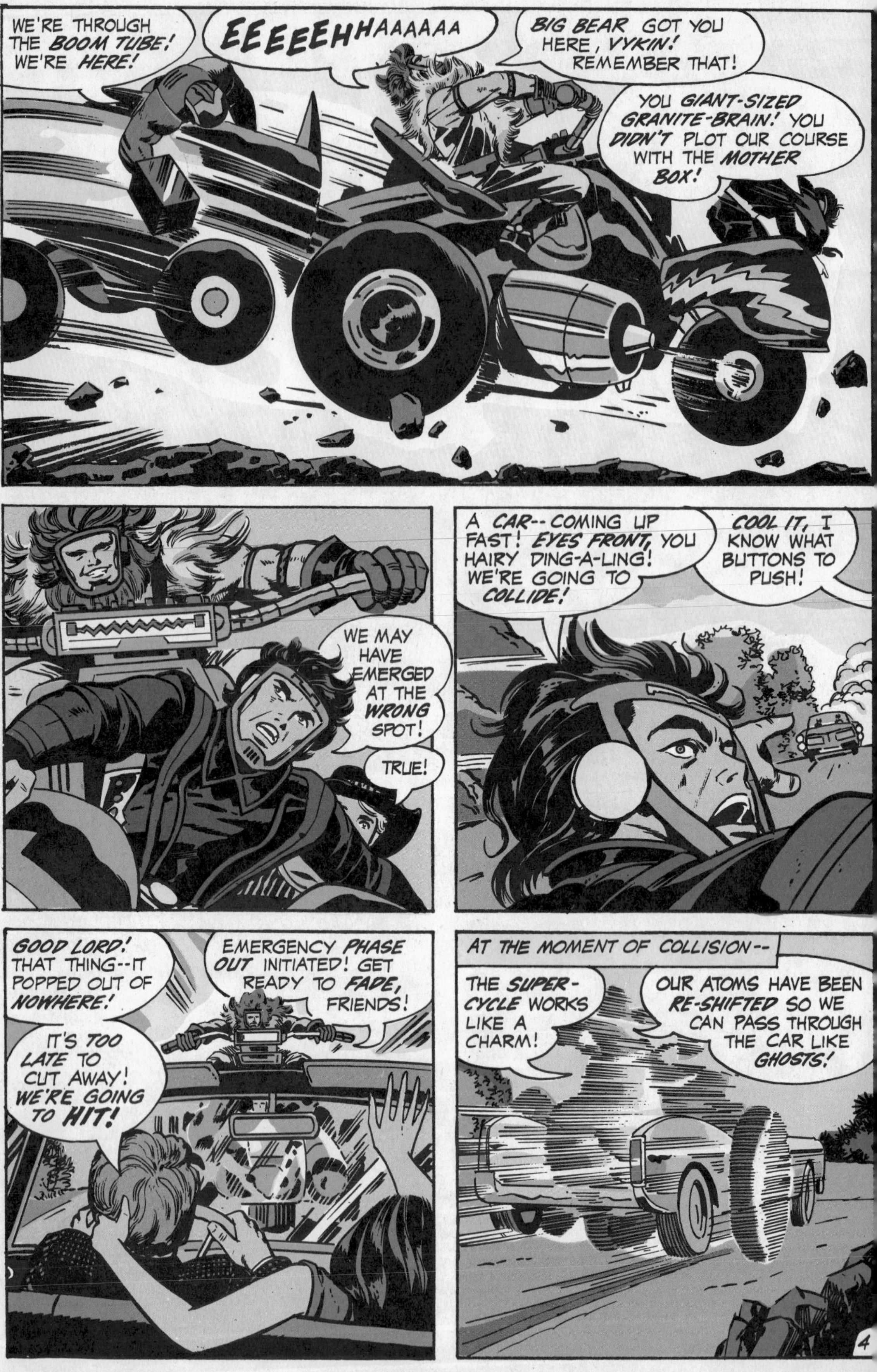
WE'RE THROUGH THE BOOM TUBE! WE'RE HERE!
EEEEEHHAAAAAA
BIG BEAR GOT YOU HERE, VYKIN! REMEMBER THAT!
YOU GIANT-SIZED GRANITE-BRAIN! YOU DIDN'T PLOT OUR COURSE WITH THE MOTHER BOX!
WE MAY HAVE EMERGED AT THE WRONG SPOT!
TRUE!
A CAR--COMING UP FAST! EYES FRONT, YOU HAIRY DING-A-LING! WE'RE GOING TO COLLIDE!
COOL IT, I KNOW WHAT BUTTONS TO PUSH!
GOOD LORD! THAT THING--IT POPPED OUT OF NOWHERE!
EMERGENCY PHASE OUT INITIATED! GET READY TO FADE, FRIENDS!
IT'S TOO LATE TO CUT AWAY! WE'RE GOING TO HIT!
AT THE MOMENT OF COLLISION--
THE SUPER-CYCLE WORKS LIKE A CHARM!
OUR ATOMS HAVE BEEN RE-SHIFTED SO WE CAN PASS THROUGH THE CAR LIKE GHOSTS!
4

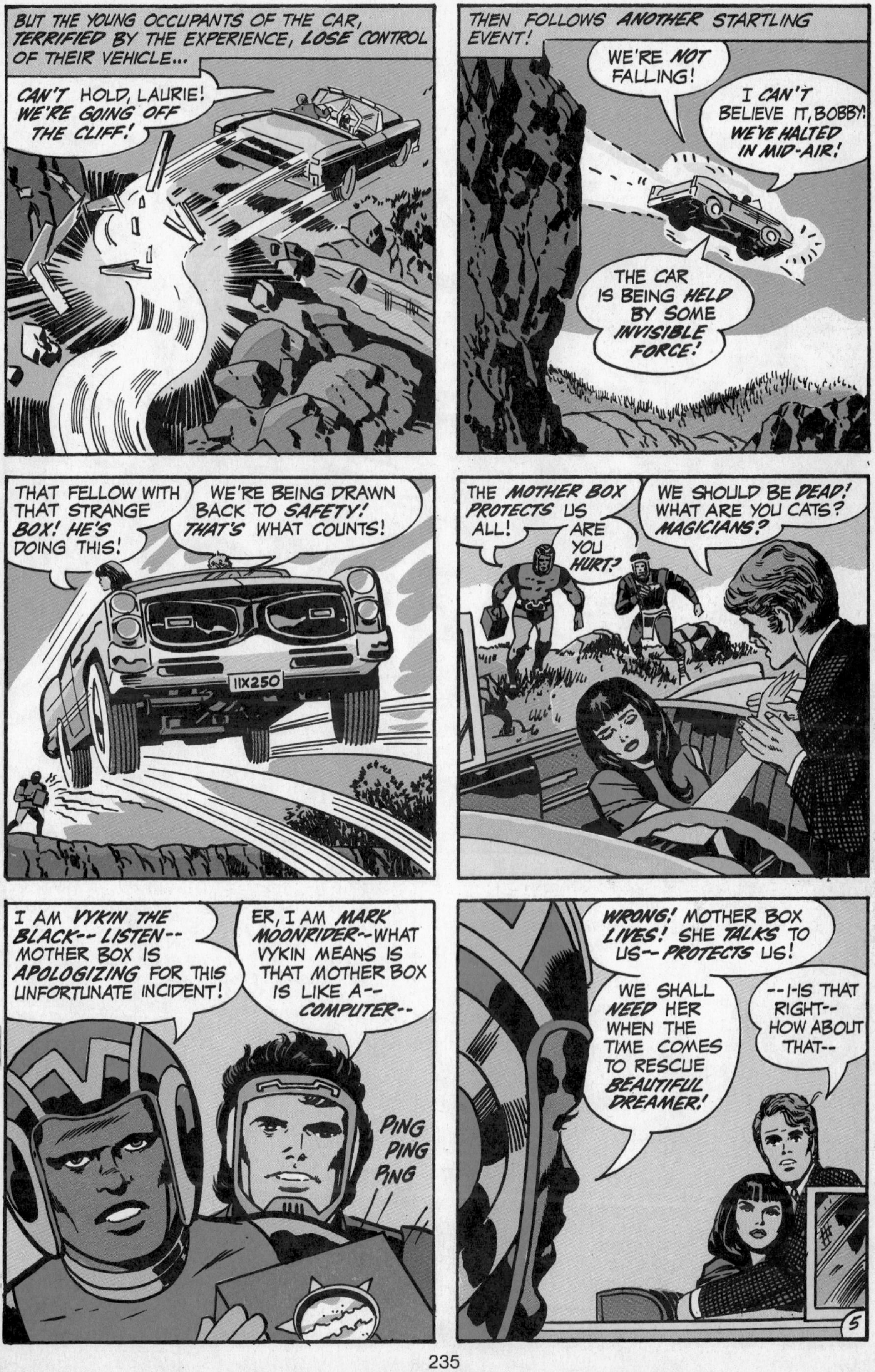
BUT THE YOUNG OCCUPANTS OF THE CAR, TERRIFIED BY THE EXPERIENCE, LOSE CONTROL OF THEIR VEHICLE...
CAN'T HOLD, LAURIE! WE'RE GOING OFF THE CLIFF!
THEN FOLLOWS ANOTHER STARTLING EVENT!
WE'RE NOT FALLING!
I CAN'T BELIEVE IT, BOBBY! WE'VE HALTED IN MID-AIR!
THE CAR IS BEING HELD BY SOME INVISIBLE FORCE!
THAT FELLOW WITH THAT STRANGE BOX! HE'S DOING THIS!
WE'RE BEING DRAWN BACK TO SAFETY! THAT'S WHAT COUNTS!
11X250
THE MOTHER BOX PROTECTS US ALL!
ARE YOU HURT?
WE SHOULD BE DEAD! WHAT ARE YOU CATS? MAGICIANS?
I AM VYKIN THE BLACK-- LISTEN-- MOTHER BOX IS APOLOGIZING FOR THIS UNFORTUNATE INCIDENT!
ER, I AM MARK MOONRIDER--WHAT VYKIN MEANS IS THAT MOTHER BOX IS LIKE A-- COMPUTER--
PING PING PING
WRONG! MOTHER BOX LIVES! SHE TALKS TO US-- PROTECTS US!
WE SHALL NEED HER WHEN THE TIME COMES TO RESCUE BEAUTIFUL DREAMER!
--I-IS THAT RIGHT-- HOW ABOUT THAT--
5

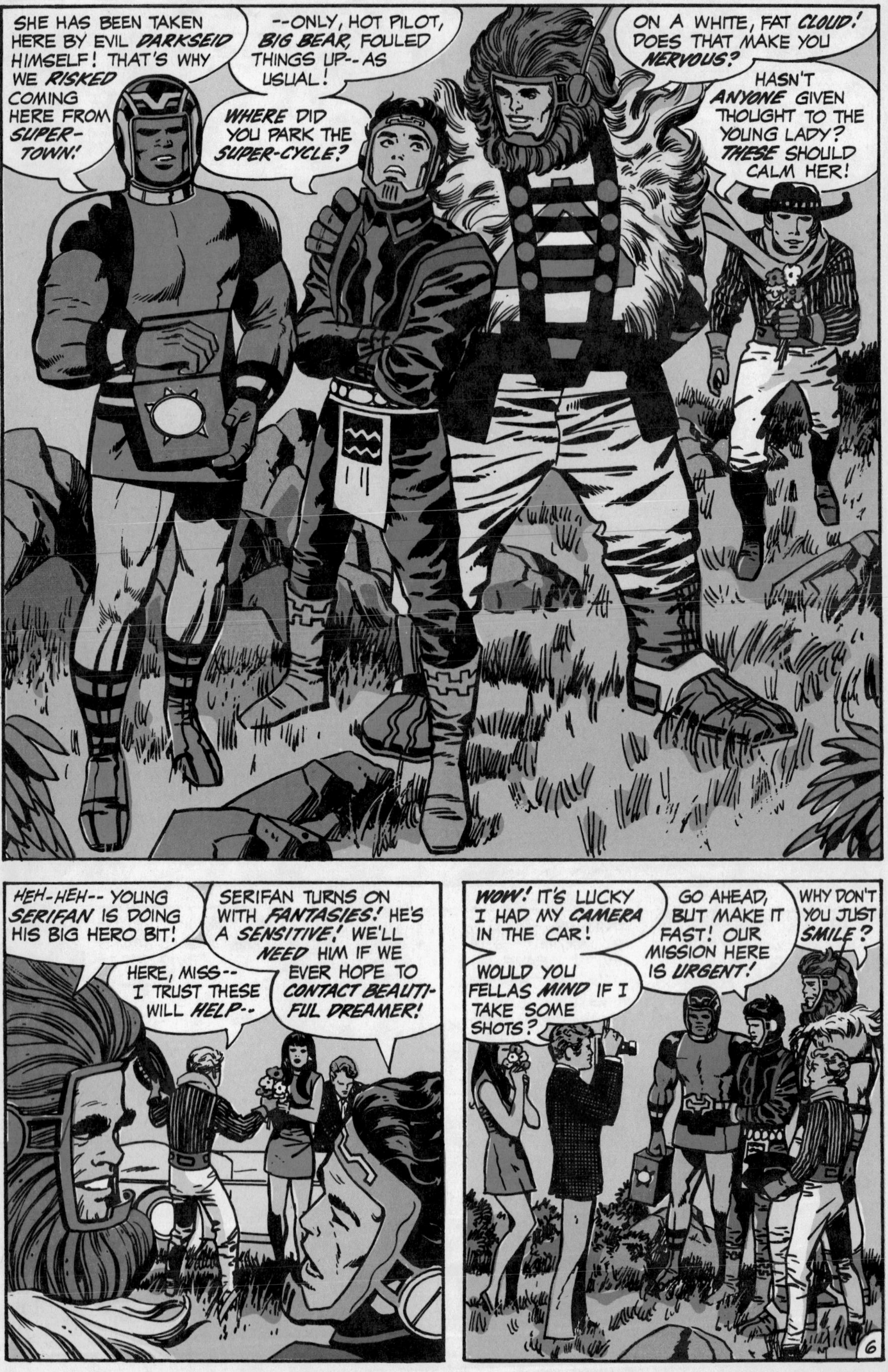
SHE HAS BEEN TAKEN HERE BY EVIL DARKSEID HIMSELF! THAT'S WHY WE RISKED COMING HERE FROM SUPER-TOWN!
--ONLY, HOT PILOT, BIG BEAR, FOULED THINGS UP-- AS USUAL!
WHERE DID YOU PARK THE SUPER-CYCLE?
ON A WHITE, FAT CLOUD! DOES THAT MAKE YOU NERVOUS?
HASN'T ANYONE GIVEN THOUGHT TO THE YOUNG LADY? THESE SHOULD CALM HER!
HEH-HEH-- YOUNG SERIFAN IS DOING HIS BIG HERO BIT!
SERIFAN TURNS ON WITH FANTASIES! HE'S A SENSITIVE! WE'LL NEED HIM IF WE EVER HOPE TO CONTACT BEAUTIFUL DREAMER!
HERE, MISS-- I TRUST THESE WILL HELP--
WOW! IT'S LUCKY I HAD MY CAMERA IN THE CAR!
WOULD YOU FELLAS MIND IF I TAKE SOME SHOTS?
GO AHEAD, BUT MAKE IT FAST! OUR MISSION HERE IS URGENT!
WHY DON'T YOU JUST SMILE?
6

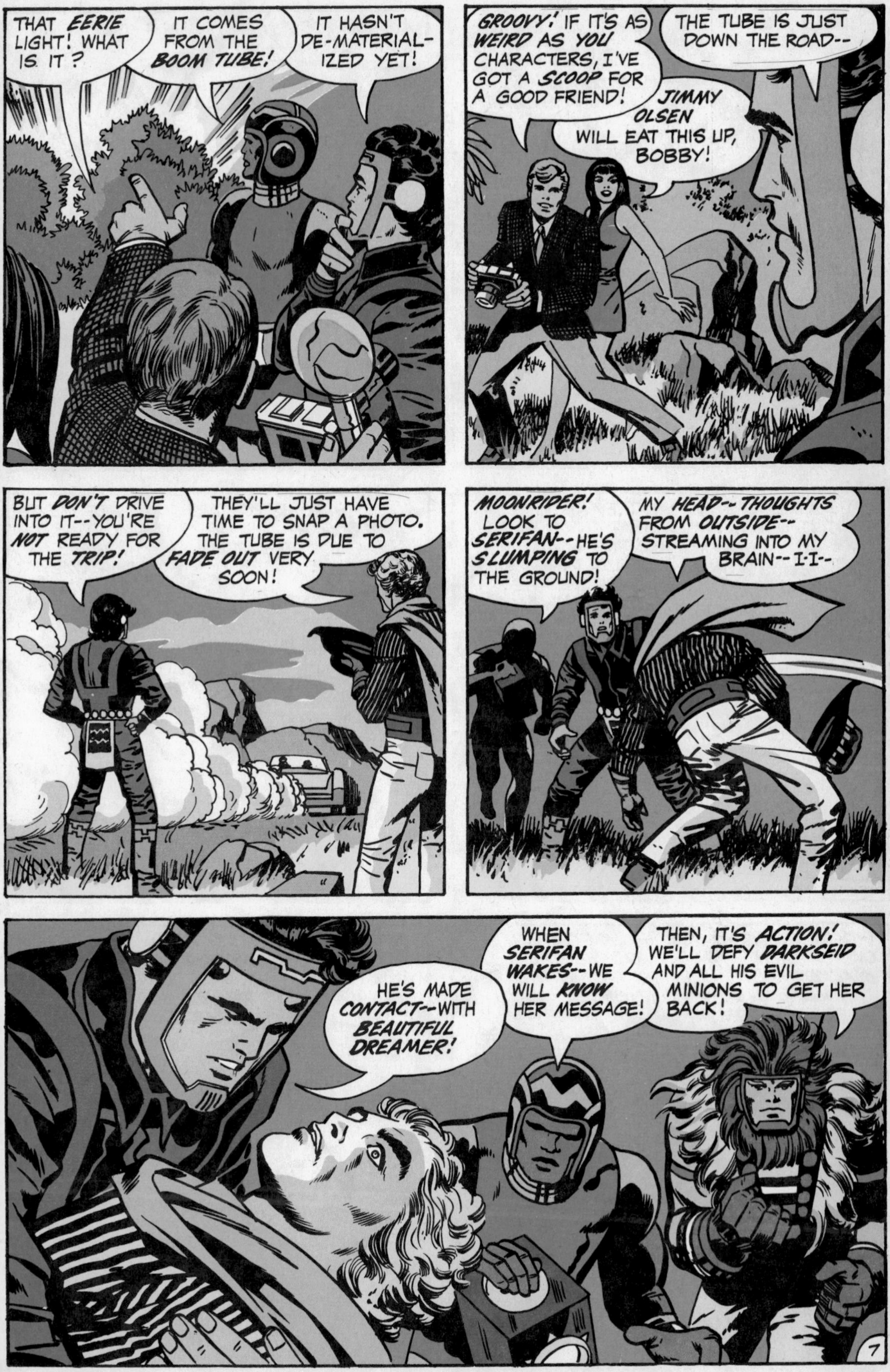
THAT EERIE LIGHT! WHAT IS IT?
IT COMES FROM THE BOOM TUBE!
IT HASN'T DE-MATERIALIZED YET!
GROOVY! IF IT'S AS WEIRD AS YOU CHARACTERS, I'VE GOT A SCOOP FOR A GOOD FRIEND!
THE TUBE IS JUST DOWN THE ROAD--
JIMMY OLSEN WILL EAT THIS UP, BOBBY!
BUT DON'T DRIVE INTO IT--YOU'RE NOT READY FOR THE TRIP!
THEY'LL JUST HAVE TIME TO SNAP A PHOTO. THE TUBE IS DUE TO FADE OUT VERY SOON!
MOONRIDER! LOOK TO SERIFAN--HE'S SLUMPING TO THE GROUND!
MY HEAD--THOUGHTS FROM OUTSIDE--STREAMING INTO MY BRAIN--I-I--
HE'S MADE CONTACT--WITH BEAUTIFUL DREAMER!
WHEN SERIFAN WAKES--WE WILL KNOW HER MESSAGE!
THEN, IT'S ACTION! WE'LL DEFY DARKSEID AND ALL HIS EVIL MINIONS TO GET HER BACK!
7

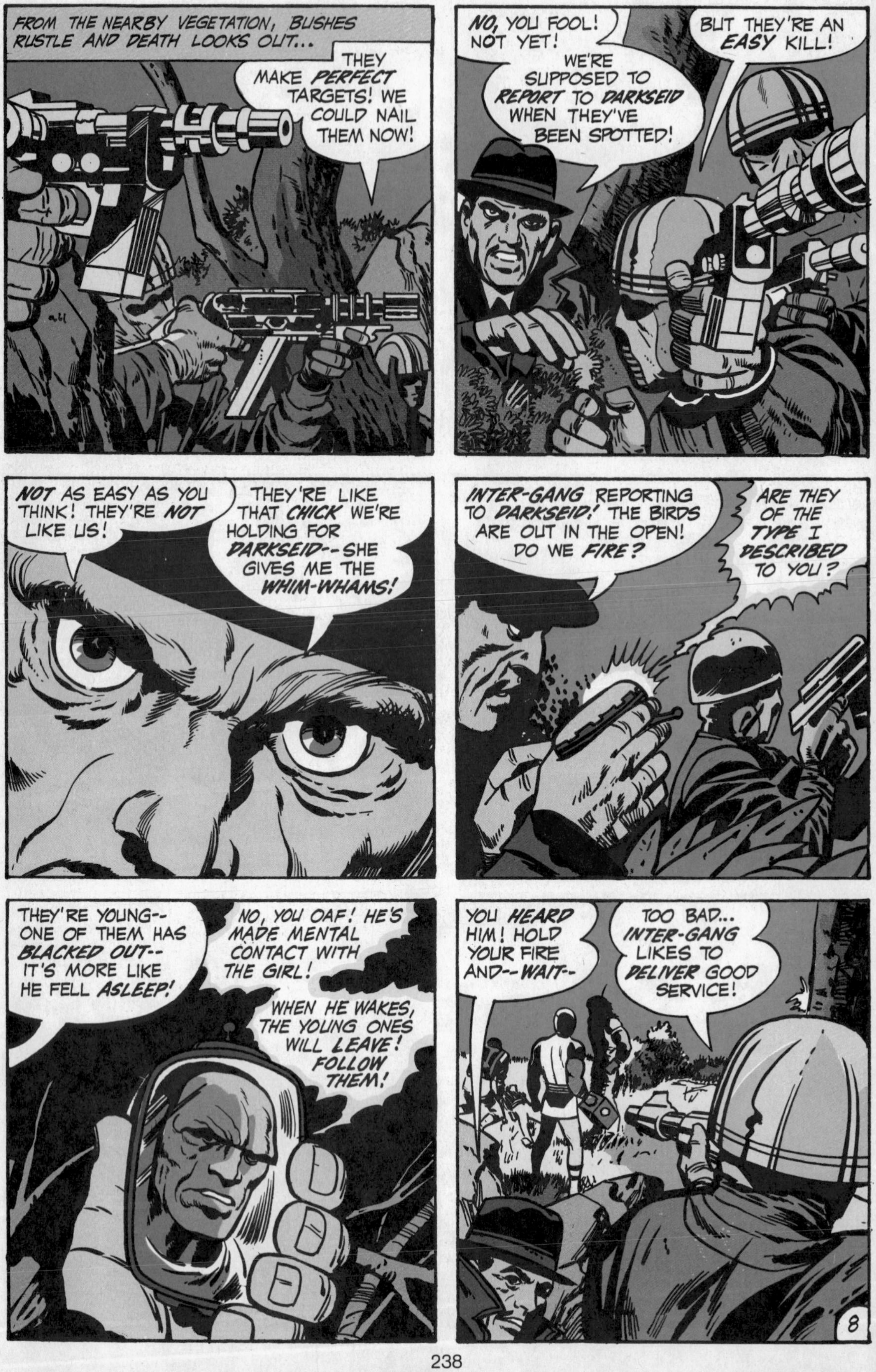
FROM THE NEARBY VEGETATION, BUSHES RUSTLE AND DEATH LOOKS OUT...
THEY MAKE PERFECT TARGETS! WE COULD NAIL THEM NOW!
NO, YOU FOOL! NOT YET!
WE'RE SUPPOSED TO REPORT TO DARKSEID WHEN THEY'VE BEEN SPOTTED!
BUT THEY'RE AN EASY KILL!
NOT AS EASY AS YOU THINK! THEY'RE NOT LIKE US!
THEY'RE LIKE THAT CHICK WE'RE HOLDING FOR DARKSEID-- SHE GIVES ME THE WHIM-WHAMS!
INTER-GANG REPORTING TO DARKSEID! THE BIRDS ARE OUT IN THE OPEN! DO WE FIRE?
ARE THEY OF THE TYPE I DESCRIBED TO YOU?
THEY'RE YOUNG-- ONE OF THEM HAS BLACKED OUT-- IT'S MORE LIKE HE FELL ASLEEP!
NO, YOU OAF! HE'S MADE MENTAL CONTACT WITH THE GIRL!
WHEN HE WAKES, THE YOUNG ONES WILL LEAVE! FOLLOW THEM!
YOU HEARD HIM! HOLD YOUR FIRE AND--WAIT--
TOO BAD... INTER-GANG LIKES TO DELIVER GOOD SERVICE!
8

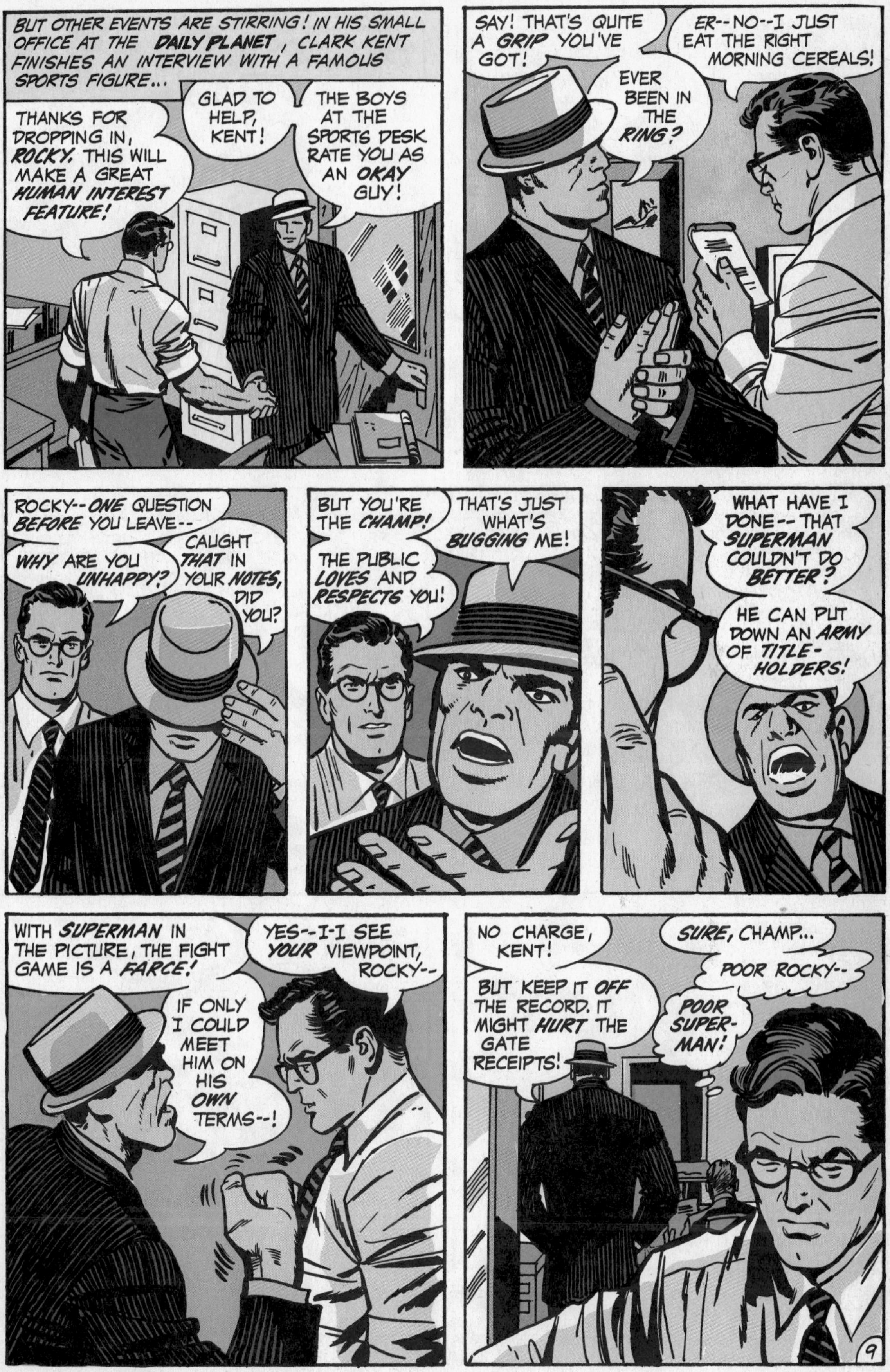
BUT OTHER EVENTS ARE STIRRING! IN HIS SMALL OFFICE AT THE DAILY PLANET, CLARK KENT FINISHES AN INTERVIEW WITH A FAMOUS SPORTS FIGURE...
THANKS FOR DROPPING IN, ROCKY. THIS WILL MAKE A GREAT HUMAN INTEREST FEATURE!
GLAD TO HELP, KENT!
THE BOYS AT THE SPORTS DESK RATE YOU AS AN OKAY GUY!
SAY! THAT'S QUITE A GRIP YOU'VE GOT!
EVER BEEN IN THE RING?
ER--NO--I JUST EAT THE RIGHT MORNING CEREALS!
ROCKY--ONE QUESTION BEFORE YOU LEAVE--
WHY ARE YOU UNHAPPY?
CAUGHT THAT IN YOUR NOTES, DID YOU?
BUT YOU'RE THE CHAMP!
THAT'S JUST WHAT'S BUGGING ME!
THE PUBLIC LOVES AND RESPECTS YOU!
WHAT HAVE I DONE--THAT SUPERMAN COULDN'T DO BETTER?
HE CAN PUT DOWN AN ARMY OF TITLE-HOLDERS!
WITH SUPERMAN IN THE PICTURE, THE FIGHT GAME IS A FARCE!
YES--I-I SEE YOUR VIEWPOINT, ROCKY--
IF ONLY I COULD MEET HIM ON HIS OWN TERMS--!
NO CHARGE, KENT!
BUT KEEP IT OFF THE RECORD. IT MIGHT HURT THE GATE RECEIPTS!
SURE, CHAMP...
POOR ROCKY--
POOR SUPER-MAN!
9

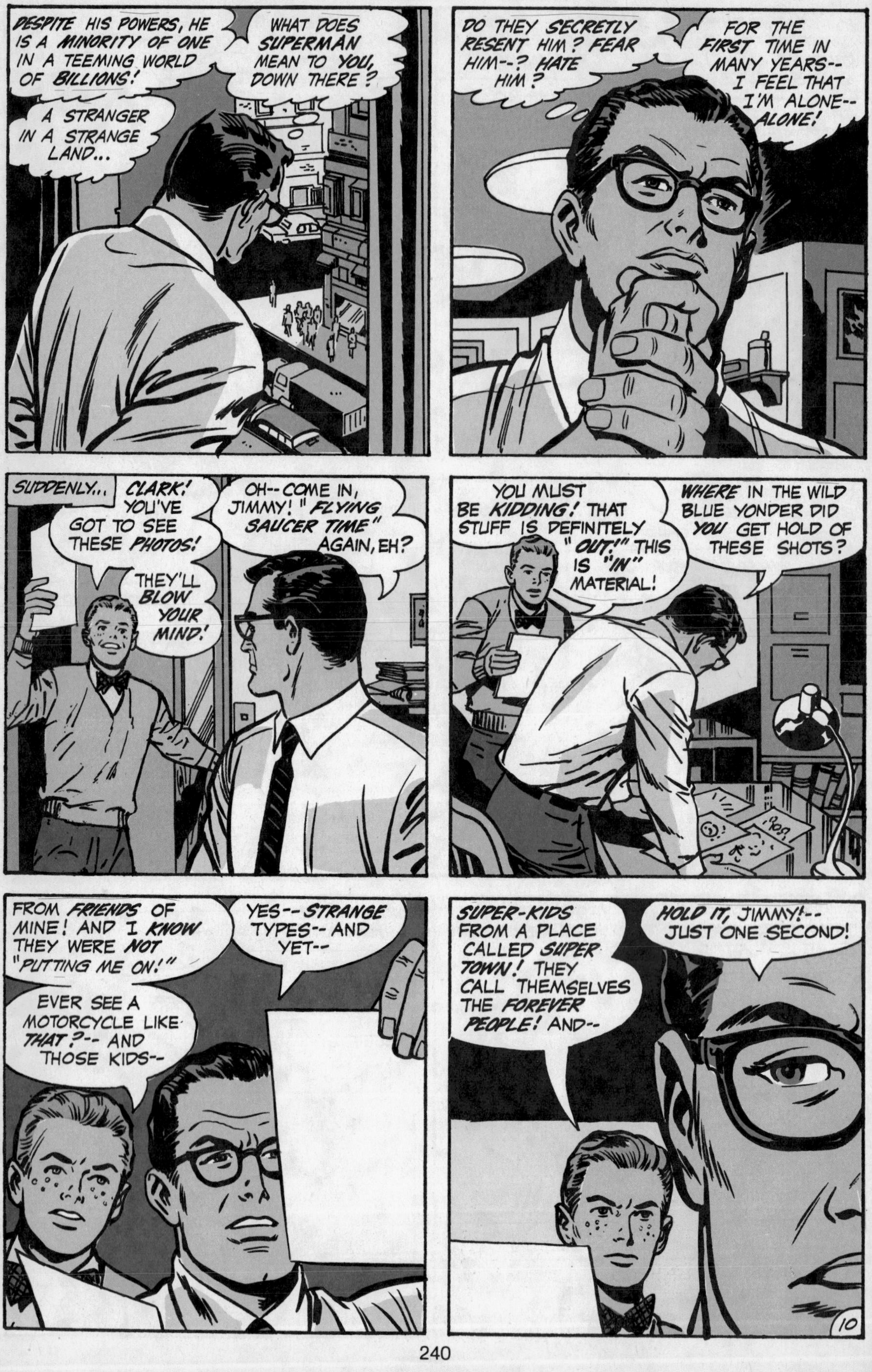

DESPITE HIS POWERS, HE IS A MINORITY OF ONE IN A TEEMING WORLD OF BILLIONS!
WHAT DOES SUPERMAN MEAN TO YOU, DOWN THERE?
A STRANGER IN A STRANGE LAND...
DO THEY SECRETLY RESENT HIM? FEAR HIM--? HATE HIM?
FOR THE FIRST TIME IN MANY YEARS-- I FEEL THAT I'M ALONE-- ALONE!
SUDDENLY...
CLARK! YOU'VE GOT TO SEE THESE PHOTOS!
THEY'LL BLOW YOUR MIND!
OH--COME IN, JIMMY! "FLYING SAUCER TIME" AGAIN, EH?
YOU MUST BE KIDDING! THAT STUFF IS DEFINITELY "OUT!" THIS IS "IN" MATERIAL!
WHERE IN THE WILD BLUE YONDER DID YOU GET HOLD OF THESE SHOTS?
FROM FRIENDS OF MINE! AND I KNOW THEY WERE NOT "PUTTING ME ON!"
EVER SEE A MOTORCYCLE LIKE THAT?-- AND THOSE KIDS--
YES--STRANGE TYPES-- AND YET--
SUPER-KIDS FROM A PLACE CALLED SUPER TOWN! THEY CALL THEMSELVES THE FOREVER PEOPLE! AND--
HOLD IT, JIMMY!-- JUST ONE SECOND!
10

SO YOU'RE GRABBED BY THE *BOOM TUBE,* HUH? ISN'T IT THE *WILDEST?*

MY FRIEND, BOBBY, SHOT THIS LAST FRAME AS IT WAS *FADING OUT!*

THERE IS SOMETHING--

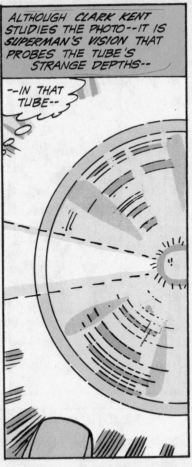

ALTHOUGH *CLARK KENT* STUDIES THE PHOTO--IT IS *SUPERMAN'S* VISION THAT PROBES THE TUBE'S STRANGE DEPTHS--

--IN THAT TUBE--

A TINY *MICRODOT* IN ITS *INFINITE* CENTER IS *ENLARGED* BY MILLIONS-- AND A *FANTASTIC* IMAGE IS REVEALED!

--AT THE OTHER END--GOOD LORD!

ISN'T THAT A *GAS?*

THAT'S HOW THE *SUPERKIDS* SAID THEY GOT HERE! THROUGH THAT *TUBE!*

--A CITY-- *SUPERTOWN* EXISTS!

JIMMY--NOW GIVE ME THIS *ENTIRE STORY--* STEP BY STEP--

--FROM THE BEGINNING!

YOU BET! EVEN AS A *LIE*--THIS YARN WOULD BE A *WHOPPER!*

AS *CLARK KENT* LISTENS-- IT IS *SUPERMAN* WHO DARES TO DREAM--AND HOPE--

NOW GET THIS--BOBBY AND LAURIE HAD THIS DATE, SEE?...

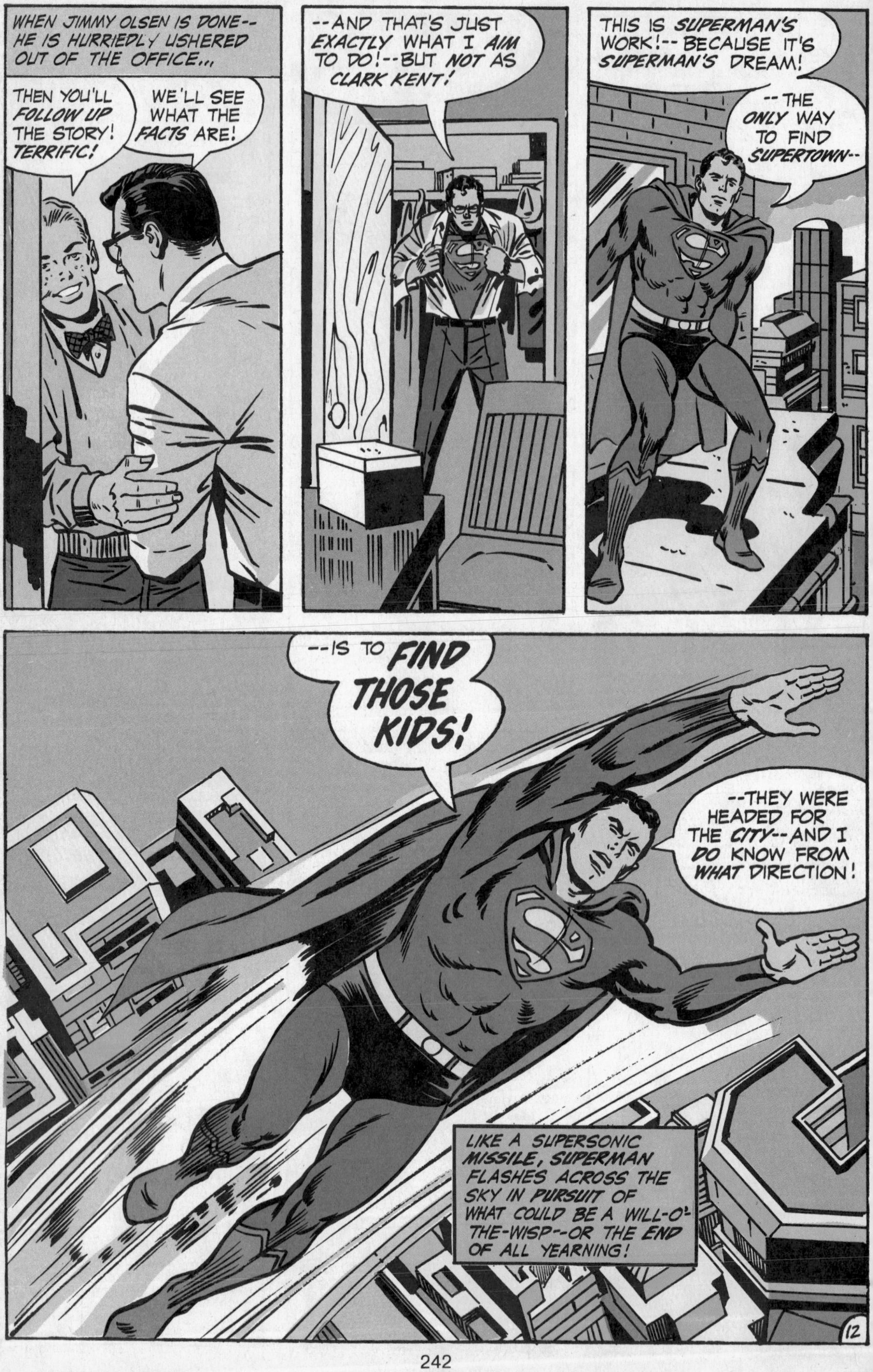
WHEN JIMMY OLSEN IS DONE--HE IS HURRIEDLY USHERED OUT OF THE OFFICE...
THEN YOU'LL FOLLOW UP THE STORY! TERRIFIC!
WE'LL SEE WHAT THE FACTS ARE!
--AND THAT'S JUST EXACTLY WHAT I AIM TO DO!--BUT NOT AS CLARK KENT!
THIS IS SUPERMAN'S WORK!--BECAUSE IT'S SUPERMAN'S DREAM!
--THE ONLY WAY TO FIND SUPERTOWN--
--IS TO FIND THOSE KIDS!
--THEY WERE HEADED FOR THE CITY--AND I DO KNOW FROM WHAT DIRECTION!
LIKE A SUPERSONIC MISSILE, SUPERMAN FLASHES ACROSS THE SKY IN PURSUIT OF WHAT COULD BE A WILL-O'-THE-WISP--OR THE END OF ALL YEARNING!
12

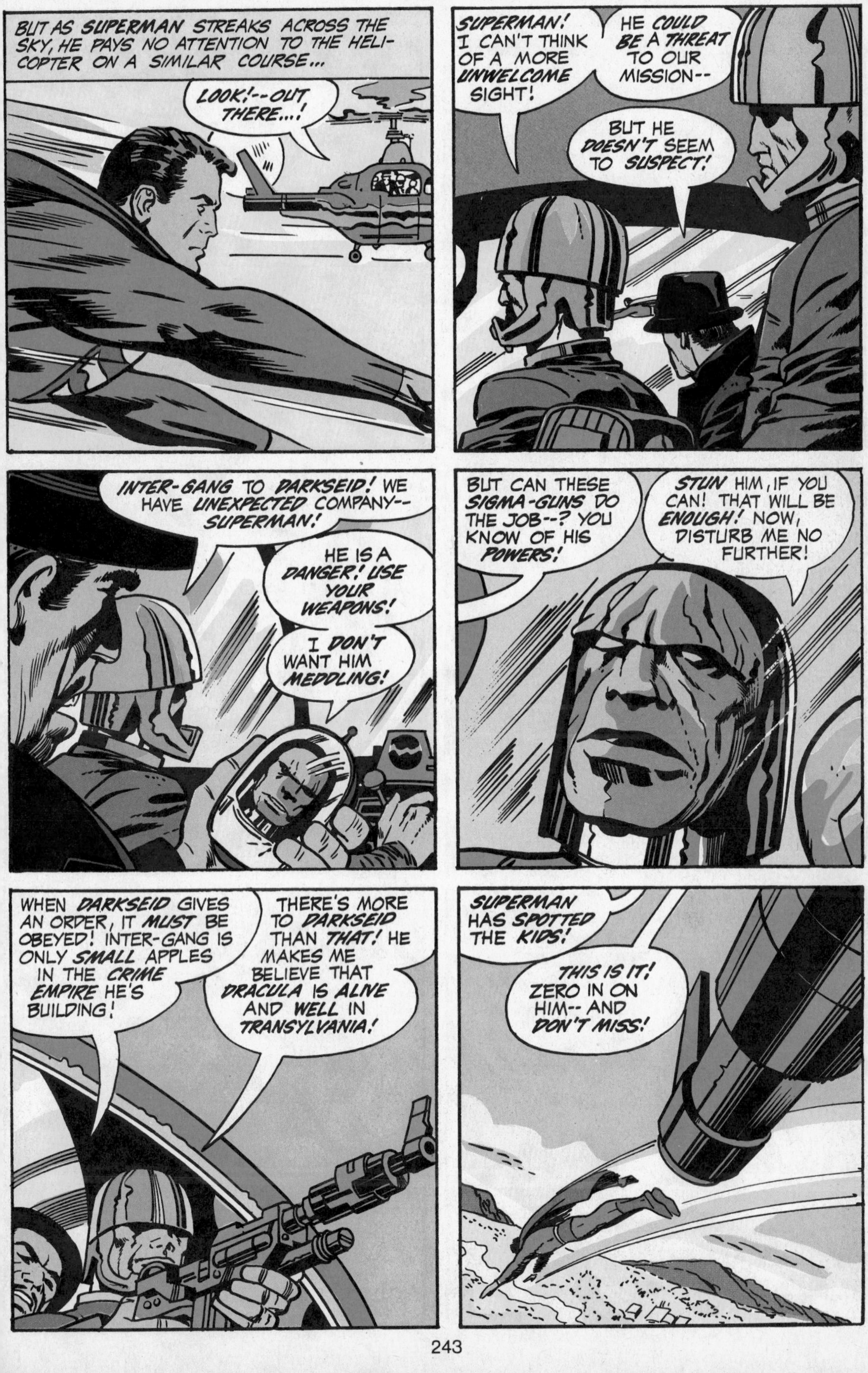

BUT AS SUPERMAN STREAKS ACROSS THE SKY, HE PAYS NO ATTENTION TO THE HELICOPTER ON A SIMILAR COURSE...
LOOK!--OUT THERE...!
SUPERMAN! I CAN'T THINK OF A MORE UNWELCOME SIGHT!
HE COULD BE A THREAT TO OUR MISSION--
BUT HE DOESN'T SEEM TO SUSPECT!
INTER-GANG TO DARKSEID! WE HAVE UNEXPECTED COMPANY--SUPERMAN!
HE IS A DANGER! USE YOUR WEAPONS!
I DON'T WANT HIM MEDDLING!
BUT CAN THESE SIGMA-GUNS DO THE JOB--? YOU KNOW OF HIS POWERS!
STUN HIM, IF YOU CAN! THAT WILL BE ENOUGH! NOW, DISTURB ME NO FURTHER!
WHEN DARKSEID GIVES AN ORDER, IT MUST BE OBEYED! INTER-GANG IS ONLY SMALL APPLES IN THE CRIME EMPIRE HE'S BUILDING!
THERE'S MORE TO DARKSEID THAN THAT! HE MAKES ME BELIEVE THAT DRACULA IS ALIVE AND WELL IN TRANSYLVANIA!
SUPERMAN HAS SPOTTED THE KIDS!
THIS IS IT! ZERO IN ON HIM-- AND DON'T MISS!

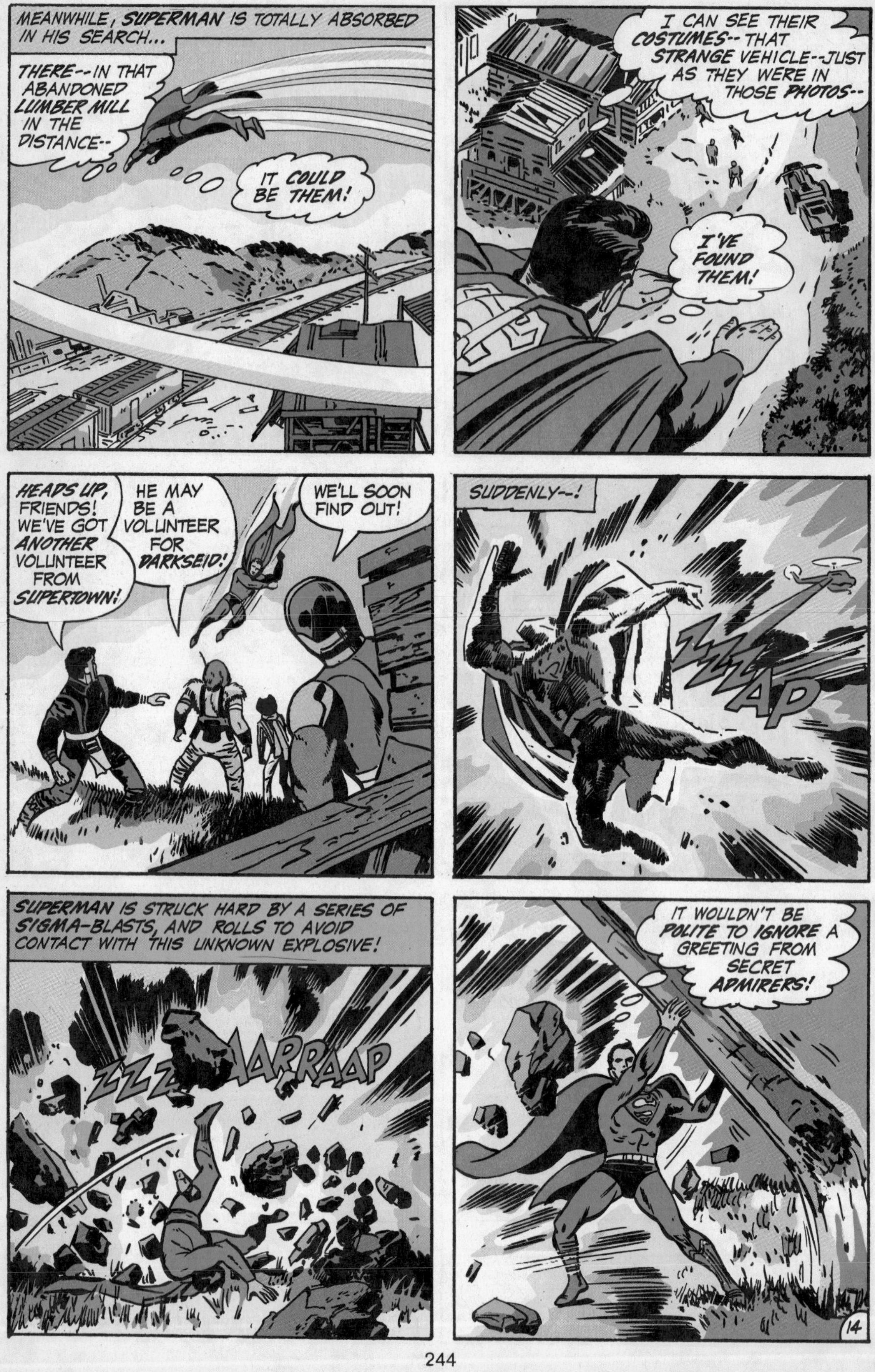

MEANWHILE, SUPERMAN IS TOTALLY ABSORBED IN HIS SEARCH...
THERE--IN THAT ABANDONED LUMBER MILL IN THE DISTANCE--
IT COULD BE THEM!
I CAN SEE THEIR COSTUMES-- THAT STRANGE VEHICLE--JUST AS THEY WERE IN THOSE PHOTOS--
I'VE FOUND THEM!
HEADS UP, FRIENDS! WE'VE GOT ANOTHER VOLUNTEER FROM SUPERTOWN!
HE MAY BE A VOLUNTEER FOR DARKSEID!
WE'LL SOON FIND OUT!
SUDDENLY--!
ZZZAP
SUPERMAN IS STRUCK HARD BY A SERIES OF SIGMA-BLASTS, AND ROLLS TO AVOID CONTACT WITH THIS UNKNOWN EXPLOSIVE!
ZZZAARRAAP
IT WOULDN'T BE POLITE TO IGNORE A GREETING FROM SECRET ADMIRERS!
14

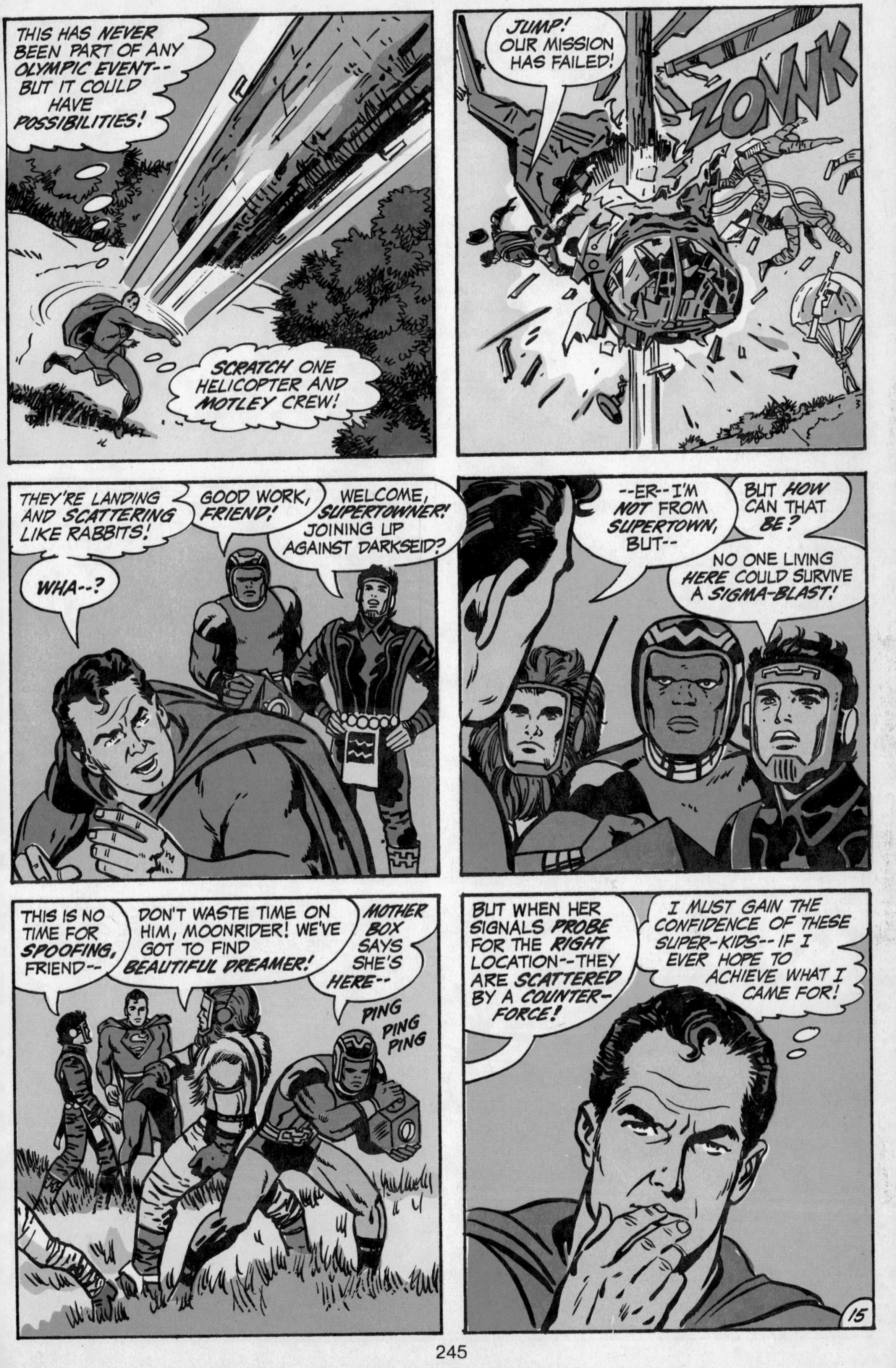
THIS HAS NEVER BEEN PART OF ANY OLYMPIC EVENT-- BUT IT COULD HAVE POSSIBILITIES!
SCRATCH ONE HELICOPTER AND MOTLEY CREW!
JUMP! OUR MISSION HAS FAILED!
ZOWWK
THEY'RE LANDING AND SCATTERING LIKE RABBITS!
GOOD WORK, FRIEND!
WELCOME, SUPERTOWNER! JOINING UP AGAINST DARKSEID?
WHA--?
--ER--I'M NOT FROM SUPERTOWN, BUT--
BUT HOW CAN THAT BE?
NO ONE LIVING HERE COULD SURVIVE A SIGMA-BLAST!
THIS IS NO TIME FOR SPOOFING, FRIEND--
DON'T WASTE TIME ON HIM, MOONRIDER! WE'VE GOT TO FIND BEAUTIFUL DREAMER!
MOTHER BOX SAYS SHE'S HERE--
PING
PING
PING
BUT WHEN HER SIGNALS PROBE FOR THE RIGHT LOCATION--THEY ARE SCATTERED BY A COUNTER-FORCE!
I MUST GAIN THE CONFIDENCE OF THESE SUPER-KIDS-- IF I EVER HOPE TO ACHIEVE WHAT I CAME FOR!
15

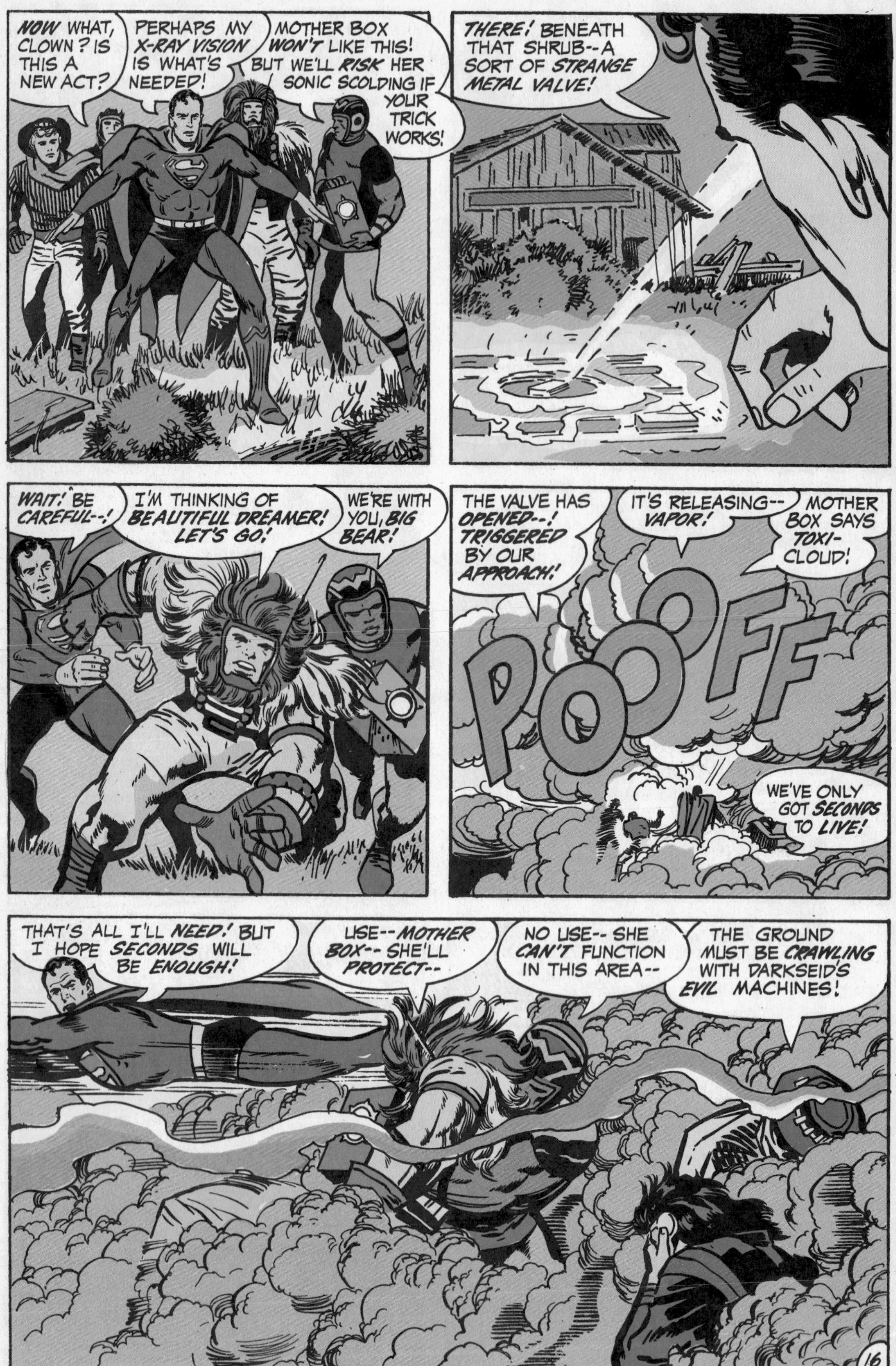

NOW WHAT, CLOWN? IS THIS A NEW ACT?
PERHAPS MY X-RAY VISION IS WHAT'S NEEDED!
MOTHER BOX WON'T LIKE THIS! BUT WE'LL RISK HER SONIC SCOLDING IF YOUR TRICK WORKS!
THERE! BENEATH THAT SHRUB--A SORT OF STRANGE METAL VALVE!
WAIT! BE CAREFUL--!
I'M THINKING OF BEAUTIFUL DREAMER! LET'S GO!
WE'RE WITH YOU, BIG BEAR!
THE VALVE HAS OPENED--! TRIGGERED BY OUR APPROACH!
IT'S RELEASING-- VAPOR!
MOTHER BOX SAYS TOXI-CLOUD!
POOOFF
WE'VE ONLY GOT SECONDS TO LIVE!
THAT'S ALL I'LL NEED! BUT I HOPE SECONDS WILL BE ENOUGH!
USE--MOTHER BOX-- SHE'LL PROTECT--
NO USE-- SHE CAN'T FUNCTION IN THIS AREA--
THE GROUND MUST BE CRAWLING WITH DARKSEID'S EVIL MACHINES!
16

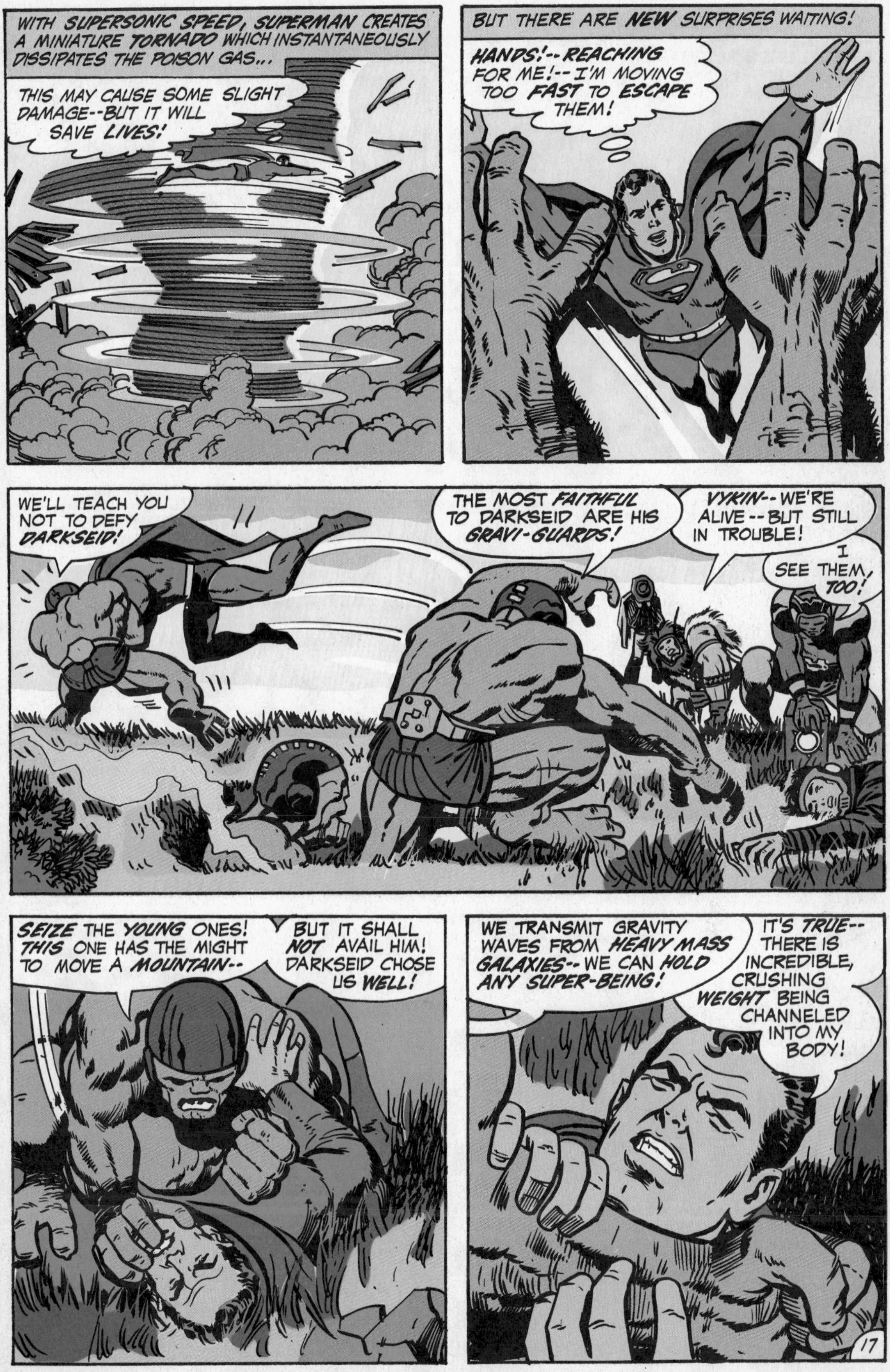
WITH SUPERSONIC SPEED, SUPERMAN CREATES A MINIATURE TORNADO WHICH INSTANTANEOUSLY DISSIPATES THE POISON GAS...
THIS MAY CAUSE SOME SLIGHT DAMAGE--BUT IT WILL SAVE LIVES!
BUT THERE ARE NEW SURPRISES WAITING!
HANDS!--REACHING FOR ME!--I'M MOVING TOO FAST TO ESCAPE THEM!
WE'LL TEACH YOU NOT TO DEFY DARKSEID!
THE MOST FAITHFUL TO DARKSEID ARE HIS GRAVI-GUARDS!
VYKIN--WE'RE ALIVE--BUT STILL IN TROUBLE!
I SEE THEM, TOO!
SEIZE THE YOUNG ONES! THIS ONE HAS THE MIGHT TO MOVE A MOUNTAIN--
BUT IT SHALL NOT AVAIL HIM! DARKSEID CHOSE US WELL!
WE TRANSMIT GRAVITY WAVES FROM HEAVY MASS GALAXIES--WE CAN HOLD ANY SUPER-BEING!
IT'S TRUE--THERE IS INCREDIBLE, CRUSHING WEIGHT BEING CHANNELED INTO MY BODY!
17

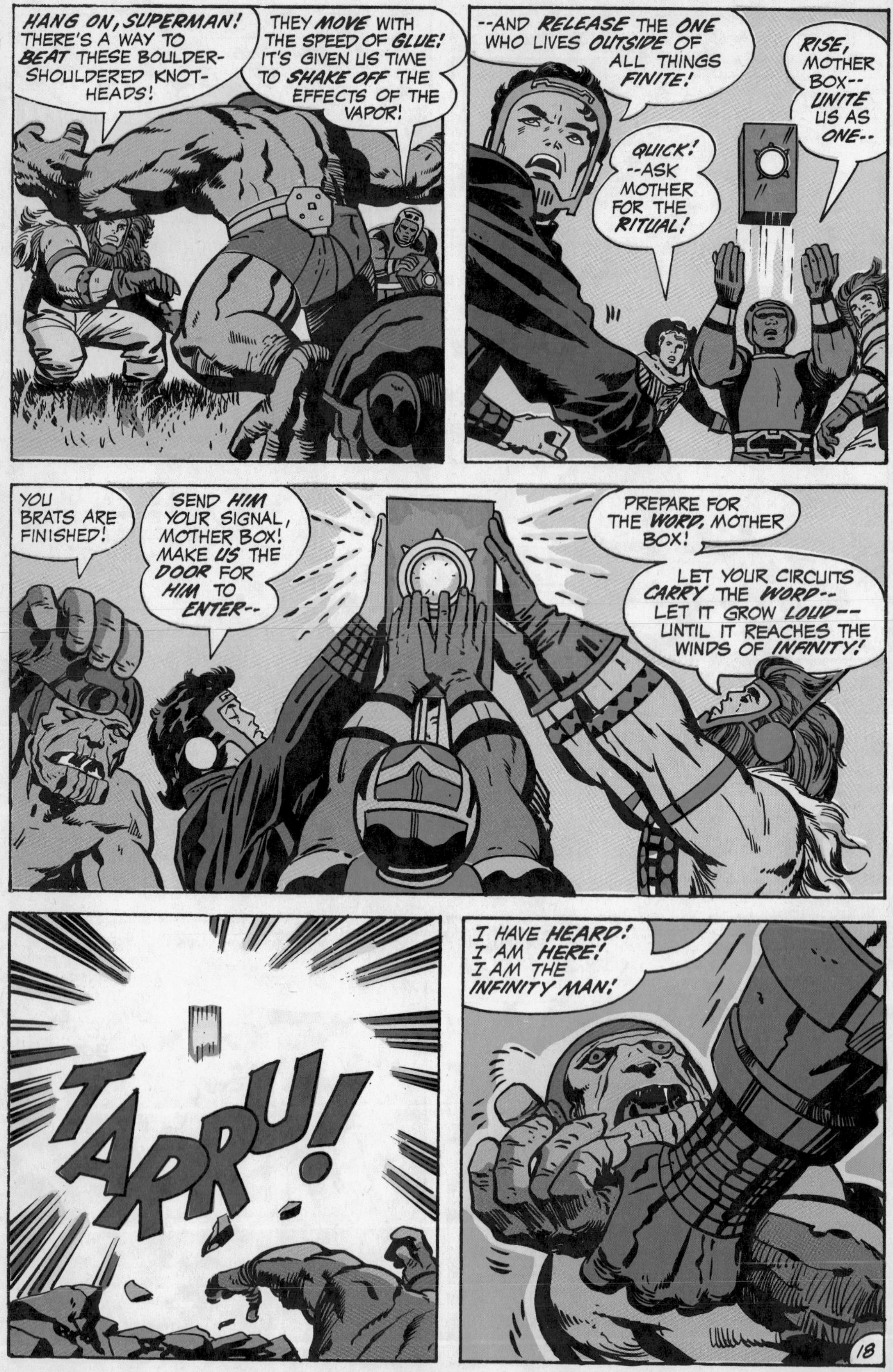
HANG ON, SUPERMAN! THERE'S A WAY TO BEAT THESE BOULDER-SHOULDERED KNOT-HEADS!
THEY MOVE WITH THE SPEED OF GLUE! IT'S GIVEN US TIME TO SHAKE OFF THE EFFECTS OF THE VAPOR!
--AND RELEASE THE ONE WHO LIVES OUTSIDE OF ALL THINGS FINITE!
QUICK! --ASK MOTHER FOR THE RITUAL!
RISE, MOTHER BOX-- UNITE US AS ONE--
YOU BRATS ARE FINISHED!
SEND HIM YOUR SIGNAL, MOTHER BOX! MAKE US THE DOOR FOR HIM TO ENTER--
PREPARE FOR THE WORD, MOTHER BOX!
LET YOUR CIRCUITS CARRY THE WORD-- LET IT GROW LOUD-- UNTIL IT REACHES THE WINDS OF INFINITY!
TARRU!
I HAVE HEARD! I AM HERE! I AM THE INFINITY MAN!
18

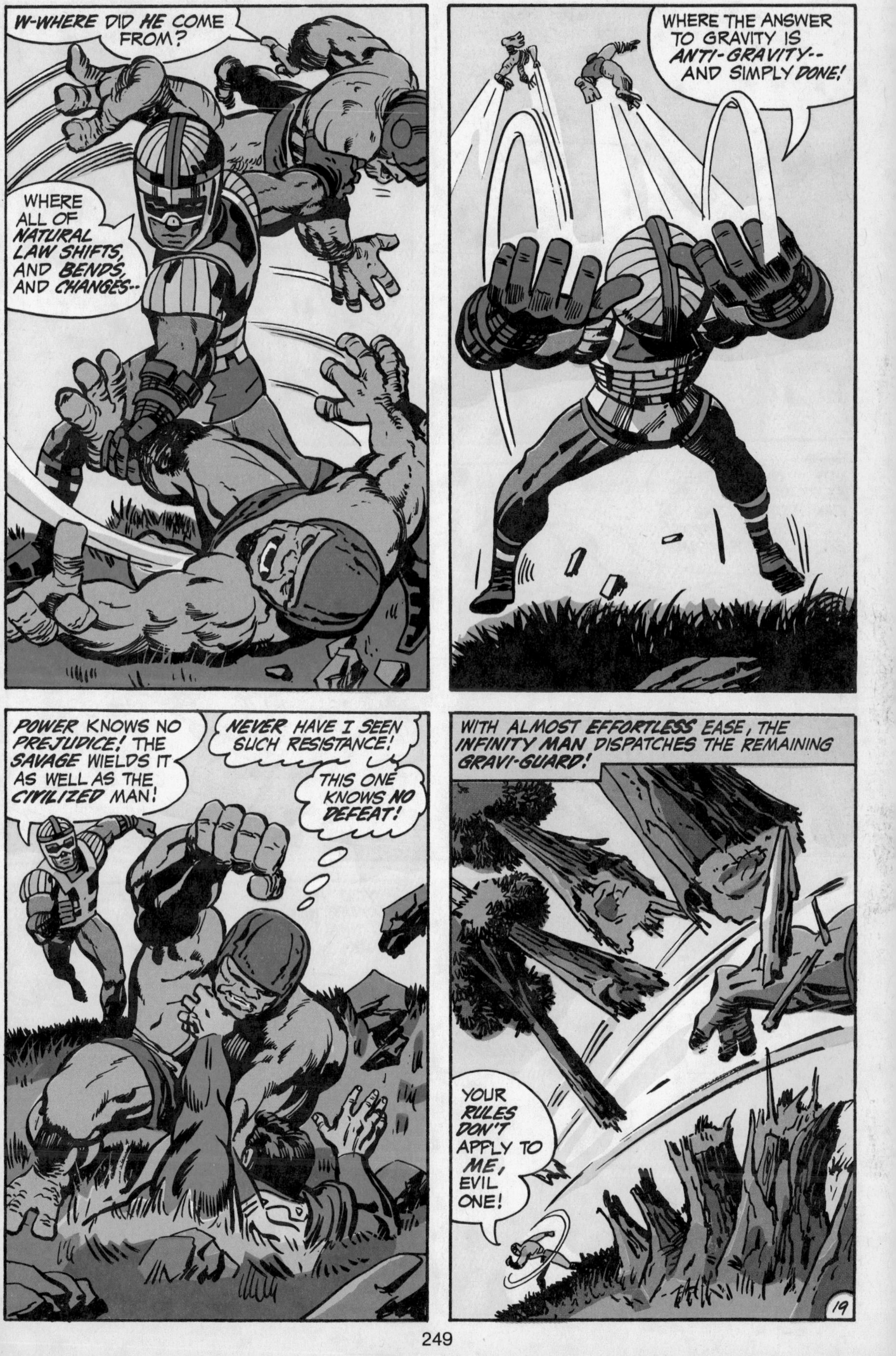
W-WHERE DID HE COME FROM?
WHERE ALL OF NATURAL LAW SHIFTS, AND BENDS, AND CHANGES--
WHERE THE ANSWER TO GRAVITY IS ANTI-GRAVITY-- AND SIMPLY DONE!
POWER KNOWS NO PREJUDICE! THE SAVAGE WIELDS IT AS WELL AS THE CIVILIZED MAN!
NEVER HAVE I SEEN SUCH RESISTANCE!
THIS ONE KNOWS NO DEFEAT!
WITH ALMOST EFFORTLESS EASE, THE INFINITY MAN DISPATCHES THE REMAINING GRAVI-GUARD!
YOUR RULES DON'T APPLY TO ME, EVIL ONE!
19

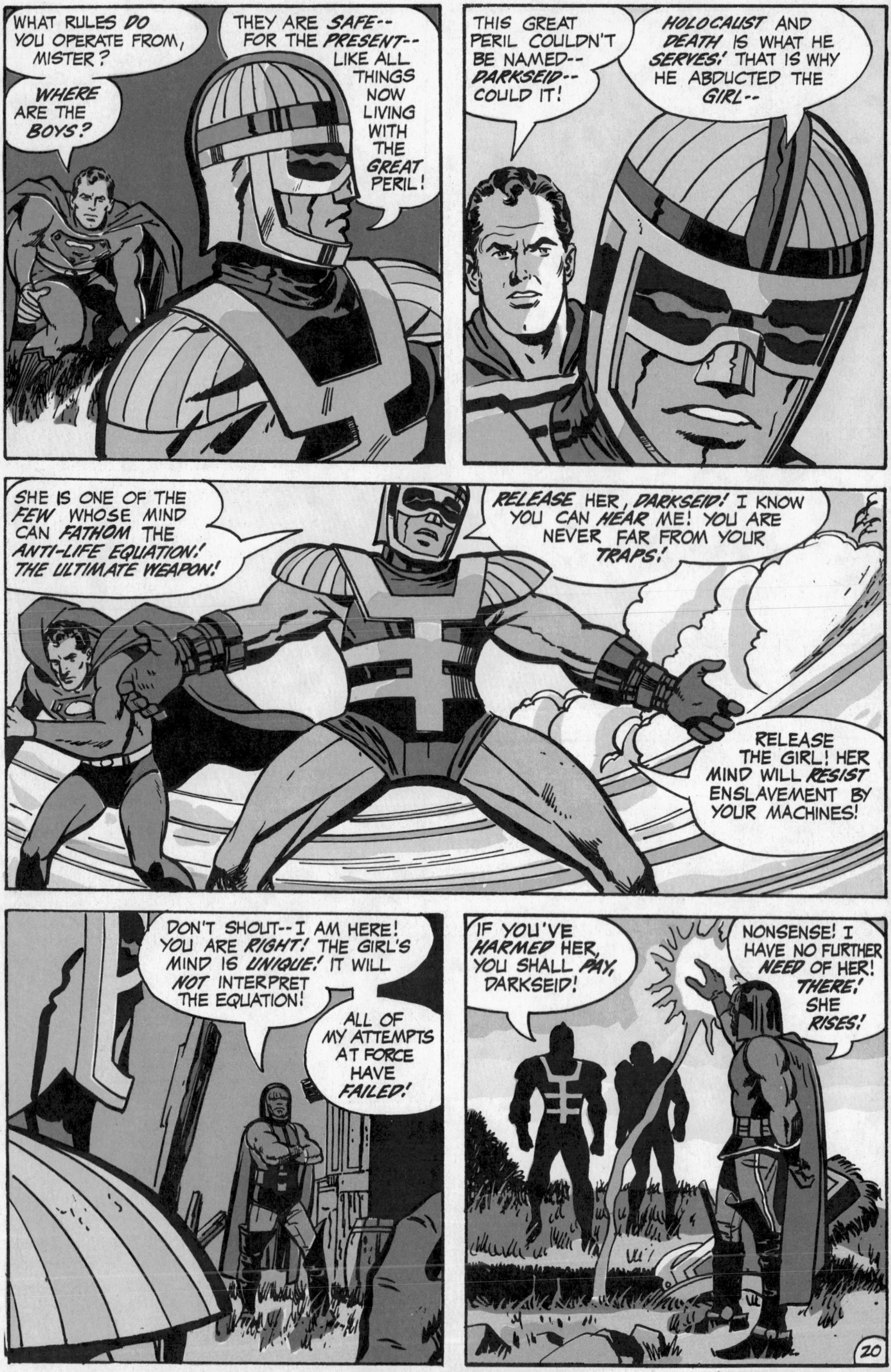
WHAT RULES DO YOU OPERATE FROM, MISTER?
WHERE ARE THE BOYS?
THEY ARE SAFE-- FOR THE PRESENT-- LIKE ALL THINGS NOW LIVING WITH THE GREAT PERIL!
THIS GREAT PERIL COULDN'T BE NAMED-- DARKSEID-- COULD IT!
HOLOCAUST AND DEATH IS WHAT HE SERVES! THAT IS WHY HE ABDUCTED THE GIRL--
SHE IS ONE OF THE FEW WHOSE MIND CAN FATHOM THE ANTI-LIFE EQUATION! THE ULTIMATE WEAPON!
RELEASE HER, DARKSEID! I KNOW YOU CAN HEAR ME! YOU ARE NEVER FAR FROM YOUR TRAPS!
RELEASE THE GIRL! HER MIND WILL RESIST ENSLAVEMENT BY YOUR MACHINES!
DON'T SHOUT--I AM HERE! YOU ARE RIGHT! THE GIRL'S MIND IS UNIQUE! IT WILL NOT INTERPRET THE EQUATION!
ALL OF MY ATTEMPTS AT FORCE HAVE FAILED!
IF YOU'VE HARMED HER, YOU SHALL PAY, DARKSEID!
NONSENSE! I HAVE NO FURTHER NEED OF HER! THERE! SHE RISES!
20

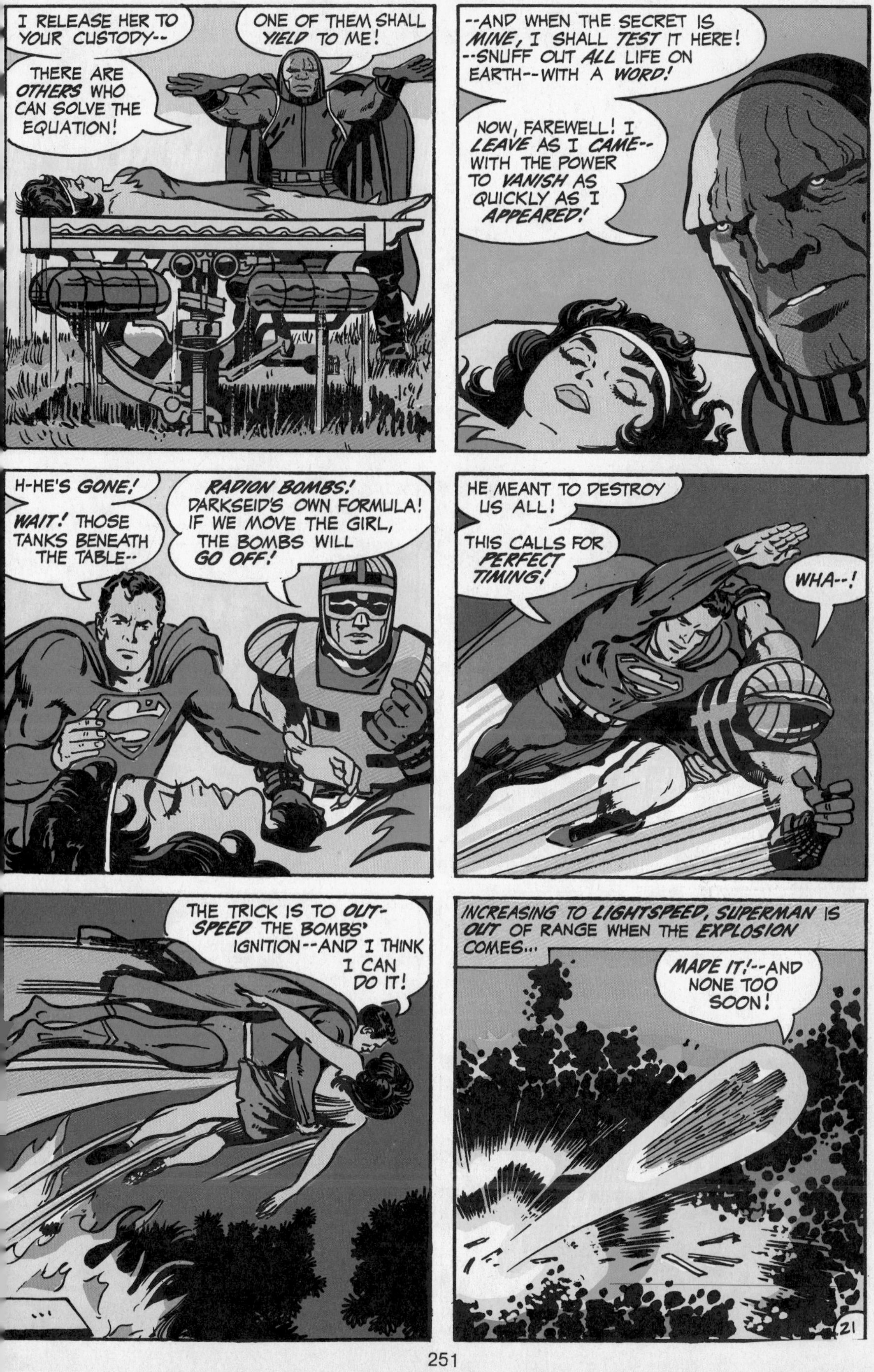
I RELEASE HER TO YOUR CUSTODY--
THERE ARE OTHERS WHO CAN SOLVE THE EQUATION!
ONE OF THEM SHALL YIELD TO ME!
--AND WHEN THE SECRET IS MINE, I SHALL TEST IT HERE! --SNUFF OUT ALL LIFE ON EARTH--WITH A WORD!
NOW, FAREWELL! I LEAVE AS I CAME-- WITH THE POWER TO VANISH AS QUICKLY AS I APPEARED!
H-HE'S GONE!
WAIT! THOSE TANKS BENEATH THE TABLE--
RADION BOMBS! DARKSEID'S OWN FORMULA! IF WE MOVE THE GIRL, THE BOMBS WILL GO OFF!
HE MEANT TO DESTROY US ALL!
THIS CALLS FOR PERFECT TIMING!
WHA--!
THE TRICK IS TO OUT-SPEED THE BOMBS' IGNITION--AND I THINK I CAN DO IT!
...
INCREASING TO LIGHTSPEED, SUPERMAN IS OUT OF RANGE WHEN THE EXPLOSION COMES...
MADE IT!--AND NONE TOO SOON!
21

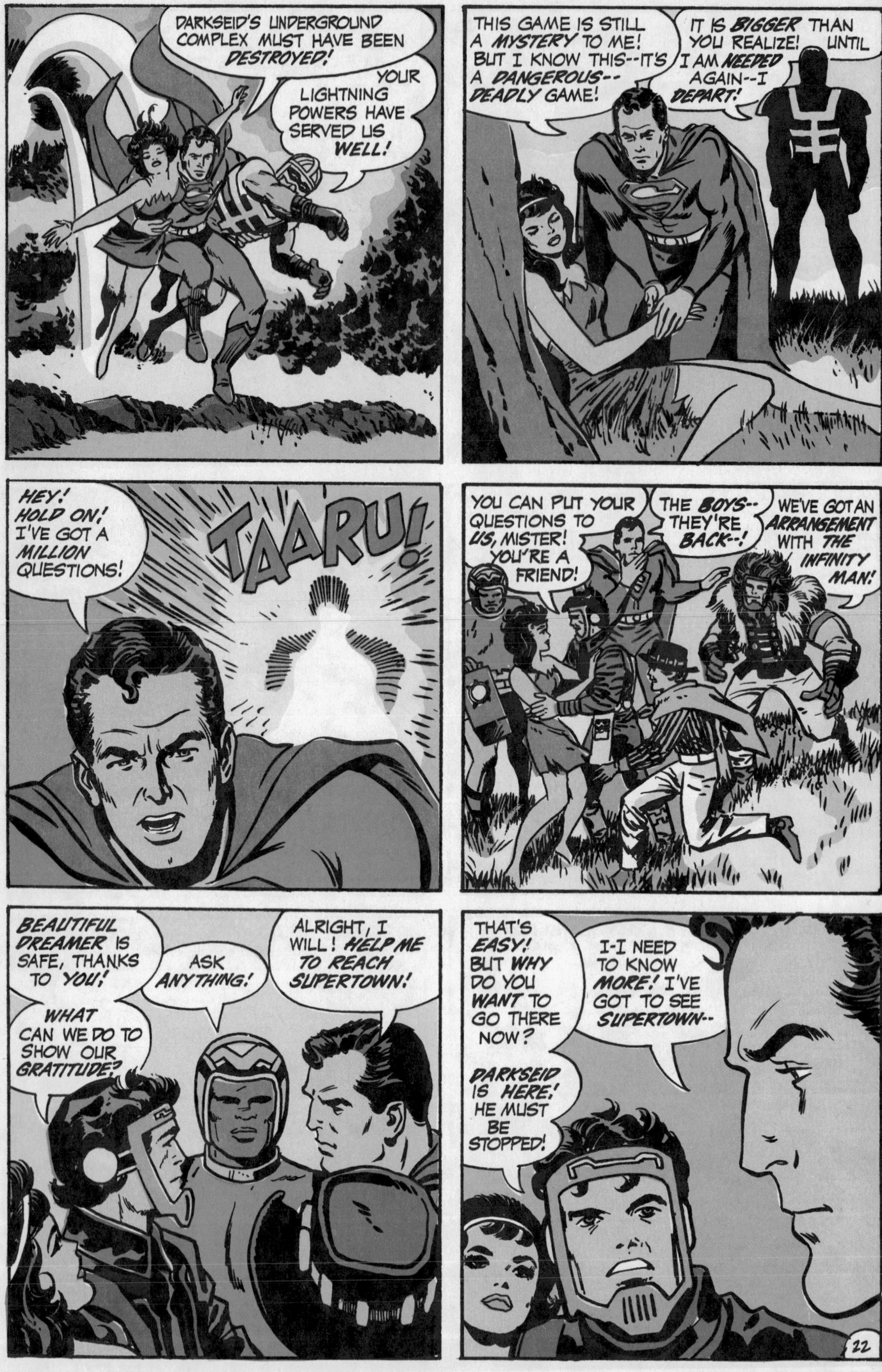
DARKSEID'S UNDERGROUND COMPLEX MUST HAVE BEEN DESTROYED!
YOUR LIGHTNING POWERS HAVE SERVED US WELL!
THIS GAME IS STILL A MYSTERY TO ME! BUT I KNOW THIS--IT'S A DANGEROUS--DEADLY GAME!
IT IS BIGGER THAN YOU REALIZE! UNTIL I AM NEEDED AGAIN--I DEPART!
HEY! HOLD ON! I'VE GOT A MILLION QUESTIONS!
TAARU!
YOU CAN PUT YOUR QUESTIONS TO US, MISTER! YOU'RE A FRIEND!
THE BOYS--THEY'RE BACK--!
WE'VE GOT AN ARRANGEMENT WITH THE INFINITY MAN!
BEAUTIFUL DREAMER IS SAFE, THANKS TO YOU!
WHAT CAN WE DO TO SHOW OUR GRATITUDE?
ASK ANYTHING!
ALRIGHT, I WILL! HELP ME TO REACH SUPERTOWN!
THAT'S EASY! BUT WHY DO YOU WANT TO GO THERE NOW?
DARKSEID IS HERE! HE MUST BE STOPPED!
I-I NEED TO KNOW MORE! I'VE GOT TO SEE SUPERTOWN--
22

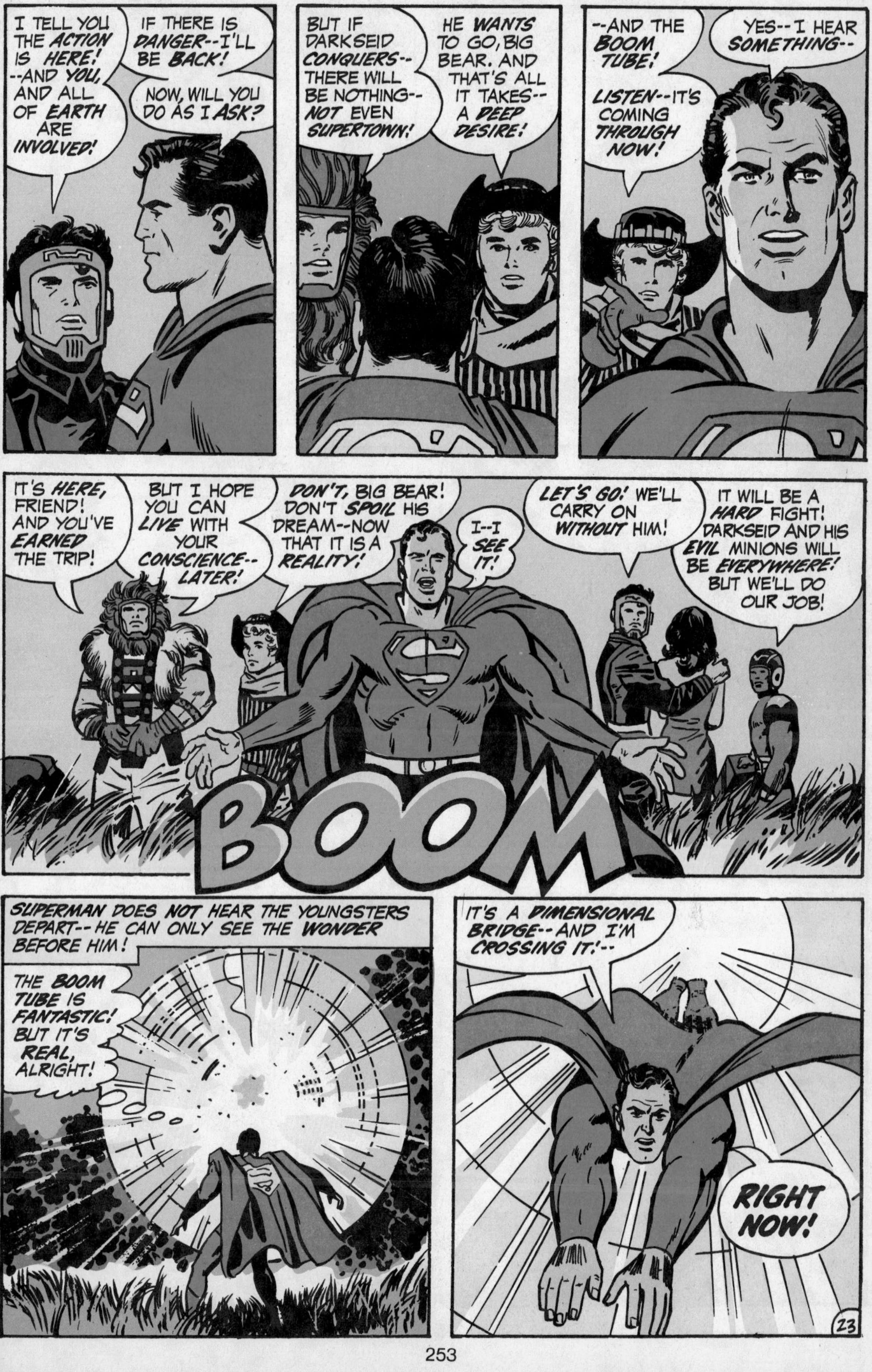
I TELL YOU THE ACTION IS HERE! --AND YOU, AND ALL OF EARTH ARE INVOLVED!
IF THERE IS DANGER--I'LL BE BACK!
NOW, WILL YOU DO AS I ASK?
BUT IF DARKSEID CONQUERS--THERE WILL BE NOTHING--NOT EVEN SUPERTOWN!
HE WANTS TO GO, BIG BEAR. AND THAT'S ALL IT TAKES--A DEEP DESIRE!
--AND THE BOOM TUBE!
YES--I HEAR SOMETHING--
LISTEN--IT'S COMING THROUGH NOW!
IT'S HERE, FRIEND! AND YOU'VE EARNED THE TRIP!
BUT I HOPE YOU CAN LIVE WITH YOUR CONSCIENCE--LATER!
DON'T, BIG BEAR! DON'T SPOIL HIS DREAM--NOW THAT IT IS A REALITY!
I--I SEE IT!
LET'S GO! WE'LL CARRY ON WITHOUT HIM!
IT WILL BE A HARD FIGHT! DARKSEID AND HIS EVIL MINIONS WILL BE EVERYWHERE! BUT WE'LL DO OUR JOB!
BOOM
SUPERMAN DOES NOT HEAR THE YOUNGSTERS DEPART--HE CAN ONLY SEE THE WONDER BEFORE HIM!
THE BOOM TUBE IS FANTASTIC! BUT IT'S REAL, ALRIGHT!
IT'S A DIMENSIONAL BRIDGE--AND I'M CROSSING IT!--
RIGHT NOW!
23

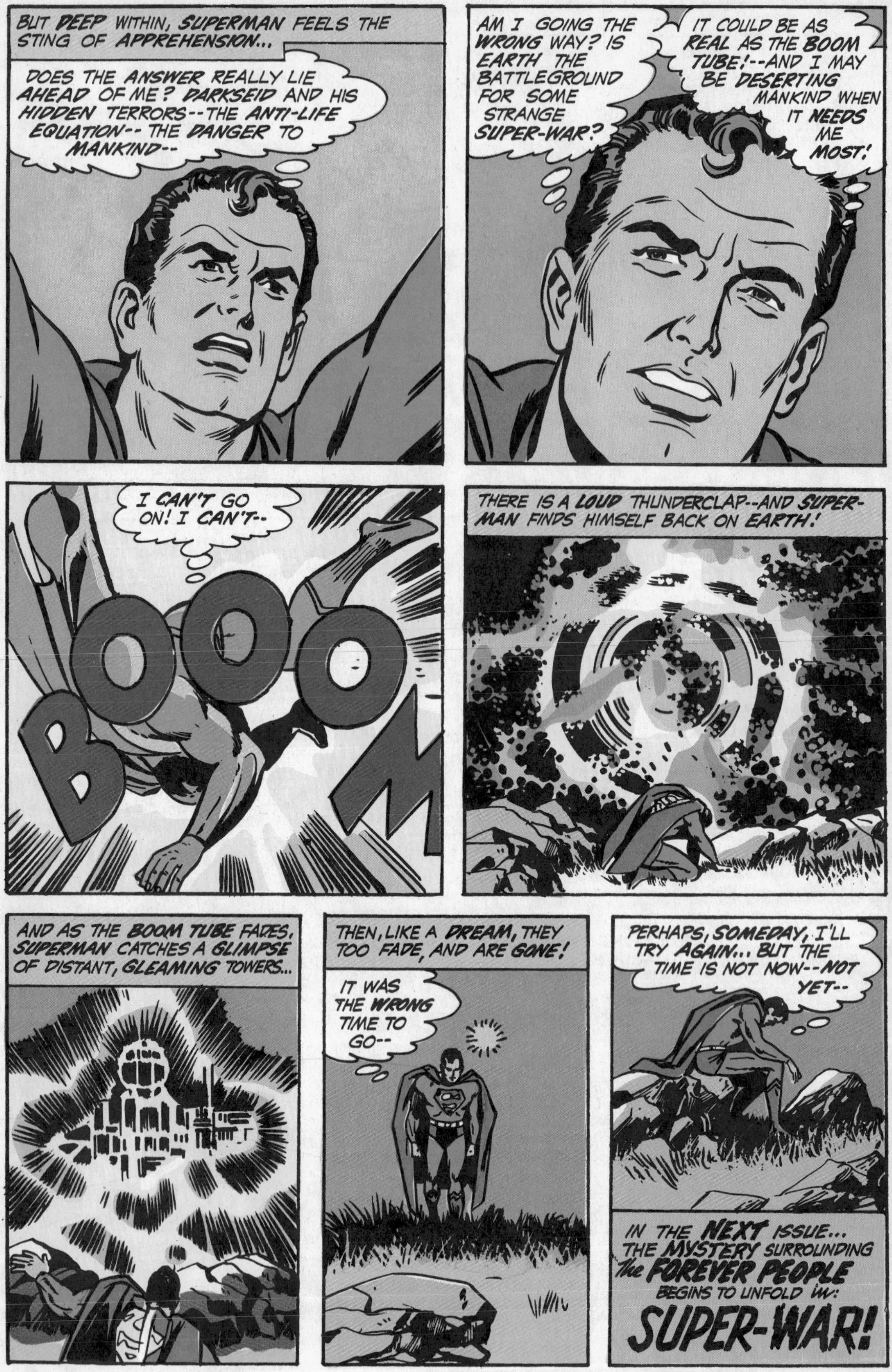

BUT DEEP WITHIN, SUPERMAN FEELS THE STING OF APPREHENSION...
DOES THE ANSWER REALLY LIE AHEAD OF ME? DARKSEID AND HIS HIDDEN TERRORS--THE ANTI-LIFE EQUATION-- THE DANGER TO MANKIND--
AM I GOING THE WRONG WAY? IS EARTH THE BATTLEGROUND FOR SOME STRANGE SUPER-WAR?
IT COULD BE AS REAL AS THE BOOM TUBE!--AND I MAY BE DESERTING MANKIND WHEN IT NEEDS ME MOST!
I CAN'T GO ON! I CAN'T--
BOOOOM
THERE IS A LOUD THUNDERCLAP--AND SUPERMAN FINDS HIMSELF BACK ON EARTH!
AND AS THE BOOM TUBE FADES, SUPERMAN CATCHES A GLIMPSE OF DISTANT, GLEAMING TOWERS...
THEN, LIKE A DREAM, THEY TOO FADE, AND ARE GONE!
IT WAS THE WRONG TIME TO GO--
PERHAPS, SOMEDAY, I'LL TRY AGAIN... BUT THE TIME IS NOT NOW--NOT YET--
IN THE NEXT ISSUE... THE MYSTERY SURROUNDING The FOREVER PEOPLE BEGINS TO UNFOLD in: SUPER-WAR!

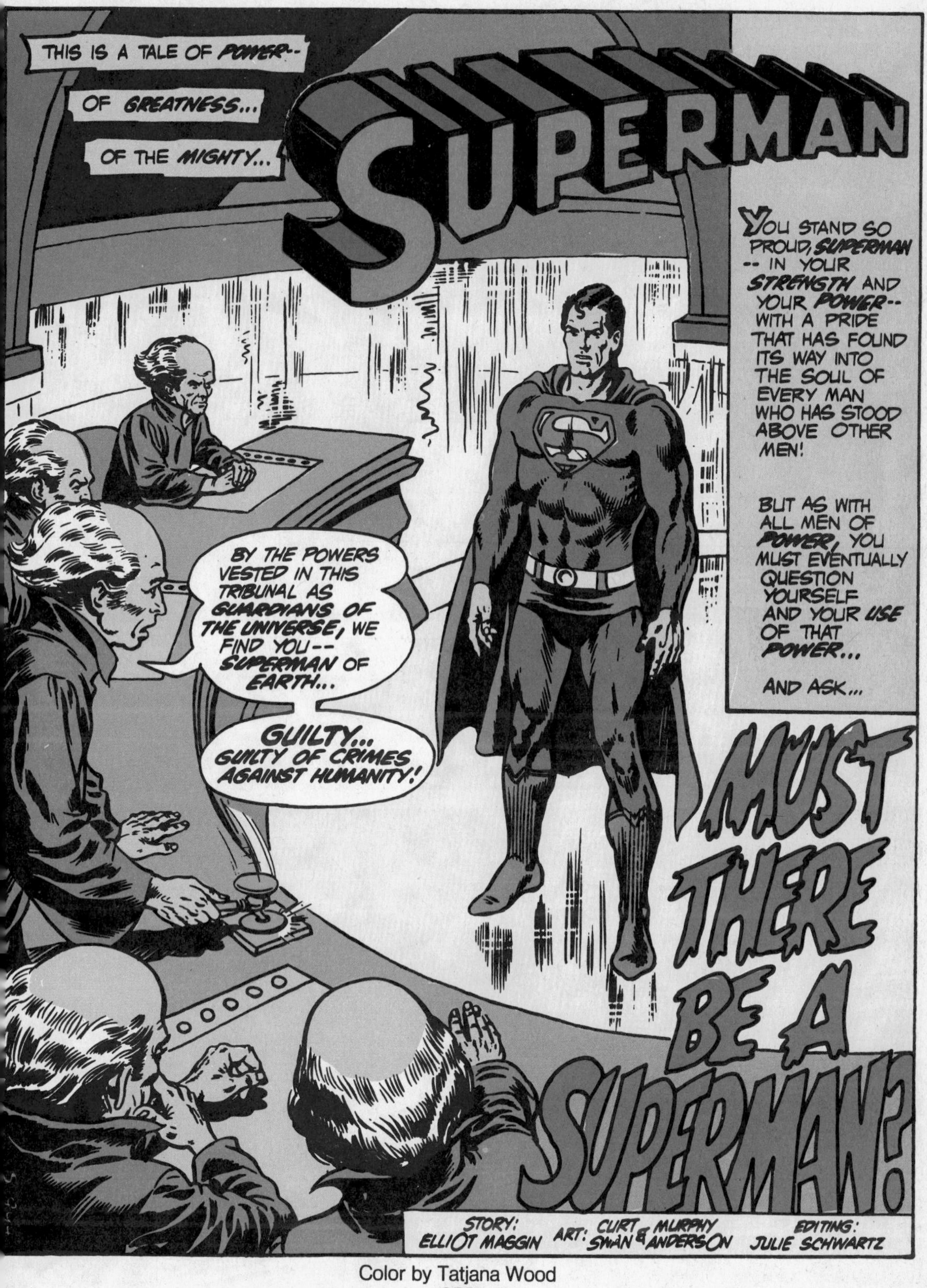

THIS IS A TALE OF POWER--
OF GREATNESS...
OF THE MIGHTY...
SUPERMAN
YOU STAND SO PROUD, SUPERMAN -- IN YOUR STRENGTH AND YOUR POWER-- WITH A PRIDE THAT HAS FOUND ITS WAY INTO THE SOUL OF EVERY MAN WHO HAS STOOD ABOVE OTHER MEN!
BUT AS WITH ALL MEN OF POWER, YOU MUST EVENTUALLY QUESTION YOURSELF AND YOUR USE OF THAT POWER...
AND ASK...
BY THE POWERS VESTED IN THIS TRIBUNAL AS GUARDIANS OF THE UNIVERSE, WE FIND YOU-- SUPERMAN OF EARTH...
GUILTY... GUILTY OF CRIMES AGAINST HUMANITY!
MUST THERE BE A SUPERMAN?
STORY: ELLIOT MAGGIN ART: CURT SWAN & MURPHY ANDERSON EDITING: JULIE SCHWARTZ

Color by Tatjana Wood

THERE IT IS-- JUST AS THE *GUARDIANS* SAID! A *POD* FULL OF *SPORES* BURSTING INTO OUR *GALAXY!*

IT WILL UPSET THE *GALACTIC BALANCE OF NATURE* IF IT IS ALLOWED TO GROW IN OUR UNIVERSE! I MUST BLAST IT OUT OF HERE!

IT'S GOING TO BE *ROUGH!* THIS PART OF THE *GALAXY* IS FULL OF *RED STARS*... LIKE THE STAR-SUN OF MY NATIVE *KRYPTON!*

I CAN ALREADY FEEL MY POWERS WEAKENING UNDER THEIR INFLUENCE!

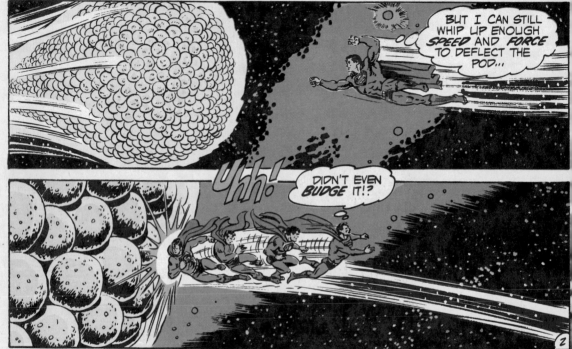

BUT I CAN STILL WHIP UP ENOUGH *SPEED* AND *FORCE* TO DEFLECT THE POD...

UHH!

DIDN'T EVEN *BUDGE* IT!?

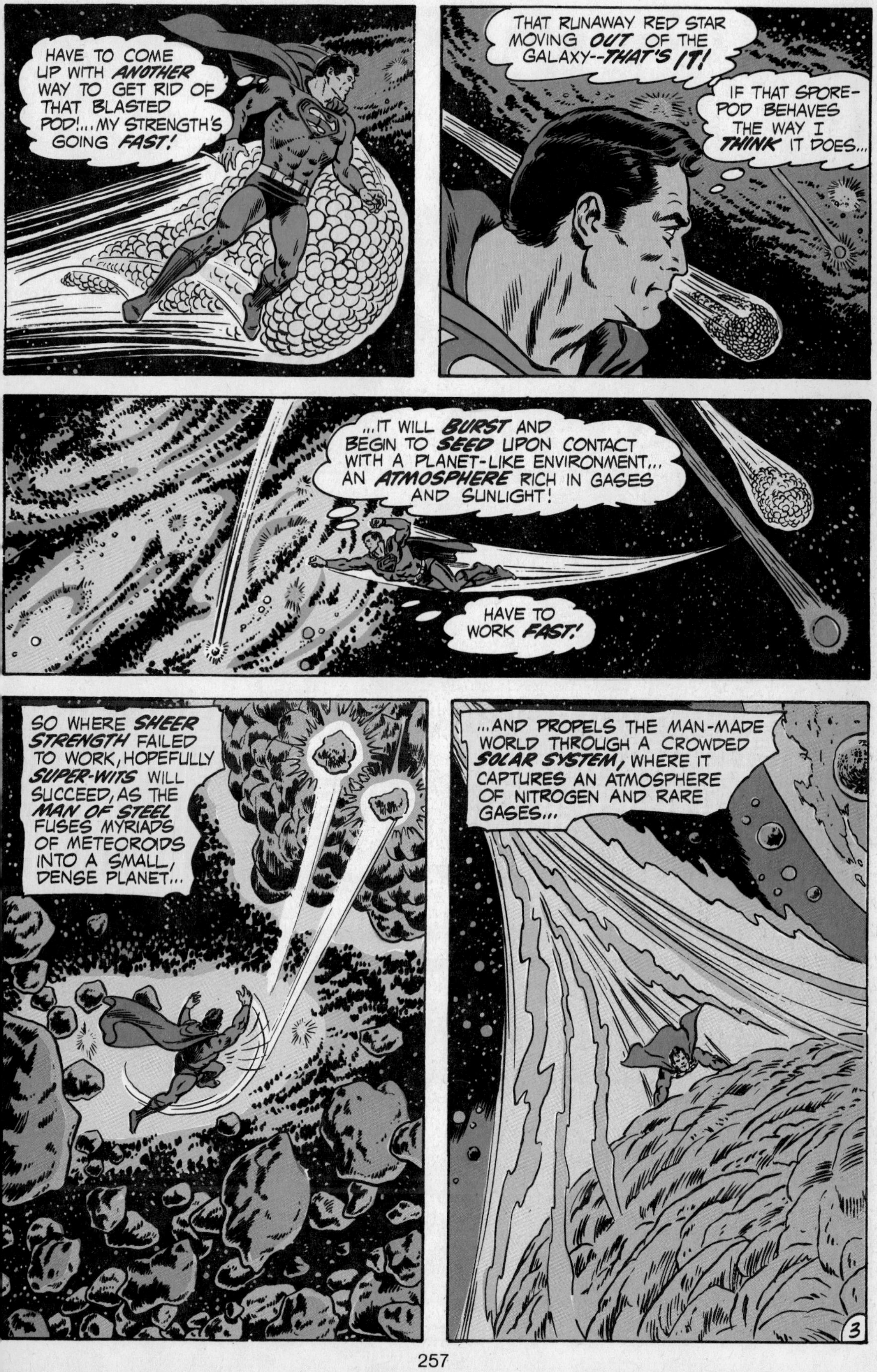
HAVE TO COME UP WITH ANOTHER WAY TO GET RID OF THAT BLASTED POD!... MY STRENGTH'S GOING FAST!
THAT RUNAWAY RED STAR MOVING OUT OF THE GALAXY--THAT'S IT!
IF THAT SPORE-POD BEHAVES THE WAY I THINK IT DOES...
...IT WILL BURST AND BEGIN TO SEED UPON CONTACT WITH A PLANET-LIKE ENVIRONMENT... AN ATMOSPHERE RICH IN GASES AND SUNLIGHT!
HAVE TO WORK FAST!
SO WHERE SHEER STRENGTH FAILED TO WORK, HOPEFULLY SUPER-WITS WILL SUCCEED, AS THE MAN OF STEEL FUSES MYRIADS OF METEOROIDS INTO A SMALL, DENSE PLANET...
...AND PROPELS THE MAN-MADE WORLD THROUGH A CROWDED SOLAR SYSTEM, WHERE IT CAPTURES AN ATMOSPHERE OF NITROGEN AND RARE GASES...
3

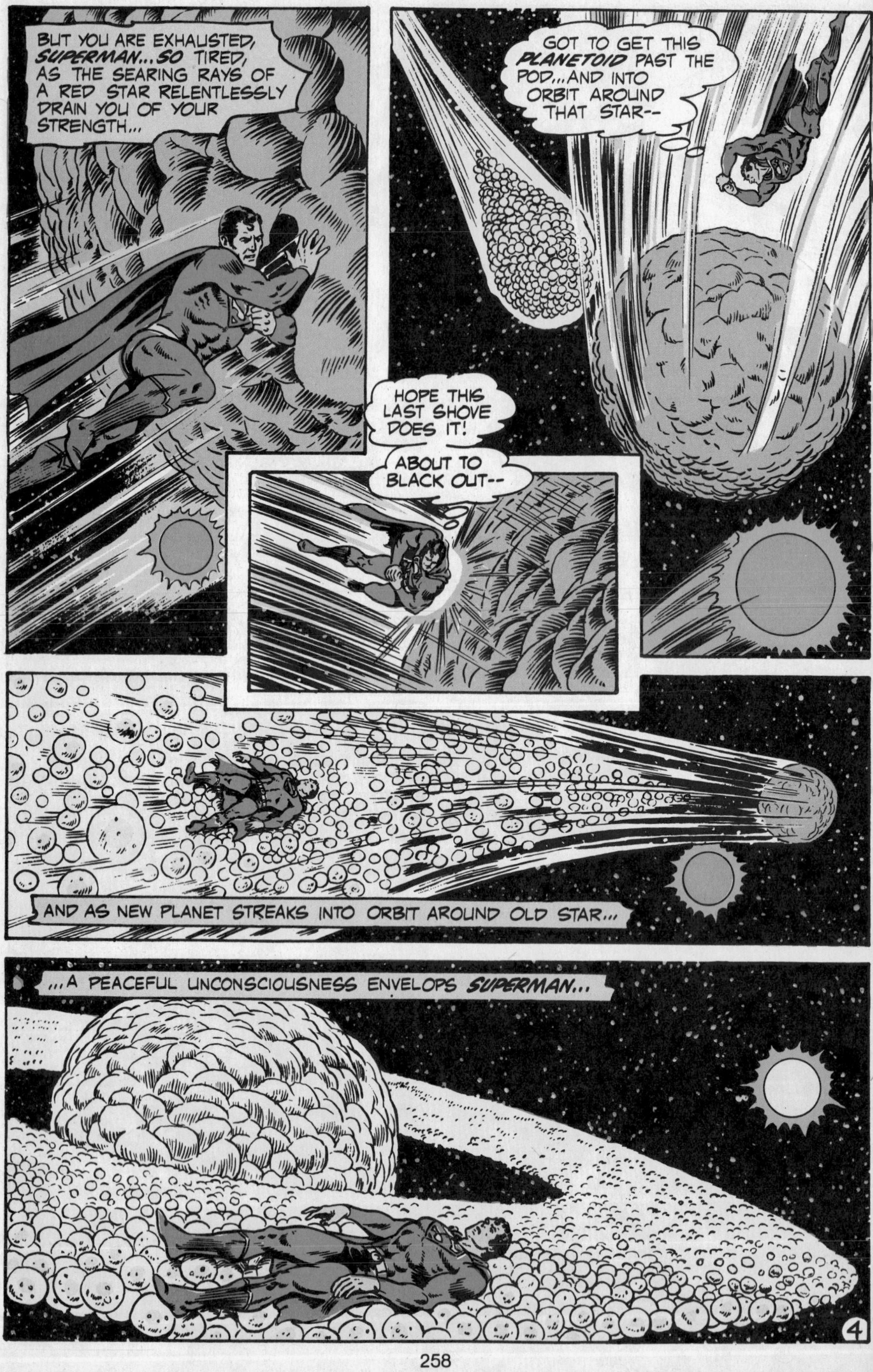
BUT YOU ARE EXHAUSTED, SUPERMAN...SO TIRED, AS THE SEARING RAYS OF A RED STAR RELENTLESSLY DRAIN YOU OF YOUR STRENGTH...
GOT TO GET THIS PLANETOID PAST THE POD...AND INTO ORBIT AROUND THAT STAR--
HOPE THIS LAST SHOVE DOES IT!
ABOUT TO BLACK OUT--
AND AS NEW PLANET STREAKS INTO ORBIT AROUND OLD STAR...
...A PEACEFUL UNCONSCIOUSNESS ENVELOPS SUPERMAN...
4

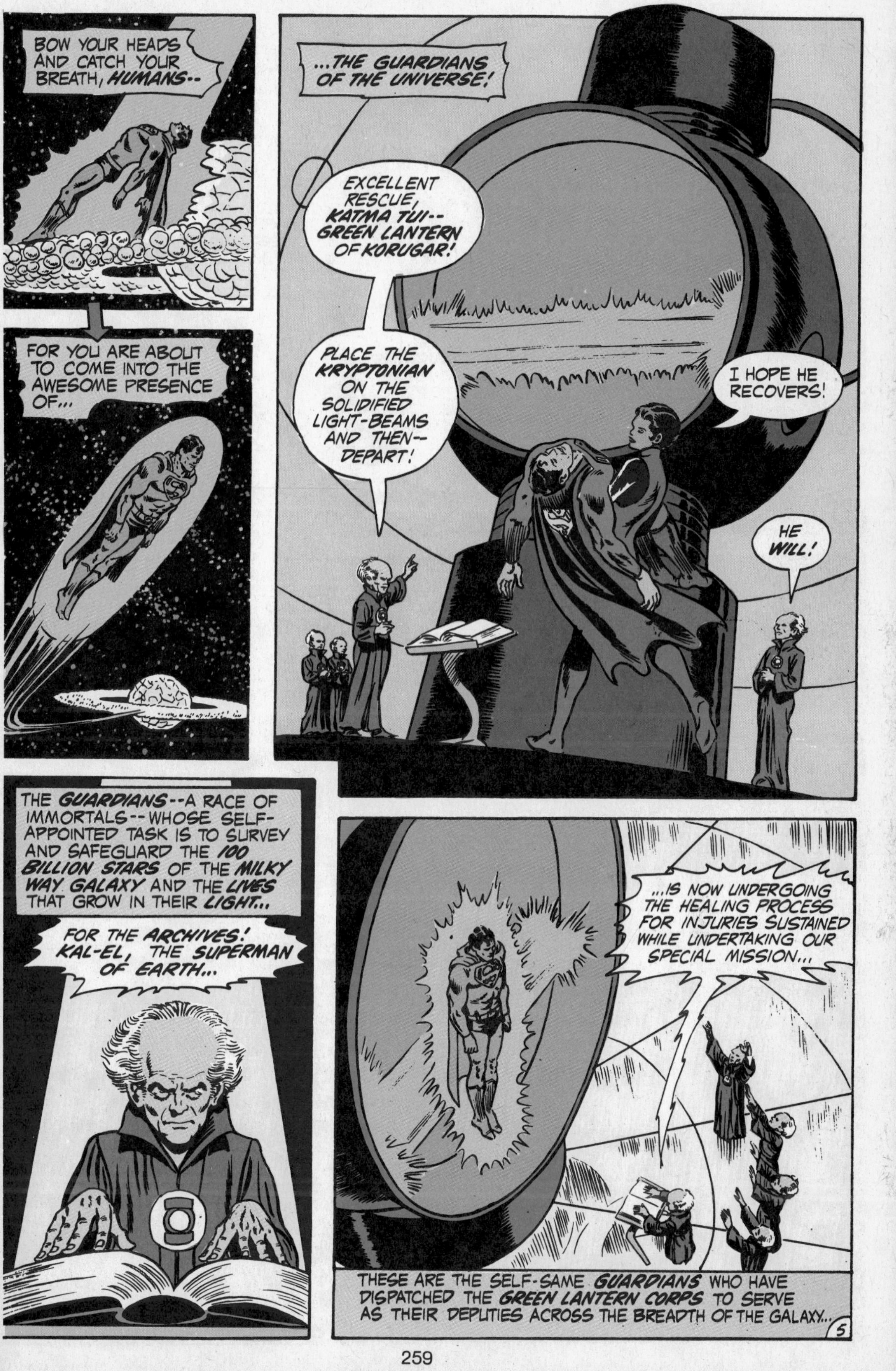

BOW YOUR HEADS AND CATCH YOUR BREATH, HUMANS--
FOR YOU ARE ABOUT TO COME INTO THE AWESOME PRESENCE OF...
...THE GUARDIANS OF THE UNIVERSE!
EXCELLENT RESCUE, KATMA TUI-- GREEN LANTERN OF KORUGAR!
PLACE THE KRYPTONIAN ON THE SOLIDIFIED LIGHT-BEAMS AND THEN-- DEPART!
I HOPE HE RECOVERS!
HE WILL!
THE GUARDIANS--A RACE OF IMMORTALS--WHOSE SELF-APPOINTED TASK IS TO SURVEY AND SAFEGUARD THE 100 BILLION STARS OF THE MILKY WAY GALAXY AND THE LIVES THAT GROW IN THEIR LIGHT...
FOR THE ARCHIVES! KAL-EL, THE SUPERMAN OF EARTH...
...IS NOW UNDERGOING THE HEALING PROCESS FOR INJURIES SUSTAINED WHILE UNDERTAKING OUR SPECIAL MISSION...
THESE ARE THE SELF-SAME GUARDIANS WHO HAVE DISPATCHED THE GREEN LANTERN CORPS TO SERVE AS THEIR DEPUTIES ACROSS THE BREADTH OF THE GALAXY...
5

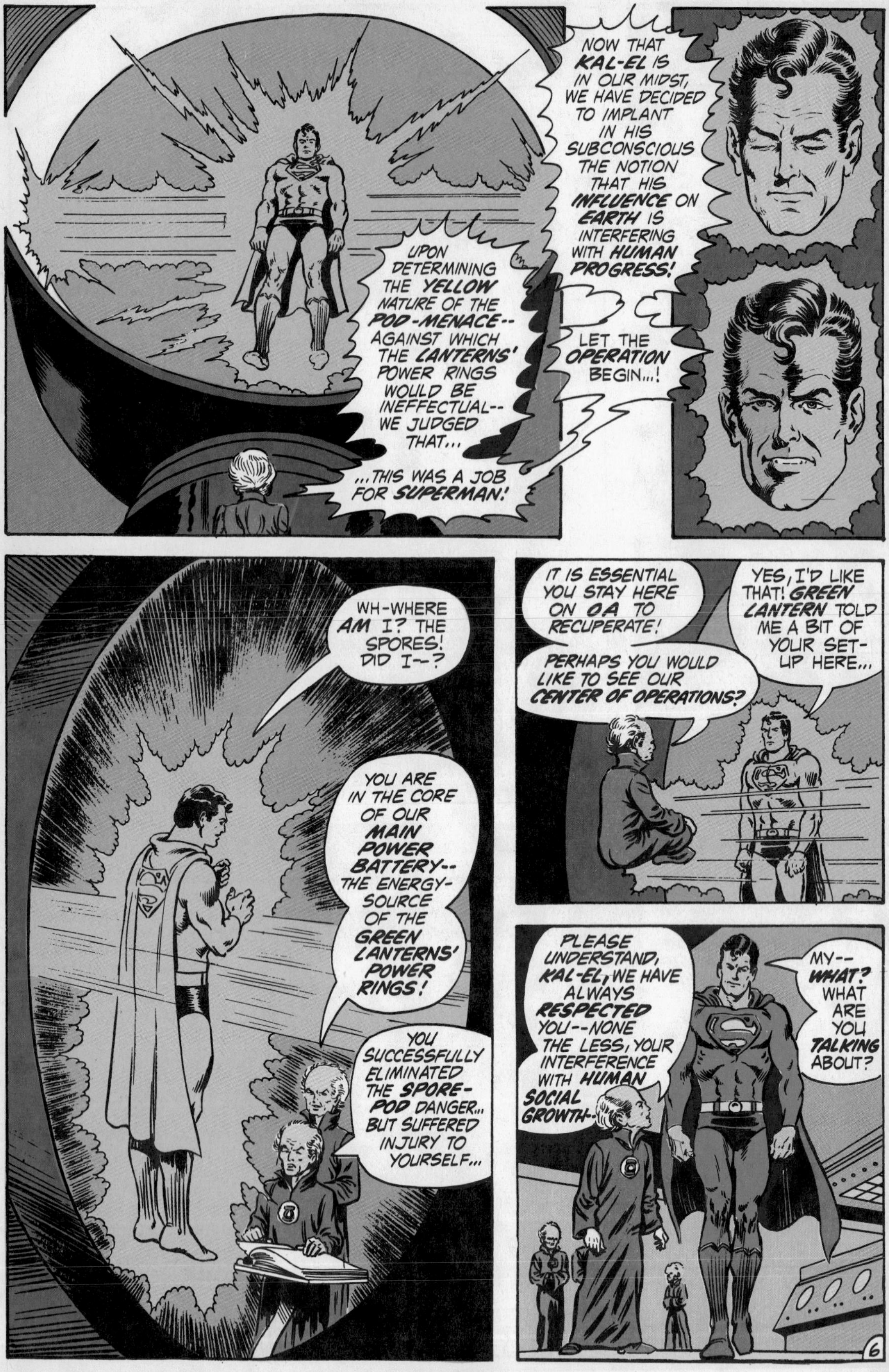
UPON DETERMINING THE YELLOW NATURE OF THE POD-MENACE-- AGAINST WHICH THE LANTERNS' POWER RINGS WOULD BE INEFFECTUAL-- WE JUDGED THAT...
...THIS WAS A JOB FOR SUPERMAN!
NOW THAT KAL-EL IS IN OUR MIDST, WE HAVE DECIDED TO IMPLANT IN HIS SUBCONSCIOUS THE NOTION THAT HIS INFLUENCE ON EARTH IS INTERFERING WITH HUMAN PROGRESS!
LET THE OPERATION BEGIN...!
WH-WHERE AM I? THE SPORES! DID I--?
YOU ARE IN THE CORE OF OUR MAIN POWER BATTERY-- THE ENERGY-SOURCE OF THE GREEN LANTERNS' POWER RINGS!
YOU SUCCESSFULLY ELIMINATED THE SPORE-POD DANGER... BUT SUFFERED INJURY TO YOURSELF...
IT IS ESSENTIAL YOU STAY HERE ON OA TO RECUPERATE!
PERHAPS YOU WOULD LIKE TO SEE OUR CENTER OF OPERATIONS?
YES, I'D LIKE THAT! GREEN LANTERN TOLD ME A BIT OF YOUR SET-UP HERE...
PLEASE UNDERSTAND, KAL-EL, WE HAVE ALWAYS RESPECTED YOU--NONE THE LESS, YOUR INTERFERENCE WITH HUMAN SOCIAL GROWTH--
MY-- WHAT? WHAT ARE YOU TALKING ABOUT?
6

SURELY YOU MUST REALIZE THAT YOUR PRESENCE ON *EARTH* DIRECTLY CONTRIBUTES TO THE *TERRANS'* *CULTURAL LAG!*

CULTURAL LAG?--I *STILL* DON'T UNDER-STAND!

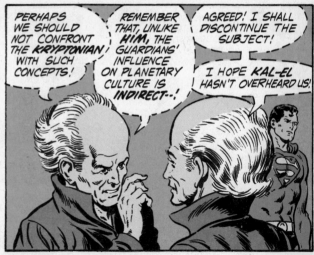

PERHAPS WE SHOULD NOT CONFRONT THE *KRYPTONIAN* WITH SUCH CONCEPTS!

REMEMBER THAT, UNLIKE *HIM,* THE GUARDIANS' INFLUENCE ON PLANETARY CULTURE IS *INDIRECT--!*

AGREED! I SHALL DISCONTINUE THE SUBJECT!

I HOPE *KAL-EL* HASN'T OVERHEARD US!

WE WILL NOW PROCEED TO THE *HALL OF RECORDS*-- IF THAT IS TO YOUR LIKING--?

HUH?-- OKAY... *SURE...*

EXCELLENT! HIS REACTION REVEALS HE *DID* OVER-HEAR US!

DIRECT CAUSE... *CULTURAL LAG...?*

IN THIS SPHERE IS STORED THE *COMPLETE HISTORY* OF THE *GALAXY...*

INDIRECT INFLUENCE ON PLANETARY CULTURES...?

WOULD YOU LIKE A DEMONSTRATION...?

WHA...? OH-- UH-HUH...

PERHAPS SOME *RECENT* HISTORY-- SUCH AS THE TIME YOU VISITED THE PLANET *KALYARNA* WITH THE *JUSTICE LEAGUE OF AMERICA?* *

FINE--!

*NOTE: THAT WAS IN *JUSTICE LEAGUE* #86!

7

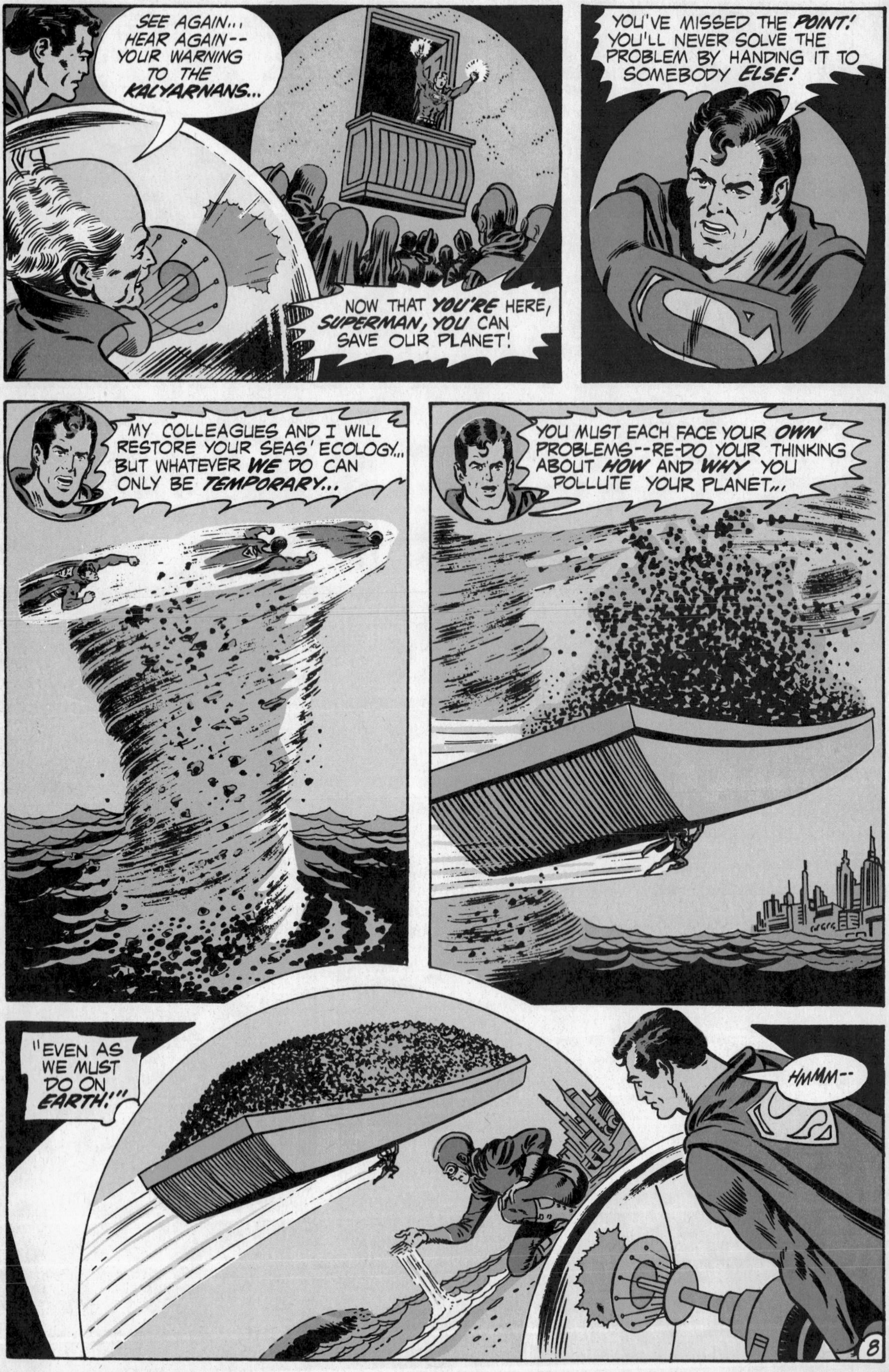
SEE AGAIN... HEAR AGAIN-- YOUR WARNING TO THE KALYARNANS...
NOW THAT YOU'RE HERE, SUPERMAN, YOU CAN SAVE OUR PLANET!
YOU'VE MISSED THE POINT! YOU'LL NEVER SOLVE THE PROBLEM BY HANDING IT TO SOMEBODY ELSE!
MY COLLEAGUES AND I WILL RESTORE YOUR SEAS' ECOLOGY... BUT WHATEVER WE DO CAN ONLY BE TEMPORARY...
YOU MUST EACH FACE YOUR OWN PROBLEMS--RE-DO YOUR THINKING ABOUT HOW AND WHY YOU POLLUTE YOUR PLANET...
"EVEN AS WE MUST DO ON EARTH!"
HMMM--
8

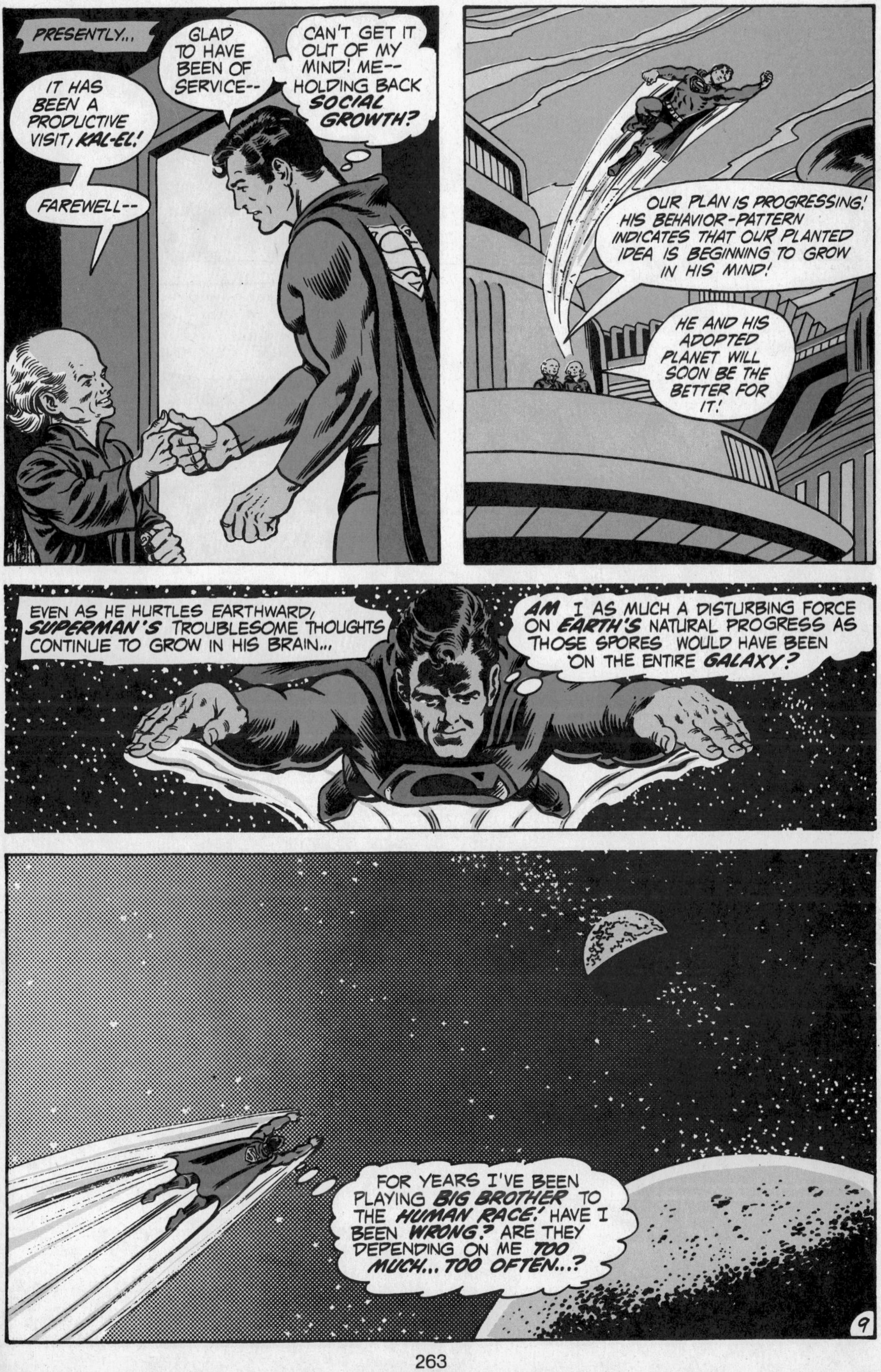

PRESENTLY...
IT HAS BEEN A PRODUCTIVE VISIT, KAL-EL!
GLAD TO HAVE BEEN OF SERVICE--
CAN'T GET IT OUT OF MY MIND! ME--HOLDING BACK SOCIAL GROWTH?
FAREWELL--
OUR PLAN IS PROGRESSING! HIS BEHAVIOR-PATTERN INDICATES THAT OUR PLANTED IDEA IS BEGINNING TO GROW IN HIS MIND!
HE AND HIS ADOPTED PLANET WILL SOON BE THE BETTER FOR IT!
EVEN AS HE HURTLES EARTHWARD, SUPERMAN'S TROUBLESOME THOUGHTS CONTINUE TO GROW IN HIS BRAIN...
AM I AS MUCH A DISTURBING FORCE ON EARTH'S NATURAL PROGRESS AS THOSE SPORES WOULD HAVE BEEN ON THE ENTIRE GALAXY?
FOR YEARS I'VE BEEN PLAYING BIG BROTHER TO THE HUMAN RACE! HAVE I BEEN WRONG? ARE THEY DEPENDING ON ME TOO MUCH... TOO OFTEN...?
9

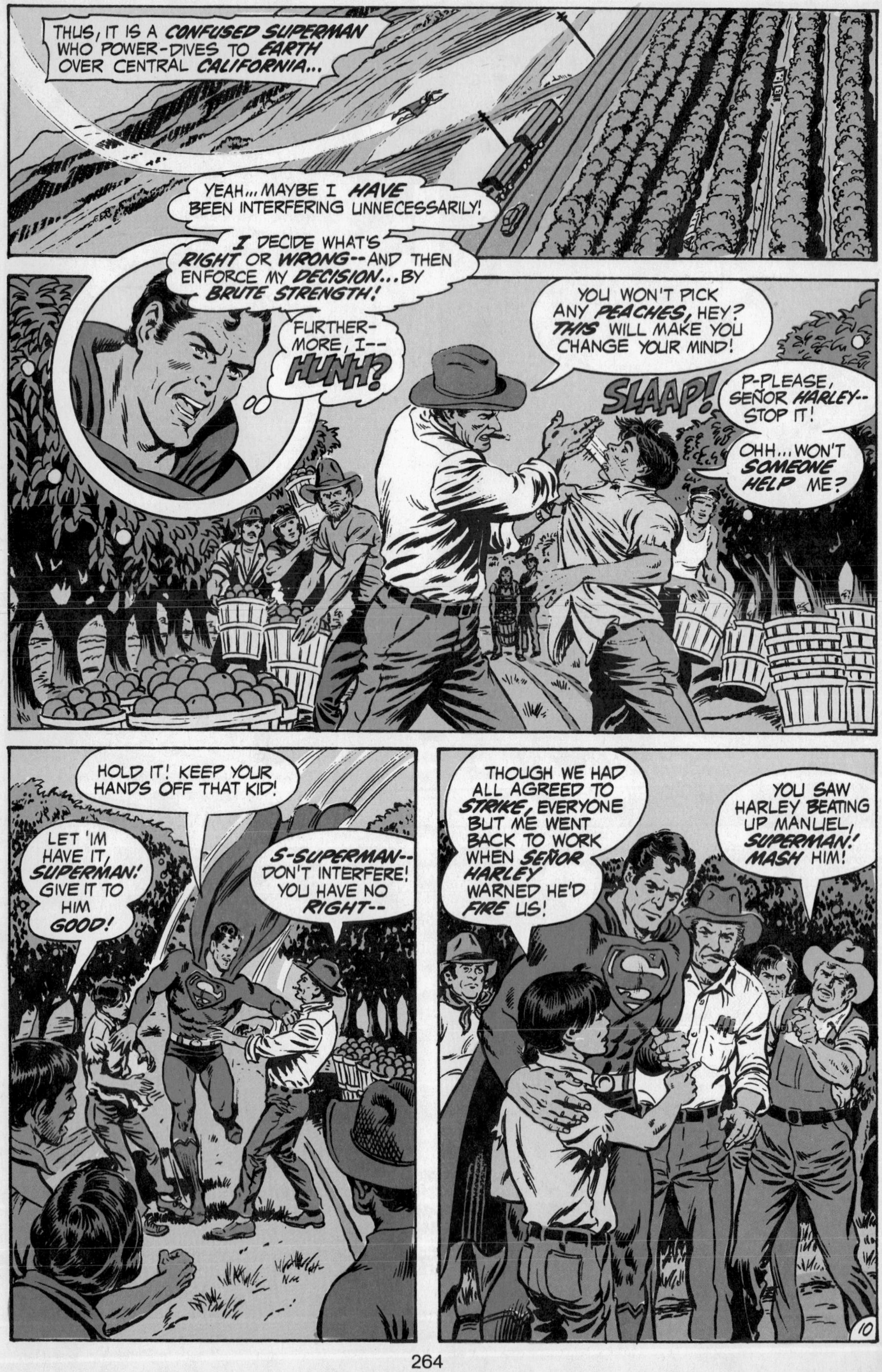
THUS, IT IS A CONFUSED SUPERMAN WHO POWER-DIVES TO EARTH OVER CENTRAL CALIFORNIA...
YEAH... MAYBE I HAVE BEEN INTERFERING UNNECESSARILY!
I DECIDE WHAT'S RIGHT OR WRONG--AND THEN ENFORCE MY DECISION... BY BRUTE STRENGTH!
FURTHER-MORE, I--
HUNH?
YOU WON'T PICK ANY PEACHES, HEY? THIS WILL MAKE YOU CHANGE YOUR MIND!
SLAAP!
P-PLEASE, SEÑOR HARLEY--STOP IT!
OHH... WON'T SOMEONE HELP ME?
HOLD IT! KEEP YOUR HANDS OFF THAT KID!
LET 'IM HAVE IT, SUPERMAN! GIVE IT TO HIM GOOD!
S-SUPERMAN--DON'T INTERFERE! YOU HAVE NO RIGHT--
THOUGH WE HAD ALL AGREED TO STRIKE, EVERYONE BUT ME WENT BACK TO WORK WHEN SEÑOR HARLEY WARNED HE'D FIRE US!
YOU SAW HARLEY BEATING UP MANUEL, SUPERMAN! MASH HIM!
10

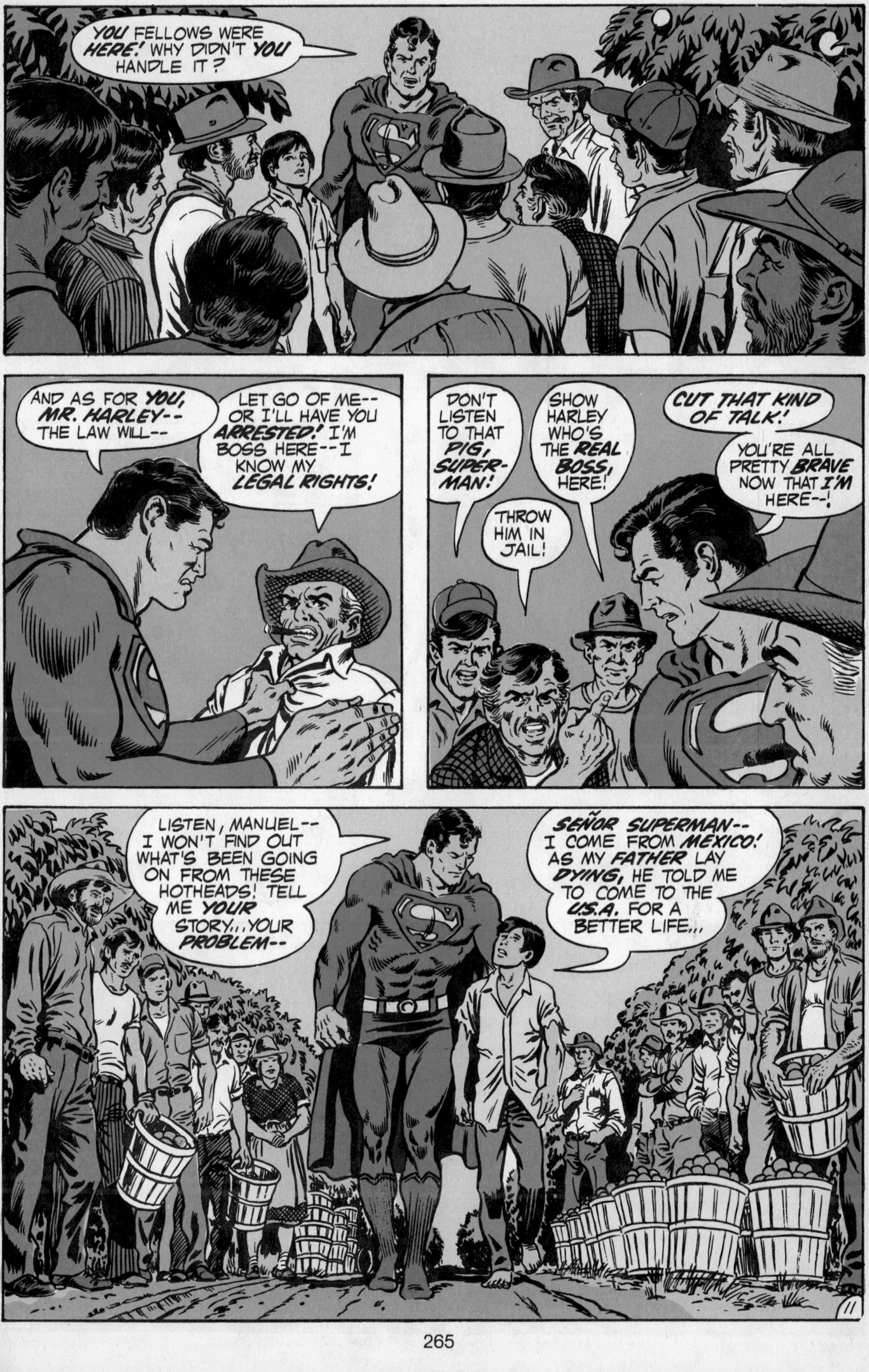
YOU FELLOWS WERE HERE! WHY DIDN'T YOU HANDLE IT?
AND AS FOR YOU, MR. HARLEY-- THE LAW WILL--
LET GO OF ME-- OR I'LL HAVE YOU ARRESTED! I'M BOSS HERE--I KNOW MY LEGAL RIGHTS!
DON'T LISTEN TO THAT PIG, SUPER-MAN!
SHOW HARLEY WHO'S THE REAL BOSS, HERE!
THROW HIM IN JAIL!
CUT THAT KIND OF TALK!
YOU'RE ALL PRETTY BRAVE NOW THAT I'M HERE--!
LISTEN, MANUEL-- I WON'T FIND OUT WHAT'S BEEN GOING ON FROM THESE HOTHEADS! TELL ME YOUR STORY... YOUR PROBLEM--
SEÑOR SUPERMAN-- I COME FROM MEXICO! AS MY FATHER LAY DYING, HE TOLD ME TO COME TO THE U.S.A. FOR A BETTER LIFE...
11

WHO KNOWS WHAT SETS OFF A *MEMORY* BURIED DEEPLY IN THE MIND OF A *SUPERMAN...*?

...A MEMORY OF ANOTHER PLACE, LONG AGO AND FAR AWAY... AND *ANOTHER FATHER--* HIS OWN...

...JOR-EL-- WHO JUST BEFORE HE DIED SAW TO IT THAT HIS *SON* MIGHT HAVE A CHANCE AT A BETTER LIFE...

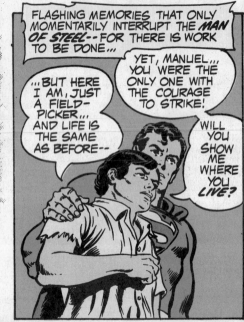

FLASHING MEMORIES THAT ONLY MOMENTARILY INTERRUPT THE *MAN OF STEEL*-- FOR THERE IS WORK TO BE DONE...

...BUT HERE I AM, JUST A FIELD-PICKER... AND LIFE IS THE SAME AS BEFORE--

YET, MANUEL... YOU WERE THE ONLY ONE WITH THE COURAGE TO STRIKE!

WILL YOU SHOW ME WHERE YOU *LIVE?*

MAMMA! MAMMA! *SUPER-HOMBRE!*

HE IS *HERE!*

SHH! DO NOT TALK NONSENSE, JUAN--

CARAMBA!

12

266

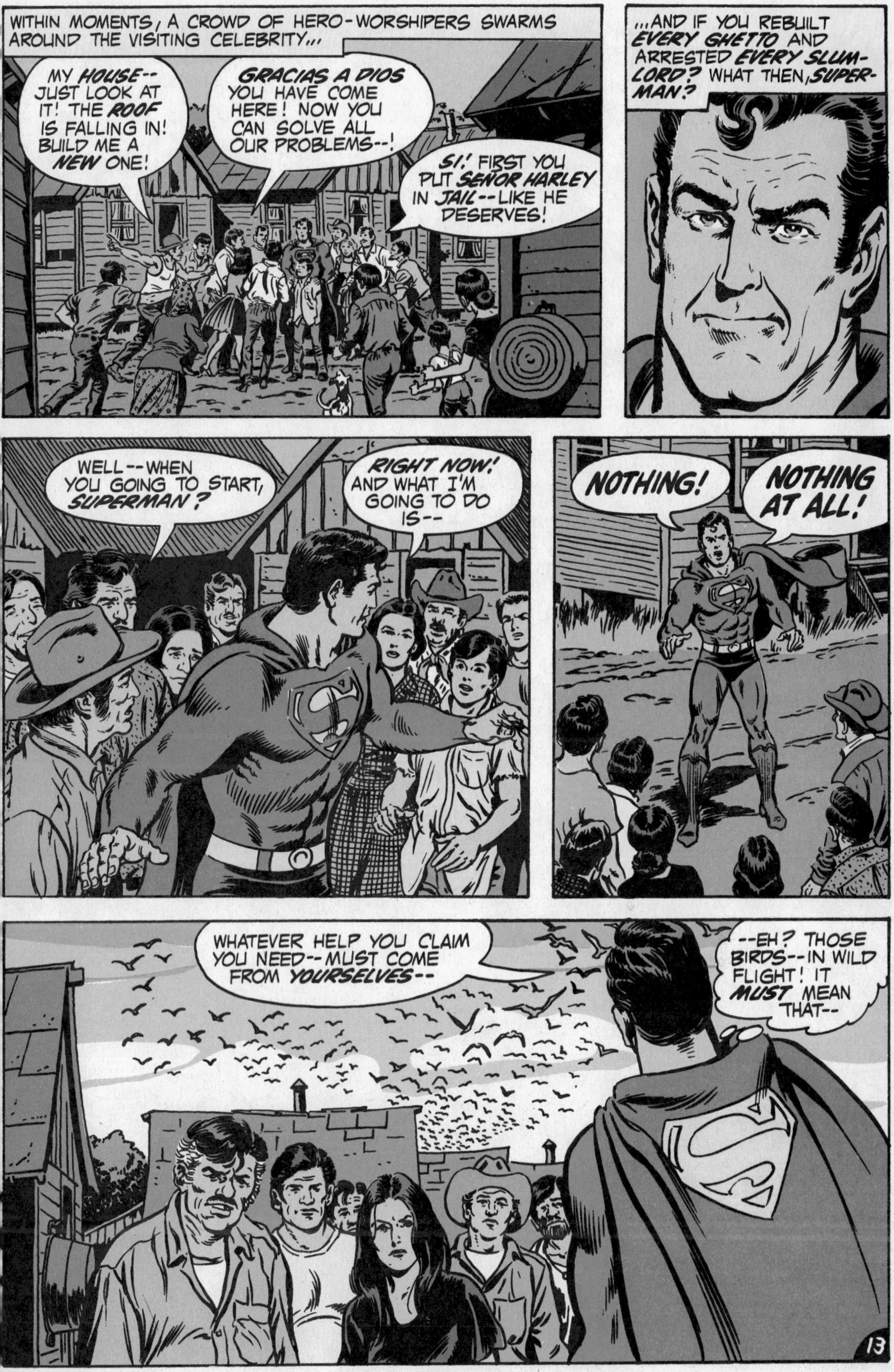
WITHIN MOMENTS, A CROWD OF HERO-WORSHIPERS SWARMS AROUND THE VISITING CELEBRITY...
MY HOUSE-- JUST LOOK AT IT! THE ROOF IS FALLING IN! BUILD ME A NEW ONE!
GRACIAS A DIOS YOU HAVE COME HERE! NOW YOU CAN SOLVE ALL OUR PROBLEMS--!
SI! FIRST YOU PUT SEÑOR HARLEY IN JAIL--LIKE HE DESERVES!
...AND IF YOU REBUILT EVERY GHETTO AND ARRESTED EVERY SLUMLORD? WHAT THEN, SUPERMAN?
WELL--WHEN YOU GOING TO START, SUPERMAN?
RIGHT NOW! AND WHAT I'M GOING TO DO IS--
NOTHING!
NOTHING AT ALL!
WHATEVER HELP YOU CLAIM YOU NEED--MUST COME FROM YOURSELVES--
--EH? THOSE BIRDS--IN WILD FLIGHT! IT MUST MEAN THAT--
13

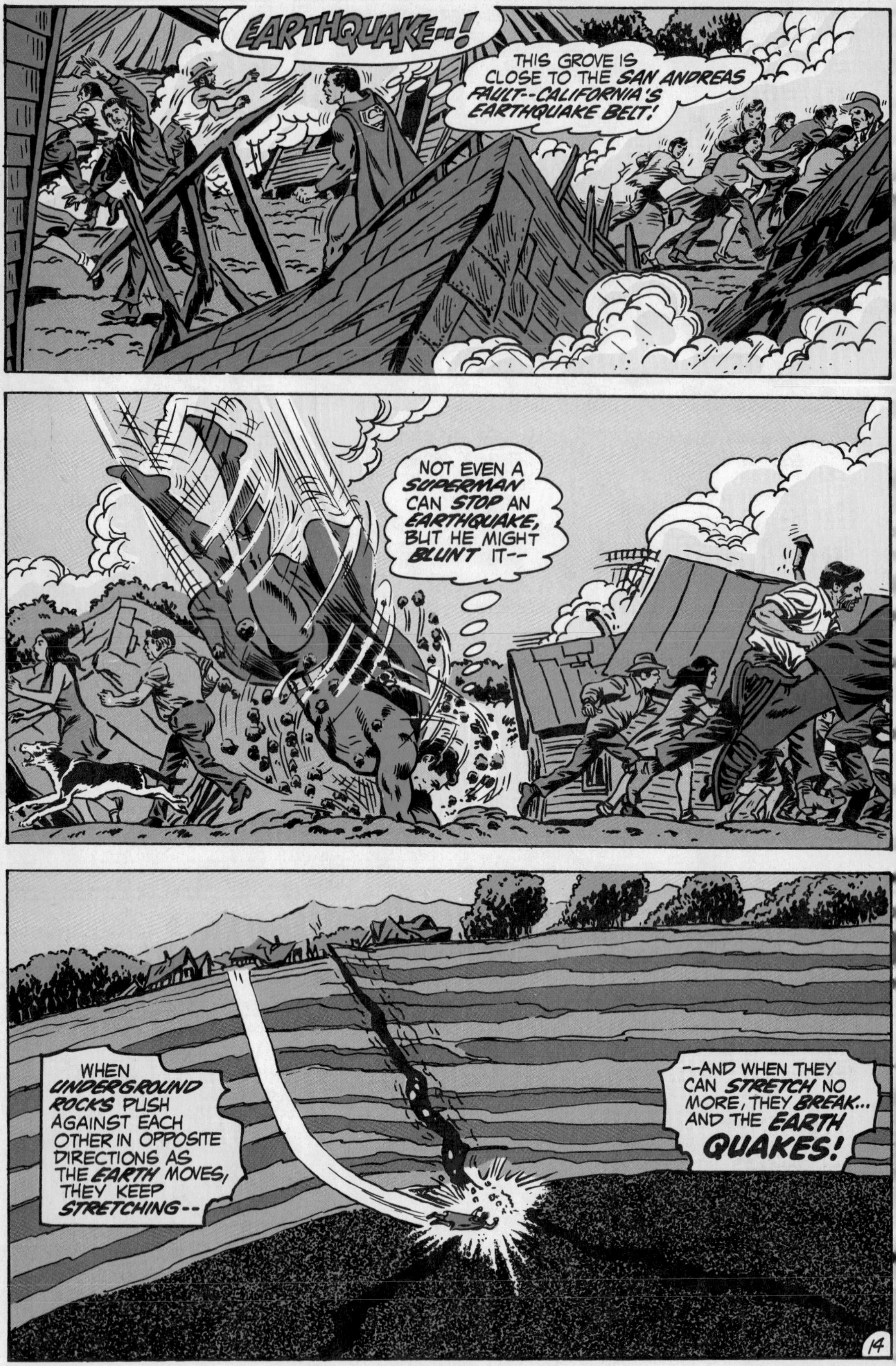
EARTHQUAKE--!
THIS GROVE IS CLOSE TO THE SAN ANDREAS FAULT--CALIFORNIA'S EARTHQUAKE BELT!
NOT EVEN A SUPERMAN CAN STOP AN EARTHQUAKE, BUT HE MIGHT BLUNT IT--
WHEN UNDERGROUND ROCKS PUSH AGAINST EACH OTHER IN OPPOSITE DIRECTIONS AS THE EARTH MOVES, THEY KEEP STRETCHING--
--AND WHEN THEY CAN STRETCH NO MORE, THEY BREAK... AND THE EARTH QUAKES!
14

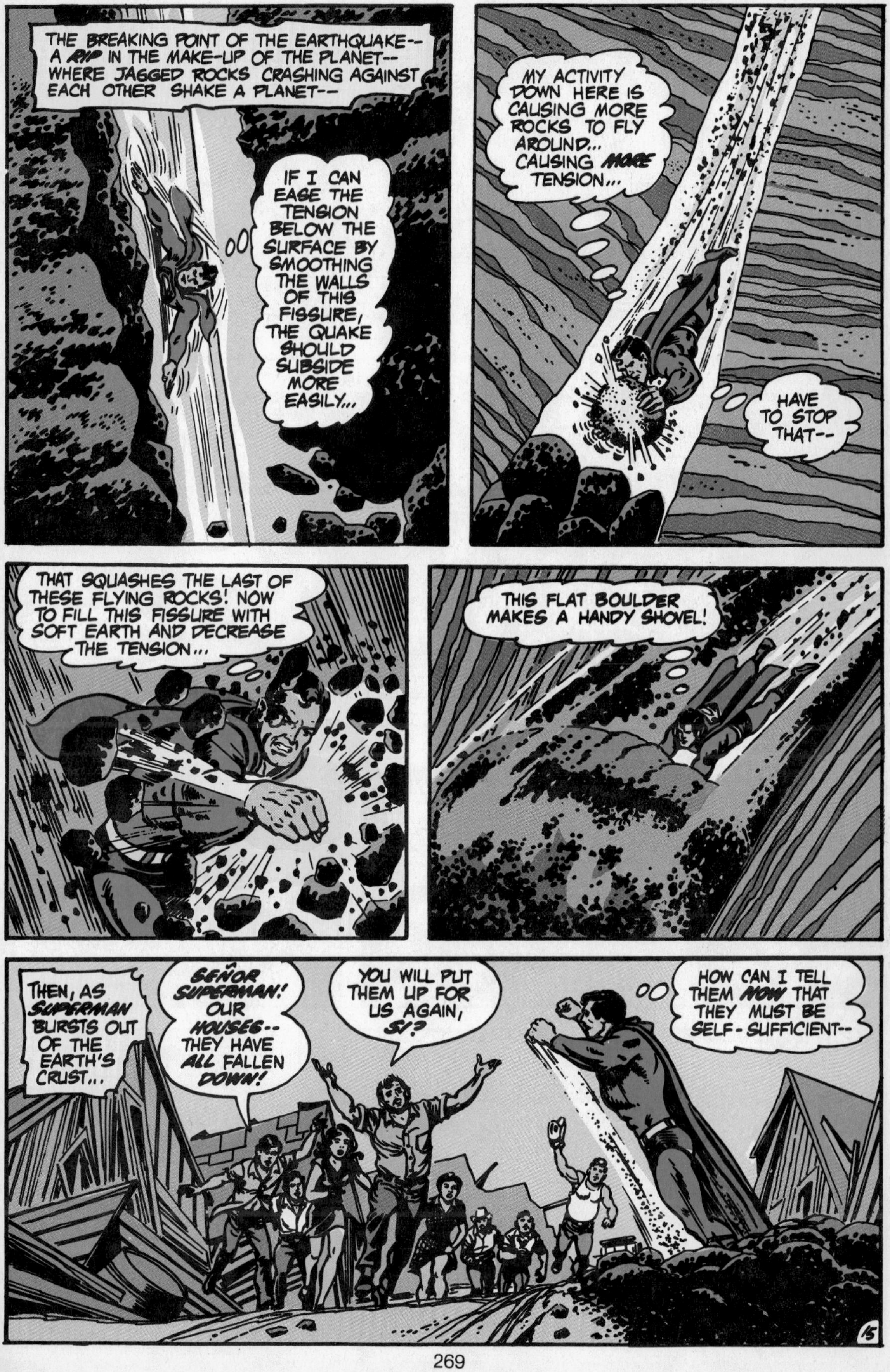

THE BREAKING POINT OF THE EARTHQUAKE-- A RIP IN THE MAKE-UP OF THE PLANET-- WHERE JAGGED ROCKS CRASHING AGAINST EACH OTHER SHAKE A PLANET--
IF I CAN EASE THE TENSION BELOW THE SURFACE BY SMOOTHING THE WALLS OF THIS FISSURE, THE QUAKE SHOULD SUBSIDE MORE EASILY...
MY ACTIVITY DOWN HERE IS CAUSING MORE ROCKS TO FLY AROUND... CAUSING MORE TENSION...
HAVE TO STOP THAT--
THAT SQUASHES THE LAST OF THESE FLYING ROCKS! NOW TO FILL THIS FISSURE WITH SOFT EARTH AND DECREASE THE TENSION...
THIS FLAT BOULDER MAKES A HANDY SHOVEL!
THEN, AS SUPERMAN BURSTS OUT OF THE EARTH'S CRUST...
SEÑOR SUPERMAN! OUR HOUSES-- THEY HAVE ALL FALLEN DOWN!
YOU WILL PUT THEM UP FOR US AGAIN, SI?
HOW CAN I TELL THEM NOW THAT THEY MUST BE SELF-SUFFICIENT--
15

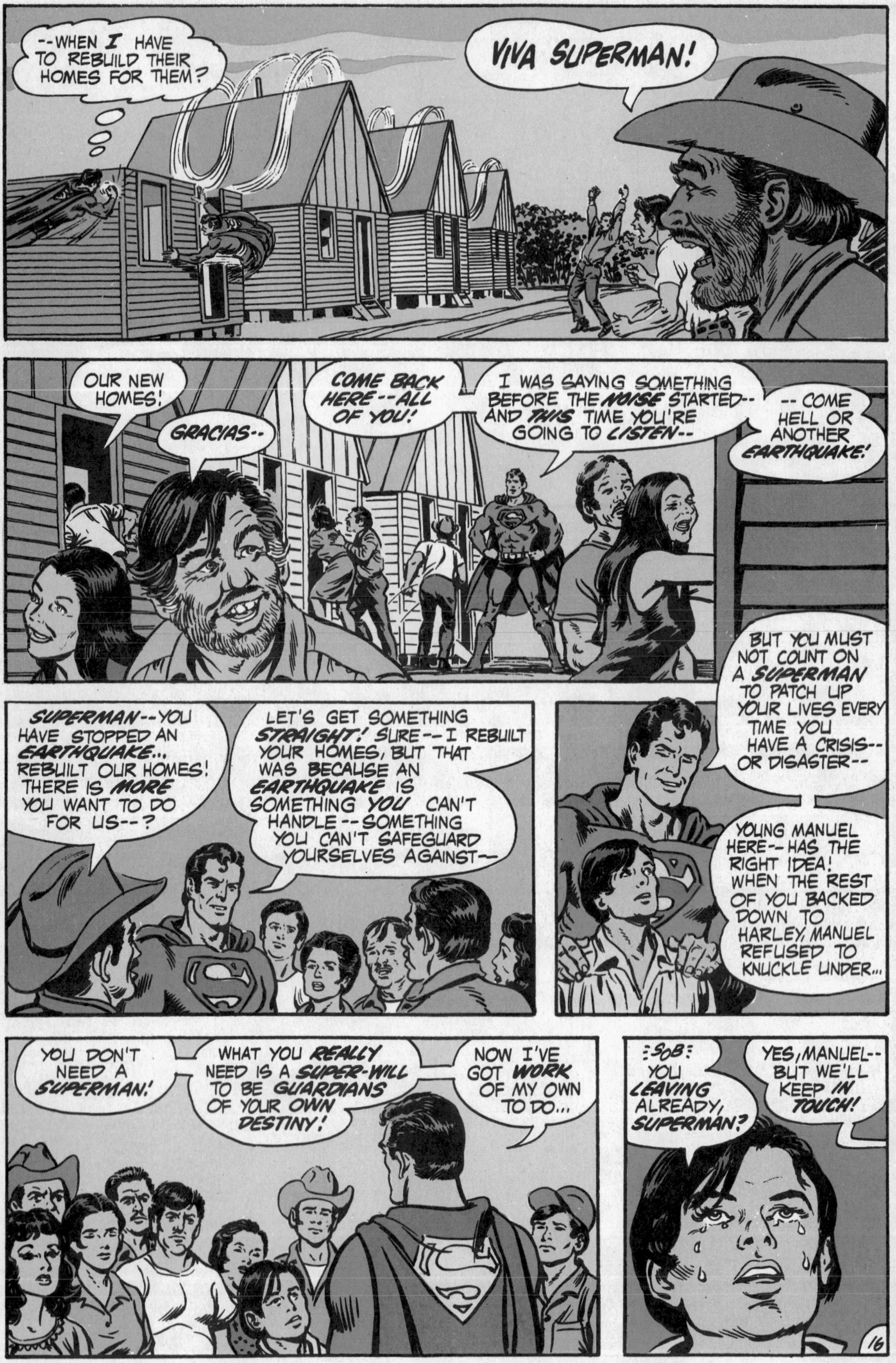
--WHEN I HAVE TO REBUILD THEIR HOMES FOR THEM?
VIVA SUPERMAN!
OUR NEW HOMES!
GRACIAS--
COME BACK HERE--ALL OF YOU!
I WAS SAYING SOMETHING BEFORE THE NOISE STARTED-- AND THIS TIME YOU'RE GOING TO LISTEN--
-- COME HELL OR ANOTHER EARTHQUAKE!
SUPERMAN--YOU HAVE STOPPED AN EARTHQUAKE... REBUILT OUR HOMES! THERE IS MORE YOU WANT TO DO FOR US--?
LET'S GET SOMETHING STRAIGHT! SURE--I REBUILT YOUR HOMES, BUT THAT WAS BECAUSE AN EARTHQUAKE IS SOMETHING YOU CAN'T HANDLE--SOMETHING YOU CAN'T SAFEGUARD YOURSELVES AGAINST--
BUT YOU MUST NOT COUNT ON A SUPERMAN TO PATCH UP YOUR LIVES EVERY TIME YOU HAVE A CRISIS--OR DISASTER--
YOUNG MANUEL HERE--HAS THE RIGHT IDEA! WHEN THE REST OF YOU BACKED DOWN TO HARLEY, MANUEL REFUSED TO KNUCKLE UNDER...
YOU DON'T NEED A SUPERMAN!
WHAT YOU REALLY NEED IS A SUPER-WILL TO BE GUARDIANS OF YOUR OWN DESTINY!
NOW I'VE GOT WORK OF MY OWN TO DO...
SOB YOU LEAVING ALREADY, SUPERMAN?
YES, MANUEL-- BUT WE'LL KEEP IN TOUCH!
16

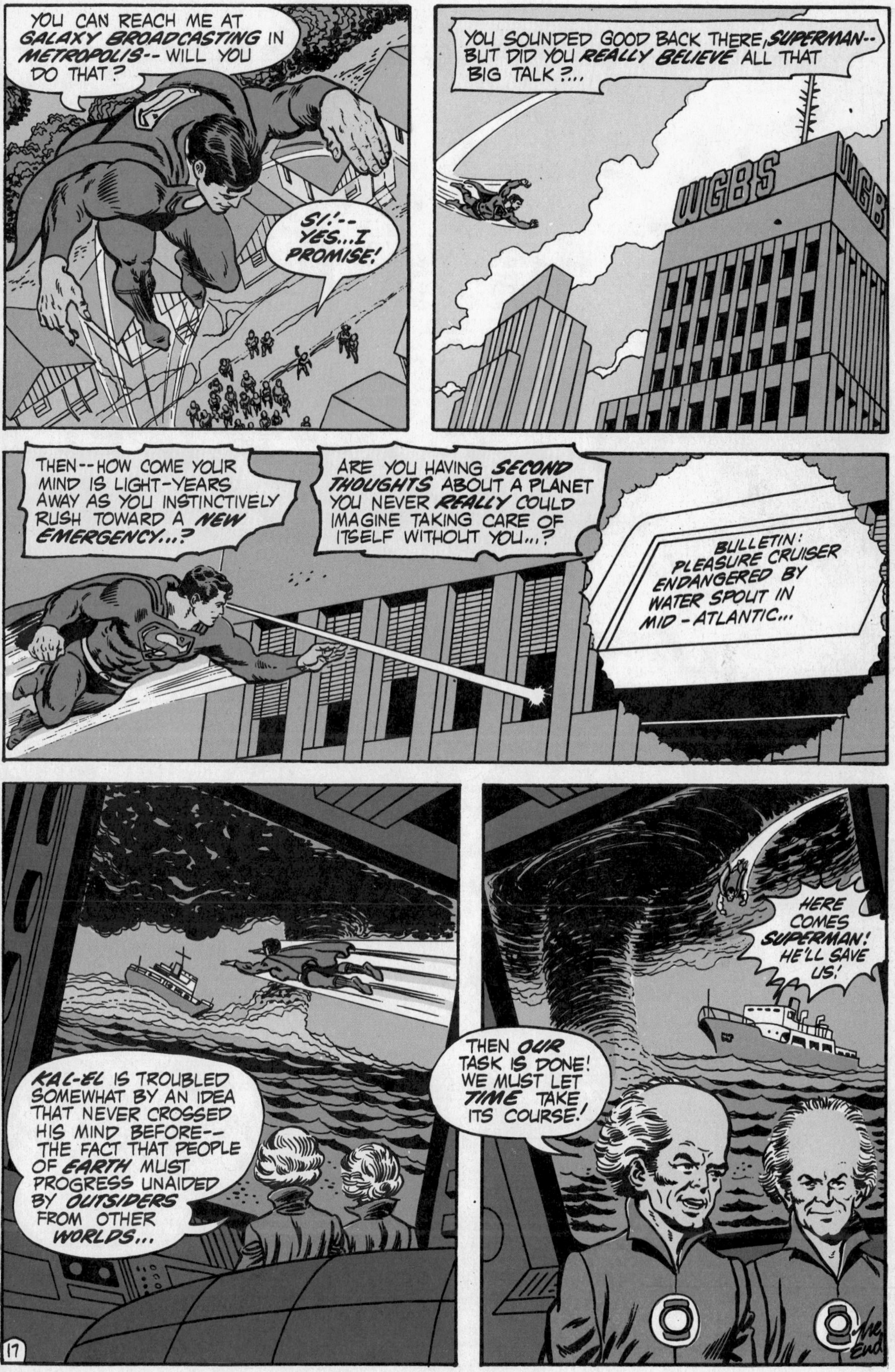
YOU CAN REACH ME AT GALAXY BROADCASTING IN METROPOLIS-- WILL YOU DO THAT?
SI!-- YES...I PROMISE!
YOU SOUNDED GOOD BACK THERE, SUPERMAN-- BUT DID YOU REALLY BELIEVE ALL THAT BIG TALK?...
WGBS
THEN--HOW COME YOUR MIND IS LIGHT-YEARS AWAY AS YOU INSTINCTIVELY RUSH TOWARD A NEW EMERGENCY...?
ARE YOU HAVING SECOND THOUGHTS ABOUT A PLANET YOU NEVER REALLY COULD IMAGINE TAKING CARE OF ITSELF WITHOUT YOU...?
BULLETIN: PLEASURE CRUISER ENDANGERED BY WATER SPOUT IN MID-ATLANTIC...
KAL-EL IS TROUBLED SOMEWHAT BY AN IDEA THAT NEVER CROSSED HIS MIND BEFORE-- THE FACT THAT PEOPLE OF EARTH MUST PROGRESS UNAIDED BY OUTSIDERS FROM OTHER WORLDS...
HERE COMES SUPERMAN! HE'LL SAVE US!
THEN OUR TASK IS DONE! WE MUST LET TIME TAKE ITS COURSE!
17
The End

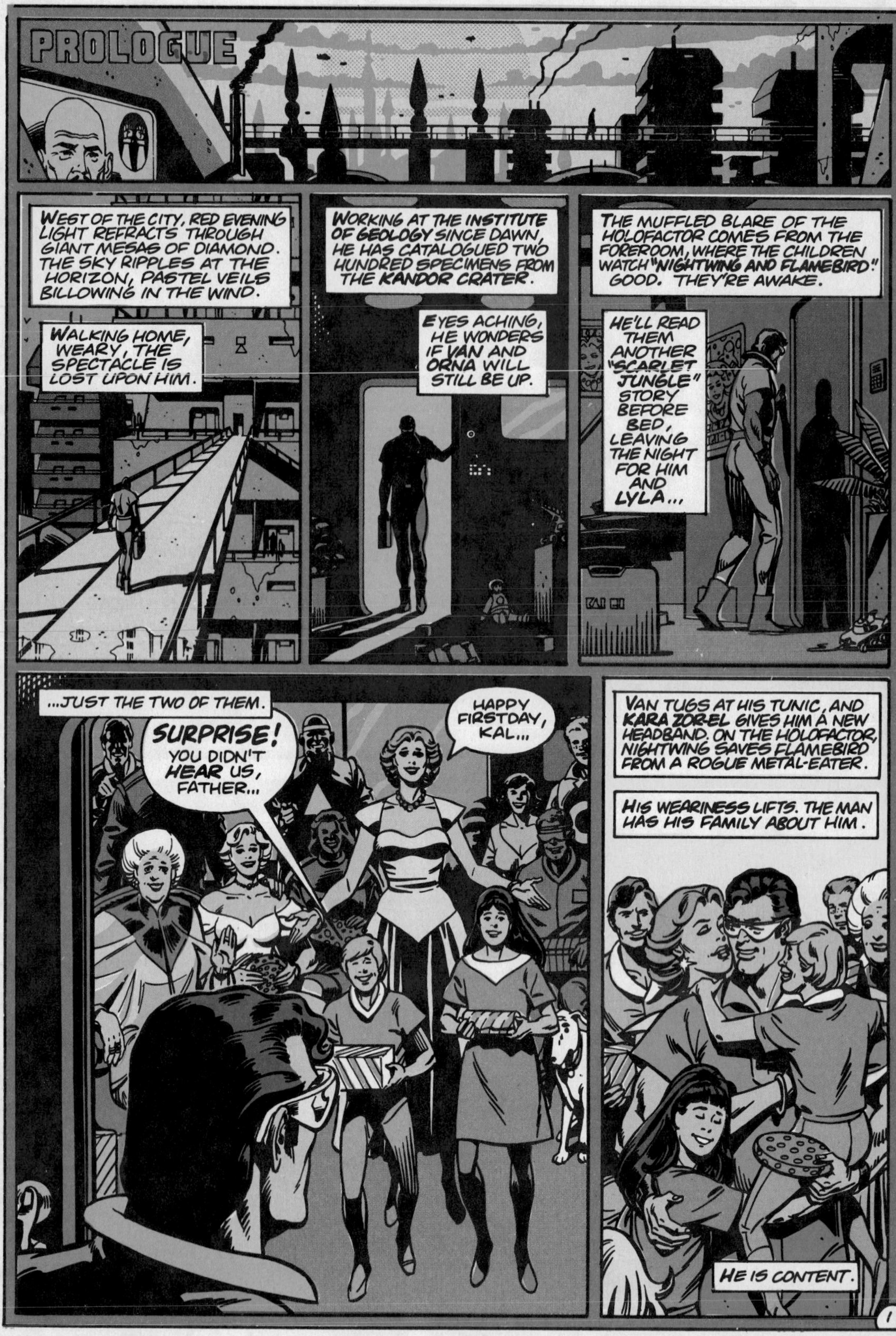
PROLOGUE
WEST OF THE CITY, RED EVENING LIGHT REFRACTS THROUGH GIANT MESAS OF DIAMOND. THE SKY RIPPLES AT THE HORIZON, PASTEL VEILS BILLOWING IN THE WIND.
WALKING HOME, WEARY, THE SPECTACLE IS LOST UPON HIM.
WORKING AT THE INSTITUTE OF GEOLOGY SINCE DAWN, HE HAS CATALOGUED TWO HUNDRED SPECIMENS FROM THE KANDOR CRATER.
EYES ACHING, HE WONDERS IF VAN AND ORNA WILL STILL BE UP.
THE MUFFLED BLARE OF THE HOLOFACTOR COMES FROM THE FOREROOM, WHERE THE CHILDREN WATCH "NIGHTWING AND FLAMEBIRD." GOOD. THEY'RE AWAKE.
HE'LL READ THEM ANOTHER "SCARLET JUNGLE" STORY BEFORE BED, LEAVING THE NIGHT FOR HIM AND LYLA...
...JUST THE TWO OF THEM.
SURPRISE! YOU DIDN'T HEAR US, FATHER...
HAPPY FIRSTDAY, KAL...
VAN TUGS AT HIS TUNIC, AND KARA ZOR-EL GIVES HIM A NEW HEADBAND. ON THE HOLOFACTOR, NIGHTWING SAVES FLAMEBIRD FROM A ROGUE METAL-EATER.
HIS WEARINESS LIFTS. THE MAN HAS HIS FAMILY ABOUT HIM.
HE IS CONTENT.
1

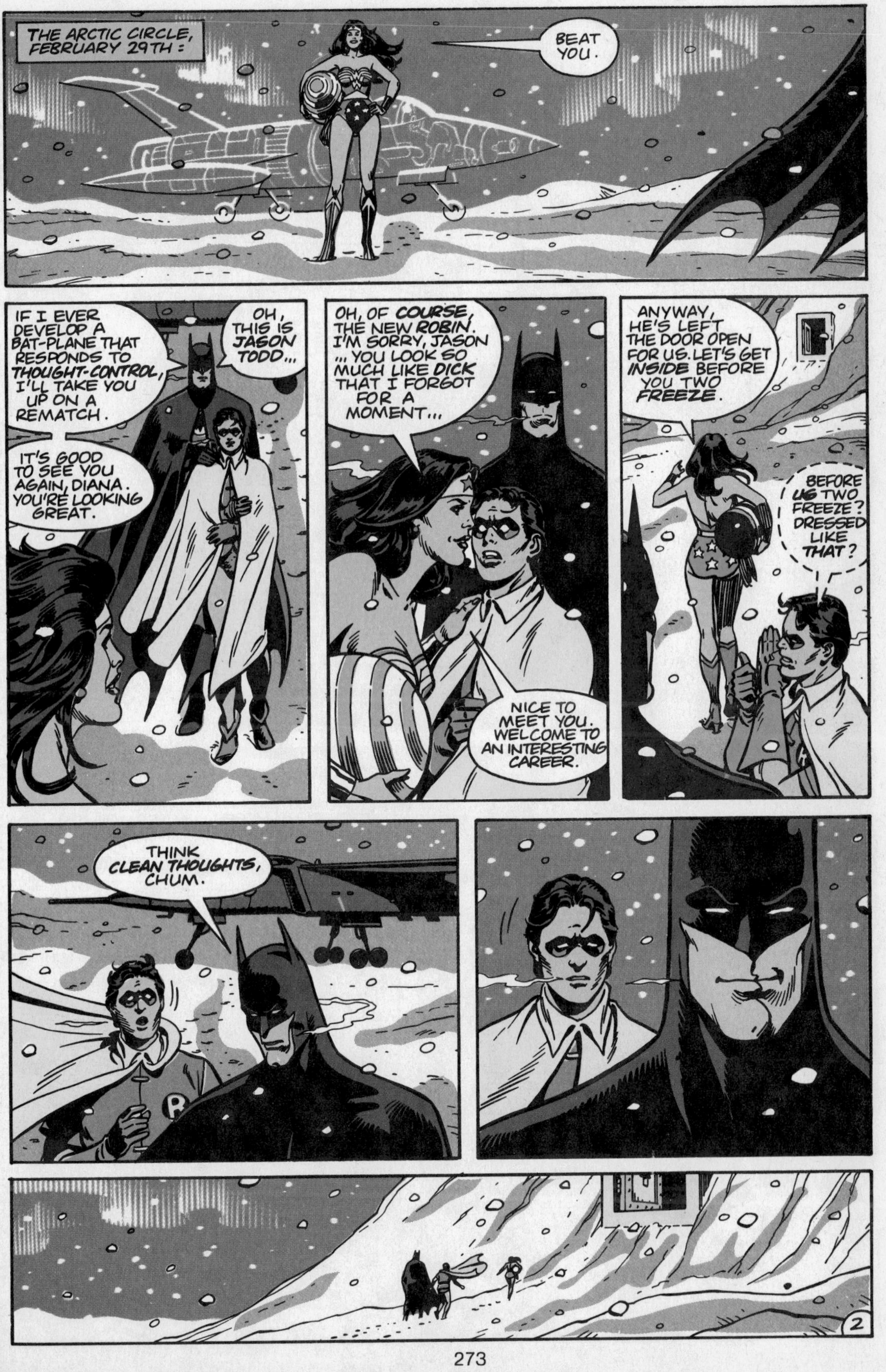
THE ARCTIC CIRCLE, FEBRUARY 29TH:
BEAT YOU.
IF I EVER DEVELOP A BAT-PLANE THAT RESPONDS TO THOUGHT-CONTROL, I'LL TAKE YOU UP ON A REMATCH.
OH, THIS IS JASON TODD...
IT'S GOOD TO SEE YOU AGAIN, DIANA. YOU'RE LOOKING GREAT.
OH, OF COURSE, THE NEW ROBIN. I'M SORRY, JASON ...YOU LOOK SO MUCH LIKE DICK THAT I FORGOT FOR A MOMENT...
NICE TO MEET YOU. WELCOME TO AN INTERESTING CAREER.
ANYWAY, HE'S LEFT THE DOOR OPEN FOR US. LET'S GET INSIDE BEFORE YOU TWO FREEZE.
BEFORE US TWO FREEZE? DRESSED LIKE THAT?
THINK CLEAN THOUGHTS, CHUM.
2

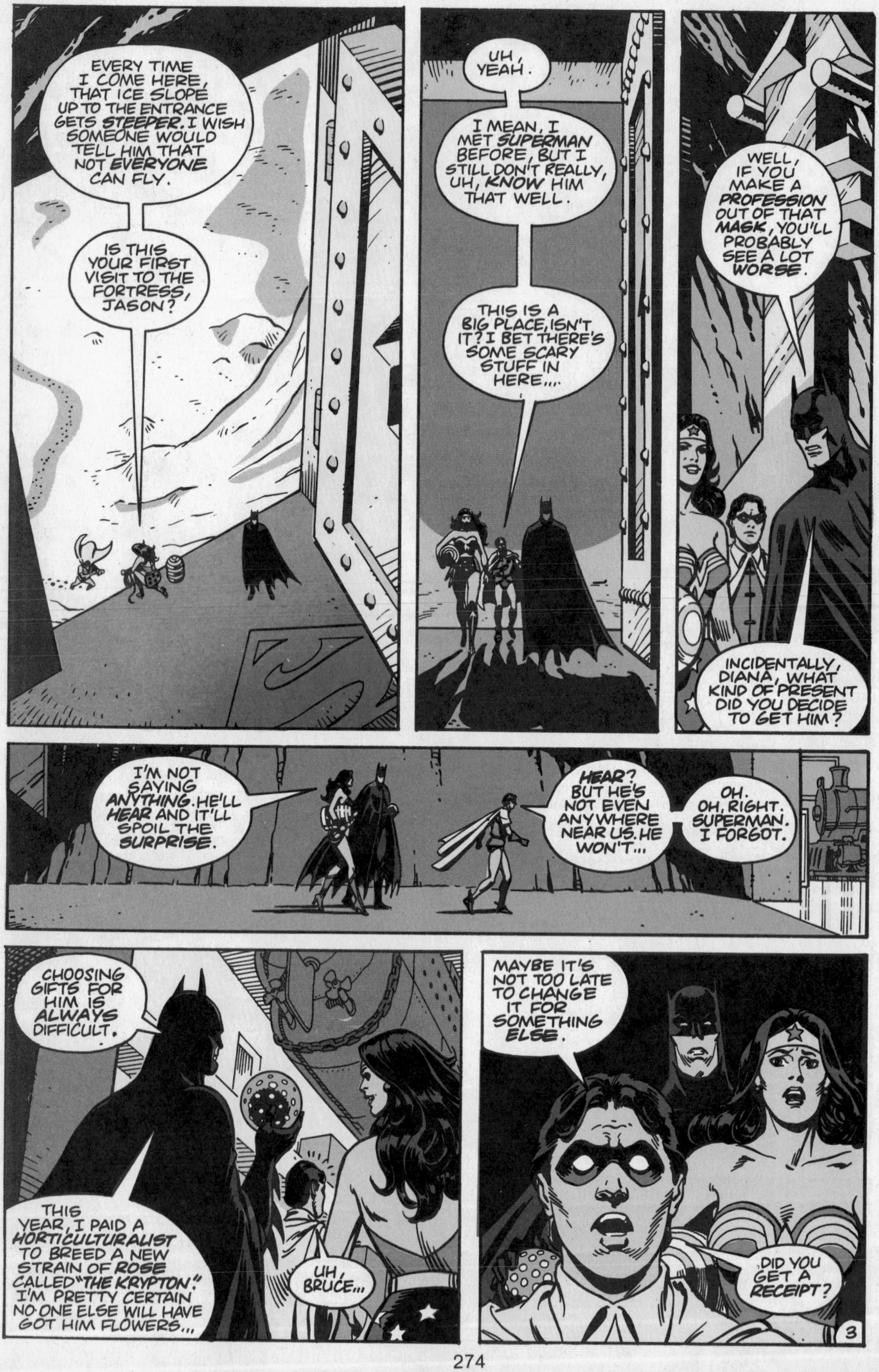
EVERY TIME I COME HERE, THAT ICE SLOPE UP TO THE ENTRANCE GETS STEEPER. I WISH SOMEONE WOULD TELL HIM THAT NOT EVERYONE CAN FLY.
IS THIS YOUR FIRST VISIT TO THE FORTRESS, JASON?
UH, YEAH.
I MEAN, I MET SUPERMAN BEFORE, BUT I STILL DON'T REALLY, UH, KNOW HIM THAT WELL.
THIS IS A BIG PLACE, ISN'T IT? I BET THERE'S SOME SCARY STUFF IN HERE....
WELL, IF YOU MAKE A PROFESSION OUT OF THAT MASK, YOU'LL PROBABLY SEE A LOT WORSE.
INCIDENTALLY, DIANA, WHAT KIND OF PRESENT DID YOU DECIDE TO GET HIM?
I'M NOT SAYING ANYTHING. HE'LL HEAR AND IT'LL SPOIL THE SURPRISE.
HEAR? BUT HE'S NOT EVEN ANYWHERE NEAR US. HE WON'T...
OH. OH, RIGHT. SUPERMAN. I FORGOT.
CHOOSING GIFTS FOR HIM IS ALWAYS DIFFICULT.
THIS YEAR, I PAID A HORTICULTURALIST TO BREED A NEW STRAIN OF ROSE CALLED "THE KRYPTON." I'M PRETTY CERTAIN NO ONE ELSE WILL HAVE GOT HIM FLOWERS...
UH, BRUCE...
MAYBE IT'S NOT TOO LATE TO CHANGE IT FOR SOMETHING ELSE.
DID YOU GET A RECEIPT?
3

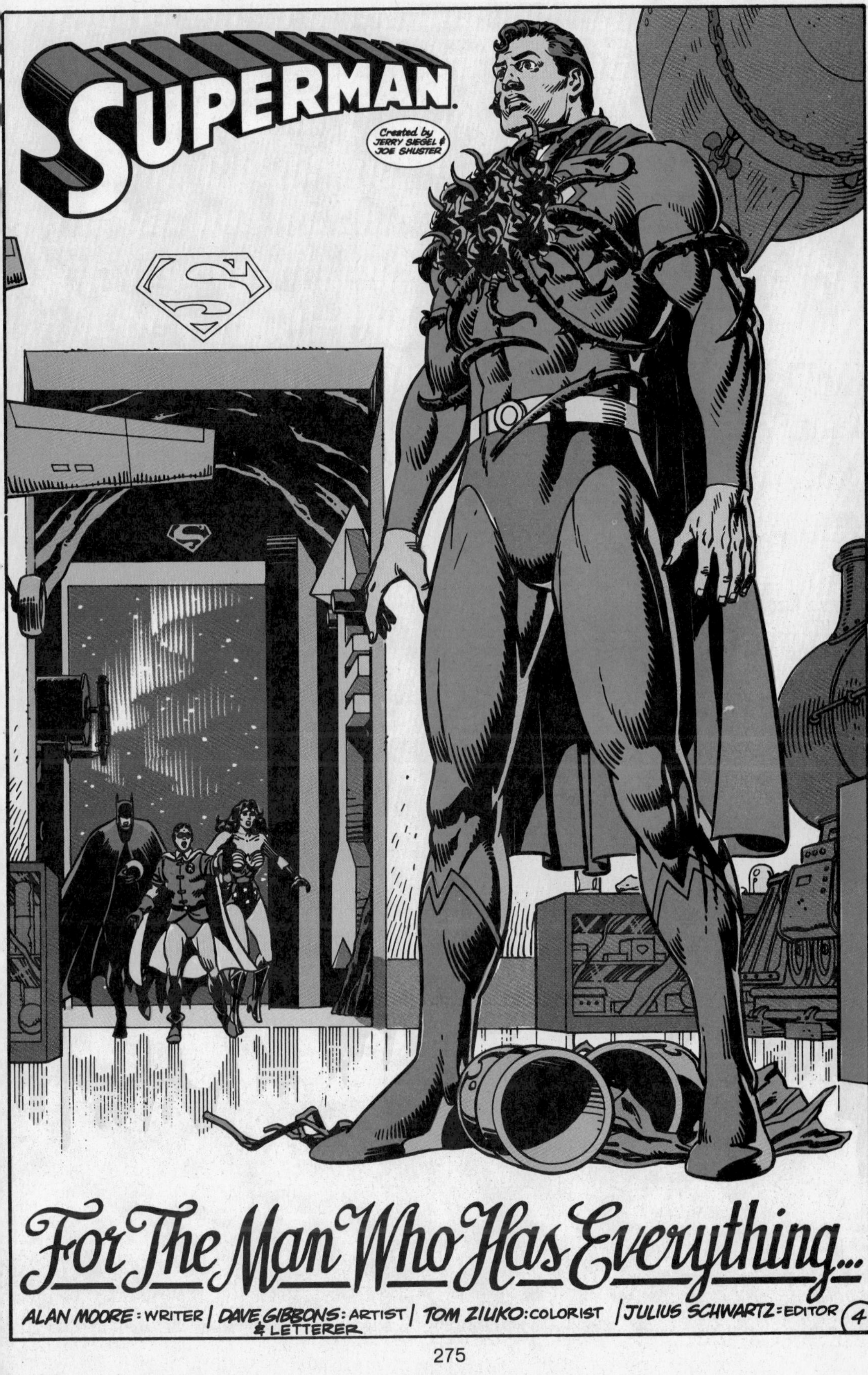
SUPERMAN
Created by JERRY SIEGEL & JOE SHUSTER
For The Man Who Has Everything...
ALAN MOORE: WRITER | DAVE GIBBONS: ARTIST & LETTERER | TOM ZIUKO: COLORIST | JULIUS SCHWARTZ: EDITOR
4

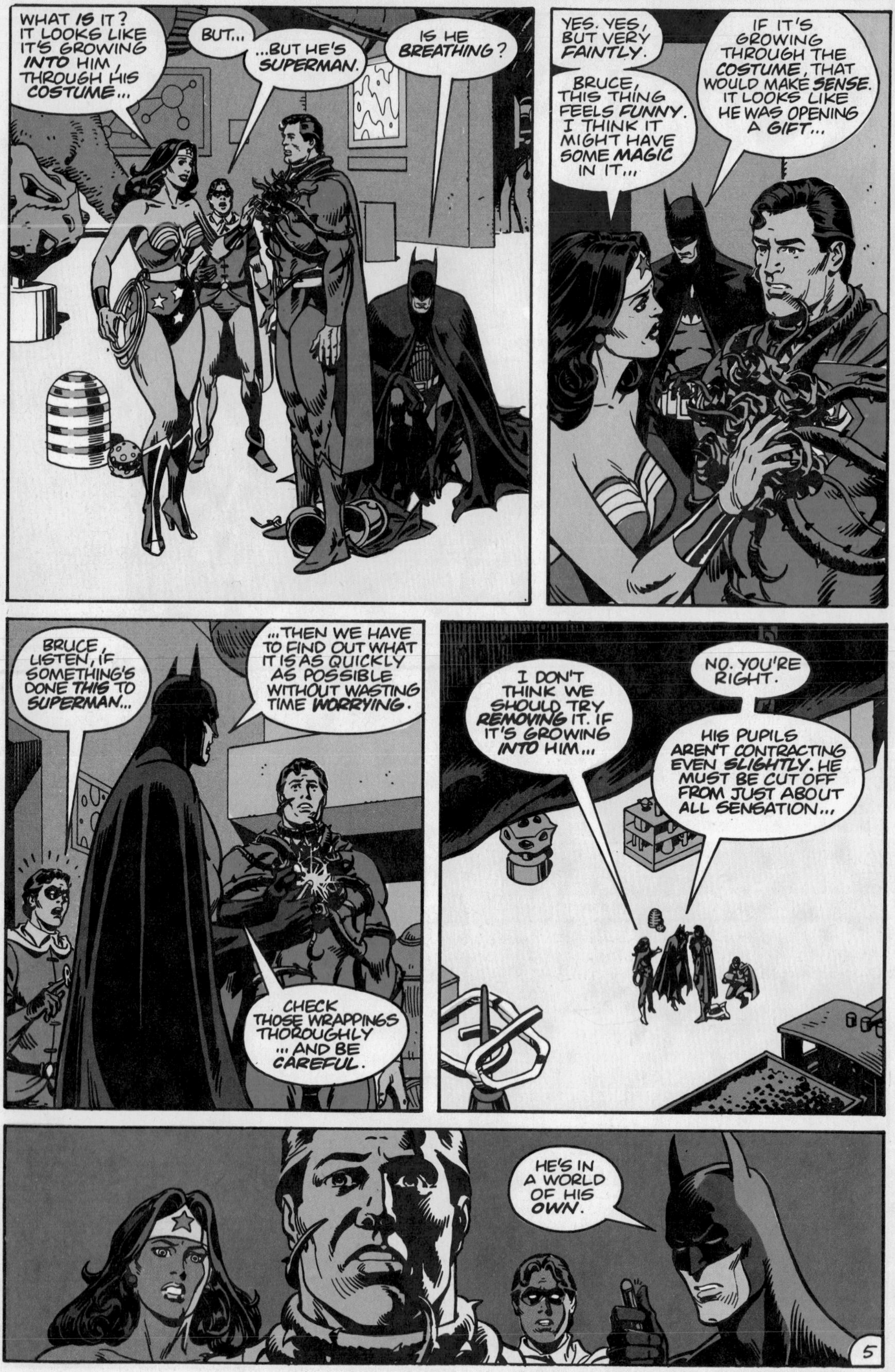
WHAT IS IT? IT LOOKS LIKE IT'S GROWING INTO HIM, THROUGH HIS COSTUME...
BUT...
...BUT HE'S SUPERMAN.
IS HE BREATHING?
YES. YES, BUT VERY FAINTLY.
BRUCE, THIS THING FEELS FUNNY. I THINK IT MIGHT HAVE SOME MAGIC IN IT...
IF IT'S GROWING THROUGH THE COSTUME, THAT WOULD MAKE SENSE. IT LOOKS LIKE HE WAS OPENING A GIFT...
BRUCE, LISTEN, IF SOMETHING'S DONE THIS TO SUPERMAN...
...THEN WE HAVE TO FIND OUT WHAT IT IS AS QUICKLY AS POSSIBLE WITHOUT WASTING TIME WORRYING.
CHECK THOSE WRAPPINGS THOROUGHLY ...AND BE CAREFUL.
I DON'T THINK WE SHOULD TRY REMOVING IT. IF IT'S GROWING INTO HIM...
NO. YOU'RE RIGHT.
HIS PUPILS AREN'T CONTRACTING EVEN SLIGHTLY. HE MUST BE CUT OFF FROM JUST ABOUT ALL SENSATION...
HE'S IN A WORLD OF HIS OWN.
5

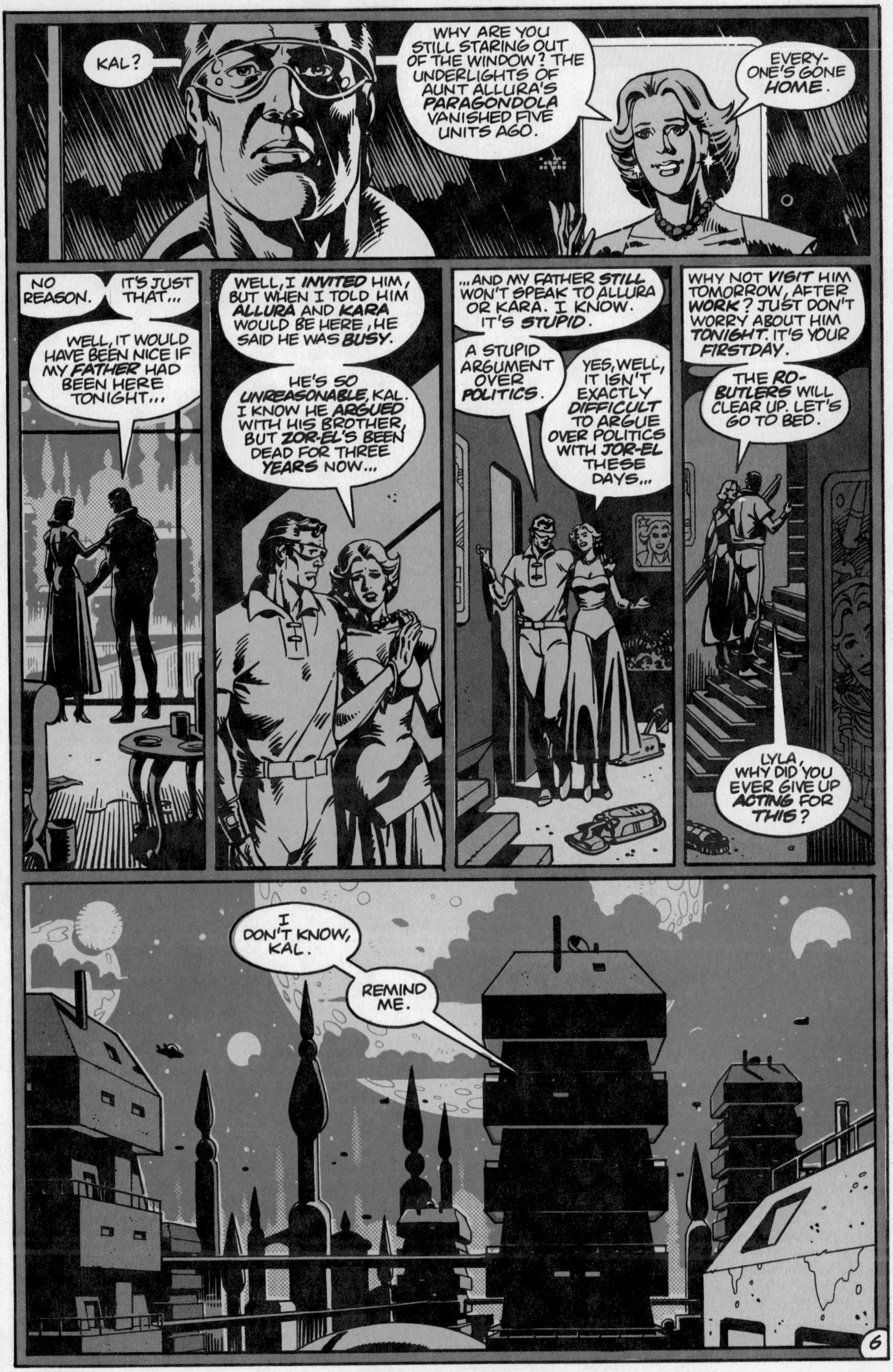
KAL?
WHY ARE YOU STILL STARING OUT OF THE WINDOW? THE UNDERLIGHTS OF AUNT ALLURA'S PARAGONDOLA VANISHED FIVE UNITS AGO.
EVERY-ONE'S GONE HOME.
NO REASON.
IT'S JUST THAT...
WELL, IT WOULD HAVE BEEN NICE IF MY FATHER HAD BEEN HERE TONIGHT...
WELL, I INVITED HIM, BUT WHEN I TOLD HIM ALLURA AND KARA WOULD BE HERE, HE SAID HE WAS BUSY.
HE'S SO UNREASONABLE, KAL. I KNOW HE ARGUED WITH HIS BROTHER, BUT ZOR-EL'S BEEN DEAD FOR THREE YEARS NOW...
...AND MY FATHER STILL WON'T SPEAK TO ALLURA OR KARA. I KNOW. IT'S STUPID.
A STUPID ARGUMENT OVER POLITICS.
YES, WELL, IT ISN'T EXACTLY DIFFICULT TO ARGUE OVER POLITICS WITH JOR-EL THESE DAYS...
WHY NOT VISIT HIM TOMORROW, AFTER WORK? JUST DON'T WORRY ABOUT HIM TONIGHT. IT'S YOUR FIRSTDAY.
THE RO-BUTLERS WILL CLEAR UP. LET'S GO TO BED.
LYLA, WHY DID YOU EVER GIVE UP ACTING FOR THIS?
I DON'T KNOW, KAL.
REMIND ME.
6

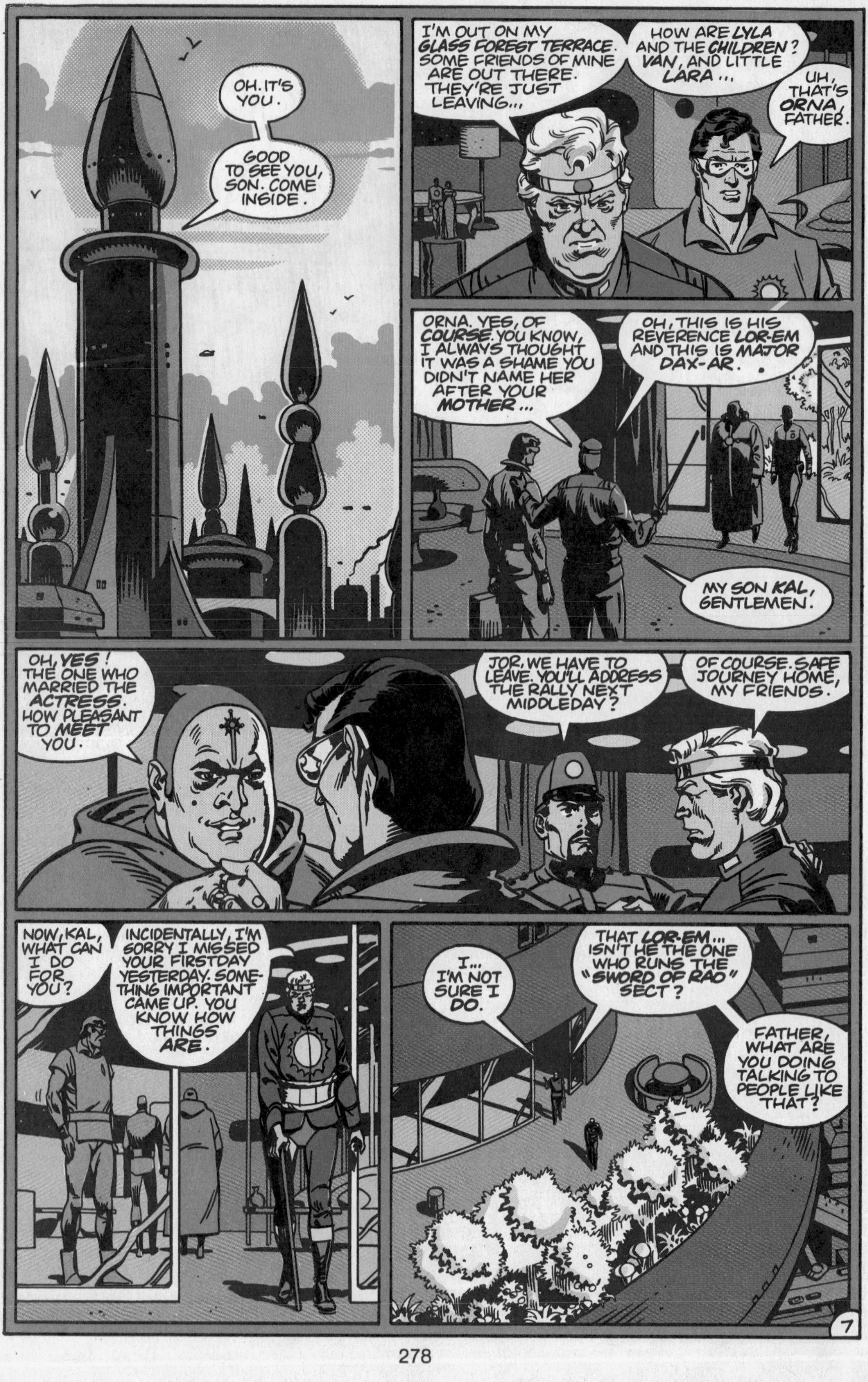
OH. IT'S YOU.
GOOD TO SEE YOU, SON. COME INSIDE.
I'M OUT ON MY GLASS FOREST TERRACE. SOME FRIENDS OF MINE ARE OUT THERE. THEY'RE JUST LEAVING...
HOW ARE LYLA AND THE CHILDREN? VAN, AND LITTLE LARA...
UH, THAT'S ORNA, FATHER.
ORNA. YES, OF COURSE. YOU KNOW, I ALWAYS THOUGHT IT WAS A SHAME YOU DIDN'T NAME HER AFTER YOUR MOTHER...
OH, THIS IS HIS REVERENCE LOR-EM AND THIS IS MAJOR DAX-AR.
MY SON KAL, GENTLEMEN.
OH, YES! THE ONE WHO MARRIED THE ACTRESS. HOW PLEASANT TO MEET YOU.
JOR, WE HAVE TO LEAVE. YOU'LL ADDRESS THE RALLY NEXT MIDDLEDAY?
OF COURSE. SAFE JOURNEY HOME, MY FRIENDS.
NOW, KAL, WHAT CAN I DO FOR YOU?
INCIDENTALLY, I'M SORRY I MISSED YOUR FIRSTDAY YESTERDAY. SOMETHING IMPORTANT CAME UP. YOU KNOW HOW THINGS ARE.
THAT LOR-EM... ISN'T HE THE ONE WHO RUNS THE "SWORD OF RAO" SECT?
I... I'M NOT SURE I DO.
FATHER, WHAT ARE YOU DOING TALKING TO PEOPLE LIKE THAT?
7

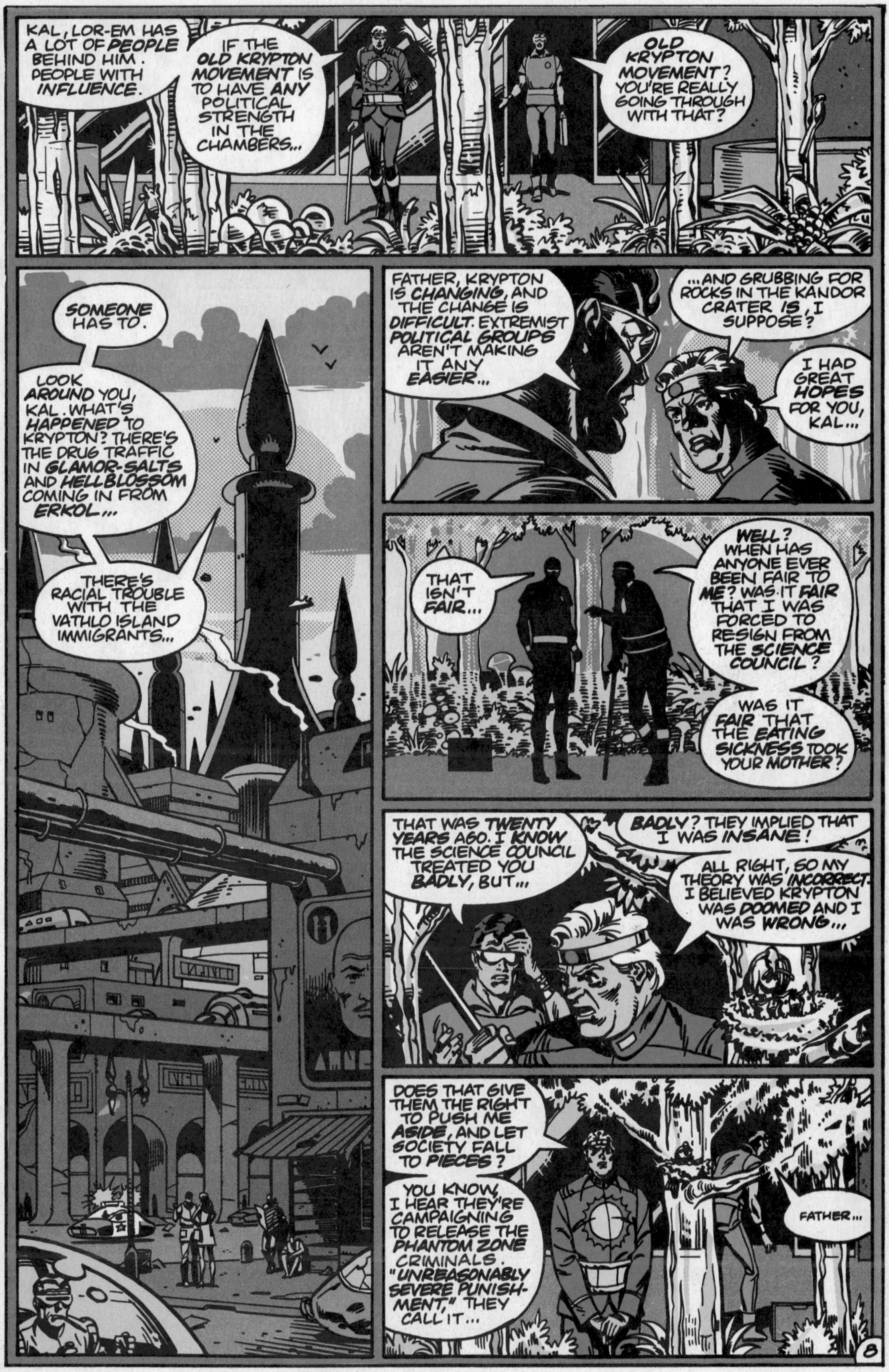
KAL, LOR-EM HAS A LOT OF PEOPLE BEHIND HIM. PEOPLE WITH INFLUENCE.
IF THE OLD KRYPTON MOVEMENT IS TO HAVE ANY POLITICAL STRENGTH IN THE CHAMBERS...
OLD KRYPTON MOVEMENT? YOU'RE REALLY GOING THROUGH WITH THAT?
SOMEONE HAS TO.
LOOK AROUND YOU, KAL. WHAT'S HAPPENED TO KRYPTON? THERE'S THE DRUG TRAFFIC IN GLAMOR-SALTS AND HELLBLOSSOM COMING IN FROM ERKOL...
THERE'S RACIAL TROUBLE WITH THE VATHLO ISLAND IMMIGRANTS...
FATHER, KRYPTON IS CHANGING, AND THE CHANGE IS DIFFICULT. EXTREMIST POLITICAL GROUPS AREN'T MAKING IT ANY EASIER...
...AND GRUBBING FOR ROCKS IN THE KANDOR CRATER IS, I SUPPOSE?
I HAD GREAT HOPES FOR YOU, KAL...
THAT ISN'T FAIR...
WELL? WHEN HAS ANYONE EVER BEEN FAIR TO ME? WAS IT FAIR THAT I WAS FORCED TO RESIGN FROM THE SCIENCE COUNCIL?
WAS IT FAIR THAT THE EATING SICKNESS TOOK YOUR MOTHER?
THAT WAS TWENTY YEARS AGO. I KNOW THE SCIENCE COUNCIL TREATED YOU BADLY, BUT...
BADLY? THEY IMPLIED THAT I WAS INSANE!
ALL RIGHT, SO MY THEORY WAS INCORRECT. I BELIEVED KRYPTON WAS DOOMED AND I WAS WRONG...
DOES THAT GIVE THEM THE RIGHT TO PUSH ME ASIDE, AND LET SOCIETY FALL TO PIECES?
YOU KNOW, I HEAR THEY'RE CAMPAIGNING TO RELEASE THE PHANTOM ZONE CRIMINALS. "UNREASONABLY SEVERE PUNISHMENT," THEY CALL IT...
FATHER...
8

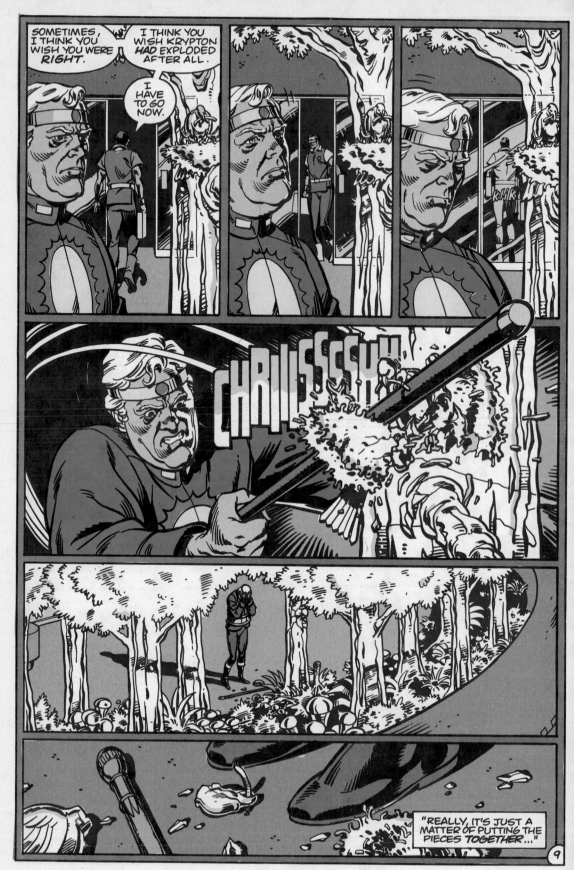

SOMETIMES, I THINK YOU WISH YOU WERE RIGHT.

I THINK YOU WISH KRYPTON *HAD* EXPLODED AFTER ALL.

I HAVE TO GO NOW.

CHRIIISSSSHH...

"REALLY, IT'S JUST A MATTER OF PUTTING THE PIECES *TOGETHER* ..."

9

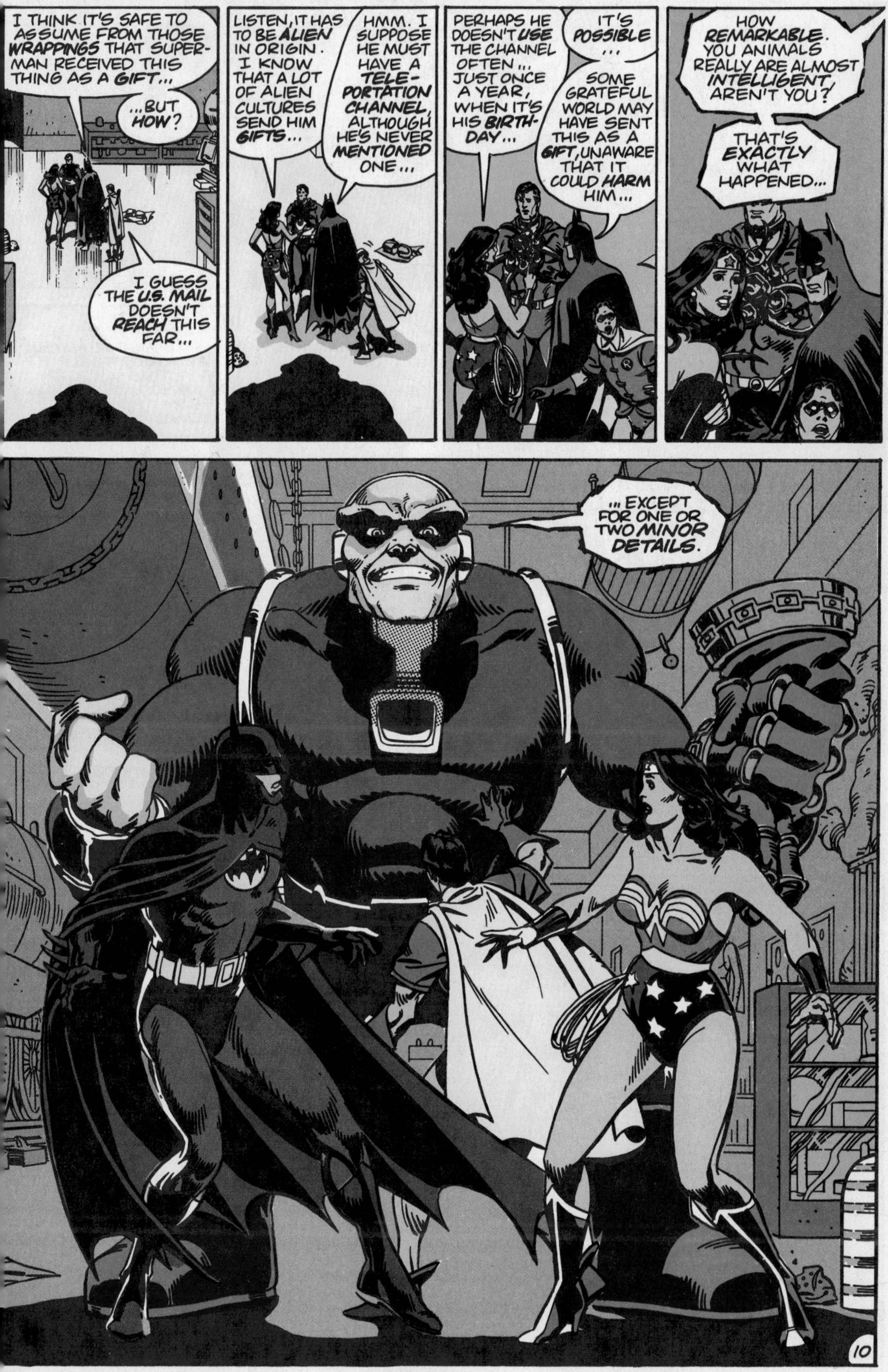
I THINK IT'S SAFE TO ASSUME FROM THOSE WRAPPINGS THAT SUPERMAN RECEIVED THIS THING AS A GIFT...
...BUT HOW?
I GUESS THE U.S. MAIL DOESN'T REACH THIS FAR...
LISTEN, IT HAS TO BE ALIEN IN ORIGIN. I KNOW THAT A LOT OF ALIEN CULTURES SEND HIM GIFTS...
HMM. I SUPPOSE HE MUST HAVE A TELE-PORTATION CHANNEL, ALTHOUGH HE'S NEVER MENTIONED ONE...
PERHAPS HE DOESN'T USE THE CHANNEL OFTEN... JUST ONCE A YEAR, WHEN IT'S HIS BIRTHDAY...
IT'S POSSIBLE...
SOME GRATEFUL WORLD MAY HAVE SENT THIS AS A GIFT, UNAWARE THAT IT COULD HARM HIM...
HOW REMARKABLE. YOU ANIMALS REALLY ARE ALMOST INTELLIGENT, AREN'T YOU?
THAT'S EXACTLY WHAT HAPPENED...
...EXCEPT FOR ONE OR TWO MINOR DETAILS.
10

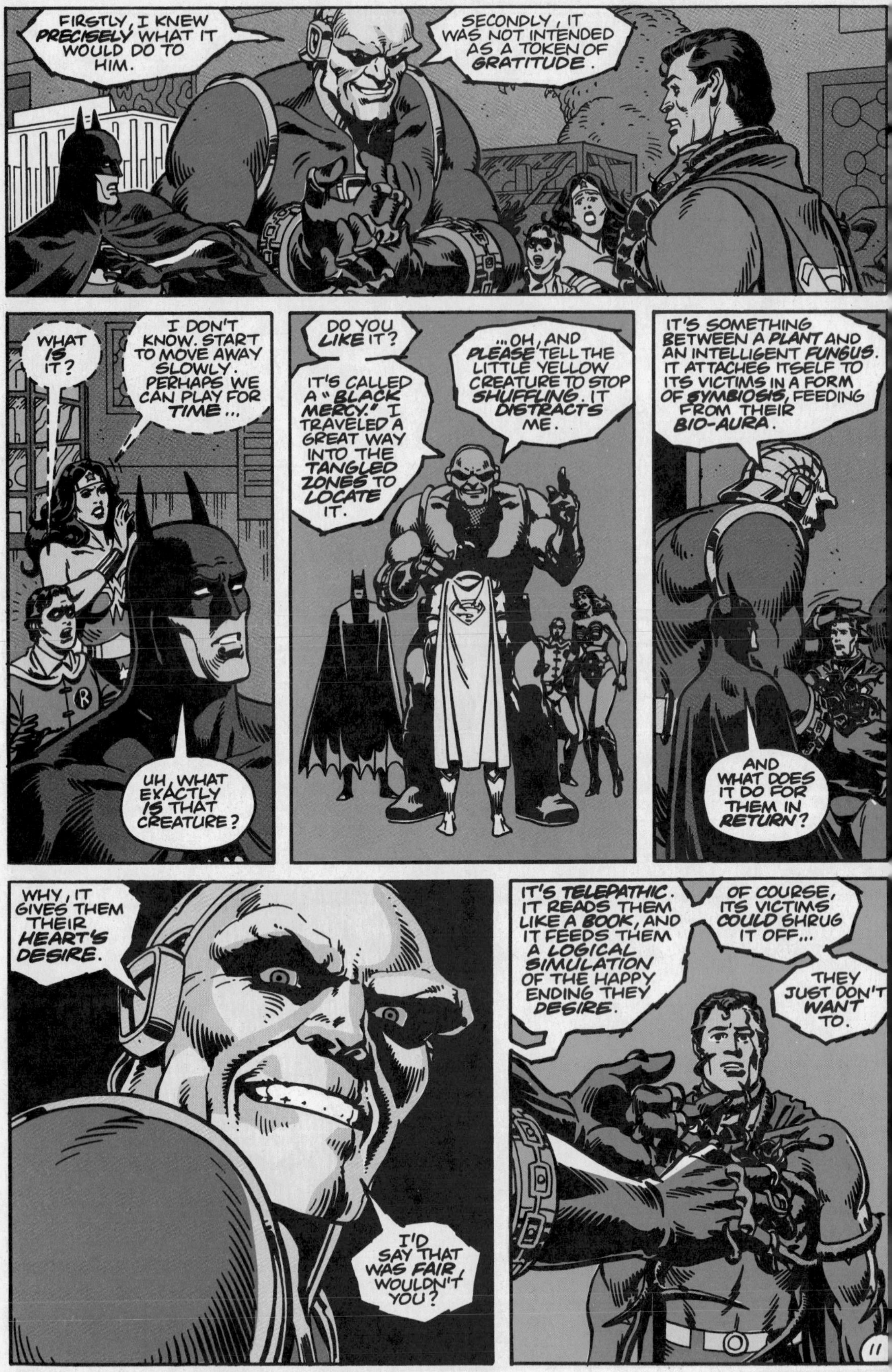
FIRSTLY, I KNEW PRECISELY WHAT IT WOULD DO TO HIM.
SECONDLY, IT WAS NOT INTENDED AS A TOKEN OF GRATITUDE.
WHAT IS IT?
I DON'T KNOW. START TO MOVE AWAY SLOWLY. PERHAPS WE CAN PLAY FOR TIME...
UH, WHAT EXACTLY IS THAT CREATURE?
DO YOU LIKE IT?
IT'S CALLED A "BLACK MERCY." I TRAVELED A GREAT WAY INTO THE TANGLED ZONES TO LOCATE IT.
...OH, AND PLEASE TELL THE LITTLE YELLOW CREATURE TO STOP SHUFFLING. IT DISTRACTS ME.
IT'S SOMETHING BETWEEN A PLANT AND AN INTELLIGENT FUNGUS. IT ATTACHES ITSELF TO ITS VICTIMS IN A FORM OF SYMBIOSIS, FEEDING FROM THEIR BIO-AURA.
AND WHAT DOES IT DO FOR THEM IN RETURN?
WHY, IT GIVES THEM THEIR HEART'S DESIRE.
I'D SAY THAT WAS FAIR, WOULDN'T YOU?
IT'S TELEPATHIC. IT READS THEM LIKE A BOOK, AND IT FEEDS THEM A LOGICAL SIMULATION OF THE HAPPY ENDING THEY DESIRE.
OF COURSE, ITS VICTIMS COULD SHRUG IT OFF...
THEY JUST DON'T WANT TO.
11

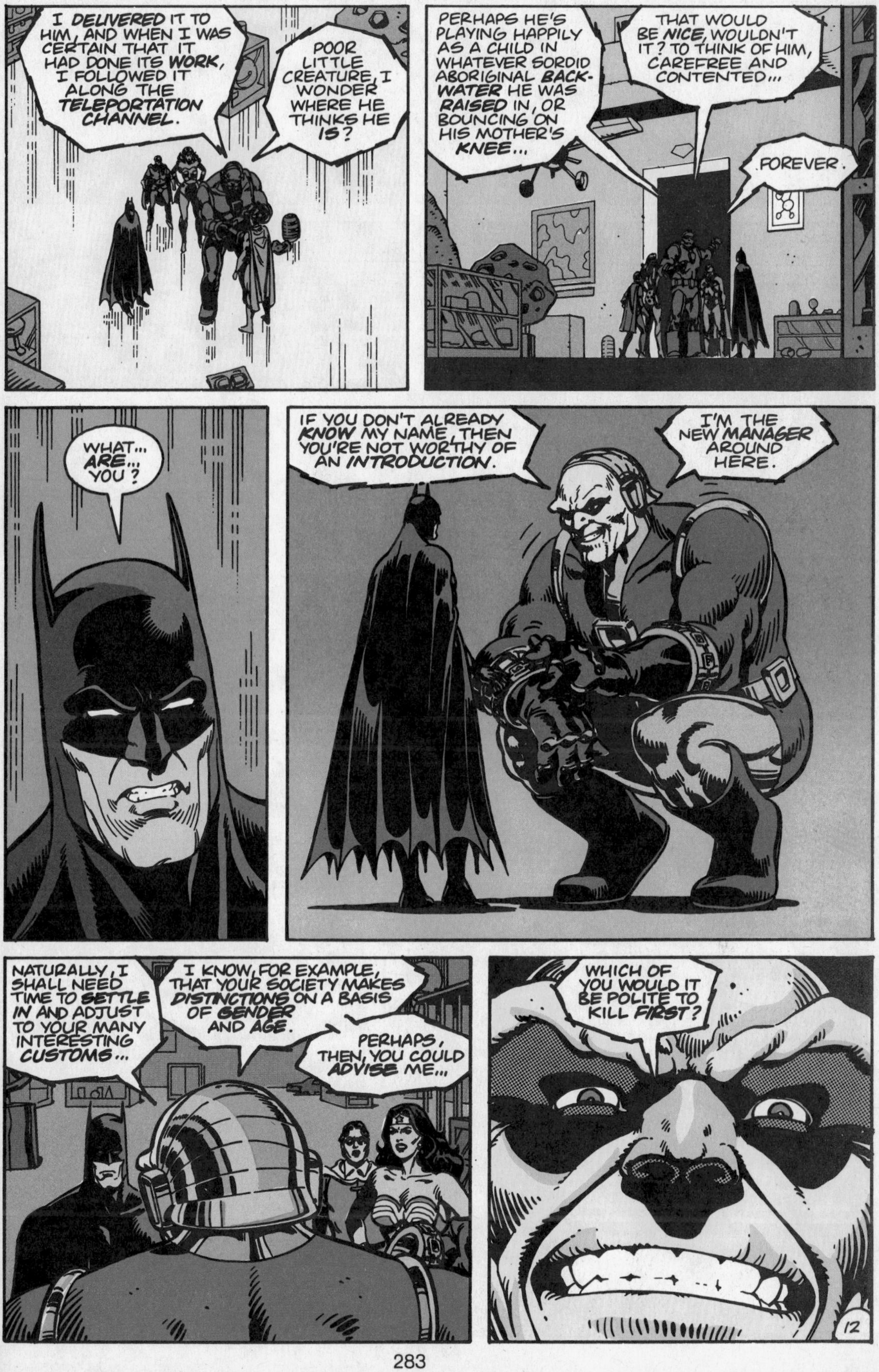
I DELIVERED IT TO HIM, AND WHEN I WAS CERTAIN THAT IT HAD DONE ITS WORK, I FOLLOWED IT ALONG THE TELEPORTATION CHANNEL.
POOR LITTLE CREATURE, I WONDER WHERE HE THINKS HE IS?
PERHAPS HE'S PLAYING HAPPILY AS A CHILD IN WHATEVER SORDID ABORIGINAL BACK-WATER HE WAS RAISED IN, OR BOUNCING ON HIS MOTHER'S KNEE...
THAT WOULD BE NICE, WOULDN'T IT? TO THINK OF HIM, CAREFREE AND CONTENTED...
...FOREVER.
WHAT... ARE... YOU?
IF YOU DON'T ALREADY KNOW MY NAME, THEN YOU'RE NOT WORTHY OF AN INTRODUCTION.
I'M THE NEW MANAGER AROUND HERE.
NATURALLY, I SHALL NEED TIME TO SETTLE IN AND ADJUST TO YOUR MANY INTERESTING CUSTOMS...
I KNOW, FOR EXAMPLE, THAT YOUR SOCIETY MAKES DISTINCTIONS ON A BASIS OF GENDER AND AGE.
PERHAPS, THEN, YOU COULD ADVISE ME...
WHICH OF YOU WOULD IT BE POLITE TO KILL FIRST?
12

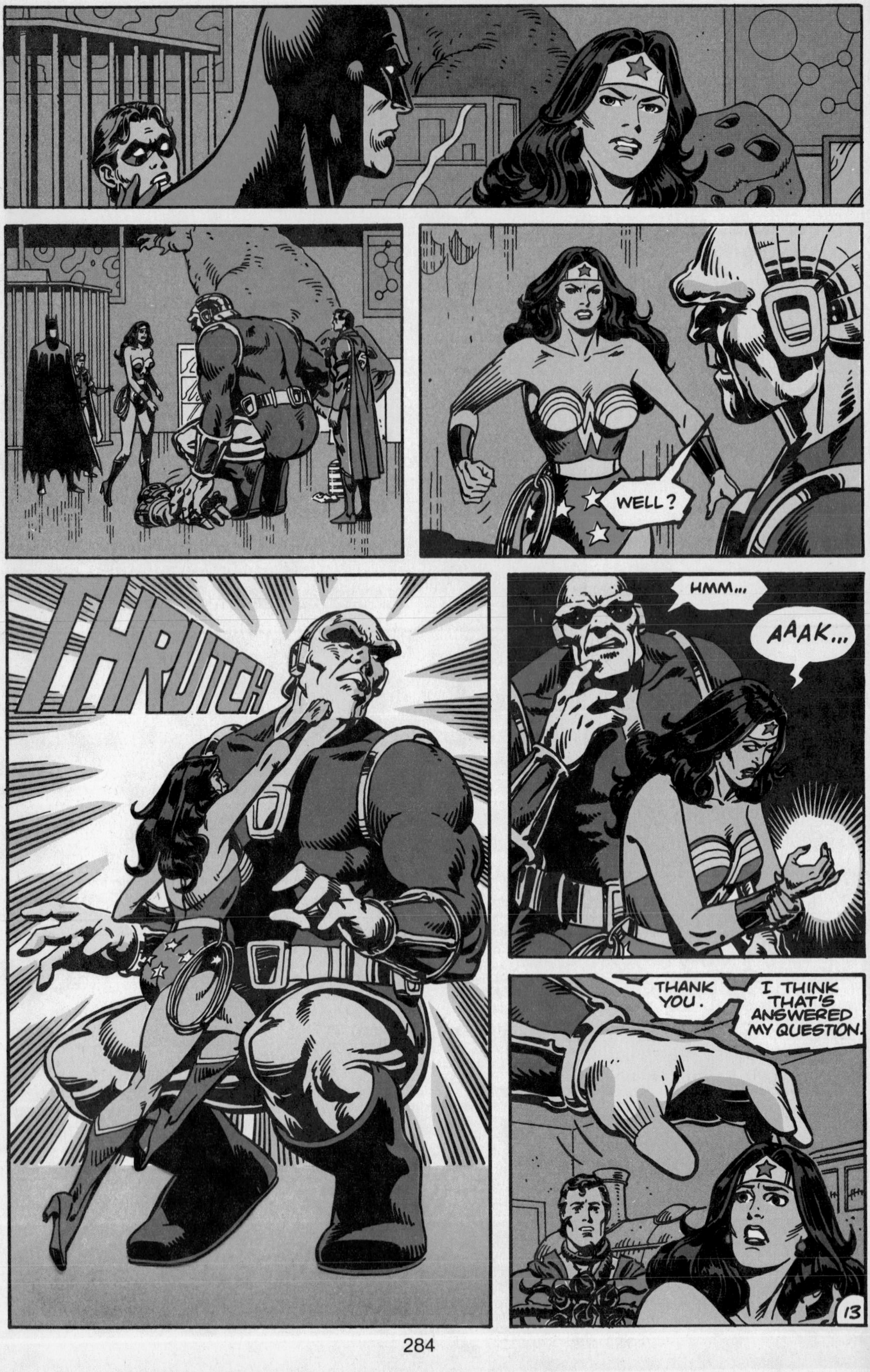
WELL?
THRUTCH
HMM...
AAAK...
THANK YOU.
I THINK THAT'S ANSWERED MY QUESTION.
13

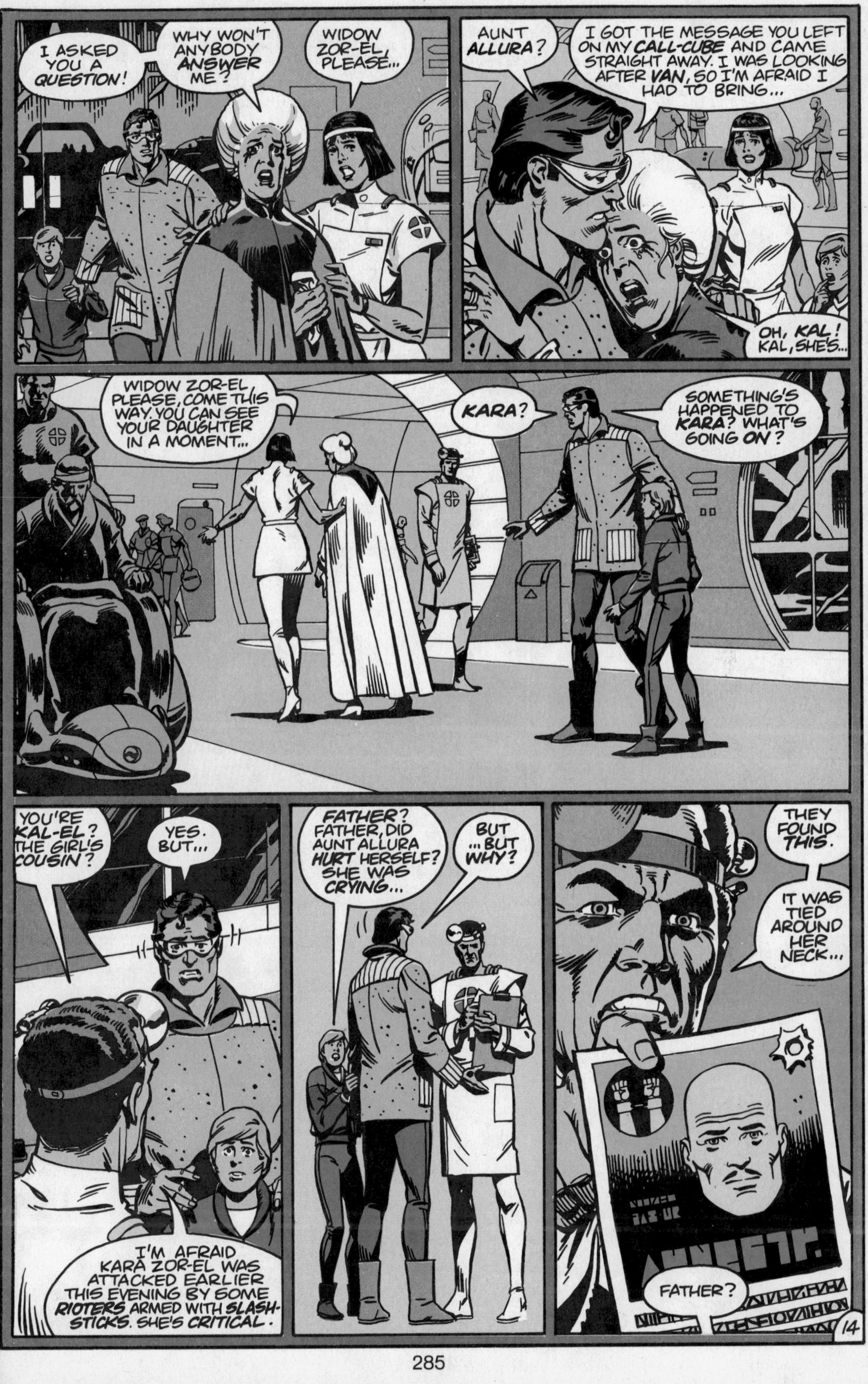
I ASKED YOU A QUESTION!
WHY WON'T ANYBODY ANSWER ME?
WIDOW ZOR-EL, PLEASE...
AUNT ALLURA?
I GOT THE MESSAGE YOU LEFT ON MY CALL-CUBE AND CAME STRAIGHT AWAY. I WAS LOOKING AFTER VAN, SO I'M AFRAID I HAD TO BRING...
OH, KAL! KAL, SHE'S...
WIDOW ZOR-EL PLEASE, COME THIS WAY. YOU CAN SEE YOUR DAUGHTER IN A MOMENT...
KARA?
SOMETHING'S HAPPENED TO KARA? WHAT'S GOING ON?
YOU'RE KAL-EL? THE GIRL'S COUSIN?
YES. BUT...
I'M AFRAID KARA ZOR-EL WAS ATTACKED EARLIER THIS EVENING BY SOME RIOTERS ARMED WITH SLASH-STICKS. SHE'S CRITICAL.
FATHER? FATHER, DID AUNT ALLURA HURT HERSELF? SHE WAS CRYING...
BUT ...BUT WHY?
THEY FOUND THIS.
IT WAS TIED AROUND HER NECK...
FATHER?
14

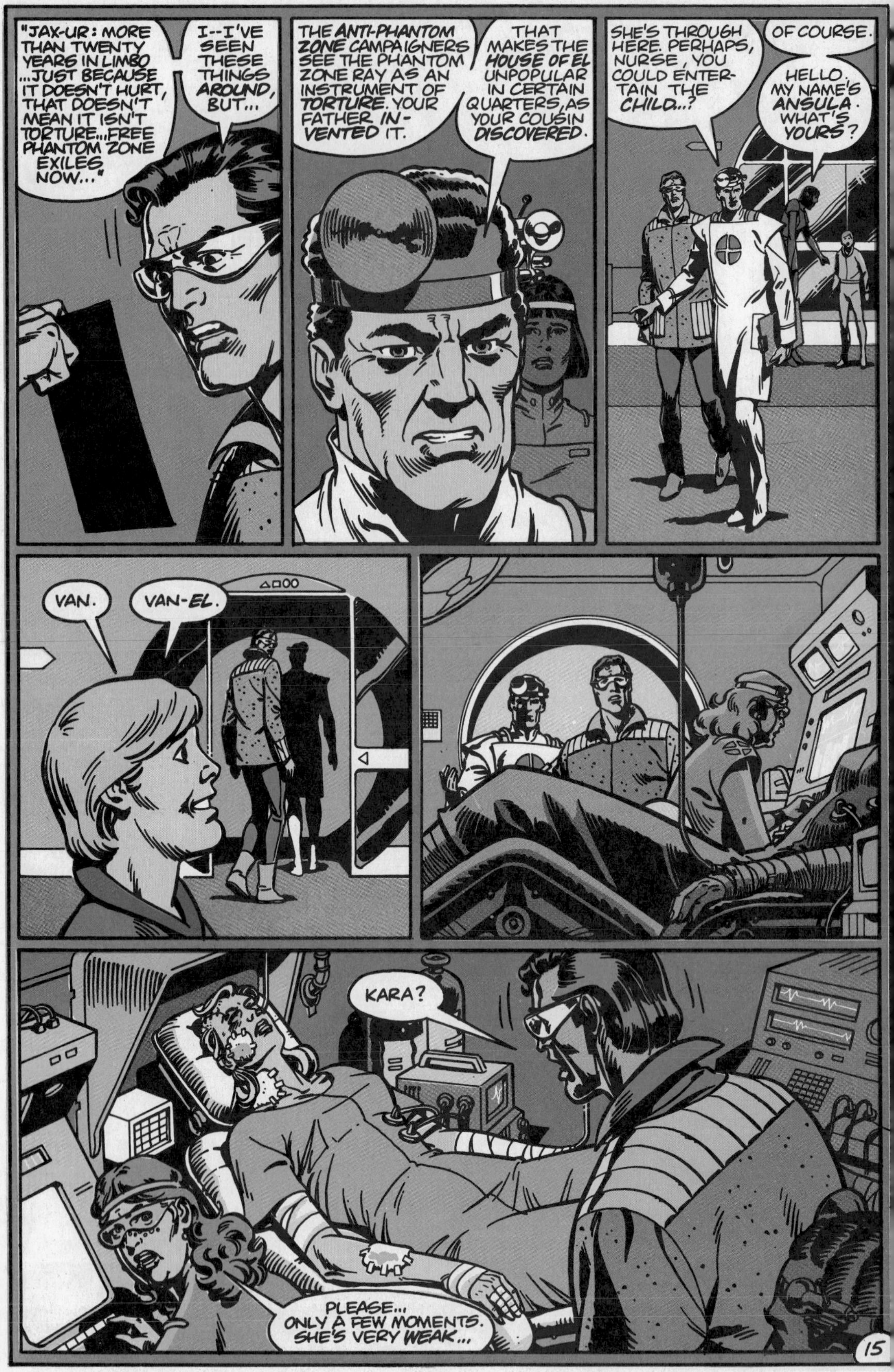
"JAX-UR: MORE THAN TWENTY YEARS IN LIMBO ...JUST BECAUSE IT DOESN'T HURT, THAT DOESN'T MEAN IT ISN'T TORTURE...FREE PHANTOM ZONE EXILES NOW..."
I--I'VE SEEN THESE THINGS AROUND, BUT...
THE ANTI-PHANTOM ZONE CAMPAIGNERS SEE THE PHANTOM ZONE RAY AS AN INSTRUMENT OF TORTURE. YOUR FATHER INVENTED IT.
THAT MAKES THE HOUSE OF EL UNPOPULAR IN CERTAIN QUARTERS, AS YOUR COUSIN DISCOVERED.
SHE'S THROUGH HERE. PERHAPS, NURSE, YOU COULD ENTERTAIN THE CHILD...?
OF COURSE.
HELLO. MY NAME'S ANSULA. WHAT'S YOURS?
VAN.
VAN-EL.
KARA?
PLEASE... ONLY A FEW MOMENTS. SHE'S VERY WEAK...
15

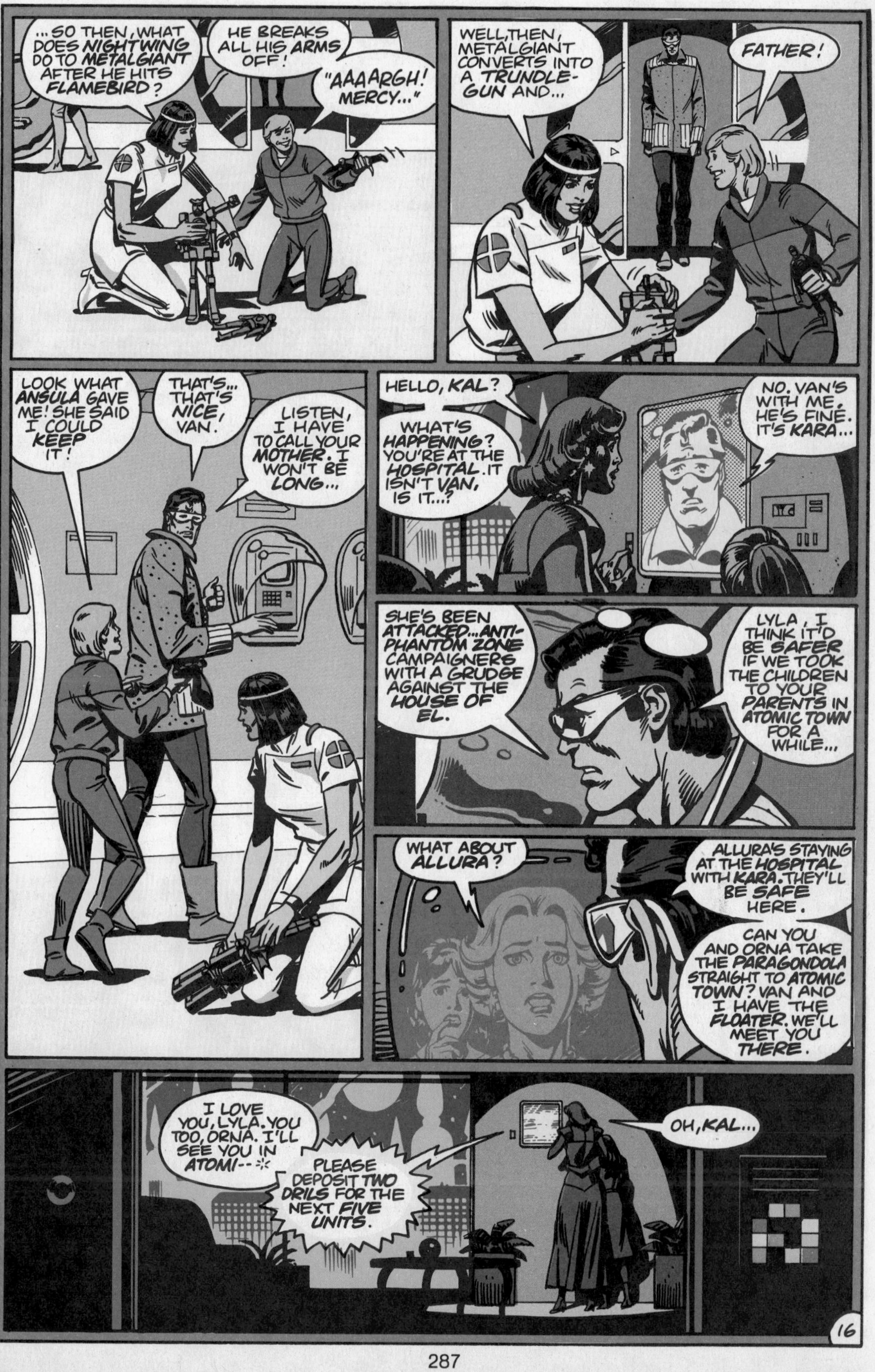
...SO THEN, WHAT DOES NIGHTWING DO TO METALGIANT AFTER HE HITS FLAMEBIRD?
HE BREAKS ALL HIS ARMS OFF!
"AAAARGH! MERCY..."
WELL, THEN, METALGIANT CONVERTS INTO A TRUNDLE-GUN AND...
FATHER!
LOOK WHAT ANSULA GAVE ME! SHE SAID I COULD KEEP IT!
THAT'S... THAT'S NICE, VAN.
LISTEN, I HAVE TO CALL YOUR MOTHER. I WON'T BE LONG...
HELLO, KAL?
WHAT'S HAPPENING? YOU'RE AT THE HOSPITAL. IT ISN'T VAN, IS IT...?
NO. VAN'S WITH ME. HE'S FINE. IT'S KARA...
SHE'S BEEN ATTACKED... ANTI-PHANTOM ZONE CAMPAIGNERS WITH A GRUDGE AGAINST THE HOUSE OF EL.
LYLA, I THINK IT'D BE SAFER IF WE TOOK THE CHILDREN TO YOUR PARENTS IN ATOMIC TOWN FOR A WHILE...
WHAT ABOUT ALLURA?
ALLURA'S STAYING AT THE HOSPITAL WITH KARA. THEY'LL BE SAFE HERE.
CAN YOU AND ORNA TAKE THE PARAGONDOLA STRAIGHT TO ATOMIC TOWN? VAN AND I HAVE THE FLOATER. WE'LL MEET YOU THERE.
I LOVE YOU, LYLA. YOU TOO, ORNA. I'LL SEE YOU IN ATOMI--
PLEASE DEPOSIT TWO DRILS FOR THE NEXT FIVE UNITS.
OH, KAL...
16

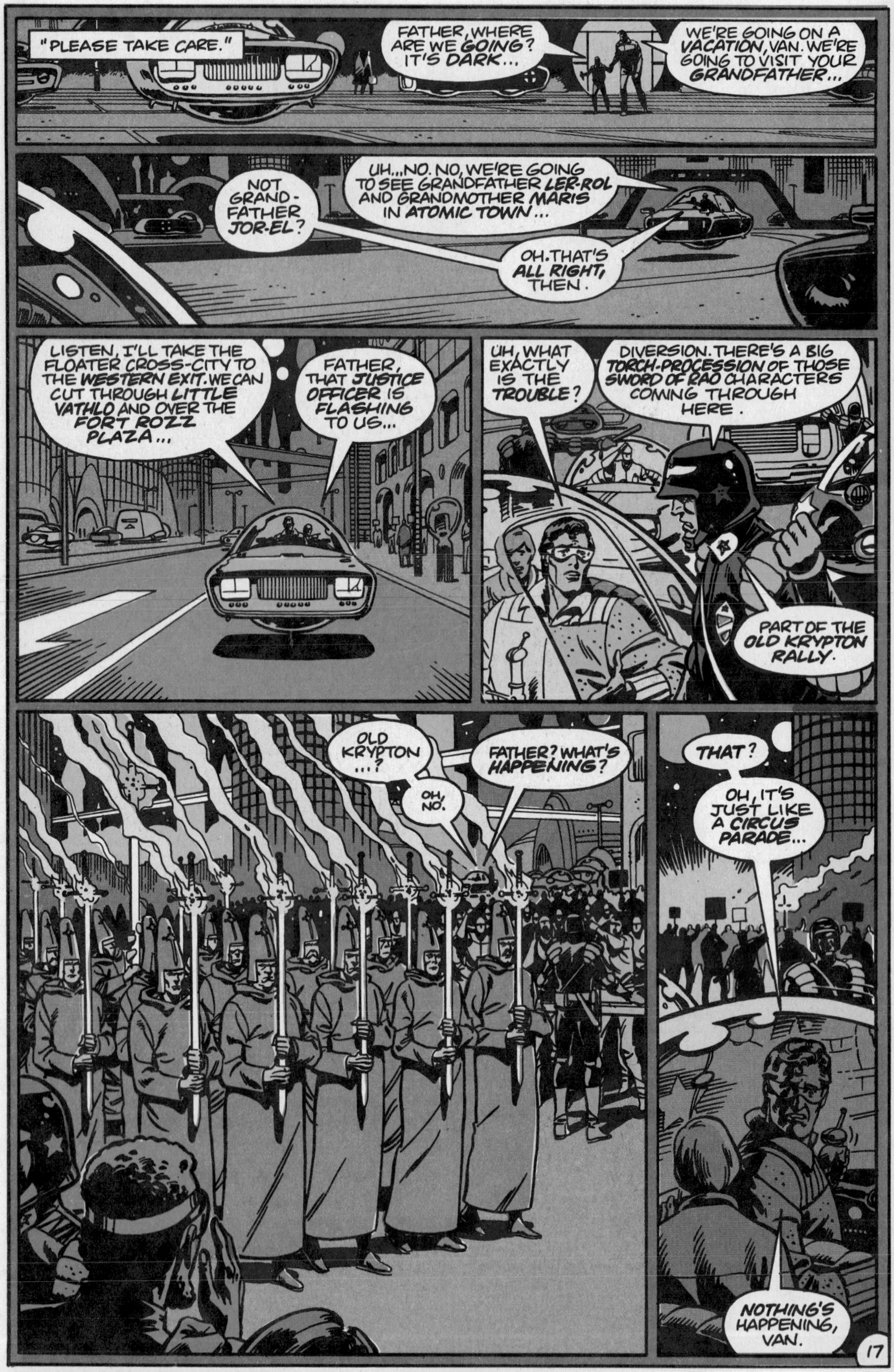
"PLEASE TAKE CARE."
FATHER, WHERE ARE WE GOING? IT'S DARK...
WE'RE GOING ON A VACATION, VAN. WE'RE GOING TO VISIT YOUR GRANDFATHER...
NOT GRAND-FATHER JOR-EL?
UH...NO. NO, WE'RE GOING TO SEE GRANDFATHER LER-ROL AND GRANDMOTHER MARIS IN ATOMIC TOWN...
OH. THAT'S ALL RIGHT, THEN.
LISTEN, I'LL TAKE THE FLOATER CROSS-CITY TO THE WESTERN EXIT. WE CAN CUT THROUGH LITTLE VATHLO AND OVER THE FORT ROZZ PLAZA...
FATHER, THAT JUSTICE OFFICER IS FLASHING TO US...
UH, WHAT EXACTLY IS THE TROUBLE?
DIVERSION. THERE'S A BIG TORCH-PROCESSION OF THOSE SWORD OF RAO CHARACTERS COMING THROUGH HERE.
PART OF THE OLD KRYPTON RALLY.
OLD KRYPTON ...?
OH, NO.
FATHER? WHAT'S HAPPENING?
THAT?
OH, IT'S JUST LIKE A CIRCUS PARADE...
NOTHING'S HAPPENING, VAN.
17

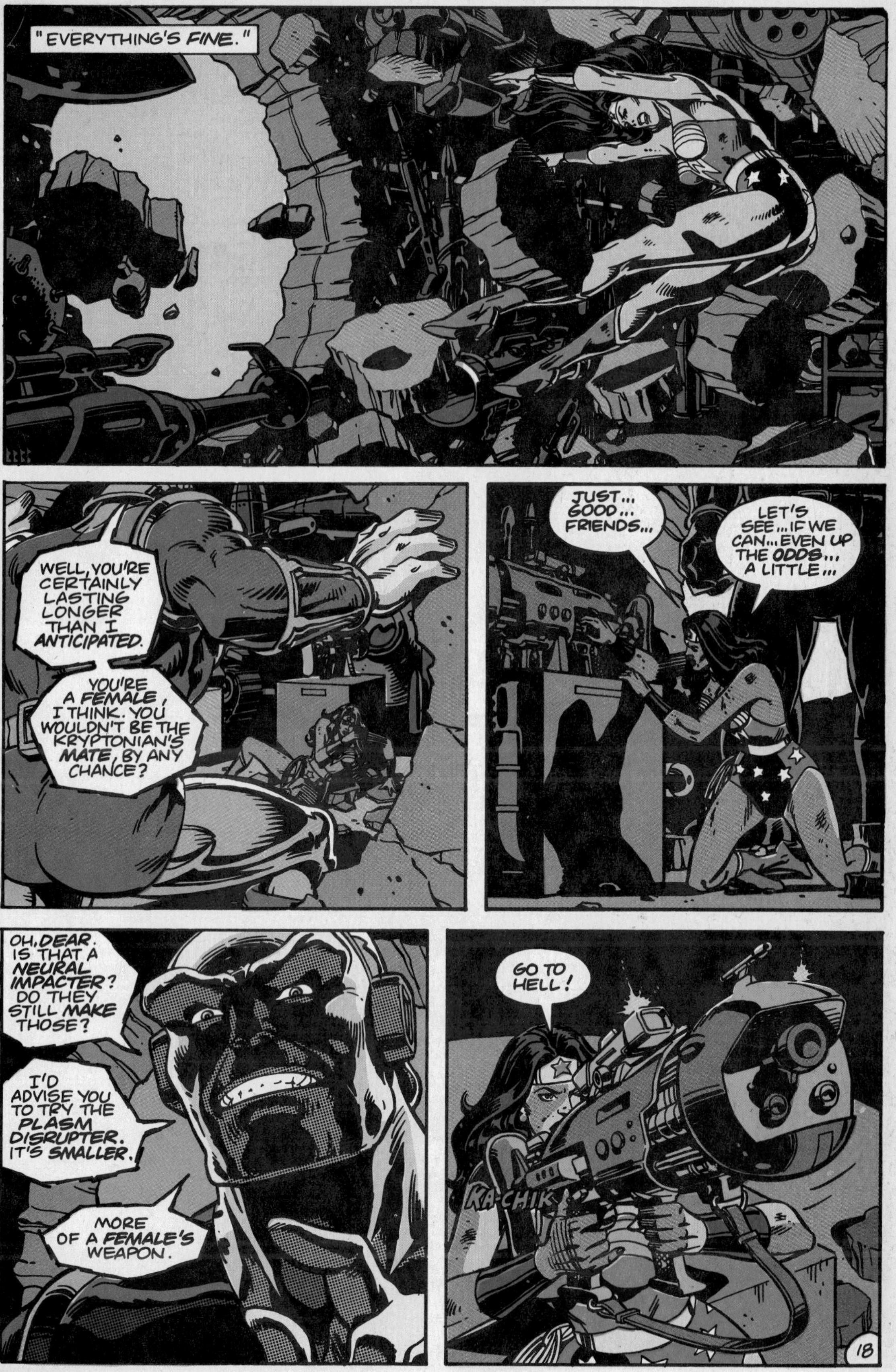
"EVERYTHING'S FINE."
WELL, YOU'RE CERTAINLY LASTING LONGER THAN I ANTICIPATED.
YOU'RE A FEMALE, I THINK. YOU WOULDN'T BE THE KRYPTONIAN'S MATE, BY ANY CHANCE?
JUST... GOOD... FRIENDS...
LET'S SEE... IF WE CAN... EVEN UP THE ODDS... A LITTLE...
OH, DEAR. IS THAT A NEURAL IMPACTER? DO THEY STILL MAKE THOSE?
I'D ADVISE YOU TO TRY THE PLASM DISRUPTER. IT'S SMALLER.
MORE OF A FEMALE'S WEAPON.
GO TO HELL!
KA-CHIK
18

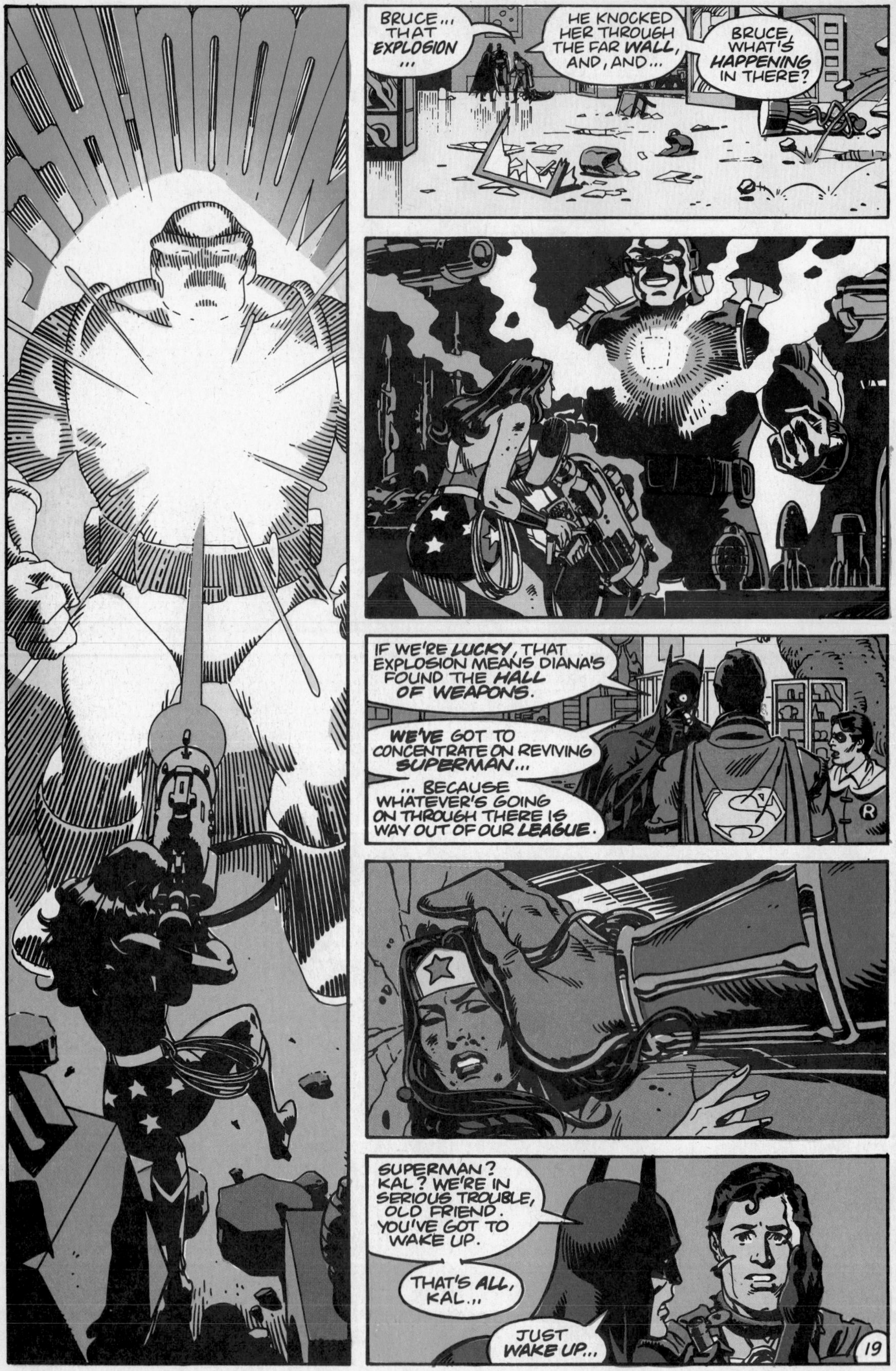
BRUCE... THAT EXPLOSION ...
HE KNOCKED HER THROUGH THE FAR WALL, AND, AND...
BRUCE, WHAT'S HAPPENING IN THERE?
IF WE'RE LUCKY, THAT EXPLOSION MEANS DIANA'S FOUND THE HALL OF WEAPONS.
WE'VE GOT TO CONCENTRATE ON REVIVING SUPERMAN...
... BECAUSE WHATEVER'S GOING ON THROUGH THERE IS WAY OUT OF OUR LEAGUE.
SUPERMAN? KAL? WE'RE IN SERIOUS TROUBLE, OLD FRIEND. YOU'VE GOT TO WAKE UP.
THAT'S ALL, KAL...
JUST WAKE UP...
19

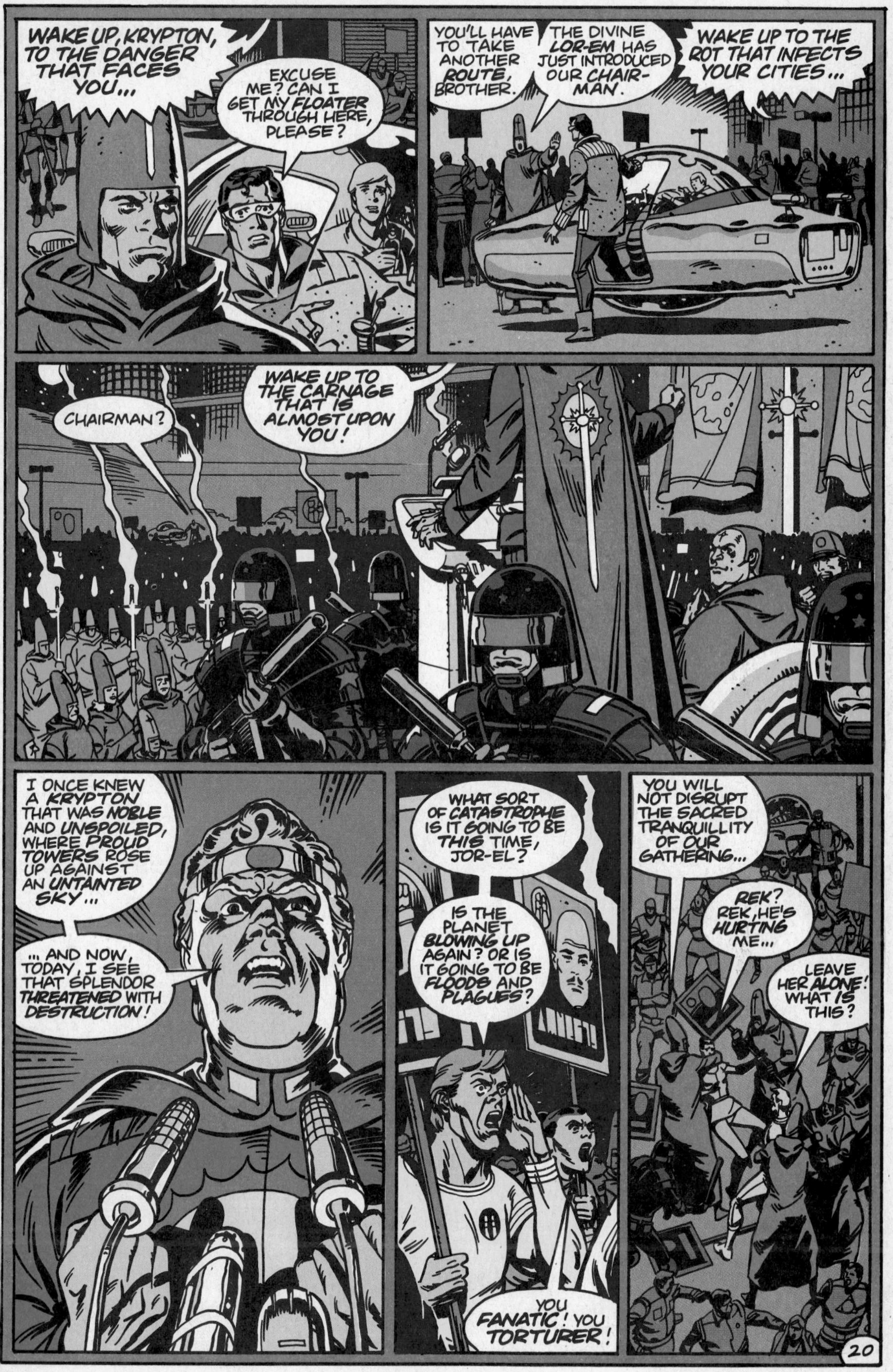
WAKE UP, KRYPTON, TO THE DANGER THAT FACES YOU...
EXCUSE ME? CAN I GET MY FLOATER THROUGH HERE, PLEASE?
YOU'LL HAVE TO TAKE ANOTHER ROUTE, BROTHER.
THE DIVINE LOR-EM HAS JUST INTRODUCED OUR CHAIRMAN.
WAKE UP TO THE ROT THAT INFECTS YOUR CITIES...
CHAIRMAN?
WAKE UP TO THE CARNAGE THAT IS ALMOST UPON YOU!
I ONCE KNEW A KRYPTON THAT WAS NOBLE AND UNSPOILED, WHERE PROUD TOWERS ROSE UP AGAINST AN UNTAINTED SKY...
... AND NOW, TODAY, I SEE THAT SPLENDOR THREATENED WITH DESTRUCTION!
WHAT SORT OF CATASTROPHE IS IT GOING TO BE THIS TIME, JOR-EL?
IS THE PLANET BLOWING UP AGAIN? OR IS IT GOING TO BE FLOODS AND PLAGUES?
YOU FANATIC! YOU TORTURER!
YOU WILL NOT DISRUPT THE SACRED TRANQUILLITY OF OUR GATHERING...
REK? REK, HE'S HURTING ME...
LEAVE HER ALONE! WHAT IS THIS?
20

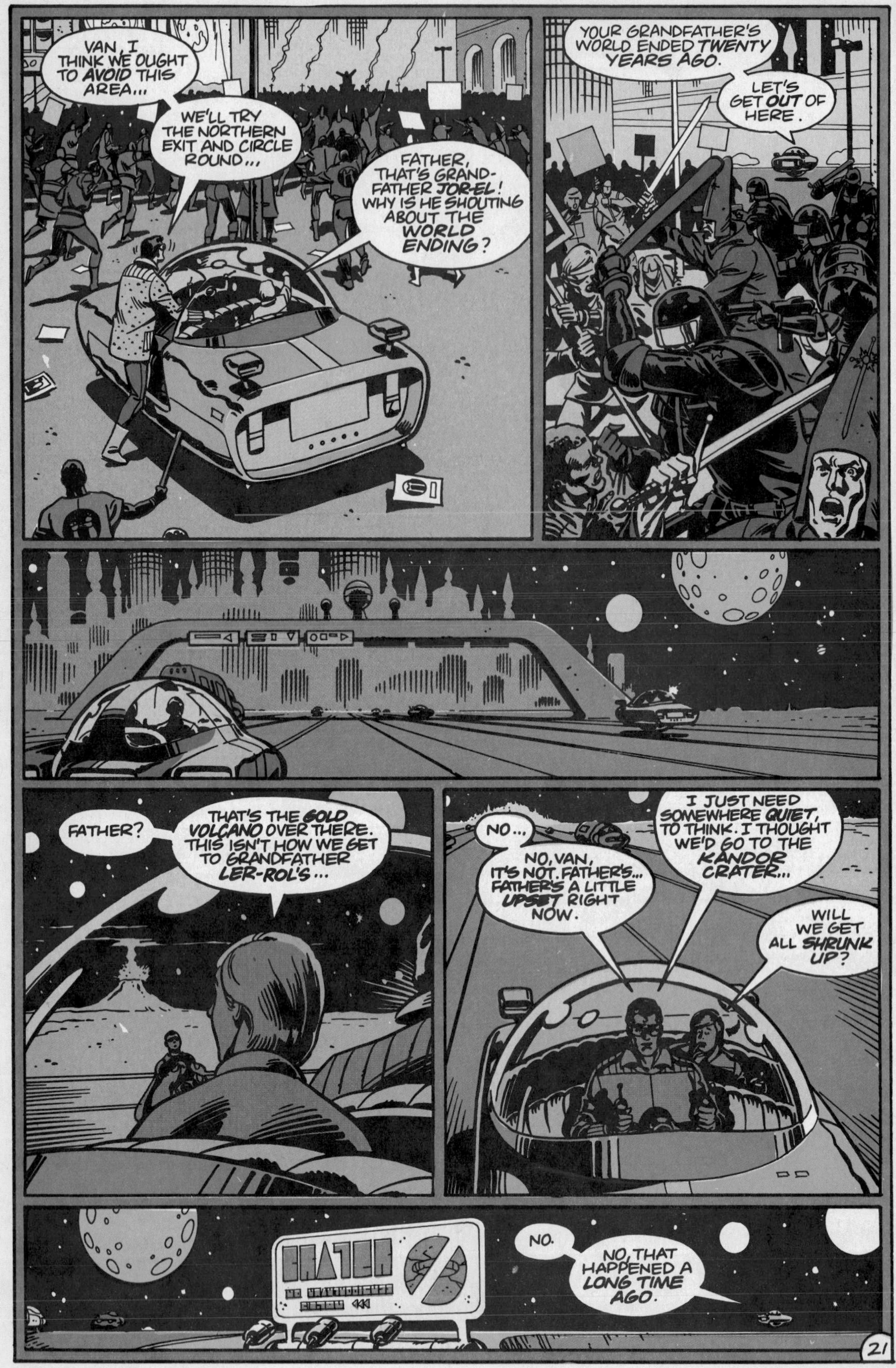
VAN, I THINK WE OUGHT TO AVOID THIS AREA...
WE'LL TRY THE NORTHERN EXIT AND CIRCLE ROUND...
FATHER, THAT'S GRAND-FATHER JOR-EL! WHY IS HE SHOUTING ABOUT THE WORLD ENDING?
YOUR GRANDFATHER'S WORLD ENDED TWENTY YEARS AGO.
LET'S GET OUT OF HERE.
FATHER?
THAT'S THE GOLD VOLCANO OVER THERE. THIS ISN'T HOW WE GET TO GRANDFATHER LER-ROL'S...
NO...
NO, VAN, IT'S NOT. FATHER'S... FATHER'S A LITTLE UPSET RIGHT NOW.
I JUST NEED SOMEWHERE QUIET, TO THINK. I THOUGHT WE'D GO TO THE KANDOR CRATER...
WILL WE GET ALL SHRUNK UP?
CRATER
NO.
NO, THAT HAPPENED A LONG TIME AGO.
21

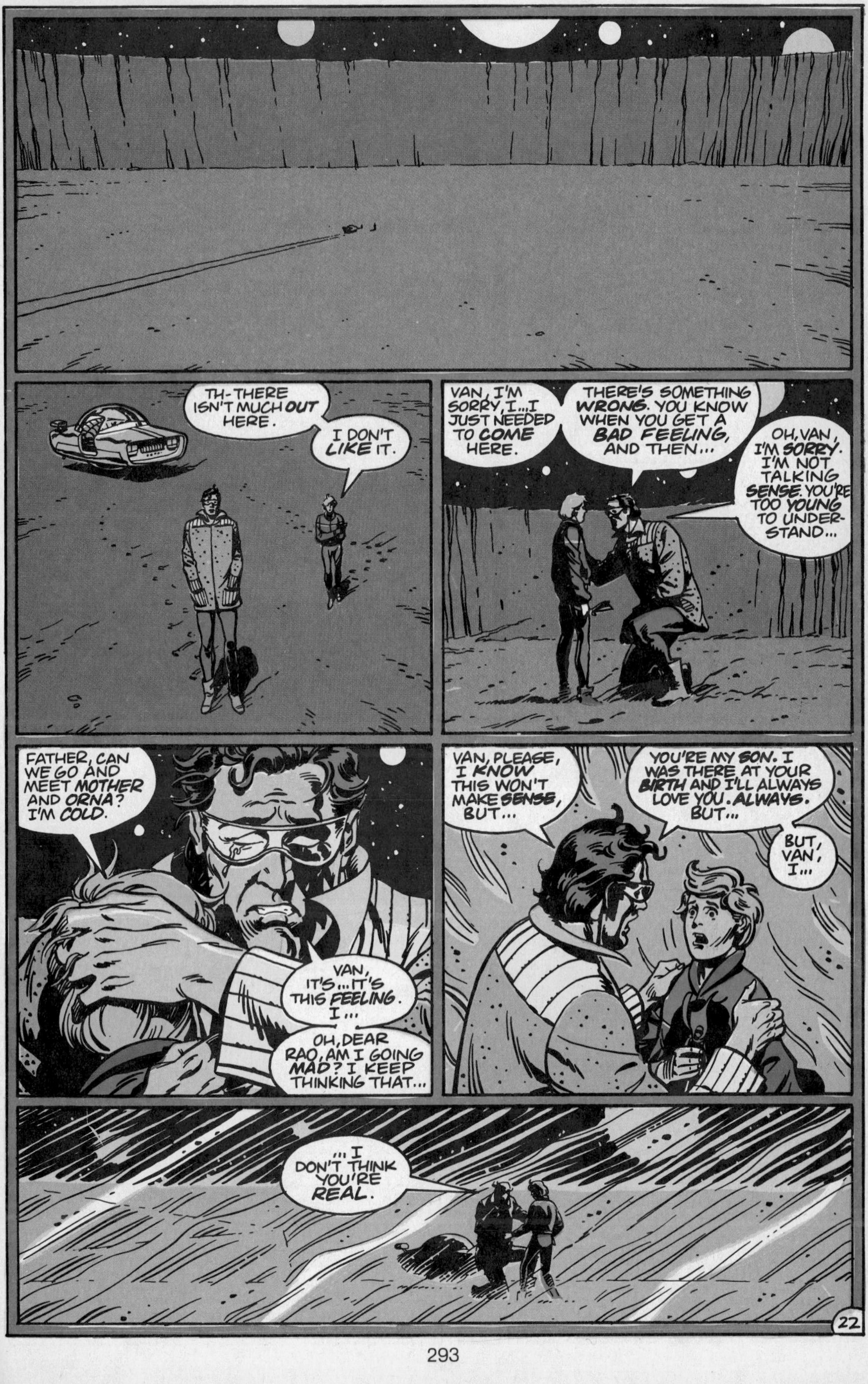
TH-THERE ISN'T MUCH OUT HERE.
I DON'T LIKE IT.
VAN, I'M SORRY, I...I JUST NEEDED TO COME HERE.
THERE'S SOMETHING WRONG. YOU KNOW WHEN YOU GET A BAD FEELING, AND THEN...
OH, VAN, I'M SORRY. I'M NOT TALKING SENSE. YOU'RE TOO YOUNG TO UNDER-STAND...
FATHER, CAN WE GO AND MEET MOTHER AND ORNA? I'M COLD.
VAN, IT'S...IT'S THIS FEELING. I...
OH, DEAR RAO, AM I GOING MAD? I KEEP THINKING THAT...
VAN, PLEASE, I KNOW THIS WON'T MAKE SENSE, BUT...
YOU'RE MY SON. I WAS THERE AT YOUR BIRTH AND I'LL ALWAYS LOVE YOU. ALWAYS. BUT...
BUT, VAN, I...
...I DON'T THINK YOU'RE REAL.
22

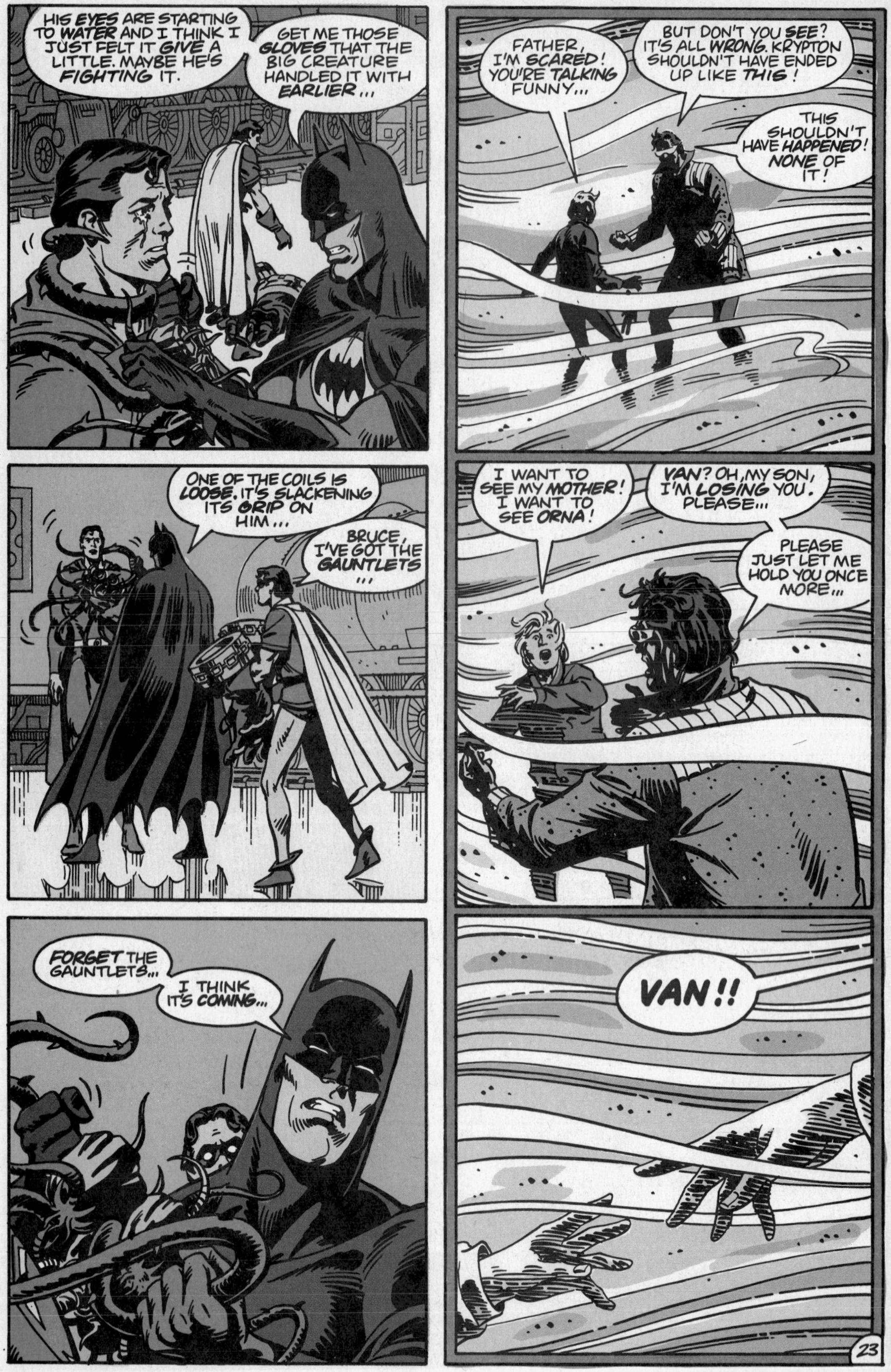
HIS EYES ARE STARTING TO WATER AND I THINK I JUST FELT IT GIVE A LITTLE. MAYBE HE'S FIGHTING IT.
GET ME THOSE GLOVES THAT THE BIG CREATURE HANDLED IT WITH EARLIER...
FATHER, I'M SCARED! YOU'RE TALKING FUNNY...
BUT DON'T YOU SEE? IT'S ALL WRONG. KRYPTON SHOULDN'T HAVE ENDED UP LIKE THIS!
THIS SHOULDN'T HAVE HAPPENED! NONE OF IT!
ONE OF THE COILS IS LOOSE. IT'S SLACKENING ITS GRIP ON HIM...
BRUCE, I'VE GOT THE GAUNTLETS...
I WANT TO SEE MY MOTHER! I WANT TO SEE ORNA!
VAN? OH, MY SON, I'M LOSING YOU. PLEASE...
PLEASE JUST LET ME HOLD YOU ONCE MORE...
FORGET THE GAUNTLETS...
I THINK IT'S COMING...
VAN!!
23

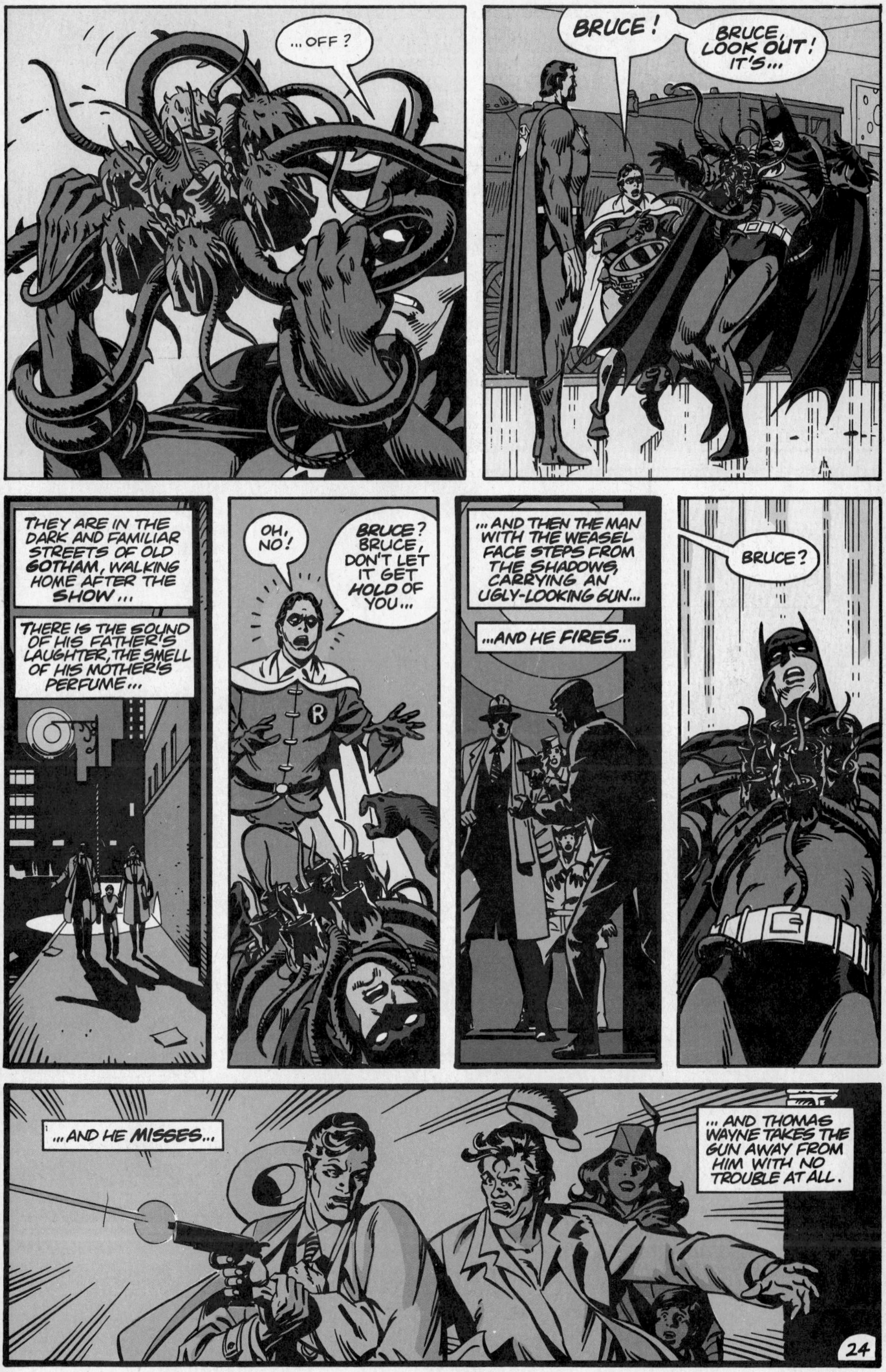
...OFF ?
BRUCE!
BRUCE, LOOK OUT! IT'S...
THEY ARE IN THE DARK AND FAMILIAR STREETS OF OLD GOTHAM, WALKING HOME AFTER THE SHOW...
THERE IS THE SOUND OF HIS FATHER'S LAUGHTER, THE SMELL OF HIS MOTHER'S PERFUME...
OH, NO!
BRUCE? BRUCE, DON'T LET IT GET HOLD OF YOU...
...AND THEN THE MAN WITH THE WEASEL FACE STEPS FROM THE SHADOWS, CARRYING AN UGLY-LOOKING GUN...
...AND HE FIRES...
BRUCE?
...AND HE MISSES...
...AND THOMAS WAYNE TAKES THE GUN AWAY FROM HIM WITH NO TROUBLE AT ALL.
24

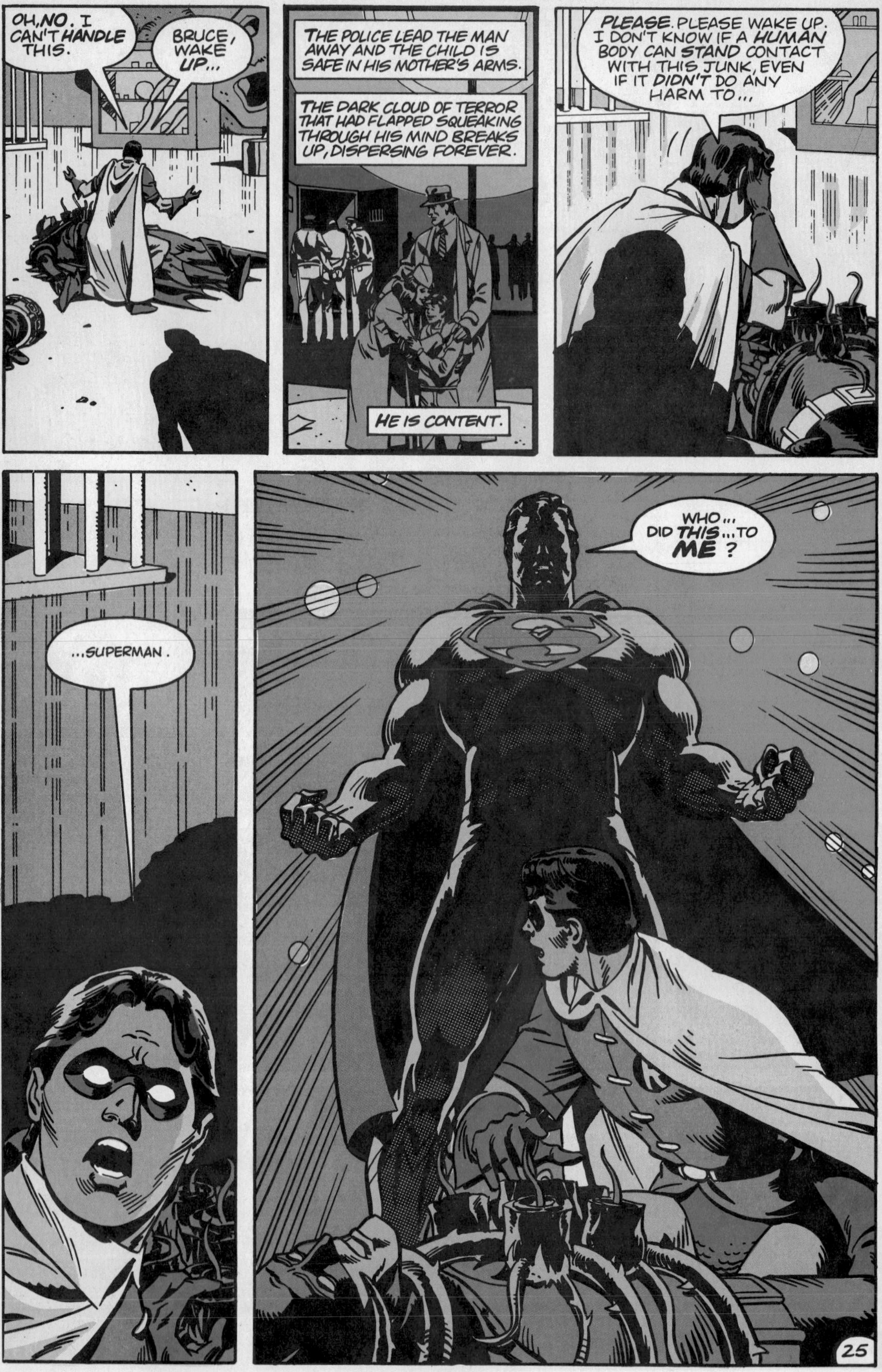

OH, NO. I CAN'T HANDLE THIS.
BRUCE, WAKE UP...
THE POLICE LEAD THE MAN AWAY AND THE CHILD IS SAFE IN HIS MOTHER'S ARMS.
THE DARK CLOUD OF TERROR THAT HAD FLAPPED SQUEAKING THROUGH HIS MIND BREAKS UP, DISPERSING FOREVER.
HE IS CONTENT.
PLEASE. PLEASE WAKE UP. I DON'T KNOW IF A HUMAN BODY CAN STAND CONTACT WITH THIS JUNK, EVEN IF IT DIDN'T DO ANY HARM TO...
...SUPERMAN.
WHO... DID THIS... TO ME?
25

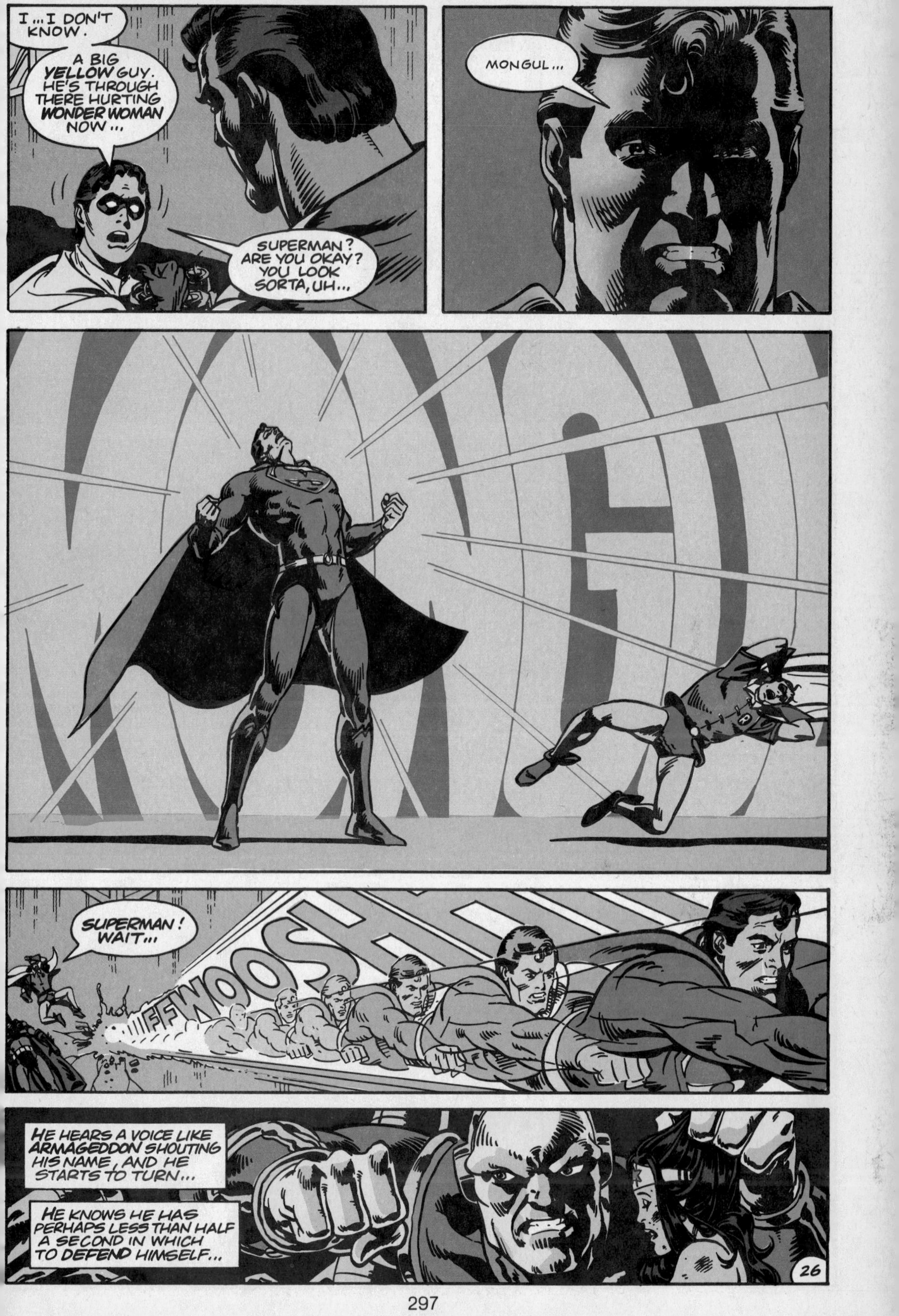
I...I DON'T KNOW.
A BIG YELLOW GUY. HE'S THROUGH THERE HURTING WONDER WOMAN NOW...
SUPERMAN? ARE YOU OKAY? YOU LOOK SORTA, UH...
MONGUL...
SUPERMAN! WAIT...
HE HEARS A VOICE LIKE ARMAGEDDON SHOUTING HIS NAME, AND HE STARTS TO TURN...
HE KNOWS HE HAS PERHAPS LESS THAN HALF A SECOND IN WHICH TO DEFEND HIMSELF...
26

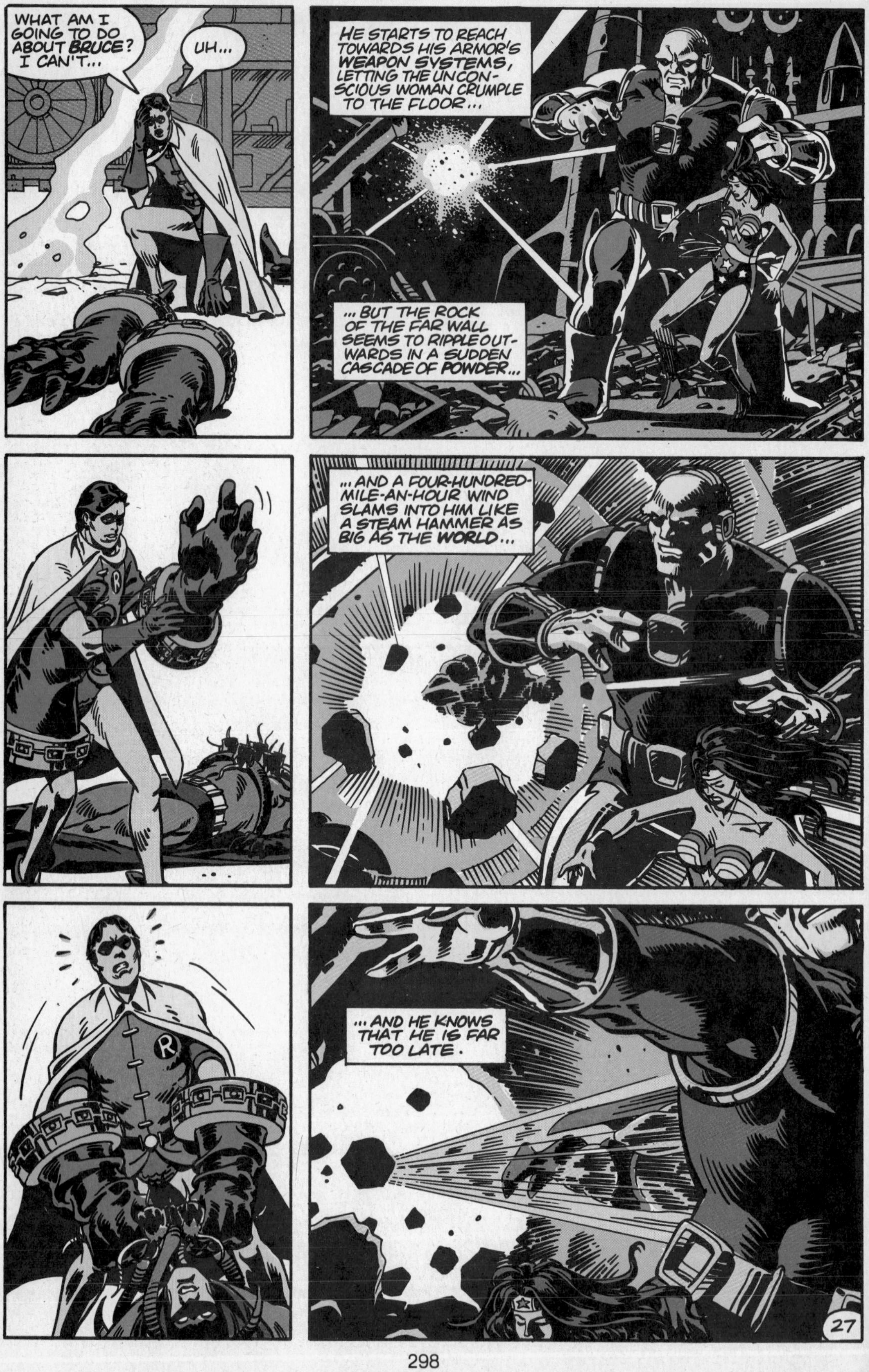
WHAT AM I GOING TO DO ABOUT BRUCE? I CAN'T...
UH...
HE STARTS TO REACH TOWARDS HIS ARMOR'S WEAPON SYSTEMS, LETTING THE UNCONSCIOUS WOMAN CRUMPLE TO THE FLOOR...
...BUT THE ROCK OF THE FAR WALL SEEMS TO RIPPLE OUTWARDS IN A SUDDEN CASCADE OF POWDER...
...AND A FOUR-HUNDRED-MILE-AN-HOUR WIND SLAMS INTO HIM LIKE A STEAM HAMMER AS BIG AS THE WORLD...
...AND HE KNOWS THAT HE IS FAR TOO LATE.
27

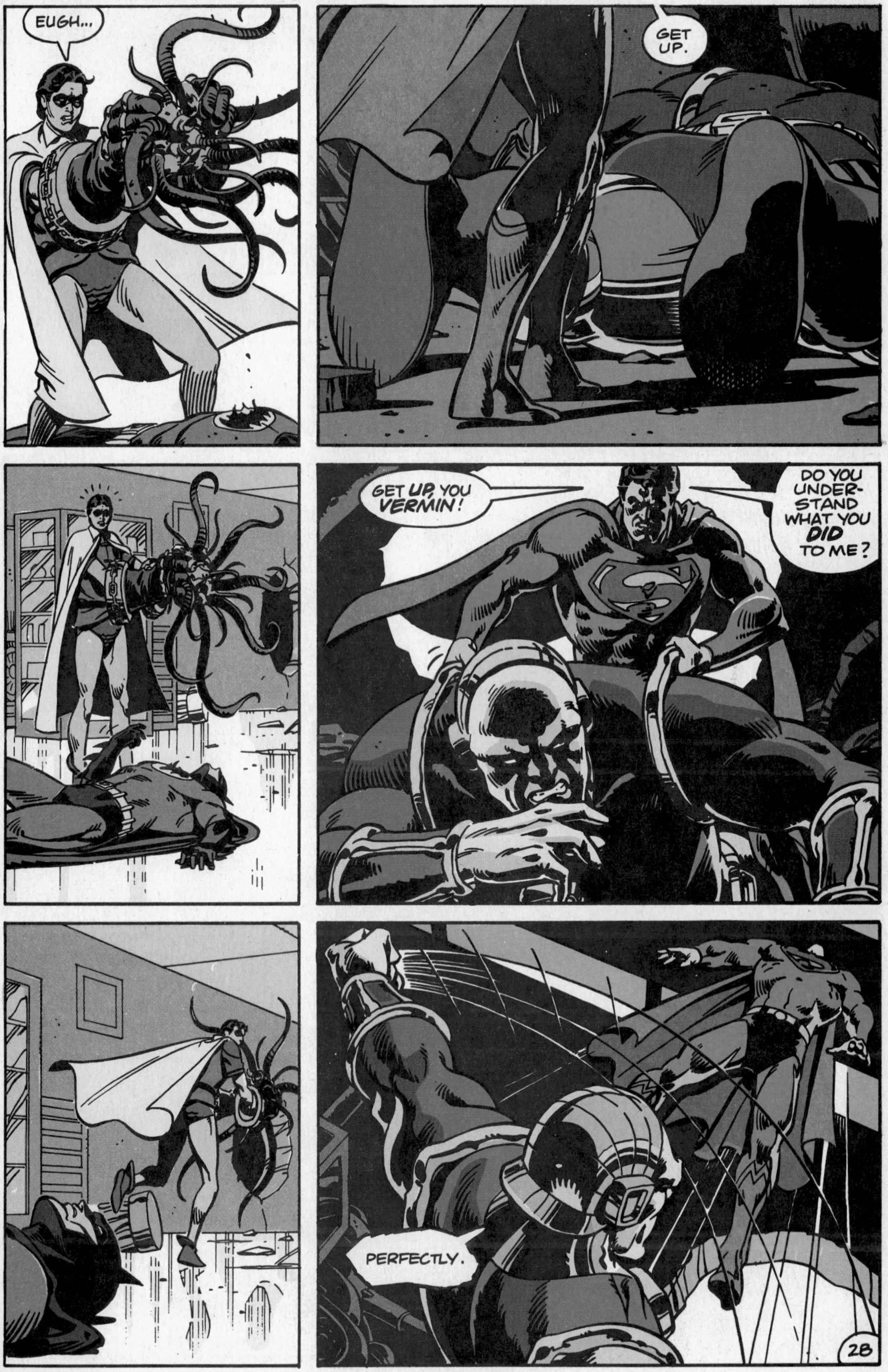
EUGH...
GET UP.
GET UP, YOU VERMIN!
DO YOU UNDERSTAND WHAT YOU DID TO ME?
PERFECTLY.
28

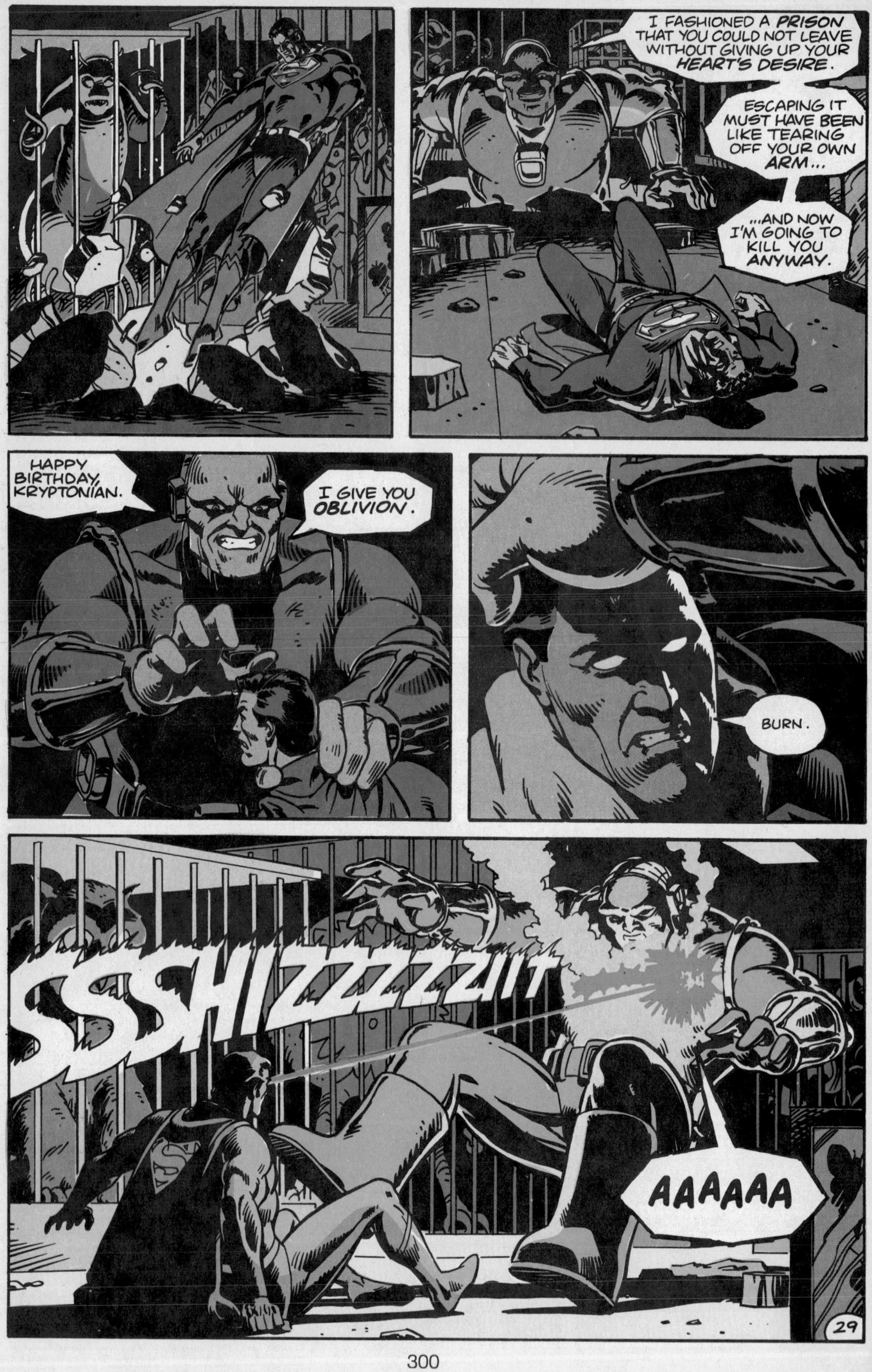
I FASHIONED A PRISON THAT YOU COULD NOT LEAVE WITHOUT GIVING UP YOUR HEART'S DESIRE.
ESCAPING IT MUST HAVE BEEN LIKE TEARING OFF YOUR OWN ARM...
...AND NOW I'M GOING TO KILL YOU ANYWAY.
HAPPY BIRTHDAY, KRYPTONIAN.
I GIVE YOU OBLIVION.
BURN.
SSHIZZZZZIIT
AAAAAA
29

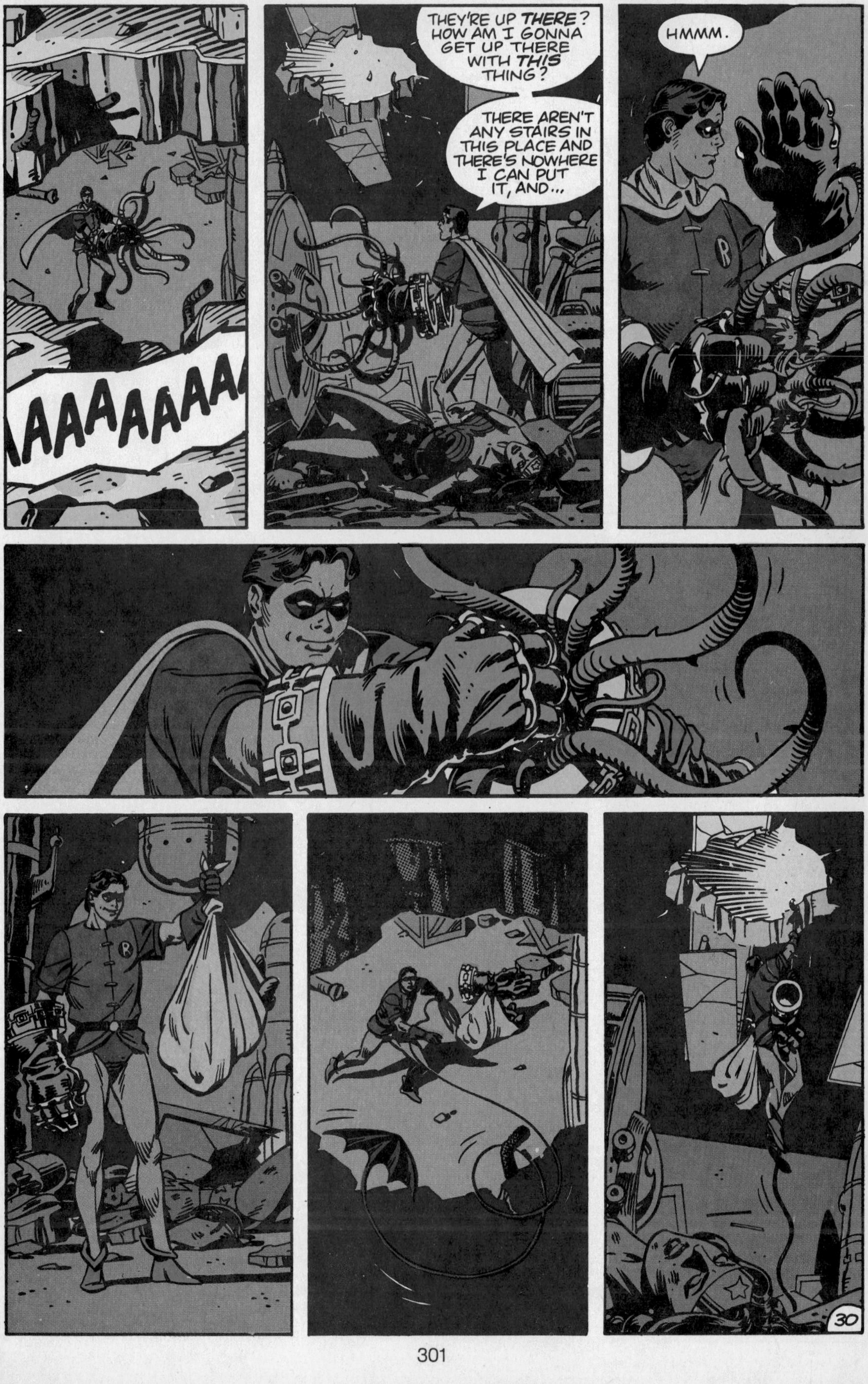
AAAAAAAA
THEY'RE UP THERE? HOW AM I GONNA GET UP THERE WITH THIS THING?
THERE AREN'T ANY STAIRS IN THIS PLACE AND THERE'S NOWHERE I CAN PUT IT, AND...
HMMM.
30

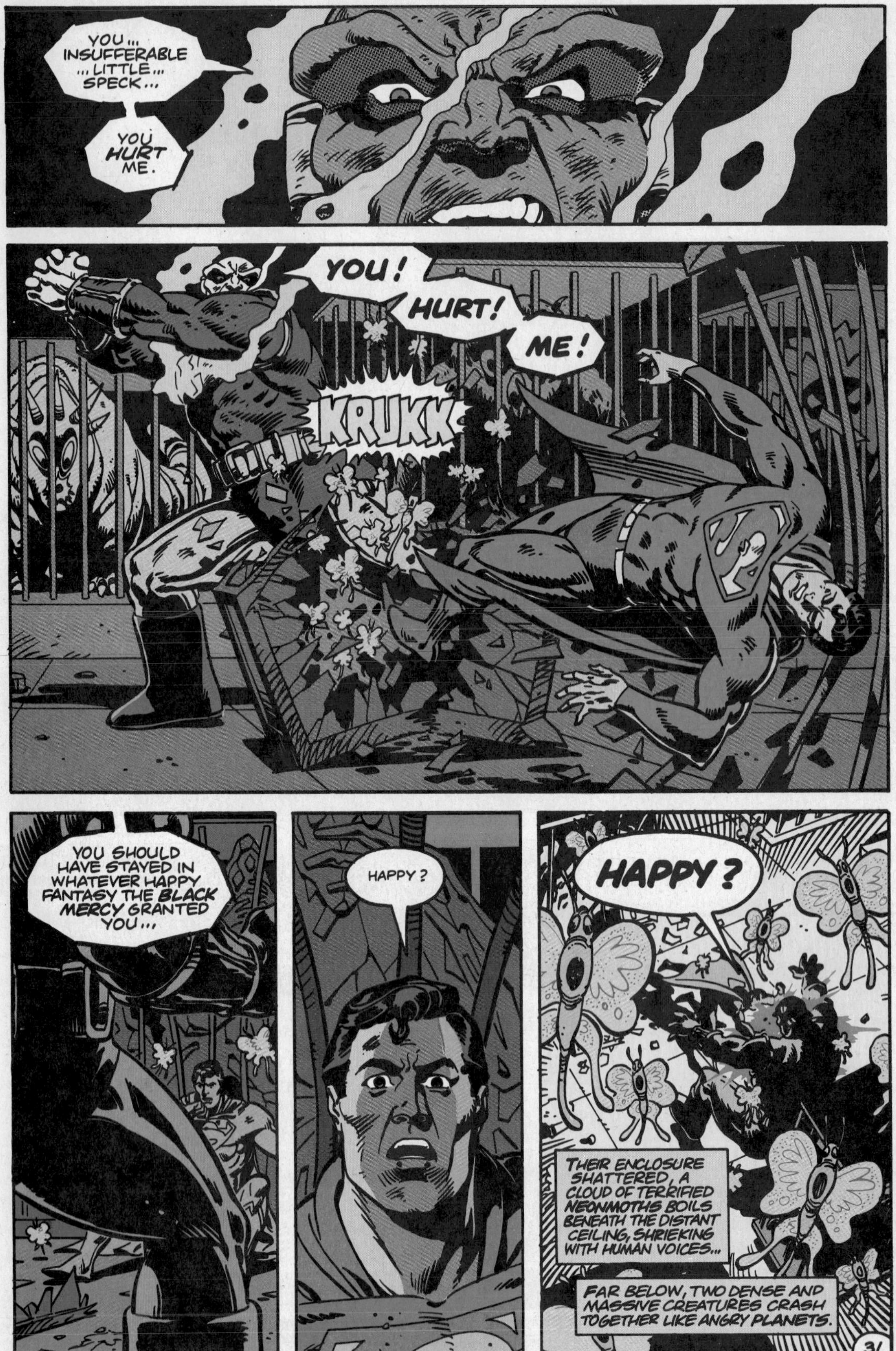
YOU... INSUFFERABLE ...LITTLE... SPECK...
YOU HURT ME.
YOU!
HURT!
ME!
KRUKK
YOU SHOULD HAVE STAYED IN WHATEVER HAPPY FANTASY THE BLACK MERCY GRANTED YOU...
HAPPY?
HAPPY?
THEIR ENCLOSURE SHATTERED, A CLOUD OF TERRIFIED NEONMOTHS BOILS BENEATH THE DISTANT CEILING, SHRIEKING WITH HUMAN VOICES...
FAR BELOW, TWO DENSE AND MASSIVE CREATURES CRASH TOGETHER LIKE ANGRY PLANETS.
31

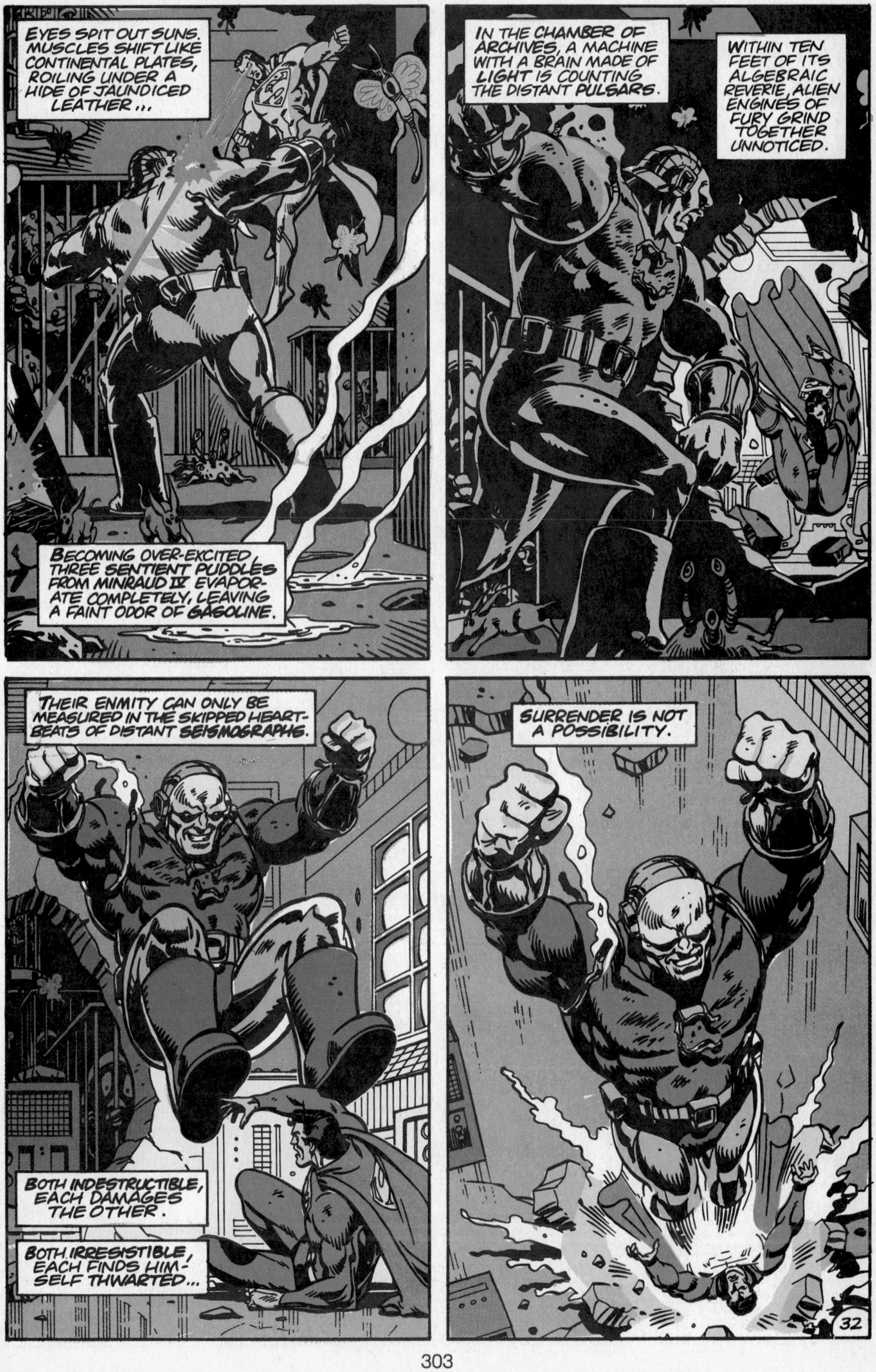
EYES SPIT OUT SUNS. MUSCLES SHIFT LIKE CONTINENTAL PLATES, ROILING UNDER A HIDE OF JAUNDICED LEATHER...
BECOMING OVER-EXCITED, THREE SENTIENT PUDDLES FROM MINRAUD IV EVAPORATE COMPLETELY, LEAVING A FAINT ODOR OF GASOLINE.
IN THE CHAMBER OF ARCHIVES, A MACHINE WITH A BRAIN MADE OF LIGHT IS COUNTING THE DISTANT PULSARS.
WITHIN TEN FEET OF ITS ALGEBRAIC REVERIE, ALIEN ENGINES OF FURY GRIND TOGETHER UNNOTICED.
THEIR ENMITY CAN ONLY BE MEASURED IN THE SKIPPED HEART-BEATS OF DISTANT SEISMOGRAPHS.
BOTH INDESTRUCTIBLE, EACH DAMAGES THE OTHER.
BOTH IRRESISTIBLE, EACH FINDS HIM-SELF THWARTED...
SURRENDER IS NOT A POSSIBILITY.
32

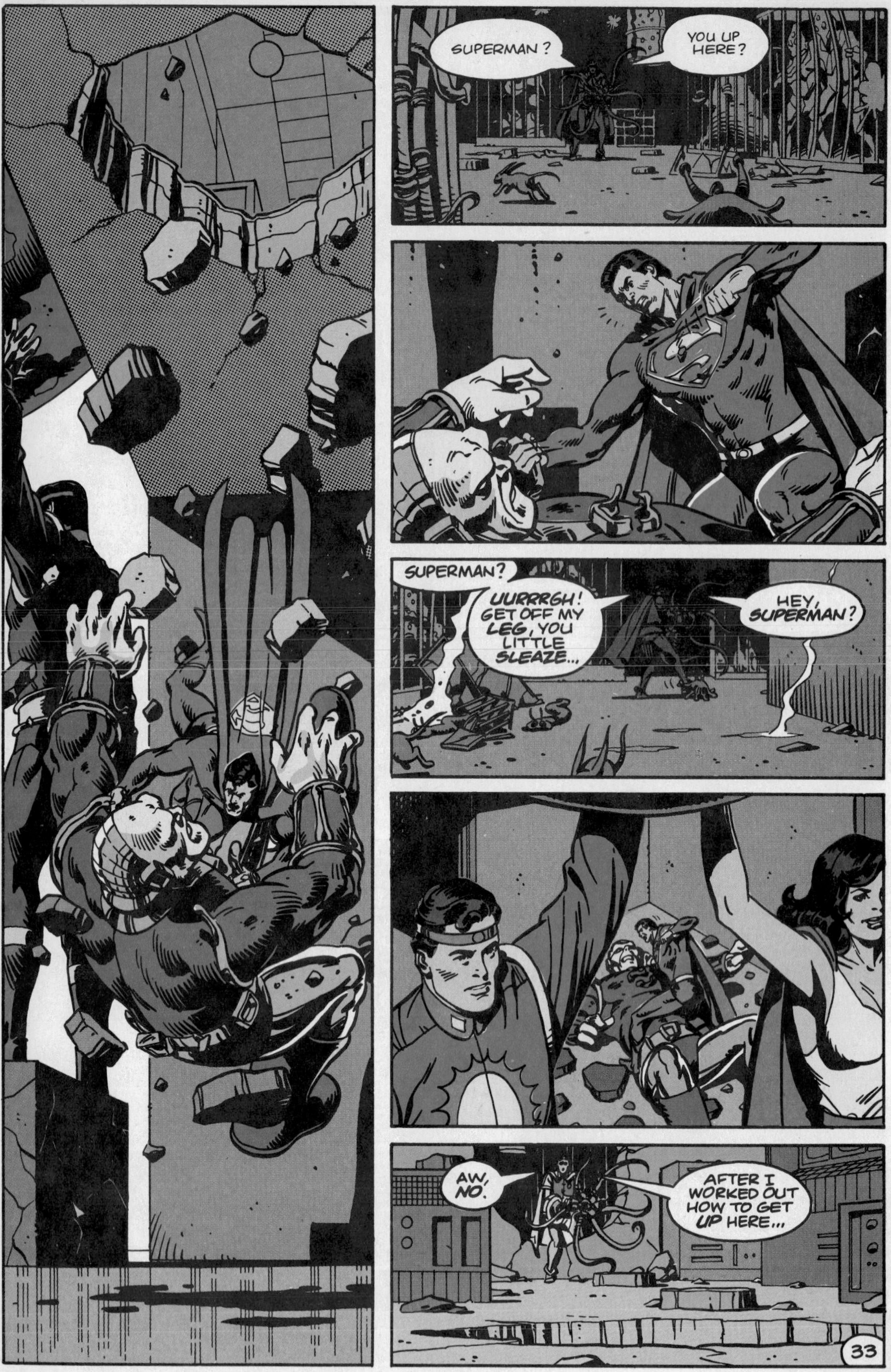
SUPERMAN?
YOU UP HERE?
SUPERMAN?
UURRRGH! GET OFF MY LEG, YOU LITTLE SLEAZE...
HEY, SUPERMAN?
AW, NO.
AFTER I WORKED OUT HOW TO GET UP HERE...
33

KRYPTON...?

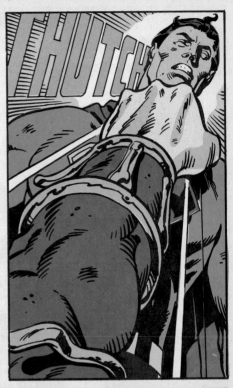

THUTCH

THERE...

DO YOU KNOW, I ALMOST BELIEVED THAT YOU WERE GOING TO KILL ME.

HOW STUPID OF YOU TO HESITATE LIKE THAT...

NOT A MISTAKE THAT I'LL MAKE, I ASSURE YOU...

UH, EXCUSE ME...

34

305

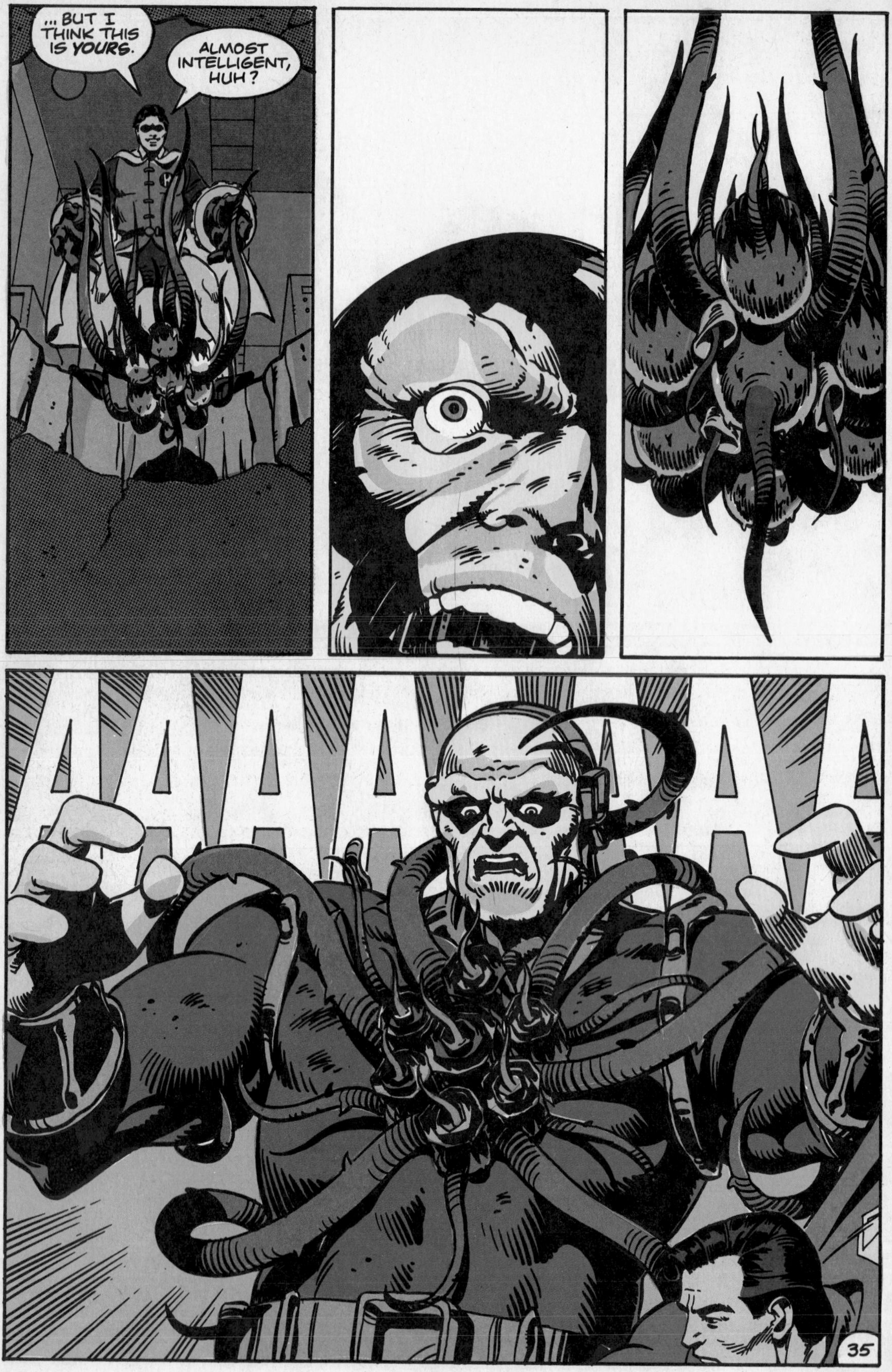
...BUT I THINK THIS IS *YOURS*.
ALMOST INTELLIGENT, HUH?
AAAAAAAAAA
35

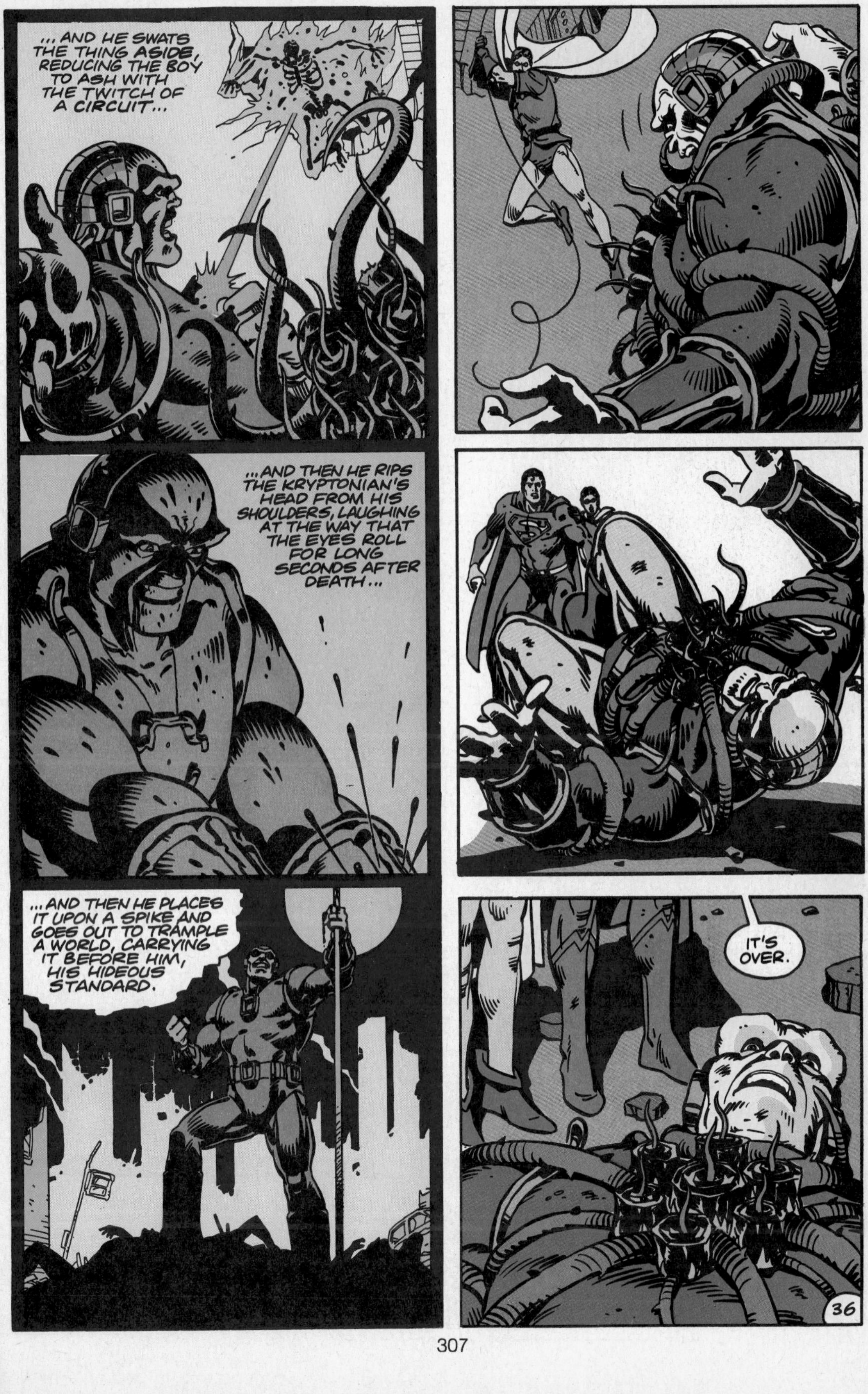
...AND HE SWATS THE THING ASIDE, REDUCING THE BOY TO ASH WITH THE TWITCH OF A CIRCUIT...
...AND THEN HE RIPS THE KRYPTONIAN'S HEAD FROM HIS SHOULDERS, LAUGHING AT THE WAY THAT THE EYES ROLL FOR LONG SECONDS AFTER DEATH...
...AND THEN HE PLACES IT UPON A SPIKE AND GOES OUT TO TRAMPLE A WORLD, CARRYING IT BEFORE HIM, HIS HIDEOUS STANDARD.
IT'S OVER.
36

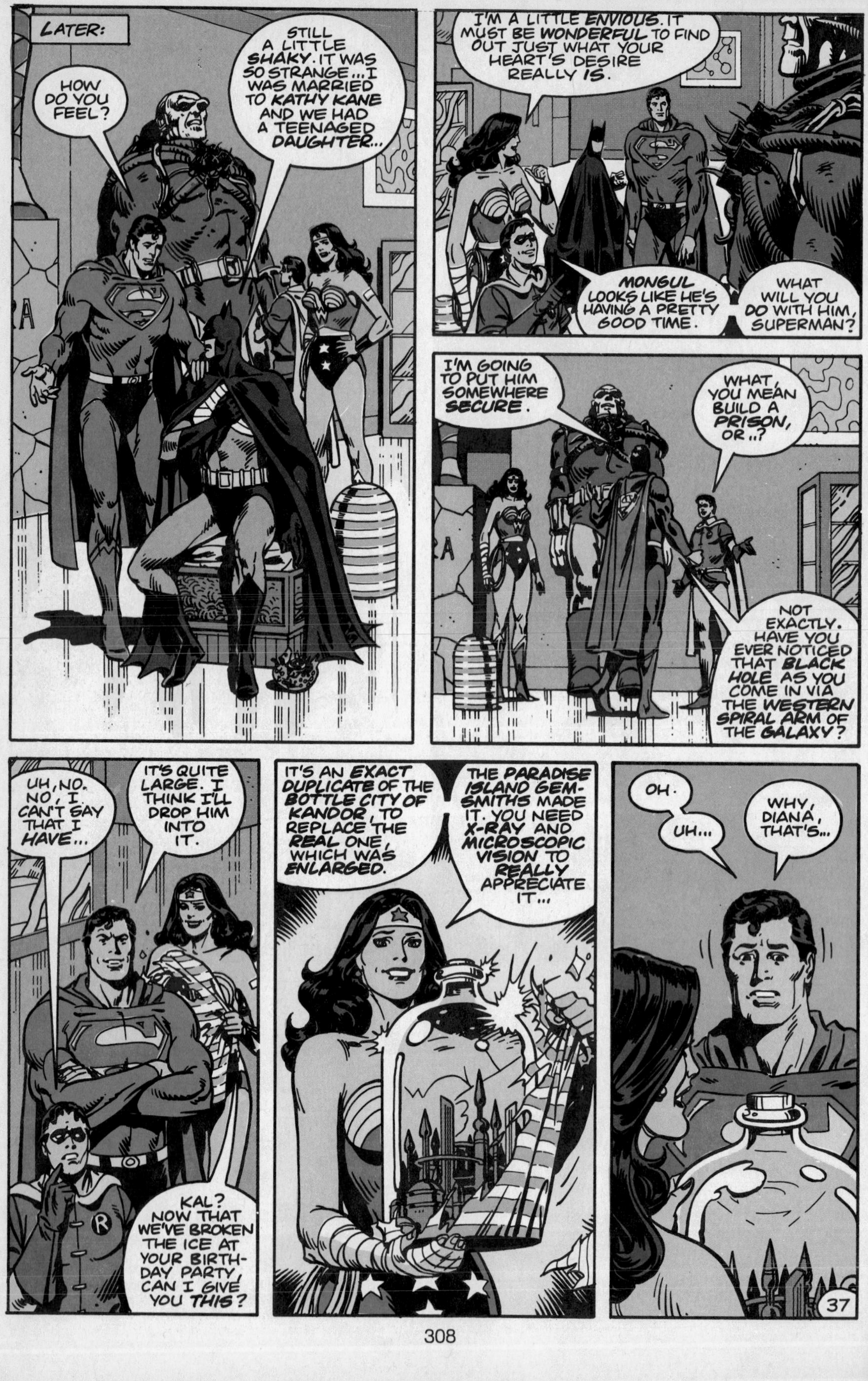
LATER:
HOW DO YOU FEEL?
STILL A LITTLE SHAKY. IT WAS SO STRANGE... I WAS MARRIED TO KATHY KANE AND WE HAD A TEENAGED DAUGHTER...
I'M A LITTLE ENVIOUS. IT MUST BE WONDERFUL TO FIND OUT JUST WHAT YOUR HEART'S DESIRE REALLY IS.
MONGUL LOOKS LIKE HE'S HAVING A PRETTY GOOD TIME.
WHAT WILL YOU DO WITH HIM, SUPERMAN?
I'M GOING TO PUT HIM SOMEWHERE SECURE.
WHAT, YOU MEAN BUILD A PRISON, OR..?
NOT EXACTLY. HAVE YOU EVER NOTICED THAT BLACK HOLE AS YOU COME IN VIA THE WESTERN SPIRAL ARM OF THE GALAXY?
UH, NO. NO, I, CAN'T SAY THAT I HAVE...
IT'S QUITE LARGE. I THINK I'LL DROP HIM INTO IT.
KAL? NOW THAT WE'VE BROKEN THE ICE AT YOUR BIRTHDAY PARTY, CAN I GIVE YOU THIS?
IT'S AN EXACT DUPLICATE OF THE BOTTLE CITY OF KANDOR, TO REPLACE THE REAL ONE, WHICH WAS ENLARGED.
THE PARADISE ISLAND GEM-SMITHS MADE IT. YOU NEED X-RAY AND MICROSCOPIC VISION TO REALLY APPRECIATE IT...
OH.
UH...
WHY, DIANA, THAT'S...
37

...JUST...

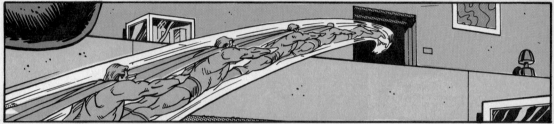

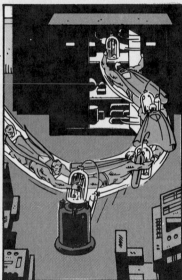

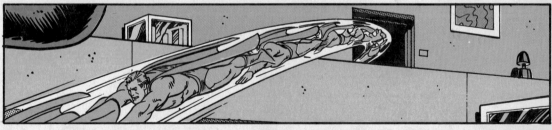

...JUST...

38

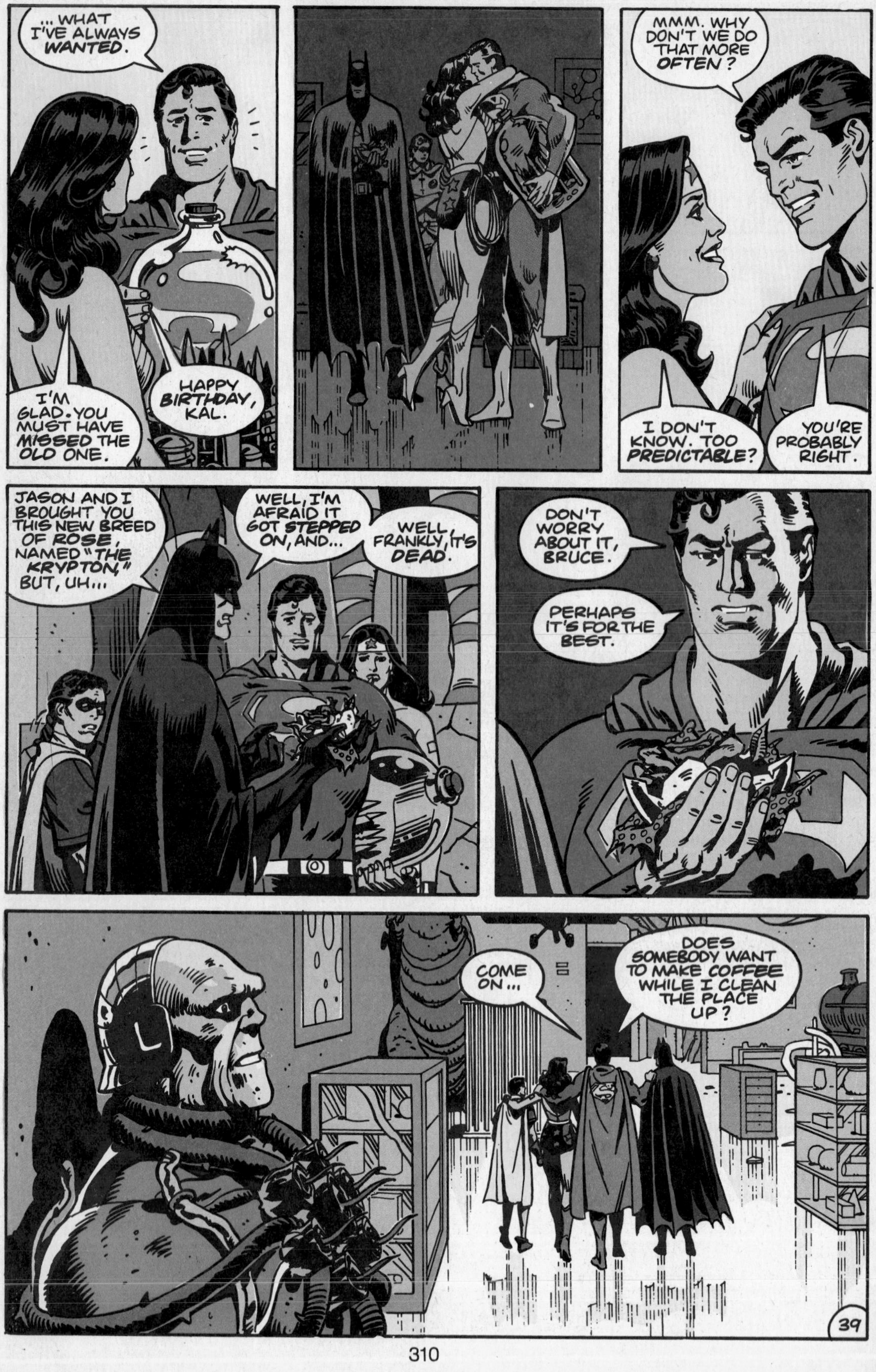

...WHAT I'VE ALWAYS WANTED.
I'M GLAD. YOU MUST HAVE MISSED THE OLD ONE.
HAPPY BIRTHDAY, KAL.
MMM. WHY DON'T WE DO THAT MORE OFTEN?
I DON'T KNOW. TOO PREDICTABLE?
YOU'RE PROBABLY RIGHT.
JASON AND I BROUGHT YOU THIS NEW BREED OF ROSE, NAMED "THE KRYPTON," BUT, UH...
WELL, I'M AFRAID IT GOT STEPPED ON, AND...
WELL, FRANKLY, IT'S DEAD.
DON'T WORRY ABOUT IT, BRUCE.
PERHAPS IT'S FOR THE BEST.
COME ON...
DOES SOMEBODY WANT TO MAKE COFFEE WHILE I CLEAN THE PLACE UP?
39

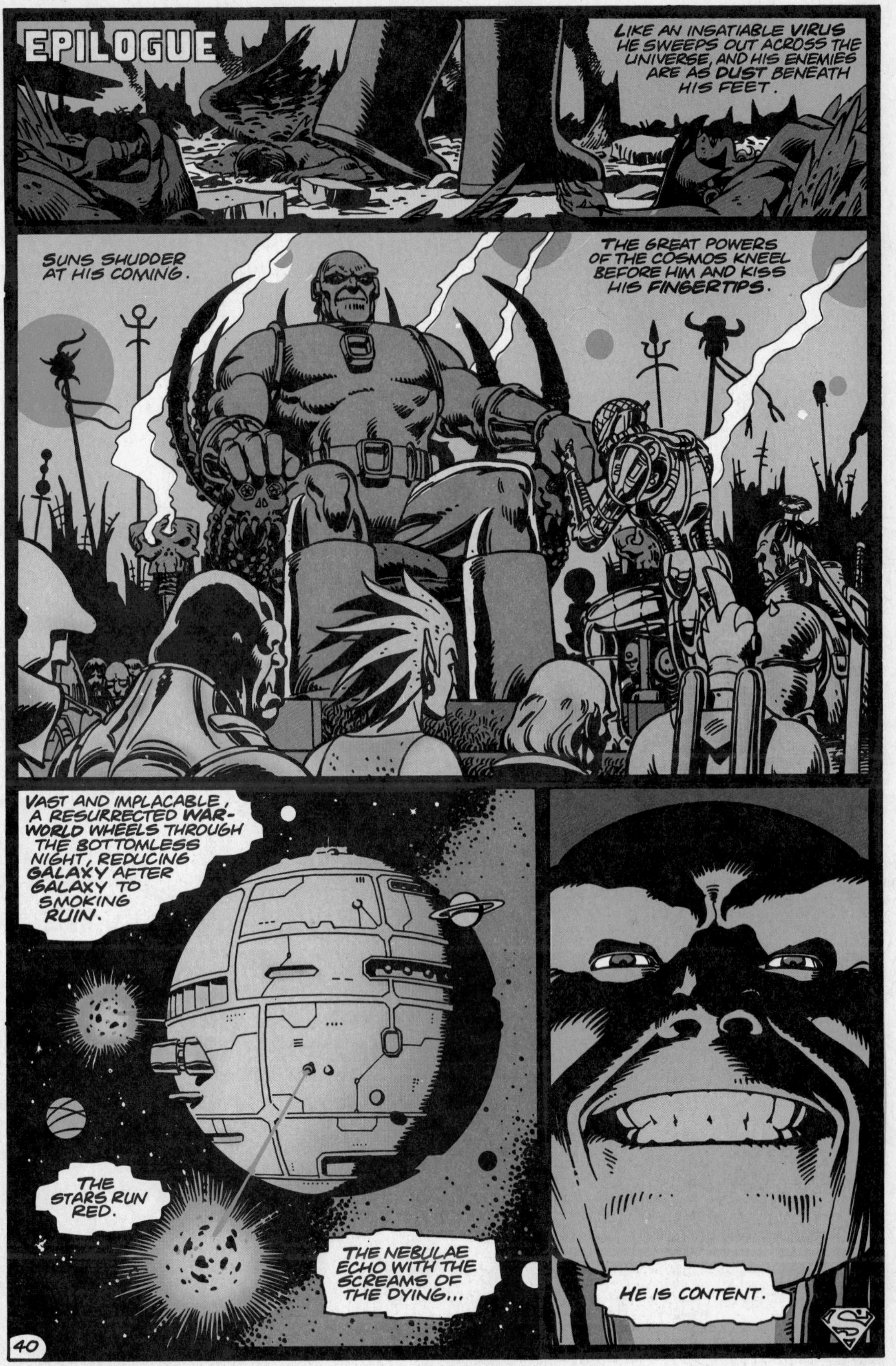
EPILOGUE
LIKE AN INSATIABLE VIRUS HE SWEEPS OUT ACROSS THE UNIVERSE, AND HIS ENEMIES ARE AS DUST BENEATH HIS FEET.
SUNS SHUDDER AT HIS COMING.
THE GREAT POWERS OF THE COSMOS KNEEL BEFORE HIM AND KISS HIS FINGERTIPS.
VAST AND IMPLACABLE, A RESURRECTED WAR-WORLD WHEELS THROUGH THE BOTTOMLESS NIGHT, REDUCING GALAXY AFTER GALAXY TO SMOKING RUIN.
THE STARS RUN RED.
THE NEBULAE ECHO WITH THE SCREAMS OF THE DYING...
HE IS CONTENT.
40

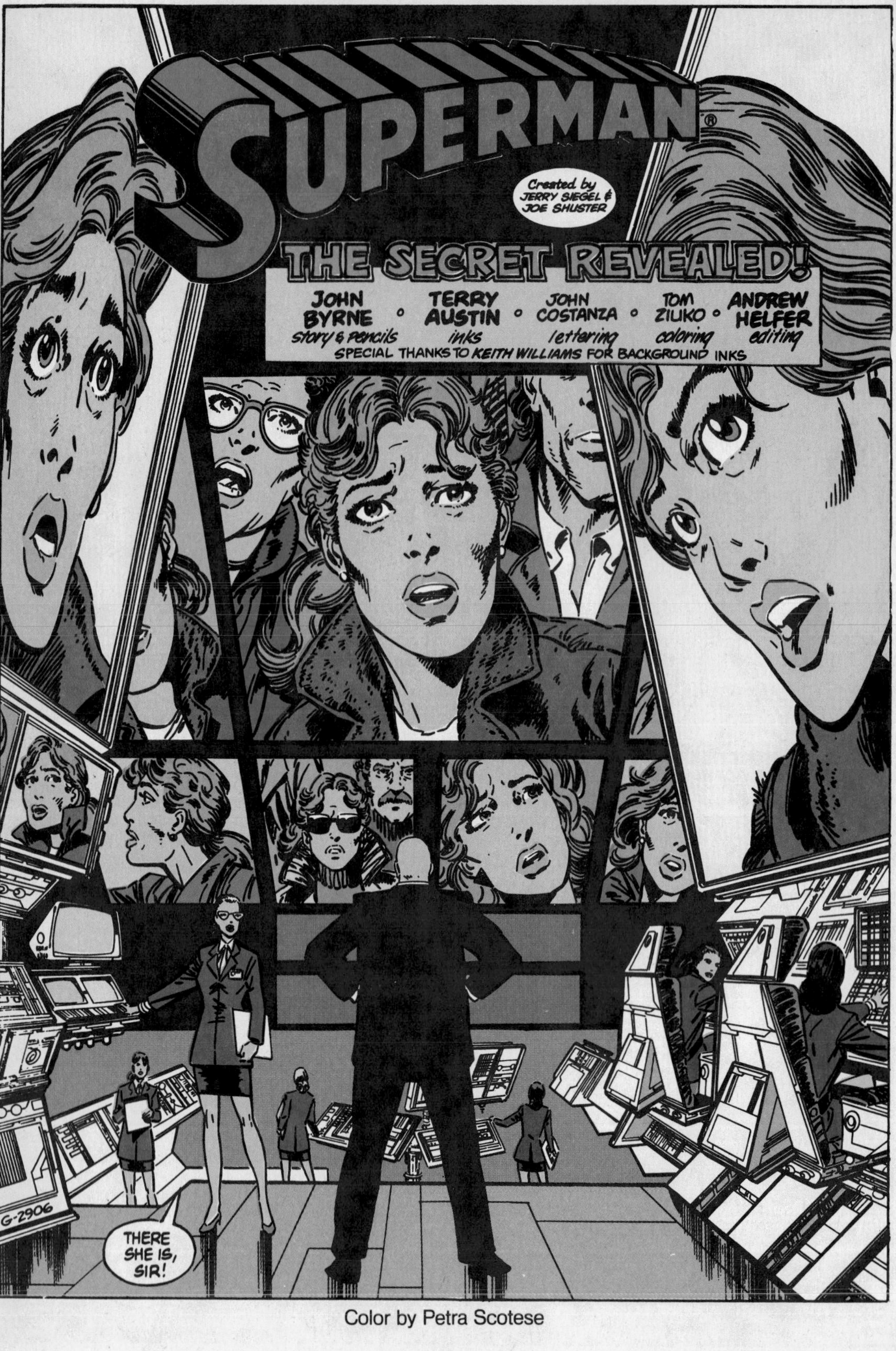
SUPERMAN
Created by JERRY SIEGEL & JOE SHUSTER
THE SECRET REVEALED!
JOHN BYRNE story & pencils
TERRY AUSTIN inks
JOHN COSTANZA lettering
TOM ZIUKO coloring
ANDREW HELFER editing
SPECIAL THANKS TO KEITH WILLIAMS FOR BACKGROUND INKS
G-2906
THERE SHE IS, SIR!

Color by Petra Scotese

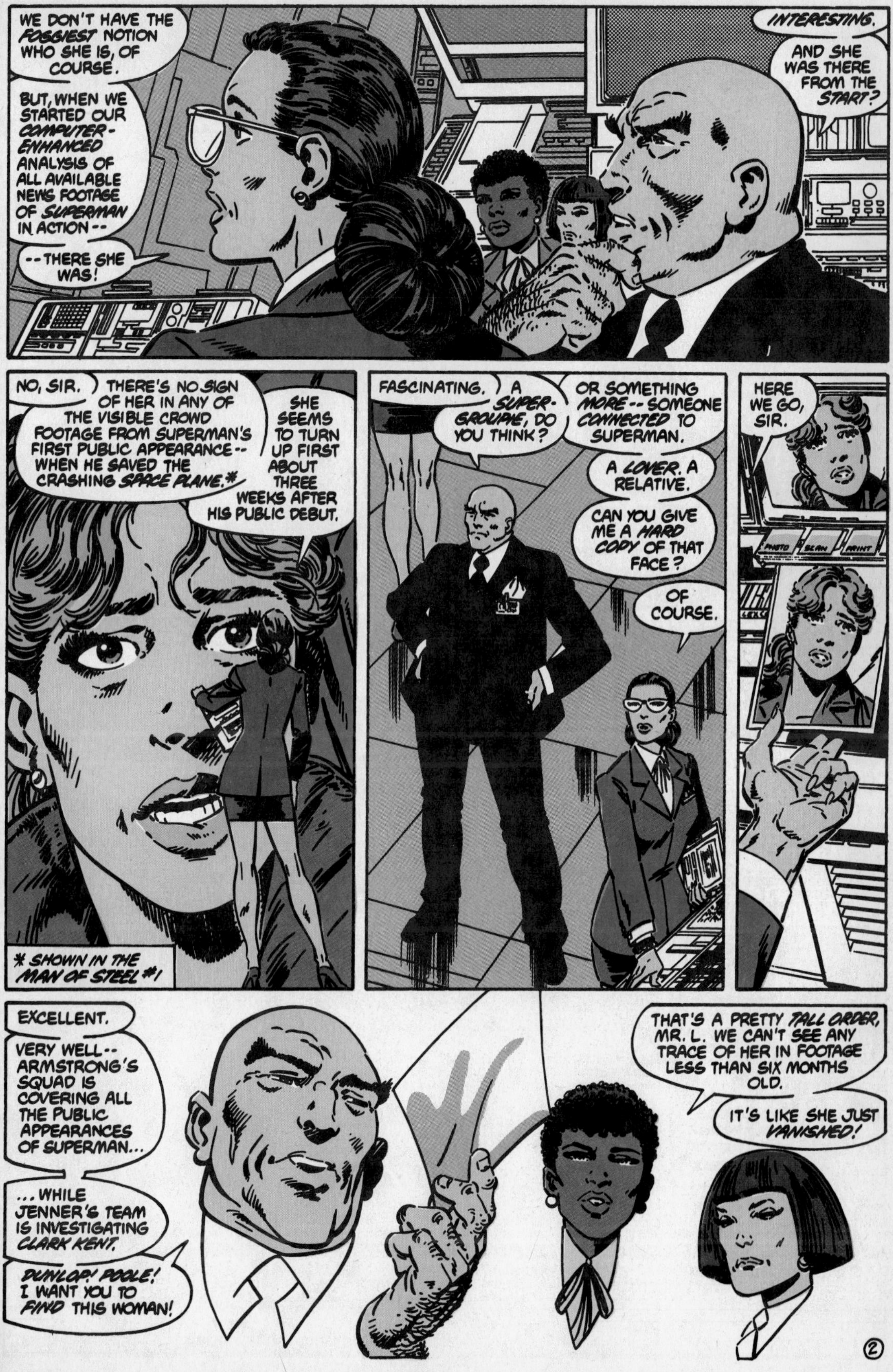
WE DON'T HAVE THE FOGGIEST NOTION WHO SHE IS, OF COURSE.
BUT, WHEN WE STARTED OUR COMPUTER-ENHANCED ANALYSIS OF ALL AVAILABLE NEWS FOOTAGE OF SUPERMAN IN ACTION --
-- THERE SHE WAS!
INTERESTING.
AND SHE WAS THERE FROM THE START?
NO, SIR.
THERE'S NO SIGN OF HER IN ANY OF THE VISIBLE CROWD FOOTAGE FROM SUPERMAN'S FIRST PUBLIC APPEARANCE -- WHEN HE SAVED THE CRASHING SPACE PLANE.*
SHE SEEMS TO TURN UP FIRST ABOUT THREE WEEKS AFTER HIS PUBLIC DEBUT.
* SHOWN IN THE MAN OF STEEL #1
FASCINATING.
A SUPER-GROUPIE, DO YOU THINK?
OR SOMETHING MORE -- SOMEONE CONNECTED TO SUPERMAN.
A LOVER. A RELATIVE.
CAN YOU GIVE ME A HARD COPY OF THAT FACE?
OF COURSE.
HERE WE GO, SIR.
PHOTO
SCAN
PRINT
EXCELLENT.
VERY WELL -- ARMSTRONG'S SQUAD IS COVERING ALL THE PUBLIC APPEARANCES OF SUPERMAN...
... WHILE JENNER'S TEAM IS INVESTIGATING CLARK KENT.
DUNLOP! POOLE! I WANT YOU TO FIND THIS WOMAN!
THAT'S A PRETTY TALL ORDER, MR. L. WE CAN'T SEE ANY TRACE OF HER IN FOOTAGE LESS THAN SIX MONTHS OLD.
IT'S LIKE SHE JUST VANISHED!
2

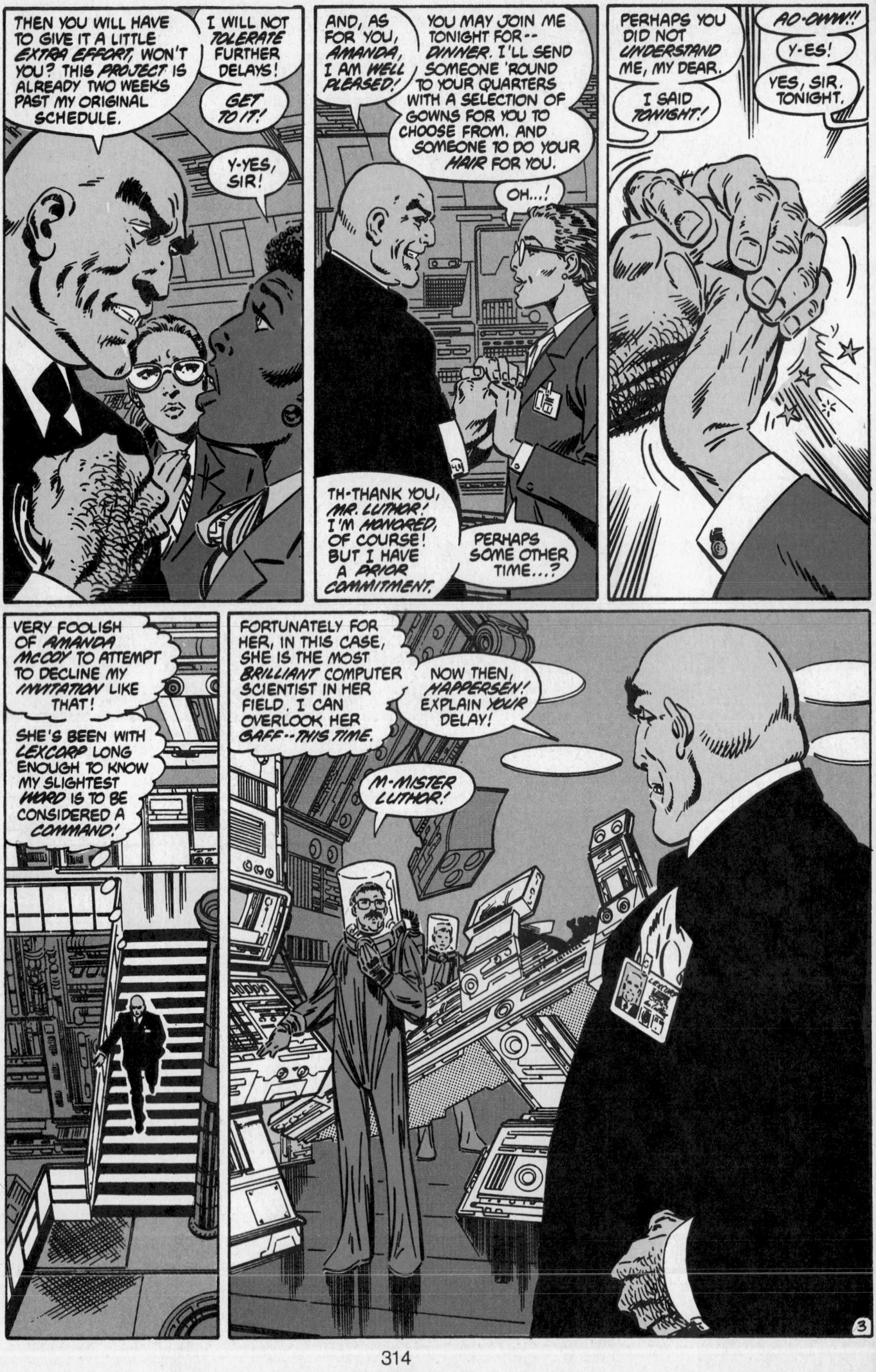
THEN YOU WILL HAVE TO GIVE IT A LITTLE EXTRA EFFORT, WON'T YOU? THIS PROJECT IS ALREADY TWO WEEKS PAST MY ORIGINAL SCHEDULE.
I WILL NOT TOLERATE FURTHER DELAYS!
GET TO IT!
Y-YES, SIR!
AND, AS FOR YOU, AMANDA, I AM WELL PLEASED!
YOU MAY JOIN ME TONIGHT FOR-- DINNER. I'LL SEND SOMEONE 'ROUND TO YOUR QUARTERS WITH A SELECTION OF GOWNS FOR YOU TO CHOOSE FROM. AND SOMEONE TO DO YOUR HAIR FOR YOU.
OH...!
TH-THANK YOU, MR. LUTHOR! I'M HONORED, OF COURSE! BUT I HAVE A PRIOR COMMITMENT.
PERHAPS SOME OTHER TIME...?
PERHAPS YOU DID NOT UNDERSTAND ME, MY DEAR.
I SAID TONIGHT!
AO-OWW!!
Y-ES!
YES, SIR. TONIGHT.
VERY FOOLISH OF AMANDA McCOY TO ATTEMPT TO DECLINE MY INVITATION LIKE THAT!
SHE'S BEEN WITH LEXCORP LONG ENOUGH TO KNOW MY SLIGHTEST WORD IS TO BE CONSIDERED A COMMAND!
FORTUNATELY FOR HER, IN THIS CASE, SHE IS THE MOST BRILLIANT COMPUTER SCIENTIST IN HER FIELD. I CAN OVERLOOK HER GAFF--THIS TIME.
NOW THEN, HAPPERSEN! EXPLAIN YOUR DELAY!
M-MISTER LUTHOR!
3

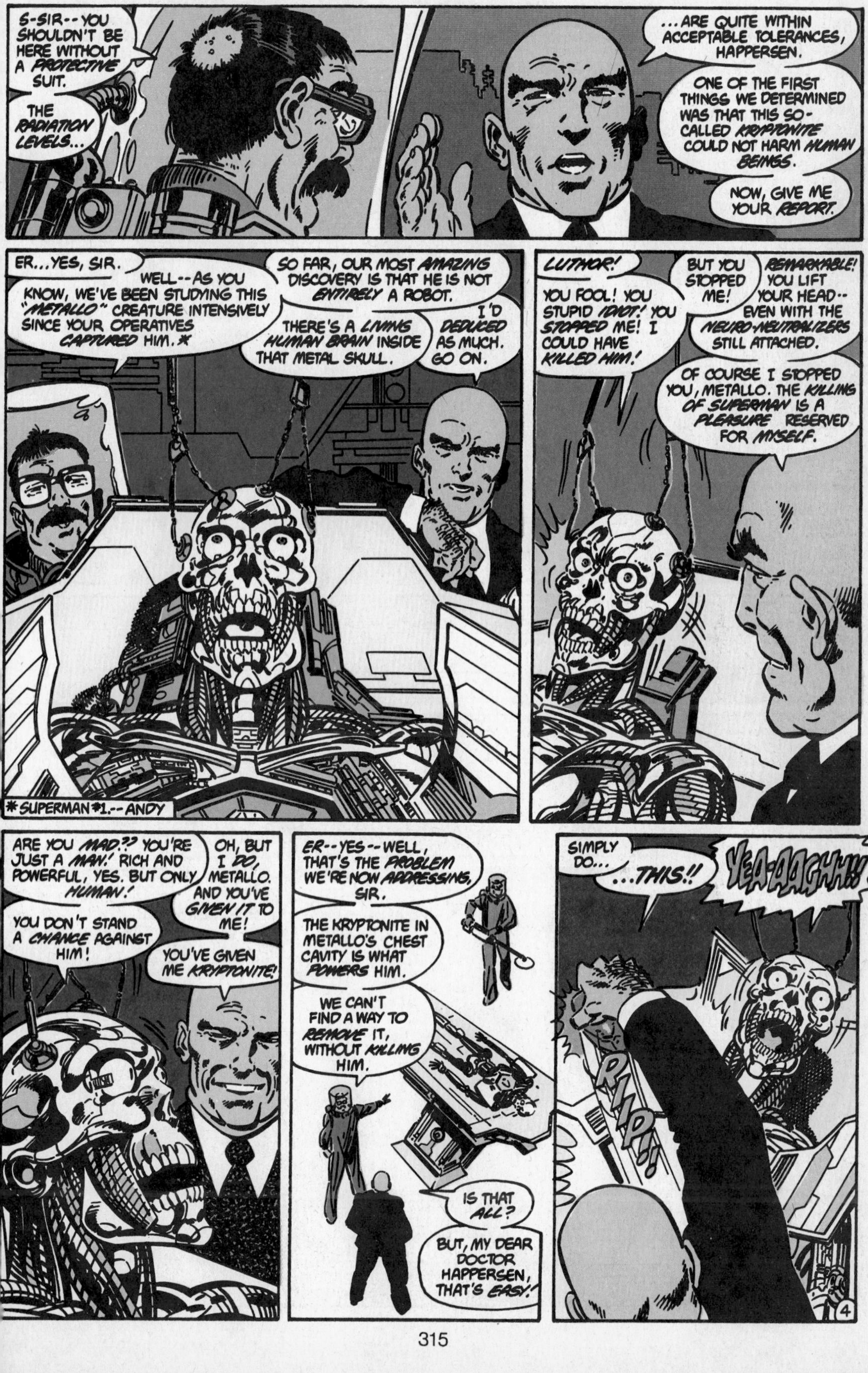
S-SIR--YOU SHOULDN'T BE HERE WITHOUT A PROTECTIVE SUIT.
THE RADIATION LEVELS...
...ARE QUITE WITHIN ACCEPTABLE TOLERANCES, HAPPERSEN.
ONE OF THE FIRST THINGS WE DETERMINED WAS THAT THIS SO-CALLED KRYPTONITE COULD NOT HARM HUMAN BEINGS.
NOW, GIVE ME YOUR REPORT.
ER...YES, SIR.
WELL--AS YOU KNOW, WE'VE BEEN STUDYING THIS "METALLO" CREATURE INTENSIVELY SINCE YOUR OPERATIVES CAPTURED HIM. *
SO FAR, OUR MOST AMAZING DISCOVERY IS THAT HE IS NOT ENTIRELY A ROBOT.
THERE'S A LIVING HUMAN BRAIN INSIDE THAT METAL SKULL.
I'D DEDUCED AS MUCH. GO ON.
* SUPERMAN #1.--ANDY
LUTHOR!
YOU FOOL! YOU STUPID IDIOT! YOU STOPPED ME! I COULD HAVE KILLED HIM!
BUT YOU STOPPED ME!
REMARKABLE! YOU LIFT YOUR HEAD-- EVEN WITH THE NEURO-NEUTRALIZERS STILL ATTACHED.
OF COURSE I STOPPED YOU, METALLO. THE KILLING OF SUPERMAN IS A PLEASURE RESERVED FOR MYSELF.
ARE YOU MAD?? YOU'RE JUST A MAN! RICH AND POWERFUL, YES. BUT ONLY HUMAN!
YOU DON'T STAND A CHANCE AGAINST HIM!
OH, BUT I DO, METALLO. AND YOU'VE GIVEN IT TO ME!
YOU'VE GIVEN ME KRYPTONITE!
ER--YES--WELL, THAT'S THE PROBLEM WE'RE NOW ADDRESSING, SIR.
THE KRYPTONITE IN METALLO'S CHEST CAVITY IS WHAT POWERS HIM.
WE CAN'T FIND A WAY TO REMOVE IT, WITHOUT KILLING HIM.
IS THAT ALL?
BUT, MY DEAR DOCTOR HAPPERSEN, THAT'S EASY!
SIMPLY DO...
...THIS!!
YEA-AAGHH!!
RIP!!
4

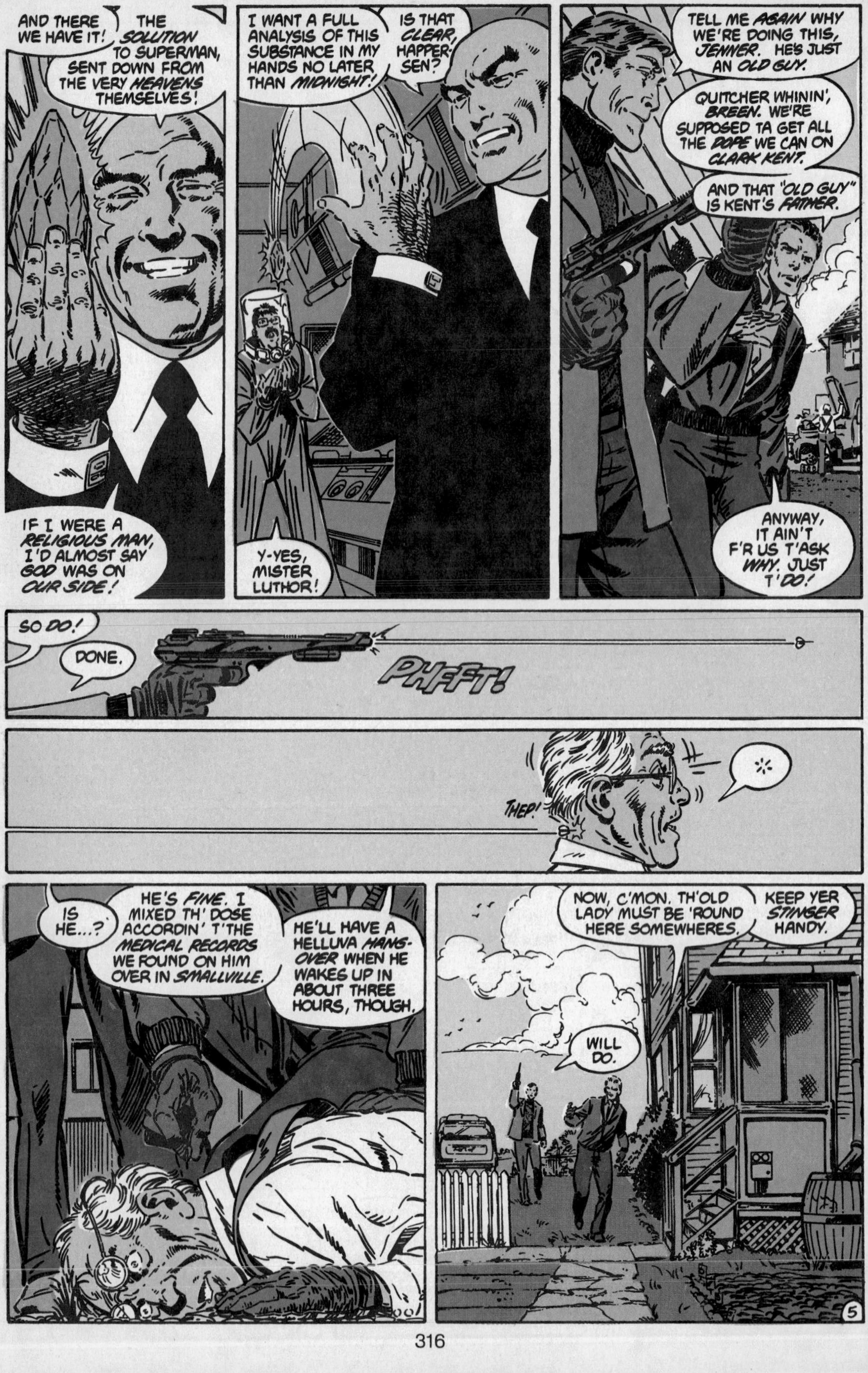
AND THERE WE HAVE IT!
THE SOLUTION TO SUPERMAN, SENT DOWN FROM THE VERY HEAVENS THEMSELVES!
IF I WERE A RELIGIOUS MAN, I'D ALMOST SAY GOD WAS ON OUR SIDE!
I WANT A FULL ANALYSIS OF THIS SUBSTANCE IN MY HANDS NO LATER THAN MIDNIGHT!
IS THAT CLEAR, HAPPER-SEN?
Y-YES, MISTER LUTHOR!
TELL ME AGAIN WHY WE'RE DOING THIS, JENNER. HE'S JUST AN OLD GUY.
QUITCHER WHININ', BREEN. WE'RE SUPPOSED TA GET ALL THE DOPE WE CAN ON CLARK KENT.
AND THAT "OLD GUY" IS KENT'S FATHER.
ANYWAY, IT AIN'T F'R US T'ASK WHY. JUST T'DO!
SO DO!
DONE.
PHFFT!
THEP!
IS HE...?
HE'S FINE. I MIXED TH' DOSE ACCORDIN' T'THE MEDICAL RECORDS WE FOUND ON HIM OVER IN SMALLVILLE.
HE'LL HAVE A HELLUVA HANG-OVER WHEN HE WAKES UP IN ABOUT THREE HOURS, THOUGH.
NOW, C'MON. TH'OLD LADY MUST BE 'ROUND HERE SOMEWHERES.
KEEP YER STINGER HANDY.
WILL DO.
5

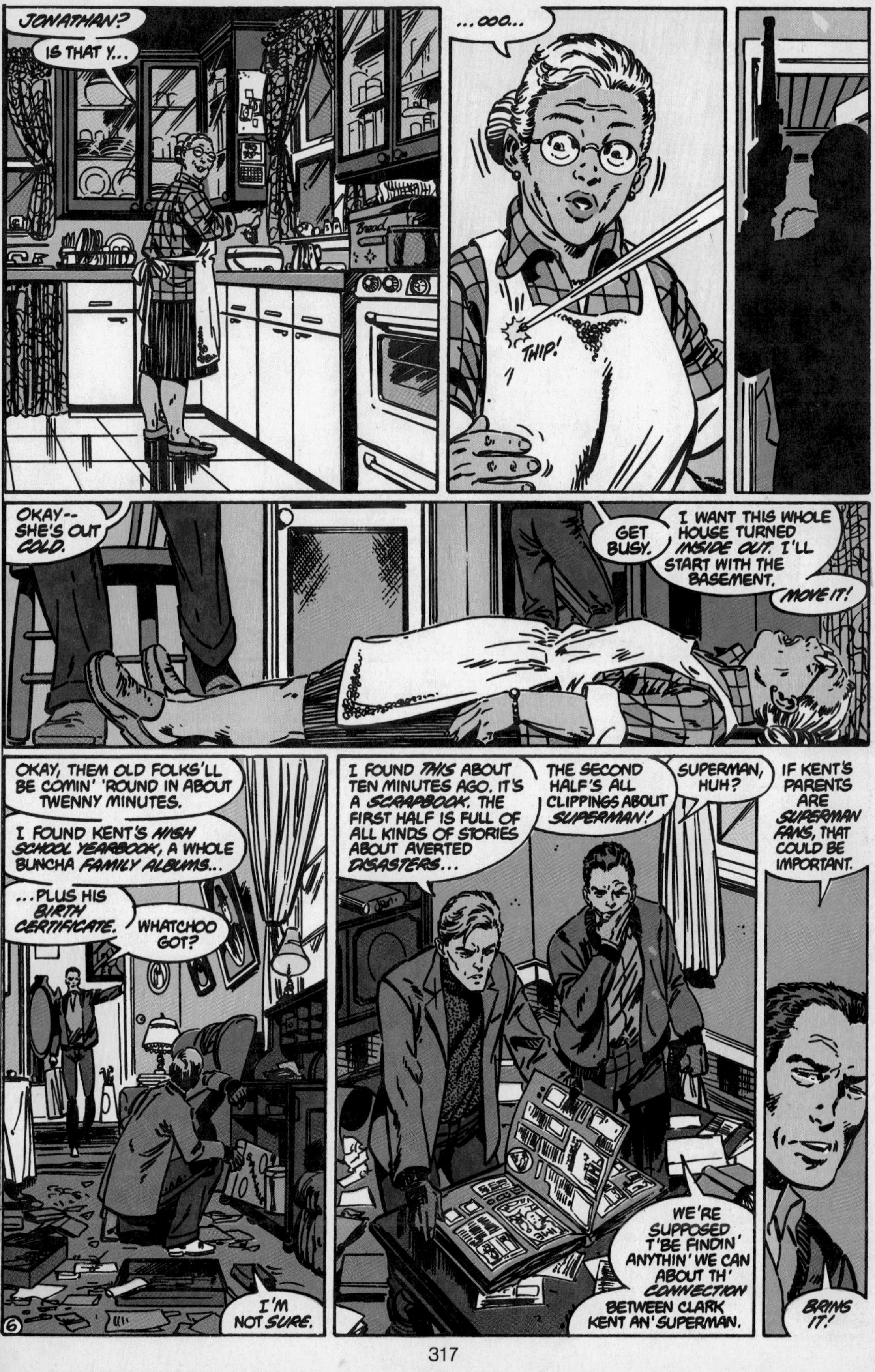
JONATHAN?
IS THAT Y...
...OOO...
THIP!
OKAY-- SHE'S OUT COLD.
GET BUSY.
I WANT THIS WHOLE HOUSE TURNED INSIDE OUT. I'LL START WITH THE BASEMENT.
MOVE IT!
OKAY, THEM OLD FOLKS'LL BE COMIN' 'ROUND IN ABOUT TWENNY MINUTES.
I FOUND KENT'S HIGH SCHOOL YEARBOOK, A WHOLE BUNCHA FAMILY ALBUMS...
...PLUS HIS BIRTH CERTIFICATE.
WHATCHOO GOT?
I'M NOT SURE.
I FOUND THIS ABOUT TEN MINUTES AGO. IT'S A SCRAPBOOK. THE FIRST HALF IS FULL OF ALL KINDS OF STORIES ABOUT AVERTED DISASTERS...
THE SECOND HALF'S ALL CLIPPINGS ABOUT SUPERMAN!
SUPERMAN, HUH?
WE'RE SUPPOSED T'BE FINDIN' ANYTHIN' WE CAN ABOUT TH' CONNECTION BETWEEN CLARK KENT AN' SUPERMAN.
IF KENT'S PARENTS ARE SUPERMAN FANS, THAT COULD BE IMPORTANT.
BRING IT!
6

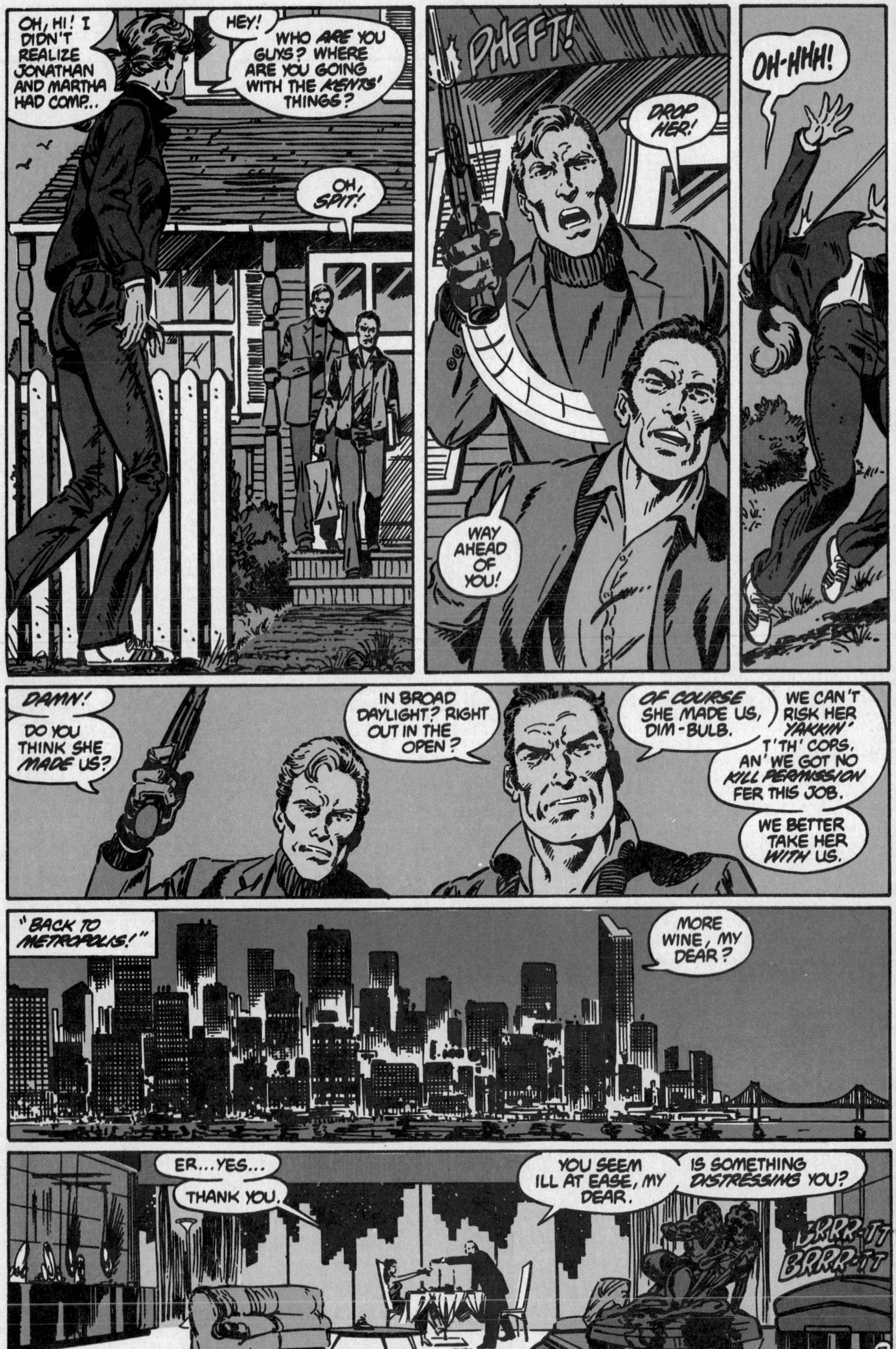
OH, HI! I DIDN'T REALIZE JONATHAN AND MARTHA HAD COMP...
HEY!
WHO ARE YOU GUYS? WHERE ARE YOU GOING WITH THE KENTS' THINGS?
OH, SPIT!
PHFFT!
DROP HER!
WAY AHEAD OF YOU!
OH-HHH!
DAMN!
DO YOU THINK SHE MADE US?
IN BROAD DAYLIGHT? RIGHT OUT IN THE OPEN?
OF COURSE SHE MADE US, DIM-BULB.
WE CAN'T RISK HER YAKKIN' T'TH' COPS, AN' WE GOT NO KILL PERMISSION FER THIS JOB.
WE BETTER TAKE HER WITH US.
"BACK TO METROPOLIS!"
MORE WINE, MY DEAR?
ER...YES...
THANK YOU.
YOU SEEM ILL AT EASE, MY DEAR.
IS SOMETHING DISTRESSING YOU?
BRRR-TT
BRRR-TT
7

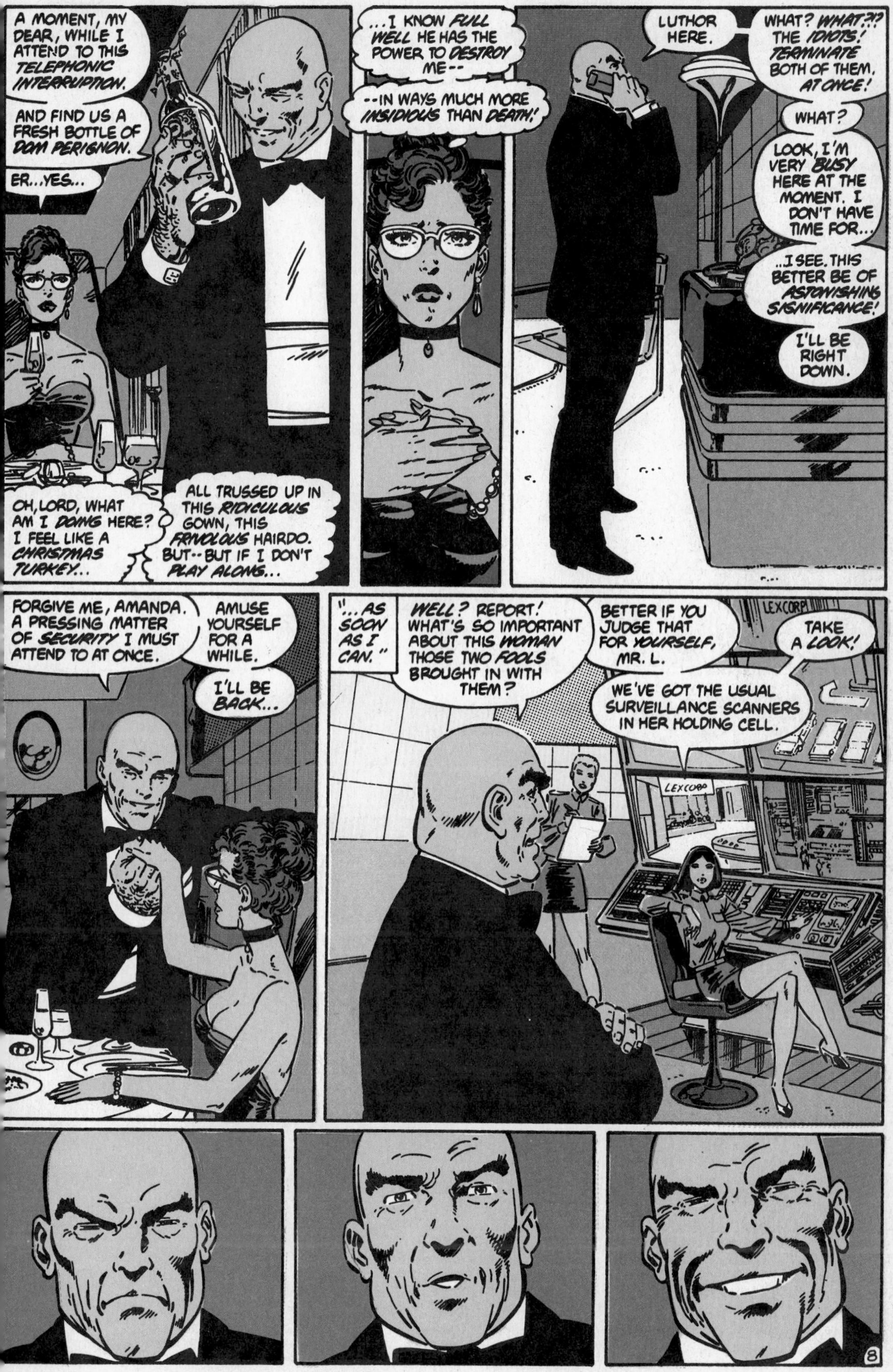

A MOMENT, MY DEAR, WHILE I ATTEND TO THIS TELEPHONIC INTERRUPTION.
AND FIND US A FRESH BOTTLE OF DOM PERIGNON.
ER...YES...
OH, LORD, WHAT AM I DOING HERE? I FEEL LIKE A CHRISTMAS TURKEY...
ALL TRUSSED UP IN THIS RIDICULOUS GOWN, THIS FRIVOLOUS HAIRDO. BUT--BUT IF I DON'T PLAY ALONG...
...I KNOW FULL WELL HE HAS THE POWER TO DESTROY ME--
--IN WAYS MUCH MORE INSIDIOUS THAN DEATH!
LUTHOR HERE.
WHAT? WHAT?!? THE IDIOTS! TERMINATE BOTH OF THEM. AT ONCE!
WHAT?
LOOK, I'M VERY BUSY HERE AT THE MOMENT. I DON'T HAVE TIME FOR...
..I SEE. THIS BETTER BE OF ASTONISHING SIGNIFICANCE!
I'LL BE RIGHT DOWN.
FORGIVE ME, AMANDA. A PRESSING MATTER OF SECURITY I MUST ATTEND TO AT ONCE.
AMUSE YOURSELF FOR A WHILE.
I'LL BE BACK...
"...AS SOON AS I CAN."
WELL? REPORT! WHAT'S SO IMPORTANT ABOUT THIS WOMAN THOSE TWO FOOLS BROUGHT IN WITH THEM?
BETTER IF YOU JUDGE THAT FOR YOURSELF, MR. L.
TAKE A LOOK!
WE'VE GOT THE USUAL SURVEILLANCE SCANNERS IN HER HOLDING CELL.
LEXCORP
LEXCORP
8

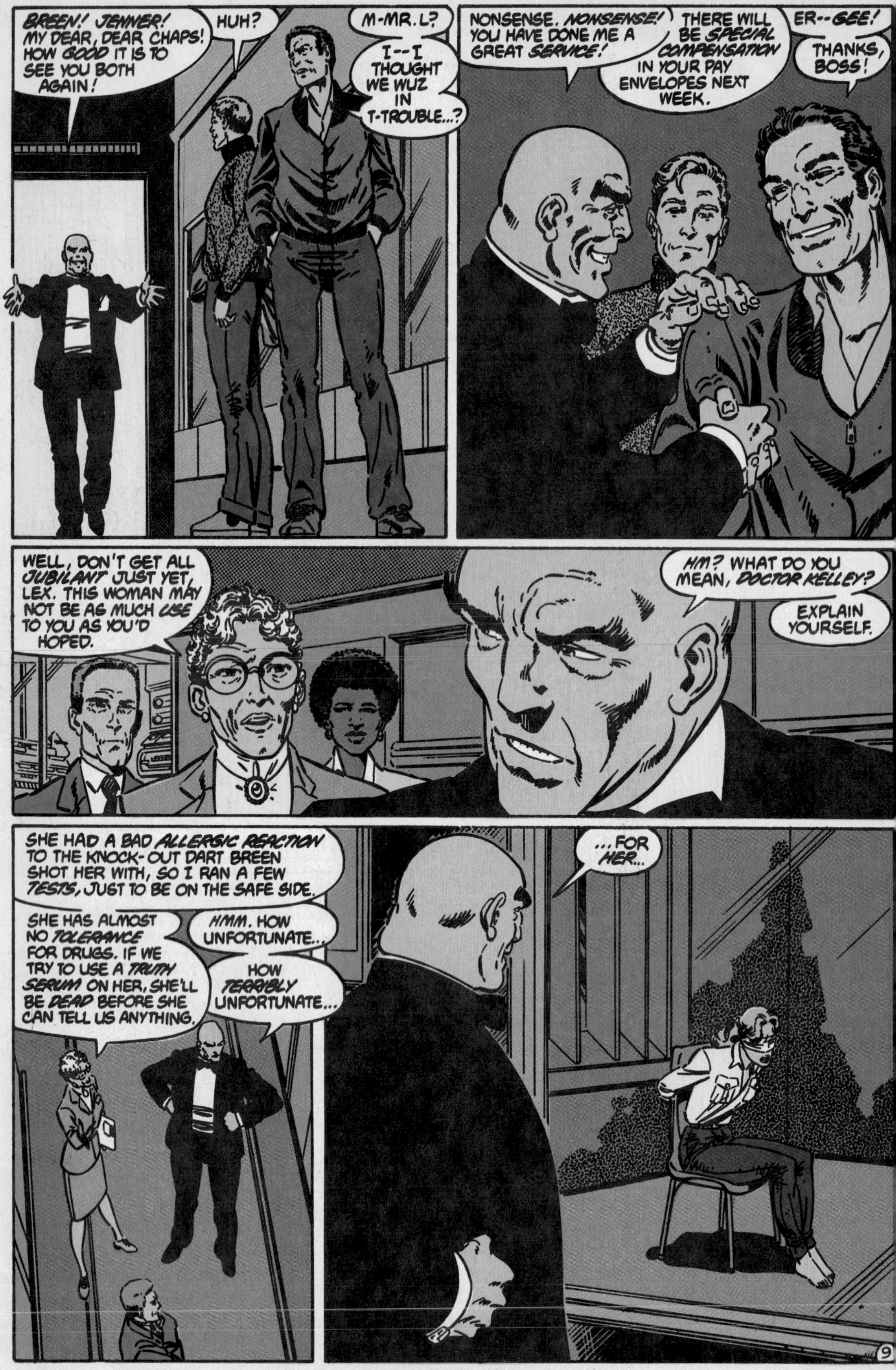
BREEN! JENNER! MY DEAR, DEAR CHAPS! HOW GOOD IT IS TO SEE YOU BOTH AGAIN!
HUH?
M-MR. L?
I--I THOUGHT WE WUZ IN T-TROUBLE...?
NONSENSE. NONSENSE! YOU HAVE DONE ME A GREAT SERVICE!
THERE WILL BE SPECIAL COMPENSATION IN YOUR PAY ENVELOPES NEXT WEEK.
ER--GEE!
THANKS, BOSS!
WELL, DON'T GET ALL JUBILANT JUST YET, LEX. THIS WOMAN MAY NOT BE AS MUCH USE TO YOU AS YOU'D HOPED.
HM? WHAT DO YOU MEAN, DOCTOR KELLEY?
EXPLAIN YOURSELF.
SHE HAD A BAD ALLERGIC REACTION TO THE KNOCK-OUT DART BREEN SHOT HER WITH, SO I RAN A FEW TESTS, JUST TO BE ON THE SAFE SIDE.
SHE HAS ALMOST NO TOLERANCE FOR DRUGS. IF WE TRY TO USE A TRUTH SERUM ON HER, SHE'LL BE DEAD BEFORE SHE CAN TELL US ANYTHING.
HMM. HOW UNFORTUNATE...
HOW TERRIBLY UNFORTUNATE...
...FOR HER...
9

HMMM...

EVERYTHING SEEMS TO BE *FUNCTIONING* AT MORE OR LESS *NORMAL* LEVELS.

NORMAL FOR *ME*, THAT IS.

I WAS SERIOUSLY CONCERNED FOR A WHILE THERE. AFTER MY FIRST EXPOSURE TO METALLO'S *KRYPTONITE* THE OTHER WEEK, IT TOOK SEVERAL DAYS FOR MY POWERS TO GET BACK UP TO SNUFF.

IT'S QUITE POSSIBLE A *PROLONGED* EXPOSURE TO THE STUFF COULD *STRIP* ME OF MY POWERS *PERMANENTLY!*

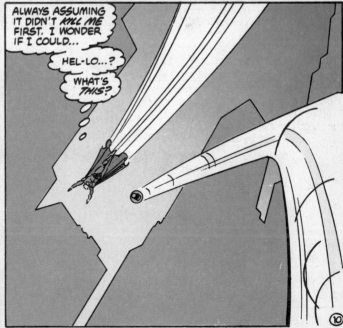

ALWAYS ASSUMING IT DIDN'T *KILL ME* FIRST. I WONDER IF I COULD...

HEL-LO...?

WHAT'S *THIS?*

⑩

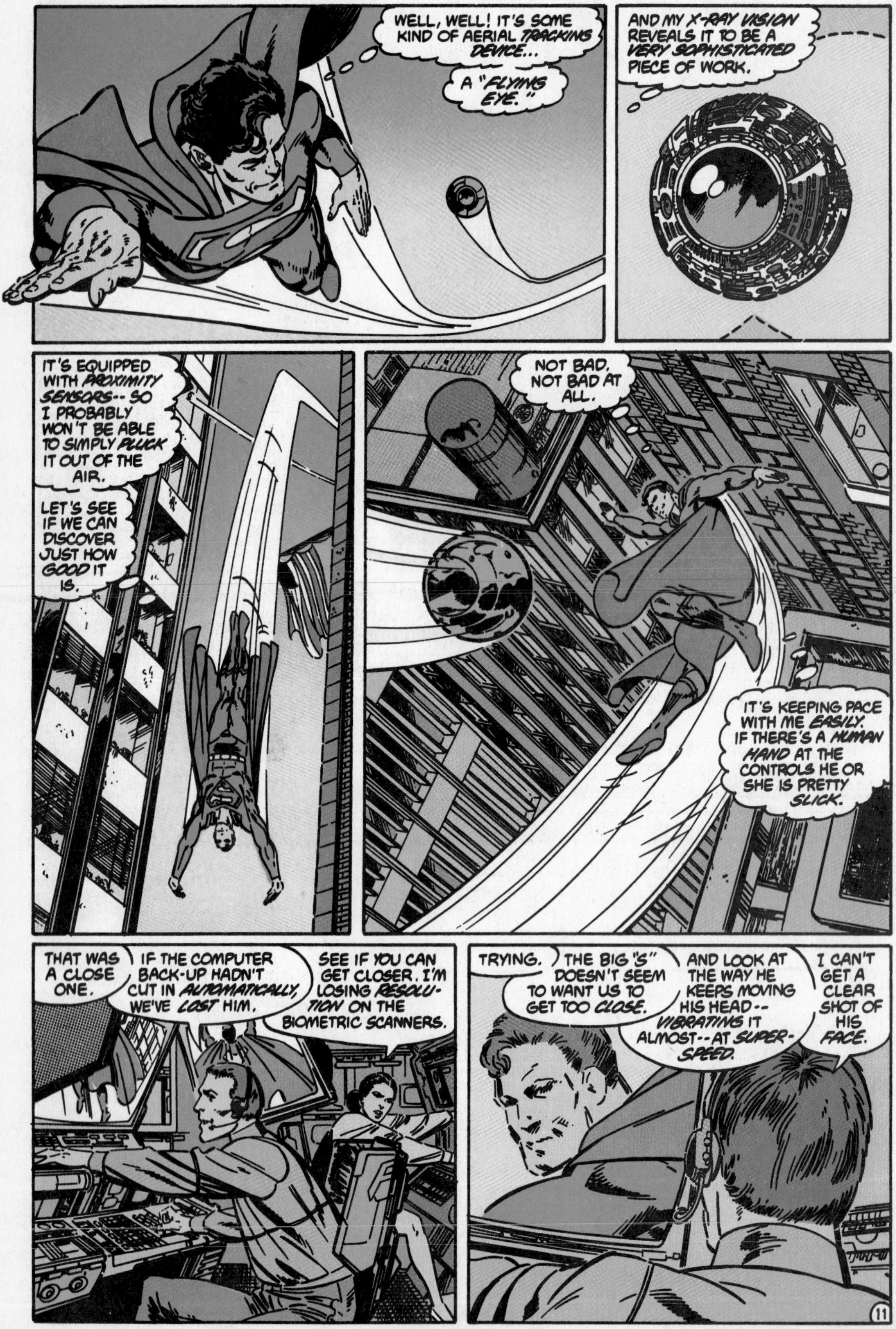
WELL, WELL! IT'S SOME KIND OF AERIAL TRACKING DEVICE...
A "FLYING EYE."
AND MY X-RAY VISION REVEALS IT TO BE A VERY SOPHISTICATED PIECE OF WORK.
IT'S EQUIPPED WITH PROXIMITY SENSORS-- SO I PROBABLY WON'T BE ABLE TO SIMPLY PLUCK IT OUT OF THE AIR.
LET'S SEE IF WE CAN DISCOVER JUST HOW GOOD IT IS.
NOT BAD. NOT BAD AT ALL.
IT'S KEEPING PACE WITH ME EASILY. IF THERE'S A HUMAN HAND AT THE CONTROLS HE OR SHE IS PRETTY SLICK.
THAT WAS A CLOSE ONE.
IF THE COMPUTER BACK-UP HADN'T CUT IN AUTOMATICALLY, WE'VE LOST HIM.
SEE IF YOU CAN GET CLOSER. I'M LOSING RESOLU-TION ON THE BIOMETRIC SCANNERS.
TRYING.
THE BIG "S" DOESN'T SEEM TO WANT US TO GET TOO CLOSE.
AND LOOK AT THE WAY HE KEEPS MOVING HIS HEAD-- VIBRATING IT ALMOST--AT SUPER-SPEED.
I CAN'T GET A CLEAR SHOT OF HIS FACE.
11

IT'S STILL WITH ME.

WELL, I HAVE MUCH *BETTER* THINGS TO DO TODAY THAN PLAY *TAG* WITH THIS NOSEY EIGHT-BALL.

AND THERE'S MY *SOLUTION!*

LUCKILY I ALWAYS CARRY A FEW *DOLLARS* INSIDE MY HOLLOW BELT BUCKLE.

GOOD AFTERNOON, SIR. I'D LIKE TO BUY YOUR *ENTIRE* STOCK!

S-SUPERMAN!!!

NOW THEN--LET'S *START* BY LETTING OUR LITTLE FRIEND GET *CLOSER...*

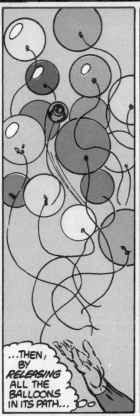

...THEN, BY *RELEASING* ALL THE BALLOONS IN ITS PATH...

...I CAN *CONFUSE* THE PROXIMITY DETECTORS LONG ENOUGH...

...TO *SNAG* IT!

12

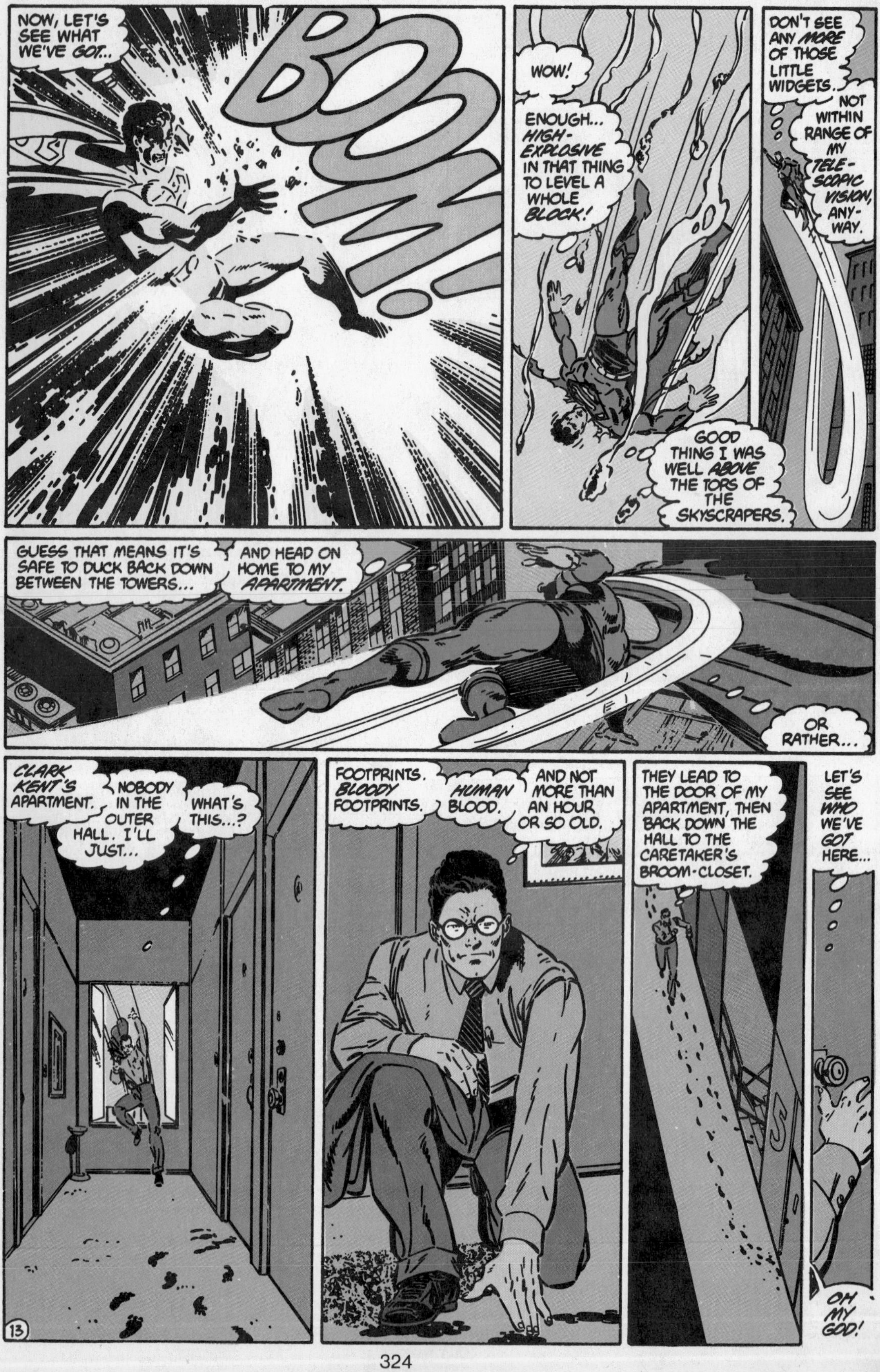
NOW, LET'S SEE WHAT WE'VE GOT...
BOOM!!
WOW!
ENOUGH... HIGH-EXPLOSIVE IN THAT THING TO LEVEL A WHOLE BLOCK!
GOOD THING I WAS WELL ABOVE THE TOPS OF THE SKYSCRAPERS.
DON'T SEE ANY MORE OF THOSE LITTLE WIDGETS...
NOT WITHIN RANGE OF MY TELE-SCOPIC VISION, ANYWAY.
GUESS THAT MEANS IT'S SAFE TO DUCK BACK DOWN BETWEEN THE TOWERS...
AND HEAD ON HOME TO MY APARTMENT.
OR RATHER...
CLARK KENT'S APARTMENT.
NOBODY IN THE OUTER HALL. I'LL JUST...
WHAT'S THIS...?
13
FOOTPRINTS. BLOODY FOOTPRINTS.
HUMAN BLOOD.
AND NOT MORE THAN AN HOUR OR SO OLD.
THEY LEAD TO THE DOOR OF MY APARTMENT, THEN BACK DOWN THE HALL TO THE CARETAKER'S BROOM-CLOSET.
LET'S SEE WHO WE'VE GOT HERE...
OH MY GOD!

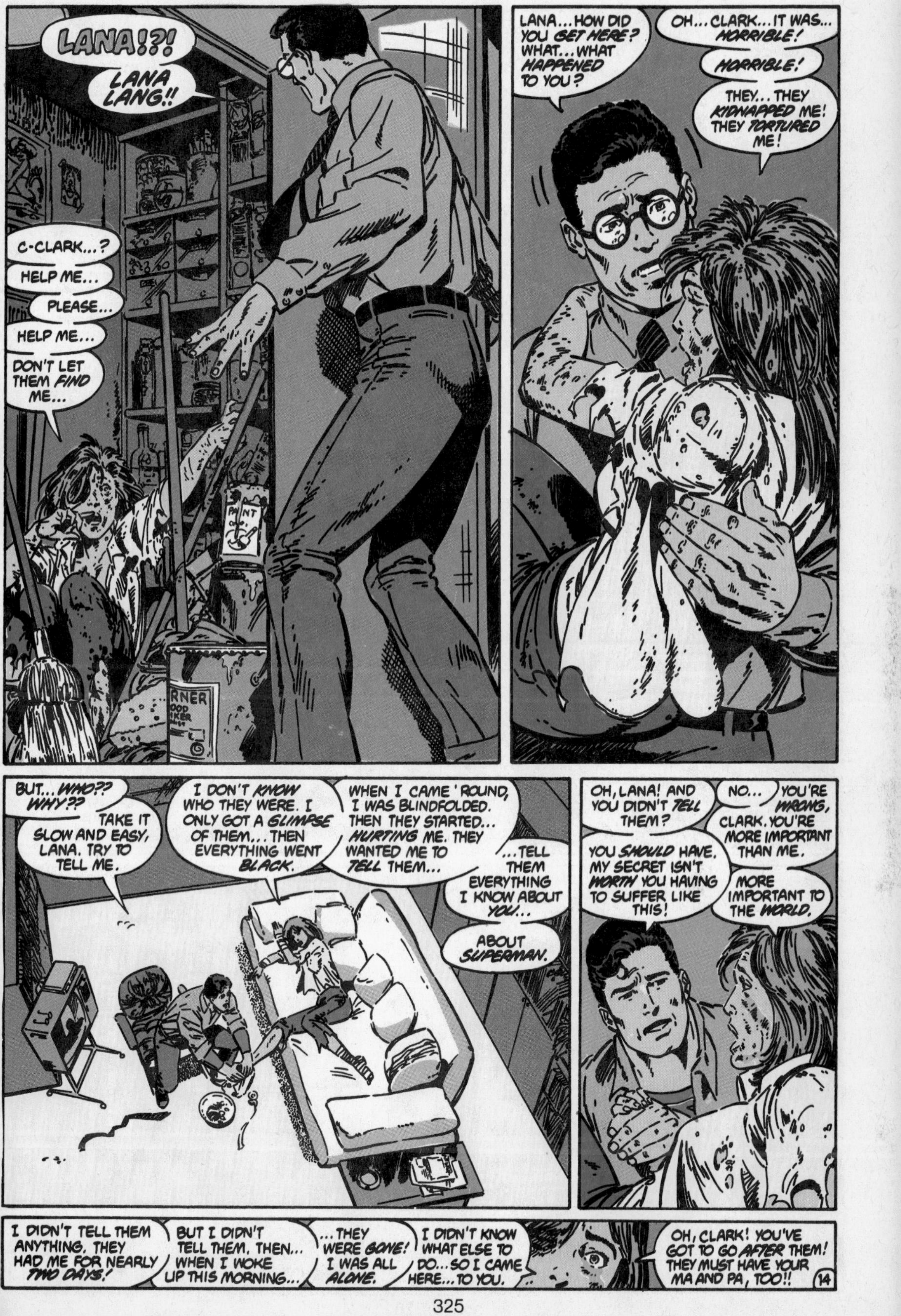
LANA!?!
LANA LANG!!
C-CLARK...?
HELP ME...
PLEASE...
HELP ME...
DON'T LET THEM FIND ME...
LANA... HOW DID YOU GET HERE? WHAT... WHAT HAPPENED TO YOU?
OH... CLARK... IT WAS... HORRIBLE!
HORRIBLE!
THEY... THEY KIDNAPPED ME! THEY TORTURED ME!
BUT... WHO?? WHY??
TAKE IT SLOW AND EASY, LANA. TRY TO TELL ME.
I DON'T KNOW WHO THEY WERE. I ONLY GOT A GLIMPSE OF THEM... THEN EVERYTHING WENT BLACK.
WHEN I CAME 'ROUND, I WAS BLINDFOLDED. THEN THEY STARTED... HURTING ME. THEY WANTED ME TO TELL THEM...
...TELL THEM EVERYTHING I KNOW ABOUT YOU...
ABOUT SUPERMAN.
PAINT
OH, LANA! AND YOU DIDN'T TELL THEM?
YOU SHOULD HAVE. MY SECRET ISN'T WORTH YOU HAVING TO SUFFER LIKE THIS!
NO... YOU'RE WRONG, CLARK. YOU'RE MORE IMPORTANT THAN ME.
MORE IMPORTANT TO THE WORLD.
I DIDN'T TELL THEM ANYTHING. THEY HAD ME FOR NEARLY TWO DAYS!
BUT I DIDN'T TELL THEM. THEN... WHEN I WOKE UP THIS MORNING...
...THEY WERE GONE! I WAS ALL ALONE.
I DIDN'T KNOW WHAT ELSE TO DO... SO I CAME HERE... TO YOU.
OH, CLARK! YOU'VE GOT TO GO AFTER THEM! THEY MUST HAVE YOUR MA AND PA, TOO!!
14

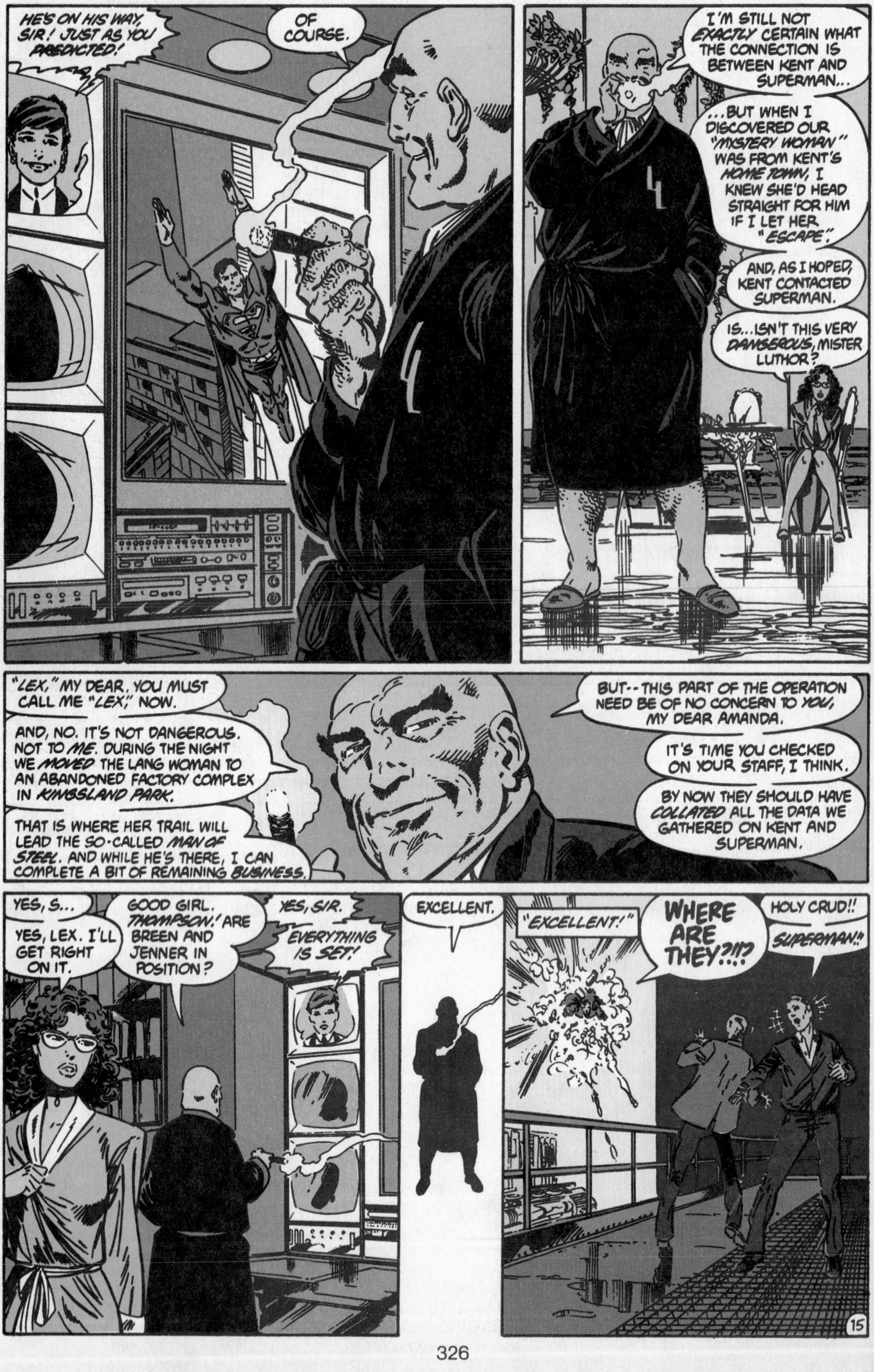

HE'S ON HIS WAY, SIR! JUST AS YOU PREDICTED!
OF COURSE.
I'M STILL NOT EXACTLY CERTAIN WHAT THE CONNECTION IS BETWEEN KENT AND SUPERMAN...
...BUT WHEN I DISCOVERED OUR "MYSTERY WOMAN" WAS FROM KENT'S HOME TOWN, I KNEW SHE'D HEAD STRAIGHT FOR HIM IF I LET HER "ESCAPE".
AND, AS I HOPED, KENT CONTACTED SUPERMAN.
IS...ISN'T THIS VERY DANGEROUS, MISTER LUTHOR?
"LEX," MY DEAR. YOU MUST CALL ME "LEX," NOW.
AND, NO. IT'S NOT DANGEROUS. NOT TO ME. DURING THE NIGHT WE MOVED THE LANG WOMAN TO AN ABANDONED FACTORY COMPLEX IN KINGSLAND PARK.
THAT IS WHERE HER TRAIL WILL LEAD THE SO-CALLED MAN OF STEEL. AND WHILE HE'S THERE, I CAN COMPLETE A BIT OF REMAINING BUSINESS.
BUT--THIS PART OF THE OPERATION NEED BE OF NO CONCERN TO YOU, MY DEAR AMANDA.
IT'S TIME YOU CHECKED ON YOUR STAFF, I THINK.
BY NOW THEY SHOULD HAVE COLLATED ALL THE DATA WE GATHERED ON KENT AND SUPERMAN.
YES, S...
YES, LEX. I'LL GET RIGHT ON IT.
GOOD GIRL. THOMPSON! ARE BREEN AND JENNER IN POSITION?
YES, SIR. EVERYTHING IS SET!
EXCELLENT.
"EXCELLENT!"
WHERE ARE THEY?!!?
HOLY CRUD!! SUPERMAN!!
15

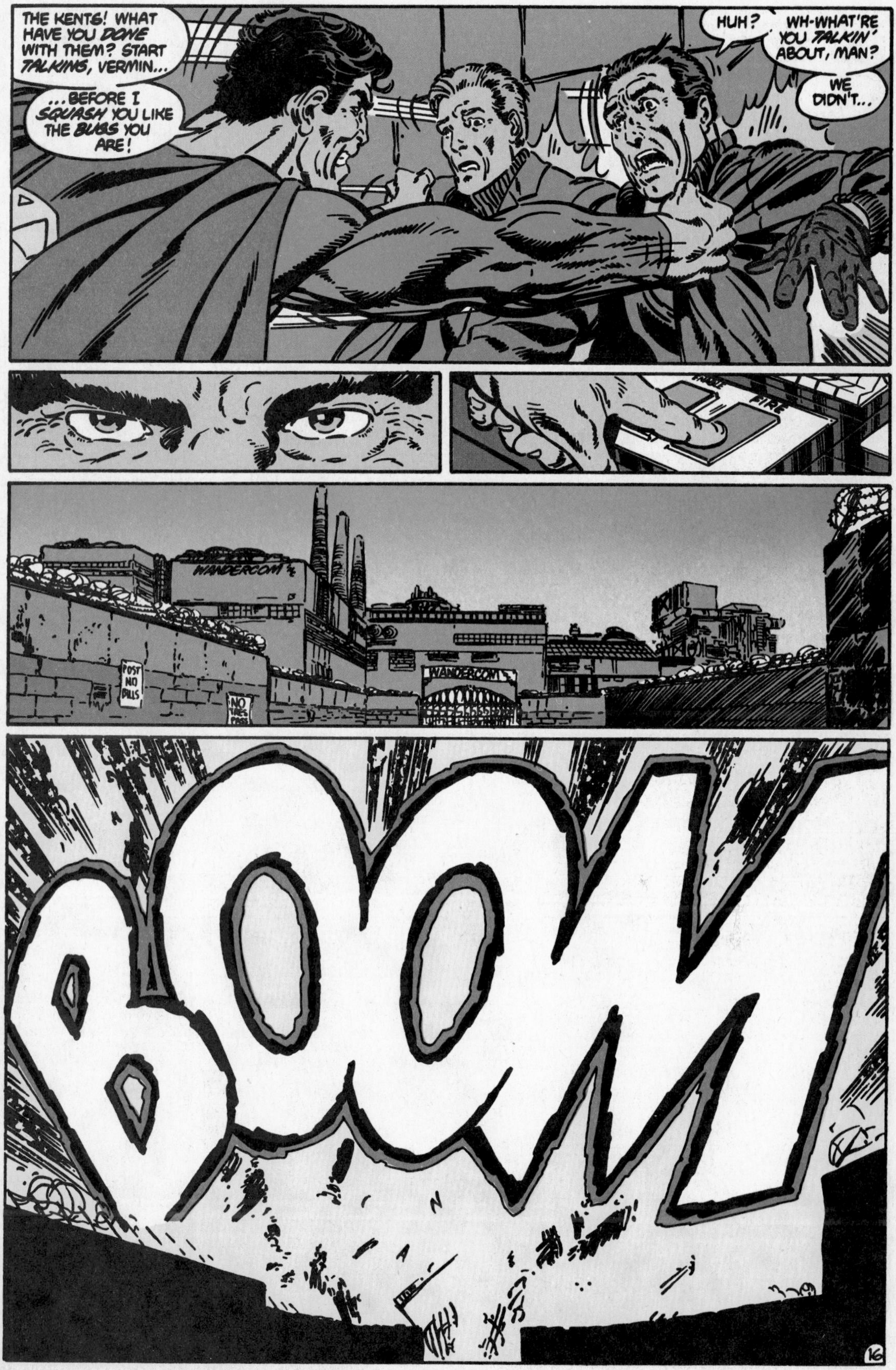
THE KENTS! WHAT HAVE YOU *DONE* WITH THEM? START *TALKING*, VERMIN...
...BEFORE I *SQUASH* YOU LIKE THE *BUGS* YOU ARE!
HUH?
WH-WHAT'RE YOU *TALKIN'* ABOUT, MAN?
WE DIDN'T...
FIRE
WANDERCOM
WANDERCOM
POST NO BILLS
BOOM
16

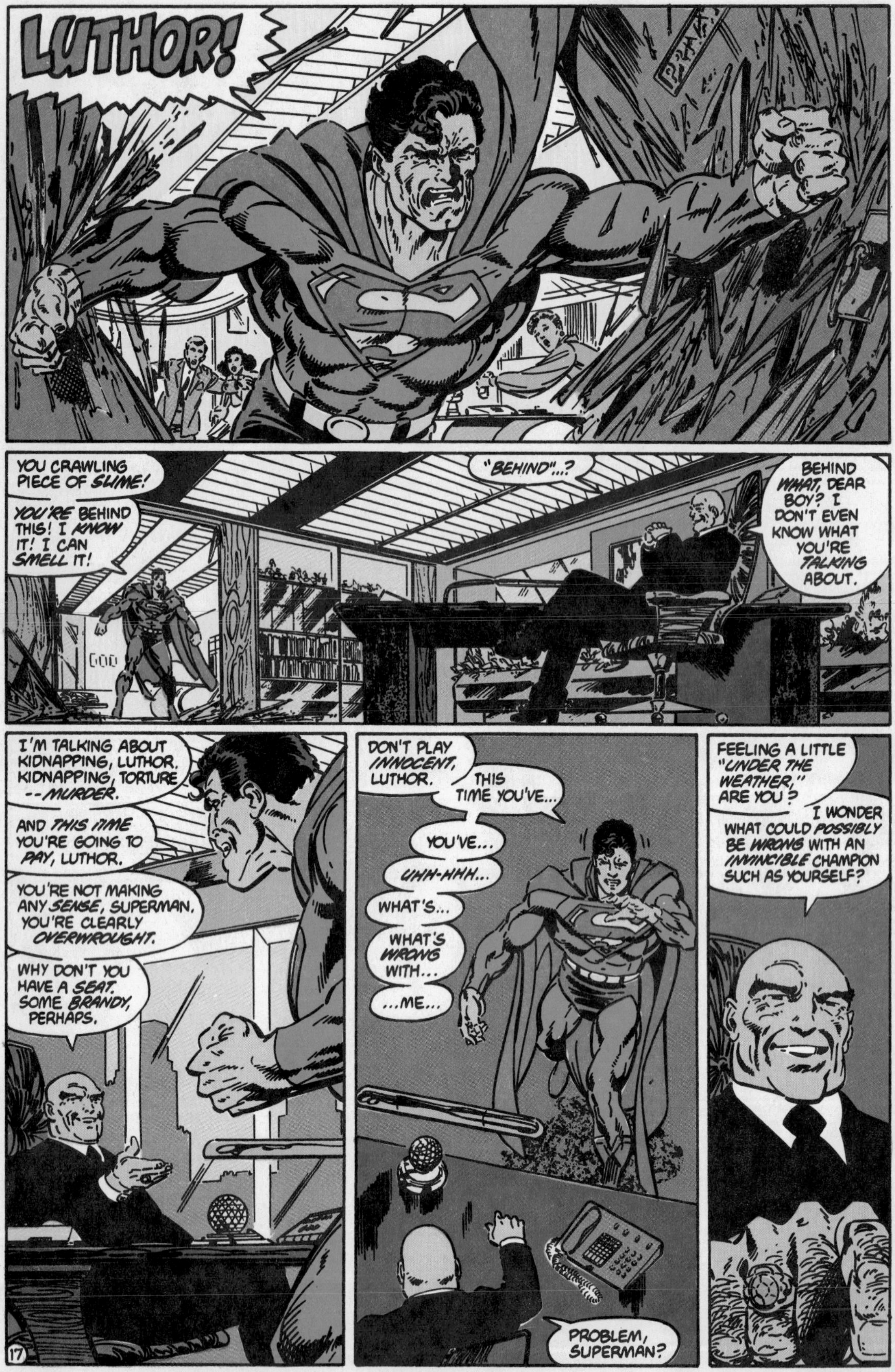
LUTHOR!
YOU CRAWLING PIECE OF SLIME!
YOU'RE BEHIND THIS! I KNOW IT! I CAN SMELL IT!
"BEHIND"...?
BEHIND WHAT, DEAR BOY? I DON'T EVEN KNOW WHAT YOU'RE TALKING ABOUT.
I'M TALKING ABOUT KIDNAPPING, LUTHOR. KIDNAPPING, TORTURE --MURDER.
AND THIS TIME YOU'RE GOING TO PAY, LUTHOR.
YOU'RE NOT MAKING ANY SENSE, SUPERMAN. YOU'RE CLEARLY OVERWROUGHT.
WHY DON'T YOU HAVE A SEAT. SOME BRANDY, PERHAPS.
17
DON'T PLAY INNOCENT, LUTHOR.
THIS TIME YOU'VE...
YOU'VE...
UHH-HHH...
WHAT'S...
WHAT'S WRONG WITH...
...ME...
PROBLEM, SUPERMAN?
FEELING A LITTLE "UNDER THE WEATHER," ARE YOU?
I WONDER WHAT COULD POSSIBLY BE WRONG WITH AN INVINCIBLE CHAMPION SUCH AS YOURSELF?

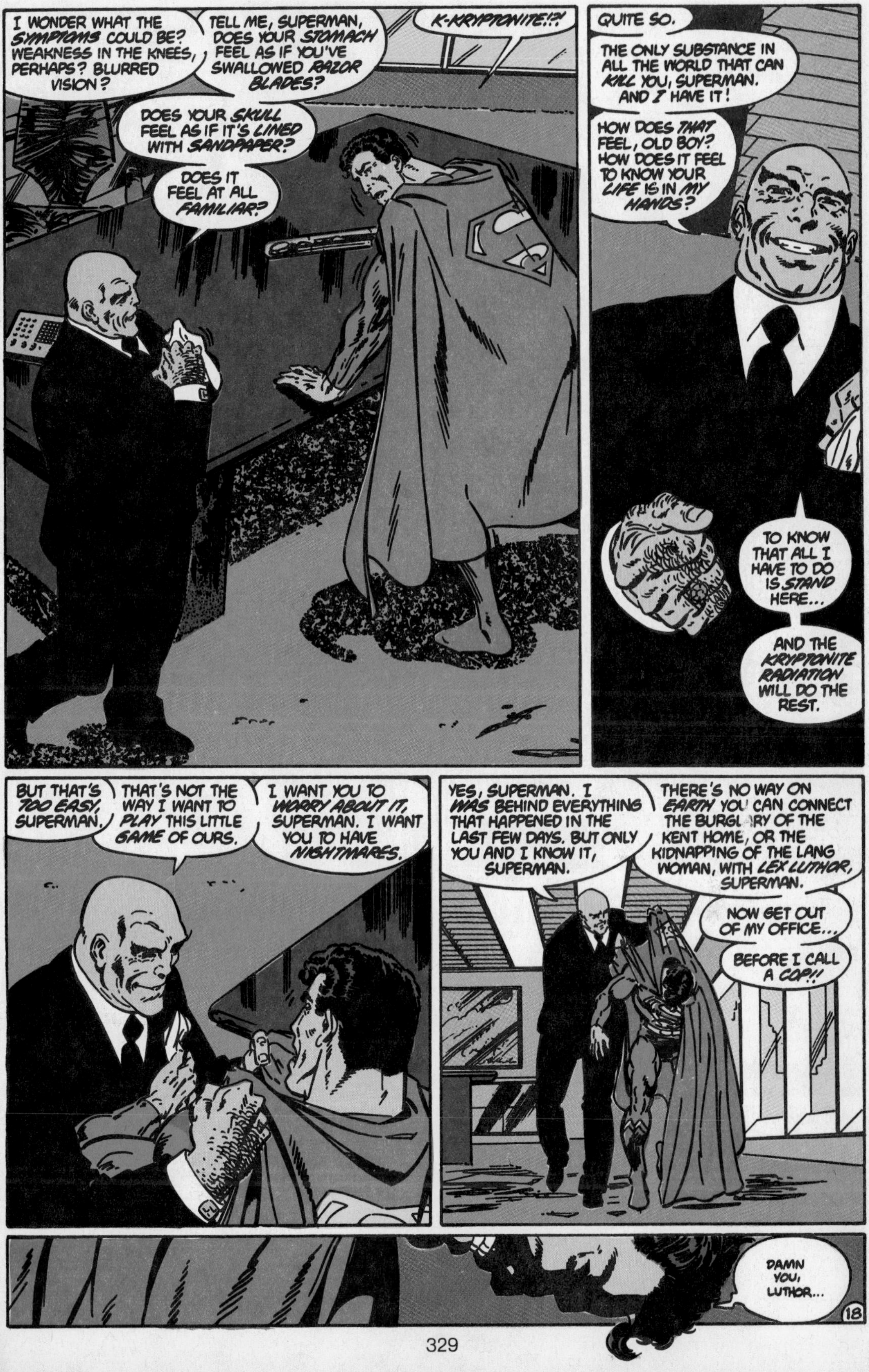
I WONDER WHAT THE SYMPTOMS COULD BE? WEAKNESS IN THE KNEES, PERHAPS? BLURRED VISION?
TELL ME, SUPERMAN, DOES YOUR STOMACH FEEL AS IF YOU'VE SWALLOWED RAZOR BLADES?
K-KRYPTONITE!?!
DOES YOUR SKULL FEEL AS IF IT'S LINED WITH SANDPAPER?
DOES IT FEEL AT ALL FAMILIAR?
QUITE SO.
THE ONLY SUBSTANCE IN ALL THE WORLD THAT CAN KILL YOU, SUPERMAN. AND I HAVE IT!
HOW DOES THAT FEEL, OLD BOY? HOW DOES IT FEEL TO KNOW YOUR LIFE IS IN MY HANDS?
TO KNOW THAT ALL I HAVE TO DO IS STAND HERE...
AND THE KRYPTONITE RADIATION WILL DO THE REST.
BUT THAT'S TOO EASY, SUPERMAN,
THAT'S NOT THE WAY I WANT TO PLAY THIS LITTLE GAME OF OURS.
I WANT YOU TO WORRY ABOUT IT, SUPERMAN. I WANT YOU TO HAVE NIGHTMARES.
YES, SUPERMAN. I WAS BEHIND EVERYTHING THAT HAPPENED IN THE LAST FEW DAYS. BUT ONLY YOU AND I KNOW IT, SUPERMAN.
THERE'S NO WAY ON EARTH YOU CAN CONNECT THE BURGLARY OF THE KENT HOME, OR THE KIDNAPPING OF THE LANG WOMAN, WITH LEX LUTHOR, SUPERMAN.
NOW GET OUT OF MY OFFICE...
BEFORE I CALL A COP!!
DAMN YOU, LUTHOR...
18

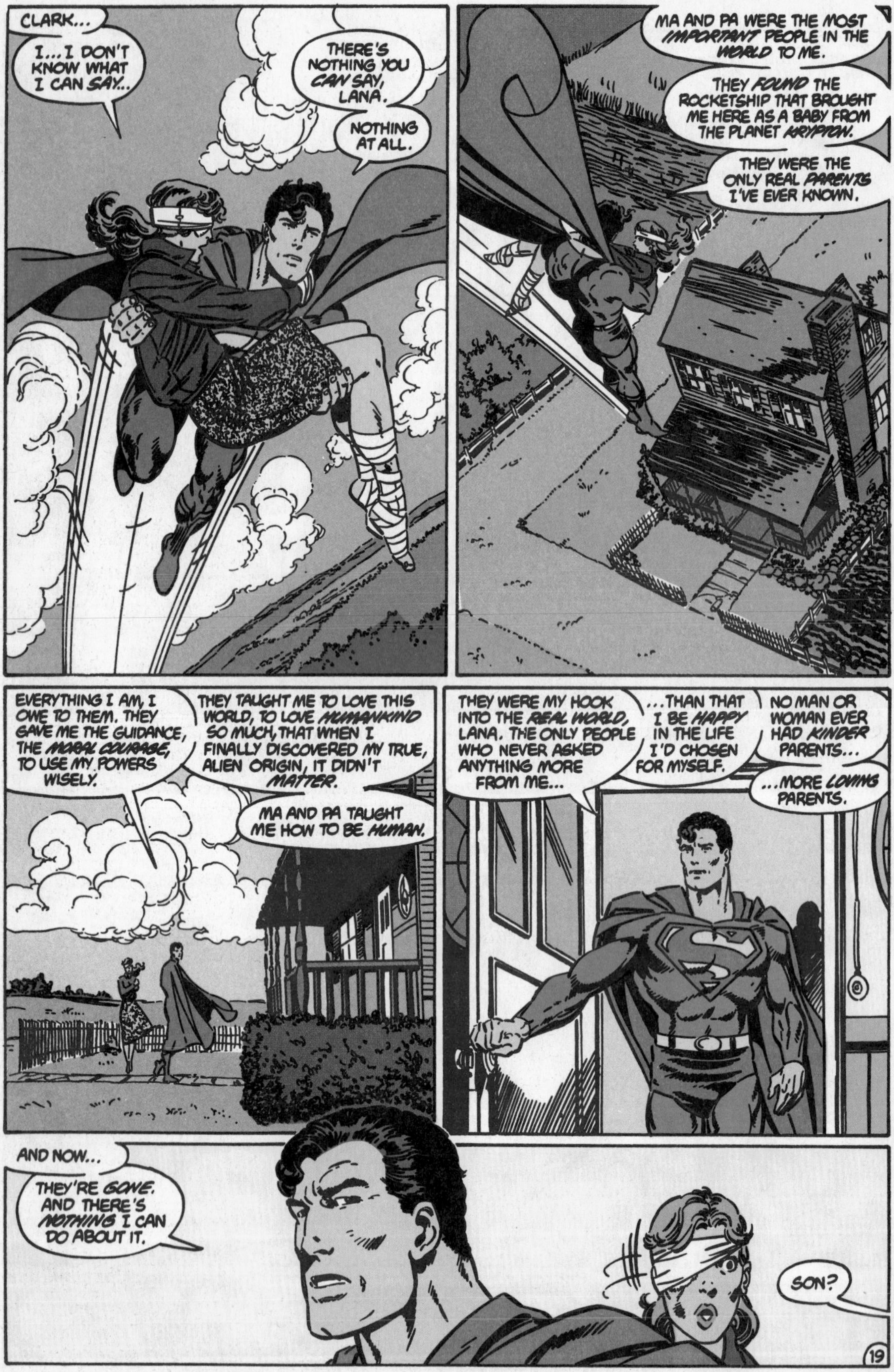
CLARK...
I...I DON'T KNOW WHAT I CAN SAY...
THERE'S NOTHING YOU CAN SAY, LANA.
NOTHING AT ALL.
MA AND PA WERE THE MOST IMPORTANT PEOPLE IN THE WORLD TO ME.
THEY FOUND THE ROCKETSHIP THAT BROUGHT ME HERE AS A BABY FROM THE PLANET KRYPTON.
THEY WERE THE ONLY REAL PARENTS I'VE EVER KNOWN.
EVERYTHING I AM, I OWE TO THEM. THEY GAVE ME THE GUIDANCE, THE MORAL COURAGE, TO USE MY POWERS WISELY.
THEY TAUGHT ME TO LOVE THIS WORLD, TO LOVE HUMANKIND SO MUCH, THAT WHEN I FINALLY DISCOVERED MY TRUE, ALIEN ORIGIN, IT DIDN'T MATTER.
MA AND PA TAUGHT ME HOW TO BE HUMAN.
THEY WERE MY HOOK INTO THE REAL WORLD, LANA. THE ONLY PEOPLE WHO NEVER ASKED ANYTHING MORE FROM ME...
...THAN THAT I BE HAPPY IN THE LIFE I'D CHOSEN FOR MYSELF.
NO MAN OR WOMAN EVER HAD KINDER PARENTS...
...MORE LOVING PARENTS.
AND NOW...
THEY'RE GONE. AND THERE'S NOTHING I CAN DO ABOUT IT.
SON?
19

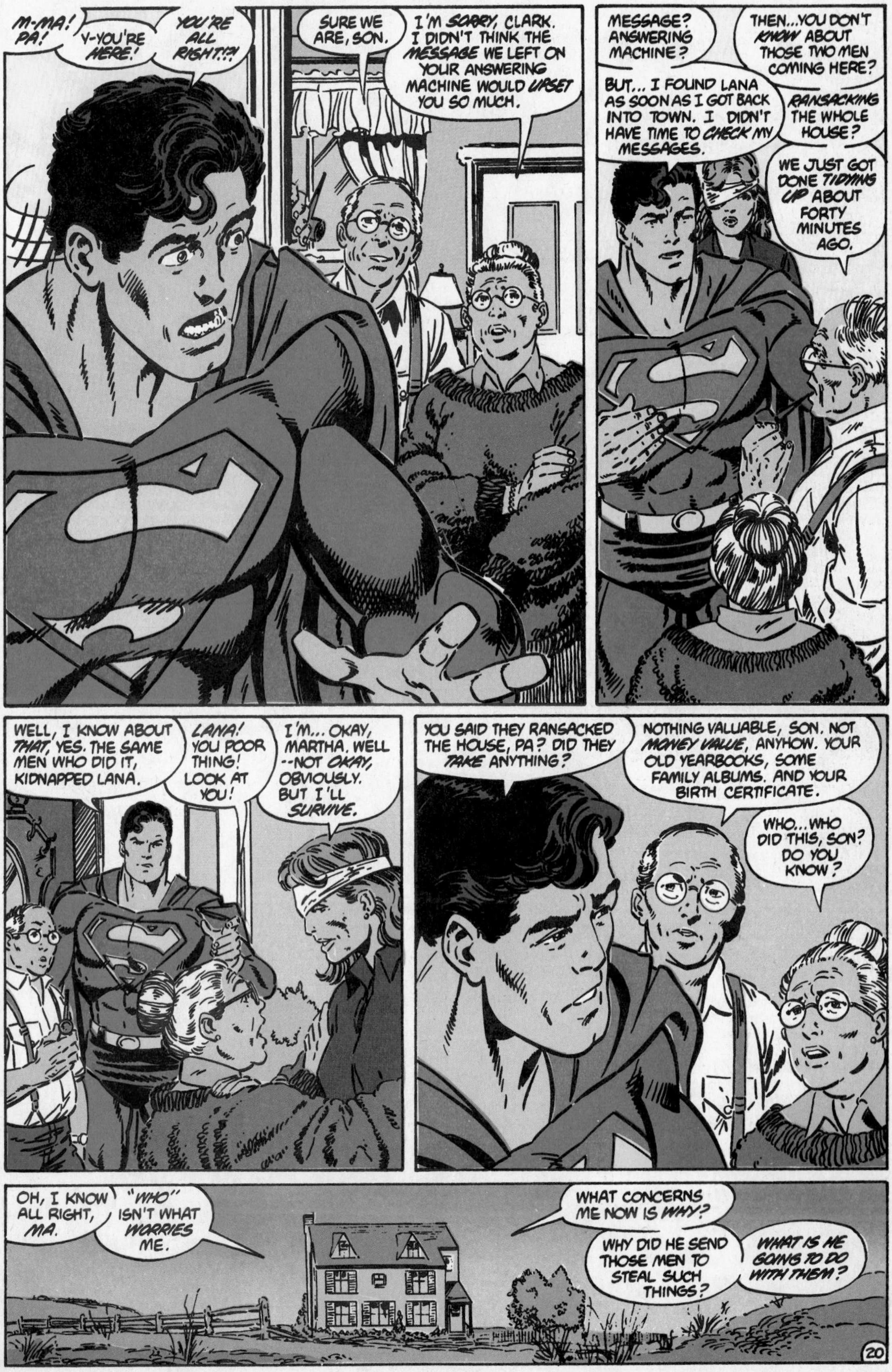
M-MA! PA!
Y-YOU'RE HERE!
YOU'RE ALL RIGHT!?!
SURE WE ARE, SON.
I'M SORRY, CLARK. I DIDN'T THINK THE MESSAGE WE LEFT ON YOUR ANSWERING MACHINE WOULD UPSET YOU SO MUCH.
MESSAGE? ANSWERING MACHINE?
BUT... I FOUND LANA AS SOON AS I GOT BACK INTO TOWN. I DIDN'T HAVE TIME TO CHECK MY MESSAGES.
THEN...YOU DON'T KNOW ABOUT THOSE TWO MEN COMING HERE?
RANSACKING THE WHOLE HOUSE?
WE JUST GOT DONE TIDYING UP ABOUT FORTY MINUTES AGO.
WELL, I KNOW ABOUT THAT, YES. THE SAME MEN WHO DID IT, KIDNAPPED LANA.
LANA! YOU POOR THING! LOOK AT YOU!
I'M... OKAY, MARTHA. WELL --NOT OKAY, OBVIOUSLY. BUT I'LL SURVIVE.
YOU SAID THEY RANSACKED THE HOUSE, PA? DID THEY TAKE ANYTHING?
NOTHING VALUABLE, SON. NOT MONEY VALUE, ANYHOW. YOUR OLD YEARBOOKS, SOME FAMILY ALBUMS. AND YOUR BIRTH CERTIFICATE.
WHO... WHO DID THIS, SON? DO YOU KNOW?
OH, I KNOW ALL RIGHT, MA.
"WHO" ISN'T WHAT WORRIES ME.
WHAT CONCERNS ME NOW IS WHY?
WHY DID HE SEND THOSE MEN TO STEAL SUCH THINGS?
WHAT IS HE GOING TO DO WITH THEM?
20

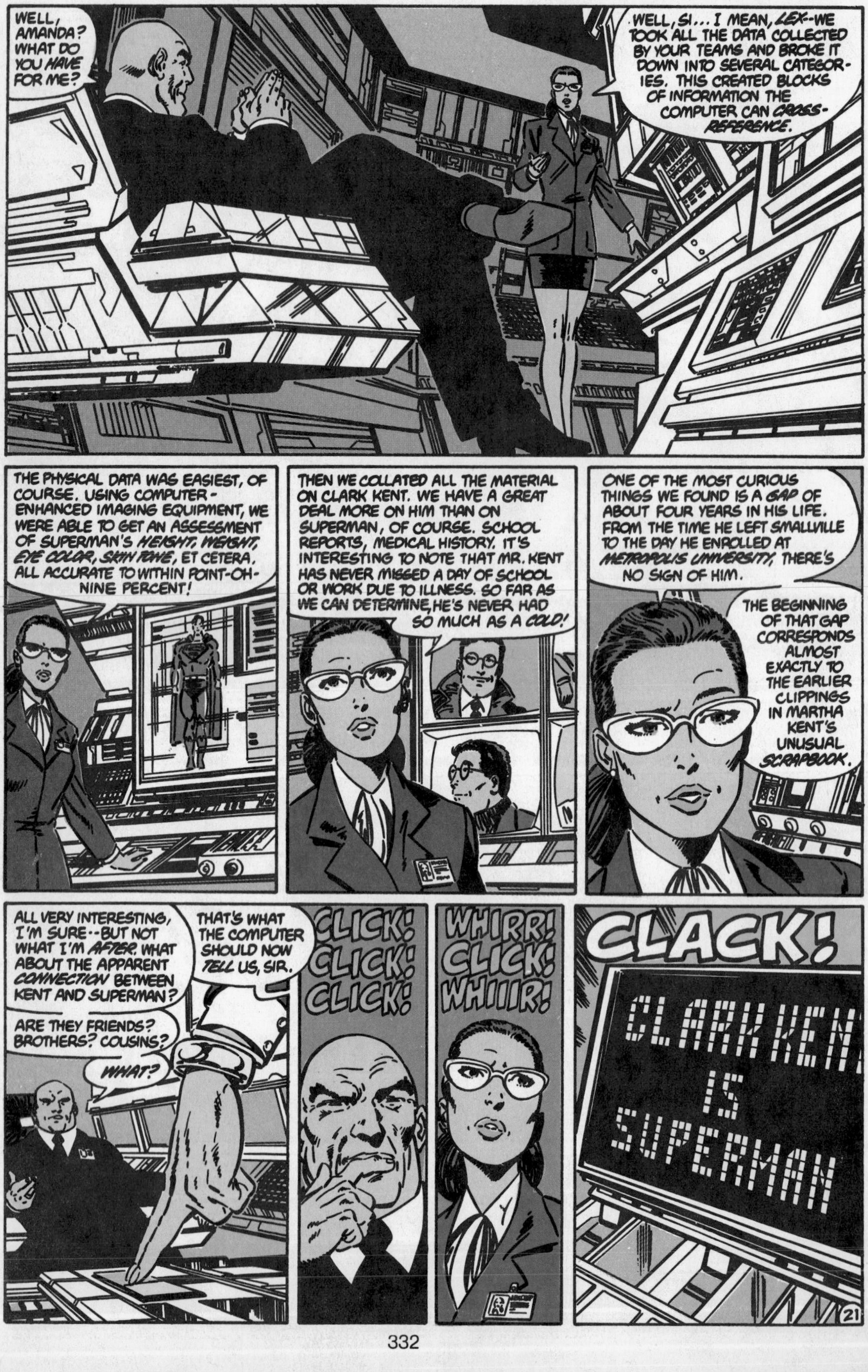
WELL, AMANDA? WHAT DO YOU HAVE FOR ME?
WELL, SI... I MEAN, LEX--WE TOOK ALL THE DATA COLLECTED BY YOUR TEAMS AND BROKE IT DOWN INTO SEVERAL CATEGORIES. THIS CREATED BLOCKS OF INFORMATION THE COMPUTER CAN CROSS-REFERENCE.
THE PHYSICAL DATA WAS EASIEST, OF COURSE. USING COMPUTER-ENHANCED IMAGING EQUIPMENT, WE WERE ABLE TO GET AN ASSESSMENT OF SUPERMAN'S HEIGHT, WEIGHT, EYE COLOR, SKIN TONE, ET CETERA, ALL ACCURATE TO WITHIN POINT-OH-NINE PERCENT!
THEN WE COLLATED ALL THE MATERIAL ON CLARK KENT. WE HAVE A GREAT DEAL MORE ON HIM THAN ON SUPERMAN, OF COURSE. SCHOOL REPORTS, MEDICAL HISTORY. IT'S INTERESTING TO NOTE THAT MR. KENT HAS NEVER MISSED A DAY OF SCHOOL OR WORK DUE TO ILLNESS. SO FAR AS WE CAN DETERMINE, HE'S NEVER HAD SO MUCH AS A COLD!
ONE OF THE MOST CURIOUS THINGS WE FOUND IS A GAP OF ABOUT FOUR YEARS IN HIS LIFE. FROM THE TIME HE LEFT SMALLVILLE TO THE DAY HE ENROLLED AT METROPOLIS UNIVERSITY, THERE'S NO SIGN OF HIM.
THE BEGINNING OF THAT GAP CORRESPONDS ALMOST EXACTLY TO THE EARLIER CLIPPINGS IN MARTHA KENT'S UNUSUAL SCRAPBOOK.
ALL VERY INTERESTING, I'M SURE--BUT NOT WHAT I'M AFTER. WHAT ABOUT THE APPARENT CONNECTION BETWEEN KENT AND SUPERMAN?
ARE THEY FRIENDS? BROTHERS? COUSINS?
WHAT?
THAT'S WHAT THE COMPUTER SHOULD NOW TELL US, SIR.
CLICK! CLICK! CLICK!
WHIRR! CLICK! WHIIIR!
CLACK!
CLARK KEN
IS
SUPERMAN
21

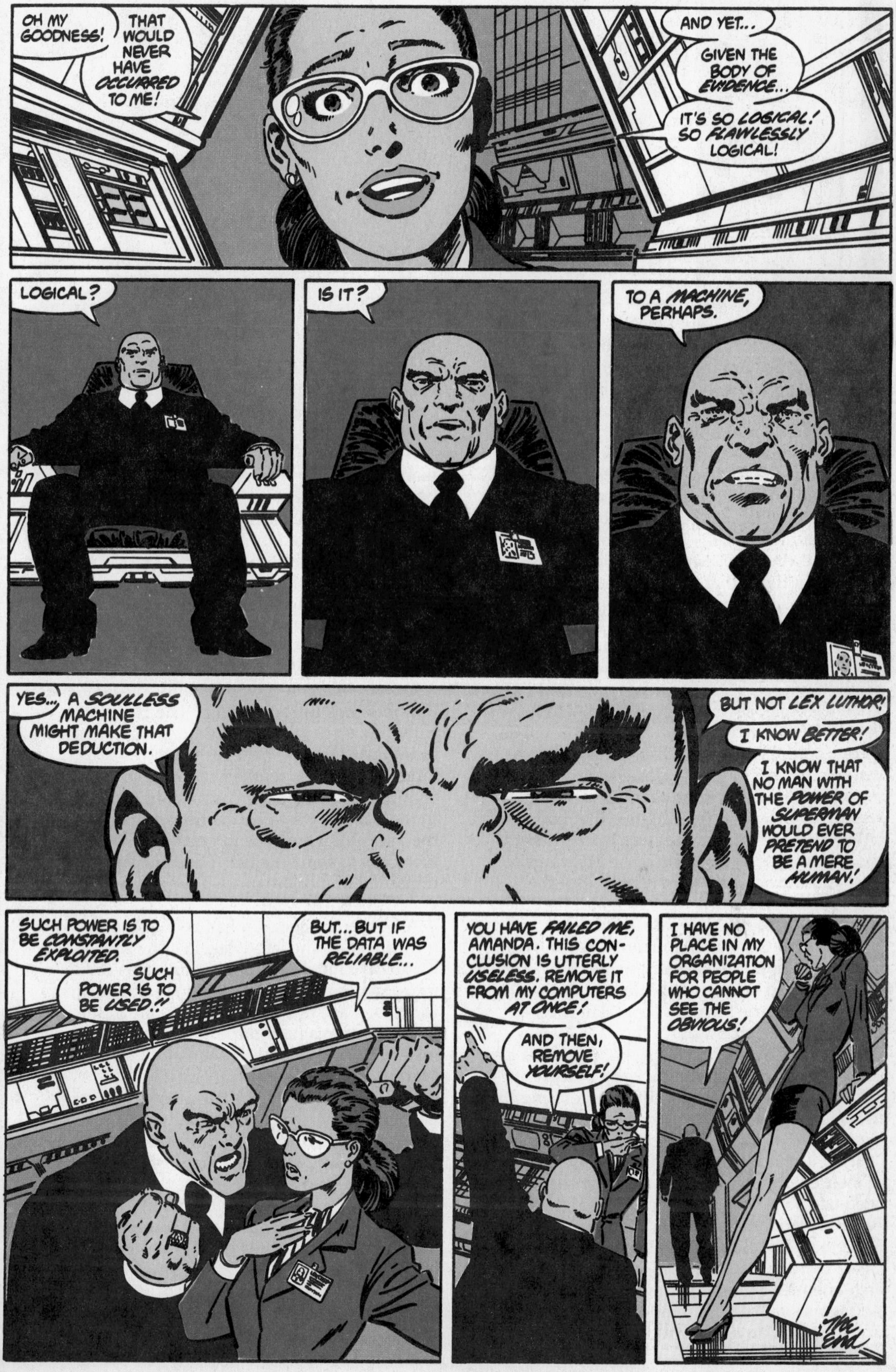
OH MY GOODNESS!
THAT WOULD NEVER HAVE OCCURRED TO ME!
AND YET...
GIVEN THE BODY OF EVIDENCE...
IT'S SO LOGICAL! SO FLAWLESSLY LOGICAL!
LOGICAL?
IS IT?
TO A MACHINE, PERHAPS.
YES... A SOULLESS MACHINE MIGHT MAKE THAT DEDUCTION.
BUT NOT LEX LUTHOR!
I KNOW BETTER!
I KNOW THAT NO MAN WITH THE POWER OF SUPERMAN WOULD EVER PRETEND TO BE A MERE HUMAN!
SUCH POWER IS TO BE CONSTANTLY EXPLOITED.
SUCH POWER IS TO BE USED!!
BUT... BUT IF THE DATA WAS RELIABLE...
YOU HAVE FAILED ME, AMANDA. THIS CONCLUSION IS UTTERLY USELESS. REMOVE IT FROM MY COMPUTERS AT ONCE!
AND THEN, REMOVE YOURSELF!
I HAVE NO PLACE IN MY ORGANIZATION FOR PEOPLE WHO CANNOT SEE THE OBVIOUS!
THE END

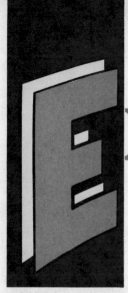

END NOTES

Superman is an inspiration to three generations of readers around the world; a select few of whom had a chance to repay that debt by helping us choose the stories to be included in this volume. There literally were dozens of stories nominated and the final selection process weighed many factors, as discussed in Mike Gold's introduction. However, the stories that did not achieve a place here certainly are worthy of mention.

In reviewing the selections, it becomes apparent that those that are most memorable are not the ones of superhuman feats of strength, but rather the stories that tugged at our emotions. They are the moving stories that we carried with us since those days we first came across them.

For example, several judges cited "Let My People Grow" by Len Wein and Curt Swan as an exemplary tale. What distinguished it was that the Bottle City of Kandor was finally restored to its full size on another world. It was an emotionally uplifting tale that had a bittersweet ending when it was learned that the enlarging method turned the buildings to dust and the city had to be rebuilt. But the entrapped Kandorians were free and had the chance to carve their own destiny.

When Julie Schwartz concluded his 17-year stint as editor of the Superman line, he commissioned a two-part wrap-up tale, "imaginary story," from writer Alan Moore, and penciller Curt Swan. "Whatever Happened to the Man of Tomorrow?" provided a satisfactory conclusion to the saga of the entire Superman family, allowing them an ending the month before John Byrne arrived to start it all over again.

Several other tales were nominated because of their emotional impact. One most frequently cited tale was "The Team of Luthor and Brainiac" from the same era as Superman-Red/Superman-Blue and "The Death of Superman." Here, the Man of Steel's arch-enemies teamed up and found a way to rid themselves of Superman via a serum unleashed on an alien world. Superman nearly died but was rescued by the Superman Emergency Squad, Kandorians who used to aid Superman when times got tough. Its cosmic scope was rare in the early 1960s, making it a popular tale.

Another super-villain pairing that received many votes was "The Terrible Trio" which brought Luthor into an uneasy alliance with the Toyman and the Prankster. In this short story, they teamed up to distract Superman while they committed larcenous acts. Luthor tried to upstage his colleagues by luring Superman into space and trapping him atop a satellite containing synthetic kryptonite. Superman, of course, saves himself and captures the trio in the act of gloating.

Other villains received several votes, such as Jim Shooter's introduction of The Parasite, a truly powerful villain. A janitor at a research facility mistakenly believes treasures were hidden in barrels marked radioactive. While trying to steal these "treasures" he is exposed to radioactive waste and is transformed into the Parasite, a creature in need of others' lifeforces to remain alive. The Parasite has remained one of the more powerful Superman villains over the years.

An even deadlier foe has been Metallo, introduced in the late 1950s in "The Menace of Metallo." Here, a common criminal is rebuilt into a cyborg powered by a kryptonite heart. Described as "evil incarnate" by one judge, Metallo has plagued Superman frequently and his kryptonite heart has nearly killed the Metropolis Marvel.

Lex Luthor is perhaps the most frequently used Superman foe and his name turns up in several stories that are included and remain on the runner-up list. An older story using Luthor involved an unusual item called the Powerstone which gave him great powers and nearly earned a victory over Superman. Because they gave Luthor powers at a time when most of Superman's adversaries were common criminals, the stories were precursors of things to come during the 1950s.

Luthor also provides Superboy a powerful

lesson in the short tale called "The Impossible Mission." Here, Superboy decides to journey through time and prevent John Wilkes Booth from assassinating Abraham Lincoln. However, Luthor also has journeyed back to the same event and shows Superboy that great as his power is, he cannot alter the course of history. Lincoln is still killed and a saddened Superboy never tries to tamper with time again.

Superman's limitations have been a part of his character ever since it was established that despite his great power, he still could not prevent his foster parents from dying from a rare tropical disease. This has plagued Superman over the years and has given us a great many tales about both his real parents, Jor-El and Lara, and his adoptive parents, Jonathan and Martha Kent.

Writer Cary Bates examined this same theme in a much-acclaimed two-part tale called "The Miraculous Return of Jonathan Kent," wherein benevolent aliens grant Jonathan his fondest wish by giving him 30 hours to visit his grown son. By the end of his visit, Jonathan has helped Superman against a new threat and approved of Lois Lane as his potential mate. After his return, the memory of Jonathan's mysterious arrival is removed from eveyone's mind and Superman concludes the tale by feeling closer to his parents than ever before.

Superman has returned to his native world of Krypton on many occasions in both "real" and "imaginary" stories. One of the most requested tales was Superman's return to Krypton and his romance with actress Lyla Lerrol. Nominated by Superman co-creator Jerry Siegel (among others), it has Superman chasing an alien through space and accidentally flying too fast and finding himself hurtling through the time stream. He finds himself trapped on Krypton and begins a search for a way home.

Kal-El is startled to find that the era he arrived in was just in time for his parents' wedding. Kal-El becomes Jor-El's lab assistant and pursues an ill-fated romance with Kryp-

ton's greatest actress, Lyla Lerrol. The story offers a unique and fascinating look at many elements of Kryptonian life. An accident sends Superman into space, far enough away from Krypton's red sun for his powers to return and he journeys back to his normal time. Yet, Lyla Lerrol remains one of his greatest loves, right behind Lois Lane, Lana Lang, and Lori Lemaris.

The double "L" in their names was originally an accident that became a pattern to the series over the years. It got to the point where a character was introduced with a double "L" name and readers knew some sort of trouble was brewing.

There was another Krypton tale that told the story of Kal-El's original fate. The Guardians of the Universe, seen in "Must There Be a Superman," realized that the baby Kal-El could become the greatest Green Lantern of them all.

Superman's place in the scheme of the universe has come into play time and again, but perhaps in no more an important setting than DC's 50th anniversary comic series, *Crisis on Infinite Earths*. The 12-part story took a lot of DC's backstory and trashed it in favor of a cleaner, more streamlined universe for DC's super-heroes. One result was the death of his cousin Supergirl.

Kara Zor-El was introduced in 1959, shortly after publication of "The Girl of Steel." She remained in training for her first few years until a memorable serial proved her ready for public action. The climactic tale, "Superman Presents Supergirl to the World," received a handful of nominations.

Supergirl was a character that went through numerous creators and creative directions, but ultimately proved unwieldy compared to her stronger cousin. When *Crisis* went into production, major events were required and her death was perhaps the most significant change to the public at large.

The Maid of Might frequently teamed up with Superman and some of those tales received nominations, including her participation in a multi-part Superman story written by

Paul Levitz and drawn by Jim Starlin that dealt with Superman on a more spiritual level.

Her final appearance, in *Crisis #7*, was also a nominated story. It didn't make this volume since its clarity would be seriously diluted by taking it out of its epic context.

Superman, being the world's greatest super-hero, has teamed up with virtually every major character DC has published over the last 52 years. A fair number of those stories were nominated, with the overwhelming winner being a tale written by Alan Moore. Here, Superman was paired with Swamp Thing, a character created by Len Wein and Berni Wrightson who again received great critical acclaim under Moore's authorship in the 1980s. The story was more than just two heroes getting together and trashing a bad guy: it dealt with the nature of being a hero and the elements of Superman's life that helped shape him into America's greatest super-hero.

As frequently as Superman has met other heroes, he has been stripped of his powers, only to prove time and again that he has what it takes to be a hero under any circumstance. One oft-mentioned story was a four-parter co-written by Cary Bates and Elliot Maggin, with art by Curt Swan. Dubbed the "Mr. Xavier" story, it featured a Superman who wearied of the responsibilities attached to having great power. Instead, he opted to remain Clark Kent for a time and allowed that part of his persona to grow. The story evolved into an examination of Clark Kent the man and led to an affair with Lois Lane which brought their characters closest to a consummated relationship. In the end, the menace of Mr. Xavier (an alien masquerading as Kent's neighbor) brought Superman back into action.

Just as Superman has dominated the comic book world, he has always been a strong element in the newspapers. His comic strip debuted shortly after his success in *Action Comics* and Jerry Siegel wrote many of the early continuities. While complete proofs from those early strips cannot be found, Siegel still fondly recalls the early origin tales, making them worthy of notation.

Of special note, Siegel also points to a handful of early comic book stories that cannot be reprinted as negatives no longer exist. There was one from *Action Comics #3* that dealt with the rights of miners and another featuring an inventor from late 1941. "A Superman story reprinted in *Superman #3* from *Action Comics* haunts Joe [Shuster] and me. In it, Joe and I forecast how the Superman character could be profitably licensed and merchandised."

Jerry Siegel, among others, also points to a handful of stories from Superman's companion titles *Superman's Girl Friend Lois Lane* and *Superman's Pal Jimmy Olsen*. Most of these are "imaginary" tales where Lois finally marries Superman or Clark Kent and the complications that arise. The Jimmy Olsen tales either have him transformed into something inhuman or pair him with Superman as the non-powered Nightwing and Flamebird from a series of Kandor stories during the 1960s.

Perhaps the common denominator amongst all the stories nominated is the use of Super-man and his supporting family. These are all stories about the human spirit and its ability to transcend all adversity. The "imaginary" stories usually end with Superman taking his rightful place as the premier super-hero on Earth or have a happy ending with Superman defeating evil and finding happiness with the woman of his dreams.

The Superman Family bulged during the 1960s with the arrival of Supergirl and a plethora of super-animals, the Legion of Super-Heroes and various survivors from Krypton. As charming and fanciful as those stories were, the family grew too large.

"Must There Be a Superman" and other thoughtful human dramas dominated the 1970s-era nominations. The 1980s nominees dealt with the Man of Steel's legend, such as Marv Wolfman and Gil Kane's "What If There Was No Superman?" Aliens have invaded the Earth and no super-hero exists to defend the human race. Two teenagers, Jerome Siegel and Joe Shuster, use their fertile imaginations to create a defender and suddenly, there was a whooshing red blur. Since there was no Super-man, they had to create one.

Whatever the story, from whatever the source, the end result remains. We desire a defender of truth, justice and the American way. We need one. That sentiment is as true today as it was 50 years ago.